from

Mum & Dad,

Christmas, 1979.

Billy Graham

Books by Marshall Frady

Wallace
Across a Darkling Plain: An American's Passage through
the Middle East
Billy Graham: A Parable of American Righteousness

MARSHALL FRADY

Billy Graham

A Parable of
American Righteousness

HODDER AND STOUGHTON
LONDON SYDNEY AUCKLAND TORONTO

The author is grateful to the following publishers and individuals for permission to quote from material noted below.

Mrs. C. A. Beard for letters by Ben Coffey appearing on pp. 20–21.

Mr. Stuart K. Hine and Manna Music, Inc. for lines from "How Great Thou Art" by Stuart K. Hine. Copyright © 1953 by Stuart K. Hine. North American lyrics copyright © 1953, 1955 by Manna Music Inc., 2111 Kenmere Avenue, Burbank, Ca. International copyright secured. All rights reserved. Used by permission.

Author's original words lines two and three are:

"Consider all the works Thy hand hath made,

I see the stars, I hear the mighty thunder."

Lillenas Publishing Company for lines from "The Love of God" by F. M. Lehman, arr. Claudia Lehman Mays. Copyright 1917. Renewed 1945 by Nazarene Publishing House. All rights reserved. Used by permission.

British Library Cataloguing in Publication Data

Frady, Marshall
    Billy Graham.
    1. Graham, Billy 2. Evangelists—United
    States—Biography
    269'.2'0924   BV3785.G69
    ISBN 0-340-24005-9

To Gudrun
Life-Giver

Author's Note

This book had its beginning as a magazine assignment in the fall of 1973 — to cover a Graham crusade in North Carolina at a time when Watergate was still fitfully unfolding forth. Very soon, though, I began to suspect that the story of Billy Graham and what had become his peculiar meaning in the life of this country might be a matter somewhat larger than a magazine exercise. It seemed to me that Graham presented one of those figures in whom something elemental in the character of a people and an age — in this case, Mid-America since World War Two — comes into a singular focus. It wasn't only that he had served for over two decades as high pastor to the proud and mighty and prosperous of the land. More than that, he himself constituted something like the very embodiment of the common American righteousness — what has lasted, really since Plymouth, as the particular American sense of the upright, the American godliness and goodness.

How I wanted to tell this story, though, was through frequencies of feeling, mood, characterization — of realization — fuller to the reality than simple blank reportage or essay-like critiquing: that is, while carefully answering to the journalistic integrities of accuracy and equitableness, to write about the entire man and the entire matter with the deepest possible registers and sensings. Through all the years that Graham has abided as a familiar presence in the nation's popular life, it seems the actuality of the man himself — his personal heft and textures and humors — has continued to be rather vaguely, flatly apprehended. He has existed in the general perception largely as a cliché, a kind of animated manikin. One reason for this, I think, is that all wider-range book takes of him have been more or less the handiwork of specially interested parties — whether diligently admiring or indicting, all principally arguments with their homiletic points to make. But the interests of neither commendation nor censure ever serve the fullest understandings, because life and human character are finally larger than all polemics, all forensics.

What I began to find was that there had accreted over the years a virtual Comstock Lode of unmined lore on Graham and his career, along with a multitudinous cast of attendant players throughout his past who had never really been engaged for a truly deep-dimensioned biography of him. At the same time, having grown up myself as the son of a Southern Baptist preacher in much the same religious barometrics that made up Graham's world, I felt in a way that I already knew him, in a sense that I'd known him all my life. One must still remain always wary of such presumptions, of course. But after tracking through all the ponderous archive of commentary that has accumulated after Graham through the years, and then passing a long time among all that material out in the field, I wanted to commence the writing as if no one had ever tried to tell it before — so that, when it was finished, both Graham's faithful and his critics, as well as those simply curious about him, would at the least know the man as they'd never known him before.

Perhaps I should indicate at the outset that the research — a more detailed record of which can be found at the close of this story — over thirty volumes alone on Graham and his career, extensive newspaper files, along with some 280 magazine pieces from 1949 to the present, but most of all a long succession of interviews ranging from Charlotte to Los Angeles to Toronto to Tampa, which included Graham and members of his family, his associates and old acquaintances, a number of whom I returned to for second and third sessions, continuing on in this live research until I reached a point where I found material beginning to repeat to a substantial degree. In some cases, I have elected to leave a source unnamed, even though it was not requested, when it seemed that specific identification might afford that party unnecessary discomfiture. In every instance possible, though, for what I considered especially pertinent or novel details, I tried to plot a coordinate of at least two sources, and often wound up with more. Certain remarks or circumstances or situations that I may have encountered first in reading I posed again to Graham and his people or other parties, not only for confirmation but for a fuller illumination and amplification. In particular, aspects and descriptive specifics of scenes in the past, if not actually mentioned in reference sources, came from direct queries — down to such details as "What do you remember the weather being like that afternoon? . . . In what tone of voice do you remember hearing him say that?" I also visited as many as possible of this story's settings that have remained virtually the same — for instance, the grounds of that moss-muffled Bible academy outside Tampa with its golf course where, one anguished late night almost forty years ago, Graham more or less relinquished the earth and gave himself up to heaven. In addition, for other particulars of description, I consulted slide collections, old photographs, private film reels dating back to around 1938, and, at Graham's World Wide Studios in Burbank, unedited footages and film documentaries going back to 1949.

The interviews with Graham himself included a first talk of perhaps two hours at his home above Montreat, North Carolina; scattered periods with him through a crusade in San Diego; but most of all, two marathon sessions over two separate days in Montreat, both of which lasted almost literally from breakfast straight through on past dusk.

It may be that, for this sort of biography, one just naturally, unconsciously, enters into a self-identification with one's subject that would be something like an experiential, Stanislavski method of biography — in a way, one *becomes* for a while who and what one will be writing about; one comes to exist *inside* of it all in a kind of suspension of one's own sensibilities and persuasions. In this instance, at least, very soon on moving into the live research out in the field, I was taken not only with a huge liking for and empathy with Graham, but with the greatest enthusiasms about everything around him. But the difficulty is that, when one arrives at the point where one has to begin the actual writing of it, one necessarily must withdraw into a detachment, a remove almost of impersonality — the only way, interposing that distance, to recognize the largest, last realities of the matter. And in this last stage of the work, one is totally alone, one belongs to no loyalties whatsoever other than the important meanings of the man and the story.

Whatever may be their differences now with the imports of this personal history of Graham and his ministry, to Graham himself and his people I would like to say that, among those final detached perspectives out of which it was written, was assuredly to measure and play everything against the nature and implications of Jesus' own ministry and message — against the original. So in that sense, it can be considered also a religious account — in fact, for it to have any real authenticity, no way it could have escaped that.

Last, I must express my great appreciation to the following: to Billy's family and his community of friends, but especially to Billy himself for his time and his openness; to Roger Donald, senior editor at Little, Brown, for both his logistical and editorial ministrations that carried this book on through to delivery, and to his wife, Diana, for her own gallant courtesies and graciousness; for a varied range of other assistances, to James T. Roe III, Sterling Lord, Robert Silvers, Berry Stainback, Steve Gelman, Jonathan Larsen, Franklin Ashley, Ed Kopeschka, Robert Sheheen, Timothy Skidmore; in a more personal way, to Anne and Jack Williamson, and Emily and Joe Cumming, simply for splendid times of congregating and talk that enspirited more than they could have supposed; a particular gratitude and appreciation, for their long and patient cheerfulness (and no slight secretarial assistances), to Eva Reuter, and Nona Reuter, and Thomas too — and to my mother and father, for their many vital solicitudes through the course of this work. A very special debt I owe to my children — Katrina, Carson, and Shannon — for all the time over the past two years they have not had with their father.

But finally, I owe more than I could ever recount here to Gudrun, my wife.

Billy Graham

But the form of Billy Budd was heroic . . . the moral nature seldom out of keeping with the physical make. . . . A virtue went out of him, sugaring the sour. . . . Much of a child-man . . . he possessed that kind and degree of intelligence going along with the unconventional rectitude of a sound human nature, one to whom not yet has been proffered the questionable apple of knowledge. . . . Nor unaware was he of the peculiar favorable effect his person and demeanor had upon the more intelligent gentlemen of the quarterdeck. . . .

HERMAN MELVILLE,
Billy Budd, Foretopman

PROLOGUE

— Then, from about two in the afternoon, I'm in the room. I go over the sermon. I have to be alone. Even my wife doesn't disturb me; I like to go to the service physically refreshed. Toward the late afternoon, I lie down to about five-thirty. . . . I dream sometimes, in a very light sleep.

— What do you dream?

— I dream . . . well, I dreamed I was in another country, and they held the presidential election here, and I didn't know who had won. I went all around asking people, but nobody would tell me who had won. . . .

He awakes, opens his eyes into the vacant and spacious hush of his dim motel suite, the drapes drawn. For an instant, it could be a room anywhere in the world — Miami, Hong Kong, Seattle, Jerusalem — the span of carmine carpet with a pair of vaguely Mediterranean lounging chairs sitting over by the veiled window, the shadowy glaze of the television screen, glasses wrapped in cellophane resting on the tiny plastic wafer of a tray atop a frail desk, on the walls the few pale indefinite scenes of wraithy gondeliers, anonymous piazzas. There is no sound, no sign of what actually lies outside beyond the muffling fabrics of the closed drapes, only a dull lurk of light around their edges. He swings up and hangs at the edge of the bed for a moment, and then snaps on the small glow of the lamp over the telephone — this is North Carolina, of course, this is Raleigh now.

He will be leaving for the service in an hour. In the bitter white glare of the bathroom, he briefly showers, moves about with small clinks and rustlings. Before finally setting out for the stadium, standing before his own towering solitary image in the dresser mirror, he sips lightly from a cup of thin tea.

Already they have begun hauling in out of the wide darkening spaces of the countryside — from all directions, an endless converging of cavalcades over the dust-hazed parking field, old school buses enameled now in candy-bright tints, heaving and wheezing in one after another, strung with banners, CALVARY METHODIST CHURCH — HONK IF YOU LOVE JESUS, IMMANUEL BAPTIST CHURCH — GOD'S IN-CROWD, steadily spilling forth a scrubbed and cheerful multitude, neatly combed and barbered, matrons in spun-glass bouffants and rhinestone butterfly spectacles nestling Bibles in their arms, their men in pastel leisure suits with binocular cases slung over their shoulders, all moving in little murmurous rills and shoals everywhere over the grass with a sedate briskness — a continuous unloading under the high white flare of the stadium lights like some systematic unpacking of population out of the far comfortable deeps, the Swiss-cupboard kitchens and pine-paneled dens, the dishwasher hums and color-TV luminescences, of Inner America. They are still filling the stands, brimming on up to the last top tiers, on up to the very edge of the empty dimming sky, with faint scattered waftings of sweet perfume, soap, Aqua-Velva, pizza and fried chicken from the supper tables they have just left, toothpaste, Juicy Fruit gum, like a mingling pleasant incense tinging the chill blue evening — as the service commences with a vast organ-billowing surf of singing over the high parapets and chasms of the stadium: *"O Lord, my God, when I in awesome wonder consider all the worlds Thy hands hath made; I see the stars, I hear the rolling thunder, Thy power throughout the universe displayed"* — mighty Christ-anthems, exultant with virtue, surging and pealing against the pale twilight sky slowly extinguishing into night, *"Then sings my soul, my Savior, God, to Thee! How great Thou art! How great Thou art! . . ."* There is about it an authentically skin-prickling pageantry, a certain fugitive Nuremberg grandeur, its effect being to somehow translate the snug tidy modest respectability of this host of ordinary citizens suddenly into a dimension of galactic splendor; it is niceness cast on a scale of Wagnerian majesty. And as the mammoth choir behind the field platform is swelling into the last celestial cascadings of "The Lord's Prayer," and everyone's head is bowed, abruptly and almost stealthily he comes striding, swiftly, over the grass along the sidelines.

Tall and preened in a shimmerous dark suit, even now at middle age he still has that look of some blond, gallant, crystal-eyed prince out of a Nordic fairy tale — young Hansel grown to a stalwart golden manhood, unaging, changeless. His Bible snuggled in one hand to his chest and his chin sturdily clamped in a resolute little smile, he moves with long rapid swipes of his legs in a small immediate space of aloneness, among an encircling bevy of security guards in sober suits, walkie-talkies cupped discreetly in their palms — an entrance curiously like a small idle reflection of the comings and goings also, in this late September of 1973, of his auspicious friend, President Nixon.

When everyone then lifts his head at the end of the choir's chorale, he is discovered suddenly and simply delivered onto the stage down there before them. All over the stadium, there is a myriad glimmering of binoculars. Among this evening's platform gallery of miscellaneous notables — a lieutenant governor, a football coach, a vaguely famed television songstress — he sits composed and motionless, his hands folded formally over the Bible in his lap, his long thin legs elegantly crossed and his theatrical, luxuriously maned Viking's countenance lifted just a little in musing abstraction into the middle air, as the current Miss North Carolina swims up to the pulpit mike in a scintillant gown to trill, "I'm so excited to be here with all these people. Listen — are yawl depressed or lonely? If you are, I've got a little song for you," and in a breathless little-girl's voice, proceeds to lilt thinly, "It's a wonderful, wonderful day. . . ."

At last, he arises, swoops to the pulpit. "I'm going to ask now that there be no walking around, no moving of any kind, no talking." His voice comes like an abrupt, startling clash and boom of bronze. "Only one person moving around in a great stadium like this can distract many people, and there are those here tonight who have great burdens that need to be lifted, sins that need to be forgiven — " He takes a step back from the pulpit and cocks one hand, palm downward, against his hip, his other arm swinging high like a windmill's blade in the air over the host banked around him. "Battles will be going on all over this stadium tonight, greater battles than are ever fought on this athletic field — battles of the soul, with all eternity hanging in the balance. And while I am talking to you, there will be another voice deep down inside speaking to you. That voice will be the voice of the Spirit of God. . . ."

From the far altitudes of the stadium, his figure is tiny and miniaturized, like a dwindled and hectically gesturing form viewed through the wrong end of a telescope, but as he circles and paces the pulpit, actually seeming to stalk it with a rapt swarming urgency, all of his movements, his long arms looping and lashing and whisking downward like a flourishing of scimitars in the air, are all minutely and precisely distinct, absolutely discernible. It's as if he had been singularly constructed, with his El Grecan attenuation of limb, to be perceived across great distances, among huge spaces. But down at the field platform itself, there is an odd intimate calm of detachment from the throng ranged panoramically around him, as if the area here were contained within some glass bell of solitude — some secret hush of remoteness and privacy, with the magnolia leaves arrayed around the edges of the platform quietly clacking in a black night wind, the pages of his Bible ruffling and slapping in stray small whispers, his vented coattails flipping and muttering as he strides and wheels about the pulpit.

— *Yes, it's a strange thing, but when I begin to preach, I feel almost totally alone. It's almost as if I'm not even aware of the thousands and thousands of people out there. I'm preaching just to the first six inches in front of my face. . . .*

His voice clangors beyond him in surreal amplification like the shout of a titan over the expanse of the stands. "We have seen during the past few weeks how morally *weak* we really are in this country. It seems almost that some sinister force has taken hold of our country and is ripping it apart. . . ." In fact, it is a period, with the Senate Watergate Hearings still in progress, when magnesium flares seem to be dropping everywhere over dark unsuspected landscapes of evil in Washington, but this is his only allusion, random and fleeting, to those successive lurid illuminations that have begun now inexorably approaching the person of the President himself, his old confidant. "Listen —" and he pulls far back from the pulpit, flinging high one arm with his Bible sagging from his hand, his other hand outstretched and tautly slicing, fanning back and forth "— if I didn't know my name was written in the book of life, you couldn't *drag* me out of this stadium tonight, I would stay in this stadium until I *knew!*" His voice, with its haughty and faintly autocratic East Shore society intonations, is like a ringing of cymbals in a canyon. "You can say of Jesus Christ what you will, you can say he was a great revolutionary, you can say he was mad, you can say he was the son of the living God —" and he lunges back into the pulpit again, smacking down his Bible, and leans urgently forward, his eagle's profile edged with a bright dazzle against the high batteries of field lights, his eyes crackling with an arctic brilliance of some icy fierceness, as he unleashes his long arms straight out in front of him with both fists desperately clenched "— but he loves you, loves you, loves you! *loves you!*"

Finally, as the choir behind him begins massively hymning "Just as I Am," he calls, "I'm going to ask you now to come. Up here — down here —" One lifted arm planes and arcs about him in the air, palm extended, as if stroking the vast spaces around him. "You, way up there in those last rows, you might say, 'But it's a long way from up here.' It ought to be a hundred times as far; Christ carried a cross all the way up to Calvary to die for you —" Already they are beginning to ripple down the aisles, to sift heavily down out of the stands, flowing on out across the floodlit Easter-green field. "That's it, that's it. A little voice down inside is speaking to you, telling you that you need to come. That voice is the voice of the Holy Spirit, wooing you, asking you to come and give your life over to Christ, who died for your sins. I want you to come. You can find a new life here tonight by a complete surrender to Jesus Christ. You may be a church member, you may not be, but you've never had that living encounter with God, something's missing in your life. Father, mother, young person — you need to come. You may never have another moment like this one. If you don't come tonight, you may never come, you could go out of this stadium tonight and have your life taken from you before the sun rises tomorrow. That's it, come on. You stand at the crossroads of life. There's still time. I want you to come. . . ."

By now, there has collected around the platform a wide lake of uplifted faces, vague of expression, as if mildly dazed. Others are still filtering across the field. The choir sings on, like the soft persistent slow concussions of tide on distant reefs, ". . . *to rid my soul of one dark blot, to Thee whose blood can cleanse each spot, O Lamb of God, I come.* . . ." His arms crossed over his Bible and his head slightly bowed with one forefinger curled over his chin, he stands finally silent, still, looming tall above the starburst sprays of gladioluses and lilies around the pulpit, alone against the blind inky sky, draped now in a pale luminous raincoat against the mist that has begun ghosting down.

Some two and a half years later, one spring morning over a year after Nixon's fall, up in the high hushed air of North Carolina's mountains, on up a narrow looping drive twining along a deep plunge of woods down through far spills of space, on beyond the fortress-like stone ramparts of his gate, at his tidy gray log-and-shingle home curled and scrolled in primroses and morning glories, he comes around the side of the house — emerging suddenly out of a glimmer of leaves with a curiously lurching and off-tilt lope, a precipitous and galumphing eagerness. He greets his visitor, a stranger who has flown up that morning, with a huge glad grin flaring lavishly under his dark sunglasses, yet there seems in his manner some vague momentary falter of abashment, distraction — his commodious handshake loose and tentative, in the cordial blare of his voice some vapor gap of light uncertainty — a furtive shyness that is faintly startling after all the awesome theatre of those stadiums over the years.

They amble on back through the archway of leaves to his sideyard, a flat glittering expanse of lawn as immaculately mown as a golf green, immediately giving off, beyond a split-rail fence, to emptiness — a giddying measureless swoop of mountain ridges heaving off into lost blue distances. Here, on the brick-floored veranda running along the side of the house, he settles into one of the rocking chairs distributed along its length that were shipped up to him by Lyndon Johnson from Johnson's own porch gallery along the Pedernales — his rambling storklike frame, garbed now in an old golf sweater limply buttoned once over his checkered slacks, arranged in the rocker in a loose lounging slouch. On a small table beside him, a Bible lies plopped open among a disarray of papers with notes, notions, phrases dappled over them in scrawls of red ink.

"Of course," he grins, the sunglasses still over his eyes, "you know we bought all the land for this place way back when we were able to get it for only about twelve dollars an acre. We'd never have been able to afford what it's probably worth now." After a few more moments, he blurts, "By all means, call me Billy, please; I'd certainly be uncomfortable if you didn't. Why goodness, man, I'm just like any other fella you'd meet along the side of the road out there," and he tosses his long arm widely out at the airy mountainscapes around him, and with that, removes his glasses at last — his eyes are strangely clear and transparent like light held in quartz, like the translucent eyes of a leopard.

A housekeeper presently materializes from the mirror-windowed silences of the house, bringing out a simple lunch of fruit salad and mint tea. He hunches over his spindly tray-table, his elbows propped on the sides of the rocker, and delivers a short casual prayer, mentioning the stranger sitting across from him — "And Lord, we'd ask you to bless him and bless his family, and be with us in our talk here this morning." It has the peculiar effect of producing in the stranger, as he hears this with bowed head, an unexpected little interior bloom of gratitude. They chat then idly over lunch in the chapel-like quiet of the late morning, a washed glistening morning in early April, with no other sound than the scattered ring of birds in the steep woods around. Hanging over his tray with his plank-end knees splayed wide underneath, he snatches another gulp of tea, swipes at his mouth with his paper napkin, and then inquires amiably, almost incidentally, "And you, what is your own spiritual standing?"

"Well, I don't know that I have accepted Jesus exactly in the sense you would mean, but I believe in him, I love him, he's a living reality to me. I'm a Christian, yes, though a terribly imperfect and faltering one."

He grins generously. "Well, I would say that's the case with all of us — we all are."

He leans back in his rocker, slinging one leg sideways over his knee, his spacious winglike hands folded now over his shallow waist, and continues his leisurely, random reflections over what has happened to him through the past thirty years: "I heard just the other day, you might be interested, there's somebody doing a study now of the effects of all our crusades in Europe. They say they've found over twenty-five different religious groups and movements all over Europe that have come directly out of our work over there. I was amazed, I had no idea there was anything like that, but that's what they tell me they've found. . . ."

Eventually he mentions Johnson. "You know, he made me stay at the White House every time I was in Washington, he just wouldn't let me stay anywhere else. He'd call me up and say, 'What are you doing over there, you know your room's waiting over here, get on over here now.' The White House became almost my hotel whenever I was up there. But that was back then before —"

And for an instant, his expansive grin goes flat: he announces then with a slightly louder and toneless clang of resolute blitheness in his voice, "But, uh, of course, never again. I mean —" and he gives a quick little cough of a laugh "— I've had my turn getting mixed up in politics, you can be sure of that. Oh, no, never again." It is no more than a momentary passing rumor of unease, a shadow's flicker glimpsed and gone in the morning's calm sunniness. "We'll be going back over to Europe next month," he cheerfully continues. "I'll be holding several meetings in Germany. Wonderful things are beginning to happen among the young generation in Germany, I think, and among the young people all over Europe, for that matter. . . ."

The aide who drove the visitor up from the airport now appears from the house to report that he has managed to arrange for a seat on a flight that afternoon back out of Asheville, a flight that the visitor had been told only a few hours earlier was fully booked. Billy tilts forward in his rocker. "I'm sorry you have to go. I wish we had more time, I really do; I've enjoyed talking with you. But I look forward to getting together with you more later on." Conducting the visitor on back around to the front driveway where the aide's station wagon is parked, he declares, "We'll be praying for you," and gives him two pats on the back. "All right now, have a good trip back. Good-bye now." He pauses a few seconds longer in the drive, wearing his gracious splendid grin as he loftily hangs there with that vague dangling awkwardness again, giving his arm one last loose wave as the station wagon pulls on away. Then he turns and disappears with his lunging lope back through the leaves.

But some touching sensation of benediction lingers on the way back down the mountain. It's as if his simple presence has the effect of a kind of blessing — leaves a mellowness afterward of a spontaneous, guileless, eager, fond absorption and regard. But more than that, one is left with a surprising sense in him of an ineffable utter innocence, as clear and blameless as that crystalline mountain morning. It prompts the stranger to turn and declare to the aide behind the wheel, "I have to tell you, I've never gotten off of anyone I've ever met such a feeling of natural goodness — sheer elemental goodness. What a wickedness it would be to ever visit mischief on a soul like that." And then one realizes—he's Billy Budd. Melville's welkin-eyed Billy. He has exactly that quality of raw childlike unblinking goodness. He could be Adam just stepped forth out of the soft flare of his own creation, strolling bright and silvery-eyed in the Garden. . . .

He has endured. Since his first exuberant emergence back in those brave sunny simplicities of America right after victory in World War Two, he has somehow kept imperviously preserved through all the attritions and abrasions of the years — the duresses of the Cold War, racial convulsions, assassinations, Vietnam, the street melees of the Sixties, finally Watergate — that chaste glamour of Sunday-morning sanctity. It has been a phenomenon not without its mysteries. An affable and vibrantly ordinary farm boy out of the bland midlands of North Carolina, suddenly glaring it seemed out of nowhere, Billy Graham has abided ever since as a folk totem-figure, virtually a mythic eminence, in the popular life of the nation: the icon, the breathing, bodied image of the native American rectitude.

The magnitude of his meaning to his vast constituency has reached registers of the uncanny. Through the little mountainside community just below his high-fenced home, there browses a ceaseless traffic of cars, station wagons, campers, church buses, passing endlessly through the seasons in private pilgrimages from all over the continent. At word some years ago that he was suffering from a small blood clot behind his retina, telegrams immediately came milling in from devotees offering to furnish him one of their own eyes, and after he underwent an operation following a kidney attack, his doctors received a blizzard of letters pleading for at least one of his kidney stones. From the multitudes that surround him in his stadium services, scrawled notes to him are slipped into the collection plates, making up a kind of unspoken collective psalming of communion between him and his masses — *"Thank you Jesus! for Dr. Graham! . . . Rev. Dr. Billy Graham, I am a Christian, baptized twice. This year I've developed a problem only God can cure and I'm waiting and praying for his help. What I have is Amyothropic Lakral Sclerosis. Please pray for my cure. . . . Please do not permit the unjust criticisms of pseudo prophets to undermine your strength. . . . We love you We hope you will honor our humble request to just meet you. God bless you. . . . God bless a very beautiful godly like person."* The reflexes of these faithful to any intimations of impoliteness toward him are instantaneous, massive, and tend toward the sulfurous: when the Charlotte *Observer* once carried a less than enchanted commentary on him by columnist Bob Lancaster, one of the letters that batted in advised briskly, "Bob Lancaster would be better off playing with lightning than someone of the spirit of God. . . . Bob Lancaster, and you people, too, had better ask God to have mercy on your souls. The Lord said, 'Touch not my anointed.' . . . There's going to be people praying — you watch."

To the conventional sophistication over the years, he has

always seemed somehow unaccountable — never much more than a kind of marceled Tupperware Isaiah. But he has simply, obliviously outlasted all the cynicisms of those particular Philistines, as if he has all along inhabited some medium, some physics of reality, finally beyond their ken. He has seemed as undamageable, unshatterable as chromium. To his own enormous congregation over the obscure expanses of the American interior, he has remained the imperishable demi-angel of the common righteousness. At the same time, not incidentally, he has acted as standing high chaplain, a kind of staunch-jawed American Jaycee Wolsey, to successive generations of the proud and powerful of the land. Whatever else, he has transmuted into a peculiar sort of megacelebrity, megastar of his age: his rangy wheat-haired form has been personally beheld, the reverberant bay of his voice immediately heard, by more people over the face of the earth than any other single human being in the history of the race.

The truth is, growing up a genial and lambently handsome but sturdily uncomplicated country youth, he simply happened to be somehow, somewhere stricken by a staggering passion for the pure, the sanitary, the wholesome, the upright — a transport has since proven, by almost any measure, epic. It has been suggested more than once that behind his highly varnished dramatic handsomeness and lordly bearing of Elijah-like authority, there dwells only a bright emptiness. But as one old acquaintance notes, "He can walk into a room full of people, there can be Senators and Cabinet officers and even a king or two in there, but immediately they're all silent for just an instant, just a little hold of breath — and then they're all humming and swatting around him like they were just popped with about ten thousand watts of electricity." If nothing else, his presence holds the mystic voltages of a certain order of greatness — a monumental certitude that, in its own way, approaches the heroic.

"The simple secret of Graham's genius," one religious commentator suggests, "is his own feeling of just a natural closeness with the reality of Jesus. He lives totally in that. That's what his prodigious certainty, his absolute unflappability owe to.

It's as if nothing whatsoever — criticism, calamities, any adversities on this earth — can ever intrude between him and that feeling of a personal intimacy with Jesus." Graham has explained on occasions his own sense of Jesus: "He was no sissy. I have seen so many pictures of Jesus as a frail, sad-faced weakling with a soft, almost feminine figure, that I am sick of it. You can be sure he was straight, strong, big, handsome, gracious, courteous," he would boom — as in Berlin's Olympic stadium once, standing tall and sun-gilded against a bare enameled blue sky with his golden hair whipping in a chill breeze — "All over the world, young people are searching for something to believe in. They want security. They want to be controlled. I believe Jesus Christ can become that controller! I'm not believing in some effeminate character. I'm believing in a real he-man, a real man who had a strong jaw and strong shoulders. I believe that Jesus Christ was the most perfectly developed physical specimen in the history of the world. He never had sin to deform his body. His nervous system was perfectly coordinated with the rest of his body. He would have been one of the great athletes of all times. Every inch a man! I can believe in that Christ! I can follow that Christ!" As he further defined him once, "One of Jesus' most appealing traits was his wide-ranging sociability. He was gregarious and companionable. . . . Among the patricians of Jerusalem he was a sought-after guest. Yet 'the common people heard him gladly.' He spoke their language — simple, forthright, familiar — not the lofty rhetoric of the rabbis and intelligentsia."

On the whole, Jesus emerges in Graham's perception of him as a figure remarkably not unlike Graham himself. And in fact, as one Baptist cleric privately muttered while a Graham crusade was underway in his town, "To most churchgoing folks in this country, Billy Graham has become nothing less than the nearest thing to Jesus on this earth. He's sort of like Christ's American son." Indeed, the singular significance of Billy Graham through the deepening disquiets of the American experience since its last great triumphant war is that he has endured as the incarnation, the very articulation into flesh of the native American ethic: he has derived directly, acted directly out of the very quick of Inner

America's sense of virtue and guilt, decency and dishonor, goodness and evil. One close associate over two decades, John Connally, has pronounced him "the conscience of America." An old friend allows, "In a way — never having really been sullied himself by defeat, or poverty, or tragedy, eternally optimistic and enthusiastic — Billy Graham *is* America. . . ."

But for all the executive suites and chandeliered chambers of power through which he moves now so easily and familiarly, he carries with him a sense that, behind his finely tended tan and ambassadorial coiffure and sleek excellent suits, there still lurks just a long and gangly country-grown Candide, plain as a cornstalk. One morning in the midst of his crusade in Raleigh, as he stood on the sidewalk outside a downtown church chatting convivially with a huddle of local ministers, he had about him the air of merely a lank and amicable hill boy arrived now at a well-cured middle age, gone only a bit gauntish, casually hugging his Bible to his chest in his folded arms with his beltless slacks gently bagging from the slightest loose sag of a paunch below his middle coat-button. From his boyhood on his father's dairy farm, there still seems a quality about him, like a lingering ambiance from all those years of milking twenty cows every day, of fresh cream and butter and custard, a certain pasteurized dairy-like mildness.

But it is no accident that he has wound up now with his image translated into a stained-glass window in Washington's National Presbyterian Cathedral. He constitutes finally the apotheosis of the American Innocence itself — that plain, cheerful, rigorous, ferociously wholesome earnestness which, to some, as one Egyptian editor put it during the days of Vietnam, "has made you nice Americans the most dangerous people on the face of the earth."

Perhaps part of it is that we are a nation that began stray-born as an urchin and foundling of history, pastless, abruptly blurting forth out of nothing but a proposition, a doctrine, and even yet have never really concluded exactly who we are. Instead, it's as if some fitful unspoken duality and ambivalence has run through our experience from our very inception: that original didactic from Plymouth's starch-collared theocracy of probity and diligence and order and conscientiousness that has ever since made up the commonplace beatitudes of our daylit world — the world of Eisenhower and Norman Rockwell and *The Reader's Digest* — all the while in dim struggle with the other half of our nature, more obscure and submerged, our night-being: a dreaming of larger and more prodigal mysteries about us, a reckless fever for adventure which is not unacquainted with the exhilarations of anarchy, that headlong yawping glee of the frontier for the far, unknown, windy margins of life, a second half of us most tellingly intimated by our lyricists and mystics like Whitman, Twain, Woody Guthrie, Kerouac, Thomas Wolfe, Hemingway. And all of our history, all of our past — from Salem through Shays's Rebellion to the Wobblies, from John Brown through Sacco and Vanzetti to Vietnam — could be read as the unending violent reenactments of that unresolved schizophrenia in the American psyche, our long and continuing travail with that primal mystery of who we actually are and what we are for: our meaning.

It remains, in the end, the immemorial dramatic game, as old as Othello and Don Quixote and Oedipus — the everlasting mirror-play between reality and illusion, innocence and evil, life and emptiness. And it continues to be the most desperately critical game in which we are ever engaged.

As he sits slumped in a wingback chair in his office, talking on in a slow muted husking voice now at the end of the day with a clock ticking discreetly somewhere, shadows of the cedars outside noiselessly stir and float in the white gauze curtains behind him, murmur in the long declining light of the late afternoon.

— I just couldn't understand it. I still can't. I thought he was a man of great integrity, I looked upon him as the possibility of leading this country to its greatest and best days. And all those people around him, they seemed to me so clean, family men, so clean-living. Sometimes, when I look back on it all now, it has the aspects of a nightmare. . . .

I

The Beginnings

OVER THE HORIZONS of Charlotte now, blank geometries of concrete and glass and asphalt have long effaced the old wilderness of the Cherokees into which the first of his people filtered — somewhere among those anonymous drifts of dour cadaverous Celts and Gaels who sifted like wind-strewn thistle down into the middle Carolinas before the Revolutionary War, themselves stragglings from those gaunt apparitions at Culloden who had come running and wailing out of the fog at the King's cannoneers and musketmen with nothing but rakes and scythes. They had brought over with them from the chill sleets of Skye and the Hebrides a wintry and implacable Calvinism as harsh and bitten as the wastes out of which they had wandered. But the countryside around Charlotte into which they grafted that fierce righteousness — a damp green midlands of mild hills and soft blowing light and fine indefinite rains — has long since vanished into a shadeless mica-glitter of shopping centers and office parks and car lots strung in a thin flickering of plastic pennants, scattered far with the white spires of colonial red-brick sanctuaries where, each Sunday, in place of that old baleful theology of their progenitors, manicured and carnationed young pastors in horn-rimmed glasses, resembling bank managers or suburban florists, deliver brief inspirational devotionals and bulletin recitals of upcoming church-league bowling matches. All that is left now of the tangled woods once of pine and hickory and red oak are scrappy shreds engulfed in kudzu at the back of the Village Hermosa Apartments, behind the rear lot of the Giant Genie Supermarket, from which possums scuffle forth at night to rummage in the dump bins. Out at the Charlotte airport, a ceaseless whine and shrill of jets passes rushing low over the power lines and Majik Marts, where, back in a time that seems as remote now as some preglacial age, there once nestled the cornfield and orchard of one of his grandfathers.

I

That was his mother's father, Ben Coffey, a tall and pallid man with brown calflike eyes, subdued and scant of word, who in 1861, a youth of nineteen, had dutifully enlisted himself off his father's modest homestead into the Eleventh North Carolina Regiment of Pettigrew's Brigade — leaving behind his sweetheart, a stout and equally placid-humored girl named Lucinda Robinson. By the summer of 1863, he was writing home in a ragged penciled scrawl, "Dear farther . . . I feel very well only my feet is rightly smartly blistered we commenced our martch on the 11 and have been martching ever since. . . . we have passed where there has been some large battles fought there is grave yards every where along the road and agreat many horses some places the men feet or hand you can see not buried more than 3 or 4 inches deep the weather is very warm and dry an the roads are very dusty I never saw the like of waggons you can see waggon for miles. . . ." Thirteen days later, under a hot sun around three o'clock in the afternoon, trampling up a tawny slope at Gettysburg in the midst of a stampeding charge among wild yelps and a clapping of rifles, he suddenly toppled. A week later, from somewhere in Maryland, he wrote with a cramped and agonized laboring of a pencil-stub across lined paper, "Dear farther I seat my self this morning to let you no how I am getting along. I am very severely wounded in the left leg it doant look like it will ever get well any more an have avery severe wound above my right eye caused by a shell I think it will cause my eye to go out an cant see any at this time. . . . I was thinking if I was over about Richmond or somewhere probably you could send after me but I am so far from home it is no use to talk about getting home. . . . it may be it will have to cut of if you never get to see me it may be you will see some one who cand give you some satisfaction about me . . ." his blurred scrawl now failing, falling down through the lines of the paper as if from the mere effort and breathless pain of writing itself, "I will rite again if I am able you truly B M Coffey give my love to all." Then, in the beginning of autumn, he wrote, "My leg is doing very well at this time it is taken of just below the knee. . . . my eye is entirely well an is closed I miss it very mutch but nothing like I do my leg." He was in a hospital in Virginia now, where he remained until the next winter — a former female college converted into a casualty ward where, it was noted over half a century later in his newspaper obituary, "he was kindly treated . . . especially by a young widow, Mrs. Mary Lee."

When he finally returned home, stump-legged, one eye blotted out, he passed the rest of his years, after that one awesome blazing instant on the slopes of Gettysburg, in an unalleviated and methodical sedateness, sedulously tending to his meager forty-five acres of vegetables and fruit trees with a single mule and one black hired man, never uttering anything afterward of the terror and ferocity through which he had passed other than an occasional dry complaint about having had to eat raw fatback once. One of his daughters would insist years later, "He had more ambition in him than a totally whole man would have." Yet it was not until 1880, when he was almost forty and Lucinda now well into her thirties — as if, after coming back marred and incomplete, it took the progression of fifteen more years before he could finally bring himself to again trust her affection and value of him enough — that he at last entered into marriage with her: her granddaughters still have the nightdress that, after all those patient static years of waiting, she wore on her wedding night, a plain, almost austere white cotton gown primly stitched with a long series of buttons up to the neck. She was installed with him then for the rest of their lives on his farm, in a small white frame house perched on brick pillars with sawed plank steps up to a bare wooden porch, its few rooms with unplastered thin-slatted walls and ceilings painted a robin's egg blue.

There followed in time a succession of daughters, among them Graham's mother, whom Ben Coffey had intended to be a son and, confounded in that, doggedly and obliviously gave her the name he had selected anyway: Morrow. . . . Finally on a warm May evening in 1915, "after two years of failing health borne with patience," as the local newspaper recorded, he died. No photographs of him have lasted — only a few dimly recollected glimpses, among his surviving kin, of him sitting with his long cloudy beard under one of his pear trees in the middle of the afternoon, his wooden leg stretched out rigidly in front of him, his one eye contemplating with a remote bland calflike calmness the play of his grandchildren in the yard.

It was Graham's other grandfather, Crook Graham — named for some passing fine-frenzied tabernacle preacher in the scruffy little town where he was born — who constitutes the sole imposing presence to appear over the generations of the family's past: a tumultuous colossus of a man with a great bristling dark thicket of a beard and bleak blue-gray eyes like sleet, who was long fabled as the county's most spectacular unregenerate. He looms alone and unrepeated in Graham's lineage like some primeval pagan Goliath — profane and uproarious and uncontainable. Raised in a shacky little raffish junction just below the state line in South Carolina, he too had fought for the Confederacy, all the way from Fort Sumter to Appomattox, losing himself in it, one senses now, not without exultation — those same high wild mad yelps of Bonnie Prince Charlie's bedraggled savages that had been heard by the Duke of Cumberland's men at Culloden two hundred years earlier, heard again by Ohio and Michigan farmboys crouched behind rail fences as ramshackle specters the color of earth came flailing toward them with not much more than rakes and scythes, spent squirrel rifles and wired-on bayonets. When it was finished, he trudged all the way back home barefoot, living on stolen chickens and scavenged field greens, a bullet in his shank which he would carry to the end of his days.

Then, shortly after his return home, during that haggard time over the gullied land of the South, he abruptly removed himself several miles over the state line into North Carolina, a migration made in somewhat hasty circumstances which were murkily involved with his membership in the Klan. There, in an empty countryside of brush and pine and bright red dirt and honeysuckled creek bottoms near the village of Charlotte, he staked himself out a spacious farm of cornfields and livestock and orchards, lumbering together a four-room house of log walls, caulked and whitewashed inside. He was married by now, and proceeded to sire a weltering haphazard spill of children, eleven of them, Graham's father, Franklin, the eighth among them. But as they grew up around him, about his only regard seemed to consist of such fitful agitated notices as, when he spied young country gallants hovering at the edges of his yard as his daughters began to ripen, snatching his rifle from over the hearth and stomping out to the front porch to let loose great thunderclaps into the air. He attended to his farm with the same hectic and manic distraction. "He worked it — rather, worked at working it — for years and years," says one kinsman, "and never got anything out of it."

Instead, he lived in a private bedlam. It was as if he had simply been too long lost in roar and bugles and smoke to ever subside back again into the quiet orderly monotonies of peace. He was compulsively pitching himself into spurious and petty fracases around the community — someone finally burned his barn for him, over which he long abysmally brooded. Most of all, he engaged in monumental bouts of swigging raw savage whiskey, "the pure stuff, white corn," recollects a family member who lived with him as a child — a lady with a manner still, over sixty-five years later, of dull pained embarrassment at the recall of him, as if the outrage and mortification of him is something they still bear. "He was really a kindhearted man deep down," she says. "Nobody realized that. But he would endorse a lot of notes for people, and then lose them, just forget about them. Now and then he would put us all in a fringe-top surrey and take us to the Methodist church — except for those Sundays when he was drunk."

He would leave in his rig on a Friday afternoon for a drugstore in town, picking up there the large jars of colorless whiskey glistening clear as water, and then would reappear at his place in the sundown's last copper lurkings of light, "already drunk. The horse'd just bring him on back home with the lines laying loose over the dashboard, him just sitting there and already beginning to sing — gone." Lurching on into his enormous log-wall bedroom, he would then proceed to whomp and wheeze away at the pump-organ, bawling out "not really songs, nothing with any melody," but, to the organ's wild and inchoate bleating, "just singing out his worry, worries about his farm, his crops, where the money'd come from, sometimes about the war" — a blank formless caterwauling to himself, out of some inarticulate unknowable woe and blind grieving, that bellowed on through the night in the grimed yellow murk of oil lanterns. His wife would gather together the children and take them all to sleep with her in another room while it lasted, on through the weekend — sometimes, in the middle of those nights, he would blunder up with one of the oil lamps and go clumping, baying on through the other rooms of house, "and we would lie there listening to him, afraid he would stumble and drop the lantern and start a fire, burn the whole house up."

His wife is now little more than a faint and faceless memory as brief and tenuous as a light breath on a windowpane. One relative recalls, "She was always afraid he wouldn't ever get saved. She was praying for him all the time. She was a praying woman." When she passed away at last, her last words to her middle son, Franklin, were, "Frank, be a good boy. . . ." After her death, Crook Graham fulsomely vowed never to drink again. "But of course," says the lady who grew up in his house, "that didn't last long." He heaved on through a number of more years before finally, in 1910, collapsing — even his dying a long and turbulent relinquishment as pandemonious as his life, at one point as he lay floundering in his bed the chimney suddenly catching on fire.

In one photograph that still lasts out of that distant time, his clan is collected, fuzzily squinting, in some wintry afternoon under bare spidery elms in front of the paintless and weathered patriarchal house, with Crook Graham himself hulking high over them on a mule, wearing a black frock coat with a tieless white shirtfront, his face sunk in his fuming white Abraham-like beard, and his eyes — in this yellowed ghost-glance of that lost winter day — shadowed under his black top hat, hidden, unseeable. He still remains the solitary being of any larger and

lustier mystery in the generations before Billy, the only instance
in his blood-past of someone given to the old, darker, reckless
furies of life.

Of his three sons, his eldest, Tom, was the closest take of him,
oversized and blusterous and impatient. Perhaps for that reason,
as if quickly sensing insupportable pressures in occupying the
same county or even the same state as his father, he removed
himself out to Oklahoma, married a part-Cherokee woman
there, and promptly became rich in ranching and oil. Billy himself still remembers his returning to their place once: only a
small boy then, he gazed at him enthralled — "He was big as a
giant. He spoke with authority. He had gone out there and married this Cherokee Indian and made a fortune in cattle and cotton and oil, and he came back home in the biggest automobile
any of us had ever seen."

But Franklin, the middle son, Billy's own father, was a surpassingly muted and unassertive soul. Says one family member,
"What Frank did most while his daddy was still alive was just sort
of generally stay out of his way." In fact, he could not have
seemed more alien to the bombasts of his father. A long, lean-
strapped youth with a bony, mildly musing face and a loose
abashed grin in the few smoggy snapshots of him from that time,
he was scrupulously measured and unassuming of temper —
seemingly spare of any passions other than a kind of general
abiding politeness. As he once pleasantly allowed, "I never hated
anyone." Whatever aspirations he himself entertained were
somewhat sere and minimal. Having passed perfunctorily
through only three grades at the local Lizard Hill school, just
enough to come by a bare initial inkling of reading and writing,
he then quit forever.

Even so, when the farm devolved to him and his younger
brother, Clyde, "it was Frank," says one of his kinfolk, "who immediately seemed to take over and manage things. It just sort of
turned out after a while that Clyde was working under Frank."
And before long, Crook Graham's shabby and neglected four
hundred acres were transformed, under Franklin's hand, into
sleek plump tidy pastures, neatly combed stands of corn, all

snugly stenciled in fences and tree-breaks. He prospered spankingly — a diligent and self-contained young country bachelor,
careful and sober, the sole indulgences he allowed himself being
an occasional small wad of chewing tobacco, a cigar now and
then at certain headier moments, and in time, a snappy buggy in
which he clopped and glittered about the countryside: a spiffy
affair, with a sleek black leather canopy stretched taut as a kite,
trace poles varnished a brilliant Christmas red. It was the single
considered extravagance, the one calculated flair and vanity that
he allotted himself — hitching it to one of his two horses, a chest-
nut and a mottled gray, both of them, a friend attests, "very
high-steppin' numbers." And it was in this dapper rig that, when
he was twenty-two years old, around the time of his father's
demise, he came flickering out of a calm lilac summer twilight at
a Charlotte lakeside park where Morrow Coffey, visiting at a
friend's house in town, had come after supper to see the lake
grounds with the lights on.

Morrow had grown up, on her father's small farm, as a decorously modulated and dutiful girl, precise of manner and cultivated in devotion and the Scriptures. She had gone on briefly
to a female academy in Charlotte, where she was further tutored
in such nicities as "expression," comportment, piano, and
voice — a grave young lady with a certain chaste vanilla fresh-
ness about her, light and trim as a willow wand, with a fragilely
handsome face. She was wearing, this summer evening, a gown
of vapory lavender voile, and it was here in the park's green
dusk, dappled with globes of light, and with a merry-go-round in
the small amusement arcade nearby twirling and piping, that
Frank Graham appeared before her, wearing a white Panama
hat — a cigar cocked in his mouth which he removed with a
flourish, tapped, and introduced himself.

Recollecting that evening some sixty years later, she sits in her
living room in Charlotte in a fading autumn afternoon with a
constant mumble of traffic passing outside beyond her filmy
panel curtains — a slight and wispy figure with cottony hair,
poised with a frail and rigid erectness at one end of her settee,
her gaze momentarily blurring off as she adds, "That outfit he

had on, those white trousers and navy blue jacket and white hat, that's what he loved to wear more than anything else. All his life, that's what he loved to dress up in. . . ." After they had chatted together for a while, he took her for a short turn over the lake in a boat, and then for a ride on the amusement arcade's roller coaster — and at the end of the lifts and swoops of that ride he asked her if he might take her home. "That's just what I wanted to hear," she reminisces now; "it thrilled me to death." She had, in fact, earlier glimpsed him several times from the front porch of her sister's house in town as he came jauntily skimming past in his buggy on his way to the bank, and "I just longed to meet him." As they were riding now back through the cricket-stitching summer evening, he further inquired if he might perhaps call on her the next weekend. And from then on, once every week, he was transporting himself in his buggy the eight miles over to her house to sit with her, patiently clopping through summer dusks and autumn frosts and ice-rimed winter nights, on through the next six years.

"The Grahams were always a dogmatic clan," says an old neighbor, "and Frank courting Morrow like that steadily through six years proves just what a dogmatic people they could be." It would usually be on a Saturday evening, he dependably appearing in his natty white Panama and a dark blue business suit, however forbidding the weather through which he had come, and then, promptly at eleven, would take his leave. It was a courtship as deliberate and ceremonious as a Japanese masque, no more than a brief clinging of hands now and then, once in a while a kiss fleeting as a brush of moth wings. "It was all so wholesome then," she recalls. "That was back before the days of parking — we wouldn't have known what that sort of thing was back then. We didn't even know there was such a thing as sin in those days."

Some two years after they met, one evening in 1912, as they were riding back from town after listening to a soprano's spiraling arpeggios at the Charlotte Opera House, he had slipped his arm around her shoulder and produced his proposal of marriage. But it was not until four years later, in the autumn of

1916, that they were formally accomplished at last as man and wife. Before setting out for their five-day honeymoon in the mountains, she carefully tucked her Bible into her suitcase — "I just wouldn't have felt like a clean person without my Bible with me." On their wedding night, at last standing alone together in a bleak and sallow-lit hotel room, Franklin immediately had his bride kneel beside him on the worn linoleum and proceeded to conduct the two of them in an extended and slightly wavery prayer there by the side of the bed, "dedicating our marriage and our family to the Lord."

Two years later, on a bright windy November day, she trudged, heavily pregnant, a quarter of a mile with a bushel basket to gather some butterbeans. That evening, almost precisely as the high clock in the hall began chinging midnight, her labor started. It lasted on through the morning, slow and anguishing, on past noon, the wind outside sinking away, a fire in the room quietly rustling on through the long wasting of the soft blue fall afternoon. At last, around 5:30, just at sundown, she gave birth to a son. In the early evening, Franklin Graham was brought in, and he lifted him up and contemplated him for a long moment in the firelight, and finally mumbled in a dull and idle amazement, "He sure does work his feet already. Look how he works those feet. . . ."

Since that dusk of November 7, 1918, the house has long disappeared. Morrow Graham, sitting in the azure-carpeted living room of the brick home they later built — this dwelling now all that is left in an encompassing proliferation of apartment warrens and branch banks and office complexes — explains, "He was born right over there where the IBM building is now."

Franklin Graham's conversion had taken place ten years before his marriage. He may have been the most circumspect of creatures, but disembodied charges of sheer guilt still hung so muggily in the general religious weathers over those communities then that, by the time he was eighteen, he had somehow contracted the sensation, sourceless and indefinite but unbearable, that he'd "committed the unpardonable sin," as he later de-

scribed it. It was an oppressiveness occasioned, as much as anything else, by his simple failure to connect in the altar calls to
penitence at a local revival, conducted by three grizzled Confederate veterans in a raw-carpentered tabernacle near the fringes
of Charlotte. An old acquaintance of his recounts, "The first
meeting he attended, he got under conviction and went down
front. They prayed with him, but he just couldn't get the message clear — couldn't feel himself forgiven by the saving grace of
the Lord. He prayed and prayed, but he just couldn't pray
through. He kept that up for nine straight nights." Frank Graham himself later admitted, "I didn't want to eat or drink. . . . I
don't think I'd have even picked up a five-dollar bill if I'd saw it
laying on the sidewalk." Finally on the tenth night, as he was riding in his buggy to the tabernacle again through a moon-mazed
Friday evening, like a small soft combustion of release, it happened — as simply and suddenly, as he recalled it later, as a
sneeze: "Just as I turned off Park Road onto Selwyn, God
saved me. When I turned that corner, the light from heaven
broke over my soul, and a great burden just rolled off my heart."

Whatever, the rest of Frank Graham's life, after that one quiet
puff of exaltation, was conducted in a relentlessly orderly respectability. His older son, Billy, would later reflect, "I never once
heard him use even a slang word, much less a profane one" — an
abstemiousness whose formidable constrictions would, in themselves, have imparted to Billy a monumental sense of the seemly,
the nice. Even while working in his fields, plowing behind his
mules and later manning his tractor in dust and sun-glower, he
would always wear a tie and a felt hat tugged down firmly and
perfectly level over his eyes. Once, recalls one of his old tenants,
"he decided he didn't want any smoking on his place. We all had
to quit smoking there for a while — even his brother Clyde, he
made him stop too. Clyde would have to slip around all over the
place, sneaking himself smokes behind sheds and trees and little
bushes all day long."

He presided as austerely over his household, abjuring any trivial embellishments in their lives of luxuries or mere whimsical
diversion, abstaining even from letting them know the extent of

his steadily accumulating prosperity. In 1933, he lost all his savings in a bank's collapse — some $4,000, "quite a sum in those days," says Billy, "and it caused him to live in discouragement for months." Before that ambush, as one friend puts it, "he and Morrow were just nominal churchgoers, but after that bank thing, they began holding Bible meetings in their house, that's when they really began to lay hold of deeper spiritual truths." At the least, it served to introduce even more of an asperity into the household. The black cook, Suzie, kept a glass jar of penny candy tucked away out on the back porch in a paper sack because, says a neighbor, "she didn't feel those children got enough sweets."

As his circumstances eventually became more substantial again, he indulged himself now and then in certain snipped little witticisms, but for the most part, testifies an old acquaintance, "there just wasn't a whole lot of levity in him. He was a right tight old Scotsman, actually, dry and proper as a persimmon." Most of his tenants were white, living in a few slatternly frame houses out beyond the barn, and one of them remembers, "I only had me thirty minutes in the middle of the day for dinner. But during tractor time, planting time, if I went back to the house to eat dinner, Mr. Graham wouldn't say anything, he'd just climb up there on the tractor and drive it himself until I was through. It kinda made it hard to really enjoy your food, I mean, having to sit there hearing him out there gunning that tractor back and forth waiting for you to finish." He was "absolutely straightbacked," declares a family friend. When he was cutting lumber once with a circular saw, "a knot of green gum hung and flew out and hit him in the mouth," relates his younger son, Melvin, "knocked his whole lower face apart, knocked out all but his eyeteeth, broke both jaws, the roof of his mouth fell down on his tongue. The surgeon who operated on him said he'd never seen a man hurt that bad; it ought to have killed him. But he just got back up and walked across the road to his brother's place and got him matter-of-factly to drive him to the hospital."

But as one former farmhand reports, with an admiring cackle,

"Man wanna cheat Frank Graham, he'd have to get up mighty early in the morning, yessir. Man'd have to go some, be busy twenty-six hours a day to get any edge on Mr. Frank. He didn't miss many licks, nosir. Back during the war, we worked a bunch of Germans out there on the place — he'd heard there was a P, O, W camp full of 'em down in Monroe, so he went down there one morning and worked out some kinda deal, and we started bringing a load of 'em up every morning and taking 'em back every night, working 'em hauling hay and gathering corn and picking beans. They was crazy, they didn't have enough sense to stop work every once and a while and get out of the sun, so he had to take 'em off of it and put 'em over in the shade for a while so they could cool. He used 'em on must of been several months. Nosiree, he didn't let much get by him." Grady Wilson, a friend of Billy's then who would eventually become one of his closest associates, acknowledges, "Mr. Graham's word was his bond, but he was awfully astute too. He was right astute, for instance, on that water-line business — he somehow managed to persuade the city to run a water line out to his place, and then he turned around and charged everybody along it about a hundred dollars to tap in. He'd go down there to those car auctions, bid on cars, and he wouldn't even move 'em off the lot after he bought 'em; he'd turn right around and sell 'em to somebody else for twenty percent profit." His younger brother, Clyde, was still living across the road from the main house occupied by Frank Graham and his family, "and it wasn't long," says one resident of the community then, "before Clyde's wife saw the handwriting on the wall. She knew if she didn't do something, Frank was going to wind up with the whole thing, the whole farm. So she insisted that papers be drawn up and the property clearly divided between them."

Despite Frank Graham's unremitting piety ever since his buggy-conversion at eighteen, Billy recollects now that "there never seemed a real joy of salvation in him. Instead, my father just always seemed weighed down with worry. I can still remember his worry. As I look back, I remember my father would stare a lot — stand in front of a window just staring into space."

As a matter of fact, declares a former neighbor, "he had reasons to worry. There were things in Frank's life that weren't exactly right. Those poor tenants who worked on his place, he hardly paid them anything at all, it was really shameful." One of them, a slow heavy man now living in a small house in a cluttered neighborhood, submits, "We stayed out there twenty-one years. Twenty-one years —" He sits heaped on his narrow couch, his bulky ankles bagged in white socks over his clumpish black shoes, the room slightly sour and overheated from a large oil burner in the corner. "I done my work while I was there, I didn't try to beat. And they was good to me, they was good to my family. But finally, I went on to the pipe company — I had to. I still wasn't making but sixteen dollars a week. But with the pipe company, I could make in about a day what I'd made in a week with Mr. Graham." Beyond that, his former neighbor maintains, "Frank Graham was always just a little too sharp in his business dealings. Like when he heard that Esso was thinking about putting up an office building on that property he co-owned with Guy Carswell. What he did was quickly buy out Carswell, without ever mentioning that particular little bit of information he had happened on."

But at the same time, he continued through the years to anguish quietly and dully about the state of his soul, his exact spiritual standing. "I can remember many times at church or Christian businessmen's meetings," says Billy, "when he was called on to lead in prayer, he would stand up there praying and the tears would start coming down his cheeks." But whatever dim dread lurked in his bones, whatever intimations of some final emptiness he would gaze into those times he stood staring out of a window, it was a woe he never once mentioned to his wife. Instead, he would sit for long hours in a car with his brother-in-law, a bespectacled and feverishly pentecostal bookkeeper named Simon Barker, and, with Billy lying in the back seat listening to them, Frank Graham would exhaustively fret about his actual state of redemption as Barker labored to reassure him. But it was an unease in him that could not seem to be assuaged. "He was always bothered, always jumping around from one church to another," an acquaintance says.

The truth is, for many years he had nurtured a vague private fancy that he himself had actually been meant to preach, to serve some call from the Lord. The night of his conversion, as he later told it, "the preacher saw me down there at the front, and he got up on the platform and said to everybody, 'This man is going to preach someday.'" From that instant on, he was afflicted with a secret suspicion of a brave possibility for himself in the future. Then, when his first son began to gain his own celebrity as an evangelist, Frank Graham's old lingering failed expectation mutated into something like a Joseph fixation: he began to consider that he was being realized, fulfilled at last, in his son. Sometime around 1951 he proposed, "My mind has been made clear on a matter which has bothered me for forty-five years. Now I feel I have the answer. The Lord had other plans for me — he put me out to plowing corn and milking cows, because my part was to raise a son who in due time would preach the gospel all over the world." This enlightenment, he said, "dawned on me when a letter came to me from the editor of the Boston, Massachusetts, *Post* — saying that no one had ever drawn as many people in that city as Billy. After I finished reading that letter, I felt that the Lord was with my boy. My burden to preach was lifted, and I now felt God had used me to give him a son."

Despite that, through all his life it was as if he and that son inhabited two separate dimensions, were caught on opposite sides of some invisible barrier like figures sealed behind plate glass, through which they only beheld each other soundlessly moving and gesturing. In the end, whatever larger gratifications Billy's work afforded him, "Daddy still never could really understand," says one of his daughters, "anyone who wanted to do anything other than physical labor." Instead, he always seemed comfortably closer to his second son, Melvin, born five years after Billy. "Now you take Melvin," he would insist on through the years of Billy's fame, "he's a powerful good dairy farmer.

He's also doing what the Lord intended him to do. He's just the same kind of Christian boy as his brother."

Over the long course of Billy's prominence in the popular eye, Melvin Graham has remained a rather solitary and inconspicious soul, a bit halting and ungainly whenever negotiating one of his infrequent appearances in public: "Whenever we'd be somewhere together," he once confided, "Billy would have to introduce me so people'd realize I was there." A chunkier, thicker figure given to the plodding deliberation of his father, with blunt hands and a hominy-plain face and, at middle age, just beginning to bald with a fringe of tan hair rippling down to his stout sun-chapped neck, they could in fact be members of two different species, have derived out of totally alien elements, ground and light. Indeed, the difference between them in a way evokes that between Esau, thick and swart, belonging to the simple bluff earth, and his brother Jacob, pale and fair and quick, his mother's cherished. Melvin comments, "Yeah, Billy was always the sweet one with Mother, but she used to whip me about every time she was awake. She'd want me to go out and water her flowers. Daddy never did whip me much, but Mother whipped me about every day." Melvin sportingly allows now, "I'm five years younger, but to look at me, most folks would think I was older. I been pretty much weatherbeaten. But Billy," he adds with a hesitant smile, "he's got that thick wavy hair and that smooth skin."

One of Frank Graham's hired men reports, "Billy, he was around 'bout half the time. Billy didn't believe in work. Soon as he got old enough, he'd be in there in his room gettin' his sermon up. In one sense of the word, I'd have to say that I sorta liked Melvin more than Billy. I mean, we'd work together all day long in the field — Melvin was a man, know what I mean." His sole enthusiasm beyond work was to close himself alone in his room and, for hours, wordlessly heft and grunt away at weights with the steady dogged application of a steam piston. "You could hear him bumping and carrying on with them upstairs," says a friend.

"Yeah, I was quiet and liked to be alone," Melvin himself

admits now. "But Billy never could stand to be alone. He thrives on being among people. We could be milking or plowing or helping pick spinach or turnip greens — Billy was looking for a call somewhere else. He was quick at that milking, all right — he could milk a cow in about four minutes, where it takes most people usually about ten minutes. That was just how much he didn't like doing it. But me, I knew way back that I wanted to be just a farmer like our daddy was. I loved to watch what my daddy did while he was working."

During the war, just when Melvin was scheduled to follow Billy on up to a religious school in Illinois, he overheard his father telling a handyman — it not unsuspected by some later, by design — "Well, Melvin's going away to that school this fall, and I think I'm just gonna have to close down the dairy. There's no way I can handle it all with him gone." Mrs. Graham says, "Melvin had already been accepted. He already had several drawers of his undies and things packed in the suitcases" — but with that, Melvin calmly and methodically unpacked everything again, and informed his mother, "I wouldn't go up there for anything now, and cause Daddy to have to close down the dairy." It was yet another despair and exasperation he afforded her, perhaps the terminal disappointment. "It was a real heartbreak," she says; "I wasn't over that one for months and months."

So he persevered on among the cornfields and barns and feed lots with his father — every now and then in the evenings, sitting in his den with his crusted brogans on the floor beside him, holding a kitchen glass of iced tea or buttermilk as he watched on television a phantom image of his brother behind pulpit microphones somewhere in India or Australia. With the dissolution of his father's diary operation in 1959, he moved with his wife out to open countryside south of Charlotte to raise cattle on a spread there. Sturdily prosperous, he has now a handsome and spacious home, where they occasionally receive company over fruit punch and cinnamon cookies.

He will agreeably confess, "In one way, it was difficult for me for a long time to be Billy Graham's brother. I wasn't jealous of 'im. I just didn't particularly want to be involved with anything he had anything to do with. I never could get it out of my mind that people would automatically be making comparisons. It sort of caused me to withdraw into a shell. Truth is, I suppose I felt far beneath him —" again a little smile "— maybe in a sense I still do. But little by little, I came out of it. I began to accept a few little Sunday-school classes, became a deacon in the church." He also undertook brief sallies now and then into the public notice in antiliquor campaigns, local Republican politics.

Then around 1975, he sustained three brain operations. Before he was rolled into the operating room the first time, Billy leaned over him, and said, his eyes dampening, "Melvin — I just want you to know. I love you." And for Melvin's part, whatever intermittent dull resentments he may have been visited with in the past, he seems to have succeeded in wholly extinguishing. "I think he's just the finest man I've ever known of," he submits. "He's always been almost perfect to me. In fact, I think he's bent over backward to make sure I didn't feel left aside — like whenever I go somewhere where he is, he'll introduce me to everybody, and make sure I have the best place to sit." His wife will proudly bring out for guests two photograph portraits of Billy that he inscribed and presented to Melvin, one of them a theatrically illuminated profile, which he autographed, "To the greatest 'guy' I know my brother Melvin With affection Billy."

Still, as Melvin offered once with a faintly poignant amicableness, "I never realized how far apart we'd grown until the other day when I heard him on a radio preaching up in Chicago, and I was down here spreading manure on a flower bed."

That same final distance also endured to the last between Billy and his father. A businessman who passed the Graham place every afternoon on his way home from his office would tarry sometimes to chat with Frank Graham while Billy could be seen working in a far field, and he once suggested, "You know, Frank, I sure hope you're planning to send that boy off to college. He really ought to go to a good college" — to which Graham replied with only a short snuffle, a scowl. In fact, for all of his son's eventual feats as an evangelist, it was as if a rigorous ordinariness always remained, for Frank Graham, the truest righteousness.

Vigilantly unpresuming about himself and his own, he once snapped, "Billy's just doing what he's supposed to be doing. If he weren't, the Lord would soon clip his wings." As for himself, "there was nothing else in life to him," reports Billy, "but church and working." During the summers, he never returned to the house from his fields until after sunset. "He never played a game in his life," Billy recites now in a peculiarly flat voice. "He never cared about fishing or hunting or baseball, anything like that. Never went swimming in his life. He would just go out a little bit and wade. He was always afraid of water." On those two or three days each year when he would take his family to the beach, he would merely roll up his trouser legs a few careful turns above his thin tallowy shins and then step out just into the shallow skimming of foam around his ankles, standing there for several minutes straight and rigid, his hands pinned to his waist with his elbows winged out, abruptly turning then and striding out again back up to the hard packings of sand.

Indeed, throughout Billy's amplifying notability, his father always remained somewhat choleric about journeying anywhere very far beyond his own premises. Once, while Billy was conducting a crusade in New York, Mrs. Graham, sitting with her husband in their front parlor in Charlotte, mentioned to a reporter who had dropped by for an interview, "I went to London to hear Billy Frank, but I've said I wouldn't go to New York if he didn't go —" pointing then, with a quick little wordless stab of her finger, in the direction of her husband, who, from the chair across the room where he had been sitting with the upright stiffness of someone posing in a daguerreotype, promptly crackled, "It's all right with me if she wants to go. But I don't like to travel." As Billy was about to embark once for a crusade in Korea, Frank Graham inquired of him, with a small clearing of his throat, "Now exactly where is this Korea?"

Rather, during his latter years, he absorbed himself primarily in industriously haggling off to real estate developers swatches of the ancestral acreage left him by his roisterous rogue-centaur of a father — the landscape of wide pastures and brambled pine woods around their house gradually dissolving, in smokes of hot tar and a fuming dust of steam shovels, into apartments and parking lots and convenience curb-stores. In 1958, when he found one prospective transaction unexpectedly sabotaged by a technicality in a city zoning regulation, "he came to my office," a city councilman related, "with tears in his eyes." As Graham's attorney entreated council members in a private gathering in the mayor's office, "He either has to give up about thirty thousand dollars' worth of land, or get you folks to approve a variance" — which the council, at their subsequent formal session, obligingly did.

So he abided on through the years of his son's magnifying renown with a kind of peaceable and oblivious remoteness — a figure as lean and plain as a yard rake, with a long flattish face and narrow age-freckled forehead under a dim patina of zinc hair, a pale cresent above his brow from the hat kept clamped there all those summers, standing for occasional photographs with his flat slabbed hands clasped clumsily together below his waist with the formality of a church usher waiting to take up the collection. With most of his farm at last transmogrified into filling stations and office parks — he keeping only one mule in his side yard, explains an old associate, "because he just wanted to be able to look out there now and then and see it" — his chief occupation during his last years seemed to be passing his day ambling amiably among the tables at the S & W Cafeteria in the nearby Park Road Shopping Center. Having remained thin and hard up to that point, he began to acquire a bit of padding now: "He'd eat his piece of apple pie over there at the S & W twice a day, every day," says Melvin.

It was, in fact, the first shopping center to appear in Charlotte, and the cafeteria there became for him — after all the years of blank exertion in sweat-reek and grime — something like a suburban Shalimar of surcease and peace at last, a sanctorum with Muzak pleasantly lilting over the monotone sibilations of the diners among potted plastic greenery and walls of pumpkin orange. "He ate two meals out every day over there at the S & W from the time they built it," says Melvin. "He would have eaten breakfast over there too if they'd been open." After disposing of his own serving, he would then mosey about shaking hands and cozily chatting with the people at the other tables. "He'd be over there most the whole day," says Melvin. "In fact, he didn't come home any more than when he used to farm."

Melvin continued to take him there even after, in his seventies, he suffered a series of small strokes, successive little gentle dimming obliterations. After his third one, recalls Grady Wilson, "he still loved to tell those few little favorite jokes of his, over and over again. I can see him now, sitting there at the dinner table saying, 'He fought a good fight, but his razor was dull,' holding his fork with his hand just shaking, food spilling off the fork down over his tie." Finally, in 1962, in a hospital room early one hot August morning just after sunrise, he quietly expired. Only his doctor was with him — "I was over in Monroe," says Melvin, "getting parts for a hay baler." The doctor, turning him over to his other side, had asked, "Now, how is that, how's everything?" and in that instant, even before the doctor had finished turning him, Frank Graham was already dead — even as the doctor heard him softly sighing, "Fine," the answer released simply in a last toneless expelling of breath.

Whatever may have been his own distances from Billy, though, during his perambulations about the tables at the S & W, he had taken to introducing himself, "How are you, I'm Frank Graham, I'm Billy's daddy." And curiously enough, Melvin recalls, several weeks before he died, "when he was home he always thought he was at Billy's. He'd suddenly look around and say, 'Well, well, Billy's got a house just like ours. How about that. How did he get a house just like ours?' He seemed real pleased. He couldn't stop wondering over it. After sitting there awhile and looking around and marveling over this, he'd say, 'Well, now, it's getting too late to stay here any longer, I got to get on back home now.' " So Melvin would dutifully take him outside, put him in the car, drive him around a few blocks and then bring him back to the house, and he would mumble happily as they pulled back up the driveway, "Now. Now. Awful nice being over at Billy's, but this is more like it now. . . ."

Years later, Billy reported that one of his first memories was of his father trying to teach him to walk in a wide grassy field out beyond their house: "It was in the afternoon. I remember him clapping his hands, opening his arms, calling 'Billy Frank, come to Daddy. C'mon to Daddy, Billy Frank. . . .'" In a certain sense, it was as if he never really closed that space; they never finally met: they remained forever, in an elusive but elemental way, irrevocably strangers to each other. As Billy stood with his family in the funeral home, he finally turned bleakly to his sister: "I wish I could cry. I wish I could, but I can't."

Afterward, he observed with a peculiarly detached affection, almost as if he were commenting on the unhappy passing of one of his close associates, "He prayed for me faithfully. It always meant a great deal to me to know that."

After "Mr. Graham went away," as his wife politely referred to the event forever afterward, she stayed contently on alone in the house. At one point, she allowed the family to persuade her to move into a nearby apartment building, but she was immediately unsettled, after a life mostly passed among hard surfaces, by the meltingly lush carpets of her rooms there. But she muttered nothing — until, one afternoon six weeks after she had been installed there, her daughter Catherine dropped by and finally said, "Mother, do you want to just move on back to the house?" With that, she quietly began to weep. She was rapidly returned then to the home along Park Road.

It sits in the collection of offices and neon signs around it, a last quiet shaded patch of the old place remaining as if in its own private bell-jar vacuum in time — a square two-story edifice of red and purple brick with a front yard of magnolias and oaks, the backyard with an antique rusted gas pump still standing slightly atilt in the grass. Billy's old bedroom at an upstairs back corner now has paper shades pulled down over all its windows, masked to the Steak-and-Egg and Pizza Hut and bowling lane that, just beyond the gas pump and the grassy plot where the scuppernong arbor once was, have accumulated along the rear flank of her property.

She has passed her days there since her husband's death in a halcyon and unruffled solitude. She still receives a few visitors, ladies from her Bible circle and her DAR chapter, but they know to call on her only in the afternoon, and they are expected to take their leave by at least six. She spends much of her time in the mornings reading, principally religious and devotional fare, though she permits herself now and then, as she crisply remarks, "a secular book. I am not immune to them. For instance, I've read four of Catherine Marshall's." Lying atop a cupboard in the kitchen is a small polished pearl-handled revolver that someone in the family furnished her somewhile ago, but she has never touched it since placing it there. She still possesses — even now well into her eighties, dwindled and frail as a figure of match-sticks — a bearing of dauntless and doughty intrepidness not so much brave as simply heedless of any possible unpleasantness or embattlement or despair. She has maintained a strapping appe-tite: "Today for lunch," she will cheerfully note, "I had a big helping of roast beef, rice and gravy, black-eyed peas, and two rolls." On the whole, she declares, "I'm not at all lonely here."

Nevertheless, she eats only a few of her meals in the tiny breakfast room off the kitchen — "I don't much like anymore to sit down and eat by myself in a dark enclosed place," she says; "I like to take a tray and sit in some bright lighted spot, or in front of the TV." But most of all, she has found over her years staying on there in the house that "when you're alone most of the time like I am, time doesn't mean what it used to. You forget the hours, even forget the days sometimes." Now, more than any-thing else, she is fond of sitting in her downstairs bedroom-den on Thursday evenings watching *The Waltons*. "I love that pro-gram," she confides with a light smile. "That's just the way we used to be. . . ."

Actually, it has become the lore among some on her side of the family that her father, Ben Coffey, had grimly resisted her mar-riage to Franklin Graham, due to the scandalousness of old

Crook Graham. Morrow herself, says a member of the community then, "was, oh, so fine, so delicate. She looked just like Dresden china." She had her father's pallor, with caramel hair and sky-blue eyes, an ethereal poise always about her, and "at the church pageants she would always take the part of the angel," a relative reports. She will note herself now, "I may not have mentioned, but I was in a lot of plays before I was married. Five or six plays, I'd say" — adding then after a pause, "I would usually play the main character."

But after she was settled with Frank Graham on his dairy farm, it became her daily lot, besides getting breakfast on the table at 5:30 every morning, to chop the firewood, haul water, hoe weeds: "Mr. Graham worked so hard," she explains, "and he taught me to work hard." Nevertheless, says one of her daughters, "she went on teaching piano and voice for a while. She was very disappointed that one of us didn't turn out to be a musician. She was always far more sophisticated than Daddy — Daddy, he'd shave maybe once a week." Through the winters, he took to wearing long underwear that he would peel off only at the end of every week, toiling in it through the days and then sleeping in it at night, this particular propensity of his producing one of the few instances of tautness between him and Mrs. Graham. Billy himself reminisces now, "They just lived in two different worlds. He was always sweating, always sweaty. But my mother was the type who wouldn't even go into the sun. She thought a suntan was something awful. She was very much a lady. I don't even think she'd ever heard the word *sex*. . . ."

Fifteen years now after her husband's passing, perched neat and spruce on the sofa in her living room in a late afternoon, she still has that blanched pallor of alum, of years spent in shade, out of sunglare, her pale circular eyes fixed like two damp nickel coins behind her glasses. She keeps the front room here dusky and shadowless and cool, the drapes drawn against the flare and fade of the days outside — a parlor of brocades and satins all in a nebulous haze of aquamarine, aqua walls, aqua carpet, aqua curtains. "I've kept the house pretty much as it always was," she says. "Mr. Graham didn't believe in changing things, and I've always been happy with it like it is." For that matter, she pronounces — speaking with a precise deliberation in a small voice like a crinkling of tissue paper, her hands folded primly in her lap — "I've never had the feeling our life would have been different *if*. I've never had to worry about any *ifs* in my life. I wouldn't have had a thing different. I loved it just the way it was, and I still do today. I would not change a thing."

She dwells on, then, in the comfortable chrysalis of a lifetime's pat and comfortable exclusion of all other possibilities. Sitting on her sofa in the dulling light of a late afternoon, the house around her is absolutely quiet save for the minute ticking of a clock by the stairs in the hall: suddenly, the phone in the next room rings with a startling clangor — but she remains sitting perfectly motionless and unblinking, oblivious, the phone clamoring again and again over the house, but unheard by her. Her hearing has now waned into an almost immaculate, serene silence.

She mostly occupies her days with "writing to nearly five hundred people a year who write to me — shut-ins, elderly people, just a lot of people from Billy Frank's ministry." And on Sunday mornings, at the Calvary Presbyterian Church, she is conducted, with her Bible and handbag bundled in one arm, down the aisle of the sanctuary to her usual seat on the end of the second pew, and she sits deposited there, composed and unstirring, through the service — a figure with the arctic whiteness of a snow queen, formed seemingly of sheer soft frost and fog, in white shoes and white dress with glassy spun-sugar hair, only a single tiny flushed pink spot on the nape of her neck under her permanent.

To Billy, at least, she has indeed long constituted a kind of winter madonna of the nice, the pure. "When Billy was growing up, he would always be bringing Mother flowers," says Melvin. "He would cross the creek and go back there to the deepest part of the woods to get flowers for her, even up to when he was fifteen, sixteen years old. He was always the sentimental type when it came to his mother." Billy himself acknowledges, "Yes, every Sunday, after we'd been to church, I'd go out by myself and spend several hours finding wildflowers to bring back and give to my mother. My greatest joy was to please her. I always considered her a beautiful woman, refined and godly. In fact, the pictures of her at thirty-five or forty are not unlike the pictures of my wife, Ruth, at that age. To me, she was perfect."

It may simply be the compulsion of certain men, the sons of vigorous and cherishing and finely mannered mothers matched to ruder and withdrawn fathers — as it was with Lyndon Johnson, Franklin Roosevelt — to create themselves on an extravagant scale into what they grew up sensing, in their mothers' disappointment, their fathers failed to be. On Mrs. Graham's part, hanging now on a wall in her azured front room is an immense gilt-frame portrait, gently illuminated, of Billy in one of his more dramatically meditative and spiritual poses, and she declares, "To me, he lives almost a divine life. My doctor said there seems like there's a natural glow about him — which I thought was really something to come from a doctor. But you know, after he was born, I prayed that God would take him and use him. When he went off to school, I prayed that every day for seven years up there in that bedroom. I don't think it could be said that my prayer was not answered."

The only time, other than that moment of despair in the apartment, that her daughter Catherine can recall seeing tears in her mother's eyes, happened one late morning in 1968 when the two of them were standing out on the side porch, waiting for the motorcade of then-presidential candidate Richard Nixon to arrive to pay a call on them. When the motorcycles and limousines finally appeared twinkling in the distance, "I looked around," says Catherine, "and saw Mother standing there crying. She told me, 'I never thought that a simple farm family like us would ever be waiting out here on our side porch for the Vice-President of the United States to come and visit us.'"

II

Near the site of the house where he was born that windless November afternoon in 1918, there is now a small memorial on the lawn in front of the IBM building — an inconspicuous little octagonal plaza set under pin oaks close to the traffic beating past in the street, with a granite tablet in its center inscribed, *"Billy Graham is one of the giants of our time, truly a man of God. The force of his spirit has ennobled millions in this and other lands. I salute him with deep affection and profound respect." Richard Nixon President of the United States,* and under a bronze bas-relief of Billy's visage, the graven epigraph, *Birthplace of Dr. Billy Graham World-renowned evangelist, author, and educator and preacher of the gospel of Christ to more people than any other man in history.* . . .

But it was still then a paveless countryside of sloping woods-skirted meadows, orange dirt roads curling under heavy trees glinting an almost molten green in summertime, with the Grahams' plank farmhouse sitting in a grassless dirt yard kept brushed ruthlessly clean with brooms of dogwood switches. In the distances around, Frank Graham's herd of some hundred Jerseys and Holsteins grazed in a shifting patternry of russet and black-and-white over the glossy grasses of his ample pastures. It was never quite a matter for them, as Billy would advertise in later years, of "acres of hard red clay where my father eked out a bare subsistence." By the time Billy was ten, the family had moved on into their more commodious red-brick country-squire dwelling, with its white-pillared front stoop and indoor plumbing.

But "as soon as I could walk," as it seems to Billy now, he began a daily laboring, from 3:30 in the black starless mornings on through to dusk again, among cows and pails and stalls, in a kind of primal steaming mire of fodder, mud, straw, milk-reek, muck, cleaning latrines and forking manure. And during those first years, he would be bathed by his mother in a galvanized tin washtub filled with pump water that had become a milky blue — "We would all have to take baths in that same water," he remembers still with a faint wince — and as she rigorously soaped and scrubbed him clean again, she recited to him a Scripture verse for him to repeat, phrase by phrase as she scoured behind his ears, his thin bent neck, "For God so loved the world . . . that He gave His only begotten Son, . . . that whosoever believeth in Him should not perish . . . ," rinsing him now, scrubbing him dry and slick and fresh again with a coarse harsh towel, ". . . but have everlasting life."

He had then rather the pale, blond look of his mother, the same porcelain-blue eyes and sharply crafted face. They called him Billy Frank. In those years, he seemed merely a gleeful and thoughtless youngling of nature, full of a careless eagerness, who would romp barefoot among the cool dirt aisles of his grandfather Coffey's orchard rummaging himself pears, figs, apples, plums from the laden sagging boughs — all the ripe earth's easy prodigal bounty his to snatch and enjoy without question. He also moved everywhere accompanied by a ganging of dogs, goats, cats — "One point, I had twenty cats," he reports. As a cousin of his puts it, "Billy Frank always seemed to have an unusually easy way with animals." More, it was as if some vital part of him were detached into a special secret mute communion with them. "He was always kissing dogs," the cousin says, "putting his mouth on their nose. I even saw him a lot of times, he'd actually put their noses in his mouth. It used to make me shudder, but he didn't think anything about it." Once, says a childhood friend, an immense white wild cat appeared on the Graham place out of the woods, "white as snow, an albino cat it might have been, and it wouldn't let any human being approach it, wouldn't let any human hand get near to touching it — except for Billy. And it would sleep with him. While Billy was reading or doing his homework, that wild white woods-cat would curl up in Billy's lap and just lie there, purring. Beat all I ever saw."

But he had "an unusual fondness for those goats of his," Melvin recollects. "He fed 'em, played with 'em all the time, almost more'n he would other children. They'd all go trotting off after him in a bunch wherever he went, jiggling along behind him even when he was riding his bicycle." Billy admits, "I always loved goats. I don't know why, but I just loved goats." He would sometimes take them to a nearby quarry and lead them back and forth over the rocks throughout the length of a whole afternoon, watching them with unwearying captivation as they rippled after him light and deft as shadows over the white-glared spill of crags. Now and then, when his parents were gone, he would even bring them on into the house, happily ushering them in to flow and shuffle at loose random among the lamps and clocks and organdy curtains, as if he were simply unrecognizing yet of the delineations, demarcations, between society's orderly forms and the free rowdy play of nature.

As Graham sits now among the arrayed plaques and ranks of books in his office in Montreat, he muses, "I do seem to remember that I liked to be alone in the woods a lot once at an early age." If each person repeats in himself the life of the human race since its genesis, boyhood would be something like each man's primordial age of gentle barbarism at the beginning of his own long history, and Billy, when he was around ten, would lose himself for hours in the deep wild-growths beyond the edges of his father's pastures, far from voices and duties and the engine clatter of the farmwork. He would plunk robins off twigs with his slingshot, later with his .22, roasting them over a small fluttering fire and then eating them, smears from the bright beaded blood on his wrists. His consuming enthusiasm during that time was playing Tarzan, clambering high into the trees to lounge hidden among the limbs, suspended in light and leaves and air above the dull familiar ground's flat and heavy claim.

He would also lead his sister Catherine, and Melvin, and his second sister, Jean, along with their friends, back into those tangled green glooms, the last shaggy vestiges of the old vanished wilderness, contriving careful trails of tattered white flakes of paper to track their course through its shadowed mazes back out again to the tamed, ordered, fenced clearings of his father's farmland.

He was taken weekly to church, but about his only attention to that occasion seemed to be, in the few minutes before the service started and before his parents had entered, skulking low among the pews with a rubber band to twang paper pellets at the bonnets of matrons already ensconced there. But it was as if he had about him then some quality of an aboriginal moralness beyond all catechisms and hymnbooks. One of his first teachers recalls, "Once, I got terribly put out with this boy sitting in a desk next to Billy Frank, and I went over and slapped this boy so hard — and I'll never forget the expression on Billy's face. Such *shock* — he just stared at me speechless with those wide blue eyes. And suddenly, I was shocked myself at what I had done." Her act seemed to her immediately reflected and judged in that appalled apprehension of it in his innocence's astonished blue gaze. "I'll never forget that look of his for as long as I live," she says. "I never did touch another student of mine after that, for as long as I taught."

He grew up, though, in a regimen of diligent pieties in his household; by the time he was ten, he had memorized all the 107 articles in the Shorter Catechism. "We had Bible reading and prayer right after supper, even before I cleaned up the kitchen," says Mrs. Graham. "We all got down on our knees and prayed, yes we did, sometimes from twenty to thirty minutes. That was the main event of the day in our house." They attended an Associate Reformed Presbyterian church, a somewhat formal fundamentalist sect, where the congregation sang only psalms, their voices gathering after the groaning of an organ. On those Sundays, Billy was forbidden to read the comics in the newspaper, to play ball, to venture into the woods — the only diversions during that day being the perusal of Scripture and religious tracts, with Mrs. Graham collecting the children into the front room in the afternoon to sit together listening, on their radio console, to Charles Fuller's *Old-Fashioned Revival Hour* from Long Beach, California. But something in the vacant, arrested stillness of those long Sunday hiatuses communicated to Billy a certain inexpressible bleakness, a sense of limitless salt flats of monotony. "It meant I couldn't go out and play; it meant there couldn't be any fun or entertainment at all. I didn't like Sundays then at all. I dreaded to see them come."

It was a discipline of decorums — devised, it seemed, to insulate life against any disarraying intrusions of rowdy spontaneity or whimsy — that was implacably sustained. His father would sometimes withdraw a wide leather belt to apply to him, once when he was discovered with a plug of chewing tobacco bulging in his cheek, another time snatching him up from a church pew where Billy had been fretfully squirming, shoving him on out into the vestibule and there strapping him thoroughly. Over all the years since then, Billy maintains, what he still remembers most about his father is the feel of his hands against him: "They were like rawhide, bony, rough. He had such hard hands." In one instance, after Billy had gained some size, his father stood over him flailing away with the belt as Billy was lying on his back, and "I broke two of his ribs, kicking with my legs."

He was also occasionally whistled with a long hickory switch by his mother — "But," he says, "I never fought back with her." Mrs. Graham reflects now, "Mr. Graham was right stern, I suppose. Perhaps we were both a little too strict, perhaps we whipped them more than we should have. But it was just that we had to work so hard then, we had little time for anything else, we had too little patience. We thought that little disobediences, you know, were terrible things." In this moral dialectic — an inflation of menial errancies to proportions of the cosmic and dreadful — Billy was systematically drilled by his mother in such Old Testament verses as *"For we are consumed by Thine anger, and by Thy wrath are we troubled. Thou hast set our iniquities before Thee, our secret sins in the light of Thy countenance. . . ."*

When he presented himself for his first day at the Sharon community school — a single-floored construction of dingy brick, set in a bald dirt yard under oaks — his teacher recalls, "he stood there in the door, this beautiful golden-blond little boy, very quiet and watchful and very, very tidy." Another teacher then at Sharon school offers, "Billy Frank never got into scuffles. Never got mussed. Wore knickers — a very businesslike little fellow. As I remember, he seemed really unusually reserved and dignified and sober for so small a child." (By the time he was ten, at least, he had become perspicacious enough to note gravely, just as he was about to depart with his family from a Christmas gathering at an uncle's house, "Mommy, I don't believe we're taking home as much as we brought, are we?") The teacher continues, "I can remember particularly that he always made it a point to sit in the front of the room, just to make sure nobody would think he had anything to do with any of the rowdiness or misbehavior further back in the rows."

The one occasion during those years when he abruptly, briefly, took on in public a different presence happened during a school pageant in which he performed, in a tall smokestack hat, the part of Uncle Sam — suddenly he seemed possessed by an exorbitant, almost antic animation, a strutting and boisterous assurance. "I recall I was right startled," says one of his teachers. From his very beginning, in fact, as soon as he could walk, he had proved fond of producing rather outsized and spectacular commotions around him: "Once in the old house, when he still wasn't much more than a toddler," says his mother, "I suddenly heard something coming down the steps that sounded like a tractor or something, and I ran in there, and Billy had somehow managed to turn this huge dresser over and send it crashing down the stairs. It didn't frighten him at all. He just stood there watching it all with this amazed expression of delight on his face."

His misbehaviors at home were composed of such small mischiefs as slinging rocks at passing cars now and then, pillaging watermelons from a patch down the road. One of his cousins relates, "Billy Frank was always getting us into trouble, far more trouble than he'd ever get caught in himself somehow. He always liked to have us skirt just a little close to danger. We would climb the silo a lot, and he was always the leader in that. When we'd jump into the hay near the pitchfork, he would just laugh — that would tickle him if someone came near danger. But it seems he never got hurt himself." But more than anything else, declares one woman who grew up in the community, "he was just a little tattletale. If you want to know the truth, he was the worst tattle-tale then I have ever known."

When a visiting minister once dropped by the Graham house for a Sunday afternoon visit, Billy suddenly paused in his spirited caperings about the room, which had been regarded by the preacher with rather frosty glances, to pipe into the conversation, "I wanna be an evangelist!" — to which the minister replied, "Why don't you run on along, little fella. You never gonna make any evangelist."

But at school he was always curiously subdued, inert, self-enclosed. In one yellowed class photograph from that time, he stands off near one end of the front row, his hands stuffed into his pockets, faintly scowling under his pale strawy hair into the sunlight. According to one teacher, he would have to be taken outside in the hall before he would recite his lessons. "In the classroom, in front of the other students, he would hardly open his mouth. He was terribly shy and timid, it seemed to me."

His fifth-grade teacher professes, "I just couldn't get him to say a word in class. I remember once, he just sat there looking at me after I asked him a question, and I finally burst out in exasperation, 'Billy Frank, don't just sit there — say *something*. Please, just say *something*.' Not a sound. He just kept staring at me. And to tell you the truth, I just forgot about him after he passed on out of school. Then, I don't know how many years later it was, I saw him for the first time on one of his television crusades. I simply couldn't believe it. His whole personality was so completely changed. He had such certainty, and the way the words were just pouring out — I kept thinking, somebody's putting the words in his mouth, he's just pantomiming it out. I couldn't get over it, I kept thinking, 'Is *that* actually Billy Frank Graham? *What in the world happened to him?*' "

Among his first memories is a faint brief furor of Billy Sunday preaching once in Charlotte back in the Twenties. "I really have only the slightest recollection of being there," says Billy, "mostly of my father telling me to be very quiet, and of sitting there being very frightened." But for anyone assiduously raised in the religious atmospherics of small Southern outback towns like Charlotte then, all the terrible and mighty stageworks of the faith soon became almost tangibly impending realities — Judgment Day, that instant thunderclap of trumpets in a calm sky, Jesus and the angels spilling suddenly out of nowhere in a vast long slow tumble earthward to end the game; and of course Hell, a smokily glaring grotto of writhing bodies and wails and gnashing teeth; and Heaven, an everlasting sunlit Sabbath morning in Easter pastels with pink cumulus clouds and rosy-cheeked choirs. When Billy was fifteen, he remembers, he stood with his family at the bedside of his grandmother Coffey — she the patient and placid woman who had bided her time for a decade and a half until the maimed Ben Coffey trusted her affection enough again finally to take her as his wife. Now, over forty years after that, she lay dying in a dusky stammering lamplight late one night, shadows wheeling over the high room, when abruptly she lifted herself up from her pillow and cried, "I see heaven! —" Billy instantly froze where he stood, gaping as she sobbed on, "Oh, I can see heaven. Yes, yes — I see Jesus! He has his hands outstretched to me. I see Ben. There's Ben —" And with that, says Billy, "she fell back. And my aunt leaned over her and then said, 'She's gone. She's gone on to heaven now.' "

At the same time, one acquired, over all those Sunday services and Wednesday night prayer meetings at church, a kind of sensation of righteousness, made up of scents of soap and hair tonic and old varnish on pews and some ancient tinge of dust and a stale chill in corners and hallways on wet winter mornings, but more than anything else, the sensation of being pent with an unrelenting regularity in tautly laced shoes and starched collars, caught in the obscure machineries of a finally incomprehensible theology for which one was abruptly plucked out of the private happy pagan boyhood sensualities of wind and grass and dirt. But over the course of that endlessly repeated weekly lacuna of Sunday school and preaching, one became intimate very early with the clashings and smoke and titans and magic of those sagas of blood and wantonness and retribution captured out of time in the filmy tissue-leaves of the black leather-bound Bibles — those names, those figures like Joshua, Gideon, old thorny Elijah with his carnivorous glare of God's judgment startling King Ahab strolling in murdered Naboth's vineyard, all became as immediately familiar as names out of one's own family past; indeed, those very geographies, Jericho, Samaria, the caves of the prophets along the Jordan, Gaza, the Valley of Sharon, became a second invisible country of one's childhood, an alter geography in which one lived on Sunday, which became in a way more real and deeply sensed than the mundane weekday one. And in the spring and summer, those Sunday mornings were not without a certain fine, lyric exaltation, the congregation singing ethereal hymns while, in the pauses, myriad soft sounds of sparrows murmured through the opened windows from the sun-blurred leaves outside, with finally at that night's service, the great long haul of the Sabbath's ruthless abstraction again arriving at its close, its benediction, with the choir behind the pulpit singing with a slow and fading sweetness, *"Now the day is over; night is drawing nigh; shadows of the evening steal across the sky. . . ."*

Baptists and Methodists and Presbyterians collectively made up then what could be called the folk church of the South, a Calvinist commonry as plentiful and uncountable as grasshoppers over the land. They were like China: there were incalculably more of them than anybody else, and they tended to regard themselves as the center of the universe. One lady who grew up in Billy's community declares, "I never even saw anybody but a Presbyterian until after I met my husband." They generally looked on Catholics as a slightly alien and gamy folk — to all appearances normal and like everybody else, but furtively dissolute, given without qualm to toddies and bingo gambling, and even a trifle sinister, answering to a cabalistic third authority beyond the Bible and the Declaration of Independence. Denominational distinctions, a sober matter even between Baptists and Methodists, were never so grim as with Catholics: on his way to his own Presbyterian sanctuary, Frank Graham would obligingly take one young couple who lived on his place to their Catholic church every Sunday morning, but each time he let them out, he would gently suggest, "Are you sure you wouldn't rather ride on with me, now?" Episcopalians were beyond serious regard, merely effete country-club mutations of Catholics conveniently conceived out of some English monarch's balked lecheries once. The fringe fundamentalists like the Holiness, Nazarenes, Seventh-Day Adventists were generally considered somewhat overheated cults, if not faintly berserk, whose turf was the mill villages, the dirt back lanes of tin roofs and chinaberry trees. There weren't enough Lutherans around to matter. As for the Jews, they were an errant, melancholy lot who had let the Lord down with a consistency finally beyond absolution, and if He had it to do over again, the folk at Central Baptist and First Presbyterian knew the people He would choose.

They were, altogether, the elemental Protestants — sparse in their worldly indulgences and staggeringly earnest in extraterrestrial matters (which an uncommon number of matters were to them), maintaining a certain detachment from the actual muddy toil of history around them, but at the same time an excruciatingly conscience-stricken folk. They were like a people of the morning — energetic, simple, fresh, wholesome as biscuits and buttermilk. Their fellowship and diversions were confined for the most part to community picnics and softball games and church suppers, all staunchly chaste of alcohol or concupiscence, with retreats every summer up into that complex of religious compounds in the North Carolina mountains — where Billy years later would make his own home — for a week of hymn singing and hikes and Bible study and ice cream in the cool, bright air.

On the whole, back in those childhoods in the small, thoroughly churched communities of the inland South, one grew up among a people who seemed rather like displaced persons on this planet. All earthly beguilements they regarded from a more or less migratory point of view, as merely transitory and incidental distractions, ranging from innocuous to treacherous, in their passage through this world to a better land, the only land that counted. One Southerner who was reared in a Baptist household that, like Billy's, was meticulously pious in the direct daily old-fashioned sense, still remembers sitting as a child on the rug amid a gathering of church folk in the front parlor of his home one winter night, everyone around him sipping hot cocoa as they listened, on an old phonograph, to a slow and deeply chambered baritone, tolling, *"Lead me gently home, Father. . . . When life's toils are ended, and parting days have come, Sin no more shall tempt me, ne'er from Thee I'll roam. . . . Lest I fall upon the wayside, lead me gently home. . . ."* and, looking up at them collected there out of the black cold night into that small lamp-lit room, he suddenly realized, with some astoundment, that behind their bland and pleasant faces, their comfortable chatter and the clinking of spoons and saucers, they were all somehow mysteriously bereaved and discontent: who they were, their lives now, was not enough for them; they had some curious profound soul-pining for some other place and some other existence still far from them.

When Billy was no more than ten or eleven, he would sit on Sunday afternoons on the front porch of his Uncle Simon's house in town, listening to him eagerly expound about the Second Coming with the same febrile inexhaustible volubility with which he had travailed with Frank Graham about his state of grace for hours in the front seat of a parked car. "The Second Coming was always on Daddy's mind," says one of Simon Barker's daughters. "Sometimes you got the feeling it was all he was really living for. Before he'd ever make a comment on anything, he'd always say, 'If the Lord tarries —'" He was a neat, negligible-sized man with a bald mushroom-pallid pate, an accountant who wore crinkly salt-colored seersucker suits with his plain face printed with the harsh twin circles of metal-frame glasses. For a time he had aspired to be a doctor, but ultimately had to make his peace with a life working as a bookkeeper for the local power company. But he was also given to a certain strangled sentimentalism that had taken the form of a high constant thrumming religious euphoria.

For years now, it was as if he had been dwelling with his whole being in that verse from First Thessalonians: "For the Lord Himself shall descend from heaven with a shout, with the voice of the archangel, and with the trump of God: and the dead in Christ shall rise first: Then we which are alive and remain shall be caught up together with them in the clouds, to meet the Lord in the air —" he passing each prosaic moment of each repeating day, driving in the morning to his office and there at his desk stooping over the unending petty addition of numbers on bills and then breaking for his lunch, always in a quiet breathless expectancy of that sudden, stupendous, supernatural intervention into the unsuspecting commonplace surfaces of daily mortal existence: housewives instantly and tracelessly vanishing from their kitchens, children in a blink gone from their playgrounds, husbands from beside their sleeping unconverted wives in their beds at night, a heavenly abduction of the saved elect that would happen as an enormous unaccountable momentary hush falling over the whole planet, followed then by uproar and wails and tumult from those left behind. "He was waiting for it all the time," says his daughter. "He always hoped to be living when the Lord came. It was probably the most real thing in the world to him — nothing else in his life was as real as that moment he was always looking for." It turned out to be his fate, though, to die in an automobile collision at fifty-four. "Yeah," says Melvin, "Uncle Simon was killed on Labor Day in nineteen thirty-six on his way home from the mountains in a brand-new Ford. Man hit him head-on, he wasn't hurt at all — he was charged with drunk driving." About all that he left behind were a few of his religious tracts, all now brown-speckled and crackly as old autumn leaves, and a will, written in blue ink, on the back of a pink meter-bill form from the power company.

But in the years of Billy's beginning, he was a presence who became something like what Eli was to young Samuel. It was in the constant thrilling of his pentecostal fevers that there transpired Billy's first actual religious charges outside his own home — the first real takes on the blank film of his life's yet unemerged vision. On those Sundays on the front veranda of his Uncle Simon's house along a narrow quiet neighborhood street, with a hedge along the sidewalk past which occasional strollers floated back and forth, the two of them sat in rockers with their

feet propped up on the banister with Billy listening to his uncle — Barker's coat off and shirtsleeves rolled above his elbows,
his tie removed but his collar still pinned together at his neck —
unscrolling forth into the drowsing light-slanted air of the long
afternoon all that awesome imminent pageantry of Resurrection
Day and Judgment, the blasting trumpets, the pitching of the
earth, the splendor in the clouds.

But in the end, what was actually at work in that righteousness
in which Billy was seasoned was the old understanding of humankind's lot — lasting still from those dour Celts who brought
it over from the wintry moors of Scotland and Ulster — as an
immutable sentence on this earth of struggle and grief, mortality
an unrelieved embattlement, life itself inalterably unfair, ultimately imponderable, with all attempts to substantially improve
or to mitigate this immemorial human condition mere instances
of fancy folly. It was a vision as old, actually, as Aeschylus, the
ancient pagan understanding of man simply disguised now as
Calvinism. One Southern Baptist minister relates how the Mississippi countryside of his boyhood bristled with "saw-briars which
were considered part of the curse of Adam and Eve's disobedience, part of what we had coming to us because of somebody's
long-ago sin which was passed on to us, became our own. So this
is what you preach: life is suffering and sorrow and the beginning of death; we are all come forth like a flower and are cut
down; we are all of us of a few days, and full of trouble; all flesh
is grass, and we are all here dying together."

At the center of this Southern religious sensibility was a kind
of sweltering romance about Jesus, and more particularly, a romance about the cross — a dark gothic business of thorns and
midnight anguish and blood and betrayal by torchlight, with
nothing in the life of Jesus, including His Resurrection, matter-
ing to the Southerner quite as much as His suffering and death.
The Southern Calvinist Jesus was an almost Pre-Raphaelite figure of a pale languishing melancholy sweetness, with a tender
grave bearded face strangely like those thin doomed faces of
young Confederate officers that peer, already like unhoping
ghosts, out of dim flecked tintypes. The final and almost un-

bearable poignancy of Jesus to the Southern soul was that, from the moment of His birth, He was Holiness caught in constant crucifixion on a cross of flesh, all for the sake of "a wretch like me," as one old hymn intones. He always had rather more to do with Prometheus than Saint Paul.

All the engines of this religious mythos came into their climactic resolution in the flare of those revival meetings that boomed like brush fires over the South in the summer, where anyone who had grown up in those spiritual climes was walloped with the realization, if he had not sensed it before then, that he existed in the midst of a pervasive, insistent acquisitiveness — a soft siege for his very being. Whatever, one's true psychic baptism took place in those summer-night services reeling with contrition and exultation, where the issues involved were such guttural matters as whoring, drinking, gambling, dread, and brimstone, and where one witnessed elemental and terrific conversions — gaunt, whiskey-scorched, reprobate fathers brought back sobbing rackingly into the fold of their families, wayfaring daughters with peroxided hair slumped in mortification, as if dealt a blow with a cudgel, at the altar — while the ancient grand hymns pealed slowly and hugely in the smoldering bulb-shined night, exerting a tidal pull that continued to bring them toppling down the aisles, *"Tomorrow's sun may never rise to bless thy long-deluded sight. . . . Be saved; O tonight! . . ."* Few there were, whatever their heavenly standing at the moment, who would not feel their knees give in the great undertow of those hymns; at the least they left one forever after with a special lurid understanding of the nature of doom — " *'Almost persuaded' Christ to receive. . . . Sad, sad, that bitter wail — 'Almost —* but lost!' " At play those nights, in fact, was a heaving moral melodrama in which there was joined, in the hot yellow tragic glare of those light bulbs, the great everlasting struggle against the flutings and blandishments of all this world's flesh, the abject furious striving against the winsome and clinging clay.

Anyone bred in that strenuous abnegation of all mere earthly entrancements would later tend to have, whatever larger circumstances and urbanities he might suppose he'd attained, still a sense of being on the outside looking in, a mild wonder at finding himself a part of consequential secular matters. Also, he would find it impossible ever to sin with any grace of aplomb, would never be really any good at it. At the same time, one was left permanently with a special, if not slightly exorbitant, sense of the dark glamours of Sin and the luxurious exhilarations of Repentance: the dynamics of guilt, contrition, atonement became irrevocably a part of one's sense of life.

For Billy at least, it was a religiousness as endemic to those locales of his boyhood as jimson weed and cornbread. Charlotte happened to be at the center of a ceaseless barging back and forth of tent evangelists through the farm junctions and mill-towns of the Carolina interior, and Billy can recall that when one of them came packing in for a week or two, "most folks spent every night singing in the choir, ushering, trying to make converts of backsliders and the uncommitted." When a revival authentically took, suddenly began to brawl through the community, the term for it then was "it broke out." One aficionado of those times in Charlotte laments now, "There really hasn't been a big one since Thirty-four." Indeed, it is a tradition and mystique of those parts with its own constellation of legendary feats and mythic names, figures like George Truett, swart Gypsy Smith with his Admiral Dewey mustache, Hyman Applemann. When Billy was around nine, he was taken to see one of these broom-sage Jonahs, a great ramshackle gantry of a man named Cyclone Mack, with long haggard soot-black hair that flung about his shoulders as he reared and tossed his massive head, a gryphon's glower in his brimstone eyes under thorny eyebrows, and a voice like the cavernous foghorn call and bellow of some sea beast risen forth out of the unfathomed darks of another unknowable past. Billy could not have been more stunned if he had been beholding a brief visitation of Vulcan among the mortals.

As it happened, though, Billy glimpsed only a few of these passing gospel-boomers during his boyhood. All the sweat and seethe and whoopings under their scruffy moth-swarmed tents was regarded by the Grahams as rather vulgar and unseemly. He was raised instead in a sanctitude composed of the strictures of the circumspect. "We were never among the more emotional of the Christian people," Mrs. Graham stipulates. "We were just never that type. There are so many cults, you know, that are — well, emotional. That was not us."

But even within these sanctitudes around him, he grew up a glad and easy country princeling, his own world simple and bright and blithe. Tall and fair, with the straight lank hair of his childhood having begun to furl over the blue blaze of his eyes, he had the rangy, loose scaffolding of a young longhorn, and through the course of the day he would come clattering into the house, the back screen door clapping behind him, to grab a whole tomato from the crystal bowl kept on the counter in the white sunlit kitchen, with a quick sling of salt chomping it down on the spot. He was disposed then to stretch himself out simply and unceremoniously full-length on the rug in the front parlor where, says his sister Jean, "he would even carry on conversations with you, lying down there on the floor." Often, sprawled there, he would nap, taking himself drafts of instant untroubled sleep as easily as he might pause to take a drink of sweet water from a dipper. "Nothing ever seemed to vex or depress him back then," says his mother. Jean declares, "I remember him always being very loud. He used to carry me around on his shoulders and sing 'Polly-Wolly-Doodle All Day' to me. I say sing — he never found out what singing was, really, it was just a sort of monotone shouting."

He seemed then so inordinately and lavishly energied that, in his early teens, his parents actually took him to be examined by a doctor. One of his relatives asserts that "even way back when he was just a little thing, as soon as he learned how to work a tricycle, he would ride that thing fifty miles an hour up and down that hallway in his house. I have never seen a small child actually move that fast — I mean, he would *zoom* back and forth, his feet working so fast you couldn't see them." He ate with the same headlong milling glee — his greatest gustos being fried okra, roast beef, which he would smack down along with creamed potatoes skillet-sizzled with a crust on both sides, and then a dessert of Jell-O with custard. Even so, "he was so tall and skinny and awkward," says Jean, "that he would literally fall into a room when he entered it — fall right in sometimes flat on the floor." According to one friend, "Billy was always a little self-conscious about being so long and narrow, the tallest guy in the class. So he'd go around flexing his muscles all the time, you know, he was always wanting to get into these gripping contests, squeezing hands until the other guy gave." But as one woman who knew him then testifies, "He just liked everybody so enthusiastically that everybody had to like him. It was just this lovable feeling that he himself seemed to have for everybody. You couldn't resist him."

He was never a notably complicated or thoughtful youth, his grades rather faltering through high school. "I could see no point in going to school at all," he admits. "I asked myself, what do I need to know about science or algebra or all that?" More, it was as if all cerebration, all intellection and abstraction beyond the immediately and spontaneously experienced, were simply alien to him — almost as if he were one of those accidental pure specimens the Elizabethans called, in that ultimate and mystic sense of the word, a Natural. "Literature in particular gave him a lot of trouble," says one of his former classmates. "We had to memorize and explain this long poem by Milton, 'Allegro,' and he was the last of everybody to get it." He also failed French. But "there was never actually any question of his graduating," his high-school principal once admitted, because by now, "his daddy happened to be chairman of the school board," despite his own minimal third-grade literacy. Nevertheless, says an old friend, "in the eleventh grade there, Billy almost didn't make it. He had to take an exam over twice to pass."

Indeed, aside from his sheer effervescence, there hardly seemed anything auspicious about him. "Melvin was always motivated to farm," he concedes, "but I was completely mindless when it came to motivation." He counted as his most extraordinary moment then "when I shook hands with Babe Ruth once when he was passing through Charlotte" — he did not wash his hand for three days. In fact, his single most desperate hankering during those years was to become a major-league first baseman. But even in this one ambition of his, he proved not particularly graced or gifted, too tall and gawky for the game's quick hard nimble precisions — "He had a good reach," says one friend, "but that was about all, there was nothing he could do with it," and for all his lurching eagerness at bat, he kept flamboyantly whiffing.

He did eventually manage four innings with a local semipro team. "But about all I remember of Billy playing baseball is the thrilled and startled look that came over his face whenever he got a hit," says a companion of those days, Sam Paxton, who himself later went on to a semipro league. "He just didn't have the build, ability, something — his legs were so long and thin, it looked like he was made out of stilts. That's why he wouldn't play basketball, he didn't want to show those long skinny legs of his in those uniforms he'd of had to wear. To tell you the truth, he just wasn't the athletic type. He wanted to be, wanted it something terrible — I have never seen anybody with their heart so set on being a ball player. But he just didn't have the moves that, well, you'd normally expect — *strange* moves, I mean. He was naturally right-handed, for instance, but somewhere along the way he got to hitting left-handed. That's right — just no feel for things like that, it seemed." A number of years later, when Billy had begun evangelistic tours around Illinois and Canada, one of his associates then reports, "From things Billy had mentioned off and on, I got the impression that he had practically played 3-I League baseball once, that he could have gotten a contract in the majors almost. It'd just be little things he'd mention now and then, casually, you know. Then he came up here for a church conference we held one summer, and he played in this ball game we held out in a recreational field — and I was dumbfounded. I mean, he actually batted cross-handed. *Cross-handed.*"

But however imprecisely executed his enthusiasms, he early evinced a rather assertive disposition for fair play — for the correct way to act. "If things didn't go like he thought they should in a game or a swap," says one of his teachers, "he'd let the offending party know about it right off. He'd really preach to them out there on that playground, waving that finger in their face." It was as if any instance of bald orneriness or inequity instantly inflamed him. After a high-school basketball game one night, a general rhubarb broke out as he was conducting his date back to his car, and the girl remembers, "suddenly he went flying over that car, going for six" — simply disappeared, pinwheeling, into the melee. As Billy himself later told it, "I was in the center of it all, and when one big fella came at me, I found a milk bottle and was able to break his head open. He left screaming with blood running down his face. I thought maybe I'd killed him, but on that night, as I recall it, I didn't mind if I had." But as the girl recollects, when he reappeared and got behind the wheel of the car, he was only slightly rumpled and scuffed, lightly brushing off his trousers as he remarked to her, "They were ganging up on my friends." For the most part, though, whenever he found himself at the center of a gathering altercation, he would tend to loquaciously abstain from any actual fists and tussling. "Billy, you know, was a leader," says a former hand on his father's farm, "and leaders, you know, they never fight — they usually manage, if it has to come right down to that, to have somebody else sort of tend to that for them."

Despite his fascination with the apocalyptic panoplies arrayed by his uncle Simon, he seemed singularly devoid of any real inclinations toward the spiritual, the devout. The religious pamphlets which his mother persisted in pressing on him he impatiently dismissed as "hogwash." At the religious retreat in the mountains to which his family sometimes dispatched him in the summers, he principally devoted himself to such merriments as emptying pitchers of water from upstairs windows on the heads of the soberer communicants there. After the communion services at church, he would plunge among the pews happily flipping down the driblets of grape juice left in the miniature thimble-size glasses in the hymnal racks. At the most, he engaged in small playful mimes and mimicries of what, unwitting, would turn out to be his destiny, his first performances of that future realization consisting of lampoonings, charades of it — burlesquing the pulpit manner of certain preachers with histrionic flingings of his arms, great bawls and brayings, antic muggings. More than once, he acknowledges now, he had vehemently vowed to himself that he would "never become an undertaker or a preacher" — so did they seem to him then more or less the same thing, both occupied in conducting one on out of life.

On the whole, he was a consummately, larkily ordinary youth. On Saturday nights, he would ride whooping in a friend's convertible through the middle of town, a girl friend of his standing in the back seat clanging a cowbell. One girl who grew up with him says, "I never thought of him exactly as worldly, but he was anything but serious. He was the type who'd have an electric buzzer in his palm when he shook your hand." Of such yoicks and hoots was his humor, his festiveness composed: he was given to such japeries as smuggling stale biscuits and chicken bones into the jacket pocket of the basketball coach, setting a wastebasket ablaze during a school exam and then yelling, "Fire!" as he vaulted out the window.

It has since become a common rumination among those who knew him then that, as one of his teachers put it, "had we had any idea he was going to be so famous one day, we would have certainly noticed and paid more attention to him. But it was just inconceivable that Billy Frank Graham would one day be preaching in stadiums and running around with Presidents and kings and queens." All of his old friends from those days still seem, in fact, vaguely mystified by what has transpired since then. Sam Paxton lives now with his wife, Laura, in a simple brick house deposited on a treeless plot of lawn close by a highway out in empty spaces of sky and fields south of Charlotte, and sitting one Saturday morning in his paneled taffy-hued den, stabbing out successive cigarettes in a tin-wafer ashtray, he smiled, "Shoot, naw, Billy was just normal in those days. We were all just country boys who carried on a lot and had ourselves a lot of fun. Wouldn't the first one of us ever imagined he would wind up what he is today — including himself. None of that was on his mind back then, I can tell you that."

Perhaps his highest delight, in those days of Prohibition, was to load his friends into his father's car on a Saturday night and go rollicking into downtown Charlotte — then only an incidental clutter of squat flat-roofed buildings — where they would drag-race bootleggers up and down the main street. "You could spot 'em a mile away," says Grady Wilson; "they'd have these cars jacked way up in the back. They must have had a special immunity worked out, 'cause they didn't think anything of riding right through the center of town. There was one of 'em in particular, always drove this black and white coupe." As soon as they spied him paused with exhaust puttering at a red light — briefly materialized out of unknowable regions of the fantastic and illicit and violent, the coupe's rump poised high, exposing an underside spattered and clotted with the dried mud of savage careenings over gullied back-country roads — they would haul around and then ease up beside him, he a reedy little cricket of a man with black varnished hair, always attired with a gaudy outrageous dandiness, hunched to his steering wheel with a toothpick pinned at a rakish uptilt in his teeth, "and Billy would call out the window, 'Hi,' and he'd turn and smile real slow," and after just a moment, one soft beat of pulse, suddenly with a great racketing roar they simultaneously barreled off side by side, the back of the bootlegger's coupe riding still raffishly high.

But that was all. Beyond his occasional light mischiefs and schoolyard skirmishes and those momentary accelerations fender-to-fender with bootleggers on Saturday nights, he ranged no closer to any deeper heats of human experience. It has no doubt been true for all the sons of men since Cain that the first true tastings of life have blurted on the palate of innocence coarsely, rank as raw garlic, and even in such small Southern communities as Charlotte then, one could come by those old rude musks by way of a nether-precinct of roadhouses and honky-tonks and pool halls. Back in that age of villages in America there could be found, even in the most prim and meager township, at least one pool hall abiding unobtrusively on some dim side street with a kind of sleazy discreet indestructibility, a solitary quality about it of being one great knell of time older than all the trim white churches, the banks, the flags, the schools. It shared this quality with perhaps only two other places in town — the jail and, if there was one, the bus station: the same bare glum walls scribbled over with infinite graffiti oddly resembling Babylonic or Sumerian script, the same circular pacing of anonymous fugitive souls in a mugginess of weary harried unflagging human quick. Even for a youth from one of the genteel neighborhoods in town, where on sunny Saturday mornings there filtered over the picket fences from swiss-curtained windows the careful plinkings of piano lessons, the pool hall provided a clandestine tunnel-entry into the darker labyrinths of his more elemental legacy as a man, those other more ancient territories of mortal experience. In such places, there often was enacted one's first rudimentary apprenticeship in the root mysteries of the race: lust, desperation, unplumbable lonesomeness, compulsion and manic risk, ruin, defeat, but also indefatigable hope and belief.

But Billy himself existed in a matrix of mores immitigably removed from all that. As he explains, "You know, pool halls back then, they weren't considered respectable. There wasn't even any hanging around a drugstore as I was growing up." He passed instead through a kind of cauled nebulous youth, in which the weekdays proceeded as little more than intervening parentheses of the duteous and perfunctory between endlessly recurring Sundays that held in them some musty chill, like a whiff of old roses in stale water, of unflinching rectitude and abstentions of the heart, a propriety refined out of all the common welterings of the earth. If almost all the great prophets have had their abandoned and pagan pasts once, there was hardly anything ever remotely Dionysian about Billy's: he answered to all the conventional sanitations, did not smoke or drink, was chaste of language. Like his father, "I never recall hearing Billy Frank once use a slang word," says his sister Catherine, and Mrs. Graham attests, "That type of language simply wasn't known in my family. We never really had those kinds of problems with the children, any of them — I will say that as their mother." Any possible fancy for spirits was effectively extinguished in Billy when his father, on the day the county voted in beer and wine, brought home a case of beer and compelled Billy and Catherine to bolt down bottle after bottle, until they retched. The same astringencies applied to the reading fare on which Billy was raised — a collation of Biblical commentaries, religious biographies, periodicals of religious prophecy, an encyclopedia, and a few romances from Protestant publishing houses detailing the staunchly antiseptic passions and struggles and triumphs of male and female missionaries in the jungles of India and the Amazon. "I did read the Tom Swift and Tarzan books and a lot of Zane Grey," Billy offers. Other than that, says his sister Jean, "I never saw a real novel in the house."

As it happened, he came by his initial epiphanies on sensual matters — which his "mother and father were reluctant to discuss" — by way of a hired hand named Pedro Evans, who had wandered there from Spartanburg, South Carolina — a scrubby, vociferous rooster of a man with a dark soot of beard on knotty jaws usually pumping away at a clump of tobacco. Billy recollects, "He was a pretty rough character, but I liked him." Along with introducing Billy to the basics of spurting tobacco, it was also in the perspective of his somewhat glandular and baldly smacking appreciations that Billy's first illuminations on sexuality came to pass — "He told me all about his experiences with women," as Billy phrases it. When the elder Graham discovered these incidental instructional services being tendered by Pedro, he promptly fired him.

Some years later, at a class party Billy attended one evening, someone produced a jar of wine that had been cached in the woods out back. "I took a few sips," says Billy, "until I started acting foolish." It was a result that profoundly unnerved him, particularly in that harrowing loss of composure, control. "Afterward," he says, "I just felt so embarrassed, so ashamed." No further than such modest extensions, then, did he ever come to know, to sense, the mixed rife pulsings of life. It was as if he were contained still in a kind of spiritual amniotic sac, comfortable, no more than shadowily touched by the actual wonder and terror and exhilaration of what it finally, fully means to be a human being. As it was, states one of his sisters, "We never expressed emotion very openly in our family. I don't remember Billy himself ever showing any emotion back then like weeping or warm affection or anything like that." The only degree to which he ever tasted anything like woe, Billy allows, "was when my father would make me stay at home and milk the cows on Sunday afternoons. I used to have the feeling I was an oddball because other people could play on Sunday."

Instead, what affected him most singularly through the whole course of his youth up to his conversion were instances when he happened to be out of compliance with the common patterns of order — such as once "when I wasn't lining up right for the school bus after school, and the principal grabbed my ear and showed me how you were supposed to line up right." When he was older then, he had come to answer undeviatingly to the larger alignments and conventions of the community: "I can remember there was a colored barbershop downtown where they gave great haircuts, real cheap," says one of his old friends, "and me and some others started going there. But Billy never would. He told me, 'Long as there's a white barbershop in Charlotte, I'll never have my hair cut at a nigger barbershop. Never.'" As close as he ever came to experiencing any great moment of awe in his youth, he recalls, was when he arrived at a community picnic once, and "I'd never seen so many people in one place in my life, there was everybody from all around, must have been as many as five thousand people there moving around under the trees, talking and eating and playing games — to me then, it was like all the people in the world had come out and collected there."

But at the same time, even in the contractions of this existence, it was curiously as if he yet lived in some vast submerged undefined eagerness and expectancy that was far larger than his actual experience and sensibilities — some sourceless urgency, a gift for excitement, an instinct for joy, a simple blind avidity for life to which his own actual perceptions and sense of life were inadequate. It was a peculiar disjunction and asymmetry of parts in him — a disparity between his barging appetites and his actual capacity to experience. Many years later, one man who had known Graham propounded, "I've always thought there are really only two kinds of people on this earth — only two races: those who were born to live, and those who were born to just get it over with as comfortably and painlessly as possible. It's the second sort who tend to look for the payoff later. Billy wound up standing for all those in that second category." But the truth is, Billy would have seemed, in his beginning, rather of an indeterminate, middle order — one of those few spirits somehow hung, half-resolved, between the other two: half of life and half stasis. In that sense, he was actually suspended in an ambivalence of nature of the most fundamental kind.

Indeed, as he grew older, as if vaguely sensing other, larger magnitudes of experience beyond the closely pent reality around him, he was visited with a fitful amorphous restlessness — an inarticulable desperation, as he recollects, almost of claustrophobia, a dim sensation of being buried alive, "on that little farm, in that little community. I understood little, and resented my parents, my teachers, my humdrum life as a farmhand and a high-school student."

He suddenly began consuming history books at a ferocious rate, as if only in those largest movements of time and consequences might he find the possibilities for a self-realization absent in everything immediately around him — going through one hundred volumes before he was fifteen, disposing of ten over one Christmas vacation, sitting cross-legged in a chair "with those knees of his sticking way out," says a sister, gnawing away at his already shredded raw fingernails. "My mother bought me a *Book of Knowledge* encyclopedia, and I read all the way through that too," he reports. Whatever his bafflement before French and algebra and poetry in school, improbably he had dispatched Gibbon's *Decline and Fall of the Roman Empire* by the time he graduated.

Billy speculates now of that period of dull frantic impatience, "As I look back, I think it was wanting to travel. I wanted to see Philadelphia, I wanted to see New York, all those far-off places." It was a restlessness, actually, that had been primarily imparted to him by his mother's own balked fancies. "She had always dreamed of going to Paris, to London, to Vienna and the opera there," says Billy, "and she was always talking to me about those places, how she wanted to go there." But as for actually venturing herself anywhere significantly beyond the environs of Charlotte, says Mrs. Graham now, "Mr. Graham just knew it was settled in his mind that we weren't going, so there was no point in ever even talking about it to him, he just didn't want to hear it." Instead, she engaged Billy in her abiding wistfulness for foreign shores and far landscapes, until in time it became for him a mystique — the glamoring of remote locales — like a electric lambency given off by that gap of tension between his directionless enthusiasms and what seemed to him the meagerness of life around him. So stricken did he become by the romance of the distant, "I even used to wonder if the land in those places would look like our land — if the very earth, the soil, wouldn't look different there."

In one of the books his mother gave him, he says, "there was this picture of the Rose Window in the Rheims Cathedral. I never thought I'd actually be over there. I would study that picture for hours — literally for hours." It was as if that celestial corona of sun-dazzled stained glass became for him the very emblem, the heraldic sign, of those possibilities of glory beyond the prosaic perimeters of his own reality. "I just know that I kept feeling that something was going to happen to me," he declares, "something was about to happen to take me out of all that, out of the farm and out of Charlotte."

During this time of restiveness, he notes, when he would feel most vividly alive "was driving my father's car just as fast as it would go whenever I could." It was a rather staid dark-blue Plymouth sedan, but Billy, released in it, would go dusting wildly over moon-pale back roads over the dark and sleeping countryside, slewing around curves on two wheels, once or twice near the outskirts of town running taxis into ditches. In his excursions into Charlotte, he would occasionally drive a short distance down a midtown sidewalk, and once, as he began to swoop into a turnaround in the middle of a main intersection, a policeman yelled to him, "Hey, hey, you can't do that!" and he yelled back, "I think I can" — "And I did," as he told it years later. He sometimes raced friends in their cars along those forsaken back roads, and one memorable evening he clocked up almost three hundred miles.

But even this exultation was suddenly nipped for him when, recounts a friend, "during a break in a play practice at school, we decided to have a quick little race down the road out front — me and Sam Paxton in my car, Billy in his daddy's car. I had pulled out in front of Billy a good distance when I went into an S-curve. Suddenly, I was going down the road sideways on two wheels — I remember looking over and seeing the pavement going by along Sam's head. It was a real near bad situation. Billy, he was behind us and saw it all — and he just immediately turned around, never even stopped to talk or check on us, just turned around and went right on back to the school, it scared him so bad."

But as much as his elation plunging over those nighttime roads, he reveled then in "kissing girls until my mouth was chapped," he acknowledges with a grin. When he was about fourteen, he had taken aside one of his girl cousins and, in a kind of hushed, amazed celebration of discovery, whispered to her. "You ever kissed a boy? Because I've kissed a girl. I actually have. . . ."

In his father's Plymouth, he would park with them at a nighttime site that had become a kind of communal spooning ground, a long driveway curving like a tunnel through crepe myrtles in front of the burned-out hulk of a brick manorial home. And the next day, says a former schoolmate, "Billy would always tell me, 'Boy, did I surprise that girl with how I could kiss! She had no idea I was such a good kisser!' He was all the time bragging about what a great kisser he was."

For all his loopy gangliness now, he had acquired the arresting look of some young country archangel — a high flaring miter-like brow whorled with honeyed hair on top, with already those cavernous incandescent wizard's eyes. And there was a certain quality of vulnerability in his ebullience which peculiarly enchanted, endeared: "He was so tall and awkward and good-looking," one girl explains, "he just struck me as somebody honest and decent and very sincere." With something of his father's youthful appreciation for spiffiness, he dressed in Crayola-bright suits with rainbowed ties. "He always seemed to make it a point to be dressed a little snazzier than the average guy," says an old acquaintance, "even if we were just going to the movies or getting an ice-cream cone. It was like he always wanted folks to be able to tell he came from a nice home, a nice family." Indeed, the particularly commending effects of fine appointments had not escaped his attention. "He had this watch he was especially proud of," one of his close friends then, Wint Covington, remembers, "and he kept telling me I ought to get myself a good watch too. He told me, 'People will see you with a watch, and they'll think you're not really that poor, however else you might be dressed. That's the great thing about having a good watch, Wint.' "

Fully as effulgent as his raiment was his effusiveness as a swain. Says Melvin, "He was always in and out of love," and his style, when he was stricken, tended toward the swooping and moony. Sam Paxton's wife, Laura, who often double-dated with him, recalls that after he would deliver his date of the evening back to her door, he would return to the car and then sag back in the seat without touching the steering wheel, leaning his head back and soulfully moaning, "Oh. I'm so in love, Laura. There's no way for me to describe it. Oh, I'm so in love. . . ." But as Melvin maintains, "Every single girl he went with, he was always in love with her. He'd sometimes date two girls, one right after the other, on the same night. That'd mean he'd been in love twice that night. That's all he thought about. Whoever the one might be that week, or that day, he couldn't keep from talking about her everywhere. At suppertime, he could hardly wait for the blessing to be finished to start talking about her some more — how beautiful she was, what a great personality she had, what she had worn that day, how this time he knew positively he was really in love, this was *it*." When he brought one of them home to meet his family, he would labor elaborately, says a sister, "to impress her for us," producing such cavalier flourishes as suddenly snatching a grapefruit and, with a wink and a smirk,

biting a plug out and sucking it dry. When his parents once essayed to transfer him out of this dizziness up to a Bible retreat in
the mountains, he quickly dispatched a postcard from there to
one Charlotte girl, "I sure hope you can come up this weekin.
Billy."

But even in these gleeful disportings, he still maintained, in
the end, a vigilant circumspectness. Whatever wayward tugs and
swimmings toward any profounder rompings, he scrupulously
contained. He would later reflect, "Those were years when I had
tendencies to become wild and go with pretty girls, but somehow
I never engaged in sexual immorality. For some reason, God
kept me clean." As one friend presents it, "Oh man, he did date
those girls. But I don't think there's a one of them he dated that,
if he saw her now, he'd have to feel uncomfortable with her —
know what I mean?" Billy himself suggests, "I was just shy, actually. It probably wasn't so much morality at all. According to my
friends, I simply didn't know what to do. But I was just held
back by a force that I don't understand. I never touched a girl in
the wrong way, and I thank God for it. I never even touched a
girl's breast. The only explanation I have now is just providence." As much as providence, though, it was a demurral, a
refraining, that seemed to hint, at the very center of his being,
some final inertness. He would later offer, "The reason I didn't
commit sexual immorality when the opportunity became so available in my teens is because my parents expected us to be clean
and never doubted that we would be." In particular, he says
now, "I never did anything that I didn't confide in my mother. I
would come back from a date and tell her, 'Mother, I was with a
new girl, she was really pretty, I'd love for you to meet her.' If
my mother had said no on any girl, I'd have dropped her in a
minute."

One of those whom she approved was a quietly studious and
conscientious girl, now a teacher in a small college. A sturdy
woman with a severe scissoring of hair, she tautly announces, "I
was just kind of his good chum. We were good friends. That's
all. We would go sledding over the Sharon golf course during
snowfalls. We'd go possum-hunting in pairs, that was one kind of

date — we'd follow the crowd through the woods, and the dogs would tree the possum. We had class parties, and we'd play post-office, yes. We did all that back then, believe it or not. We'd choose a partner with spin-the-bottle, yes —" and abruptly she declares, "This sounds terribly silly, doesn't it?" giving a wince of a smile, as if suddenly ambushed by embarrassment at this lapse into the sentimental. Of another of Billy's sweethearts during that time, she readily acknowledges, "She was pretty, very pretty, very feminine and gracious and charming, had a lot of poise. Whereas I — I was very athletic, played basketball, but otherwise I was awkward. Which might be why I would have remembered all that about her."

But one seems to sense in her still some faint lasting exaspera-tion at his later infatuations with all those other girls — "some of the others were kind of fly-by-night" — and when it is suggested that Billy himself must have resembled back then a kind of young Gabriel, she briskly retorts, "No, he didn't look like that to me at all. He was just nice and sincere, it seemed to me. He was not very articulate, either. In making talks in class, he was not at all expressive or impressive, I thought."

She continues in a voice like a flat ring of ironware, "But of course, my own life has completely changed since all that silliness way back then. I never took it seriously. Oh, I do get a Christmas card from him now and then — his organization, that is, they send out Christmas cards for him, which I suppose he signs him-self. I'll get one of them occasionally, but I certainly don't feel it's personal. Of course not. I'm not silly enough to really take it seriously."

As it happened, throughout the array of his enamorments then, the only one whom he did not bring home to present to his mother was a slim dark sprite of a girl named Pauline Presson — and it was she, by all accounts, who became indisputably the transport of his life during that time. She was one of those bouyant young camellia belles of the small towns of the South of that era who seemed always possessed of a slightly feverish ela-tion — with extravagant brown eyes and long maple-brown hair and a certain amber lucency to her skin. Living now in a Char-

lotte condominium with her husband, a retired oil company avia-
tion manager, she is still a lissome woman with a neatly snipped
thatch of mercury hair, still with the splashy and winsome brown
eyes of her girlhood. "It wasn't that I was really all that pretty,"
she insists now with an aslant little smile, "but the boys did seem
to like me, I noticed."

At the least, she held a particular devastation for Billy. As he
attempts to reinvoke it now, "I don't know, she had a sort of
gypsy look, and just this tremendous personality. I mean, she
just knew how to weave the boys around her little finger, it
seemed like." More precisely, his sister Catherine explains, "Pauline was always far more sophisticated than most of the other
girls — in her looks, her manner. She was more citified. I remember her dressing real nicely, wearing more makeup than
any of the other girls. But not flashy. Just like a sophisticated
woman."

Her family was of the town gentry — her father an affluent
contractor, with a gusty ruddy-faced heartiness. "The Depression didn't bother us one whit," she says. "I don't think we ever
noticed there was one." In one faded snapshot, she poses beside
her black Buick convertible, lounging against a fender with an
elegant coy languorousness. Indeed, there was about her then
not a little of one of Fitzgerald's diaphanous young debutantes,
that blithe recklessness for the magical and romantic. "All my
family were musicians, but me, I danced the music instead of
playing it. They tried to make me take piano lessons. They
would lock me in that room with that piano, and as soon as the
door was shut, I'd go straight out that window and climb on my
bicycle and be gone. I would get physically sick whenever anybody tried to control me." She was only nominally and politely
religious. "Sure, I had my gold pin for fifteen years of Sunday-
school attendance and that sort of thing. But I grew up believing
in a quiet Methodist kind of religion, you know." As Billy's close
associate now, Grady Wilson, describes her with a vague air of
lament and regret, "Pauline was just built for this world. She
loved fun, pleasure, dancing, and that was about all."

Nevertheless, more than a few who knew Billy then still

suggest, as one relative of his puts it, "If you ask me, Pauline was the greatest love to ever hit him. She really sent him into somersaults." They had first met at a mountain religious retreat the summer before Billy turned seventeen — the summer, as it happened, just after Pauline's father had died, when, she says, "I nearly lost my mind. I had worshiped him, and it just about wrecked me." When she first glimpsed Billy loping across the assembly grounds, "he stuck out like a brass band. Lord, he was good-lookin' — tall and blond with that winning grin. That very second, I just flipped over him." That evening, they took a walk down to the stone wall surrounding the assembly area, "and before we even got there, he kissed me for the first time. We didn't waste any time, believe me." In truth, it was as if they immediately fell into a daze with each other. During the preaching services each evening, they would sit together in a pew holding hands, a stealthy delicious mingling of fingers through the steamy surging of the old hymns, the soul-shivering gales of oratory, after which, says Pauline, "we'd absolutely shoot out of that church, still holding hands," to go sit once more along the stone wall in the darkness.

After that summer, says Pauline, "Billy and I were always together." Around her, there continued the customary stir of other suitors, but "Billy was just so nice to be with. He was an easy person, you know — he wasn't *rough,* if you know what I mean. He just fascinated me. He didn't do any of the things the others did. He didn't cuss, he didn't dance. He was just tall and good-lookin'. He wore clothes like a prince —" she remembers it again in a low voice that has in it a sound like a moving of deep grasses "— those navy slacks, that white jacket, white shoes, and a tie; he was never in blue jeans. *Goood*-lookin' — umh! the *best*-lookin' thing!" Her mother, and especially her spinster aunt who had been a minister herself once, "they thought Billy hung the moon." Returning her home from a movie one night — "It could have been *Gone with the Wind,* I'd never have noticed" — he was kissing her on the front porch "when suddenly the light flashed on. He didn't lose any time in getting off that porch. Not a word of farewell — he was off, sailed over that hedge, and was gone."

Billy himself reports, "We'd go to church parties, things like that" — but afterward, they would park along that long circular driveway under crepe myrtles in front of the gutted and weed-grown mansion, and in the muted glow of the car radio, listened to the gauzing music of bands like Tommy Dorsey, Glenn Miller, Woody Herman, coming from the far penthouse ballrooms of Chicago and Manhattan and Kansas City, and playing quietly in the car on through long fumbling sweetly-panging hours of ex-quisitely tentative grapplings. Says Pauline, "Hell's bells, yes, he was spirited. It was all natural with Billy. He may have always been the finest of boys, but he was no sissy. I can tell you, that boy never for the first minute talked religion to me. Unh-unh."

Billy concedes now, "Yeah, we'd park there for an hour or two and listen to the radio and hold hands, kiss, neck. But that was all. Nothing more than that." Still, it was as if the earth itself had suddenly, momentously stirred under him. She was shimmer-ingly alive, and it was the first time that he had come truly close to spilling on into more lavish lyricisms of life. With her, it was as if he were lost in some luxurious dream obscurely fraught with distant and exotic portents, intimations of another whole un-known continent of voluptuous possibilities.

III

On a warm silvering May dawn in 1934, with Charlotte then languishing in the deep gulch of the Depression, a group of some thirty local businessmen had gathered at Frank Graham's farm to conduct a day-long session of prayer down in a pine grove on his place. "I remember seeing and hearing them down there when I left for school that morning," says Billy, "and when I returned that afternoon, they were still at it." While he was pitching hay with a handyman, they continued to arrive in their dusty coupes and black boxy Fords to disappear into the stand of pines across the road, from which there periodically floated faint shouts. When the handyman finally asked him exactly what was taking place down there, Billy, blushing slightly, muttered, "Aw, probably some fanatics talked Dad into letting them use the farm."

It was a time when the nation was passing through the greatest vertigo in American life since the Civil War — that frenetic smoke-hung pause before its second great war abroad, its streets washed with food riots and strike brawls, with sun-dimming dust storms out of which there proceeded a forlorn pilgrimage of wired-together vehicles creeping to California impossibly laden with what seemed the hasty salvaged debris of a cataclysm, mattress springs and tubs and splintered mirrors. Over a land of foreclosed mortgages, sourceless solitary men in bagging clothes the color of ashes, with shabby hats yanked low over gaunt vicious faces, wandered through an endless yellow-afternoon loneliness of weeds and empty scrappy highways and hot glinting railroad tracks. All over North Carolina itself, banks were collapsing daily, and there were clatters of gunfire now in the strikes underway at its monolithic textile mills, with several workers already killed.

In the midst of all these dislocations and forebodings, it became the inspiration of a brotherhood of Charlotte laymen called the Christian Men's Club — one remnant left from Billy Sunday's passage through in 1924 — to mount a succession of all-day prayer meetings out in the secluded locust-rasping sun-stricken stillness of cowpastures and cedar groves about the countryside. For the most part, "we were not prominent men in business," one member asserts. "Most of us were just humble businessmen with deep religious convictions." One survivor from that time, a small prim man in his eighties with a grandmotherly face, remained largely lost in the evangelical swoons and fervors of those days — subject to sudden constricted wheezes of rapture, soundless sobs, swampings of joy and wonder, when reminiscing about those distant times of pasture pentecosts as he sat years later in the basement den of his suburban home. "I feel we're very near the coming of the Lord," he announced at one point, and seemed to gag then — sitting absolutely motionless on the couch, turned slightly sideways with his gnarled and stubby

hands folded daintily to one side of his crossed legs — and then
went on in a tiny squeezed voice, "Yes, we are now in the final
great advance of the Holy Spirit to finish the work of the Lord in
preparation for His triumphal return. . . ." He was wearing on
this early winter morning a coat tightly fastened with two buttons
around his middle, and as he talked on he kept insistently tug-
ging down his coattails about him, fretfully tucking himself tidily
together. Seized by another noiseless combustion of glee and
weeping, he continued on with his folded hands wringing and
twisting at each other, his voice thinly kiting upward in a soft ecstatic whine, "Like the Samaritan woman who went back to tell
her men friends about having met the Messiah, I have meat to
eat that the world knows not of. That was the conviction of all of
us when we came together for those prayer meetings in those
meadows."

At that day-long stand of prayer on the Graham farm, leaving
their wives at the house to sit with Mrs. Graham, they trudged
on down a dim twin-rutted path to the pine grove, and as Frank
Graham himself would later relate it: "We fasted all day, didn't
eat a thing from sunrise to sunset, first one praying, then another, sometimes several of us praying at once." One farmhand
recollects, "I toted water to 'em down there all day long. Man,
they was having a time down there." Kneeling in loosened ties
and white shirt-sleeves on quilts spread over the pine needles,
their faces reddening and polished with sweat through the long
gnat-humming burn of that spring day, "we got bolder and
bolder," one of them remembers, "in what we asked of the Lord
as we prayed on." Finally, one of them stood and bayed, "O
Lord! Out of this very city, out of Charlotte itself, may You raise
up such a one as will go out and preach Your gospel to the ends
of the earth!"

As another member of that group explains, "We weren't the
top business and professional leaders at all, a lot of us didn't
have anything left by now, and we were just struggling. But it
was like things went on falling apart all over the country, there
just didn't seem to be any bottom to it." It was, in fact, like a
gathering mute ragged hysteria among them — as indeed over

the nation that whole harried population of modest, water-combed, celluloid-collared merchants and tradesmen were approaching a dull frenzy of despair. And at last, some of those at the pine-grove prayer session convened for a council in Charlotte's First National Bank building to plan a wholesale community-wide revival late that summer with a peripatetic evangelist out of Kentucky called Dr. Mordecai Ham.

A tall, strapping, rigid figure, bald and fractious-tempered and florid of face, Ham had something of the antique look of a Roman proconsul, with a thin white frost of hair fringing his marbled dome, a white glisten of a mustache under rimless pince-nez spectacles ornamenting a permanent irascible glower. He was "full of smoke and flames," testifies someone once in his audiences, and he bawled back and forth over the small cities and mill-burgs of the South with an accompanying pianist by the name of Rawley Tredway, preaching in timber tabernacles and ball parks and shoe factories and textile plants. He derived directly, in fact, out of the old furies of those brush evangelists of the frontier, having presided once at a bonfire of dubious literature in Mineral Wells, Texas, and in general railing at bootleggers and other assorted sinners with the combative vigor of those old-fashioned Virginia City free-for-alls that left ears and fingers missing: as it happened, street altercations often attended his presence in a town.

Not incidentally, he also served in that long unspoken collaboration in America between gospel drummers and the baronies of commerce. In particular, he was one of his era's most gaudy and livid anti-Semites, fulminating against "apostate Jewry" and "the wicked Jews who killed Jesus," brandishing the Protocols of Zion and reciting from some of Henry Ford's more squalid anti-Semitic cantos, for which he had more than once been dinned out of towns by city councils and newspapers, even while he would receive cordial notes from executive assistants in Dearborn, Michigan, "More strength to your arm. I am showing your latest letter to Mr. Ford." One of Ham's later apologists, a nephew of his, explained in a biography that his uncle merely meant to demonstrate how "a tightly-controlled, highly-sub-

sidized agency in International Jewry had set out to throttle all
expressions of public opinion which are unfavorable to atheistic
communism and International Semitism." The truth is, the
miasma of dingy dread and desperation brooding over the
United States at that time was much the same sullen weather that
held in Germany then. It was hardly remarkable that Ham's
boisterous anti-Semitism afforded those beleaguered and pious
petty burghers of Charlotte no measurable discomfort. One of
them admits, "We had a little trouble with some of the Jewish
people about bringing Ham in. There was a Jew on the city
council name of Kahn, he jumped on a train up there in New
York when he heard about it and came down and tried to stop
it." But all that this local churchman will still allow is "Ham, he
may have been a little off there on that thing about the conspir-
acy to control the finances of the world."

One day some forty years after Ham's revival, this same elder
took a visitor to show him the site, humped intently over the
wheel of his car with a hat now planted snugly on his head this
cold November morning. Driving there, he seemed in some distracted float halfway between then and now, meandering slowly
and peacefully through the barging of other traffic around him
as if only incidentally noticing it as he blissfully told again about
those vanished days of glory. When he arrived at last at the
downtown corner where Ham's revival had rampaged on
through those weeks in 1934, a site since inherited by the asphalt
lot of a Glidden Paint store, he gently trundled his car up under
a pin oak tree in a dirt clearing across the street, and got out. A
brick liquor shop was sitting about on the spot where Ham's pulpit had been erected. But this surviving elder seemed not to really see that either. He simply stood musing for a few moments
in the thin November sunshine, and then pointed and declared,
"There it is, right there. That's where Billy Graham got saved."

It was late that same summer when Billy had met Pauline that
Ham arrived in Charlotte to commence his revival. Setting up a
lumber tabernacle on that downtown corner, then an empty lot
of red clay strewn with straw not far from the Seaboard Railway

tracks, Ham proceeded to storm on night after night, through the singed-out shank of the summer, on into the fall.

But through most of the revival's course, Billy was parking in the evenings with Pauline, vastly indifferent to the whole affair, until Ham suddenly managed to create a sensation in the community by blaring one night, a Charlotte native recollects, that "fornication was rampant among the high-school students at Central High in Charlotte. I'm not quite sure how he happened on that particular piece of intelligence, but it served to sufficiently scandalize the whole town." At the least, it immediately and enormously intrigued Billy. As he explains it now, "It made me very angry, his attack on the integrity of the high-school students." Whatever, reports an old acquaintance, "the very next night, ole Billy was sitting right there, sticking up straight and alert in the middle of the crowd."

As it turned out, the sheer array of the occasion itself utterly mesmerized him — that huge collection of people out of the night, some roosting on produce crates and car fenders outside, while inside the tabernacle, which had been clapped together out of raw yellow planks with a winy tang of pine rosin lingering over the sawdust aisles, people were packed everywhere in a fluttering of paper fans in the damp shine of bulbs strung along the bare rafters overhead, the choir in white dresses and white shirt-sleeves with faces shellacked with sweat, a little tinny but glad and lusty of lung, galloping on through gospel choruses to the lickety-split whanging of a piano. "I'd never seen anything like it in my life," Billy recounts, "the big crowd, the singing, the excitement. I know they said in later years that Ham took on anti-Semitic overtones, and I'm sure there was some of that while he was in Charlotte, but I never noticed it. I didn't even have any idea what anti-Semitism was anyway. I was just caught up in the services."

Now in those last nights of Indian summer, with a heavy moon hanging low and orange over a dark countryside adrift still with fireflies, he began journeying regularly into town for the services in the tabernacle. There, to a faint clash of freight trains shuttling past down the hill, there unfolded each night under those direly glaring bulbs that dramaturgy of doom and salvation, the terrific striving against the sweet entwinings of this world. "I began to have thoughts," as Billy puts it now, "that I'd never had before." At one point one evening, Ham suddenly flung a long flagging finger directly at Billy's wide blue gaze — "You're a sinner!" — at which Billy instantly ducked behind the billowy hat of a matron in front of him, "like he'd been shot at," says Grady Wilson. After that, he decided to position himself in the choir, despite the gate-hinge squawk of his own singing, to escape the sweep and rake of Ham's cannonading. But even there, he was stricken again when Ham bellowed another evening, "There's a grea-a-a-at sinner here tonight!" By no measure could his night-time scrimmagings with Pauline in the parked car and his bewitchment with that aura she carried of other realms of life have been considered approaching anything like the dimension and complexity of great sin — there was hardly any heaviness of a Rasputin or Faust in his nature — but so compressed were the registers of his conscience that, on hearing Ham's proclamation, he groaned in his soul.

In the meantime, Pauline herself had attended one of Ham's services with a friend. But she had been merely appalled, stirring to leave when Ham suddenly called down a young couple quietly stealing out. "Said they'd be struck dead if they went on out," says Pauline, "so I had to keep sitting there, I was too terrified to get up." But Billy would return home after those meetings, retreat immediately up to his room, with its plain wallpaper and pair of iron-frame single beds, and simply lie for a long while in the moonlight, propped up with his hands behind his head and gazing out of his window to those woods through which he had romped and tracked in his boyhood, now only a depthless stretch of darkness under a full moon. And "as I lay there, I would feel a kind of stirring in my breast that was both pleasant and scary."

At last, late one afternoon toward the end of October, Albert McMakin, the burly and zealous son of one of Frank Graham's tenants, called to Billy, "Hey, let's go in to the meeting tonight," and in the McMakins' pickup truck, they rode through the dusk back again to the tabernacle downtown. At the invitation at the close of Ham's bombardments, the choir began hymning "Just as I Am." Billy stood with Grady Wilson, singing in a stammerous murmur, when suddenly there appeared at his elbow a fastidiously groomed and boutonniered figure with a tomato-pink face — the owner of a local men's haberdashery, J. D. Prevatte — who husked to him, "Billy Frank, wouldn't you like to be a Christian?" Billy paused and then gave a stifled little nod, while nudging Grady in the ribs. Prevatte whispered then, "So why don't you boys settle it? I'll go down with you — " And Billy lurched with Grady on down out of the choir, his head hung and dangling, and on across the sawdust to the altar, joining the congestion of other penitents there, now and then taking furtive peeks at the others around him. Afterward, he and Grady shuffled back to sit with McMakin, and a moment later, says McMakin, "Billy's daddy came over and put his arm around him there for a minute."

But Billy's New Birth that evening was a curiously sedate event, in which there was a calm blankness of any mystic flares or fevers. "I can't say that I felt anything spectacular," he would later acknowledge. "I felt very little emotion. I shed no tears. In fact, when I saw that others had tears in their eyes, I felt like a hypocrite, and this disturbed me a little." Indeed, he only vaguely recollects now the actual particulars of the moment. "I'm sure I had a tremendous sense of conviction, the Lord did speak to me about certain things in my life, I'm certain of that — but I can't remember what they were." As he was riding back home that night with McMakin in the pickup truck, he was strangely wordless and subdued. He only remarked once in an abrupt, quiet, level voice, "Now I've gotten saved. Now whatever I do can't unsave me. Even if I ever killed somebody, I can't ever be unsaved now."

He was already home when his parents arrived. As they came in through the kitchen door in the back, "he was in the breakfast room pretending to make himself a sandwich," Mrs. Graham remembers, and as soon as he heard the slap of the screen door, he came pitching into the kitchen and slung his arms around his mother; "I'm saved, Mother, I got saved!" There was a bit of eye-blurring, a few sniffles. She told him, "Son, I'm so glad for what you did tonight."

But back up in his room again, lying in the pale heatless glow of the moon, he found himself still oddly vacant of any passion or exhilaration. He merely occupied himself for a while in compiling a systematic ledger, a kind of balance of accounts between his indiscretions and vulnerabilities and fortitudes, to determine what would need to be revised now. And presently, he slipped on into sleep. . . .

If, in fact, some sudden interior detonation of soul has been common in the pasts of almost all the great evangelists and prophets and saints, Billy's particular metaphysical flash seemed hardly on the order of that of Paul on the Damascus Road or St. Augustine in his mother's garden in Milan. He concedes, "I did wonder if it was even real, because I didn't seem to have that emotional shock other people seemed to have." As he would later struggle to define what happened, "It was the majesty of God, I think, that hit me as I heard Ham preach about it." For all the timorousness of his own trespasses, "anyone approaching the holiness, the greatness, the righteousness of God will automatically think of himself as a great sinner, just as the closer you get to a mountain, the smaller and more insignificant you seem to yourself." Whatever, it had served to bring insupportable if obscure cargoes of guilt unpacking on him. "It was just a sense that I had sinned grievously against God and needed salvation. How? I can't recall exactly — I just felt a tremendous need to escape the judgment depicted so clearly in Ham's preaching. And it was to know that this guilt, this guilt that absolutely *destroys,* it would all be forgiven. That everything's forgiven, it was to know that." Specifically, of course, there was that simple heart-impaling drama of Jesus, the inexpressible sweetness of that self-willed anguish and slaughter of divine innocence "all for the sake of a wretch like me" — no slight headiness, too, in the attachment of that cosmic saga directly to one's own person, "the fact that he, the son of God," as Billy explains, "would go to such lengths to save *me.*"

But in later years, he would resort to accounting for the phenomenon by proposing, "Of course the New Birth is a mystery — it is not something you do for yourself, it is something that is done for you — but in all life, there is an element of mystery," citing then, with rather a banalizing clunk, "for instance, who can explain which came first, the chicken or the egg?" He also offered once, "Certainly the concept of conversion is not unusual in our society. Any good salesman knows that he must convert prospects to his product or his way of thinking. The business of advertising is to convert the buying public from one brand to another."

As a matter of fact, while it has always been assumed, by Billy himself and in all the commentary that has collected after him over the years, that his conversion took place that night in Ham's tabernacle, the real probability is — to the extent that he ever experienced a New Birth — it did not happen to him then at all: it was more a false dawn. The true event still awaited him. It would be some four years later that the authentic agonies and exaltations of transfiguration would befall him.

When he awoke the next morning, he says, "There was both a kind of song and dread in my heart. I remember the world looked different — even the trees, the grass. Suddenly it all had a purpose. I felt there was a meaning to life, whereas before, it was flat and meaningless." That would not seem to have altogether been the case, given his captivation then with Pauline. But it was as if, suspecting perhaps his final unfitness for actually becoming a part of the life those tantalizations whispered, he had been presented with another deliverance out of that impasse between his huge free-floating undefined eagerness and his own apprehensions of the meagerness that mortal existence seemed to come to. This new purpose now, at least, promised a larger experience, a larger reality — indeed, one could not stand to live otherwise.

But at the most, it seemed at that point simply a commitment to the beatitude of decency and niceness. "I think it was something he really had in him all that time," says one relative, "and that revival just brought it on out of him." In fact, says Grady, Billy was confronted now with a somewhat peculiar conundrum: "Ham had preached on 'The Devil's Big Three' — dances, card parties, and booze. Billy felt he had to give 'em up even though he didn't do any of 'em, and he kept trying to figure out some kind of way he could do that." But the only immediate discernible difference it made in his manner, says his sister Catherine, "was he treated me a little nicer." As Billy himself terms it, "Ethics crept into my life. During the day, I tried to be courteous and kind to those around me. For the first time, I tried to apply myself to my studies, and my grades improved somewhat." In the meantime, J. D. Prevatte presented him with a coat from his men's shop: a natty white jacket with vertical stripes. "He looked like a stick of peppermint candy walking around in that thing," says a friend.

Once, while Billy was waiting with Grady in a Charlotte garage to have a blown tire repatched, the mechanic banged his thumb and yelped, "Christ!" Billy instantly intoned, "Sir, don't do that. I'm a Christian. Don't you ever take the Lord's name in vain again." The mechanic gave him a long glower: "This is a free country, sonny. I can do what I damn well please and say what I damn well please." Billy crowed, "Not around me, you can't!" At that, the mechanic hefted up a tire iron, and Billy quickly announced, "I'll tell my daddy if you do that. My daddy's Mr. Frank Graham, and he brings all his Deere trucks in here." The mechanic paused, and then sank back on his haunches and resumed scrabbling away at the tire, "just gruntin' something," says Grady.

Indeed, Billy's conversion — with Ham having departed shortly thereafter for other campaigns — did have the effect of producing in him a certain studied priggishness. He took to berating his old friends for what he considered their improbities of language and conduct. "Suddenly, we weren't serious enough for him," says one. At a class party once at a girl's home in town, Laura Paxton remembers that she had begun dancing with the girl's father when she felt a sudden, savage finger-stab at her shoulder, and turned to find Billy glaring at her, pale — "Laura,

you stop that," he hissed. "What do you think you're doing? Stop
it." Not long after that, when she became engaged to Sam, she
says, "To this day, I'll never forget how Billy came up to me and
just bawled me out. Said, 'Laura, why do you want to destroy
your life and Sam's too? You're both too young; you'll ruin both
your lives. It's just not God's will in your lives, and you know it.' "

One of his cohorts of those jubilant nights of slewing over
moonlit back roads and drag-racing bootleggers through town
recalls now, "We all knew he had gotten saved, of course, and he
started acting real concerned about his friends and classmates.
He started telling us all the time, 'You're just not gonna be saved
until you confess your sins and admit Christ as your savior.' He
almost had what you might call an obsession with getting us converted too. Like he wanted company in it, wanted us to follow
along with him. He got awfully concerned that I was running
around with some older guys — he'd tell me, 'You shouldn't be
running around with those fellas; first thing you know you'll
become weak, you'll take a drink. You know they're a bad influence on you.' " Finally, he says, when he showed up one evening
for a revival service in a community church, Billy was there to
seize his arm immediately, demanding, "C'mon, now, you come
sit down with me, the Lord's gonna speak to you tonight." And
"sure enough," this old friend reports with a brief and not entirely convincing smile, "it happened. I was saved that very
night." He works now in a small unadorned office with white
walls the texture of an Alka-Seltzer tablet, an amiably deferential
and slightly shy man with a round rosy face, who, though he insists he has "surrendered my life to the Lord," yet has a suggestion in his dark moist eyes of a susceptibility still to worldly blandishments and the mildly and harmlessly sybaritic, a faint air of
having wound up strayed into some vague misrealization of his
nature, as if had he not happened to come into accidental conjunction once with Billy's eager overwhelming solicitudes, he
would have passed an agreeable life of light toddies in the evening and a little poker now and then — a gentle propensity to
party that, if not wholly purged in him, has been successfully
submerged.

But despite his conversion, he says, "We began to drift apart that last year or two Billy was home. He started going with another set that some folks called the Preacher Boys, the Wilson brothers and a bunch of others. Later on when I started college, they thought it was just terrible I was taking geology. They kept trying to tell me it was against the teaching of the Scriptures. Billy kept telling me it was 'too scientific.' To be frank, I never could exactly understand what all they were talking about." Not everyone, for that matter, was enchanted with Billy's enthusiasms after his decision in Ham's revival. One teacher at his high school, says a fellow student, "was a little perturbed that he was falling into this evangelism, always going around at night to these testimonial meetings and things." Out of some peculiar, profound exasperation, she insistently railed at him in class — "called him 'Preacher Boy,' once told him there in front of everybody that he'd never amount to anything." Her distemper over his new directions somewhat baffled Billy. "She just seemed terribly upset about it for some reason," he still recalls; "I don't know why."

Melvin remembers of that time that "Billy seemed to kind of feel he wanted to be a preacher, but he wasn't sure where and what kind." His first congregation consisted of a conscription of the children of the tenants on his father's place. Says a former hand, "He'd take my kids and the colored kids of the cook, and he'd herd 'em all down to that creek and sit 'em down, and then he'd get up and preach away to 'em from a rock." But already he had begun to assume a certain boggling unblinking certitude, announcing matter-of-factly to a girl cousin whose fiancé had been injured in a wreck, "Augusta, I prayed all night last night, and he's gonna be all right." His cousin says now, "I'm sure he did just that, he probably stayed on his knees all night long to make sure he got the job done right. That's the way he'd do things — whatever it was, foolish or serious, once he decided on it, he had to do it to the finish."

At the same time, though, he continued to see Pauline. Even yet, he could not bring himself to relinquish her. "There wasn't any difference in him at first," she says. "None at all. He was the same ole Billy." They would still park in the evenings, nestled together in the radio's glow, in that slow dreaming of music from unseen ballrooms.

But, Pauline reflects now, "After he was converted, he never really looked back." One gray winter afternoon, she happened to glimpse him standing alone on a downtown street corner, preaching to passersby — a forlorn and faintly panicky figure, bareheaded and without a topcoat in the sharp cold, furiously flurrying away to the unheeding swarm along the sidewalk. From a distance, unnoticed by him, she stared at him stunned. "Can you imagine — there he was, he'd gone down there and was just preaching away all by himself on that sidewalk in front of Belk's Department Store to all those people going by" — and she gives a small shudder — "all of them totally ignoring him, businessmen just wanting to get on home and have a cocktail before dinner, and there he stood raving away at them. It was awful —"

When he graduated from high school in the summer of 1936, a year and a half now after Ham's revival, he struck out for South Carolina as a drummer of Fuller Brushes, with a pack of his fellows that included Grady Wilson and his brother, T. W. "Billy just couldn't wait to get out of Charlotte and see a little bit of the world," says a friend, "and that was one way he figured he could do it." Under the supervision of Albert McMakin, who was now a full-time Fuller Brush agent, they coursed along the narrow tar-seamed highways all over the piny sandy flatlands of South Carolina's tobacco and cotton country, the rowed fields monotonously flickering past the windows of their car as they proceeded through a succession of identical little towns, such places as Cheraw, Marion, Latta, where on Saturdays the sidewalks around the square were thick with coveralled men and their sunbonneted women moiling past the rusty-marqueed movie theatres and dimestores. They tarried a few days in each of these towns, quartered in slightly frumpish dollar-a-day boarding houses mostly occupied by a Depression flotsam of miracle-tonic salesmen, day laborers, anonymous roustabouts. Over the supper tables, there would sometimes occur little tiffs and bristlings as the general banter waxed a bit briny, Billy reddening and scowling about him until someone paused and said, "What'sa matter with you, kid?" He would then snip, "I'm a Christian." "Oh. That so. That why you seem to be having a little trouble digesting your biscuits?" After supper, they sometimes occupied themselves back up in one of their rooms with sessions of prayer and Bible-reading. But just as often, actually, Billy and T. W. would set out to drive awhile around the town with local girls that T. W. had earlier managed to scout up. "While they were out tooling around with those gals," says Grady, "Albert and I would stay back at the boarding house praying for 'em."

Billy would begin his rounds each morning with a prayer, and then in a peacock-hued tie and a gabardine suit of bottle-green with thin yellow piping — "Most of my suits were gabardine then," he says, "I liked 'em 'cause they were slick" — he would go clomping on with his sample case from house to house, continuing, says one of his companions then, "to pray before each call for sales success. Then, if he got a chance, he'd witness about Jesus to the customer."

Grady recalls that, on the whole, "we sorta got disillusioned with the human race that summer. We were supposed to give out these little sample brushes first off when somebody answered the door, you know, and some of those women would snatch those things out of your hand and slam that door shut again in your face without so much as a howdy." But as it happened, Billy — due to his almost preternatural capacity for an indiscriminate fanatical enthusiasm in any enterprise that engaged his fancy — wound up the top Fuller Brush salesman in the two Carolinas that summer. The area sales manager, says Grady, "was absolutely overwhelmed at the Fuller Brushes that Billy sold those few weeks. He couldn't quite believe it, in fact. He didn't quite see how just one single human being could possibly sell that many brushes in that space of time." Billy himself professes, "I believed in the product. Selling those little brushes became a cause to me. I felt that every family ought to have a Ful-

ler Brush as a matter of principle. I would even sell them
sometimes at night, that was when you could catch the whole
family there." So effusive was he in this particular evangelism,
one beleaguered housewife finally had to empty a pitcher of water
on him from a second-floor window. But Billy maintains, "Sincerity is the biggest part of selling anything, I found out —
including salvation. And I was sure sold that those were the
greatest brushes in the whole world." According to Grady, "He
was especially keen on those pure Russian boar bristles in those
toothbrushes. He brushed his teeth so many times with those
things, his gums started receding. That's right. He'd use up
about four or five of 'em a week. He'd brush until his gums were
actually bloody."

Grady suggests, "One big reason why Billy did so well that
summer was that Albert went around with him in his rounds. It
was really the two of them against each one of the rest of us." But
more than an interest in Billy's sales performance, McMakin —
having conveyed Billy to that service of his conversion — had
now taken it on himself to attend him so closely because, says
Grady, "Albert thought Billy still needed a little supervision and
help in getting his life straightened out. Just that Billy still
seemed to like dating all those girls, you know." Over forty years
afterward, McMakin, heavily plopped in an easy chair in his living room, his hands comfortably folded over the flaps of his tie
on his ample midriff, still takes on a certain proprietorial tone in
explaining his attentions to Billy during that summer of 1935.
"You see, it took a little time for Billy to get his life really sorted
out there. I could tell he wasn't wholly committed to the Lord
yet. He was still just a little wild in some things, y'see. . . ."

When he returned to Charlotte on weekends, he would still
see Pauline. But she recalls, "He was just running off all the time
now. He had to run off and sell that silly Fuller Brush that summer. He just kept running away, it seemed like."

Off and on through that summer, he would also tag about
with a young evangelist out of Alabama named Jimmie Johnson — a thin, darkly glittering chap with a certain debonair

languor about him, always hatless. "All the girls thought he was just so unusually handsome," says Billy's sister Catherine. Pauline herself entertained a pronounced aversion to him: "I thought he was spooky. But Billy was fascinated by him. He thought he was such a tremendous speaker, such a powerful personality. Billy, my God, he was so *dumb* then. He was still so much a country boy, I could have cried."

In the religious mystique of those parts then, it immediately became the communal anticipation whenever a singularly vibrant and promising youth appeared among them that he would eventually be a preacher or missionary or evangelist: it meant approximately what performing as a matador in the bullrings of Madrid means in the back provinces of Spain. Sometimes, says Grady, "a few of us beginners, before Billy came along, we'd all go out to these jailhouses, and what we'd preach on was Paul and Silas in the Philippian jail. Just what those pore prisoners in there wanted to hear about, somebody else in jail. Or we'd go to the home for unwed mothers — the Industrial Home, they called it — and we'd talk on the woman taken in adultery. We figgered that was what would be *appropriate* in those places, you know." But when Billy essayed his own first street-corner apostolics, says Grady, "he was just scared and rattly. He'd stand there and just twist his coat in his hands, you know, like he was in pain. He couldn't even give a sensible testimony. He'd go out there on that street corner and try to give his testimony and he'd twist his coattail in both hands until it looked like a rope."

But in the righteous mythos of those prosaic locales, the Preacher Boys constituted a dashing lot, the gifted young rookies, intense, vigorous, touched with a certain glamour. The house of a pious stationery salesman, Vernon Patterson, was usually full of a rush and whooping of them, the local aspirants along with the others lodging there while passing through between revivals. Billy began dropping by there with increasing frequency, enthralled by them: they seemed to move in some special galvanic field of excitement and portent, already a sheen of incipient stardom about them. And while he was over there among the clamor of their comings and goings, he would often pause in front of a mirror to execute a brief hand flourish, a head angle, an arm swoop, raptly pondering these tentative images and gestures of his own possible future. The beguiled maidens who were always fluttering about the Patterson house when Preacher Boys were collected there would twit him, "Billy Frank, what you keep lookin' at yourself in the mirror for?" But he would be unable to resist any mirror that offered itself, searching it with extravagant gesticulations, sweeps of his arms, for some glimpse of who he might be, a first glimmer of the image of his destiny.

Jimmie Johnson was touring then with a portable tabernacle that Patterson and a group of other patrons had contrived for him — a contraption of collapsible wooden sections which, after a stand in one town, would be folded like an accordion and trucked on to the next town, the next ball field or vacant fair ground. "That thing was hauled all over North Carolina," says Patterson, "and thousands were saved." Whenever possible, Billy trailed along after Johnson "just to hear him preach," and it was on one of these outings that he produced what could be considered his first full-blown preaching performance — on a Sunday afternoon in Monroe, North Carolina, where Johnson was then conducting a revival.

The night before, he and Grady and T. W. had taken a room in a dumpy back-street hotel in Monroe, and around three in the morning, says Grady, "I woke up and said, 'Billy, I can't seem to get to sleep, I got sumpum in my eye.' I turned on the light, and it was a bug. They were crawling all over that room." They rapidly evacuated the hotel and, carrying only their Fuller Brush sample cases, they proceeded through the empty streets to Johnson's tabernacle several blocks away. There, stretching out in the sawdust below the pulpit, they spent the rest of the night, Billy sprawled in the pine shavings in his yellow-striped green suit. A little while after dawn — in a fresh summer Sunday morning with stray savors of breakfast coffee in the air — they stirred awake, a trifle rank in their clothes now. At a spigot nearby, they bent to splash their faces with cupped handfuls of water, while in the town's churches around them, they could hear, faint and surging like a rumor of a familiar surf, the hymns already beginning.

Then that afternoon, they filed after Johnson into the Monroe jail, where Johnson was to conduct a service. It was a dim and sleazy kennel holding only a few prisoners, "most of them black," remembers Grady, "and most of them in there for bootlegging, drunk, razor fights, things like that." They were huddled behind the bars in a sour murk, the walls dank as if with the dingy residue of the desperations and griefs of those refuse souls pent here over the years. Indeed, Billy, still holding his sample case, was suddenly in the presence of the elemental sediment and sweat of the truly lost of Man's Fall: they moved before him, shifting and muttering behind the bars, like vague and faceless apparitions of the doomed. And while Billy was staring at them, Johnson startled him by announcing, "We have a young fellow here with us this afternoon who's only been converted a short time himself, and who I'd like to step forward now and give his own testimony."

He stood paralyzed for an instant, then let his case plop to the floor and took a step forward. Says Grady, "He just stood there a minute wringing his coat a little bit." What he finally blurted as a beginning was, "Well, I'm awfully glad to see such a nice crowd out this afternoon, it's good to see all of you here" — proceeding then to make a few remarks about Paul and Silas in the Philippian dungeon. But then, gradually — still humming with a slightly feverish and giddy incandescence from only a few hours of sleep, with a look of antic and famished gauntness in his rumpled suit — he began to stalk and honk, "I was a sinner! And no good! I didn't care anything about God or the Bible! Or people!" He was striding and swooping back and forth now in an implausibly exercised animation for the occasion, popping his hands, hunkering almost double, lunging — the first rude gutterings of his pouncings and pacings and hand smacks in those stadium pulpits of his future, the dim shapes before him the first foreshadows of all the multitudes later to come. "But Jesus changed my life! He gave me peace and joy! He will forgive your sins as he forgave mine! Just let him come into your heart! When

I accepted Jesus as my lord and savior, the very trees looked different! The flowers looked different! The birds were singing!" Such poetries may have been a bit alien to his audience's circumstances, but Billy remembers he began to hear low mumbling *Amens,* and "a great thrill filled me." He ended abruptly, and stood panting a little, flushed, looking around him quickly with a glare of surprise and wonder.

He then stooped, with a kind of clumsy violence, to snatch his sample case back up. When Johnson finished his own message, Billy, still trembling, still lost in a peculiar disembodied euphoria, lurched on after him out of the jail.

His own inclinations had been to enter the University of North Carolina after that summer, but at the insistence of his mother — who had heard Bob Jones, a former Methodist back-bush evangelist of the same chloleric pietism as Ham, speak once at the local high school — he dutifully set out for Jones's small fundamentalist academy in Cleveland, Tennessee. "I didn't have the slightest idea what kind of school it was," he says now. "All I knew was that it was Christian." Actually, it was more a kind of evangelical boot camp, grim brick barracks with long low corridors lit with drab glares and posted with notifications like *Griping Not Tolerated,* and it was presided over by the autocratic and irascible figure of Jones, a chunky badger of a man with a face weathered raw and livid under a white hummock of hair, whose manner it was to discourse out of one side of his mouth in a harsh, strangled, raucous blare. They did not take altogether benignly to levity there. Jones himself once advised a restively capersome student, "You're possessed of demons. I can see it in your eyes."

But Billy still had about him that quality of an unsubdued and jubilant child of nature. Jimmie Johnson submits, "He was a totally liberated personality. I mean, he would just do the most unexpected, fascinating things — like once, when he was driving us all back from Charleston, the sun visor kept falling down in front of him, and finally he just reached up and snatched it right off and threw it out the window. Those kinds of little things." As it turned out, Johnson had entered Bob Jones with Billy, and, he reports, "His room was never orderly, he just never seemed conscious of such things. He ate a lot of grapefruits up there — he would suck them like oranges, and then just pitch them into the corner. Along with pecan hulls and everything else imaginable. There would be this heap there after a while, a midden of old grapefruit rinds, banana peels, peanut shells, and he would just leave it there while two, three weeks went by." Johnson then muses a moment. "You'd certainly never have thought in those days that he'd be able one day to run such a large and complex organization as he has now. We knew he was no run-of-the-mill person, but we would have been absolutely staggered back then to think that one day Billy Graham would be preaching to two hundred and seventy-five thousand people. Billy was no genius, by any stretch of the imagination. Yet he had a — a magic about him. I was — we were all — charmed by his youthful nature. He was just a tall jaunty young man with a loose careless way about him, and he always had a large group of fellows around him, everywhere he went."

As it turned out, Billy's expansive nature soon came to pose an affront to that order of sedulous disciplines of the spirit at Bob Jones. As one Bob Jones stalwart puts it, "He just had too much charisma for one body. He was charming, overwhelming, irresistible. And it began to be recognized that he was beginning to have too much influence on the other students." It was hardly anything deliberate on Billy's part — simply the subversive effect of his exuberance in that stringent campus society. Some of the school's faithful even contend now that he was actually asked to leave. At the least, something in him seemed to accost them, prompt and prick almost a lust to subdue and mute him. "He never liked discipline, he never liked to be told what to do," says one of his contemporaries there. "He was just still unsurrendered up there. Especially in his unruly, headstrong, going-to-get-the-best-out-of-life nature."

For that matter, he still had not been able to bring himself to disengage from Pauline. Billly insists of all that now, "I make a distinction between love and infatuation," and even at the time, he had begun to declare to friends, "This is just not the one for me." But one of those friends suggests, "He wasn't talking to us when he was saying that. He kept saying it trying to convince himself." It was becoming, in fact, a torment for him. Even while he sensed that she belonged irrevocably to that life that he had decided to abjure, he would moan to Grady, "Unless she becomes a Christian, I just can't go on. I just don't see how I can make it." When he had left for Bob Jones that fall of 1935, she had dated Wint Covington a few times, and Billy, on one of his returns to Charlotte, found a handkerchief of hers in Covington's car: at the private school in Raleigh where she was now installed, she received a plaintive little note from him, entreating her, she remembers, to "please send him a handkerchief too with perfume. . . ."

In the meantime, in the Dickensian bleakness at Bob Jones, he began to pale and droop, came to feel an obscure despair that at times approached panic. "I never did fit in," he now glumly allows. "I couldn't believe the rules there. It shocked me. There were demerits for just about everything, including what they called 'loitering in the hall.' You couldn't even speak to girls, couldn't even hold hands. About once a week, you could only sit for fifteen minutes in two opposite chairs in a parlor. They even monitored your mail." His single reprieve from that regimen was selling shoes every Saturday at the Belk's store in town. And now at Bob Jones there first began to visit him that harpy of insomnia which was to harrow his nights for the rest of his life.

Before long, he had begun involving himself in what he would later term "several escapades" — once, as he narrates it, "cars of people from town came through the campus on Halloween night throwing firecrackers and rocks at the windows of our dorms. We knew they were going to be coming back, so the next night, a group of us boys hid behind some trees, and sure enough, here they came again, and as they were driving past us, we jumped out and let 'em have it with those rocks. I think we broke every window in those cars and cut those people all to pieces. But they never came back." Another time, he made an unauthorized excursion off-campus with his roommate, Wendell Phillips, who had a preaching engagement in a nearby community, they having to wade across a creek with their shoes and socks in their hands to reach the church, but when Billy returned and was sitting in the dining hall for supper, Dr. Bob spied the mire on his shoes: "Billy told 'im everything, immediately," says a friend. "It was like he couldn't have cared less one way or the other. But then, Billy always has been transparent. He just never knew what dissembling was." During a convocation once of men students, Jones inquired, "How many of you fellas don't feel as spiritual now as when you came here?" Only one in the whole assembly lacked the wit not to disclose such a discontent to Jones's fearsome ill-humor — Billy instantly lofting up one long arm.

He was writing home now at least three times a week, and at last, almost as a last frantic recourse, he sank into a dreariness of the flu. At least, "when I came home for the Christmas holidays, I told my parents it was the flu"; it was mostly a case of miserableness, he acknowledges. About that time, he received a letter from a friend who had transferred to a small religious school outside Tampa, Florida Bible Institute — a letter enthusing over the palmy pleasantness of that setting, which reached Billy, in the stark barracks of Bob Jones, like a sudden promise of waiting Elysian deliverance. It happened that, during that Christmas break, Frank Graham had allowed his family to persuade him to drive them down to visit relatives in Orlando. With all six of them piled into his new green Plymouth, they traveled the gravel roads, on down the coast of South Carolina, Georgia, at last into Florida. "It was exciting to see the lakes," Billy relates, "the palm trees" — in fact, he was transported. Whenever the car stopped, he would tumble out and go striding about with great sweeps of his arms, shouting "Just look at those flowers! Look at those oranges! Look at that sunset — just look!" Indeed, after the bitten chills of Bob Jones, it presented itself before him like a flush balmy vista of Paradise.

He returned then to Bob Jones after Christmas to apprise Dr. Bob, with some discomfort but a stubborn adamancy, that he was going to defect. With winterlight glancing off his glasses that afternoon, Jones barked, "Look here, if you're a misfit at Bob Jones College, you'll be a misfit anywhere, Billy. You leave and throw away your life at a little country school like that down there, chances are you'll never be heard of again. Best you'll ever amount to is a poor country preacher somewhere out in the sticks." He went on, Billy says, "to tell me how he could have been governor of Alabama if he'd wanted to, how lonely that little school down there in Tampa was going to be." But he could not be dissuaded. The truth is, says T. W. Wilson, "when he left for the Christmas vacation after he'd gotten that letter about that place down there in Florida, he just happened to take all his clothes with him. He already knew then he wasn't coming back."

Even so, Pauline remembers that when he returned to Charlotte from Bob Jones that Christmas, he had the spectral look of a convalescent from a siege of tuberculosis. "He had become a little strange," she says. "He was far more religious, almost fanatic, but it still didn't seem natural in him somehow. He was really all tangled up, whether he knew it or not." He came over to her house one evening, and the two of them sat off talking in low tense tones in an anteroom as Christmas company passed with gay tinkling voices back and forth beyond the door. As he recounts that night now, Billy alleges that "I told her my life had taken a different direction, that we couldn't go on together. I told her I couldn't do it." But as Pauline recalls, it was not quite that concise an exchange. "He wanted me to say I'd marry him. He carried on for over an hour, demanding I say I'd marry him. If you want to know what I think, at that point Billy was just looking to get married to almost *anybody,* for some reason. I got the feeling that at that time he'd have married the first girl who said yes, just like that — You wouldn't believe how he sat there and pleaded, pleaded, pleaded with me.

"But I wasn't about to tell him I'd do anything like that now. I told him it seemed like he was getting it more and more in his mind that he had to be a preacher, and I just didn't want to be a preacher's wife. It was the most dismal thing I could imagine. I said, 'Billy, I can't even play the *piano.*' But he said I didn't need to play the piano, love was all that mattered. Love, love, he kept saying, love would take care of everything. 'Well,' I told him, 'I'll probably love you forever, Billy — but I just can't be a preacher's wife, for God's sake. I've just got too much of the heller in me, I just enjoy life too much.' I told him, 'Billy, you're probably gonna make one of the finest preachers in the whole world someday. And I don't want to wreck your life. And that's just what would happen if I were to marry you.' "

When he finally left her house that evening, she walked with him back to his car. "He was stumbling and fumbling around like he didn't really notice where he was going. I felt so sorry for him all of a sudden that I hugged and kissed him and told him he was darling." He toppled on into the car, and he admits now, "I remember as I drove down that long driveway that night, I could hardly see it for the tears in my eyes."

Still, "he kept bringing me all these presents," says Pauline, "just like he was always doing back when we were going together. Huge boxes of candy. That big box of Evening in Paris stuff, the biggest box they sell with everything in it. That summer he was down there in South Carolina, he'd brought me all those Fuller Brush items, and now when he went on down to that school in Florida, he'd bring me back those shell lamps they'd make down there." After a while, she says, "he even started trying to get me to go to those Bible schools with him too. As if I could even begin to visualize myself at some Bible school. He wanted it both ways."

Whatever, he was a long slow painful time in releasing her at last from his hopes — as if she still remained to him somehow the angel of that distant dimly sensed country of rich possibility that he would irretrievably lose if he lost her, too much yet in him of that sheer instinct and compulsion for joy and adventure to be able easily to relinquish her and that country of promise forever. At the same time, though, he realized now he could not "save" her. It was simply not in her nature. He would later report, "I think she tried, yes, she tried a couple of times, actually. But she was never able to do it." But this confoundment — the impossible inconsonance between her own spirit and the "salva-

tion" he had in mind — seems to have told him nothing, indicated nothing to him of what that salvation might actually mean,
or that it might hold something less than a universal validity.
And to Pauline, it was as if he had finally elected to surrender up
himself and his life irredeemably to some incomprehensible and
faintly repellent eccentricity, a perversity. He was finally lost to
her.

Several years later, after Billy had gone from the school in
Florida on to a religious campus in Illinois called Wheaton, he
returned one week to hold a revival in a small tabernacle just
across the street from the site of Ham's revival back in that summer of 1934. "I saw in the paper that he was preaching there,"
Pauline remembers, "and I was just drawn to go to that church
that night for some reason." Sitting on a back row with a friend,
she watched him — and he was a stranger, transfigured, withdrawn now into some unreachable distance of intensity, and he
was not a little forbidding. "He got up there and preached this
terrible death-and-go-to-hell bit, saying those things about sin
and judgment and damnation and all. Somehow, I felt this great
sorrow again watching him up there, that same feeling I'd had
when I happened to see him I don't know how many years before down on that street corner in front of Belk's. The difference was, he was a little frightening now. I've always won-
dered if he noticed me in there — he was probably preaching
straight to me, in fact. Anyway, all of a sudden, I just got all
choked up. I started believing everything he was saying, I told
myself, you know, I really *do* need to be saved — saved somehow
from something, I realized that, I just wasn't quite sure what yet.
But I really got choked up. So I decided I'd let Billy save me,
and I went down there to the front when they gave the invitation. . . ."

Billy affirms now, "Yes, I remember that night. It was a New
Year's Eve service in the little mission church there, and I remember it thrilled me greatly to see her come forward." In fact,
says Pauline, when the service was over, "he was out of that
church like a shot, and found me as I was getting back in the car,
and we stood there talking a little while. I could tell he was

tickled to death. It was in his voice, he had that big smile of his."
Billy recalls, "She told me, 'With all my heart, I want to accept
Christ, Billy.' She seemed to really mean it." They parted then,
Pauline riding back off into the night with her friend, Billy returning to his home, where his mother was waiting with a girl he
had brought down from Wheaton — Ruth, whom he would eventually marry — "and the three of us had a prayer for her," he
says.

"But for some reason," he ponders now, "she was just never
able to make that last complete surrender of her life to God."
Pauline says, "I told him that night I'd try, like I had told him
other times before. And I did. But I just couldn't do it. It just
wasn't in me. Maybe I just loved life itself too much, I *wanted* life
too much. . . ."

She eventually married an army aviator, who returned at the
end of the war as one of the highest-decorated flyers in the
South Pacific, with the Distinguished Flying Cross, and who soon
thereafter joined Cal-Tex Oil. Her life with him then proceeded
as an uninterrupted thirty-year gambol of champagne receptions
in Singapore patio gardens, sundown parties on the jasmine-
spilled terraces of Kuala Lumpur. "I have to say that it would
have been one of the saddest things if I had missed knowing
Billy," she declares now, "but it was a great life. I can truly say
that." She still has about her a vivid and unvanquished vivacity,
most of all now in her avid warm eyes. "Sure, I still think of
him," she says, "maybe because it was the first real love of my
life. We were both so young then, so free and happy. But there
never was another one quite like Billy. It was awfully hard for
me to get married after that. Afterward, I compared every man
I met to Billy — even to this day, I still find I do that a little. I
don't think there's a man I've ever met so alive as he was then.
There's no question, we sure did love each other there for those
two or three years. But then he just started running *off* — first
with that ridiculous Fuller Brush that summer, and then up to
that Bob Jones place, then it was down to Florida. I would have
gone stark crazy sitting home waiting for him. I just couldn't
have missed all those dances. But I sure loved Billy. Lord, how I

loved that boy. And in a way, I suppose, I still do, sort of — I mean, I don't think you ever get over those first loves completely, do you? It never happens quite like that again; you're always still a little in love with that first one for the rest of your life, aren't you?"

In a sense, over the years uncountable other women have tended to be smitten with Graham, from however far a distance and however subliminally, in much the same way — actresses, socialites, wives of governors and press barons, who seem to behold in him the palpable image of what they somehow missed in their own men through their lives: that lost bright man-angel of their sweet American maidenhoods back in that brief nebula in time when they were good, and pure and undamaged, their whole life a soft pastel shimmering of possibilities, and they knew and believed in a potential of love as they never would again. Pauline herself reflects, "The nicest memories I've got, actually, are those memories of courtin' Billy. But so much has happened since then, so much has changed. My life, when I look back on it sometimes, seems so messed up in a way — wild, crazy, anything but peaceful. Of course, I wouldn't have had it any other way. But it was so sweet back then with Billy. I was sweet. And I'm not quite so sweet any longer."

Occasionally, she will turn on her television to discover him preaching in some crusade in Toronto or Taiwan, "and I sit down and watch him for a little while, and I feel very proud of him." Then in 1968, she was invited to an honorary reception for him in Charlotte. While she watched him from their table being swarmed by the other guests, her husband suggested she make her way over and at least say hello, and she sniffed, "You think I'd push and scratch my way up there? Not for anything. Look at all those other idiots all over him — I'm not going to be a part of that." But after another moment, she declared, "Aw, fiddle-faddle — let's go." When Billy spotted her, says Pauline, he immediately shouted, "Ruth! Ruth! She's here!" and came plowing toward her and, she says, "he threw those long ole arms of his around me." But she realized in that instant that he was greeting her with merely the same easy hearty but detached affability with which he would have greeted any other friend or acquaintance out of his past.

IV

One mild February afternoon in 1937 on the campus of Florida Bible Institute, which was now mostly deserted during the break between exams, the dean of the school happened to glance out a back door of the administration building to see a green Plymouth pull up in the yard below him, the doors open, and a youth unfold his lanky frame like a carpenter's ruler out of the back seat, "this tall, clean-cut young fella, who stood there a minute just stretching" — a long racking stretch with his spread hands reaching astonishingly high in the air.

A Bible academy of some seventy-five souls located several miles out of Tampa among the sprawling orange groves of a community called Temple Terrace, it was a campus that had formerly been a wintering preserve for wealthy Northern migrants until falling a casualty of the Depression, when it was inherited by a stocky revivalist out of North Carolina named W. T. Watson. "Here was its owner," Watson still marvels, "this Jewish fella in New York, who owned about a third of the Empire State Building, a man not even of our faith, and you know what a deal the Lord helped us put over on him? He let us have the whole place, furnished, sixty thousand dollars, and no down payment for ten years and no interest. Now, to deal with a Jew and get the place for that, no interest even, that was a miracle how the Lord made that happen." Flanked along one side by a golf course tapering off under high moss-hung pines, its central building, which had been the hotel itself, was a hulking tapioca-pale stucco confection with a slightly shabby Alhambra-like ornateness among the royal palms and tennis courts, in one wing of which there continued to be installed about ninety guests, "upper-middle-class church people from the North," as Graham recounts. Behind this turreted rococo edifice, a small complex of

other stucco buildings with red tile roofs was distributed along a
slope beside the narrow calm running of the Hillsboro River, a
flat sluggish purling of black water glinting tea-gold in late afternoon sunlight, easing under long tatterings of moss from the
cypresses along its edges.

It was a rather curious affair — this fundamentalist lyceum established in what resembled the vaguely tawdry government
buildings of some minor tropical republic, beside a swamp river
of hyacinths and palmettos with a certain savage prehistoric look,
where Watson's modest aggregation of students was instructed in
such matters as Prophecy, Modern Missions, Bible Geography,
Hymnology, and a course called Gospel Magic. But as one friend
whom Billy met shortly after his arrival there, Roy Gustafson,
testifies, "after Bob Jones, Billy landed on that campus like he'd
just been let out of jail."

After his father had delivered him over to the dean that February afternoon, Billy spent his first few days simply galloping
over the school's green grounds like a young giraffe, exultant,
sprinting with great whoops up and down the mown fairways of
the golf course in clopping brogans and chartreuse trousers,
with a Boy Scout knife dangling from his belt, says Gustafson,
"like some overgrown schoolboy." The months that followed
turned out to be perhaps the most lyric season of his life. He will
still mention now and then as he muses back over the years,
"That time down there, that's when I was the happiest. . . ."

The days began with a doctrine class at seven on a cold stomach before breakfast, with a chapel service around eleven, and
his general curriculum consisted of not much more than Bible
history, the life of Christ, something called Bible Customs — but
he fared rather feebly even in these minimal academic rigors.
Mainly, he dolphined through delight there — paddling canoes,
gleefully whacking away at tennis and, with his odd cross-handed
grip, at golf. He would even go about his turn at washing dishes
in the dining hall with a huge clattering zest. Enlisted once to
drive some guests from the other wing of the main building on a
tour through Tampa in a station wagon, "I took off with them
and went around for several hours explaining all the wonderful

things about Tampa, which I myself had never seen before until that afternoon, but when I brought them back, they all seemed happy." He bounded about the campus in radiant bow ties, pin-stripe suits of primary colors, suede shoes in maroon and rust and purple, which lent him something of the look of an ambulatory aurora borealis. "Billy was always turned out sharp as a tack," says Gustafson. "Unlike most of the rest of us down there, he always seemed to have plenty of money on him, too." But he was also given to sudden bargings of eager generosity, presenting Gustafson with the white double-breasted jacket with black piping that Prevatte had furnished him after his conversion, bestowing on friends others of his suits.

He was, altogether, an engagingly open-hearted and credulous young naïf — Gustafson himself managed to hustle him a book for a dollar that Gustafson insisted was required for courses there, but that turned out to be merely a handmade direct transcription of the entire text of Romans. As the school's dean, the Reverend John Minder, describes it, "Billy realized he didn't know everything there was to be known, so he learned early in life to listen to advice from others and then take it. He was always open for advice and counsel, and then he'd do *exactly* what you told him to do. That's one thing that was so unusual about him."

He eventually undertook a few preaching exercises in town. But at the same time, during those first idyllic months at Temple Terrace, he began to find for some reason, he said, "The urge to preach was revolting to me." He came to be visited with vague suspicions of "preachers as weak, not contributing. I began to feel I just didn't want to be one. I thought there were more — well, more masculine things to be." There occurred one brief grim intrusion into his ongoing celebration of spirit in the golden air of that setting: once, on a street in Tampa, he saw a man hit by a car, "and the fellow started screaming, 'I'm lost, I'm lost, I can see Hell, I can see Hell!' " — Billy stood transfixed with horror. But it was only like an instant's chill from an open dark cellar door one might pass on a summer afternoon. On the whole — among the palms and orange groves and golf greens of that small gospel campus with a warm breath of the sea coming off the nearby Gulf — it was as if he were at play now in the gardens, the Eden of his innocence.

Then, trampling with a friend down a hallway one afternoon, he paused to be introduced to a deftly crafted figurine of a girl named Emily Cavanaugh with coal-black hair — and instantly swam into love with her. "One look," he still grins, "and I was gone." The daughter of an oil businessman in Tampa, she was an effervescently pretty creature, bright of face but chaste of makeup, and carried a delicately spun nicety of manner. She also happened to be possessed of a high religious earnestness. But a certain God-thralled conscientiousness was not the least of the subtle aphrodisiacs at play in the somewhat rarefied atmosphere of such a campus as Florida Bible Institute. Spirituality mightily attracted; along with any approximation of earthly comeliness, it tended to ravish the heart.

When Billy is asked now what it was that so smote him about Emily, he professes, "She was a deeply spiritual girl, beautiful, brunette, highly dedicated." At the time, she was singing, with her two sisters, named Inez and Pleasant, in a gospel trio, performing in churches and on radio stations all the way from Miami to Canada — renditions in close trilling beelike harmony of such numbers as "This World Is Not My Home, I'm Just A-Passing Through." Emily herself had first noted Billy as he was standing in one of his pinstripe suits in the lobby of the main building, looming over a collection of students around him with his blaze of blond hair, talking with a wide flurrying of his hands. Later, in the small student gatherings convoked to pray for missionaries in the fields abroad, she was considerably taken with the energy and urgency of his delivery — "I was very, very impressed with the way he prayed."

It was a courtship that demurely proceeded, then, as a kind of minuet of decorousness through their work together with the Tabernacle Youth, playing Ping-Pong, talking in the lamplit student lounge every evening before dinner in an evanescent patter of spiritual sentiments against a running counterpoint of lingering gazes and blushings — "going to religious meetings," as Billy

describes it now, "and stealing a kiss now and then." They par-
took of ice-cream cones together and, at Emily's house, servings
of Jell-O — that chill translucent abstraction of fruit that had
always been Billy's most passionately cherished of savors. Occasionally, most sublimely, when he set out on some preaching
stint, she would go along to play the piano for him.

He was convinced now she was to be his Rachel, his Rebekah.
He wrote home, announcing to his mother that he had found
the one who would be his wife. And in fact, after his loss of
Pauline, it was as if Emily presented to him, on that campus of
orange blossoms and sanctity, a wondrous reconciliation after all
between the ripe earth and the consecrations of heaven. Sober,
soulful, she was if anything even more exactingly devout than
he, and yet she held for him a plush loveliness, her eyes sweetly
spangling in a face with the clear glow of a candlelit chapel
madonna: she seemed the utter fulfillment of all his heart's glad
and simple poetries. Sometimes, with her mother packing a
lunch for them, they would travel out for a solitary picnic along
the beach — talking there, now and then tilting gently to a brief
kiss, alone by the long sounding tide of the sea, with blowing
calls of gulls in a blue immaculacy of sky.

He brought her home at last to meet his mother. Mrs. Graham, as it turned out, was agreeably impressed. "She was a very
lovely, very serious girl," she says. "She seemed to have so much
common sense. She was very poised, and a deeply dedicated
Christian girl." For his part, Billy was almost manic with jubila-
tion. A friend of the Grahams remembers, "That time Billy
brought Emily here to meet his folks, he couldn't wait to run
down to the Belk store and tell us, 'C'mon, I want to show you
my girl.'" Finally, during the summer of 1937, while she was in
Toronto singing with her sisters, he wrote her asking if she
would marry him. After their return to the campus at Temple
Terrace, some six more months passed in suspended and delicious inconclusiveness. Then — on a warm January evening
after they had attended a service in a local black church, with the
congregation in the plank-floored sanctuary clapping and singing and stamping through their surging hymns — when they

paused on their way back to the school at a drugstore, she informed him over their scoops of ice cream, "I have something to tell you, Billy. I want to say yes to your letter last summer."

He fairly cartwheeled now through the next few months. But then, toward the first turning of spring, Emily began to evince certain signs of restiveness. Also on the campus then was a young ministerial student named Charles Massey, and as Emily explains it now, "I had always noticed Charles." Once, in fact, at a church meeting where she was to play the organ and Massey to lead the singing, the organ had suddenly gasped out, and Massey had crouched beside her as she resumed the hymn's stately refrains to the vigorous pumping of his hands at the bellows pedals. The son himself of a dairy farmer in lowland Georgia, he was a few years older than Billy, with a certain sturdy matinee-idol handsomeness, a fondness for bow ties — rather a Lancelot among the church lasses of those parts. "Frankly," says Emily, "I was a little afraid of him." On the other hand, says Grady Wilson, "Emily had sort of a motherly affection for Billy, it always seemed to me."

Whatever, it began to strike her after a while that "Billy seemed really kind of unsettled, you know, not knowing which way he wanted to go, what he actually wanted to do with his life." But to Emily, Massey owned an assurance and self-possession against which Billy began to assume aspects of an unlicked calf. "Gradually," she says, "I just began to feel very uncomfortable about Billy and I." At the same time, unnoticing, he was ceaselessly buffeting her now with gales of his own excitement — an enthusiasm that tended to take away the breath of her own feelings: there was something gustily appropriatory about the sheer heedless energy of his assumptions. "On a class trip once," she says, "I got piqued with him about something — I don't remember what it was — but I didn't want to ride back with him. I remember he asked me, 'What'sa matter with you — you seem sorta changed."

At last, she says, "I decided that I ought to be fair to him," her manner of imparting this to Billy being a suggestion that perhaps they should pray about the whole proposition. It was a recommendation that instantly knelled with a cold ominous clanging in his heart. His response was to plunge into hours of feverish praying each day, kneeling on the dank cement floor of a basement storage area that he had staked out, he says, as "my little hideaway," and imploring the Lord, among the pails and mops and wooden crates there, to let this happiness happen.

One afternoon in May, before a class party scheduled for that evening, he rode into Tampa with Dean Minder and some other boys, and as Minder relates it, "Billy asked me on the way in, 'Mr. Minder, do you know where we might get a corsage?' I took them to this little corner florist, and all the other boys got twenty-five-cent corsages, but Billy said, 'I want a fifty-cent corsage. Emily's got to have the best.' " But at the party that night, his bouquet was agonizingly absent from her blouse. Presently she led him outside to a swing under some palms beside the river, and there, as they floated back and forth in a creaking pendulum-like suspension in that spring evening, with a quiet rasp and clacking of palm blades over them, she told him, "I think I ought to give you the ring back, Billy. I'm just not sure we're right for each other" — indicating that he seemed, unhappily, a bit spiritually frivolous to her — "I just don't see any real aims or purpose in your life yet," and allowing that, in any event, it seemed she had wafted into at least a special affection, if not love, for someone else: Charles Massey.

The expression on Billy's face was that of a harpooned seal. And, "suddenly," says Emily, "we both began to cry." He quickly stood and, after a moment, managed to stammer to her, "Well, I will always love you. I will always remember for the rest of my life what you've meant to me. *I* won't ever forget —" and then abruptly wheeled and lunged off. Emily arose and walked across the school's moonlit lawns to the music practice room, and sitting there, began to play the piano to herself, singing in her thin high feathery contralto, while tears glimmered on her cheeks, "all those grand old sad hymns like 'Take Your Burden to the Lord and Leave It There.' "

But Billy was blasted. He stumbled on to rouse Minder at his house, and "that's where I lost control," as he puts it now. Sitting like a collapsed lattice of knees and elbows on a couch in Minder's living room, he sobbed for almost two hours, while Minder — a large carrot-haired man with a bluff amicable face — administered clumsy cuffs and pats to his bony shoulders, providing him the somewhat scant consolation, "Now, Billy, it'll all work out for the best," along with the rather thin gruel of the Scripture verse, "Blessed be . . . the Father of mercies, and the God of all comfort; Who comforteth us in all our tribulation, that we may be able to comfort them which are in any trouble."

On through the following days, Billy seemed caught in a kind of skittering hysteria: Jimmie Johnson, who also happened to be at Temple Terrace, remembers, "He'd cry. Then a few minutes later he was laughing. The next thing you knew, he was weeping again." As his sister Catherine recalls, "It was like a death in the family. I mean, we really felt like they were going to be married, and he was so in love with her." Actually, no small part of his bludgeoned astonishment and suffering, as one of his cousins notes, was "he just couldn't understand how Emily could have given him up, how any girl could throw him over, how it was she didn't realize what she meant to him. He kept telling his mother, 'But she just doesn't realize how I *appreciate* her.' " It was as if he were as deeply devastated by that sudden inexplicable refusal of the dazzling and extraordinary gift of himself and his heroic cherishing. He groaned to Grady, "She just doesn't know how much I love her, how much I *treasure* her. I just don't see how I can make it now. It's like it just wasn't of any worth to her."

Emily contends now, "I never really expected how it was going to hurt him, what a bomb I was dropping on him — honestly." Nevertheless, she took the precaution, she says, "of never talking to him alone again after that night. All my roommates were afraid that if I spoke to him, or I was alone with him again, I'd give in, I'd go back with him, I wouldn't be able to resist." She ventured from this deliberate self-cloisterment only once, to ask him if he would return her picture — "and he wouldn't give it to me. He said he was at least going to keep that much of me. And he never did give it back." For a while, the relationship between him and Massey was somewhat prickly and taut: Billy announced to him once, "I'm going to get her back. You wait and see. I will."

As the spring welled on toward the heavy glut of summer, he abandoned the iron-frame bed in his cinder-block dormitory room, besieged again by that insomnia that had ransacked his nights at Bob Jones, and took to wandering through those warm opulent evenings in a soft amorous blandishing of breezes from the Gulf, in a sleepless anguish. He had arrived at a moment, as he would later say, "when I learned something of the crucified life." In fact, he came to have about him now almost a look of carrion — his brow hugely bulbed like a skull, his faint grin wasting back from a glaring loom of teeth. A tall, slouched, solitary figure, he stalked for hours — "grieving in his heart and soul," as Grady tells it — up and down the moonlit fairways. Some nights, he roamed the dirt aisles of the orange groves, as he had once wandered among the boughs of his grandfather's fruit orchard back in his careless boyhood, lost now in a strangled praying: *God, I have to have her. It has to be.* . . .

He would also pace the vacant streets of a nearby housing development that had been quickly assembled during the boom in Florida in the Twenties — a perfect and intact suburban neighborhood of tidy villas with small front lawns and driveways and picture windows, complete with street signs, only absolutely deserted, everything there but the people, like a premature construction for a yet unemerged and unrealized society, awaiting now only its occupants. In those late nights as he wandered the phantom streets of that peopleless suburban neighborhood, "I would pray by the hour," says Billy, "and then, in the most unusual way, I'd have the oddest feeling of some great multitude around me."

Finally, late one night touched now with the shyest hint of autumn's cool quiescent weather, after hours of walking the golf course he sank down on the edge of the eighteenth green, at the crest of the fairway's long moon-pale incline. He sat there for some time, his head hung. And then he was breathing in light rapid shallow pants, as if his lungs were stunned by some sudden blow, and looking up, his eyes blurred, starred, and in an instant his gaunt jaws were wet with tears. It was there, on the eighteenth green of the golf course, that Graham experienced at last his true climactic Gethsemane — "That's when I surrendered," he declares. His hands twisting together, he called out in a hoarse voice, "All right, Lord! If you want me, you've got me. If I'm never to get Emily, I'm gonna follow you. No girl or anything else will ever come first in my life again. You can have all of me from now on, I'm gonna follow you at all cost." The echo of his cry dimmed off down the fairway. He stood, and walked back to his room in the dorm.

At that spot some thirty-five years later, there are still only the intermittent dry snicks of golf balls, the idle voices of golfers in the calm and empty mornings as they trundle past in canopied electric carts, with no more memorial of that protean night in Graham's past than the green's small nylon orange flag muttering and flickering in the wind. But that eighteenth-hole catharsis of heart constituted, if anything ever did, Graham's authentic conversion at last. It was as if, at that point, he said farewell to the earth forever. As Jimmie Johnson perceives it, "I think that despair and suffering of his over Emily was the last tie that bound him to the things of this world, to childhood and innocence." Billy himself would later propose, "How does one know God's call? How do you know you are in love?" That, indeed, seems to have been the transfer. As one friend says, "God became his only passion."

He took now to praying through the nights with a clutch of other fervent young men on the campus. As Grady relates it, "Before that thing with Emily happened, Billy had been pretty much a lovesick chicken. But after that, he got down to business." Mrs. Graham herself declares, "It meant the making of a *man* when they broke up. He had really believed in Emily, he had so much confidence in her. He wrote us so many letters telling us about his heartbreak. But after it happened, he began reading the Word and reading good books about what so many others had gone through, and he began to recognize it was a chastening. He began to understand that verse in Hebrews —"

and she pauses to pluck a Bible into her lap, her frail fingers fluttering through its leaves for a moment "— here, in Hebrews twelve:eleven," and reads then in her parchment-thin voice, " 'Now no chastening for the present seemeth to be joyous, but grievous: nevertheless afterward it yieldeth the peaceable fruit of righteousness unto them which are exercised thereby,' " she looking up then with a pale smile, "so you see, God taught Billy a lot in that experience." Indeed, it was a razing of his spirit that afforded a number of parties — in particular, those at Bob Jones who had considered him rather too extravagantly alive — a special measure of gratification: "That girl's comments to him down there about his inadequacy as a spiritual person," one of them says, "changed him around wonderfully. It had a splendid influence on him — it reined him in. He simply had too much of an ego before that happened to him. He'd never appreciated discipline, and that experience gave him discipline in his life for the first time."

But Billy maintains now, "I don't think I ever really got over that hurt. I think I felt it until I met Ruth. I simply forgot about girls for a long time after that, two or three years maybe." Actually, he continued to date others around the campus, if anything more frenetically than ever before — but it curiously seemed also a part of his renunciation of all this world's allures. "You should have seen some of those things he started taking out," Grady declares. "Man, I didn't understand why *anybody'd* wanna go out with bags like them after he'd been dating somebody as beautiful as Emily. They were wholly unlike the sort of girls he'd always dated. I told him that — but he didn't want to hear it. And I mean, some of 'em were plum awful. I wouldn't have been seen with 'em on a dark corner at midnight." A few of these girls he brought back home to Charlotte, one of them — whom Jean and Catherine, from a window, watched him conduct up the front walk as they uttered unbelieving moans — a somewhat sepulchral figure, by their account, with a pallor of lilies and a certain cachet of aged sardines to her presence: "Mother felt so sorry for her because of the way she was dressed that she even made a dress for her while she was there." Grady finally suggested gently to Billy, "Boy, look, this one is sholy not the one for you." But if she seemed surpassingly indifferent to all customary earthly charms, that was precisely why Billy had so quickly, abjectly clung to her: she was a part, an act, of his passionate abnegation.

He gamely attended Charles and Emily's wedding, enduring through the ceremony with a slain grin sprawled across his face: "They sat me with her family, and everybody in that church knew." Later, as if still obsessed with a relentless exertion to directly cauterize that old hope and pain out of his life now, he visited them in their home when Emily was pregnant with her first child, and Massey recollects that "the three of us knelt together in our prayer room." But over the years, a number of Billy's original enthusiasts in Charlotte never quite forgave Emily and Massey for according Billy all that torment. Vernon Patterson, for one, reports with a chortle how Billy and Grady were once watching the crowd throng in during an early crusade in Boston, when Grady suddenly grunted, "Billy, look a-there who's coming in," and Billy staring at Charles and Emily making their way along an aisle, finally muttered, "Praise the Lord, they can't seem to find a seat" — and Patterson goes on with some relish, "and you know, Charlie Massey came to see Billy while he was up there and said, 'Billy, pray for me.'"

Massey, who allows now, "I did very much want to be a missionary once," actually wound up serving for most of his life as an army chaplain, with only intervals as a pastor here and there. He has since returned to the Tampa area as a member of the faculty at Watson's new campus across town from Temple Terrace. He and Emily live in a long, low home in a cul-de-sac, with a cineramic picture window in their rear sitting room looking out over a far sweep of lawn descending under the mossy vaults of live oaks down to a stretch of the Hillsboro River — they passing their lives now along the continuing changeless running of those same peaceful olive waters beside which it all happened over thirty-five years ago. Massey — his thin ink-black hair receding now, but with mildly rakish sideburns and a debonair little flick of a toothbrush mustache — has come to be faintly testy about the curiosities they continue to be confronted with regarding that episode in Billy's past in which they happened to be so critically involved: "Just seems like every Tom, Dick, and Harry in the world," he complains, "comes through here and pesters us about that." Emily herself —still a neat and compact dovelike figure with a doll-bright face, her black hair bobbed short, still with that fine preciseness of poise and movement — is also rather snipped about such inquiries: "I don't mean to be obnoxious about it, but there's just so much one has to say about it, and that's all, there's nothing more really to say." But aside from this occasional nettlement, they entertain a mellow amiability about the way circumstances have turned out since then. Charles agreeably offers, "Yeah, Billy called us from the White House one time — that's what I call rubbing it in, huh?" And Emily herself delicately submits, "I would have to say that Billy is much more refined now than he was then." They have, in fact, even visited Billy and Ruth at their mountainside aerie in Montreat, and at a testimonial dinner for Watson in Tampa which Billy attended in 1976, Emily took to the lectern at one point in the program to melody, "The Lord has been mighty good to me. It's been great to be loved by two wonderful men" — and she turned to Billy and smiled, and he produced one of his billboard grins, flushing only slightly.

As it happened, around the time of his rejection by Emily, Billy was dealt yet another profound clobberment, when a man and a woman — "two Christians he had greatly admired," says a friend, "and learned a great deal from" — were discovered in what appeared to be, as one of Graham's more deferential biographers daintily puts it, "serious moral defections." It was, actually, a pathetically burlesque and dubious scandal. But so diphtherial was the alertness to impropriety over that small pentecostal enclave that, as Billy recounts it, someone enterprisingly took it on himself to follow the couple as they left the campus one morning and drove out to a nearby residence. Their tracker than rushed back to the school, rounded up a general posse of male students, and they returned to storm, in effect, the house. The woman was gone — as Billy says, "She was later found back at the school, lying down on a bed in the women's dorm" — but the man had the misfortune to be finally discovered hunkering in a closet, wearing nothing but an expression of calamity. There followed a mass hearing back at the school, and Billy, who had been off campus during the episode, says, "I can still remember how the man's hands were trembling."

It seemed not impossibly a mere vaudevillean mishap of appearances. However, the incident staggered Billy. As to the tatty moral vigilantism of that commando strike itself, he remained unperturbed. Instead, "he was shaken to the core," as one friend states it, by the indication of an unsuspected corruption — in much the same way, in fact, he would be stunned decades later by another sudden intimation of an unimagined evil glimpsed behind what seemed demeanors of intrepid respectability. But if that incident in Florida constituted the first trauma visited on the simplicities of his vision of goodness and his sense of the human heart, even then, instead of prompting at least larger suspicions about the true measureless complications of the human condition, his instant reflex was to contract more fixedly into the certitudes of his simplicity. "It caused me for a while to wonder if anyone was totally true to Christ," he concedes. Beyond that the effect of that disillusionment, along with his disaster with Emily, seemed to be a calculation, a determination never to trust to flesh again — to cast his lot irrevocably now beyond mere men and the life of this world.

The truth is, those ordeals simply acted to complete what had always been the inclination in him anyway — a carefulness to hold himself at a final remove from the moil and strivings of mere mortality. It was like a dim aversion and dread that absorption into that earthly welter of human experience amounted in the end to meaninglessness, nothingness, death. While he still owned that exorbitant vitality and expectancy which this lesser sense of life could not answer, the tension of that long ambivalence, that impasse, was now broken. "It was the best, if most difficult thing, that had happened to me so far," he would later pronounce. "I learned what victorious living meant. As sons and heirs of God, Christians have conquered the things of this world. They are free in a way which no non-Christian can ever be."

Not the least powerful of the properties of Christ's crucifixion and resurrection is that it has always posed the ultimate dramatic metaphor for each Christian's individual conversion and new birth. For Billy, it was indeed like his own personal crucifixion of the flesh, a passage through a shadow world of desolation and abdication of all the soft delights of the earth, and then his resurrection into a purged and transfigured being. Many years later, as he was hiking one morning in Switzerland to a high Alpine village, a haze of flies began to gather and hang about the brilliant red shirt he was wearing, shimmering ever more densely after him as he strode on faster and faster, until finally, without stopping, he snatched off the shirt and flung it aside and plunged on with his bare back glistening pale in the thin morning sunshine, leaving the shirt lying on the ground behind him with the flies mumbling over it — so, in a way, did he more or less shed his mere humanity after that golf-green commitment.

He had given himself up now to a passion only for sublime possibilities of goodness that he was unable to perceive in the life around him — that is, for a superlife, which took for him the person of Christ: "Christ is perfect goodness — the perfect, the pure." There is a photograph of Billy, not long after that night on the golf course, standing alone now on that beach where he and Emily had come once for their picnics: he is thin as a taper candle, an ascetic flame-licked emaciation about him, and in a white shirt and tie with his billowy trousers sagging from his frail waist, he is reaching high with his long lank hands in a winging whirl everywhere around him of white gulls, his head thrown back with a look of glad exaltation against a blank fierce blue sky.

He was to remain transfixed in that eighteenth-green epiphany for the rest of his years — salvation is a matter of rigorously sanitizing oneself out of all the sweats of the earth. Towering resplendent on spotlit platforms in coliseums and amphitheatres from Manila to Glasgow to Chicago to Rio de Janeiro, he would proclaim, "When I was seventeen, eighteen, nineteen, I was interested in sex, yes. Human nature is so built that it cannot resist these temptations when they are thrown from every angle. But you'll never make it to the top until you lick this thing, and you'll never lick it without Christ."

Still, through his sermons there would run rather enfevered litanies on that particular temptation — he citing Vashti, queen to Xerxes, commanded once to perform a dance at the end of a revel, "and she refused," cries Graham, and then after a long uncertain hang, " — to show her body before — before those people, all those leering men," or on Joseph in Egypt, alone with Potiphar's wife, "he was tempted all right, he desired her, the temptation was overwhelming, but *he ran out of that house!*" As he goes through these evocations of "the earthly, the sensual, the devilish," there seems a certain extra smack and vibrancy in his enunciation, a higher vigor in his movements; but he then shouts, "But Joseph, Moses, they chose the joy of following God rather than the pleasures of Egypt. And there's a joy in that! The joy! The joy! Deep down inside, *a Joy!*"

In these preachments, he would always insist, "There's nothing dirty, there's nothing X-rated about sex, there's a depth in sex you can never imagine outside of God. But sex is sacred, not an instrument of self-indulgence. Misused, it can become a terrible tyrant — " That would, in fact, become an ever-recurring allusion with him, sexuality as a tyrant: "If you aren't careful, if it gets out of control, it will damn your soul quicker than any other sin." It was almost as if he would come to sense in it some primeval demonic energy of chaos that could consume all — the soul, civilization. "It's interesting to me," he would offer, "that in the Soviet Union, Cuba, China, they're trying to build a strong society, a revolutionary society that they hope will ultimately conquer the world, but they don't allow this kind of free promiscuous open sexuality." To contain it, to fortify oneself against it, "watch your eyes. You cannot help the first look, God does not hold you responsible for seeing something which might engender impure thoughts, but he holds you responsible for that second look. Watch out! Watch your thinking. Don't dally with your thoughts." Instead, he would urge, "sex should be used wisely.

Before your marriage it can be a driving dynamo that will take you to the top," and he would testify, "I am true to my wife. I do not think about other women. I am not attracted to other women. That's the way of happiness. It's the way of joy. It's the way of peace. It's the way of success!"

It has been a matter, as one of his associates remarks, of keeping himself always armed with Paul's admonition, "I keep under my body, and bring it into subjection." But beyond distractions of the flesh, it has really been against all the lures of this world — pride, the pretty wiles of sophistication — that he has been constantly tensed: according to a colleague, "he has always run scared, under perpetual alert." As he began to prosper in later years, he came to be inordinately haunted by the story of Samson — anointed at birth as a Nazarite to be "used mightily of the Lord," eventually violating the chastities of that consecration, whereupon the blessing and the power were instantly removed from him; it became an allegory of what, through doubt or vainglory, might happen to him — says Graham, "It's been almost an obsession with me."

In fact, his life since those events in Florida has consisted of one long feat of certitude — a steadfastness against all embattlings or enervations of doubt. Not the least of his fortitudes in this effort has been his own capacity for an utter self-mesmerization with his message — practicing altar calls on a river stump off the campus at Temple Terrace, he would even feel himself pulled by his own appeals. Too, that lifetime's struggle of certainty may have been considerably facilitated by the circumstance, as one of his critics points out, that "to be sure is a blessing reserved for the simple." But as his wife, Ruth, would later observe, "Of course, he has doubts, but not for long — because he never really *entertains* them." A fellow cleric propounds, "You know, he never did attend a theological school. He was just never instructed in all those excellent complications and equivocations. He more or less came straight up out of the grass into the pulpit. He's sort of God's own divine bumpkin."

Always at the center of this certitude, there has remained the revelation he came by that midnight in Temple Terrace — that

"if Jesus Christ is who he claims to be," as he later explained it,
"then nothing else matters. Nothing else counts. If we can live all
our lives as a preparation for the moment when we are going to
meet God, that is the important thing." It is that peculiar discontent of those Calvinist folk among whom he grew up, that feeling
of displacement and only transitory tenancy in this life: "Don't
get your bank account too large here, keep loose, keep your bags
packed — you're going on a trip!" It tends to produce, among
other things, a kind of romance of death; at the least, Graham
would hardly rage against the dying of the light: "Death is just a
departure, not to oblivion but to a new horizon. In heaven, we'll
look like what we were at our best on earth, I believe. The Christian attitude toward life beyond life pierces the confusion and
darkness like a shining beacon." For his part, it's almost as if he
were half in love with that last easeful ceasing of strain and
breath: "Many times I look forward to death. I have no fear of
death whatsoever. I go to bed at night and sometimes one of the
last thoughts I have is *Well, Lord, maybe it'll be tonight, maybe you'll
be coming tonight.*" From this, there results a certain inversion of
values: one lives to die, life is for death.

Yet at the same time, even in his repudiation of the passions of
the world, there still survived that appreciation for its tokens of
prestige and position which had prompted him, as a teenager, to
effuse to Wint Covington, "Boy, you really ought to get you a
good watch. People will see you with a fine watch on, and they'll
know you're not poor. . . . That's the great thing about wearing
a good watch, Wint." In that sense, while he had renounced the
diversions of the flesh, the tension of his youth between the
celestial and the worldly had not really been broken — that old
duality had merely translated into another, this one in fact to
prove far more critical in his life than the other: an ambivalence
now between his commitment to Heaven and his lingering
captivation with the impressive appointments of station and
power — a captivation of far larger implications than those
simpler indulgences he had forsworn. And it was likely for that
reason, sensing this unquiet conjunction of impulses in his na-

ture, that the metaphor of Samson's vulnerabilities was to become a troubled fixation with him.

In the last analysis, Graham was to become over the years an evangel engaged in a certain unspoken but immemorial cultural battle — an apostle in a conflict of cultural differences like that between the Roundheads and the Cavaliers, as indeed so much of politics and history has always been a sublimated cultural warfare, a struggle between different sensibilities, different languages of feeling and being, different dialectics of life. It was an imperative of his life's long striving of certainty that his vision of the human condition would be the most minimal and practical one. It has been an evangelism of the economical, the sure, the efficient in life — which has the effect, in the end, of reducing and trivializing life, of depressing consciousness. In later years, he would even tend to diminish the actual circumstances of his golf-course surrender to his mission: "What happened was, I heard another preacher preach. He challenged the young men in the congregation to go out and spread the word of God. It troubled me. And that night, I went out on a golf course and, as it were, struggled with God. Finally, I told Him I would do it. I certainly didn't start preaching just to show a girl. Of course, my pride was hurt, but I'd forgotten her in a week, and was dating other girls in two weeks." Thus he succeeded in etherizing the true pain and passionate definition of even that experience.

In the same way does the perspective and didactic of his message war against the fullness and mystery of human experience, against awareness. He would discount most of the great dramatists of man's condition of his time — Camus, Sartre, Faulkner, Shaw — as "pessimists," who had "thrown up their hands in despair and said there is no answer to man's dilemma." In any event, he would declare, "I don't think the function of the playwright, the author, the artist, is to reflect what's going on, any more than I should reflect what's going on. I think their function ought to be to lead, to direct." Instead, the central presumption of his ministry was the unfailing efficacy of "a decision for Christ" wholly to transform any personality, no matter whose —

Caligula, Khrushchev, Eichmann, Nietzsche, even Lee Harvey Oswald ("What would have happened to Lee Harvey Oswald if he had known Christ?") — "Every human problem can be solved and every hunger satisfied and every potential can be fulfilled when a man encounters Jesus Christ and comes in vital relation to God in him. Optimism and cheerfulness are the products of knowing Christ!" — thus are Macbeth, Hamlet, Karamazov all accounted for, disposed of: they need never have had any problems. One religious observer has remarked of Graham's message, "Barbarism comes in many forms, some of them exceptionally polite, and among them there is certainly a pious barbarism. The effect of them all is the classic one of barbarism, though — a debasement of wisdom, of understanding, of beauty, of all the sensibilities of the truly civilized life."

Indeed, over the decades, there would accumulate many who would hold an almost visceral antipathy toward Graham, virtually an allergy to the very mention of his name. But for all that, one of the curious ironies that has abided through the course of Graham's career is that, personally, he always strikes one as immeasurably more refreshing and large-spirited than his message and the bulk of those devotees who have made up his supporting cast and constituency through the years: he seems, himself, oddly better, by a quantum difference, than those who in fact have comprised his effect, his meaning. The fact is that — out of what despite all has remained his simple huge goodwill and sheer compulsive affection for people — he has always been stricken with an authentic desperation for salvaging what he deems lost and unhappy souls. "You were made for God," he will appeal; "you were made in God's image for fellowship with him, and you're lonely for him, and you don't know why." It's an urgency that derives, of course, out of that dire fundamentalist orthodoxy of man's willful sin in the Garden that caused the original schism between God and mankind, with man ever since born into an alienation from God, while Christ — taking upon himself on the cross all the guilt inherited from Adam — was God's offer to man of a reconciliation with him, which man may accept or refuse, the true life or eternal damnation hanging in that choice. It is, in fact, Graham's quite literal sense that every single human being is caught at the center of an actual ongoing cosmic contest between God and Satan that has lasted through the ages ever since Lucifer was cast out of heaven — a universal competition for each individual's very being that is still underway at every instant right down to the most ordinary daily levels of each person's experience: "It's a question of who we submit to," Graham says, "and I feel a constant battle with the Devil when I am preaching the gospel. I feel as though, sometimes after I've spoken, I've been whipped with a rubber hose."

He cries from his stadium pulpits, "The Bible says you and I are sinners. We have broken the laws of God, we have continued Adam's sin and disobedience in our own lives, every day. We have kept our backs turned to God's love and forgiveness. We deserve judgment. We deserve death. We deserve Hell. But Jesus said, 'Wait! Not yet! I'll take your place!' And he gave himself up to be nailed to a cross. How could any man look at Christ shedding his precious blood in that horrible death, hammered to a cross, and still, *still*, have such a hard heart that he could turn away from him?" In these persuasions, one of his fellow evangelists declares, "Billy just has this longing, this enormous longing in his heart, to bring lost souls into the joy of redemption and reunion with their Lord. I can tell you, there's a terrific sense of fulfillment to see people make that decision and come to Christ through your bringing them the message, to have people come down and whole lives turned around — that's the fizz on the Pepsi. But that consuming longing for souls — that's the uniqueness of the great evangelist. I heard Billy tell another young evangelist once, after he'd been sitting out in the audience listening to him, 'Joe, when you gave that invitation, I felt something well up inside of me, and I wanted to get up myself and plead with them to come forward.' "

During one crusade in Sydney, having to confront yet another immense audience after an especially battering day, he had an associate kneel with him as he prayed, "O God, you know I'm not prepared for this service again tonight, and there'll be all those people out there who need thee. I read in your word of the reward for labor and service, but Lord, just forget about any rewards for me tonight — but please, don't let my unreadiness and my inadequacy cause you to blot out your blessing from these people." In his own way, Graham himself indisputably partakes, in some measure, of that limitless and unaccountable compassion that impelled Jesus, sitting one night overlooking Jerusalem, to begin weeping for those who were soon to murder him. In Graham's case, it may be a rather collective and blandly unparticularized affection. But there is no question that Graham does in fact actually love the people — or his sense of those people — to whom he preaches. Out of this omnivorous passion of his for souls, he will implore in his invitations, his voice pealing, cracking, "Father, mother with gray hairs and bifocals and bunions and bulges, have you given yourself to Christ? He loves you, he wants to save you, he died for you. . . ." Indeed, in that grand competition for the heart of every individual, it is a kind of effort of seduction. And "at the invitation," he says, "in the five minutes or the ten minutes that this appeal lasts, is when most of my strength leaves me. I seem to be drained of strength. I don't know what it is, but something is going out of me at the moment." And it is not a little compelling to be placed at the center of such an awesome event as Christ's self-sacrifice and to be so urgently wooed to accept that divine solicitude by so commanding and splendid a figure.

For the rest of his time on that campus at Temple Terrace, he pitched himself into preaching forays at local trailer courts, downtown derelict missions, on street corners. "He'd preach to a stump if there was nothing else," says Watson, "anything that'd just stand still for a minute." It was on a gloweringly hot Easter Sunday that he had preached his first pulpit sermon, in a tiny clapboard church out in the scrub pines and palmettos of a north Florida community called Bostwick, where Billy, clamping his Bible to his floral tie, had to wade through a swim of hounds and beagles in the sandy yard outside, and when he arose at last to address the congregation of sawmill hands and cattle farmers, he proceeded to career his way through his total repertoire of four sermons in about eight minutes. But it was not long after this somewhat slam-bang debut that, in the Gulf Coast village of Venice, he tried his first single-handed invitation call — in a sanctuary that was a converted meat market — and when some thirty-two people came forward, it left him bedazed for several days.

He had then a slightly hectic style for which he soon came to be referred to as "The Preaching Windmill' — his voice a high and helter-skelter blaring, he a little white around the eye. They were exercises, recalls Roy Gustafson, who has since become one of his associates, which involved much slapping of the hands, high kicks of his legs: once, narrating the long progression of Hebrew history before the fulfillment of the prophecy of the Messiah, Billy cried, "One thousand years went by — and there was no Christ," giving then a clap, a kick to one side, "two thousand years — " another slap, a kick to the other side " — and no Christ! Three thousand years —" whap! kick back to the other side, a kind of pulpit cancan "— no Christ! Five thousand years, no Christ! *Six* thousand years, still no Christ — " Caught up now in the sheer lick and lilt of this litany, he might have gone on indefinitely if, when he reached, "Eight thousand years, and no — " a friend on the rostrum had not frantically whispered, "Billy — it was only four thousand years, Billy."

Scheduled to conduct the first revival meeting of his life in a remote swamp community, whose more recalcitrant natives had regularly engaged the local preacher in fistfights in the front yard of the church, Billy nevertheless had a thousand flyers printed up for that settlement of no more than two hundred and fifty souls — "Hear! Dynamic Young Evangelist! Billy Graham!" — and was jubilantly tacking them up on loblolly pines and fence posts along a dirt road when a passerby advised him that a deputation from down at the filling-station general store was "comin' up here, they said, to clean your plow, young feller." Billy was waiting beside the front steps of the church when they appeared, a rather gristly bunch in gallused coveralls with no shirts. He immediately notified them, "Now I believe God is with me, and you can do with me what you will, but be careful —

harm me, and God will strike you dead." That proved sufficient to send them shuffling, with only a guffaw or two, on back to the store, but Billy determined it would be more prudent perhaps to cancel the revival.

Still, he reminisces now, "I was much more bold back then. I wish sometimes I were still that bold." In downtown Tampa, he would materialize in the door of a saloon, a long cranelike apparition, and begin railing at the clientele roosting in the gloom inside, and when finally shooed on off down the sidewalk, would simply go around the block and reappear in the door a few minutes later, resuming his fulminations — with the result that, at least once, "a gang of rowdies threw me down on the sidewalk outside," as he reports, "and ground my face in the gutter filth. I got my clothes all messed up, but I felt I was suffering for Christ's sake, and I jumped right back up and pronounced the judgment of God on them." Actually, he came to acquire, after flinging himself with that reckless audacity so often at such inhospitable inner precincts of the unregenerate, a certain frayed and harried fitfulness of demeanor. Once, staying at Minder's home while Minder was away for a revival, he was startled late one night by an abrupt battering on the front door, a voice shouting, "Lemme in. I'm Billy Graham. Lemme in," and as Billy tells it now, "I kept a rifle with me there all the time, a twenty-two that my father had given me when I was ten, which I'd used a few times down there to shoot a few 'gators. I figured this fella out there hollering he was Billy Graham had come to try to beat me up or something, was drunk or something, so I shot through the front door. It must have scared him when he found out I had a gun, 'cause he went on off then."

But for all that, he was possessed of an excruciating earnestness. He once came lunging into Watson's office to blurt, "I want you to pray for me, Dr. Watson. When I was preaching the other night, I added some things in one of my examples that weren't really like it happened — I felt I had to embroider it, and I've come under great conviction." They knelt then by Watson's desk, "and we prayed," says Watson, "that the Lord would help him keep his illustrations correct." Billy had come now under the special tutelage of Dean Minder, who operated his own church downtown, called the Tampa Gospel Tabernacle, where Billy frequently preached — a cavernous revival hippodrome of oyster-pale stucco under ragged palms, that had somewhat the look of a livestock show barn at a state fair. But it was in a little plank Baptist country church set in a bare sand clearing that Billy conducted his first actual revival, and after the first night, Minder asked him, "How'd it go, Billy?" Billy replied bleakly, "Those people up there, they just don't want to hear me preach. Hardly anybody came forward." But the next night, Billy arrived to find the church packed. Enspirited, he orated spectacularly, apprising the congregation they were destined for the same perdition as bootleggers and racketeers if they did not repent their faithlessness, and from then on, as Minder puts it, "things began to happen, that revival really broke out."

But at some point, it came to the attention of the deacons that Billy was still a Presbyterian, and he was advised he could not continue unless he agreed to agreed to become a Baptist. It was thus he came by his denominational reconstitution. At the end of the revival, on a balmy spring Sunday afternoon, he was escorted by another minister down a sloping white beach to the glittering waters of Crystal Lake, where, along with his week's accumulation of eighty-one converts, he was himself immersed and lifted back up, baptized a Southern Baptist now. . . . Actually, it was his third baptism by then. Minder reports, with a sly chortle muffled behind one large mitt of a hand, "Billy'd already been baptized by me earlier, back in my church. He'd come to me and said he'd been sprinkled as a Presbyterian, but he felt he ought to be baptized by immersion. But he just sort of never mentions that time. Billy has a way of making the story better over the years. He starts remembering it the way he'd like it to have been, which isn't always the way it necessarily was, y'know."

Most importantly, during all this time there had been periodically passing through the campus of Florida Bible Institute certain mighty old evangelistic grizzlies, gone only slightly mothy and foggy of eye now, out of a recent vanished grand era of revivalism in the country — Gypsy Smith, H. A. Ironside,

Homer Rodeheaver of Billy Sunday's entourage, even one of the legendary Dwight L. Moody's stalwarts, William Evans. But "evangelism had fallen on such hard times around then," says Billy, "that they had to be put up in Bible colleges whenever they moved around." Even so, those worn but still imposing behemoths out of that classic age of revivalism, which had receded just before he had reached awareness, imparted to Billy a sense of the mythic and epic in his vision of evangelism, the sense of some past glory. Watson himself nostalgically reflects, "We just don't have any giants these days like we had then. There was just an aura about those old fellows that you don't find now." They were the Paul Bunyans, the Dempseys and Babe Ruths, the Pattons and Wellingtons of the faith, and when they came through Temple Terrace and spoke at chapel assemblies, says a student there then, "all the Preacher Boys would be sitting together in a row right down there at the front, furiously taking notes." Some of them were costumed still in rusty black cutaway coats, magnificent relics in their high collars and string ties with their histrionic plumes of hair. And all of them, says one religious historian, were possessed now by one urgency. They had all "seen the fires die down," and it had become their last and single obsession: somewhere, a man must arise "to call America back to God." For his part, Billy was transported by the visitations of these old titans out of a distant larger braver time; and after hearing them preach, he would rush back to his room and there effusively re-perform their sermons. If it was true, as Watson also noted, that "Billy had always wanted to do something big, he didn't know exactly what yet, but he couldn't wait just to do something big, whatever it was," then this impatience — his impulse for some greater reality beyond the ordinariness around him — found now in those hoary dramatic figures a final focused personalization of that possibility.

According to Charles Massey, "Most of us were rather timid around them, but Billy — he was always a little bolder than we were. He always seemed to have access to them somehow. A number of us, in fact, felt a little jealous of him because of that." Mrs. Graham recalls, "Billy would do anything for them; he would carry their bags, would literally polish their shoes." When Gypsy Smith came through, Billy asked for his autograph, and Smith, then in his seventies, grunted, "Now, son. If I sign it for you, then I'm gonna have to sign 'em for all these other fellows around here." Says Watson, "That made Billy feel somewhat badly," and after that, he was inspired to plot with a secret delicious expectancy that, as he confided to Watson, "I will never decline to accept a request from anyone for an autograph." When another of these patriarchs arrived once in a taxi, Billy quickly and brightly presented himself at the curb to chirp, "Can I take your bags for you?" and after he had hefted the luggage up to the room, the evangelist extracted a dollar bill from his wallet and extended it to Billy with the announcement, "Here, young man, take this. Apply yourself, and someday you'll be able to tip also. There is a great deal more where this came from, believe me."

Indeed, along with these formidable old gospel fire-horses, Billy witnessed certain other memorable phenomena during his three years at Temple Terrace. Once, when the school suddenly found itself in terminal need of $10,000, Watson called a campuswide day of prayer, which convened in the main lobby of the administration building around nine in the morning: "All the students fasted, Billy right there among them, and we prayed on through lunch, all of us down on our knees there in that lobby. Then, sometime in the early afternoon, my secretary touched me on the shoulder and said, 'Western Union has a message for you.' It was from a businessman up north. He said that just as he was about to step in a cab about a half-hour before, he'd suddenly felt a great burden on his heart for Florida Bible Institute. The telegram said, 'I'm mailing a check to you today for ten thousand dollars.' I came back and told the students. We had an old-fashioned shouting Praise-the-Lord meeting right there, I can tell you."

For some reason, though, Billy's insomnia continued to burn through his nights. Sometimes he would go to the school's garage, and there, standing on a crate with a single light bulb dangling over him from a drop cord, utterly alone among a clutter of engine tools and mowers and gasoline cans over the oilblotted dirt floor, he would lose himself in crescendos of preaching. Now and then, some student out strolling late across the campus, hearing that vague uproar coming from the shed, would pass by and discover him there on the crate orating to himself, and would shout to him, *"Amen!"* And he would turn with a small start, a wide sheepish ambushed grin on his face, but with barely a falter would keep on, his arms slinging.

It was while he was at Temple Terrace that he happened to deliver his first radio broadcast — took on, briefly, his first electronic amplification, on a gospel program from a small coastal station with a sputtering range of no more than thirty miles. When he blinked on the air, there was a gulp of silence, and he then clamored, "Folks, pray for me, this is Billy Graham, and this is the first time I've ever done this sort of thing, and my knees are knocking together here. . . ."

In the late sundowns now, he would canoe across the black still water of the Hillsboro River to a cypress stump some distance away from the campus, and there, he would preach in a loud clangoring voice in the hush of the day's dissolving, frogs chittering, his only congregation an occasional alligator regarding him with a flat yellow lidless gaze in a moment's soundless emergence from the river, a raccoon scuffling past. And sometimes, in that primordial solitude, after tolling out his call for sinners to come forward and accept Christ, as he listened to the last ringing of his voice across the water, he also seemed to hear, he would later disclose, the faint insinuations of a voice sighing, *One day, there'll be many. One day* — and, he says, "I'd have the strangest glimpses then, just for a second, of these great crowds I now preach to. It wasn't exactly clear that I was actually preaching to them; I seemed more involved just as an assistant in it all. But as if in a dream, these vast multitudes, they'd flash across my consciousness."

Catherine remembers that, the first time she heard him hold forth from a pulpit, she and some friends sitting on a back pew began to snigger incredulously — "I felt so embarrassed. I mean, he was just preaching so loud, waving his arms around and everything." She turned to whisper to one friend, "What in the world has come over him? He's preaching like he thinks he's preaching to ten thousand people."

V

By the summer of 1940, Germany had already begun its iron brawl through the shattering glassware of Europe, the Japanese armies were shrilling in smoke down toward Indochina now, but it was all a phantasmagoria, a ferocity still abstractly contained, in America, in the muted measured intonations of Gabriel Heatter, H. V. Kaltenborn, on fluted Philco consoles among the tasseled lampshades of quiet after-supper living rooms over the land — no more yet than an occasional dull intimation of thunder off beyond the serene daylit courthouse squares and baseball parks and white spired churches of the nation's life then. Billy spent much of that summer painting the house for his father. That May, he had finished at Florida Bible Institute — president of his class, editor of what passed for the yearbook — and in the fall, he would leave for Illinois to enter another, somewhat more auspicious religious school, Wheaton College.

This felicitous development had come to pass through the good offices of a couple of affluent businessmen of pious enthusiasms from Illinois who had visited Temple Terrace that past winter. It was while Billy was caddying for them one morning, on that same golf course of his midnight travail, that they made their proposition: having already beheld the energy of his preaching, they were so taken with his personal agreeableness that they offered to subsidize him at Wheaton with a year's board, lodging, and tuition. A doctrinaire evangelical conservatory set in the tawny plains south of Chicago, Wheaton was a considerably more urbane and academically ambitious campus than Florida Bible Institute — the difference between them about comparable to that between a tub band and a chamber ensemble. Billy was elated only a little less than his mother. After a consultation with Jimmie Johnson on a preaching jaunt to Virginia that summer, he determined he would major in anthropology — Billy says, "He told me it would help me in any Christian service because it was the study of man, and also it was easy."

But when he delivered himself on up to Wheaton in the fall — he still a rather gawky country youth with his North Carolina uplands twang, in his implausibly gorgeous pinstripe suits and flowered neckties of lime and chartreuse and mauve along with clomping plowboy brogans — he immediately felt, on that more staid campus of pince-nez sanctitude, abysmally misplaced. As it struck him, "They were all real sincere Christians of high intellectual capacity up there, and it was like going from — I don't know, Eskimos to New York City for me. I was inexperienced socially, and found it difficult to make friends." As it was, his sole academic investiture after two and a half years at Temple Terrace was a certificate called a Christian Worker's Diploma, and at Wheaton he found himself now, at twenty-two, lugubriously a freshman again. He labored to muster his old buoyancy, even flung himself into some intramural wrestling for a while — at which, he says, "I made out indifferently" — but so dislocated did he feel that he was even prompted once to write Watson, "Often my mind wanders back to those blessed days spent in those halls and to the fellowship that I had while attending the school there. . . ."

In fact, for all the brutal disillusionments he had experienced in Florida, he was still given to a precipitous and almost touchingly naïve gusto in his admirations. As Johnson says, "I'm afraid he's always been terribly gullible. There was a young man who came to Wheaton who completely fascinated Billy — wore a cowboy hat and cowboy boots and had a great vitality about him, and Billy began telling us, 'Now, *that's* the way I'd like to be.' It was really an incredible mistake to attribute such great goodness and great strength to this guy — most of the rest of us could easily tell he wasn't for real, and sure enough, he did soon go down,

Ruth Bell, then in her second year at Wheaton, was the daughter of Presbyterian missionaries in China — a tall girl with black-
brown hair primly barbered, a sharp handsomeness of face, her
hazel-brown eyes curiously like Graham's in their deep-set and
faintly hawkish intensity, but with more than a hint of replete
lushness to her lithe figure. Again, it was that breath-snatching
combination of piety and prettiness. After his first glimpse of her
that fall afternoon, she was advertised to Billy as "the most devout girl on campus." But even in that enclave of sober religiousness, she kept herself nicely preened, lightly dabbed with lipstick, because "Mother had always hoped we wouldn't look like
the pickings out of a missionary barrel. It didn't seem to me a
credit to Christ to be drab." Billy himself would later rhapsodize,
"I remember the light in her face! And I had been told that she
got up every morning before dawn to pray." Indeed, she arose at
five to pass two hours, before any taste of breakfast, conducting
herself in a private devotional in her room. But she was also of
cheerfully sensible sentiments: what had drawn her to one casual
beau at Wheaton, she says, was that she "was so impressed with
his sanity and saintliness combined." Majoring in Bible, she was
minoring in art; her devoutness was additionally graced with a
disposition toward painting and a deftness for composing little
arias of private pensive verse. She was, on the whole, a singularly
ethereal and conscientious soul: as a small girl in China, her sister once reported, she "used to pray every night that the Lord
would let her be a martyr before the end of the year. She wanted
to be captured by bandits and beheaded, killed for Jesus' sake."

Born in the muddy provincial city of Tsingkiangpu in the
wind-raked reaches of northeastern China, she had grown up
there in a sturdy and commodious gabled brick residence with a
spacious veranda, blue floral wallpaper in the main parlor, and
an upright piano among shelves of her father's medical texts and
religious commentaries and detective mysteries — a citadel of
Presbyterian probity among the flyblown churn and reek of the
unenlightened Chinese masses everywhere around them: fetid
alleyways in which women with puckered faces hunkered with
shriveled babies at their bare breasts, other babies discarded in

ditches and fields to be eaten by dogs, with a ceaseless butch-
erous gusting of bandits back and forth over the countryside,
Ruth later recalling, "I can never remember going to sleep at
night without hearing gunshots somewhere in the distance."
Against this savage bedlam, Ruth's father, Nelson Bell — a tall,
lean, erect, bespectacled medical missionary, an unflinchingly
correct and bishop-like figure — maintained a household of fastidious proprieties transported over whole from his staunchly
sober origins in Waynesboro, Virginia. Whenever they journeyed beyond the compound, they carefully thumbtacked newspapers over the grimed walls of their rooms in Chinese hostels,
and in the evenings in their family parlor Bell would read aloud
to them from Dickens and Sir Walter Scott, *Little Lord Fauntleroy*,
Uncle Remus in its molasses dialect, while his wife and two
daughters sat knitting. According to an elderly erstwhile Anglican clergyman named John Pollock, who from Rose Ash, England, has somehow wound up as Graham's most exhaustive
house-chronicler and laureate, what larger diversions the Bells
allowed themselves in Tsingkiangpu also tended to be of
Virginia import, they congregating with other Southern Presbyterian Mission workers from neighboring districts to put on, in
full costume and blackface with mandolins and guitars, their
own minstrel shows.

These polite insulations were only sporadically infiltrated —
once or twice, Ruth and her older sister, Rosa, after forgetting
to scrub their hands before going to bed, awoke howling with
rats coiling over them. And ever so often, Mrs. Bell would
mutely retire to her room with a slamming migraine headache,
lying immobile behind a closed door for several days in a hot
stale shuttered dimness. But in that far locale, they were fortified
most of all by their robust Calvinist assurances: when the Bells'
ten-month-old son, Nelson, Jr., died of amoebic dysentery, at
the funeral they sang, "Praise God from Whom All Blessings
Flow," and Bell himself wrote afterward, "It was so sweet and
peaceful, no struggle and no evidence of pain, just quietly leaving us and going back to Him. His going has left an ache in our
hearts, and our arms feel empty, but, oh, the joy of knowing he

is safe . . . we know it was His will that he should go. There is no repining. . . ."

In this scrupulously preserved Southern small-town asperity, then, was Ruth quarantined throughout her eighteen years in the Orient. On Sundays, like Billy himself growing up in Charlotte, she and her sister were forbidden any secular reading, music, entertainments — only devotional literature, Bible games. If one of them failed to make it downstairs before the end of the first hymn of their morning breakfast devotional, she was denied sugar on her porridge. Mrs. Bell vigilantly scrutinized all new books shipped over from the States, and any novels she found of suspicious character were simply consigned to the cozy and pleasant flames of their fireplace — so disposing of *The Grapes of Wrath,* even *Gone with the Wind.* Ruth's Chinese amah had herself been a supplier of small girls to the teahouses of Shanghai before her conversion, but after her own spiritual fumigation as a Christian, she would squat on a small stool with her worn shabby Bible and a hymnbook, singing in the dim orange glare of an oil lantern, in a high wobbling whine, *"There is a fountain filled with blood, drawn from Immanuel's veins; and sinners, plunged beneath that flood, lose all their guilty stains. . . ."*

Reared in such a running hyperbolic moral dialectic between their own churchly decorums and the lurid brutishness around them, Ruth and her sister were instilled somewhat precociously with a rather livid sense of righteousness and perdition: Ruth's sister, when she was only three, suddenly began wailing once after being put to bed, and when Bell hastened to her room, she sobbed to him, "Daddy, I'm such a sinner." Ruth herself, when she was nine, wrote to her grandfather in Virginia, "The chinese have not changed very many of their old habits women still smoke they still gamble and play cards drink and do all other things which we do not do."

By the time she arrived at Wheaton, a young lady of nineteen, she had resolved to spend herself as a spinster missionary out in the windy rock-rubbled wastes of Tibet. She had about her now an air of detached high seriousness, which exerted no inconsiderable entrancement on Billy's heart. Indeed, while having managed to sustain a kind of pert chipper blitheness against all the monstrousness she had beheld growing up, she had a slight touch of Draconian equanimity to her nature. Billy, expounding once on how the conversion experience was not necessarily a phenomenon that happened all in one grand flare, explained, "For example, my wife — she has just always been that way."

But the truth was, in contrast to Billy, she had assumed at least enough sophistication to have already indulged in a passing flirtation with doubt during her first year at Wheaton: a boy whom she dated there, as she narrates it, "had gone on up to school for a while in Chicago and lost his faith. When I saw him next, he told me, 'Ruth, you ought to lose your faith; it's the greatest feeling in the world.' Well, that was my first encounter with an atheist — or I think he called himself a pantheist or something. But after talking with him, it was as if the light had gone out. All of a sudden, you believe nothing. This went on for months; it was a devastating summer. I argued with everybody. People dreaded to see me coming. But I didn't want anything to do with emotion, I wanted cold, hard facts. I'd tell people, 'No, no, I want you to give me cold, hard *reasons* for the faith I used to have in me.' Though I knew Jesus had died for our sins, I somehow couldn't feel included in that." After a while, it became something like a retroactive struggle to acquire a sufficient portion of guilt, despair, sensation of lostness, for that atonement actually to register and be realized. "I wasn't arguing to win; I was arguing to lose." In time, of course, she succeeded — through a deliberate process of rational demolition, wound up bereft enough then to be able to make the leap of faith that alone would reconfirm and consolidate her religiousness. "I won by losing," as she puts it.

Then on that autumn afternoon, as she stood watching Billy grapple the heavy chair into the boardinghouse and come battering back down the steps past her — "leaping those steps two at a time, just a blur," rumpled and ebullient in a shine of sweat — she remembers that it occurred to her, "There's a young man who knows where he's going." Shortly after that, they were introduced in the student cafeteria, Billy somewhat

stammerous. But at least another month elapsed before Billy
could rummage forth enough bravado — all his old élan in such
matters having been thoroughly sacked by the episode with
Emily — to ask Ruth for a date. In the library one Saturday
morning, he sat hunched forward, staring at the distant table
where she was bent over her books, while "Howard Van
Buren — he developed open-heart surgery in later years, you
know — he kept saying, 'Go on, Billy, ask her. Ask her.' " Finally
he arose and made his way over to her table, to mumble, "Hey,
Ruth. Could I take you to the concert next Sunday afternoon?"

It was snowing when they emerged from the college chapel
— where they had sat together still and wordless as the glee club
pealed forth the icily splendoring paeans of Handel's "Hallelujah
Chorus" — and as they walked now through the whitening hush
over the campus, headed toward a professor's home for a cup of
tea, they paused for a while under a tree. There, they quietly
talked together, for the first time, in that dim snowing Sunday
twilight, a weather that was far, far now, from those sensuous
anguished spring nights in Florida. . . . That night, Billy
scrawled a letter to his mother, "I have just met a wonderful girl.
Her name is Ruth Bell. She looks a little like you and even her
voice sounds like you. This is the girl I am going to marry."
(When the letter reached Charlotte, says his sister Jean, "we
thought, well, this is just another one; here we go again.") As for
Ruth, when she returned to her room that evening, though she
was still poised in a remoteness from anything like love yet, she
nevertheless proceeded to propose in a short prayer with a considered deliberation, "Oh, Lord, if you wish to give me the
privilege of sharing my life with this man, I could have no
greater joy."

It struck her, she later reported, "Billy just had something no
one else had. I had heard he was one hundred percent sold out
to the Lord, and he seemed to want to please God more than any
other man I'd ever met. There was that purpose about him that
I had noticed the first time I saw him, that he meant to go
somewhere — and I felt that maybe I'd like to go along with
him." Actually, even while it had been her determination to pass

her life unwedded dispensing the gospel in the emptiness of
Tibet, well before she had met Billy she had indulged in at least
one demure little poem of a certain timorous, tentative speculation in the form of a prayer that if there should be a man, he
might "be like Thee," with a face radiant with "character," who
when he came, would approach "with quiet eyes all aglow."

It became a courtship continuing through the next two years
as a kind of sober ceremony of chasteness in a constant halo-
glow of unuttered exquisite expectancy. As Billy himself once
described their gravitation toward each other, "Before Ruth and
I were married, much of our attraction was spiritual. The ecstasy
of passionate love developed after marriage, not before." For
that matter, at times he appeared to Ruth a bit forbiddingly austere. "He was so very serious about life in general. He didn't
have enough time to go to ball games or anything like that.
Every date we had, it seemed, was to a preaching service of some
kind. We didn't really have a very well-rounded dating life, because he was so wrapped up in the church. It was mostly preaching."

On one of their first dates, he took her to hear him preach,
placing her right on the front row, but became so exercised in
his delivery, braying loudly with antic flailings of his long arms,
that she began to mull, as she later confessed, *How can I ever sit
through all this?* His manner still tended toward much swooping
about with smacks of his hands, a certain improbable peppiness
of phraseology: "Daniel was prime minister of one of the most
powerful countries of the world, and a pal of the boss — the
King of the Medes and the Persians. Some jealous guys were out
to get him. So they trained their spyglasses on him one morning
when he was praying and had his venetian blinds up. They
tattled to the King, and the King was on the spot, so he said to
his lawyers, 'Find me a couple of loopholes so I can spring my
pal, Dan.' But they couldn't, so the King had to send his buddy
Dan to the lions. . . ."

But she found him, out of the pulpit, nowhere near so spirited. After a while, she complained to one friend, "He's being
awfully cautious, and that's just no way to court a girl." Billy

explains now that, so benumbed was he still from his capsizing in Florida, "I had told God, 'God, if you mean for this to happen, you do the courting. I'm leaving it up to you this time.'" It became a curiously oblique romantic commerce between them, made up, among other things, of much mutual twitting and light raillery. "They used to tease each other all the time back then," says his sister Jean, "almost fiercely sometimes."

Over the months, as they appeared to be approaching inexorably closer to the culmination of marriage, Billy seemed to become progressively more distracted and listless. At last, Ruth began dating other boys now and then. With that, as Billy was walking her back to her room one evening from the library, he suddenly turned to her and expostulated that she would either date him only or — flinging his arm wide then over the expanse of the campus — she could date the whole load of them and forget about him entirely. "That's when he got a little bossy," she recalls with a smile. Not long after that, in the late spring of 1941, as they were sitting one dusk in the backyard of the home where Ruth was rooming, he notified her that he considered she belonged in a home as a wife and mother rather than in the barrens of Tibet as an unfamilied female missionary — and asked if she would commit herself to marry him. For another month or so, she engaged in an interminable recital of instances of other women who had quite happily forsaken themselves for God. "But that's not you," he insisted, "you weren't made for that — "

Finally that summer, while he was in Florida conducting a revival, he received a short and somewhat terse note from her, informing him that she had decided to accept his proposal: "She said she still wasn't sure that she loved me, but she felt led of the Lord, that she felt sure it was God's will for her life."

She was staying that summer with her parents in Virginia, they having finally evacuated themselves from Tsingkiangpu with the onslaught of the Japanese. In August Billy drove up to meet them. When he pulled into their front yard, he says, "Ruth came running out of the house to hug me — " but even now, affianced at last after almost a year of abstemiously keeping company, he could bring himself at that moment to greet her with no more

than a brief and circumspect dab of a kiss to her forehead. Ruth
was not a little distraught — "She never forgot that," admits
Billy. "She thought I should have at least kissed her on the lips."
The Bells, for their part, received him heartily. But it was not
until a few evenings later, as the two of them were standing
alone atop a knoll in the nearby Blue Ridge Mountains — just as
a brimming late-summer moon was lifting over them in the
pearl-green sky — that he at last gathered his will to give her
their first full kiss. Somehow as portentous an event during that
visit, it seems from his report of it, was that, during a short trip
on up to Washington with the Bells, "we all stayed one night at a
motel — it was the very first motel I'd ever seen."

But almost immediately after contracting the matter with
Ruth, Billy's nights were again flayed by insomnia. As it happened, he saw her only once again, fleetingly, over the next six
months, she having gone to Albuquerque to attend her sister,
who was recovering from tuberculosis, not returning to Wheaton
until January. It turned out to be a rather protracted and bristly
engagement. "We began to have a few difficulties," Ruth delicately concedes. These usually took the form of little tiffs over
points of doctrine. Billy, who at that time still affected a blunt
fundamentalist disdain of all the establishment denominations,
once advised Ruth, she says, that "Daddy couldn't be in the will
of God because he was a Presbyterian. I almost gave him his ring
back right there." With the eruption then of Pearl Harbor, Billy
briefly considered volunteering for combat duty, but shortly allowed himself to be dissuaded from that, he explains, "by my
professors, who argued that God had called me to preach and
that my war effort should be in the moral and spiritual realm."

Finally, though, two years after arriving at their understanding, on their graduation from Wheaton in the summer of
1943, it was concluded. On an August evening — a Friday the
thirteenth — in a stone chapel in the small mountain community
of Montreat, where her parents now resided, Billy and Ruth
were married. With what was becoming by now a curiously recurring circumstance, this took place, like the night of his conversion at Ham's revival and then his golf-green commitment

and even the first kiss he gave Ruth, again under a full mild pale moon — Billy grinning somewhat flatly and fiercely in a white dinner jacket.

Their honeymoon consisted of seven days at a tourist boardinghouse in the mountains of Blowing Rock, North Carolina, at two dollars a night — an aged white frame structure with filigreed Victorian eaves. After a breakfast of Branflakes, they would take long brisk walks through the steep sun-slanted woods of fir and cedar, discreet little dews of sweat on their temples and upper lips. Ruth remembers that the clematis twining and furling about the front gallery of the hotel was in bloom that week, a frilling of starry blossoms, immaculate, bright, odorless. As it was, at least since Billy's days in Florida, "I had been sleeping always on the floor," he maintains, "I just couldn't sleep in a bed for a long while. It was something I learned," he adds a bit abstrusely, "from an Indian chief." And that first night after the wedding service, in their plain wainscoted room in the tourist hotel, "I spent the night sleeping on the floor — I don't mean right away, of course. But I could just sleep better down there, on a hard surface without a pillow."

Around this time, a matronly lady from Charlotte remembers, her father sat with Billy on their front porch for an hour or two, urging him, "Why don't you go on now to a really good seminary like the one at Davidson?" But Billy seemed, to her, seized with a plunging and almost abject impatience — "He kept saying, no, no, he wanted to preach right away. He had to start now, he said, he just couldn't wait any longer."

During those first months of marriage, Billy, now twenty-four, was acting as pastor to a congregation of some thirty-five souls who worshiped in the sunken basement of their unfinished church in the outlying Chicago suburb of Western Springs, Illinois. He had been invited to take on this first charge by the chairman of the church's board of deacons, who had been beguiled by him on a visit to Wheaton — a man named Robert Van Kampen with a face like flatly hammered copperplate, who also happened to own an industrial printing company that he has since transmuted into a vast religious publishing house. Indeed, as Billy had so quickly caught the fancy of the Illinois businessmen on the golf course at Temple Terrace, he continued now, with a multiplying frequency, to come by the patronages of persons of substance. Part of the magnetic at work in this peculiar conjunction may have been that Billy so eagerly and affably returned their regard. Whatever, under the auspices of Van Kampen, he began effusively to blandish other substantial business executives — over three hundred of them eventually — into a devotional society called the Western Suburban Professional Men's Club, which regularly convened at a local dining retreat called the Spinning Wheel. Says a colleague, "Those businessmen around there, for some reason they'd come out to hear Billy when you couldn't have dragged them to hear any other gospel preacher."

And before long, from the basement sanctuary of his church, amid a rigging of red, blue, and amber stage lights, he began to broadcast late every Sunday evening a religious program called *Songs in the Night* — "coming to you from the friendly church in the pleasant community of Western Springs." For these broadcasts, he had acquired as a soloist from another Chicago radio station, a bassoon-throated, gentle soul named George Beverly Shea. It was the beginning now of his ultimately massive public amplification.

In the meantime, he and Ruth were installed in a somewhat pinched upstairs apartment in the nearby suburb of Hinsdale, with an hourly uproar of freight trains battering past their windows. "It was a rather dreary little place," Ruth says, "and I was struggling to learn how to keep house there." Her cooking then consisted mostly of a repertoire of simulations of Chinese dishes. "Bill was very patient about that," she declares. Despite all her persistent gingerly suggestions, though, he obliviously continued to leave his desk and closet in a ragged dishevelment, used the top of the bathroom door as a rack for his limp damp towels and washcloths. And there began to develop, after a while, a certain vague and fitful disquiet between them. Particularly in Billy's case, it began to take on aspects of some obscure desperation.

He reflects now, "That's the way I thought my life was going to be from then on — just a pastor, preaching on Sundays, maybe with a radio ministry, holding revival meetings now and then. But a quiet pastor's life." But as he indicated in an autobiography once in *McCall's,* "We did have a difficult time adjusting to this new life and to each other." He would eventually resort to the reassuring computation, as he will sometimes profess in his crusade messages, "I believe that if you are a Christian, God has the ideal person picked out for you. This means, whether we even loved each other, much less agreed on everything, we knew God's will — and this is the soundest barrier against separation and divorce anyone could have." Nevertheless, he acknowledged in *McCall's,* "We had come from different backgrounds, and suddenly we were on our own. It was hard, and not just because of our different temperaments."

The truth was that, with Billy, it seemed almost a disconcertment arising out of his final aversion to the merely temporal life. During the unoccupied intervals in his pastor's schedule at Western Springs, instead of returning to that upstairs apartment, he would pass much of his time in coffee shops and diners loudly discoursing with other young ministers. Then, in 1944, he applied for a chaplain's commission. Finally, that fall, after a year of marriage now, he acquired a sudden violent case of the mumps. For six weeks, he lay in the bed in their apartment, the trains hourly storming past while he pitched in hot churned sheets with a wild fever, at times delirious.

When he emerged at last from this long siege, he had about him once more that purged gauntness of those nights in Florida. . . . Not long afterward — toward the close of the war — Billy was convalescing in the thin winter sun of Florida, on a hundred-dollar stipend provided him by a commiserative radio listener, and another Chicago divine with him, a flourishing revival impresario named Torrey Johnson with a bespectacled choirboy's face, posed to him the prospect of joining in his new evangelistic movement in America and Canada called Youth for Christ. Though he had served only a year as minister to the church in Western Springs, Billy agreed with alacrity. He immediately wrote the chief of chaplains asking that he be released now from his commission. "I felt I could reach more servicemen and accomplish my ministry a great deal more than if I went into the chaplaincy."

No incidental exhilaration of this enterprise was that it meant he would be off, on the wing all about the country, something like 75 percent of the time — a glee, actually, to some degree lasting from that compulsion that had sent him dusting through the night over those moonlit back roads as a teenager. And Ruth, not altogether uncheerfully, "simply packed her bags," says Billy in his *McCall's* autobiography, "and moved down to Montreat to be with her parents. She decided she would live there permanently." Ruth herself explains, "I realized that it was going to be like this from now on, that he was going to be gone most of the time. In a case like ours, I believe the family is the Lord's business, but a husband should have his wife settled where she's going to be happy." Their home, for the next three years then, consisted of the room on the second floor of the Bells' house, where Ruth was lodged. "Since some of my work would be in the South," Billy says, "we could see each other between rallies and during vacations."

In 1945, he got the news from her, in a one-sentence note that reached him just as he was scrambling to catch a train in Chicago, "We are going to have a baby in September." He managed a hasty call, had a large bouquet wired to her, and then after his arrival in Peoria where he was to preach at another rally, in the bedroom of the home where he was staying, "I got down on my knees and gave thanks," he relates. Finally, he says, "That summer I went home." It was during this brief tarrying in Montreat that, at a Youth for Christ service in nearby Asheville, he happened upon Cliff Barrows, who would become his hymn director in the crusades of the future — then, as soon as the summer was done, he took to the road again. He was in Mobile when the pastor of a local fundamentalist church phoned him at the dumpish little motel where he was lodged to tell him that his father-in-law had been trying to locate him, and then read to him a telegram apprising him that Ruth's labor had begun. By the time he got back to North Carolina, though, his first child — a daughter — had already been born.

By 1946, he had forged through about every state in the Union and most provinces of Canada. Over one twelve-month span, journeying by plane now, he logged some 200,000 miles. Ruth was still installed in that second-floor room at her parents' when she found she was pregnant again. They then purchased a summer lodge directly across the street from the Bells, where they were to be established for the next ten years. Over that course of time, though, Billy was there no more than two or three months out of each year. When he returned from one prolonged sojourn, his small son, William Franklin, Jr. — their fourth child now after three daughters — shrilled, "Who's him?" and scuffled behind his grandmother's skirt. Once, on one of his early tours, another minister with him began to puzzle over Billy's serene casualness to such extended and far-flung separations from his young wife: "I couldn't understand how he could be away from Ruth so much and not have it seem to worry him at all. I remember inquiring about this several times — and he just said it was something they had both agreed on."

It was an arrangement, actually, that seemed, after Hinsdale, somehow to their mutual relief. For that matter, it was as if Ruth began to flourish sumptuously in the thin oxygens of those long limbos of isolation, took on a fresh lustrous excellence of face, mellowed into a strikingly luxuriant figure: even to the eye of Graham's mother, as she once confessed, "Ruth looks just like a movie-star." At the least, she proved an eminently patient Penelope during his odysseys. Graham once was quoted in a Charlotte newspaper as to this rather abstinent understanding between them, "My wife and I have both had to be dedicated on this point — and Ruth has great gifts for it." If nothing else, she had become, by now, well adept at loneliness. When she was thirteen, she had been dispatched to a school in Korea for missionary children, which, she says, "was an absolutely traumatic experience for me. I adored home." Her first Christmas there, she had written her parents that, after considerable prayer, the

Lord had made it known to her that it was His will she return
to Tsingkiangpu at least for the Christmas season, to which her
mother promptly replied, "Neither your father nor I feel He is
leading us to bring you back to China for Christmas" — she
wound up staying there, in fact, for the better part of five years.
She offers now, with a crafted niceness of phrase, "I think that
God was —" a slight pause "— preparing me for a lifetime of
good-byes." Whatever, with her hardihood for loneliness, she
came to be flawlessly accomplished in the business of farewells.
Her children remember that, when Graham would leave again,
they never once saw her betray even a blink of a tear — his
departures always kept perfunctory and matter-of-fact events, almost as incidental, he said in his magazine autobiography, "as
running down to the village store" — and for the weeks or
months that he would be gone, they never noticed her brood or
droop. When Ruth was once asked by a Charlotte reporter about
the toll possibly exacted on her by all those separations, she retorted, "You get used to it. You keep busy. The best thing for
any of us is keeping busy."

She was of a rather crisp and clipped temperament anyway.
"She's very stoic," says Billy's sister Jean. "She makes very little
over pain. Her reaction to pain is to tease." Once, when Billy was
taken to the hospital with one of those maladies that have persistently waylaid him throughout his life, "really in great pain," says
Jean, Ruth presently came bustling into his room to chirp, "Aha!
So you think you're sick — you're just here to loaf off, that's all.
Don't expect any sympathy from me." And says Jean, "He was
lying there really suffering." But it was as if pain or affliction
somehow uncomfortably accosted her, she was reluctant to admit
or entertain any serious instances of distress; whenever she was
confronted with anything truly amiss in someone, it instinctively
produced in her some strange impatient brisk blitheness. "She
has tremendous inner discipline" is the way Jean describes it. Indeed, for all the vestal tremoring of that girlhood ode she had
composed before meeting Billy, she had never been notably disposed to sentimentalism after their marriage; what testimonials
of affection she allowed herself more often took the form of dry

little tweaks at Elizabeth Barrett Browning lines, such as, "I love you like the hog loves slop. . . . I love you like the chicken loves mash. . . ."

The secluded home up the mountain, to which they finally removed themselves in 1956, Ruth herself had conceived and designed like some missionary child's greeting-card dream of an unseen sweetly mythic America: as if to salvage now some semblance of her lost American past, she had begun a ceaseless inquiring at country stores and filling stations about forsaken log cabins she might buy up for wall timber, prowled alone bumping in a jeep over the surrounding mountains for months, tanned after a while to an autumn-leaf brown in her ragamuffin jeans and gingham shirts, at the same time rummaging through secondhand stores and antique shops for fixtures that, as she later put it, "were typical of our forefathers' ingenuity and art." It materialized ultimately as a snug neat log-plank abode with a studiously folksy prettiness about it, ivy ruffling over its flanks and a lantern hung on an old post at the entrance, an old spinning wheel set on the flagstone porch with a stone-slabbed chimney and bright blue shutters, checkered daffodil-yellow curtains inside, hooked rugs on floors of wide boards from those mountain shanties, stained-glass lamps and calico rag dolls in miniature rocking chairs, a beam affixed over the living-room fireplace with the inscription in Gothic German script, *A Mighty Fortress Is Our God*.

Her life there was made out of Billy's absences. She passed her years alone on that mountainside with the children — five of them eventually — and a tumble of large dogs with Biblical names like Peter and Belshazzar, some of which had to be chained whenever visitors happened by. It fell to her, of course, to administer the discipline to the children as they grew up, with switches, rulers, even a shoetree once or twice — "I played them like a xylophone," she admits. She would have them read aloud the letters Billy would send from San Francisco, New Delhi, Seoul, Nairobi, and pray for him at the dinner table and when she put them to bed in the evenings. On the long calm hanging Sunday afternoons, she would gather them together to listen to him on his *Hour of Decision* broadcasts, and then in the evening would bring out Bible games and Bible coloring books for them. But, as she readily professed once in a Charlotte newspaper profile, "There's nothing greatly stimulating about wiping noses or cleaning muddy shoes and the dirt they leave. A mother just must realize that God put her there." She occupied herself in sewing and reading, gardening around the house, writing letters constantly, taught a Sunday-school class made up of college students for a while. All through the day she kept an open Bible somewhere nearby, on the kitchen counter, atop a porch table, even carrying one with her from room to room as she vacuumed and collected laundry, repeatedly pausing to commune briefly with some verse, some passage flipped to at random. "Since I don't enjoy housework anyway," she commented, "it lightens the load." Her children would later recall that her light would be burning behind her closed door early every morning when they got up, burning again late into the night, "as she studied her Bible and prayed."

She did have a maid and a caretaker, and her parents were still living down the mountain at Montreat. But in 1969, a stroke left her mother confined to a wheelchair, and Nelson Bell devoted himself for the next several years to tending to her. In 1973, he died, and a year later, Mrs. Bell. "But they helped wonderfully in making up to the children what they missed by their father being gone," Ruth declares.

In a sense, though, it was as if she had wound up after all spending a solitary life of devoutness and self-abnegation in an isolation like those remote plains of Tibet. When she was asked if she did not sometimes resent Billy's long absences, she cheerfully replied, as in *The Ladies Home Journal* once, "Well, you know, all my life I had felt called for mission work there in China, and I only came to college to prepare myself for that work. But I think the Lord must have given me that intense longing for a purpose, so that I could have the understanding and the sense of fulfillment that I receive now from Bill's work. I knew from the very beginning that I wouldn't be in first place in his life. Christ would be first. Knowing that, accepting that,

solves an awful lot of problems right there. So I can watch him
go with no regrets, and wait for him joyfully."

Billy's own perspectives on a wife's meaning, actually, have
remained largely those of Genesis and Leviticus. While he asserted once in a slightly beatific exchange with Debbie Reynolds
for *Redbook,* "I believe I love my wife in a dimension and on a
plane that the average couple outside Christ cannot understand," on the whole he was of the mind, as he would announce
from his crusade pulpits down through the years, that "of the
woman God said, 'I will greatly multiply thy sorrow in thy conception.' As a result of sin, God cursed the woman, and the fact
that she has suffered in childbirth is a result of the fall, that first
sin of her disobedience. God said, 'In sorrow shalt thou bring
forth children, and thy desire shall be to thy husband, and he
shall rule over thee.' That has never changed; that has never
been revoked. The Bible uses six expressions to give the responsibility of the wife to the husband. The Bible says, 'Submit to, be
subject to, be in subjection to, be obedient to, reverence and
love.' In the governmental arrangement of the family, the wife is
to fit into the world of the husband."

Only now and then would Ruth accompany him on his treks.
On one of their first expeditions together, to England and
Europe, she seemed to apply her time principally to polishing
the shoes of the other ladies in their party. Occasionally she
would agree to being on the stage while Billy was preaching,
smiling up at him fixedly over her corsage, but for the most part,
she asserts, "I just have an antipathy to platforms." After attending the first night of Billy's 1957 New York crusade, she quickly
returned home to the four children they had then: "It's not right
to go off and leave them. They're little such a short time, and
especially with their daddy gone so much, I should be with
them."

Once, on a voyage to a crusade in London, she began to watch
a tall and bountiful black girl on board, "a striking-looking girl,"
with a bearing always of impassive remoteness, who Ruth shortly
learned, with a startled fascination, was a strip-teaser. Then,
when they arrived in London, she discovered the girl was also

staying in their hotel. Over the next few days, Ruth found herself increasingly intrigued by her, even writing about her to her parents, "She is rather aloof and I can imagine why. With a hotel full of us preachers and what have you, she probably feels: 'Ye Jews have no dealings with us Samaritans.' I can't help liking her. . . ." It became, for Ruth, almost like some curious intimacy, tenuous and unspoken, a random brief interpassing with another galaxy of life. Ruth, in her demure white cap swathed in dotted tulle and white gloves clasping her Bible, encountered her in the lobby or elevator a few times, "and we'd smile and say good morning. I think we were trying to make friends — but it was too difficult; there was just a chasm there." Finally, Ruth wandered one afternoon out onto the street to listen to a Salvation Army band thumping and bleating away on the sidewalk, "and suddenly I looked up and there on the opposite corner stood the Negro strip-teaser. I watched her closely. She never moved. . . . I started back slowly, hoping perhaps she would catch up and I could just pass the time of day. But she kept behind me. . . ."

Still she has remained, over the decades of her long solitudes in that picture-book home on the mountain, unflaggingly vivacious, enthusing at her happiest, "Oh, just wait till we get to Heaven!" But more than anything else now, she says, "I love quiet." Whenever she takes a trip these days, to visit her married children, to attend a crusade, "I return physically refreshed, but mentally and spiritually depleted," and to recollect herself, she undertakes a systematic exercise of reading — "One book to stimulate me. One book then to relax me. One book for information. And one book for conversation." More than reading, though, more than voices in conversation, "I just love to hear the wind in the trees. I love to hear birds. And mostly, I just love to listen to silence."

As Ruth's father once observed of Billy, "Although he has unquestionable physical charm and is good-looking by any standard, he is primarily a man's man. All his close personal friends are men." Ruth herself acknowledged to a newspaper interviewer, "I should like to see Bill oftener, to cook his favorite dishes and help him buy his clothes — but all that sort of stuff is done by the staff." Indeed, from those first eager, barging years of his Youth for Christ tours, virtually all of his days — his life, really — was to be spent in the company of those aides and confidants he termed "the team": a retinue of similarly effervescent fellow devouts whose names seemed to run to short, snappy, chummy monosyllables like Bev, Ted, Cliff, along with a transient assortment of other retainers with names like Bill Bright, Larry Love.

At that service in Asheville the summer of 1945, when he had asked for a volunteer song-leader from the audience, Cliff Barrows — himself a Bob Jones graduate, there on his honeymoon with his wife Billie — had bounded forth to become thereafter Graham's cheerleaderish songmaster and general emcee. Husky, brilliantined, his square face with a cartoon-crisp handsomeness — a somewhat "over-presentable young man," as A. J. Liebling once noted — Barrows could pass as the relentlessly radiant host of some television game show. He conducts the stadium throngs through revival anthems with an almost maniacal animation, his feet spraddled wide and his shoulders extravagantly heaving, lashing his arms in spirals over his head, his face as he sings along with the congregations, cupping his mouth in large circles, miming the ecstatic excitement of someone just plugged into a 220-volt socket.

Presiding over the preliminary proceedings at crusade services, he will happily interject at times in a sturdily ringing voice, "You know — God is great and God is good!" In fact, as a farmer's son in California's vegetable valleys, Barrows had been converted when he was only eleven years old and seems to have remained more or less arrested in that moment and spiritual take ever since. After his salvation experience, Barrows had nourished for a time his own hopes of becoming an evangelist, but soon subsumed those visions in what he came to recognize as Billy's obviously larger calling. From then on, with the same faintly frantic gladness with which he conducts his crusade choirs, he performed his other speciality — delivering little sermons, as "Uncle Cliff," to children's groups, acting out such Bible stories as Naaman, the Syrian leper who was told by Elisha to dip himself seven times in the river Jordan, narrating it all with an energy bordering on berserkness, strenuous muggings. And it was to these audiences of eight- and ten-year-olds now that he would give his own altar calls: as one account reported, "Again God moved over these children as Cliff Barrows gave the invitation. Over 500 streamed into the basement prayer room. . . ."

Billy asserts now, "Cliff is almost the most perfect human being I have ever known, aside from my wife and my mother." Cliff will counter — the mutual accolades exchanged among the group become after a while like watching extended badminton matches — "I've spent as much time with Billy as I have with my family. In a way, of course, the team *is* a family. But after all these years, he is as warm and friendly and sincere, and totally dedicated to delivering God's message, as he ever was." Barrows's own ethereal devoutness, like Billy's, results from his conclusion, as he will sometimes announce, "There is no escape from life. There's no escape — except to Christ."

Billy's durable organ-toned soloist, George Beverly Shea, whom he had come by in Chicago, was the oldest of the lot — seamed and somewhat homely of countenance, but with dark sentimental eyes, an almost painfully shy and deferential soul. Born the son of a Methodist minister in Ottawa, every morning of his boyhood he had been swiftly and thoroughly awakened by his mother's soprano abruptly ringing out, with a decisive lick of chords on the piano, "Singing I go along life's road, Praising the Lord, praising the Lord. . . ." He wound up eventually putting in nine years as a medical records clerk with the MONY offices in Manhattan, the most significant experience provided him by that tenure seeming to be, he has said, "how impressed I was by the life-expectancy charts. These statistics made Dad's sermons about the transience of life more impressive than ever."

In the meantime, he was cultivating, singing in choirs and gospel quartets, the deep burlaps of his bass-baritone, and while in New York, he finally mustered the pluck to present himself for an audition with the Lynn Murray chorale at CBS. Somehow the lore has developed among Graham's faithful that Shea actually renounced an opera career with the Met for his lifetime of unfurling sacred songs at Billy's crusades; more exactly, he was offered a salary with the Lynn Murray Singers but then declined it when he discovered he would be required to sing, from Friml's *Vagabond King,* "a line which made me uncomfortable. It read, '. . . and to hell with Burgundy.'" Later, when he moved on to Chicago to render hymns on a religious radio station there, he himself auditioned an aspiring songstress who "had considerable singing talent. For sacred singing, however, her voice had a distracting sultriness." He advised her, "If you could eliminate some of the blues quality in your voice, I think we could find a spot for you." And three months later, Shea proudly reports, "Her voice held only a trace of the blues, and we put her on the air."

It was while Shea was dispensing his lanolin-lubricated solos on a network devotional program called *Club Time* that Billy conscripted him into his entourage. Over the decades, he has gone indefatigably calliopeing on through crusade after crusade, ladling forth his orotund tones over gladioli pulpit sprays with the steadily pumping dependability of a steamboat paddle wheel.

Ted Smith, the team pianist and sometime organist, also wended into Graham's repertory from Canada — a slight, somewhat reedy figure who studied at Toronto's Royal Conservatory of Music, he would still daily browse through a little Bach and Beethoven to prime himself for his accompaniments at crusade services. Serving as the most obscure and incidental figure of Graham's company, he has essayed in the past two "folk musicals," one of which he entitled *Requiem for a Nobody.*

Grady Wilson's brother, T. W., a strapping figure who is also an ordained preacher, eventually came to act informally as Billy's bodyguard. Given sometimes to quick blusters of temper, he has a hearty face that could have been lifted directly out of a Breughel painting, a round bulb of a nose and round eyes that widen large as two poached eggs with emphasis. His father had been a plumber, and when asked about his own ambitions growing up, he remarks, "I didn't have any particular thing in mind. I just knew there was one thing I *wasn't* gonna be. That was a plumber. I promised myself that every single time I'd be helping my daddy, crouched down there in somebody's basement holding onto a pipe with that stuff running down my arm." He is usually attired now with a starchy nattiness, a vaguely buccaneerish fringe of long locks scrolled low in his neck, with something of a city-hall politico's chesty strutfulness about him. When he pauses in his barrelings about for a moment of banter with someone, he likes to stroke and strum at his coat lapels, one elbow wagging out, tilting then sideways to deliver his punch line in close with a round pop and rolling of his eyes. Like most country-reared sorts, in his peregrinations among hotels all over the world, he is a fanatic about air conditioning: "It just can't get too cold for T. W.," his wife sighs; "he's got to have that air conditioner going all the time." But T. W. and Grady, for all their boisterous and cornbread-fed good nature, happen to be an intricately canny and wary pair in their attentions to Billy's well-being, generally proceeding in their commerce with all parties of the world according to the Biblical enjoinder, "Behold, I send you forth as sheep in the midst of wolves: be ye therefore wise as serpents. . . ."

But longest at Billy's elbow — more or less ever since they had trudged together to the sawdust altar at Ham's revival — has been Grady Wilson. A ruddy, squat, amicable chap, as simple and unpretentious as a turnip, Grady was ordained as a youth as a "licensed preacher" at the Gum Springs Baptist Church near Charlotte, under the special patronage of a combination preacher-and-train-engineer named "Happy Dick" Brothers, who liked to end his runs, as he came swinging around the last curve, by hooting out the doxology on his locomotive whistle, "O happy day . . . when Jesus washed my sins away. . . ." Grady's father, after losing his post as the city plumbing inspector, had barely managed to scrap out a sustenance for himself and his family, and a somewhat more genteel lady who had been a native of their community sniffs, "Oh, those Wilsons, we looked on them back then as just so *common*." But as Billy will maintain to audiences now, with Grady sitting nearby plumply grinning, "I had a secretary once, and she said, 'You know, I never did figure out why you had Grady Wilson with you.' And after she had been with me for a year, she said, 'You know, he has more practical sense and more knowledge, and knows how to handle things better than anybody in your whole organization.' And — uh, Grady has been with us since the very, very beginning of the earliest crusades that Cliff and I had; Grady was with us before there ever was a BGA."

One afternoon in his own suburban brick ranch home in Charlotte, just having blown back in after several days of preaching out in Omaha, Grady sat wearily plopped in his easy chair in the long family room he had just added to his house, artificial logs glowing rubily in a tangerine-hued hooded Danish fireplace set at one end. Reposing with one stubby leg thrown over the other with black cowboy boot waggling, he sipped from a dainty cup of coffee brought in to him on a tray by his jovially proportioned wife while he listened raptly to a tape replaying, for perhaps the fortieth time, a particularly successful introduction of Billy he had delivered several months before, cackling to himself now and then at certain droll lines, "Thass right, exactly what he did once, thass exactly what happened. . . ." Grady seems only occasionally, vaguely restless about the somewhat peripheral position in which he has wound up beside Billy's own celebrity. Recounting a crusade he had conducted years before in the Appalachian back reaches of Kentucky, he offered, "It got more written about it in the press, you know, than anything Billy ever did. That's the truth. Fella with the AP went around with me everywhere I went for three or four solid days. Few weeks later, when Billy and I went over to Frankfurt, the commander at the base there met us with a copy of *Stars and Stripes* in his hand — said they'd all been reading about my crusade up in Appalachia; it'd been all they were talking about over there before we got there. Didn't mention a thing about what Billy'd been doing lately."

With his great beaming possum's grin and small sly eyes, Grady has served as something like Graham's Falstaff, his San-

cho Panza, his Bottom — "He keeps Billy in touch with the
earth," says one colleague. For his part, he has remained
thoroughly country-cured. Standing on the new yellow carpet of
his family room — a little blowsy of face and smoggy of eye from
having caught a flight at four that morning, his hands hiked by
his thumbs in his trouser pockets with one pants-leg hitched up
over the top of his boot — he fell to discoursing about a novel
called *The Education of Jonathan Beam* that had appeared some
seventeen years ago, a tale, written by the public relations director at the North Carolina Baptist campus of Wake Forest, about
a young farm boy, aspiring to be a Bible-and-brimstone
preacher, who arrives at a Baptist college and shortly enters into
adolescently hedonistic apostasies. A rather slight and shrill lam-
poon, it nevertheless prompted a lively scandal among the area's
Baptist establishment at the time. And somehow, even seventeen
years later now, it seemed to have improbably endured as a hyp-
notic captivation with Grady. "Yeah, I read the whole thing,
'bout this country fella, you know, wants to be a preacher. Awful,
awful — I still got it in there in my study with a lot of the things
underlined in red. It has him —" Grady took a couple of sideways shuffling steps closer, and his voice dropped to a stealthy
husk "— for instance, he'd dream about runnin' around bare-
footed over these fields of — titties, you know — wigglin' his
bare toes in 'em and all. That's right. And standin' out on his
porch at night, and —" Grady's hands briefly clasped into a cup
below his belt-buckle and swung back and forth "— and pissin'
figure-eights out in the yard. Yeah." His full round face was absolutely solemn. "Things like that, that kind of stuff. I can show
you. I've got it right in there right now with all those things underlined."

This inner troupe of attendants — Barrows, Shea, Smith, the
Wilson brothers — Graham has managed to keep about him
through almost three decades, and their fellowship together,
beyond the prayerful and spiritual, inclines toward the compulsively prankish, hilarities along the order of boys' summer-camp
japeries, short-sheeting each other's beds, contriving mutual
gullings and embarrassments, spoofs, little masquerades, fun-

nings like the time Billy lathered the inside of Grady's new ten-
gallon hat with shaving cream, which Grady discovered only
when he removed the hat to commence a radio broadcast. Nothing delights them so much as inadvertent pratfalls, awkwardly
mistaken identities, little contretemps. The practical jokes they
are constantly performing on each other, in fact, tend now and
then toward the savage. After Grady had widely advertised during one sojourn in California the magical properties of some new
sleeping pills he had acquired to help him snooze away long
stretches in the air, someone promptly smuggled mustard
powder into the capsules, and when their flight began on toward
Honolulu, to furtive peeks and sniggers around him, "I took one
of those things after another," says Grady, "thinking, 'Maybe I'm
immune to them or something.' Then I started getting a little
heartburn, a little indigestion. I thought it was that steak sauce
I'd poured on so heavily back there in Hollywood." A few minutes later, as he bent over in his seat croaking, weeping, Billy and
the others around him erupted into guffaws.

VI

It began in the loud and livid glares of those Youth for Christ
campaigns which, at the cessation of the nation's four-year exertion of war, came blustering out of the interior spaces of the
American Midwest — Saturday-night evangelical extravaganzas
with bands, banners, magicians, ventriloquists, once even one
hundred pianos all thundering away in unison, all in a swooping
of floodlights. As Billy has described the style of those events,
"We used every modern means to catch the attention of the unconverted — and then we punched them right between the eyes
with the gospel." Mounted out of a bare little office on Chicago's
North Wells Street by Torrey Johnson, that industrious revival
entrepreneur with the look of a strawberry-lipped pixie, these
fundamentalist rallies were ostensibly addressed to the new generation that had emerged during America's absorption in global

struggle. But that struggle had also left in its immense wake not only an uneasiness about the newly gathering shades of yet another menace, this one from Russia, but more than that, a suspicion that there had taken place, in the course of the war's colossal and uncomprehendible experience, some profound rearrangement in the life and identity of the country: that, in fact, some old native veil of innocence had been forevermore rent, and we had suddenly been loosed onto the open dark seas of a journey whose destination was beyond all sight and knowing. Racketing forth in this troubled aftermath of victory, there seemed something about the Youth for Christ phenomenon — with its indistinguishably virulent compound of religious and patriotic pentecostalisms in an operatic fanfare with vast hosts — that carried a peculiarly disquieting, very recent, hallucinatory familiarity. Those disquiets were not much dispelled when the movement began to attract before long, the conspicuous sponsorships of such interests as William Randolph Hearst and his complex of newspapers.

But Billy and the platoon of other young pulpit swashbucklers in Youth for Christ — freshly hatched provincial gospelteers, somewhat dandified in attire, with little jeweler's chain-loops over their plaid ties — were breezily unsuspecting of any such larger implications. One of that corps of young evangelists, a Canadian named Charles Templeton who has long since arrived at his own terminal disenchantment about it all, recalls now, "We were just these dynamic, handsome young guys, you know, full of incredible energy, full of vitality, and we were totally committed about the damn thing, every one of us. We really thought we were involved in a dramatic new resurgence of revivalism over the country."

Templeton himself first encountered Billy as the two of them were waiting on a stage just before the start of a huge rally in Chicago — and as they began to chat, sitting together on that dais isolated in the dazzle of a spotlight before the throng assembling below them, they contracted an instant enthusiasm for each other. It was an affinity that led to their being called, after a while, the Gold-Dust Twins. Templeton himself was an imposing presence. Towering as tall as Billy, he had about him the same electric intensity, with a tangle of black hair and a hot glare of urgency in his darkly tufted eyes, a fuguelike delivery, but also with a twinkling of the puckish in his apple-cheeked face. "He was the only guy I ever saw," declares someone who heard him then, "who could compare to Graham, who could have challenged him as the great American evangelist. He was formidable then." Billy will still declare, "Chuck was the most brilliant, able man I've ever known. He was a true intellectual. He could do almost anything — he'd been an artist, an actor, an inventor. He was a genius probably, I think." And for his part, Templeton remembers, he was taken with Billy as "this tall, thin, quite striking-looking, very blond guy with an absolutely uncanny platform ability." Indeed, when Billy stepped up to a pulpit, alone in the ultrabrilliance of stage lights, it was as if in that instant he suddenly came into his natural absolute apotheosis.

He had begun systematically styling his delivery after the clipped allegro syncopations of Walter Winchell and Drew Pearson, and as he had first raptly comtemplated his reflected gestures years ago in the mirrors at Vernon Patterson's house in Charlotte, he now rehearsed his pulpit poses wherever he could find a full-length mirror. He had also been lugging around with him a whole suitcase of books — "Michener, Steinbeck, especially historical-type books, anything that was popular at the time," along with Bible concordances and theological commentaries — to which he would sedulously apply himself at stray moments, undertaking, to ingest them all, a fitfully dogged regimen to invest himself with some wider intellectual dimension, more articulateness and authority on the larger affairs of the world.

But most of all, Templeton recalls that he noticed with some awe that "when Billy stood up to speak to a college assembly, and the crowd was hooting, laughing, booing at every little provocation — well, Billy told some of those awful jokes he still tells, you know, but just his simple likability had the whole audience lapping out of the palm of his hand in no time at all. It was the transparency of his spirit, I think. Here was a guy with absolutely no guile, no pretenses or defenses at all. Just this tremendous, endearing sincerity and goodwill, and his simple yearning for lost souls. One thing about Billy was that he would never kid past a certain point about spiritual matters — for instance, he never much liked any witticisms about any seeker who came forward, however comic or bizarre someone might seem who came down to the front, he wouldn't make any fun of them afterward. They were all dear in his sight. And maybe that's the thing that always distinguished Billy from the rest of us, including me — I could certainly preach circles around Billy, there was just no comparison in that regard, and even today the actual thinking in his preaching is simply dreadful — but somehow, when it came to the altar call, nobody could touch him. Billy would invariably have more people come forward than anybody else would. It would amaze us."

Another of Billy's confreres during that time remarks, "His genius was that his style of delivery was completely without decoration. You'd never hear him use an adverb, an adjective just for the sake of embellishment — for polishing things up. The only time or two he tried throwing in some fancy phrase or adjective, the result struck him as well as everybody else as ludicrous. Because, you see, an evangelist can't be complicated. They are great persuaders, not explainers. And all Billy ever really had was passion. All the great evangelists have that — extraordinary passion — which is why most of them are so virile in their preaching. They give themselves, not with intellect, but just with tremendous passion to their message." In that sense, Billy's life now had come to consist of engaging, in each service, in an act of wooing, making love to whole multitudes — "and he was already matchless in that, I admit, rather curious transference of energy," says Templeton.

Even so, Templeton reflects, "It began to bother us a little, especially Billy and me, that there seemed too much of a facileness to the way we were operating. I mean, at the services there was a kind of rushing them through each evening — these converts making what was supposedly the most drastic decision of their lives — and then afterward, we'd all go out and eat steaks. We were both just enough bothered in our Calvinist consciences about the glibness of it all."

Nevertheless, those larger interests in their campaigns from such parties as Hearst had accumulated to the point that, by 1946, means had been provided for the amplification of Youth for Christ abroad. "The first motion I made when I was elected vice-president of Youth for Christ International," grins Templeton, "was that we hire Billy as international evangelist — a motion I made, of course, with Billy's full knowledge and joy." They happened to be accompanied, in their first excursion to Europe, not only by a Hearst reporter but a *Life* photographer, and before their departure from a Chicago airport, Billy had his entourage, including Templeton, kneel with him on the tarmac by the ramp of the plane for a brief prayer meeting, the photographers around them barking, at every *Amen,* every pause, "Keep praying! Keep praying!" which they obligingly did, the wind flapping their ties in their faces, while the plane crew and other passengers waited, gawking. He finally clambered with his fellows on up into the plane, and as soon as they were airborne — actually on his way now to those far locales and landscapes of his farm-youth fantasies, *I would wonder even if the very earth over there wouldn't look different from ours,* and not only that, but trailed in this adventure by a camera of Mr. Luce's and a notebook of Mr. Hearst's — Billy began striding up and down the aisle whooping and grabbing hands in a kind of frenzied euphoria.

There was a layover, due to murky weather, at an American airbase in Newfoundland, where it turned out the commander assumed somehow they were all a vaudeville troupe. "He was talking to Torrey," says Templeton, "and he kept asking him, 'Who are you people, exactly?' All Torrey would tell him was, 'We're headed for Europe.' He asked him, 'Are you with the USO, or something?' Torrey just said, 'Yeah.' " The commander thereupon decided to arrange for them to perform in a base hangar that evening after the movie. "Torrey came rushing back to us all out of breath, 'Guys, we're gonna have a big meeting here, get ready.' He'd chosen not to disabuse the commander of his illusion, but instead to avail himself of it. He was thinking, too, of course, how we had this *Life* guy and the Hearst guy with us, and how grand the whole thing would look." They immediately began scrambling together a program. "We decided that Stratton Shufelt would come on first and sing two songs: the first would be 'Shortnin' Bread,' and then he would follow that with 'The Old Rugged Cross.' We just hoped that before anybody really caught on, we'd have them in a revival meeting. It was a very ticklish matter of gradually alternated phasing. So Shufelt went out there, and they all started clapping and stomping and whistling — they were just waiting for us to bring on the women. Shufelt starts with 'Shortnin' Bread,' really belts it out. It works great, fantastic, everybody's applauding, yelling. Then, instead of the girls, out comes Torrey in his little bow tie. There's a little groan over the audience. Torrey then quickly, in the most gauche kind of way, trying to imitate some emcee on a Hollywood game show, starts enthusiastically calling out, 'How many of you fellows from Ohio? That's great, that's just wonderful. Now, how many of you from California?' — They start booing now, whistling, hollering, 'Where are the girls? Show us some legs. Where those legs?' Torrey's gotten through only a few states, he's blushing pink, and he just gives it up, dives offstage and wildly waves for poor old Shufelt to go back on. Shufelt walks out and starts singing 'The Old Rugged Cross' — it's bedlam. Boos, howls, roars, bellows for those girls they're fast suspecting now might not actually be back there at all. Torrey tries to push me on then, but I tell him, 'Are you crazy? I'm not going out there. It ain't working at all, Torrey, it's just not going to work, they're going to kill us all, don't you realize?' About that time, the base commander appears backstage. His face is red as a beet. 'Just who the hell are you guys?' he shouts. Before we can finish explaining that we're actually an evangelistic team with Youth for Christ on our way to hold revival crusades in Europe, he's demanding that Torrey come with him for a meeting in his office. They were going to throw us in the brig. The only thing that saved us was the intercession of that Hearst reporter who was with us."

On their landing in England, London was not unlike a large mausoleum, a city of shadows still in a brownout, and the Continent was everywhere pocked and rubbled from its seven years of holocaust and sunk now in siftings of winter snow. Arriving amid these ashen wastescapes, Billy and his party of young revivalists nevertheless went about their mission, to a people just having passed through unutterable havoc and tragedy, with an improbably bouncy and gaudy perkiness. As one clergyman later remarked to one of Graham's biographers, "If they had realized what the war had meant in Britain, they wouldn't have come with that happy, cheer-us-up idea." Templeton himself admits, "One of my strongest memories from that trip is of Billy moving through all that desolation in pastels." But he insists, "I don't really think we affronted the people over there then, curiously enough. They expected ebullience from Americans. I'm not so sure they didn't welcome it. We were sort of a spot of color and life on the landscape, you know. We were all so full of bloody energy, we were just irresistible — bow ties, white shoes. We certainly didn't look like any other preachers they'd ever seen, I'm sure of that."

Templeton recounts, "As soon as we hit London that first time, we booked ourselves into the Dorchester. That would have been like putting ourselves in the Plaza in New York. But we had no idea. We were all still pretty much country boys. We just thought it was an awfully nice hotel. It looked like a palace to us, but the prices seemed very reasonable. When they took Billy and me on up to our room, the place looked big as a park to us." They stood hushed, motionless, as the bellman put away their luggage, and then as soon as he closed the door on them, they began romping about under the chandeliers, yodeling to each other, "Man, isn't this something? What a place!" Billy went vaulting on into the bathroom, whereupon there ensued a sudden silence. Then he called, "Chuck, c'mere a minute, look at this thing —" and when Templeton came hurrying in, Billy pointed to a fixture on the floor. "What's 'at? What in the world is that for?" Says Templeton now, "We'd never seen a bidet before in our lives. We'd never have been able to even imagine that something like a bidet existed. So I studied it for a second, and then I said to Billy, 'Man, it's the place where you wash your feet.' " Billy flung his arms out in wonder, and cried, "I tell you, this place has got *everything!*" About that instant, their room phone rang — Torrey Johnson, calling from a room nearby, to report with the same amazement his discovery of the same enigmatic luxury there: "Now, what do you figure that thing's supposed to be?" Billy happily shouted, "Man, don't you know? That's what they have for you to wash your feet in."

They preached then in soccer fields, churches, entertainment halls, across the haggard expanses of Europe, "mostly to young people's meetings," says Billy. Between 1946 and 1949, he was to make six forays to Europe, traveling in all some 750,000 miles. In London once, he came very near being heaved out of a pub where "we were handing out tracts," he says, "with a great deal of zeal." But they were days of high elation. In Amsterdam, Billy and Templeton rode about the narrow cobbled candy-box streets along the canals in the back of a carriage, bowing with flamboyant flourishes of their arms to everyone they passed, and to an English businessman at one reception who remarked on Billy's nickelodeon-hued tie, Billy burbled, "You like it? It's yours!" and immediately whipped it off before the gapes of the whole assembly and presented it to him. Ranging on down along the southern coast of France, "which was still pretty grim from the war," recalls Billy, they passed Christmas in Monte Carlo, where "we paid our way with stockings — one pair of nylon stockings a day was all it cost us for room and board."

At one point, Billy found himself stranded at some frowsy hotel in the glum drizzles of Troon, Scotland, his funds abruptly dwindled almost away, and he took to his bed with another onset of one of those sudden maladies that always seemed to befall him at such moments. Finally — such instructive instances as Watson's campus-lobby prayer meeting down in Temple Terrace never having been exactly lost on him — he sent an appeal to a

millionaire Texas churchman named R. G. Le Tourneau, a manufacturer of construction machinery whom he had met in
Florida. Shortly thereafter, he was restored with a check for
seven thousand dollars.

On the whole, Billy negotiated his way in these revival expeditions through Europe with a kind of pulp-romantic zest somewhat suggestive of Tom Swift or Dink Stover abroad: in Copen-
hagen, says Templeton, "we wanted to walk around and see the
town, but I told Billy, 'You know, I hear it can get a little hairy at
places here at night.' So Billy said, 'I'm going to get me a knife.'
I thought he was kidding — but he went out and bought himself
this Boy Scout hunting knife. When he brought it back with him
to the room, I said, 'Aw come on, Billy, you can't be serious.
What in the world would you do with that thing?' And he said,
'If they come after me, I'll just go —' and he gave a big yell and
jumped on the bed and plunged that knife right through the
mattress."

During one stopover in Paris, Templeton relates, "Billy and I
suddenly decided one night we wanted to go out and see some of
that city too," and as they ambled down the sidewalk, they began
to be repeatedly waylaid by brightly smiling nymphs of the evening. "We were immediately spottable as Americans, I guess.
With the way we dressed in those days, we couldn't have been
anything else." Every ten yards or so, yet another girl would
noiselessly bloom forth out of the sweet spring night, to cling
briefly to their arms, their wrists, with low liquid murmurings,
releasing them with last lingering strokes. Making his way
through this gentle gauntlet, Billy at first affected a kind of thin
heedless jauntiness, his laugh only a little quick and high and
clattery, but at each encounter, he grew progressively more rigid
and white of eye — "began walking just the slightest bit faster,"
says Templeton. "And then one of 'em stood right in front of us
and threw open her coat, by Jove, and had nothing whatsoever
on under there." By now, Billy, as he lurched on, seemed
numbed into absolute voicelessness.

At last, they plunged down some steps into what they took to
be a small basement cafe — a grotto with a whomping of music

in a murk of candles, where, almost as soon as they had fumblingly settled themselves at a table, two girls appeared to ask if they could sit with them — "very, very attractive girls, I mean really lovely creatures," says Templeton. "What did we know? We were both green as two ears of spring corn. We just thought they were being friendly — like it was some kind of student canteen." The night tapered on, and when the girls finally asked if they would take them home, "we both jumped up and said, 'Sure.'" They emerged back onto the sidewalk into the warm flush of the late night, and it developed that the girls lived in opposite directions — "They could just barely speak English, actually, but we finally understood what they were trying to tell us."

Noticing only a quick glance of something like dumb despair from Billy as they parted, Templeton walked his girl back to her apartment building. He was slightly startled by its tawdriness, and as they were ascending its stairs, Templeton was not so much a bumpkin that it did not occur to him that perhaps he should pause a moment in the hall toilet to tuck his wallet up over the water tank. "Then when I got in her room," he says, "I found out why she'd gone ahead and brought me up there." He bade a farewell, retrieved his wallet, and expeditiously decamped. Arriving back at the hotel, though, "when I opened the door to our room, Billy wasn't there.

"So I sat down to wait. An hour went by — no Billy. Two hours, three hours — still no Billy. Finally, about four o'clock in the morning, all of a sudden, he comes bursting through the door — sweat all over him, panting, his face as white as a ghost. I said, 'What in the world happened to you, man?' He just stood there for a minute or two staring at me, his eyes wide as saucers. Then he said, 'You wouldn't believe what happened. She said we had to catch a cab. So we found a cab, and got in. And we rode. And rode. And rode. It turned out she lived way out somewhere on the edge of Paris. When we got there, I took her on up to her room, and she asked me to come in. And Chuck — you're not gonna believe, just as soon as I shut the door, you know what she did? She went right over and lay down on her bed, and she threw her skirt up over her head right there in front of me, and

Chuck, *she didn't have a single thing on her underneath.* And I ran out of there — just straight out. And I kept running. I ran the whole distance all the way back here." Ever since that evening — his bolting stampede down the stairs and back out into the night, running on then, pounding blindly down long sidewalks under the successive fleeting flares of streetlights, a tall solitary flapping apparition disheveled and swamped in sweat, his hair webbed like seaweed across his brow, but running on, past discreetly lighted window-shutters, faint tatters of laughter and sourceless rills of music, fleeing on alone through that warm winy Parisian spring evening — through all the years since then, Templeton has always brought a start from Graham, a quick uneasy smile, by twitting him with the greeting, "Hey, it's the Midnight Runner."

But while he was in England, Billy had attended a church conference near the Welsh mining town of Pontypridd, where a local young evangelical, a diminutive and spiffy man of rapturous fervors named Stephen Olford, preached at one service on the text *"Be ye not drunk with wine . . . but filled with the Spirit. . . ."* "It was one of those nights," Olford still enthuses, "when heaven came down, and glory filled our souls." In fact, so shaken was Olford himself by the transports he had loosed in his preaching, that when he finished, he dropped back into his seat with bowed head sunk in his hands. After a few minutes, he says, "I suddenly sensed someone standing there over me," and glanced up to discover the long rigging of Billy's figure hanging above him. "I really believe," Olford recollects, "it was the first time in my life I ever saw anybody in a pink suit." But Billy exlaimed to him with an air of desperation, "Mr. Olford, I just want to ask you one question — why didn't you give an invitation? Because I'd have been the first one to come forward. You've spoken about something that I haven't got. I want to know the fullness of the Holy Spirit in my life too. I want what you've got." They arranged then to meet a few days later in a small hotel in Pontypridd — where they wound up closeted, in a marathon session

of tracking through the Scriptures and flailing away at heaven
with prayers, for a full two days.

Olford happened to be possessed by a constant pulsing beatific
glee, a small brisk man with a bright-coined handsomeness, who
had been the son of Christian Brethren missionaries to Angola.
When Olford had migrated back to England to study engineering, though, he says, "in my wilfullness to follow my own way, I
turned my back on the church. But I was miserable." He took to
racing motorcycles until, returning from one race, he capsized
on a deserted lane. Lying in his hospital bed, "I knew my dear
mother was praying her head off for her wandering boy" — he
was then twenty — "and I personally sensed that something momentous was about to happen to me." However unprepossessing
his prodigalities, actually, still his sense of remorse grew so "devastating," he says, "that I finally slipped down to my knees there
by the hospital bed and prayed to God to forgive me, and with
that, I sensed such a peace in my soul, such a glow, an assurance — it was an absolutely revolutionary experience." He
was to be consumed by that ecstatic of sanctity from then on.
After serving as a chaplain during the war — "I spent seven
years trying to cope with those boys" — he graduated on into an
evangelism "in dance halls, in cabarets, on crowded beaches — I
have done the most fantastic things!"

Full of a kind of passionately celestial sentimentalism, after a
long pastorate in later years at New York's Calvary Baptist, he finally had to remove himself down to Florida because of a disorder, evocative of one of Tennessee Williams's fragile divines, involving some strain and fraying "of the nerves in my heart."
Now, out of a small blank white building in a little sun-dazed
beach town near St. Petersburg, he operates his own free-
lance evangelistic enterprise, through mail and radio and cassette
tapes. Still a sprightly and dapper bobolink of a man, he effusively reminisces, his small hands vigorously whisking, "Something happened in that Pontypridd encounter with Billy that just
knit our souls together. And now, it doesn't matter how many
years have intervened, Billy and I never get together again with-

out a feeling that we want to discuss spiritual things — we never engage in small talk. Ever since that time at Pontypridd, we've just been —" and he clutches his two small fists together in front of his face, fingers interclenched, and gives three quick light tight shakes "— *so close!*"

In that aged stone hostel huddled up in a valley of Wales, they retreated to a small drab room with tatty curtains, and there, through two gray and drizzling days in late October, with a gas heater muttering in a corner, they lost themselves in what Olford describes as "prayer and praising and wrestling with the Lord." Billy notified him at the outset, "This is serious business — I have got to learn what this is the Lord has taught you," and kneeling then, he announced, "Lord! Lord, I don't want to go into the ministry without knowing this anointing you've given my brother." There was almost a peremptory rapacity in his urgency. He abstained from eating, had no appetite, at the most took a gulp of water now and then, while, says Olford, "I explained to him that where the Spirit is truly lord over your life, there is liberty, there is release — the sublime freedom of complete submission of oneself, in a continuous state of surrender to the indwelling of God's Holy Spirit. I told him about my own experience of total abandonment to God's will when the Lord completely turned my life inside out, and I experienced the Holy Spirit in all His fullness and anointing. And I can see Billy now, those eyes filled with tears, and he cried, 'That's what I want. That's what I want too.' "

Olford continues, "So from talking and discussing, we went to praying. And from praying, we went to praising. Until suddenly, somewhere around midafternoon of that second day, like Jacob of old laying hold of God and crying, 'Lord, I will not let Thee go except Thou bless me,' the crisis came — it seemed as if all Heaven broke loose in that dreary little room, and we began alternating between crying and laughing, until finally we came to a place of rest and praising." Olford remembers Billy after a few minutes lunging to his feet, swinging back and forth across the room on his long legs, crowing, "I have it! I'm filled! I'm filled! This is the turning point of my life! This will revolutionize my ministry!" And that very night, says Olford, "he preached on Belshazzar's feast at a large Baptist church nearby. As he rose to speak, he was a man absolutely anointed. As he preached, the heavens opened up. When he gave the invitation, there was chaos! Practically the enire audience came rushing forward!"

Templeton himself admits, "I began to notice after a while that Billy seemed to be taking on, more and more, a largeness and authority in the pulpit, to be going now for a certain magnificence of effect. It became fascinating, really impressive, to watch him."

Between those sorties to Europe, Billy also continued to trail about the United States with Youth for Christ. "About every town we'd go into," says Grady, "the business folk would tell us, 'We'll look after you boys, don't worry about anything.' The car dealers would always furnish cars for us, just like they still do." But more than that, Billy began to find now, wherever he put in a performance, that local ministers seemed to evidence a particular enthusiasm about him personally and the prospect of his returning again on his own. This discovery soon pricked his imagination to more expansive speculations. . . . Then, in 1947, that circle of Christian burghers in Charlotte who had conducted those cow-pasture and pine-grove prayer meetings through the Thirties that had culminated in Ham's long revival stand downtown, phoned Billy while he was in London to ask him to hold two weeks of services there in the late autumn. "We waked him up over there about two in the morning," says Vernon Patterson, "but he said right away he would come."

It was to turn out to be his first full-fledged personal crusade, for which he arranged to import Barrows, Grady Wilson, Bev Shea, for the first time all together. But as the date approached, "he got so afraid he might flop in his own home city," says Patterson, "that he started trying to bring in every prop he could think of." By the time the revival got under way — in Charlotte's old armory auditorium, a sooty brick warehouse of a building which could seat some five thousand — Billy had assembled a veritable Ted Mack revue of miscellaneous accessory attractions, including a profusion of soloists, a xylophone player, and a championship indoor-mile runner named Gil Dodds, who was scheduled to perform before one evening's service by sprinting six laps around an improvised track. "Man, back then, we'd do *anything* to get 'em in," says Grady.

"We'd gotten out letters to all the colleges in the state to send all their runners to compete with Dodds," says Patterson, "but the only one who responded was this cross-country runner from UNC named Jimmy Miller." The turnout had proved so heavy for the first few services that the revival was transferred to the more spacious accommodations of the American Legion field, but the day before Dodds's exhibition race, a pelting rain had left that site a puddled mire, so that evening's service was relocated back in the armory — "We had to rearrange the chairs in there to make a track all the way around the edges of the seating area," says Patterson. After the invocation, a few prayers, a few hymns, Dodds and Miller then knelt in place, an usher posed over them with an uplifted pistol, it popped, and they were off — their rubber tennis shoes slapping on the wooden floor around the seated congregation with its slowly and unanimously turning heads, circling again and again, the voice of Miller's wife crying over the rustling of the crowd, "Take 'im now, Jimmy, take 'im, take 'im now, Jimmy. . . ." Gradually, though, Dodds began to float on ahead on his evenly scissoring legs, crossed the finish well in front of Miller, and then, says Grady, "he climbed up to the pulpit to give his testimony, puffin' and blowin', told 'em, 'Now I wonder how many of you here tonight are doing your best in the race for Jesus Christ.' " No testimony was heard from Miller. Grady now reflects, "I sat there that Saturday night watching the thing, the whole audience quiet with those boys just streakin' around and around and I remember it came to me, *This is awfully silly. This is really a little absurd.* But you know, when we gave the invitation that night, we had an incredible number of young people to come forward. That just showed us, God can use just about anything."

At the end of those two weeks, Billy had drawn some twelve hundred penitents down the aisle to the altar. Before he left, he jubilantly presented himself at Patterson's business-forms sales office to propose, "Mr. Pat, as you know I brought Bev Shea down here all the way from Chicago to be with me, and I promised to pay him one hundred fifty dollars, but I've been wondering — I want to have him with me from now on, and I want to keep him happy, so — I wonder, with the wonderful job he's done for us in these meetings, if you could, say, double that salary for him." Patterson cheerfully consented.

But about this time, Billy happened to fall into the somewhat incongruous digression of serving as the twenty-eight-year-old president of a religious campus in Minnesota called Northwestern Schools. Its founder, William Bell Riley, was now a rickety eighty-six-year-old one-time gashouse-gang revivalist, a lofty-hung figure with a long patrician face, large gently slabbed lips under an imposing nose, curly cottony white hair, who had been one of the stalwarts of the great fundamentalist wars of the Twenties against "modernism," of which the Scopes trial in Dayton, Tennessee, was the most notable pitched engagement. In the Thirties, Riley had phased into a rather raucous anti-Semitic and anti-Catholic evangelism in concert with such parties as Gerald L. K. Smith and Gerald Winrod. He had first been taken with Billy during a visit to Temple Terrace, and hearing him later hold forth at a Youth for Christ rally, he expostulated to an organization official, "Where did you get that young man? He's a comer!" Finally, in the summer of 1947, as he lay expiring in his home in the Minneapolis suburb of Golden Valley, he had Billy summoned to his bedside.

When Billy appeared, Riley lifted a fluttering bony finger directly at his wide stare, and with a shattering of thunder and blue blares of lightning against the bedroom windows, he cawed, "You are the man to succeed me, Billy. I've known it for some time. You'll be disobeying God if you refuse this. I'm leaving this school to you as Elijah gave his mantle to Elisha — as Saul appointed David king of Israel, so I appoint you head of these schools, and I'm going to meet you at the Judgment seat of Christ with them." It becomes a propensity of souls like Riley, who have dwelt perhaps overmuch with the prophets and patriarchs in the Scripture, to lapse into such cross-muddlings of casts and occasions — but Riley's pronouncement, delivered to such a hair-raising percussive commotion of the elements outside, worked enough of a hoodoo on Billy that, despite all his instant deep disinclinations, he quickly dropped to his knees by Riley's bed and accepted the commission.

After presiding at Riley's funeral shortly thereafter, he addressed himself to the unlikely responsibility into which he had been impressed with a certain game zest — hailing the school trustees in letters as "Dear Gang." But he was largely miserable. For one thing, "as an administrator, there were just a lot of things I didn't understand. For instance, the librarian came up to me once and told me what she was making and said she had to have a raise, and I immediately told her, 'Why, you certainly do, you can certainly have it.' Just like that. The finance board went into a state of shock when they heard what I'd done." Besides this awkwardness, Billy by now had already acquired an exquisite sensitivity to the general respectability, an instant suspicion of anything with the faintest taint of the eccentric or aberrational, and the rather dowdy unstylishness then of his institution's grim fundamantalism began to give him some discomfiture.

Most of all, though, he simply could not resist the old lyric winds of being on the road: it was something like a guerrilla horseman's restlessness to be always on the move, to strike in yet another new terrain of possibilities. Says Grady, "He could hardly wait until we set out on a train again, climbed in a car or caught a plane to take off again somewhere." Astute to this compulsion, Ruth herself "didn't want to move when I went to Northwestern," allows Billy, "she insisted in staying on at Montreat with her parents." And in fact, he finally contrived a compromise at Northwestern whereby the actual management of the school was left to the aides he had collected there — including, by now, T. W. Wilson — while he was out beating back and forth over the country some ten months out of every year.

But for all his uneasiness about Northwestern's reputation for a boiler-plated fundamentalism, his own preaching still was made up of such rudely primitive theological blusters that "there were a lot of ministers," reports one colleague, "who simply wouldn't let him in their churches. In the beginning back there, we just couldn't hardly book him — we had a very tough time getting a church to take him and help pay the freight." There occurred one especially disastrous ten-day stand in Altoona, Pennsylvania — "a bust if we ever had one," says Grady — where the local ministers were singularly croupy about the whole proposition. Actually, the affair had gone hopelessly amiss from the very first meeting, on a Sunday afternoon in the Masonic Hall, owing to the fact, Grady contends now, that "we had this demon-possessed woman there. She was sittin' right down at the front, close as she could get to everything — had stringy hair, dressed real shabby, her eyes right yellow, with this wild stare — and before things even got started good, she suddenly let out a whoop and fell on the floor and said, 'I see 'em! I see 'em! The Indians are comin' to get me!' Billy and I both grabbed her and toted her back in a side room, and she became perfectly calm. She brushed herself off and informed us, 'I have these little spells occasionally.' Then she announced, 'I think I wanna go back and sing in the choir now.' I told her, 'No, ma'am, I'm sorry. You can't do that.' She looked at me a minute, and then screamed, 'You go to hell,' and got down on the floor again and commenced to kick and roll and holler. She was a wildcat. I'm tellin' you, it all went downhill from there. There were some of us who began to wonder if Altoona might not turn out to be the end of the line."

At a Bible conference that same summer in Michigan, after one late session Billy wandered with two friends — one of them Roy Gustafson from the days at Temple Terrace — out into an open meadow, where they stood for a while watching the ghostly wavering of another aurora borealis across the midsummer evening sky. "We began to talk about the Second Coming," says Gustafson, and after a few moments, Billy murmured, as much to himself as to them, "If only I could do something for the Lord before it happens. If only he would use me just a little bit before he comes —" So immediately did they all live in the suspense and imminence of that sensational event, it was as if Billy were caught now in a dread, almost a panic, that those majestic possibilities he had begun to sense might actually be denied him, it would only be a succession of Altoonas before it would all be foreclosed by Christ's return in glory. They decided then to hold a short impromptu prayer meeting there in the middle of that large meadow, Gustafson withdrawing a voluminous handkerchief and delicately arranging it like a napkin over the dew on the grass before kneeling. After a minute or two, he suddenly heard an odd, smothered groan from Billy. Gustafson opened his eyes to find him sprawled out full-length on the ground, face downward, his long arms outstretched in the classic posture of utter abasement and supplication: and he moaned, in that muffled voice, "Oh, Lord — let me do something. Trust me just to do something for you before you come."

The presence of a light coolness moved in the air of that northern evening. It was only a few months now before he was to begin another revival, that autumn of 1949, in Los Angeles.

But also during this period, Billy happened to be passing through the private throes of a last ragged skirmish with goblins of uncertainty about the literal authenticity of the Scriptures. This interlude of disequilibrium he had been lured into, he would later explain, by a friend who "was enamored of intellectualism" — as it happened, Charles Templeton.

Actually, in all their rangings over the country and abroad for Youth for Christ, Templeton had begun entering into a deep distraction of his own about the fundaments of the message they were carrying. Jimmie Johnson recalls, "Chuck Templeton always had this certain magic about him, as much as Billy had then — the same great confidence, great assurance, that same extraordinary charisma. They were like brothers in this special gift they both had. But I was always a little wary of Chuck for some reason. I think it was his — well, some underlying detachment in him. You finally felt you couldn't ever really get close to him. He was carrying some secret all the time within him."

Raised in Toronto, Templeton had dropped out of school in the ninth grade, after his father abruptly vanished, leaving Templeton's mother with five children, and he had proceeded to develop a precocious urchin nimbleness for survival and opportunity. While still only a teenager, he was already prospering as a sports cartoonist for one of the Toronto newspapers. But for all his emerging varied dexterities — in drawing, acting, writing — once when he was about seventeen, after returning home from a roisterous party in the black empty hours of an early morning, he stood looking at the reflection of his face in his bathroom mirror for a long minute — the face, it suddenly seemed, of some vaguely ominous stranger — "and I was seized with a terror then that my whole life was going down the drain." With that, "I had an absolutely overwhelming experience. It was like I was knocked to my knees. It was the quintessential conversion experience — tears, shaking, everything. It was extraordinary. It was quite real." Not long after that, he began trying occasional turns of preaching here and there, mostly for the Church of the Nazarene sect, and shortly realized that he held virtuoso wizardries in this medium too — one incomparably more exhilarating than any of the others.

A religious wunderkind around Toronto soon, with his own flourishing independent church downtown, signed on by Youth for Christ and then meeting Billy on that stage in Chicago, forging on with him through Europe, nevertheless Templeton after a time began to be plucked at by the feeling that "we were all getting along just by personal magnetism, just on speaking ability. We were just these good-looking young guys, you know, young bucks with this animal energy — that's all there was to it. And I began to realize that we couldn't get by forever on sheer pizzazz and charisma. I knew that I, at least, had to get some buttressing." Despite his ninth-grade education, he was accepted for seminarial studies at Princeton, and resigned his pastorate.

He then journeyed down to Montreat to exhort Billy to accompany him to Princeton. "I told him, 'Billy, c'mon, look now — the day's gonna pass when we're as prepossessing as we are. The day's gonna pass when we have the passion and the magnetism and the glamour — we need some *sinews*. We've got to go *deeper* than all this. Why don't you come up there with me, then?' And

Billy said, 'Chuck, I know that's all true what you're saying — but man, I'm the president of a Bible college. How can I go off to a theological seminary now? The president of Northwestern Schools entering as a student in Princeton Theological Seminary? I just can't do that. But look, I'll make you a deal. If you'll go with me somewhere out of the country, I'll do that — if you'll go with me to Oxford, in England, I'll go, I can do that, and I will. How about it?' " And, continues Templeton, "he walked over to me where I was sitting, and stuck out that big hand of his — and you know Billy, he keeps his word at almost any cost. All I'd have needed to do was take his hand. With that shake, we would have been two years at Oxford. His life would have probably gone in a totally different direction. But I didn't — for some reason I hesitated, and I didn't."

By now, actually, Templeton had already come to be haunted by second sights on it all — glances into some strangely enervating mirror of other-consciousness, a secret double vision, as if somewhere along the way he had been subtly abstracted out of it all to find himself at a peculiar extra remove, watching himself. It assumed for him the appearance of a frenetic mummery, really a matter of all those people, woeful for something to answer the dull vacancy in their lives and in their hearts, drum-majored and razzle-dazzled into a romance with Jesus.

While he was at Princeton, he and Billy began to hold periodic exhaustive binges of discussion, prayer, debate, in a small wan twin-bedded room at the Taft Hotel in New York, sessions that were like reversed reflections of Billy's two days with Olford in that hotel room at Pontypridd. Contending together over the literal verity of the Bible and the efficacies of faith and reason, Templeton was as much trying his new skepticisms — disillusionments of a somewhat elementary and sophomoric order, actually — against Billy's certitude, as Billy was laboring to affirm and sustain that certitude. The two of them would flounder on with this through the length of a whole day and then on through the night. . . .

"But Billy, there is no way, *no way*, it's possible to just dismiss the arguments that we're all here because of evolutionary processes. How do you manage to just wave away all that overwhelming evidence? —"

And Billy, smiling amiably, "The arguments you make, Chuck, no, I don't know how to answer them, I can't answer them. But wiser men than you and I will ever be, they have already encountered and examined all those arguments, and they have concluded that the Biblical record can be completely trusted, and these are men far wiser than —"

"Who? Like who, for instance? You mean you just give up the whole question, the whole decision, to —"

And Billy then, his voice ringing a little fuller, "But more than that, Chuck, more than that — I have learned something in my own preaching. I have observed that when I preach only the word of God, when I preach the Bible straight, no question, no doubts, no hesitations, then I have a *power* — I'm telling you, Chuck, a power that's *beyond me*. It's something I don't completely understand. But I just know I've found that when I say, *The Bible says!* — God gives me a power, this power, this incredible *power*. So that's why I have made a decision simply not to think about all these other things anymore."

"*Not to think?* What kind of power is that to rely on, man?"

"I don't know. All I know is that it comes from God. Because it is something totally beyond me —"

"Well, that's fine, but tell me then how you deal with this, Billy. What is the Great Commandment?"

"C'mon, Chuck—"

"What is it, Billy? It's to love the Lord thy God, not only with all thy heart and all thy soul, but all thy *mind*. All thy mind! And not to think, Billy, is a sin againt the Great Commandment. Deliberately, I mean to *decide,* not to think — that's a sin against God's will, against his word, that's disobedience, that's rebellion, that's *unfaithfulness.*"

And Billy pausing then for just an instant, hanging forward on the edge of the still-made bed, lifting one hand for an absent snicking of his teeth at his already tattered thumbnail, then shaking his head, "Chuck, I just can't answer that either, except I know I just believe. I just know what belief, without question, without reserve, has let God do in my life, and I know what God's done in others through that commitment to believe. I have decided to believe —"

At one point, Templeton finally shouted to him, "You really want to know what you've done, Billy? You've committed intellectual suicide — that's what." Billy simply stared at him then with an astounded and mildly stricken look, his wide brilliant eyes utterly blank — he uttered nothing: merely gaped in silence at Templeton out of eyes as clear and bright as an empty October afternoon sky.

But through those months, the complications visited on his sureties by Templeton slung him in a disconcertment that produced, after a while, "a terrific pain at the base of my skull." Only a month before his Los Angeles campaign, as he was driving with Grady across Utah's Great Salt Lake Desert on his way to a religious conference in the San Bernardino Mountains, Grady suddenly realized that he had remained wordless for miles, and glanced over to discover "he was driving along there with these great tears just running down his cheeks. I said, 'Hey, what'sa matter, buddy?' And he said, 'Templeton told me I've committed intellectual suicide. He told me I wasn't intellectually qualified to be going into a big city like Los Angeles. And maybe he's right. Maybe I'm not. I don't know.' Well, I told him real quick, I said, 'Look, there's a little jeep trail up there going out into the desert, why don't we just turn off there and drive out a little ways and have a little prayer?' " Billy eased his green Buick off the highway and bumped down the rutted path for a short distance and they got out, shutting the car doors with small flat trivial claps against the sudden far spaces of solitude. And alone in those sun-ringing wastes of bone-bleak rock and scrub, they began to pray, presently peeling off their shirts and, their bare backs palely luminous in the white glare of the high sun, prayed on loudly for almost two hours, until finally Billy climbed up from his knees, his shallow chest gilded in sweat, his face crimson, and "like an old war-horse again," says Grady, "he cried, 'All right, let's go! Let's go!' "

But this regalvanization lasted not much longer than it took them to arrive at the youth conference in the cool altitudes of the San Bernardino Mountains. A retreat operated by the First Presbyterian Church of Hollywood, meetings there were held at night around large brush fires where "you'd hold up a burning brand one by one and give your testimony," says Grady, "and then when you finished, pitch your brand into the fire," and as one enthusiast later recorded, "much confession was made, but all of it under the restraint of the spirit, with not a regrettable utterance." But one of the speakers there turned out to be Templeton.

Billy relates now, "Of course, Chuck was still going through that, you might say, a great period of intellectual stimulation and activity. He and some professors there began discussing higher criticisms. I just listened to them. I was fascinated — but they asked me questions I couldn't explain." These exchanges again left him so conspicuously unsettled that, Billy allows, "a friend came up to me and said, 'Billy, I can see you're disturbed by what those fellows have been talking about, but don't you worry about it, don't you mind them — you just go on as you've been going.' " After that, Billy says, "I went back alone to the cottage and read in my Bible for a while, and then I decided to take a walk in the forest." Presently, he sat down on a stump, surrounded by tall pines darkly lifting into a secret murmuration of night wind under the sky's frost of stars.

And brooding there, he managed to deliver himself through at last to a resolution of his crisis — by reducing the matter of belief in the prodigious mystery of God to the terms, as he formulated it, of how a brown cow could eat green grass and produce white milk, which, despite this considerable puzzlement, he nevertheless drank. "I cried, 'Lord, help me. I don't have the knowledge. I'm placing myself completely, heart *and* mind, without intellectual reservations, in your hands.' And I remember, the tears started coming down my cheeks —" And he stood then, and lifted his Bible in the faint icy starlight, "and I said, 'Oh, Lord, I *do!* accept this as your word! Come what may, without question or falter, I *believe* in this as your holy word.' "

With that, his commitment in Florida reached a further consolidation: on that evening almost ten years later, there was accomplished the final perfection of his certitude. He gave himself up, in effect, to the liberating, formidably energizing fallacy of "the preacher is only the messenger, not the author of the message," as he later explained. "He is not accountable for that message, he is simply called on to proclaim it. It is the Book speaking, not he; it is God speaking, not the speaker." He was thus loosed, as he has described it, "to preach with a voice of commanding authority, dissolving every 'if,' every 'I suppose,' every 'maybe.'" Billy declares now, "I never wavered from that moment to this. I know that some said I committed intellectual suicide, but I never felt such *power* —" and he clenches one large fist in the air, wags it, squints as if peering into distant horizons "— such power as after I made that decision. I felt confident from then on that what I was quoting *was* the word of God. It gave me a lasting, unassailable strength."

In this triumph over doubt after his strivings with Templeton, he began to rail with uncommon frequency in his messages against "the so-called intellectuals," against Nietzsche, Freud, Dewey, proclaiming with great vigor, "I don't care what the scientist has to say. I'm not dependent on what the scientist tells me to believe about this Book. Every time some big-shot scientist comes along and makes a statement complimentary to the Word of God, we rush out and say, 'Boy, look what So-and-so said — look what Dr. So-and-so, a Ph.D. from Oxford, had to say.' I don't *care* what any scientist says. It doesn't make the slightest difference to me. The Word of God is enough." As he would announce during a later crusade back in Charlotte, "Well, I want to tell you, you may laugh at me down here, you may say I am not an intellectual. You may say it is all speculation. Say anything you like; it does not disturb me in the slightest. Because there's no doubt. Not one doubt!"

Since that victory over all uncertainty that evening in the high pines of the San Bernardino Mountains, "they have dedicated the spot," Billy reports, "not a statue, actually, but there's a monument up there on that spot where I accepted the authority of the Scriptures in my ministry."

But as for Templeton, "what drove Billy on in his ministry and gave him his power," he recounts, "was precisely what drove me out of the ministry. I was unable to accept that you can refuse to think."

After a season at Princeton, he toured for a while as a speaker for the National Council of Churches, but he was only going through the last expiring motions of his old wasting passion. Finally, while he was at Yale for a series of lectures, the captain of the debating team asked for a conference after hearing one of his discourses. "He was a tall, very commanding-looking guy, very assured and articulate. The first thing he said when he came in was, 'I want to let you know before we begin that I am an atheist, and I would like to be able to interrupt whatever you're saying as we go along if I have a question.' He was a thoroughly brilliant young fellow. But of course, theology was my specialty. On theology, he really couldn't touch me. It was no contest. When the hour was over, he told me, 'Well, I can't say you have finally changed my convictions on this — but you have certainly tilted me in a very different direction. I find myself more inclined now to consider the possible truth of what you've been telling me.' Well, the truth about that was, of course, I happened to be in very serious trouble myself right then about all those beliefs I'd been pitching to him. After he was gone I told myself, 'Hold on a minute here — *you're* not sure of those things you were telling him. Have you the right to blunder around then in that promising young man's life?' And I knew then I had to get out of it, for good."

Settling himself back in Toronto, and divorced now from his wife, he became for a while a newspaper pundit, writing editorials for the Toronto *Star,* and finally passed on into his present electronic mutation as a radio and television commentator. Yet, as he and Billy kept in touch over the years, Templeton seemed to continue to exert a peculiar thrall on him somehow. During a 1957 crusade in New York City, with eight years having elapsed since Billy's ordeal of uncertainty, he spent several hours talking with Templeton again in a hotel room, and according to Stephen Olford, "it left Billy so rattled and shaken, he literally could barely preach that night. I was sitting with Chuck up on the platform, and Billy literally had to struggle through his message that evening, and I think it was because he knew Chuck was there." (In the same way, after Billy agreed once to hold a colloquy with a clerical critic on a Toronto television show before a crusade there, an aide quickly canceled the appearance with the explanation that the critic would present "a point of view to which Dr. Graham should not be exposed before going onstage.")

Ruth, for her part, has long maintained a somewhat tart humor toward him. "I feel sorry for the man, actually," she asserts. "Even while he was at Princeton, I felt there was something wrong in his life. He was one of the most extraordinary people I'd ever met, I agreed with Bill about that, one of the most gifted, an artist, actor, and exceptionally good-looking. But he abdicated. He deserted. He gave up." But Billy himself still insists, "I love Chuck to this very day. He's one of the few men I've ever loved in my life. He and I had been so close. But then all of a sudden our paths were parting. He began to be a little cool to me then. I think —" and he pauses, and then offers with a faint little smile "— that Chuck was always sorry for me."

Templeton still protests, "Don't get me wrong; Billy was bright as hell about certain things, he had a native shrewdness about how people felt about themselves, situations with people. But Billy also happens to be an almost genetically nice guy. He was just born a nice guy, he grew up a nice happy healthy fellow. There's not a mean or devious — or subtle — bone in his body. He is all goodwill." Indeed, after their hotel-room encounter during that 1957 New York crusade, Billy still could not seem to relinquish Templeton to his apostasy — this lingering wild hopefulness even impelling him to dragoon Templeton into delivering a prayer at that evening's service in Madison Square Garden. "He indicated he was going to do that, and I told him, 'Billy, don't. It's mad. I'm not a Christian any longer. Don't do it.' But he went ahead anyway, whether out of loyalty, nostalgia, or the crazy possibility out of concern for my soul that standing up there going through that I might somehow be reclaimed by the Spirit again. Whatever, it was a dumb thing to do. I've never felt more like a farce than when I was standing up there leading those thousands of people in prayer."

The truth is, though, Templeton never really succeeded in completely extracting himself out of those absorptions of his past. He later produced a compilation and synthesis of all Jesus' utterances — "I just thought they ought to all be brought together in one book, whereas they're scattered now through the four gospels — for which he entailed Billy into writing an introduction. But shortly after Richard Nixon's election, Billy happened to be passing through Toronto and dropped by Templeton's apartment for dinner one evening, "and things, for the first time, just weren't the same between us. I'd never thought, for all our differences, that we'd ever tire of each other's presence. But Billy sat there that night just singing Nixon's praises — how he admired his great mind, his knowledge of government, how nobody else had ever gone into the presidency as prepared as Nixon. I was absolutely stunned at how really enraptured with the guy he was — a guy I'd always considered a thoroughgoing creep, a jerk of the first class. But I didn't want to have an argument there with my friend in my house, who'd come by to have dinner with me. But something happened that evening that had never happened before. As he kept on with this unbelievable raving about Nixon, I remember thinking that we just didn't really have anything to say to each other anymore. It wasn't so much that I had changed or he had changed, as it seemed he had — I don't know — sort of finally glazed over into his pulpit attitudes. He was somewhere I couldn't reach him now — this truly blind excitement about the most dismal and thoroughly underwhelming creature. At the end of that evening, I found I was not unhappy to take him back to his hotel — I remember feeling very sad about that. It was like a small death had taken place. On the way back to his hotel, there were these long stretches of silence, which had never happened before when we saw each other. But we had simply run out of rapport. It was exhausted."

Over the years since he forsook the ministry, Templeton himself has become a personality of some celebrity around Toronto, something of a liberal Paul Harvey with a regular radio show of snappily conversational commentary — a man still of variegated facilities, inventor, novelist, television Brahmin, and on the whole rather a boulevardier, a bon vivant. He lives now in an apartment-tower suite thirty-seven floors over the far spread of the city, his large sitting room embellished with spiny Mexican flora distributed among much chrome and glass and aluminum and molded vinyl. From this spacious salon, he can still look down, through his gauzy papyrus-pale curtains, to the drab red roof of his old church far below.

Called on here of a winter afternoon by a television crew filming for a special on the modern state of religion, Templeton sits turned on his couch to the interviewer, propounding in his sonorously timbered voice, "I'm completely distant from the church now, in the sense that I have great sympathy for it, but I'm an agnostic. Intellectually, I could no longer accept Christianity. I could not call God father. . . ." As he delivers these mellifluous pronouncements, he lounges sideways on the sofa, a large bulking man with theatrically coiffed frosty hair and gray horn-tufts of eyebrows, with a touch of roguish liveliness in his ruddy face somehow suggestive of Pan — attired this afternoon in grape velveteen jeans and Japanese-like slippers, his transformation now at middle age into an urbane mandarin seemingly complete, but yet with some fugitive quality about him too of a displaced person, a kind of obscure casualty. Over the couch where he sits, there hangs an immense and oddly uneasy mirror of multiple oblique-canted panels of glass, giving off a scattered infinite fracturing of reflections, in which Templeton's own face is continuously disassembling amid a multiplying of camera lights, while he goes on in his resonantly electronic intonations, "It seems to me the universe is completely indifferent to us. I think we are in the beginning of what the historians will call the post-Christian era. I think we are in the beginning of the end of the long Christian phase of Western history. . . ."

After the crew has looped up their cords and recased their equipment and departed, Templeton shrugs on a buff topcoat, bundles a scarf about his neck, and, descending in the noiseless weightless calm of an elevator, sets out through the scraps of slush and snow and whistling wind-slaps of a black Toronto winter evening for a light dinner at a small restaurant nearby — a place with the look, as he bustlingly swings in through its heavy glass doors, of a set out of *Clockwork Orange:* like his apartment, all of chrome and glass and cast plastics, a kind of abstracted cerebral elegance of hard frictionless surfaces. Seated here, he resumes his reflections on that distant incarnation of his in the long-receded past. "That animal energy we all had then, especially I think Billy and I, I think it's just something that some people are born with. But I've never enjoyed life like I do now. I'm only sorry it took me so long to be free." He contemplates his wine for a moment. "Still —"

And he looks up with wide eyes under his wisped eyebrows: "— I have to tell you that it's a very exciting thing to have thirty, forty thousand people out there in front of you, and you know you can control them, hush them till you can hear a clock ticking in the back of the auditorium, just by dropping your hand, like this —" and he leans forward and allows his large outstretched hand to fall just slightly, just perceptibly, over the delicate transparent glitter of the wine in his glass "— just like that. Thirty thousand people, and every one of them stops breathing for just a second, all over that auditorium." He leans back again with a short smile. "Without a question, it is the highest kind of performing available to man. You begin really preaching to yourself, and then this interplay starts with the audience, they begin responding to your every tone, your every movement, *your* every breath. It becomes like all these people — thirty thousand people — they are amplifying everything you're feeling, everything you're saying, they are amplifying *you.* You become magnified to the size of all that huge crowd — thirty thousand people, and *they have become an extension, an enlargement of you* — and when it's right, when it begins to work like that, it's the closest thing to ecstasy on this earth.

"But of course, Billy, now —" Templeton lifts his glass in cradled fingers for a quick sip "— Billy, he simply wouldn't analyze what was actually happening at such moments. It was just 'I felt

God on me! I felt the power of *God* come over me!' When he felt like he hadn't preached well, that's when those slightly hypochondriacal tendencies he's got would really go to work — like one time I remember when we were walking along the boardwalk there at Atlantic City's beach after he had preached a service, and he started grumbling after a little bit, 'I didn't have any sense of God being with me tonight, Chuck. I didn't feel well — felt bad, my brain was bad.' What he really wanted me to say, of course, was no, no, he'd been great — that's when you needed to hear those reaffirmations from others, when you hadn't been so good. But he kept on, 'God just wasn't with me, I felt bad, I couldn't think; I think I might be coming down with the flu.' He would be totally miserable those times, start wondering if maybe he shouldn't see a doctor. But when he had come from a meeting where he felt God was on him — then, he was full of excitement, his spirit was really flying, you couldn't contain him. There was nothing you could have said to either reassure him or get him down then. When it's gone good, when you were really good, you didn't need to hear anything from anybody. I'm telling you, that was a feeling that few men ever know in their lives. . . .

"Well, we both knew that power then, Billy and I, that extraordinary communion that can take place between you and those great crowds of people out there. But I've never lived life so fully as I do now. Now, I believe in this —" and he momentarily places his palm over his wineglass, with a curiously measured soft grave formality as if administering some sacrament of consecration "— I believe in this. And I believe in life. I believe in love. I believe in beauty. I believe in kindness. And I do believe in moral laws. But I don't believe in God the Father. I don't believe that anymore. Now I'm not saying I'm joyful about that — it's nothing I'm particularly happy to have lost. But I'm free now. I've never loved life more. My only regret is that it took me so long."

He muses then for a second or two, among the subdued silvery scattered sibilation of voices at the other tables around him. "But you know — my God, it's strange to think back, but just here in Toronto, I once *owned* this town religiously. For a while there, in all of Canada and the United States, there probably wasn't a stronger preacher to be found. I could have — well, anyway," and he shrugs, and lifts a forked morsel of his trout meunière from his plate. "Say! This is excellent!"

VII

In the months before that Los Angeles campaign of 1949, Billy still amounted to little more than just another spirited but obscure young gospel-slinger among all the other free-lance evangelists batting back and forth with their ragamuffin tents over the land. He was perhaps a bit more incandescent than the usual run, an engagingly electric young man with corn-bright hair and startling eyes, his tall slatlike frame loosely bagged in sherbert-tinted suits with polychrome hand-painted ties. But that same summer of his luckless sally to Altoona, he mounted a revival in Baltimore's Lyric Theatre, an opera house with the names of legendary virtuosos scrolled around its plump ornate balconies, and for all his exertions, its expanse of 2,800 seats had remained only middlingly occupied; it had been like a windmilling into indifferent depths of fog. When he set out in the fall for his scheduled three-week stand in Los Angeles — at the invitation of a committee of Christian businessmen there headed by the president of a sportswear company called Hollywood Toggs, Inc. — there hardly seemed, for all his energetic earnestness, anything conspicuously portentous about him.

Nevertheless, he arrived in Los Angeles to a brave overture, advertising himself in a medley of newspaper billings as "America's Sensational Young Evangelist" with a "Dazzling Array of Gospel Talent" in a "Mammoth Tent Crusade . . . The Largest Tent in the World . . . a Canvas Cathedral." It was still then much the Los Angeles of Raymond Chandler, of *Day of the Locusts* — a kind of soft-focus, spoiled Hesperides of bougainvillea and Technicolor oleander blossoms under slack stringings

of telephone lines, an immeasurable afternoon flatland of
stucco bungalows in stale candy pastels dissolving off endlessly
under the tall stilts of palms in a strangely unbright sunlight. On
a vacant corner lot in a somewhat sallow quarter of the downtown district, Graham pitched his Canvas Cathedral — a voluminous triple-spired tent with bolted rows of wooden chairs ranked
over sawdust in a thicket of poles and masts like a frigate's rigging
— with a long banner outside running the length of the tent,
*Something's Happening Inside   6,000 Free Seats   Dynamic Preaching
Glorious Music,* and Billy's own visage peering out of a large oval
with the slightly spooky intensity of some young florist-turned-
swami, a harsh primitively painted likeness with violently bright
lips not unlike the brazen illustrations along carnival midways.

At the opening service on a Sunday afternoon, a sudden
sluggish unloading of warm rain left the seating area inside a
steamy bog of sawdust, but Cliff Barrows in his milk-white suit
blared doughtily away on his trombone, flourishing it about in
the air with a football half-time vivaciousness, on night after
night — presenting a motley bevy of other revival entertainers,
the Collins Twins' sacred-harmony duet, a tenor with the Haven
of Rest Quartet, along with the elaborately whinnying renditions
of an organist, a gospel violinist, Bev Shea — and finally then
bringing on Billy himself. He would sweep forward to an abrupt
stilling of hand fans over the congregation, tapering before them
thin and clean and shining as a scythe blade over the plank pulpit with a large cinnamon-hued portrait on its front of a lantern-
lit, lambently gazing Christ.

Opening the top button of his collar, as he began to preach he
tended to assume, with his blossoming breast-pocket handker-
chiefs, a fascinating but slightly disconcerting resemblance to
some dandily appareled young department-store floorwalker
caught in gales of epilepsy: eyes glaring, fists clutching air, his
long frame convulsing in apostolic ecstatics in his droopy bal-
looning suits, he would bray with a balefulness a touch infla-
tionary in one yet so fresh and callow, "If we're not guilty of one
thing, we're guilty of another! Tonight — tonight, there are
hundreds of people all over this great city of Los Angeles who

would not stoop to immoral depths — " and he would suddenly pounce from the pulpit to the very edge of the stage " — but they *sin!*" this like a trumpet's blast, one arm lashing across the air " — they *sin,* and in the sight of God, there is no such thing as a little sin, they are all terrible in the eyes of God. You go to church on Sunday and during the week you slip down to the cocktail lounge and listen to those dirty, filthy stories, and you laugh, and you're just as guilty as if you'd told the story and committed the act!" It was a Götterdämmerung of such prim and modest scruples, such unpresumptuous iniquities, that he delivered: a kind of apocalyptic Sunday-school niceness. "Yes, you'd cast a stone at a harlot tonight, you'd cast a stone at a drunkard tonight, but let me tell you Jesus said *you're just as big a sinner,* all men have violated the Ten Commandments! 'Thou shalt not murder' — so you say you haven't. Well, there are hundreds of husbands in this city who are *killing their wives by neglect.* There are boys and girls out there who are *killing their mother and father* with the wild life you are leading. *You are guilty of murder! . . .*"

Pausing then, sinking back behind the pulpit, he would pitch open both arms, his Bible sagging heavily from one hand, and peal now in a voice like a solitary bugle floating taps over the choir behind him stealthily gathering into "Just as I Am," "I wonder how many there are tonight who say, 'Billy, I know I'm guilty. I'm not sure I'm saved. I'm not sure if I died tonight, I'd go to Heaven. Tonight I want to give myself to Christ. I want to be sure. Right where I am, I'm going to let Christ come into my life. . . .'" And he would wait poised for an instant, glancing about with his scintillant eyes, his jaw jutting valiantly with a light parted smile, as the slow shedding of people began into the aisles, and then would drop his head and close his eyes and hug his Bible to his chest with a forefinger curled over his lowered chin.

But it went on rather perfunctorily like this, once every afternoon and again every evening, through three languishing heat-heavy weeks. There occurred then, toward the end of the scheduled run of Billy's stay there, a succession of slightly novel conversions, somewhat marginal celebrities whose metamorphoses nevertheless provided new gusts of public curiosity. Among those tugged into the doings in Billy's tent was a local radio personality named Stuart Hamblen — a convivial country boy out of Texas with black oil-combed hair and a flushed face like a well-battered catcher's mitt, who after ambling out to California and winning a Pacific Rodeo, had somehow wound up conducting a daily broadcast in Los Angeles called *Cowboy Church of the Air,* going on from that to become a kind of small-caliber Arthur Godfrey in the area. As the son of a Methodist preacher, Hamblen had been seasoned in the same homespun religious sentimentalisms as Billy himself, but had since lapsed into a casual waywardness — gambling, boozing, directing dance bands on Saturday nights, acquiring a stable of racehorses. It was a wickedness not precisely of cosmic dimensions — more that honkytonk order of sin defined in the simple righteousness of his boyhood with its hymns like "Where Is My Wand'ring Boy Tonight?" a sinfulness of the style in one of the songs Hamblen himself had crafted: *"I won't go huntin' with yuh, Jake, but I'll go chasin' wimmen. . . ."*

Nevertheless, for anyone raised in those pump-organ moral dramaturgies, a scenario that remains foreverafter irresistibly poignant and compelling is that of the Prodigal Son. It never fails, long years and sophistications later, still to clobber the heart; it simply endures as an elemental part of one's emotional hydraulics. In the middle of one of Billy's volleys one night — "There's a man in this tent tonight who's heard this story many times before, but again he is stiffening his neck, he is hardening his heart, he is turning his back, he is saying again, *No! No! No!* to God" — Hamblen arose and stomped out. For several hours, he wandered alone through the late-night neon shoals of the city, during which now and then, slouched in a dim booth of some bar, he would emit a brief dull lowing, his eyes momentarily blearing.

Finally, around three in the morning, the phone rang in the little efficiency suite where Billy and Grady were lodged. When Grady fumbled the receiver to his ear, he heard Hamblen, thoroughly sloshed by now, sob, "I'm coming over there. I'm 'bout to blow my whole life. I just got to find God — " and Grady began to mumble, "Well, Stu, old boy, that's wonderful, but couldn't it sort of wait a little bit? It's four in the morning here, you know — " but at that instant, Billy came plunging in from the other bedroom in his pajamas and snatched the phone, "This is Stuart Hamblen? Listen, buddy, you just get in your car and come right on over here, we'll be up waiting. . . ."

In a short while, Hamblen came blundering through the door, trailed by his long-patient if slightly ravel-edged wife, Suzy, and demanded, "Billy, pray for me. That's all I need, just for you to pray for me." Billy, dressed now in crisp slacks and a golf shirt, retorted, "No, that's not all you need. You need to go all the way and let Jesus Christ become Lord over all your life." After some disputation on this point, reports Grady, "suddenly down on his knees Hamblen went with a thud." They began to pray then with a full-lung gusto, one after the other, through the next two hours, Hamblen intermittently socked with sobs. "Once while Suzy was praying," says Grady, "Hamblen starts crawling over the carpet toward her, crying out, 'Oh, God, thank yuh for this little woman.' " At last, at dawn, it was done — Hamblen wauling, "God, I been tryin' to get you on the line a long time, but I never been able to make the connection. But I feel like I finally got you on the other end of that line now. And Lord, this may look like the same old Stuart Hamblen kneelin' down here, but you listenin' to a new voice talking to you. . . ." They arose then, shouting, cackling, whapping Hamblen on the back, he smacking them on the back, and with the sunrise through the venetian blinds striping the room now in buttery light, Hamblen sat down and quickly dispatched two helpings of grits cooked by Grady, bolted down with gulps of strong black coffee.

"Boys," he yelped, "I got to let people know about this," and immediately got on the phone, to actress Colleen Townsend among others: "Coke, honey, I just want you to know you haven't been wastin' your breath praying for old Stuart Hamblen — honey, the Lord Jesus Christ has just taken holt of me and changed my life right here in Billy Graham's hotel room!" And on his radio show later that day, Hamblen, still caught up in that celebration of his own salvagement that held in it certain hints of a profuse self-regard, proclaimed his conversion to his listeners, "I've quit smokin', I've quit drinkin'," and vowed he was going to divest himself of his racehorses.

Following Hamblen then, the crusade's fortunes were additionally facilitated by bagging a long-distance runner from the 1936 Olympics named Louis Zamperini — a rather tensely earnest young man who had come by a brief notability in Berlin, not so much for his performance on the track as for taking it on himself one afternoon to haul down the swastika over the Reichstag. After the war, he again found himself momentarily in the popular eye as a survivor of forty-seven days on a raft in the Pacific and captivity in a Japanese detention camp. But after those two short flashes of fame, he had promptly receded back into unnoticeability, adrift in the war's hangover years, broke, blotting himself out with the bottle. At last, having just the day before "lost my car, the last thing I had," he wandered into one of the tent services, where Billy struck him instantly, mightily, as "more like an athlete than a man of God," a magic déjà-vu vision of his own lost noble innocence, and with a nausea in his spirit of remorse and grief for that bright lost self, at the invitation he fairly sprinted down to the front.

The public regenerations of Hamblen and Zamperini were followed by the yet more exotic curiosity of the conversion of a moderately noted "electronic specialist" for gangster Mickey Cohen — a somewhat dour, suet-faced gentleman named Jim Vaus, who also happened to be the wayfaring son of a minister. After being expelled from a Bible college, Vaus had eventually trailed into such arabesque occupations as phone-tapping racetracks and bordellos for Cohen, but it was all a gaminess and irregularity in which he never finally felt quite comfortable. The evening that he made his own pilgrimage down Graham's revival aisle, he emerged from the tent into a sheet lightning of flashbulbs, headlines the next morning announcing, *Wiretapper Vaus Hits Sawdust Trail.*

As it turned out, he did not fare unfelicitously from his repentance. After making open confession to a versatile range of malfeasances, he was sportingly cleared by the courts and offered an array of jobs. It was his inspiration for a while to set up a foundation to provide electronic equipment to remote missionary outposts. Zamperini himself happened to fall into some precarious wobblings after his own dash down the aisle, but found his footing at last presiding over a refuge for errant boys in California. As for Hamblen, he tromped about for a time as a lay evangelist, composed a series of uplifting tunes — "It Is No Secret What God Can Do," "Open Up Your Heart and Let the Sunshine In," and perhaps most successfully, "This Old House" — and once ran for President on the Prohibition ticket. But as much as anything else, the religious renovations of Hamblen and Zamperini and Vaus were of a pattern that would largely characterize the hundreds of thousands of conversions to follow in Billy's crusades on over the years — proceeding from a kind of stricken nostalgia of soul for that vanished clear young morning once in their past of untroubled simplicity and goodness and wholeness. In a way, as with all the others after them, it was a matter of simply going back home again. One religious writer long familiar with Graham's career suggests, "Humankind's whole story and predicament is, we are all probably born with that old memory of Eden still somewhere in our hearts. And that's been much of Graham's incredible effect over the years — without all those people really knowing it, without even knowing it himself, it's been that old memory in everybody that he's been speaking to."

Despite the mild sensations of those conversions, though, the revival again seemed to be gasping out, after what had been a fairly respectable but by no means extraordinary four weeks. But in his messages then, as Grady recalls, "Billy was also right strong on that anti-Communism stuff of those days."

As it happened, only two days before the revival opened, Truman had announced Russia's detonation of its own atomic bomb, and it had been in the sudden doomful sky-glare of that shock — which was to loose the nation on into the Manichaean melodrama of the Cold War — that Billy came flurrying forth in Los

Angeles. On that very first Sunday afternoon service, he cried, "Today, Europe, the Far East, and America have heard the radio story of Mr. Truman's Friday morning message. This nation now knows that Russia has the atomic bomb! Today Moscow announced that Russia has been piling up bombs for over two years, and gigantic plants have been turning out atomic bombs! Radio warnings have been issued from behind the Iron Curtain, and our own President declares, 'We must be prepared!' " It was like a special dramatic field of force provided him now — imminent cataclysm — in which he could preach, invoking its ominous reverberations through service after service. "Do you know the area that is marked out for the enemy's first atomic bomb? New York! Secondly, Chicago! And thirdly, the city of Los Angeles! Do you know that the Fifth Columnists, called Communists, are more rampant in Los Angeles than any other city in America? God is giving us a desperate choice, a choice of either revival or judgment. There is no alternative! If Sodom and Gomorrah could not get away with sin, if Pompeii and Rome could not escape, neither can Los Angeles! Judgment is coming just as sure as I'm standing here! . . . The world is divided into two camps! On the one side we see Communism. On the other, we see so-called Western culture, and its fruit had its foundation in the Bible, the Word of God, and in the revivals of the seventeenth and eighteenth centuries. Communism, on the other hand, has declared war against God, against Christ, against the Bible, and against all religion! . . . This may be God's last great call! It was a dark hour when John Wesley and George Whitefield preached the gospel, but England had a great revival! That country was saved from the fate of the French Revolution. Unless the Western world has an old-fashioned revival, we cannot last!"

In all this, he did not neglect to report, "I have been in Europe six times since the war! And I have seen the devastated cities of Germany and the wreckage of war," proposing from that, "I believe the only reason that America escaped the ravages and the destruction of war was because God's People prayed. Many people still believe that God can still use America to evangelize the world!"

Expanding on that particular prospect — hunching his shoulders and bringing both hands slicing downward in the air to a V just above the page of Scripture — he went on, "I want you to see Amos, the simple shepherd and gatherer of sycamore fruit, as he trudges to the King's court. Perhaps Amaziah, the priest of the golden calf at Bethel, stands at the King's chapel. Amaziah says, 'Hillbilly, what do you want?' Amos says, 'The Lord God told me to come deliver a message to the King of Israel.' 'Oh, so you want to preach, aeh? Well, you go back to the hillbillies and preach. This is the King's court, and we don't allow any hillbilly preachers up here telling the King what to do.' But Amos, with his faith and obedience to God, *pushes* Amaziah — " Billy wheels and spanks his hands to one side, skimming one hand on out in a wide swoop " — just out of the way, and stalks right on into where the King holds court. There is something about his walk!" Billy struts from behind the pulpit, his head thrown back " — something about the *snap!* of his eyes — " and he flings his own blazing glare about him " — the set of his jaw and the squaring of his shoulders — " and his chin rams forward, his back whips straight " — that makes them all stop as they see Amos standing there, filled with the Holy Spirit — " He smacks his hands again to the other side " — and looking the King squarely in the face, he points his finger at the King and says, 'Oh, King of Israel, thus saith the Lord — *Prepare to meet thy God!*' " Slapping his Bible back on the pulpit, he leans forward then at the very edge of the stage, over the sprays of fern and lilies, his hands on his knees, his hair wetly tattered across his pale brow, his eyes absolutely bituminous: "And let me tell you something! When God gets ready to shake America, he might not take the Ph.D. and the D.D. and the Th.D." He lunges upright again, clamping the knuckles of one fist against his waist and lofting high his other long arm with forefinger spearing at the tent top: "God may choose a country boy! God may choose a man no one knows, a little nobody to shake America for Jesus

Christ in this day. A hillbilly, a country boy! who will sound forth in a mighty voice to America, 'Thus saith the Lord!' — " and he begins striding back and forth over the stage now, his forefinger swiping and slashing the air over the audience: *"Thus saith the Lord! Thus saith the Lord! Thus saith the Lord! . . ."*

On a fine autumn morning some twenty-five years later, Graham stood in the pulpit of a church in a North Carolina city — a figure now immaculately manicured and excellently tanned, a sedately elegant composure about him among the blond panelings of that suburban sanctuary — and confided with an easy smile to the convocation of local ministers filling the polished pews below him, "But the crowds at that crusade had been getting smaller and smaller with every service. We didn't know exactly what we should do; it seemed like we were going to have to go ahead and wind it up when the schedule came to its end. It was along about that time that I was having some considerable problems about the Bible as the literal and complete word of God. Finally I went out one day and sat on a stump out there in the desert, and I said, 'Lord, I don't care what any others say, as for me, I'm going to accept this as your infallible word from now on' — " At this point, Graham brandished his Bible high over his head. " — And I'm here to tell you, there is *power* in this book. Because suddenly, a whole change took place in those services, people started thronging in — and it ended up, brethren, on the front pages of newspapers all over the country!" to which there then sounded over the pews a low rolling of *Amens.*

Aside from the imprecision of sequence and occasion in his recollection of the event that morning, it happened more exactly — and more improbably, for that matter — to be the direct hand of William Randolph Hearst, unexpectedly extended forth out of San Simeon, that translated Graham at last into an instant figure in the pop-mythic life of the nation. Hearst having earlier bestowed the benign attentions of his journalistic combine on the Youth for Christ campaigns, his notice had been called to Graham's effort in Los Angeles, so legend later had it, by his maid. Whatever, as Grady himself notes, "Old man Hearst, you know, he was interested in just about anybody who was talking out

against Communism in those days." Even at eighty-six, some fifty
years after Havana Harbor and *The Maine,* now ponderous and
filmy of eye, withdrawn into his own private American Xanadu
along the misty sea cliffs of northern California, he was still
given to vagrant gutterings of that old Faustian hubris to personally choreograph the destiny of the whole Republic. And as it
turned out, this one last stroke of his, executed almost offhand-
edly only two years before he died, was to prove perhaps his
most monumentally successful conjuration since his Spanish-
American production. In that sense, carrying in it as it did old
pulsings from the palmy age of McKinley and Sousa and Teddy
Roosevelt, Billy's apotheosis in Los Angeles was a classically star-
spangled American one.

That nova burst came just as the crusade was tapering to a
monotone and desultory finish, on the final Sunday night's service. When Graham arrived at the tent, as he later recounted, "I
suddenly noticed reporters and cameramen crawling all over the
place." Not a little giddied by this abrupt inexplicable clamor out
of nowhere of flashbulbs, he finally managed to tug aside one reporter to inquire what it all meant: he was informed it had all
been set off by a memo just delivered down from Hearst — *Puff
Graham.* And with no more than that, he happened. His genesis
took place. He combusted forth.

"The Hearst papers gave me tremendous publicity," he later
related, "and the others soon followed. Suddenly, what a clergyman was saying was in the headlines everywhere, and so was the
box score of commitments made each night." The crusade was
extended another week, then another, was shortly picked up in
the chatter of the AP, then UPI, INS, Billy himself on November
14 materializing for the first time in the pages of *Time,* then
Quick, then *Newsweek,* then *Life* — he had taken.

That his transfiguration happened to be effected through this
somewhat less-than-celestial medium did not seem to afford Graham any discernible misgivings. As he would later enthuse, "I am
convinced that God uses the press in our work, and it has been one
of the most effective factors in sustaining public interest through
the years." Indeed, in his very inception, he was, in a sense, con-

summately a creature of the pop reality — assumed his definition, his life, his import in the din and flare of the media meaning. Delivered forth by those simple syllables, *Puff Graham,* it was an event that improbably evokes that moment by Michelangelo on the ceiling of the Sistine Chapel when the grandfatherly Creator's fingertip casually reaches to touch blank Adam's witlessly dangling hand. As one newsman congratulated Graham that night of his transubstantiation, "Well, you've been kissed by William Randolph Hearst!"

At the same time, in Graham's congregations now there began to appear such diverse notables as Gene Autry and the mammothly mammalian film nymph Jane Russell, who, the press soon discovered, had arranged a private devotional reception among a few of her friends for this golden young evangel. Perhaps inevitably, before Graham finally left town, he was offered a screen test by Cecil B. DeMille.

Graham has come leagues since his rude and spangly popular inception in that 1949 Los Angeles crusade. But it held even then the pattern, the genetic-code imprint, of his style over the next thirty years: the same embellishments of random celebrities attached to the proceedings like Christmas-tree ornaments, the same brassy acoustics of publicity, but most of all, the same breathless dramatic of Armageddonal crisis — "Judgment Day is fast approaching, this civilization is gone, it's just as if it were burned already!" — of that moment in Los Angeles as the nation was passing into its long witch-night of the Cold War. As he effused then, "Very rarely do I find an atheist now. People aren't so smart-alecky anymore. Why, in Los Angeles, one of the two worst centers of sin and crime in the land, they're embracing religion and changing their lives. Why? They're afraid of a third war." In a sense he was to remain in that instant of his annunciation ever after, preaching in that same atmospheric of emergency, enacting the same crusade again and again with only elaborations and amplifications of technique, politer modulations of manner, but without real progression of difference, finally outside all time and circumstance. Self-intact, changeless, only magnified to a continental scale, magnified into the whole life of the nation over three decades, he was then "puffed" by Hearst in the most awesome sense of the word.

It seems now almost mystically appropriate that Graham's advent, his popular conception in a blinding shimmer of flashbulbs, should have come in California — that furthermost hazed longitude at the continent's end which became like the nebulous climax of our destiny: where our continuing lunge after the sun, impelled by some everlasting *Not Yet* in the American psyche, had arrived at last, after all the fierce prairies and deserts, at a sudden, luxurious cessation among mild honeyed hills. It was as if those violent ambivalences in the American past were abruptly suspended, unresolved, there at that seasonless shore, where we nevertheless had to begin haphazardly arranging an identity at last. And ever since, in that cool sunlight, we seem to have been dreaming our future: our styles, our dreads, our diversions, our mythologies. It was from out there at the land's edge that the country first got its signals of what was actually about to happen to it — the first glimpses of the next episodes in our ongoing struggle for the secret truth of who we actually are. Even while Graham was flaring forth in that tent revival in Los Angeles as the new apostle of the old Plymouth rectitudes, up in the fogs of San Francisco's North Beach, where Jack Kerouac and Allen Ginsberg were quartered, another American order was emerging, what was to become through the Fifties and Sixties a whole subterranean population, garbed in the regalia of Apaches and A.W.O.L. soldiers and Billy the Kid, who were descended out of those darker, more anarchic fevers running through the American past.

It is out there, where the land ends, where there is endlessly appearing what we are forever becoming. And in 1949, California was immediately issued out of the most recent Promethean event in the life of the nation — the War — with a bemazing vision everywhere of America's new being: airplane factories, oil refineries, military bases, and a limitless rampancy of suburbs populated by a migratory tumbleweed people, a pastless people with minds washed memoryless by gasoline and the expressway winds of ceaseless speed, all of them accumulated in a waste plain of shopping centers and power lines and radar towers, beyond which the ultimate sunset of all sad and lonesome American sunsets burns out of the far edge of a blank sea.

During those last weeks in Los Angeles, Billy was dwelling in a high vivid transport out of himself — that exhilaration of a final weary release, abstraction out of self: "A strange thing happened," as he later reported it. "The weaker I became physically, the stronger I became spiritually." But as the revival boomed on in a furor of newspaper ads, "Visit the Canvas Cathedral with the Steeple of Light! All-Star Supporting Party — Held Over by Popular Demand — Sixth Great Sin-Smashing Week," with the crowds now brimming on out into the streets around the tent, Graham found himself, in the hot nights back in his hotel room, again pacing long caverns of insomnia. The sudden surge and blare around him now seemed to leave him, even in his exultation, vaguely unquiet — as if he dimly sensed he might have somehow been delivered into enormous, alien energies beyond his ken. "What I said was being quoted all of a sudden," he later recalled, "and I knew I wasn't really all that qualified. I didn't really have the experience yet to say the right things, but the people expected me to speak with that authority. I was just scared to death, frightened to death, and I was in the middle of all this attention and publicity all of a sudden, which I couldn't figure out, and I felt like it might get loose from us in some way. I was terrified, frankly." He finally phoned a colleague back in the Youth for Christ offices in Chicago: "You better get out here fast. Something's happening, and I don't know what it is. It's way beyond me."

When the revival finally closed in late November after a full eight weeks, the attendance had totaled some 350,000 people, with about 4,200 of those having made their way on down to the sawdust kneeling ground at the front of the tent. As it happened, the day Graham departed Los Angeles, the heaviest smog in the city's history moved in to hang like a deep coma over its streets for weeks. Graham himself was borne from the blaze of his popular incarnation there, in a kind of stupor now of terrific and speechless exhaustion, back across the breadth of the country by train — the level traceless deserts of old unknown violences and endurance skimming past the sealed windows of his coach, fence-stitched prairies and simple white modest towns blurring evenly by under the continuing dip and flow of telephone lines. There was a short stop in Kansas City, where he was startled by another brief gust of his new fame, a swarm of waiting reporters — clacking on then into the wide fields of evening, tiny pricks of light in distant farmhouse suppertime windows glinting like sparks and then gone, clacking on across the immense sleeping face of the land, at last arriving back in Minneapolis in the deep pit of the night. . . . Then the next afternoon, as he was addressing a hotel luncheon of Northwestern faculty members and local ministers, the clarion reverberations of his voice suddenly faltered, his throat numbed with a blow of stupendous realization and wonder, and with his eyes abruptly aswim, he mumbled a word or two more and then sank back down, shaken — still grinning bravely but with tears flicking down his cheeks.

After all the years now — lying on the living-room rug of his home in Charlotte longing over those pictures of far landscapes and distant splendors, those first fitful street-corner evangelisms, his torment through those nights in Florida, his struggles with Templeton over his commitment — now, incredibly, it had all actually come to a fulfillment. He had arrived. It was beginning.

II

The Power and the Glory

Fɪʀsᴛ ᴛʜᴇʀᴇ ᴡᴀs only the blind drifting of Indians back and forth like a trackless blowing of leaves over a continent still without time, without memory. Then, abruptly, a figure appeared for an instant: a fantastic apparition in a dark robe with a pinched face under a cowl, standing briefly on a bare white beach, a bead chain mingled in the fingers of one hand from which, as he raised it for a moment, there dangled a crucifix — and with him then, simultaneous with that gesture, a surge of horses and banners and clanking iron-plated men, blundering on through the green engulfing woods, across mottled canyoned deserts. And immediately after them came the ones without crucifixes, a certain berserk haste about them, moving along the tangled banks of nameless rivers in harlequined remnants of finery from courts and drawing rooms three thousand miles away to harvest now the skins of raccoons and otters and weasels, leaving no more trace of their quick passage than had the Indians over those uncalendared centuries before them. Finally, after the first arrival of Anglo-Saxons on the thin shore of the continent at Plymouth and Virginia, etching the first pale print of Protestantism and authority on the edge of the dark unconsumed wilderness, there presently appeared a curious specter somehow more terrifying to the Indians than all the others: a sallow ferret-like man with scanty hair and a long bony avid face under this broad-brimmed black hat, wearing a black frayed frock coat glazed with a faint green shine, mounted upon a mule with a Bible clutched to his chest in one horny fist — the frontier evangelist, a scruffy, irascible Calvinist with a chapped red lip under his ax-blade nose, sniffling with a permanent cold, but his voice ringing furious, imperious, shrill, in great rapt unscrollings of Jehovah and Judgment Day among the pine hollows and brambled ridges, roaming this fenceless wildland mapping out here the New Jerusalem, a Kingdom of Heaven — that obsession, still, of the very first ones, the cowled friars of the Conquistadors, then the Cromwellian Puritans, to appropriate and make out of the tumultuous voids of the New World a City of God.

The mule-borne frontier revivalist moved from camp meeting to camp meeting among the scatter of muddy little clearings — many of them named out of another past four thousand years earlier in prophet-ridden wastes on the other side of the globe: Salem, Bethany, Shiloh, Sharon — flimsy and tenuous outposts of simple Celtic and Anglo-Saxon and German settlers grimly sustaining now some token semblance at least of the familiar theology of the village churches left behind to fortify themselves against the savage and indifferent solitudes into which they had ventured, preserving those old reassuring patterns of faith and worship and hymns to order the nihilistic chaos of the wilderness around them. It was out of that simple, single-dimensioned struggle to contain and manage somehow the furious maw of the wild, that the rigors of the native American piety began.

From the brushfire phenomenon of the Great Awakening in the 1740s, with the peripatetic George Whitefield executing his pulpit hoedown-jigs while the howl of his voice whip-cracked over pasture congregations of twenty thousand people writhing and gabbling in tongues, and the jackdaw figure of Jonathan Edwards distributing over New England the cold brimstones of sermons like "Sinners in the Hands of an Angry God," it was a harsh folk righteousness whose "uncomplex message," as Reinhold Niebuhr has observed, "was particularly relevant to frontier conditions." For one thing, it was a Calvinism necessarily involving a permutation of the original with its doctrine of predestination, that assumption one was finally powerless to alter one's preordained direction and end. This fatalism of classic Calvinism was a perspective that could hardly be afforded in the struggle of the frontier. Thus the new American Calvinism, while still belonging to that austere conscience of guilt and judgment, took on a variant inflection, an inclination more to the efficacy of individual will and action in winning one's salvation and determining one's own destiny — thereby envigorating the contest against the wilderness and, not incidentally, with the Great Awakening, bracing the spirit of the American commonry for the impending adventure of the Revolution.

In the same way, with the frontier vision of man's lot as one of direct and elemental embattlement, there could be in that struggle little allowance for complication, nuance and equivocation, introspection: that would be to invite the very demons — uncertainty, disorder — one was striving, on those far faint fringes of society just beyond the Bostons and Philadelphias and Williamsburgs, to survive and subdue: an effort all the more desperate in that, so immediately contending against those primeval freedoms of deep woods and mountain gorges, one was at the same time all that more intimate with their wild and pagan singings to the soul. That has been the tension in the American spirit ever since. And ever since, religion in America has continued to be a kind of war against the wilderness.

Sudden epidemic seasons of national revival like the Great Awakening have seemed to recur at regular forty-year intervals on down through the course of the country's experience, and the commanding figure in each one of them has tended to present the essential image of his age. Charles Finney was the utter embodiment of the briary disputatious sockdolagizing pioneer lawyer during the spectacular outbreak of back-country evangelism in the 1830s and '40s, with its summer-long camp meetings in oak groves — a wholesale religious shivaree over the land that produced such indigenous American eccentricities as Mormonism, the Millerites, who on October 22 of 1843 were found roosting atop barn roofs and haystacks awaiting their momentary ascent at the Second Coming, and the Reverend Sylvester Graham's impassioned apostleship against white bread, out of which issued his famous cracker; but a general fervency eventually prompting, as the Great Awakening had seemed to charge the nation's nerves for the Revolutionary War, the righteous thunderheads of the abolitionist movement. Then in the 1870s and '80s, another great gale of evangelism went rushing through the brown-grimed cities of the factory age, with Reuben Torrey, Wilbur Chapman, Sam Jones, and possibly the single mightiest colossus in the annals of all revivalism, Dwight L. Moody — a thick and stumpy man with the mossy look of that time's dense-whiskered political eminences like Hayes and Garfield, its Victorian sentimentalists like James Whitcomb Riley and William Ernest Henley, Moody also with the brawling industry of the mercantile caesars then like Carnegie and Gould and Morgan. And then forty years after Moody, that jaybird pulpit stuntsman, Billy Sunday, came bawling out of the carnival of the Twenties, a firecracker salvation-hustler in white spats and straw skimmers, with his hot-jazz hootings against "hog-jowled, weasel-eyed, sponge-columned, mush-fisted, jelly-spined, four-flushing Christians."

Curiously, though, all these national contagions of revival in America's past seem to have transpired, not in periods of actual tribulation, during wars and economic derangements, but in the interludes between those turmoils. It has been as if, after those intermittent convulsive episodes of violence and peril, in which life comes at least into quick bright critical clarity, the nation has been spilled out into yet another frontier of new realities. It was in the plump complacencies of the Gilded Age, after the cataclysm of the Civil War, that Moody's evangelism took on its steams, a time that held in it, amidst the tasseled plushness of America's new urbanized industrial society, an uneasiness about some deep shift in the familiar arrangement of things — not only socially but metaphysically, Darwin like some distant rumored explosion in the atmosphere after which nothing would ever really be the same again. Then, forty years later, when Billy Sunday had come crackling forth, it had been out of the equally flush Twenties — that carousel of holiday and euphoria that came after our first full extension, with World War One, beyond the calm shores of our innocence. It was as if, after committing ourselves to grand exertions like the Civil War and the two World Wars, we found ourselves afterward in some brackish backwash of spirit — after such huge national adventures, there set in a reflex of alarm over those reckless elations in our nature the experience had betrayed to us, and we ended by quickly lusting for regularity and ordinariness again.

The new wilderness into which World War Two heaved us

may have been far more impalpable than the original one of the frontier, but in its way, it was incomparably more harrowing: a chaos now in America's actual sense of itself — intimations, so immediately after so proud a feat of self-assertion, of our own mortality. By then, the nation had undergone something like fifteen years of systematic mayhem on its orthodox optimism about the universal and enduring sufficiency of its democratic and economic theologies: first the Depression, then the uncontrollable gathering and riot of global war, instantly after that the malevolent loom of Communism, and finally the lingering vicious confoundment of the Korean War, an unendingly inconclusive American endeavor which worked no small frayings in the general sense of well-being. It had all left suspicions now of, if not a national impotence, some loss of steadiness in our historical meaning.

In a particular sense, nothing had quite blasted the old securities like those two dreadful illuminations of Nagasaki and Hiroshima — those two quick astonishing glares of a brightness that man had never seen before on earth, like flares from the creation of the world. Afterward, we found ourselves suddenly implicated in a complex of alliances as the principal protagonist in the whole planet's history, our lives abruptly enlarged to the scope of the entire globe, involved in an incalculably vaster theater of danger and possibilities than that before snugly enclosed within our own shores: anything imaginable could happen to us now.

In this new abyss into which we had been spirited by World War Two, the calls for evangelists over the country actually outran, for the first time within anyone's memory, the cast available in the field. And thus there ensued — after Edwards and Whitefield, after Finney, after Moody, after Sunday — America's fifth great popular religious resurgence. Ranging on through the Fifties, it took the form, this time, of the chatty television unctions of Bishop Sheen, the ice-cream platitudes of Protestantism's cherubic Good-Humor Man, Norman Vincent Peale. But the definitive figure of this particular renaissance of the American righteousness was to be Billy Graham.

Like all the others before him, Graham came forth with a

voice that seemed to conquer and order that new chaos in the American experience. "He preaches the life of certitude," reported one religious analyst at the time. "There are no doubts, no real choices to be made, no expanses of experience where right and wrong, the nourishing and the corrupting, the healing and the killing, cannot be easily distinguished." Thus he addressed the bewilderments and disquiets of the hour without complication, nuances, qualifications: *The Bible says, ye must be born again! The sinfulness of man's heart is the source of all this world's woes.* He was to reach his full realization with the massive suburbanization of America during the bland-witted clime of the Eisenhower years — as he would later declare himself, "The Eisenhower era was a time of spiritual awakening in America. The example he gave contributed much to this revival. Under him, I believe Americans felt a degree of security unknown under other Presidents." But he was himself generically made to his time — almost supernaturally telegenic, a clinically hygienic prophet who seemed somehow completely processed out of any distracting musts of the glandular.

At first flush, his message seemed to derive directly out of the dour frontier theology of Edwards and Finney: "God could have just come and patted man on the back and said, 'You're reconciled.' But God would not have been just, and God is primarily and basically a God of justice and holiness. If He had done that, He would have been a liar. He said, 'If you break my law, you'll die!' Man had to die. He disobeyed, and so death came upon the world — physical death, spiritual death, eternal death!" And with American society finding itself after the war entering the peculiar ennuis of affluence — that vague flatness left in life by having ceased to have to struggle — there still remained at least a wince of the old Puritan conscience. Graham answered that dull prick of anxiety: "Like the rich fool in Luke, we say, 'Soul, take thine ease — drink and be merry. You've laid up enough goods. You've got economic security now. You've got money in the bank. You've got good insurance policies. You've got a good business. Take it easy. Go and get you a little cottage in Florida and take it easy,'" leaning forward then over the pulpit to toll the warning, "But there's a voice deep down inside whispering to you, *Thou fool, this night thy soul shall be required of thee!*"

But in the end, it was somehow an oddly denatured variety of the harsh vinegars of frontier Calvinism — reconstituted into a kind of mild mass-consumption commodity, a freeze-dried instant sanctity, a rather sensible and efficient salvation. As some critics then observed, "The yearning remains for something deeper than the pallid, reasonable spiritual diet offered by most religious institutions today. Nevertheless, no one wants to be scorched by this fire of religious conviction, no one wants it to burn away his hard-won security and comfort. And Billy offers a solution — it is possible, he says, to enjoy the religious fire even in air-conditioned Madison Square Garden. You must 'surrender' — but you may be sure your surrender will never subvert the good American values you already cherish. . . . It's all for a Baptist uneasy in his Buick of a Sunday."

The piety it produced has tended to be a curious conjunction of the decorous and the fearsome, the gothic and the sanitary. In one midmorning devotional of Graham's staff in his offices now at Montreat, a young girl sat with her hands demurely nestled on her Bible and her feet politely tucked together as she delivered a few inspirational little thoughts, reporting in her small cheerful voice, to the soft ticking of a grandfather clock in that muted carpeted quiet, that she had recently imagined "going down to Hell in a long elevator," which had opened to "horrible flames and terrible suffering," out of which a figure, the unrepentant thief on the cross, "comes slowly staggering forward with agony on his face and cries, 'Oh, I almost escaped Hell.' And I thought, what an awful thing, now he had to burn forever." It was a somewhat bizarre invocation, this Hieronymus Bosch vision of fire and torment and damnation, in surroundings that looked like a photograph of an Early American den out of *House and Garden*.

But with that national unease after World War Two lasting through the racial convulsions of the late Fifties and the Sixties, and then Vietnam, there finally began to hang over the country, worst of all, forebodings of some actual loss of our own native rectitude, of America's constitutional decency. Perhaps no one is finally so dear as he who returns and restores to us assurances of our goodness. And that was to become Graham's ultimate service as a prophet to Middle America throughout the decades after the war: his effect was to affirm rousingly, not only for America's proprietorial estate, but for the savings-and-loan manager in Wichita and the real-estate developer in Anaheim, that they were, in fact, fundamentally good: despite the new wilderness of social and moral complications into which they found themselves abducted by history and perhaps even more by technology's quantum expansions of experience and consciousness, he assured them they need not feel dread. What they had always assumed was their essential worthiness — their Main Street beatitude of respectabilities — was indeed still authentic, still the operative goodness: not only that, but immortally good.

I

Following his accomplishment that autumn of 1949 in Los Angeles, he surged through a succession of crusades that became like a long Palm Sunday procession of celebration and arrival. He seemed uncannily blessed through those early days — more than once, when thunderstorms had been forecast on the day he was to hold an open stadium service, the sullen brows of dark clouds would hang piled at bay off beyond the stands while, in a sunless wind with his hair whisking, he finished his preaching. It was his splendid luck to arrive in Boston just as the newspapers there were engaged in a circulation free-for-all, they consequently competing in advertising his rallies as a sensation. One newspaperman recollected then that "he called on us up in our editorial office once, and as he sat there in a big easy chair with his legs crossed, he struck me like any sharp young successful businessman who likes a splash of color in his attire." He came to be variously termed, "Barrymore of the Bible," "Gabriel in Gabardine," "Beverly Hills John the Baptist." He presented himself for one crusade in Albuquerque in a sapphire-blue twill suit with a cowboy belt and silver buckle, later appeared in San Francisco outfitted in a ten-gallon sombrero, a pearl-buff sports jacket with a lushly illustrated tie, and blue suede shoes. When a reporter once inquired why he arrayed himself so radiantly, citing the Scripture verse about "Why take ye thought for raiment? Consider the lilies of the field, how they grow," Graham buoyantly rejoined, "There is nothing in the Bible which says I must wear rags. Slovenliness is one of the deadly sins."

Caught up in the great headiness of his deliverance now into his mission of mass sanctitude over the land, he would arise in the early dawns wherever he was, and propel himself with an unflagging exuberance on through to midnight — while managing to take, compulsively, four or five showers or baths each day: "It gets the poison out," he once explained. He would also pack down four meals daily, never particularly mindful of the cuisine: as one intimate attested then, "He never cares what he's eating — it could all be hamburger for what it matters to him." It was an expeditious indifference, since he was to pass most of his life from now on subsisting on the drab matter brought up by room service to his hotel suites. "He was happiest back then just hurrying around, in front of those big crowds, or when he was alone," says a friend. During the afternoons, he would stalk and pace about in his pajamas in the panoramic litter of his motel rooms, constantly snapping his fingers, gnawing at his nails, a green baseball cap wedged on his head — "His hair tended to bush way out," says another associate, "so he wore that baseball cap all the time to subdue it" — as he rehearsed that evening's sermon before the mirror over the room's dresser or on the bathroom door. He would partake only of a thin soup, a light tea, before setting out for his decathlon exertions of soul and passion each night.

In the phosphorescent brilliance of a spotlight, he preached still with those headlong, unrelieved syncopations of his tabernacle beginnings, while Grady, sitting squat and amiable and sly-eyed behind him with something of the look of Huey Long in his smoked-ham face, would discreetly play the mike cord in and out as Billy stamped back and forth around the pulpit. In film footages from that time, Billy's two front teeth seem slightly more prominent, giving him a bit of the look of a handsome young hayseed, and his voice still had a certain raw-textured country boy's hoarseness to it, a strained husking that would crack now and then in his pealings — only in later years did it acquire its deep-bronzed gildings. The order of his wit also tended toward such home-baked guffaws and jollities as an anecdote about a man whose mother-in-law had been kicked to death by a mule, with a huge throng then showing up for the funeral, and when someone mentioned they had never realized she had been so widely known and esteemed, the man replying, "That's not why they're here. They're all trying to buy that mule."

But he had continued his tenacious labor to acquire larger intellectual garnishments, having his assistants supply him with digests of the current high meditations on issues, pursuing through "painful cultivation," as he acknowledged, some appreciation of cultural matters, setting out to read biographies of Beethoven, Gershwin — "I just made myself do it." Even so, in his eagerness to enhance his messages with such eruditions, there would sometimes occur little blips, slight miscarryings, such as, "Now, T. K. Chesterton says. . . ." Recalls Grady, "The problem was he'd try to incorporate into his sermons everything anybody important had ever mentioned on the subject, as a result of which he'd get right harelipped sometimes. Once he decided he'd add him a new word to his vocabulary — *eschatological*. He stood up there one night and was preaching along, and finally I could tell here it was coming. He said, 'Yes, ladies and gentlemen, it was just one eschat— one eschat— eschat— aw, shucks, folks, I've never been able to get that word right.' "

For all his cosmopolitan flourishes, though, his message itself was still made up of the rudimentary elements of pentecostal fundamentalism. He maintained then that Heaven was a cube-shaped affair precisely 1,600 miles wide, 1,600 miles high, and 1,600 miles deep, "with walls of jasper, streets of gold, gates of pearl, palaces of ivory, and trees that bear a different fruit each month. What a glorious place Heaven will be! Think of that, you farmers — twelve crops a year!" It was also his notion that "we're going to have a new body when we get there. I've never been able to sing down here, but I'm going to ask the Lord to let me sing up there. I have never been able to do some of the things that others do, but one day, the Scripture says, I'll have a new body, and I'll sing with the best of them and play with the best of them; I'll play as good football or baseball as all the rest of them." As for Hell, he declared, "There will be weeping and wailing and gnashing of teeth. I believe that there is a literal fire in Hell, but if there is not, then the Bible is talking about some thing far worse when it speaks of the flames of Hell. Whatever, it is going to be so horrible that it cannot be expressed in the language of man."

And with his tie loosened but the coat still buttoned, belling out from his chest as he threw one palm back on his hip and pranced from the pulpit to fan the air with the pointed finger of his other hand like a windshield wiper, he would cry with that hoarse croak in his voice, "A sense of hysteria is sweeping all across this country tonight. I believe we're facing judgment and destruction right now unless we can turn back to God. If we don't have a revival all across this nation in the next month or the next year, we might not have any more time. Like Israel in the time of Isaiah, America is drifting away from God. And in a nation's wandering from God, God chooses a prophet, God chooses a man to call that nation back to him. Today the message has not changed from Isaiah's time. It is the same. *Repent ye! Repent ye!*" And as the choir behind him slowly swung now into "Just as I Am," he would call, "That's it, c'mon quickly, all over the place, up here, over here, come quickly. . . . That's it, c'mawn, now, others are comin'. . . . That's it, many are comin', you come. . . ." He would then suddenly bow his head, wrapping his arms around him with one hand lifted and cupped in a fist over his mouth, his eyes tightly closed, only now and then glancing up as if to surprise himself delightedly with the discovery of how many more had collected there before him while his eyes were shut. And finally, in his exhausted elation back in his motel room late that night, he would spank down another stout meal.

Registers of the actual effect of his crusades then, as in one six-week stand in Seattle in 1951, proved somewhat less than staggering: in a survey afterward, it turned out that, of the 6,354 decisions that had been reported by Graham's organization, only 3,349 referral cards had been received by churches in that city, and a third of them — 1,155 — were children under fourteen. About half of the 3,349 were also prior church members. But if his true impact in a city seemed by such statistical measurements slightly ephemeral, it was, in a way, incidental to the simple energies and panoply of the occasions themselves. Graham had come to employ by now the accumulated legacy of techniques and strategies left from the great evangelistic offensives before him, particularly those of Moody and Sunday. It had been Moody who had first developed such devices of mass evangelism as extensive and robust advance publicity, advertisements in newspapers and on billboards and posters, the mobilization of local churches across denominational lines, the elaborate deployments of ushers and choirs and counselors at the services, publishing afterward audited accounts of each crusade's financial intake and expenses. From Billy Sunday, Graham grafted the pattern of businessmen's luncheons and prayer groups and work committees, the idea of a corps of associates to attend to all the multiple phases of a campaign, the stagecrafts of gargantuan choirs and accessory entertainments, the adornments of celebrities and politicians on the platform with him, personal appearances at state legislatures and civic events out in the community, and the ploy of reserving vast sections of seats for prepackaged delegations to insure a full house. It was an old veteran revival manager from the days of Billy Sunday, Willis Haymaker, who even furnished Graham the term crusade. Haymaker once rounded up so many reserved advance church parties for one campaign that, after a few nights, he had to suspend the system when ordinary citizens began hotly complaining that they were being crowded out of the services.

It was in a crusade in Portland, in the summer of 1950, that Billy's own personal consolidation into a corporate institution first began to take shape. He produced there his first full-blown movie — a promotional documentary in flower-garden color of the meetings, which was then supplied to other prospective hosts he learned were considering extending him an invitation. Also, for several weeks, a pair of admen, Walter Bennett and Fred Dienert of Chicago's Walter Bennett Agency, had been tantalizing him with a proposition of a Sunday afternoon radio program on the American Broadcasting Company network, but Billy had remained disenheartened by the required stake of $25,000. Bennett and Dienert presented themselves to Billy again one afternoon in his hotel room in Portland, and Billy, in his pajamas, finally dropped to his knees and called, "Lord, you know I'm doing all that I can. You know that I don't have any money, but I believe we ought to do this. I feel the burden for it, but it's up to you. I want you to give me a sign — twenty-five thousand dollars, by midnight tonight."

Then, at his service that evening, he apprised his congregation of the radio possibility and what it would take to realize it: "Now we won't be seeking you out, but if you think this is God's plan, you can seek us out after the service tonight. I'll be in the back office back here for any of you folks who would like to be a part of this wonderful opportunity." After the close of the service, a long file of people shuffled past the office door where Grady stood holding out a shoebox: the collection came to $23,000, and two envelopes waiting for Graham back at the hotel made up the rest. Grady stuffed the shoebox in the top dresser drawer of his room that night — "Man, I don't think I slept a wink," he recounts — and the next day, George Wilson, Graham's tubby bubblingly enterprising business manager at Northwestern Schools, flew out with legal papers for incorporation to avert tax tolls. It was thus out of that shoebox of bills and coins and checks tucked into the shirt drawer of Grady's hotel-room dresser that there eventually unfolded the Billy Graham Evangelistic Association.

Most significantly though, Graham at Portland had added, to his custom-constructed aluminum tabernacle barn, two special sections that neither Moody nor Sunday had ever included: a master control center for all the electronic ganglia of camera lights and recorders, and a pressroom complete with typewriters and telephones. Since his Los Angeles annunciation, he had remained eminently a being of the media semantic. Graham's final wand stroke of blessing was that he happened to occur at the beginning of the pop age — he coincided not only with the electronic communalization of America but with the arrival of the Madison Avenue mass-mythos and the Nielsen metaphysic: that assumption that the more widely and spectacularly an appearance manages to take in the popular eye, the more real and consequential it is. In Graham, the man and the moment had truly met. Not only did he belong almost instinctively to the time's mass-sense of the meaningful, but he seemed a figure to the magazine cover, the film lights, the new mass-advertisement esthetic of glazy handsomeness, ultimately to the lamina of the television screen, utterly born. When one of his associates was asked in later years what might have transpired if Billy had been short and podgy and scrappy of hair, he smiled, "Well, but he wasn't, was he? The Lord worked it out so that he wouldn't be."

By the time he installed that media room in his revival gymnasium in Portland, he had already come to be accorded an extraordinary notice, for a fundamentalist evangelist, by the regular hard-news press. At each crusade, the local newspapers would expand on every conceivable aspect of the occasion, from interviews with the parking attendants to accounts of the diverse whimsical items in the lost-and-found booth, all the while transcribing the seeming changes in Billy's own temperament from night to night. One reason for this peculiar dithyrambic attention was that Billy did not neglect to call on the publishers of the newspapers in every city, and he was always, in these casual visits, resoundingly impressive and engaging. He was, sensationally, a contrast-gainer, in Saul Bellow's term for the effect: he always agreeably surprised, with his simple personal likability, what were often the initial cursory cynicisms about him. Despite his arresting presence, he seemed wholly guileless and winsomely, if not exorbitantly, self-effacing. "I have read the reports in the press, and I thoroughly agree that I am a very ordinary speaker," he would gallantly offer. "I have severe intellectual limitations." There was about him a simple invincible goodwill that seemed impervious to insult. As one of his colleagues puts it, "Billy just has this God-given ability to disarm." And in truth, it had not escaped his notice over the years that "all people," as he mentioned once, "will respond to a smile and affection."

But his strikingly winning effect, in corporate board rooms as well as in the offices of newspaper publishers, was largely unpremeditated — merely his natural large generosity of heart and spirit: he was instantly, genuinely taken with whomever he encountered, quickly dispelling any discomforts they felt in the company of so authoritative an evangel of godliness; he had a way of giving whoever happened to be in front of him at the moment the sense that he was completely, enthusiastically fascinated by them. At the same time, after paying his respects to the local publishers and editors before a crusade, neither did he neglect certain gracious attentions to the reporters assigned to cover his services, mentioning their names to his mammoth stadium congregations and even declaring now and then that he knew of individuals who had found salvation and eternal life on the basis of a reporter's dispatch of his message: "I think everybody here tonight ought to write the newspapers a letter and thank 'em for what these fellas have done."

More than anything else, though, Graham and the press co-acted out of much the same appreciations and excitements, the same sensibilities. He lived in their world: the journalistic reality of polls, trends, public personages, public commotions. He would report in his sermons, "I was asked by a very high official the other day if I thought the coming of Christ was near," as if the curiosity were somehow more authentic, more serious a testimonial to the possibility, since it came from "a very high official." In one Easter message, he declared, "When one hundred prominent Americans were asked a few years ago to name the most significant fact of history, the number one event listed was the death and resurrection of Christ." In the course of just one evening's sermon during a crusade in the early Seventies, one way or another he variously invoked — as if eagerly to corroborate the legitimacy and relevance of his message through such random auspicious associations, through such haphazard appropriations out of the whole conglomerate pantheon of pop-consequence — the names of Winston Churchill, Barbara Walters, the Archbishop of Canterbury, Erich Segal, Martin Luther King, Bobby Riggs, President Kennedy, Jimmy Stewart "when he played the part of Charles Lindbergh," Dr. Jonas Salk, the Shah of Iran "when I had the pleasure of visiting with him, and he told me . . ," and Colonel Sanders: "You know, the first thing I saw when I arrived in South Africa was a Kentucky Fried Chicken!"

Accordingly, the notice of the media seemed for Graham, whether or not out of some simple lingering provincial country-boy credulity, the final validation of anything's import and authenticity. As he still happily proclaims in appearances before other clerics, "We have lived through a period when we have seen a tremendous religious resurgence — for instance, when I first came along, neither *Time* nor *Newsweek* had a religion section." He has always cast his own effort, his own meaning, in the context of the journalistic significance, observing once when he returned to Los Angeles, "It all started here fourteen years ago, when nobody had heard of Khrushchev; Castro was just a teenager." In fact, his documentary film of his 1950 Portland crusade was styled after the manner of a kind of animated *Time* magazine format, with each principal of his team, Barrows, Shea, introduced on the screen as a subject in the pages of a *Time* profile, as if this were the legitimacy they aspired to — Billy's photograph finally appearing, in this particular conceit, with the cut line "Voice of the Century." Graham himself would allow, "I make it a point to keep up with the news of the day, and much of my preaching has been against the backdrop of the events of our time. This is the pattern followed by the Old Testament prophets." In his enthusiasm to lend it all that journalistic currency, to be a kind of Gabriel Heatter Hosea or Edward R. Murrow Obadiah, he would have himself brought on in his radio broadcasts as "a man with God's message for these crisis days," and announce, "We shall keep you abreast of fast-moving events and try to interpret them for you in the light of the Scripture." In 1960, he produced a retrospective documentary of his ministry that set itself in the theater of that decade's more momentous pomp and furors, coronations, the Korean War, the Hungarian uprising, and concluded with a single isolated snapshot, against a blank backdrop, of Graham seated next to President Kennedy at a Washington prayer breakfast — as if that were the focused moment to which the whole decade had come.

In any event, the commerce between Graham and the media evolved into a curious symbiosis. With his 1957 New York crusade, *The New York Times* reserved three pages for coverage of his opening night, and wound up printing the entire text of his sermon, which had run for some forty-five minutes. In the *Journal-American,* the intrepid Dorothy Kilgallen warbled, "Billy has come to save the city from sin, but the city knows him not," and even the immaculately civilized Murray Kempton was beguiled to accede that he would "make no sport of any honest prophet of Christ."

Meanwhile, the first broadcast of Graham's radio program, *Hour of Decision,* was carried on some 150 stations, and in a little over a month, it enjoyed the largest audience of any other religious program in history. By 1954, five years after Los Angeles, he had acquired a radio audience of around fifteen million people, with a thousand stations in the United States and thirty other short-wave stations around the planet — Graham signing off each broadcast, "And now, until next week, good-bye, and may the Lord bless you *real good!*" By then, his newspaper column, *My Answer,* was in some seventy-three newspapers reaching at least fifteen million people, and he had produced his first volume of contemplations, *Peace with God,* which sold thumpingly. Also by 1954, he had engaged every major metropolis in the nation in a crusade, preaching altogether to some eight million souls, with around three hundred thousand respondents tabulated. His choirs alone had come to number more than his original audience in that Los Angeles tent.

But over these years, as he proliferated on into a kind of personal syndicate, his nights continued to be harried by insomnia. Sometimes, when he was back in Montreat, he would slip out of the bed to kneel beside Ruth's still-sleeping form, in long mute sessions of prayer. As he would profess to assemblies of ministers then, "I had read *Elmer Gantry,* and I realized from the beginning that three things had usually tripped up evangelists. The first was money. I must say, I soon realized I had certainly hit upon a very good thing if I wanted to go into this as a financial proposition — I mean, I was beginning to get some *very* large love-offerings. So, to avoid any trouble on that point, I organized into a corporation, got a board of directors, made the finances public, and put myself on a salary. The second downfall has been pride, and all I can tell you about that is, every single time I have been tempted to think I was anything, the Lord has — " and here, he would give a sudden slap of his hands " — *cut* me right down. And then, of course, the third downfall has been morals. So I determined I would never walk alone with my secretary, never have lunch or ride alone in a car with her. And I never have, to this very day. . . ."

Indeed, with Billy's tall and splendid look then of a young Lancelot of the Lord, fully 60 percent of his congregations were women. Once, when Ruth was assisting with the counseling down front during the invitation at one of his services, she noticed one young woman "just standing there staring up at the platform, and when I asked her, 'Could I help you?' she kept on staring up there where Bill was standing. Finally I said, "Why did you come down?' and she said, 'I was just wondering what it would be like to wake up in the morning and find yourself married to that man.' I told her it was something I'd been doing for a number of years now, and it was quite pleasant." This particular effect Billy himself was not unaware of, and it accorded him some discomfort. Against the hazards invited by his cinematic glamours, he devised a meticulous security system: "He'd never go anywhere alone," says Grady, "never enter a hotel room without a male companion going in before him to check it out."

So impenetrable did this traveling bufferment prove, Graham insists now that "I don't think I've ever even had a prostitute come up and proposition me. — Ah, there was once, while I was in London, we had a little incident; I had been invited to Soho at ten in the evening by some club there to hold a street service, and I didn't realize they were planning a plot. I was on top of a car with a bullhorn, preaching the gospel to this huge crowd, when suddenly I noticed them passing up this woman — over their heads, you know, from hand to hand — up toward me. I learned later she was supposed to unzip her dress there in front of me, and pictures were going to be taken. I jumped down off the car, and we began driving off, but she fought and beat her way through the crowd for four blocks. She was on drugs, she was demon-possessed — she had the strength of ten men. It's moments like that I feel like I've acted the fool, though. It was all a plot to trap me."

In fact, even as his ministry magnified through those early years of the Fifties, his obsession with the parable of Samson — that mighty agent chosen of God against the iniquitous and profane — became, for Graham, almost a complex. He recited the story repeatedly in his sermons: "First of all, he was handsome. The girls turned around and looked at him. And that became one of his great problems — girl trouble. Secondly, Samson was strong. He had all the energy of a young man. Strong, handsome, young, vigorous! He also had godly parents. God had announced his birth; God said, 'I want this boy to be reared for me.' And he had taken the Nazarite vow. That meant that no razor could come near his hair. He could not take any alcoholic beverages. He was to live a clean life!" But Samson eventually "sinned against the Lord" — violated the sanctities of his anointment. And when Delilah had his mane sheared off as he slept, "all his strength went from him." When he awoke, though, all still seemed the same — he had no inkling the grace had been removed from him, that in fact he had become now the same dull clay as everyone else. And in private, Graham would brood to friends then, "That could happen to me." He came to dwell increasingly in a vague chill dread that "God could take his hands off my life" — he would never know the actual instant the blessing left him, everything around him would still seem the same, the mere patterns and momentums from what he had been would carry him on for a while, "but my lips would turn to stone," and the immense collapsing would begin around him, until "all that remained of the whole thing would be ashes."

But if Graham himself had come to live as something of a Nazarite, it was not so much the possibility of carnal sabotage which haunted him: the great nemesis against which he found himself constantly skirmishing now, as his organization magnified around him, was the thrall of vanity. It occasioned fleeting colics of depression and ill temper, when he would abruptly belabor his aides and himself for allowing too much pomp and circumstance to surround him, suggestions of vainglory. This was all that seemed to truly vex him, but that deeply, darkly. "My name has been printed and publicized until I'm sick of it," he would constantly insist. "I'm no big person. I'm only a servant of God, unworthy to preach his gospel, but called by his grace. Everytime I see my name up in lights, everytime I'm praised and patted on the back, it makes me cold at heart. It fills me with horror. Because God said he will share his glory with no man." He cultivated, in fact, an almost savage modesty. In one of his African tours, after confusion in an introduction resulted in some two thousand listeners leaving the site of a service before it had actually begun, Billy snapped icily to the chairman of the rally, "You share a great responsibility for what happened here this afternoon." But almost instantly, out of that constant excruciating wariness of his about somehow dispelling his blessing through self-importance, he recoiled at his remark, and later informed an associate, "Yes, I wrote that dear brother asking him to please forgive me, lest I should grieve the spirit of God and he take his hand off me."

"Since I can remember," he says now, "while I'm sitting up there on that podium before I give my message, I may look relaxed and be smiling and nodding at others on the platform, but I'm feeling like I'm nothing but a worm. My soul is in terrible agony. It's almost like Jesus in Gethsemane — because I know that someday I'll have to give an accounting for the message I give that night." It is, one senses, the unrelenting tension of sustaining this implacable interior staunchness, not only against the sirens of vanity, but all the earth's soft towings and tugs, that has largely produced Graham's sheer formidable energy through the years. What he seems to mean when he says, "When you do not feel liberty, you have the most power," is that one is most effective, most dynamic, in the constrictions of humility. And indeed, there is finally no power so forbidding, perhaps, as the terrific pent compressions of such a lavishly tempted but unremitting modesty.

As he was being driven one morning back to his motel from a television appearance, Graham was accorded some casual compliment by an admirer riding with him, and as if even such small flatteries were like arrows carrying threats of some mortal wound, he quickly declared, "Oh, I sin, I sin. I sin every day. But even in confessing your sins, there's a danger. There's a very fine line between humility and pride, you know."

Through those flourishing years of the Fifties, he was also rapidly proceeding on in his ascension into the high sanctums of the country's management estate. While he was conducting a crusade in Pittsburgh in 1952, the president of his old school in Temple Terrace, W. T. Watson, was startled by a call from a millionaire industrialist and financier, Russell Maguire, then vacationing in Palm Beach, who inquired, "How can I get in touch with this young fella, Billy Graham? What he's doing is the hope of the country right now. Understand he went to your school over there, and I'd like to talk to him about how I might be able to help him out."

Maguire, originally a Wall Street broker until the SEC plucked his license for "flagrant violations" of its codes, had gone on to make a fortune anyway of $100 million from oil investments and manufacturing Thompson submachine guns during World War Two. He also happened to be one of the more acrid anti-Com-

munists and anti-Semites of that time. That same year he
phoned Watson about financing Billy, he had also funded the
distribution of a volume entitled *Iron Curtain over America,* which
was termed by a major Methodist church journal "the most extensive piece of racist propaganda in the history of the anti-
Semitic movement in America." In such ideological enterprises,
he worked in a casual conjunction with one Allen Zoll of American Patriots, Inc., a society designated by the Justice Department
as a fascist sect. Maguire himslef had just purchased the *American
Mercury,* and was to preside over that once-legendary journal's
last seedy years, with the splendid railleries of H. L. Mencken finally reduced, in Maguire's own editorials, to such prose as "a
well-known segment of the New York press, stronghold of
Jewry, have persisted in a relentless hostility toward General
Franco. . . . The anti-Christ forces are making progress. . . .
An omission in the Bible published by Simon and Schuster deals
with a Jewish invention which they would like very much to
forget: The extermination camp, complete with gas chamber
and ovens for incinerating their victims. . . ."

But Billy had manged to remain strangely insensible of the
anti-Semitic stridors that had become by now unusually common
and recurrent through the sources and progress of his ministry — beginning with the invectives of Mordecai Ham, continuing with the solicitudes of Gerald L. K. Smith's compatriot, Dr.
William Bell Riley at Northwestern. In his response to Maguire's
invitation he seemed, again, if not oblivious, not notably distracted by Maguire's character at the time as, by almost any measure, one of the nation's more gargoylish Yahoos. Watson, with
considerable glee, brought Billy down from Pittsburgh and
ushered him into Maguire's bayside home in Palm Beach. There,
in the Baghdad-like ornateness of Maquire's large sunny lounging den, they conducted their negotiations. Maguire — a bulkish
man with a receding fringe of yellow hair and a pinkish chapped
complexion, long nose, and small eyes — posed to Billy, "I want
to subsidize you. I want you to get together ten more fellas just
like you; I want you to pick 'em out, and I want you and them to
go all over this country holding revivals and preaching the kind

of things you're preaching now. I think it's just what this nation needs. Whatever it'll take, you tell me, and I'll finance it."

Watson still yelps at the memory, "Man, anybody else offered something like that, we'd have thought the millennium had arrived!" But as Watson relates it, Billy himself, after only a momentary blush, submitted, "Mr. Maguire, I can't tell you how I appreciate that, but we're getting in fifteen thousand, twenty-five thousand letters every week in our office up in Minneapolis — every one of them with a dollar or two, and every one of them saying they're praying for me. If the word were to get out that you were actually underwriting my work, I'm afraid we'd lose that support, and we'd lose those prayers. They'd stop praying for me, and I can't afford to lose that." Maguire said, "Well, look, tell me — anything. I want to help you. Just name it." Billy then quickly proposed, "Well, I've been thinking a lot here lately about beginning to make some movies. It's something I've reached a conviction we really ought to move into. Whatever you could do to help us in that, I'd certainly appreciate it." Maguire replied, "Fine. Let's talk some more in a week or two about exactly what sort of pictures you have in mind, and we'll work it out. . . ." And not long afterward, Maguire mentioned with some satisfaction to an editor at the *American Mercury*, "This young evangelist Billy Graham, I just sent him seventy-five thousand dollars."

Actually, Graham by now had already produced his first two feature-length films, *Mr. Texas* and *Oiltown, U.S.A.*, somewhat lumpish religious melodramas whose climaxes turned on the principals listening to a Graham message — the latter narrating the conversion experience of a Houston millionaire and advertised as "the story of the free-enterprise system of America, the story of the development and use of God-given natural resources by men who have built a great new empire." The source of sponsorship for those two efforts was more than a little suggested by the curiously identical setting chosen for both of them. In fact, when Graham initiated a Sunday-night television edition of *Hour of Decision* in 1951, it was funded by a $50,000 bequest from two enthusiasts in Texas. Beyond sorts like Maguire, Billy began to attract more auspicious patrons, among them Sid Richardson — a one-time Texas wildcatter with the body of a barrel cactus and a predilection for poker and bourbon and yellow terminology, who had become one of the wealthiest, if more reclusive, boyars in the Republic, with a cordial detestation for most politicians and the entire lot of the press. But he took a special fancy to Graham. He began introducing him around his private company of other Texas grandees, including then the promising young squire John Connally. When Richardson died in 1959, Graham was imported in to conduct the funeral on Richardson's private island in the Gulf, and proclaimed there, "He was willing to go to any end to see that our American way of life was maintained."

Graham himself once proposed, in regard to the remarkable interest increasingly taken in him now by such parties as Richardson, "Whether the story of Christ is told in a huge stadium, across the desk of some powerful leader, or shared with a golfing companion, it satisfies a common hunger" — he did not go on to speculate on exactly what common hungers tended to be found in such premises as the offices of government leaders and executive golf courses. But ever since 1949 — when he happily reported as he sat in his Montreat home, "Why, just a few weeks ago, a prominent Asheville businessman came to me, and we knelt and prayed together, and when we got up he told me, 'I feel like a new man,' and he has been just that since our prayer" — his ministry seemed to be particularly involved with those more prominent citizens of substance. As Billy himself enthused once during a 1952 crusade in Washington, "I'm appealing to a higher-type social strata."

One commentator then averred, "Americans have a perpetually guilty conscience about inconsistencies between their ideals and practices, their piety and their pragmatism." In a rare way, Graham provided an incalculable blessing to members of the nation's community of circumstance — he had a transparent and almost reverent admiration for them, an esteem that, simply coming from this luminous young divine with his bearing of noble righteousness, pronounced its own sanctification upon them. In fact, he seemed to like them almost mawkishly.

In turn, those business figures to whom he personally ministered seemed at times almost abjectly appreciative of his attentions. One of these had been given to periodic open dissipations
and debauches, which not only humiliated his wife but scandalized his community, but after attending a Graham crusade in the
late Fifties, he enthusiastically undertook to rehabilitate himself.
Graham inscribed the flyleaf of a Bible for him, saluting him as a
Chosen Instrument of the Lord. More, Graham even took him
along once on a tour abroad to tutor him in Bible study. People
in the community, at the mention of his name, still grin and
shake their heads, "Yeah, he just likes to keep trying that 'saved'
business; it's one of his hobbies, but it's harder on his wife than
anyone else." But Graham has remained a flushed fanaticism of
his over the years, he having collected, on a long shelf in a
sprawling room of his spacious patrician residence, a veritable
archive of biographies and commentries on Graham and his career.

He was found in his office one winter afternoon amidst a clutter of paraphernalia for a local *I Found It!* religious campaign in
which he happened to be frenetically swept up at the moment.
Once, in his scamperings about, he hesistated to finger thought-
fully some papers on his desk, and then abruptly inquired of his
visitor, "You aren't Jewish, are you?" Reassured on that count,
he commandeered by the elbow a supervisor of the *I Found It!*
operation, "Walter, tell our friend here what happened when
you found the Lord! G'on, tell him how you were saved!"

Later that afternoon at his house, while he was clattering
together a standing screen to show his visitor slides of his trip
with Graham, his wife appeared in the room. A woman with a
mellow attractiveness, but looking a bit tousled and harried at
this late afternoon hour, she lamented, "What in the world are
you doing now? I thought you were supposed to be at the office — " He muttered only a distracted syllable or two while skirmishing with the slide projector and a pooled scramble of cords.
A moment later, he called, "Hey, you don't know where that
pamphlet of Billy's is, do you?" She turned, seeming to sag a
weary degree more, and appealed, "What pamphlet? We've got

thousands, *thousands,* of pamphlets on Billy Graham around here, you know that." He coughed — "But the pamphlet, you know, he wrote about our trip. I can't find it anywhere, I used to have it — " and she shrilled, "But that was *fifteen years ago.* Why should I know where a pamphlet fifteen years ago is in all that other stuff you have in there on Billy Graham?" He merely grunted. Then after driving back into town, as he let his visitor out he leaned across the front seat for an instant to exclaim, "You know, I had two children — and then I got converted, and we had four more! You see? The Lord just doesn't stop blessing you!"

Most of all, Graham sturdily affirmed, for the nation's affluent and proprietorial, their own sense of the fitness of things. In general, his more prestigious benefactors were themselves men from the remoter communities of the country's interior who had managed to deliver themselves into the loftier empyreans of national power — "poor boys who crossed over, like Eisenhower," as someone once described them. But they still nurtured a nostalgia for the simple orderly white-picket-fence world of their origins, still aspired to confirm, on a national scale now, their *Saturday Evening Post,* Horace Greeley romance of American life. One of them, George Champion, board chairman at Chase Manhattan and a sponsor of Graham's 1957 crusade in Manhattan, would later explain that in his hometown of Normal, Illinois, "there was the highest of moral principles. Everybody knew each other, everybody went to church, everybody's life was an open book." Billy himself eminently answered to the small-town ethic of the nation's custodial community then — as Moody some eighty years before him had been promoted by J. P. Morgan, Jay Cooke, Cyrus McCormick, for his efforts to bring churchliness "to the urban masses"; as Billy Sunday was commended by John D. Rockefeller before one New York revival as "a great power for good. I don't think it's any one thing he does or says that counts in particular. Mr. Sunday is a rallying center around whom all people interested in good things may gather."

What has placed other, more pyrotechnic figures like Carl

McIntire, Aimee Semple McPherson, Father Coughlin finally outside the pale as exotic eccentrics has been precisely their volatile inadaptability to the decorums of the general respectability. As more than one annalist of evangelism in America has concluded, one can never really challenge the consensus righteousness. That is why the great public evangelists like Moody and Sunday and Graham have never really proved to be protean prophets, like Wesley or Luther, recreating the popular religious consciousness of their times. Instead, in those disequilibriums of transition through America's past, they have served to revalidate the old religious precepts that have endured as the lodestars of the American ethos — precepts making up something more like Rousseau's notion of the civil religion: "A purely civil profession of faith . . . not exactly religious dogmas, but social sentiments without which a man cannot be a good citizen or a faithful subject." And in the Fifties, Graham rousingly verified those sensible virtues that made up the Christian canon of the chambers of commerce and offices of authority over the land: still that Puritan covenant with the integrities of duty, hard work, soberness, discipline, as the way not only of redemption but prosperity, well-being. In identifying Christianity as the Protestant ethic and that ethic with material felicity, a certain amendment of Christianity's other-worldly implications was obviously entailed. But Graham succeeded heartily in transublimating his Christian gospel into a sanctification of America's capitalist articles of faith — as he concluded an address once to a convention of motel managers, "God bless you and thank you, and God bless the Holiday Inns."

In fact, "for the best blueprint of government or business ethics," he once stipulated, "go to your New Testament . . . call it how you will, a divine policy paper, a memo from the Big Boss, a heaven-sent management manual." As he explained in an essay he composed for *Nation's Business* in 1954, "We have the suggestion from the Scripture itself that faith and business, properly blended, can be a happy, wholesome and even profitable mixture. . . . Too long have many held the idea that religion should be detached from life, something aloof and apart. . . . Wise men are finding out that the words of the Nazarene: 'Seek ye first the kingdom of God and His righteousness, and all these *things* shall be added unto you' were more than the mere rantings of a popular mystic; they embodied a practical, workable philosophy which actually pays off in happiness and peace of mind. . . . Thousands of businessmen have discovered the satisfaction of having God as a working partner. It puts integrity into their organizations, sincerity into their sales, and spiritual and monetary profits into their hearts and pockets. . . . A good slogan might be: 'The plant that prays together profits together.' It is difficult to imagine labor trouble in such an atmosphere." More particularly, Graham once described the Garden of Eden as a paradise blessed with "no union dues, no labor leaders, no snakes, no disease," and he also indicated that any Christian laborer "would not stoop to take unfair advantage" of his employer by aligning himself with a union.

At the same time, he still maintained his incessant projections of imminent apocalypse — "America at this moment is under the pending judgment of God, and unless we have a spiritual revival now, we are done as a nation. The hour is far later than we think." Yet these grim conjurations were oddly absent of any element of the disagreeably fatal, the theologically unappeasable; rather, they were posed patriotically in the rather congenial and compatible terms of the Cold War conflict — a context not all that discommoding to the interests of the nation's executiveship. It was an evangelism of an American Cold War Jonah. In fact, his preaching answered, more deeply than he might have supposed, to the Crusader tradition in its most classic historical sense: that burly compound of pious and patriotic militancies. As early as 1947, he was declaring in a Charlotte revival, "Communism is creeping inexorably into these destitute lands, into war-torn China, into restless South America, and unless the Christian religion rescues these nations from the clutch of the unbelieving, America will stand alone and isolated in the world." Specifically, after Chiang Kai-shek's final flight to Formosa, Graham was constantly urging that the Generalissimo and his "crack troops" be turned loose to dispose of Mao's regime, and professed that, along with a national revival, "I am definitely in favor of building the strongest possible military force."

He was apprised in 1951 in a letter from Eisenhower, "The thing you fellows are doing is the hope of America." As Graham would sometimes insist, "The United States needs a spiritual revival, or we'll be licked before the Communists get here," more precisely he recommended in 1960, after Japanese demonstrations had snuffed a scheduled visit by Eisenhower there, "Christianity needs a show of strength and force. . . . We must maintain the strongest military establishment on earth." In his eagerness of those days, no possible disparity between such stout martial sentiments and the Sermon on the Mount seemed to occur to Billy; rather, he was not a little invigorated by the reflection, as he mentioned more than once, that "the preaching of Paul was influential in breaking the back of the pagan Roman empire eventually."

He even wound up presenting, in Maguire's *American Mercury* in 1954, a singularly energetic exposition, composed out of his sermons, in which he announced, "Either Communism must die, or Christianity must die, because it is actually a battle between Christ and anti-Christ. . . . Satan began his revolution in the Garden of Eden. With Cain as his first devout follower, and with his brother Abel as a blood sacrifice upon the altar of totalitarianism, he has slaughtered, plundered and bludgeoned his way through the centuries. . . ." How Cain's murder of Abel parsed out as the primal blood sacrifice to totalitarianism had not occurred to a great many other theologians or pundits, but what Graham may have lacked in conceptual precision he made up for in sheer strenuousness. About the Communists, he asserted, "the Devil is their God; Marx, their prophet; Lenin, their saint; and Malenkov, their high priest. . . . Karl Marx — a subtle, clever, degenerate materialist — having filled his intellectual craw with all the filth of Europe's gutters, and garbling perverted German philosophies and half-truths, spewed this filthy, corrupt, ungodly, unholy doctrine of world socialism over the gullible people of a degenerate Europe. Europe became a colossal inferno of lies and deception; and that wild, false fire has spread through the world. . . . Communism, Satan's version of religion, has humanized almost every doctrine of Christianity which pertains to man." To contend with this demonology, he advocated "old-fashioned Americanism. Through the ideals of early Americanism we built the greatest nation ever to exist in all history. . . . Civilization stands at the crossroads. If it turns to the right and takes the way of the Cross, we well might be entering the greatest economic and spiritual renaissance man has known."

Billy has since come to feel a bit sheepish about such exercised rhetorics from those early years. But somewhat more unpleasantly, in that same exegesis in the *Mercury*, he maintained that "the mysterious pull of this satanic religion is so strong that it has caused some citizens of America to become traitors, betraying a benevolent land which had showered them blessings innumerable. It has attracted some of our famous entertainers, some of our finest politicians, and some of our outstanding educators." In 1951, as a kind of national phobia was setting in about infection of the body politic by foreign ideological contagions, with Joseph McCarthy hauling forth as yet another manifestation of that thick brutish primitive always slouching in the darker keeps of the American character, Billy himself was widely tromboning about "over eleven hundred social-sounding organizations that are Communist or Communist-oriented in this country. They control the minds of a great segment of our people." When McCarthy demanded that the Fifth Amendment protection be suspended for witnesses before his committee, Graham concurred on an *Hour of Decision* broadcast one Sunday that if it would take such an improvisation on the Constitution to flush out Communists and their sympathizers, "then let's do it!" He did offer that "in a sense, men like Senator McCarthy have gone too far; false accusations can be dangerous," but he pointed out that "Communism is far worse than we realize. With termites in America and barbarians outside, we are beginning to crumble apart." Finally, when McCarthy was condemned by the Senate, Graham complained that the action was comparable to Nero's fiddling while Rome burned, the Senate had plucked at "trifles"

and brought "disgrace to the dignity of American states-
manship." And he hailed the other current Congressional inquisitions into subversives, thanking God for "men who, in the face
of public denouncement and ridicule, go loyally on in their work
of exposing the pinks, the lavenders, and the reds who have
sought refuge beneath the wings of the American eagle."

In his interludes between these public apostleships through
the Fifties, he did not exactly withdraw like Elijah or John the
Baptist into the desolations of the wilderness; increasingly now,
as the guest of corporation executives and political dignitaries, it
was to the mown groomed fairways of golf courses that he repaired, the carpeted locker rooms of country clubs where he
could often be found, standing in his shorts, discoursing to ball-
bearing manufacturers and textile-mill magnates on the exhilarations of prolonged Bible study. He even exclaimed about
Heaven, "Boy, I sure hope they have a golf course up there!"
Anointed honorary chaplain of Charlotte's Quail Hollow
Country Club, he happily quipped, "The Apostle Paul, you
know, said, 'I have finished the course,'" and further expounded, "There's no game which opens a man's personal life
like golf. It illustrates an individual's honesty, integrity, intelligence, and character. Golf demands control of temper, concentration and integrity. You can tell a lot about a person by
playing a round of golf with him. In golf, you cope with the
same troubles as you do in life." In his own game, he was consistently impressive in swooping off tee shots of spectacular long
yardage, but a bit flounderous when it came to the final definitive precisions of detailing it on into the cup. Someone who
played with him frequently remembers he would wail, "I can't
putt, I just can't putt, I've *five-putted* this green." But he flailed
dauntlessly on at it. And rather in that way in which bleak moun-
taintops and desert caves served to charge the souls of the Old
Testament prophets, it seemed now that golf courses, ever since
his midnight surrender to Heaven on that eighteenth green
down in Temple Terrace, had come to serve Billy: it was where
he continued to come by his epiphanies and spiritual inhalings.

Even during crusades, he would return from playing nine holes to dictate his evening's sermon.

For that matter, neither did those diverse notables in American society whom he continued to beguile precisely skulk to him in the pit of night as did Nicodemus to confer with Jesus — "obviously not wishing to be seen visiting him," as Malcolm Muggeridge puts it in his study, *Jesus.* "Anyone who has associated himself with causes considered to be unfashionable or disreputable will be familiar with such nocturnal visitors of distinction." Instead, Graham was constantly being produced to ornament such occasions as, once, Southern Airline's inauguration of a new schedule of flights from Chicago to Memphis, in which Graham, from a pulpit in the passenger aisle of a plane flying in circles seven thousand feet over Memphis, conducted a devotional service carried on local radio below. At the dedication of a $2 million Standard Oil building in Charlotte on the old pastures of the Graham farmland, Esso President William Naden proposed after Billy's benedictory prayer, "I just had a most unreligious thought. What a great combination it would be to have Billy Graham associated with Esso Standard Oil!" Of course, in a sense, he already had been for some time — in his progressive assimilation into the national order of influence. Feted as America's "Salesman of the Year," he later went on to be presented, at a ceremony in New York, the Horatio Alger award — along with a doughnut tycoon, an Italian entrepreneur of Chinese food, and the eighty-year-old founder of a drugstore empire.

It was in April of 1950 that Graham delivered his first devotional in the marbled chambers of Congress, praying then, "Our father, we give Thee thanks for this greatest nation in the world. We thank Thee for the Stars and Stripes that wave above the land of the free and the home of the brave. We thank Thee for the highest standard of living in the world. . . ."

He had also caught the notice by now of House Speaker Sam Rayburn — who declared, "This country needs a revival, and I believe Billy Graham is bringing it to us" — as well as Bernard

Baruch, venerable earl of Wall Street and Washington since World War One. Even more propitiously, in 1950 while Graham was conducting a crusade in Columbia, South Carolina, Henry Luce, who was staying at Baruch's plantation retreat in the South Carolina low country, was persuaded by Baruch to make a trip up to Columbia to scrutinize for himself this young religious sensation. Then-governor Strom Thurmond had eagerly quartered Billy in the governor's mansion with him, and learning of Luce's arrival, Thurmond availed himself of that august happenstance by installing Luce in the mansion with him also. Thurmond's industrious officiousness reached such a point that, according to Grady Wilson, Luce finally took Billy aside and remarked somewhat dryly, "You know, I've never seen a governor actually get down and pray on his knees before." Billy himself recalls that Luce "finally had to let Thurmond know that he wasn't really interested in hearing about South Carolina anymore."

Instead, with his thin mineral eyes under his dark briary bishop's eyebrows, Luce "watched Billy like a hawk," says Grady. Billy recollects now, "We stayed up each night until one or two in the morning, talking alone, for two or three nights. I think he was trying to pull me out to see if I was genuine or honest. At that time, frankly, I didn't really know who he was. But boy, did I respect him."

Out of those midnight sessions between Luce and Graham in the library of the governor's mansion, there shortly ensued another story on Graham's crusades in *Time,* then one in *Life.* Luce provided now a fulfilling continuum of the initial attentions of Hearst. "*Time* and *Life,* they began carrying about everything I did, it seemed like," says Billy. "They gave me a tremendous push. Through Mr. Luce, people heard about me, people at universities and in the business community and places like that, that would have never considered our work seriously if it had not been written up in a sophisticated magazine like *Time.*" It became an enduring concord. A few years after Columbia, Luce happened to be in India while Billy was touring there, and Billy recalls, "I met him at the airport once around two or three in the morning." At a dinner for Graham that evening, says a friend,

"Whenever Billy would say anything, I could see Mr. Luce turn his eyes on him immediately — those eyes of his just glowing." Billy recounts now, "I never went to New York that I didn't call on him. I think he took a sort of fatherly interest in me almost. When he appointed Hedley Donovan to begin running everything, he called me up there and took me in and introduced me to Donovan and said, 'Now, when there's anything you want, you come to him just as you would to me.'"

Asked now how he felt in those early years to find himself so suddenly moving in such imposing company — Sid Richardson, Rayburn, Baruch, Luce — Billy admits, "Astounded, and quite frightened at first. Of course, I discovered after a while that many times I could shift the conversation to my field and put them on my ground — I feel much more at ease in all circles now. But back there when it all started, my first reaction, when I met somebody like Mr. Richardson or Mr. Luce, was just to start praying." Of this abrupt and seemingly unaccountable interest taken in him then by the mighty of the land, Billy once suggested, "They are beginning to realize that evangelism's a tremendous factor, not only politically but from the moral and spiritual point of view, which will make a contribution to the country. Because the Communists are dedicated to Communism, and we need the same dedication to the principles on which this country was founded."

But when he is asked now if he ever reflected on the possibility that he was, perhaps, being used — that whether calculatingly or unconsciously, he might have been conscripted by those parties to serve what they themselves may have considered the worthiest of national interests, but ends somewhat apart from his own gospel purposes — Billy pauses, lightly clears his throat behind his fist, and then says, "Well, I usually *thought* I could tell. Now, I always believed in the sincerity of Kennedy, for instance, because of the way his mother treated me, the way his father treated me. But with some of the other politicians, if it was an election year, yes, there would be a lot of free-lance photographers around, it seemed." But whatever misgivings he may have felt on this account, Graham arrived at a final computation: "I felt God had

given me a great open door. Because of my friendship with people like Luce and the others, Rayburn, eventually even Presidents), it would open doors that otherwise wouldn't be opened.
For instance, when I went to Italy, the ambassador would meet
me, and I would meet people whom I otherwise wouldn't have
been able to meet. . . ."

During those early crusades, he was still technically serving as
president of Northwestern Schools and "I was in a very great
struggle whether I should resign or not, whether I should go
into evangelism totally with no other responsibilities whatsoever.
I was still thinking that I might be able to combine the two."
During the Christmas season of 1951, he pondered this absolute
commitment to public evangelism while wandering mountain
paths around his home in Montreat, shuffling through fallen
leaves among silences of fog. And what finally concluded the
matter for him was "the interest of Henry Luce and people like
that. I realized it had opened up now, that I would probably be
moving around a lot. Telegrams and letters were pouring in
from all over America. I had addressed the Southern Baptist
Convention for the first time. I had even been sent for by
Eisenhower."

So it was that — by striking his own private contract with what
appeared to be promising means for accomplishing a higher,
truer mission — Graham entered into a classic tragic equation.
With that decision, the plot was laid. As Dostoyevsky illustrates in
the encounter between the Grand Inquisitor and a reappeared
Christ in *The Brothers Karamazov*, Satan's last and most lethal
tantalization of Jesus in the wilderness was to take him to a
mountaintop and offer him the arrayed dominions and principalities of the earth — the temptation to fulfill his message, his
kingdom, through the expediting devices of authority and government, so entailing him then in the instruments of temporal
power and thereby effectively negating his far more radical
meaning of simple uninstitutionalized love. But Graham's vulnerability was that, while he contended that he looked on all his
associations now in government and commerce as mere openings
for a fuller propagation of his ministry, at the same time he also

was given to a compulsive entrancement with all those larger affairs and offices of the world. He seemed helplessly infatuated by the various appointments of earthly importance. By 1958, he was flourishing to visitors a gilt-inscribed card entitling him to a room in any Hilton Hotel without a reservation, proudly beaming, "There are only forty of these cards! The only other religious figure to have one is Bishop Sheen!" It became that perverse scenario of even the best ambitions of men: the means consuming the end. Specifically, as Graham was to become progressively digested into the American complex of power and consequence, he would seem to become, after the pattern of that tragic formula suggested by Dostoyevsky, only more estranged, more remote, from the reckless extravagancies of the gospel's original vision of love.

Thus now, some fourteen years after his repudiation in Florida of all the world's allures, it finally turned out to be the world only half-relinquished after all. It was as if he had wound up in an unsuspected abortion of that original exalted resolve, suspended now in some indefinite spiritual zone halfway between the world of St. Francis and that of the Florentines. For an evangel presumably deriving out of the austerities of Amos and John the Baptist, yet he would seem constitutionally unable to resist, over the following years, being very much a part of the more conspicuous occupations of society.

In 1955, he briefly maintained a six-room "permanent national headquarters" on Pennsylvania Avenue only three blocks from the White House, explaining, "I just want to lobby for God," and by 1970, he had even installed a UPI teletype in his mountain home. At the same time, he would engage in a ceaseless extemporaneous free-form punditry on public developments, from the U.N.'s intervention in Katanga — "The U.N. is not willing to unite Korea or Vietnam, but the U.N. is anxious to fight in Katanga, which is not related linguistically or culturally to the rest of the Congo" — to the Common Market: "United States businessmen had better get on their toes, because there really will be some competition coming up, and it could really hurt

American business if they do not meet the competition." He even felt called upon eventually to deliver his own testimony on bomb shelters, announcing it as his careful, solemn conclusion that "I have made this judgment. After much prayer, I have decided not to build a private shelter at this time. . . . It is true that in the face of world destruction, Noah did build an ark to provide safety for those who would enter with him. However, Noah acted in obedience to specific instructions from God. . . . I have received no such instructions from the Lord, as yet."

This preoccupation would produce, over the decades, a rather boggling duality in his ministerial perspectives. In 1964, he would remark, "Sometimes I think the church is getting too involved in politics. The more we stay out of politics, the better." But in one of his Charlotte crusades, he declared that it was "the church's duty to lead" in establishing "civic righteousness," and pointed out that there were enough church people in Charlotte to put any any man they wanted in office. In 1972, he was still insisting, "I have really stayed out of politics purposely. It's pretty hard to do, since so many of my friends are in politics" — as earlier he had averred, "You must remember that the worst part of history was in the Dark Ages, when the church ran everything. Too many ministers think they're social engineers. They even want to get into the business of deciding where highways should go." But almost simultaneous with that estimable pronouncement, at the behest of Asheville's Chamber of Commerce he was phoning Transportation Secretary John Volpe, an old acquaintance, to urge construction of a disputed open-cut highway through a local mountain.

In fact, he was regularly involving himself in civic controversies, ranging from a zoo bond issue in Charlotte, which he lustily promoted, to the more immediate interest of petitioning Charlotte's planning commission for a rezoning change to accommodate a proposed Almart Variety Store on his family's land, a prospect bitterly fought by adjoining residents and eventually rejected by the commission with the observation that "it would degrade the neighborhood a tremendous amount," despite a personal letter from Graham to the commission explaining,

"Land taxes make it imperative that we convert to yield income."
He once appeared with a local delegation of business leaders at a
meeting with North Carolina's state highway commissioner in a
bank office in Black Mountain, the village just down the slope
from Montreat, to appeal for the paving of a road up to the top
of nearby Mount Mitchell — where a radio station of Graham's
also happeed to be located. As Graham presented it to the highway commissioner, "It takes me two hours now to get up there
by car, but only ten minutes by helicopter." The commissioner,
with a small smile, politely retorted, "Well, it would be cheaper
for the state just to buy you a helicopter, Dr. Graham." He then
suggested to Graham that perhaps he could explore among his
large collection of acquaintances in Washington the possibilities
of some federal funding to pave the road. To that, Graham
mused, "Well, you know, Wally Hickel's a good fried of mine —"
and then added the disclaimer, at which the commissioner
started to chortle but then checked himself, "— but I just don't
know anything about politics. How are you supposed to go about
these sort of things?"

As a matter of fact, in his running commentary on the more
towering public considerations of the time, he would consistently
float out rather ponderous blimps of misapprehension, as when
he once heatedly chided the U.N. for having listed the United
States as one of the world's pagan nations. When Adlai Stevenson, then U.N. ambassador, crisply refuted this, reporting that it
simply was not the case, Graham promptly offered, "I retract the
statement. This has taught me a lesson to check my facts a little
closer." It would turn out to be a lesson he never succeeded in
quite mastering, but out of his sheer urgency for agreeableness
no matter what, he would regularly dispense peculiarly contrite
and perfervid apologies — as, for instance, to a columnist who
took a particularly spirited umbrage when Graham once remarked that, in contrast to pleas then from the nation's ghettos,
his family had never needed government agencies or programs
to help them rid themselves of rats: "Please feel free to kick me
in the seat of the pants whenever you feel like it. I need it sometimes. You really know how to hurt a fellow. The reason it hurts

is because you are at least in part right. I will have to be more careful from now on."

The truth is, an elemental condition of Graham's whole nature — which largely accounted for his eager compact with the media reality and notables of his time, as well as for his curiously erratic yawings in public professions over the years — seems to be that in the very vitals of his being is an almost poignant desperation to be approved of. As his pastor at Montreat notes, "Most politicians and dignitaries admire Billy greatly, but they're also just a little puzzled by him. They can't figure out what he's really after, what he really wants. What they don't realize is that, for one thing, like any other public figure, like they themselves, he just has this great desire *to be liked*." His alertness to any possible intimations of antipathy toward him is so actue that, despite the constant impossible clamoring of appeals for his presence at occasions, he is instantly pitched into a gloomy foreboding if, for instance, some church leader requests a member of his team instead of himself to appear at an event — inquiring of mutual friends if the churchman is irate with him, laboring over what could have provoked such a mysterious disaffection. Inexhaustibly ingratiating, he will hastily assure a Jewish interviewer, "I am very pro-Jewish. We Christian gentiles have committed our lives to a Jew, you know." During his 1957 New York crusade, he was even inspired to confide to one Jewish journalist that Israel was destined to expand until the nation included the entire territory promised to the descendants of Abraham in the Bible — that is, from the Nile to the Euphrates — and after the Six-Day War in 1967, he heartily encouraged Israel to hold steadfast against demands she return seized territory, declaring that Jerusalem must be reunited as a Jewish city. But when he was once denied a visa by Jordan for "propaganda activities for Israel," he seemed genuinely bewildered and aghast, insisting, "I'm sure if they had done this, they would have notified our Minneapolis office."

Accordingly, out of that same avidity for general approval, the impulse of his ministry has always tended toward the maximum adaptability. In his more uncertain beginning years, he finally had his troupe of assistants compile a ledger of the complaints most often directed at revivalists, and thereupon set about systematically adjusting his evangelism to avert those aspects they saw as "difficulties" — which included not only embarrassments over money and morals, but "emotionalism" and "anti-intellectualism." In fact, he modulated his ministry to such a fine point that he soon began outraging the grizzled patriarchs of that smoke-snorting pentecostalism out of which he himself had issued — redoubtable fundamentalists like Bob Jones, Sr., and Dr. John R. Rice inveighing now against Graham for his apparently amiable consortings with "liberals, modernists, who do not believe in salvation by the blood of Christ, the virgin birth, the bodily resurrection, the absolute deity of Christ." By 1966, when Graham held a crusade in Greenville, South Carolina, where Jones had relocated his fundamentalist academy, Jones proclaimed that Graham, because of his commerce with the likes of the National Council of Churches and Bishop James Pike, and his wholesale distribution of converts back to local churches outside the fundamentalist pale, was "doing more harm to the cause of Jesus Christ than any other living man." But Billy continued to maintain, with his unvanquishable affability, "I really do love Bob Jones Senior, and Junior too."

He remained deathlessly hopeful and cordial with all parties. To the occasional suggestions that this indiscriminate sociability led him at times into what seemed like a helter-skelter cacophony of public professions, Graham merely submitted a citation from Paul: "I am made all things to all men, that I might by all means save some." While he would also accede, "In every generation, a few or many may be saved, but it is only a minority," he still seemed congenitally unable to settle for that, out of his urgency for the widest possible approbation, for the validations of a mass effect in his ministry. One commentator noted in 1958 that "it is a peculiarly American brand of evangelism that Billy Graham offers — an evangelism eager above all to be popular. It seeks the friendship of all political parties, supports all churches, bids for the goodwill of intellectuals, and refuses to have anything to do with bigotry. It provides a simple answer to all problems, with the assurance that 'surrender' will not affect the convert's status in the community — indeed, will not even make him lose his friends in the crowd."

Whatever, he had become by then a familiar fixture in the national pop-Elysium of the eclectically famous, beginning to show up regularly in the annual ten-most-admired lists. As he reports, not without some elation still, "Why, in nineteen fifty-six, -seven, you'll find my name in the news more than any other single public figure. There was more copy published on me than even the President. I received the award as the most publicized person in the United States for two years running. It's just amazing, I was on the front cover of *Life* four times, cover of *Look* must have been seven or eight times. I've been on the cover of *Time* just once, I think, but they've had me on the cover of *Newsweek* at least six or seven times." He was a phenomenon that one newspaper scribe, during Graham's 1957 New York crusade, undertook to explain as "To many, once afraid to mention God without being ridiculed, Billy Graham has made the contemplation of religion 'the thing to do.' Searching the soul and Bible for answers has become almost as popular as consulting a psychiatrist." With his lofty and glistering figure, he had reached a kind of stardom of his own — appearing regularly on Bob Hope and Jack Benny television specials — while the only television programs he himself tended to watch now, aside from westerns, would be interviews and performances of those other celebrities whom he had personally counseled.

But during the high meridian of Graham's rapport with Richard Nixon in the early Seventies, a Baptist minister in a city where Graham was conducting a crusade — a lean and slightly blowzy man with skimpy hair fluffed askew — sat one raining Sunday afternoon in a motel restaurant, sipping from a plastic-tip White Owl cigar between gulps at his cup of coffee, and propounded with a creak of pain in his voice, "Look, it's supposed to be the obligation of the church to pronounce the judgments of God on the state — that's been true ever since the Old Testament prophets, Nathan, Ezekiel, Hosea. But what is Graham doing? This whole nation still has the idea somehow that

we're the Sir Galahad of the world. In the midst of all the mayhem we've worked, we've still managed to remain political and
historical virgins. For instance, how did we get all this wealth?
Because we're good? Well, that's the message we get from Graham — we've been blessed like this, not because of an exploitative economy locked in with military muscle-flexing, but because
we're really pure of heart — and we're going to lose it all if we
don't stay good. What we have right now is the most powerful
man religiously in this nation, Billy Graham, giving the government and its policies and the power community in this country
his conspicuous blessing — not just in his preachments, but
through all his friendships, all those pleasant little prayer breakfasts, but more than anything else, all his silences in the face of
the most arrant outrages by that government. He has especially
become a spiritual sanction to this particular administration.
What we've got is almost a Graham-Nixon axis. I don't mean to
sound intemperate. But the truth is, Jesus went to the cross
because he alienated the powers of his day. Not for nothing do
the Scriptures say, *'Beware when all men speak well of you.'* What I
want to know is, how can a man spend thirty years preaching the
gospel, and with maybe only two or three exceptions, not have
one mayor, one governor, one banker, one chairman of the
board, one president of a Chamber of Commerce, one Defense
Department official, one political party chairman — *not one!* —
speak a single ill word against him. You ask me if there's anything finally tragic about Graham in all this? Lord knows, it's
tragic."

With an insuppressible fascination and excitement, Graham
oscillated ever closer to the precincts of power in the Washington
of the Fifties — that strangely drab period of sack suits and bow
ties and sallow bureaucrat faces all faintly dampish, it seemed, in
the general funk then of a dull glum mania of suspicion, of hot-
lit hearings. To Graham, though, it was like moving among the
colonnades of Ilium. After a 1952 crusade in Washington's National Guard Armory, he delightedly reported of the turnout,

"As near as I can tell, we averaged between twenty-five and forty Congressmen and about five Senators a night."

By the end of the decade, he had become a frequent and familiar fixture at Capitol Hill luncheons, his hosts such unlikely acolytes as Senator Everett Dirksen and Lyndon Johnson. He enjoyed a special affinity for a time with Tennessee governor Frank Clement, efflorescent orator of the 1952 Democratic Convention's keynote address, who himself drummed Billy about as "a brilliant spark, full of drive, zeal, and dedication, who inspires others to their best efforts." In fact, Billy found himself somewhat deliciously having to discount reports that he had inspired, in particular, Clement's keynote peroration. "I helped him write the speech that he was first going to deliver, getting as much spiritual content into it as I could, but he chucked that one," Billy says now. "And, uh, I don't know, but people say that in discarding that one, that cost him the vice-presidential nomination."

Before the Fifties were out, Graham was able to protest luxuriously, "I make every effort not to let it appear that I favor one party over another. I count Secretary Dulles a friend, but Senator Humphrey is also a good friend of mine," whom he had first met, he cheerfully related, "when we were both swimming in the nude at the YMCA pool in Minneapolis where he was running for mayor." Also, "Representative John McCormack, a Catholic, is the best friend I have in Washington. If I'm seen with Nixon, I try to be seen as soon as possible with Harriman." To later sarcasms about his conviviality over the years with certain of the more dubious spirits in Washington's covens of power, Graham now contends, "Look at God calling Nebuchadnezzar 'My servant.' God was using him on the chessboard of history, and the prophet Daniel was his prime minister. Which shows you that, like Daniel, you can go to Washington as a Christian and still live a Christian life." Indeed, to a question once as to what figure in all history, other than Christ, he was most taken with, Graham replied, "I would say Daniel, because he was prime minister of the greatest empire in the world. Daniel was a combination of prophet and political leader, and he wrote about many of the things that are now happening in the world."

In Billy's case, though, what was largely at work was simply that abiding country boy's awe which had him still marveling, even in the Sixties, "Never could I have dreamed I would some-day visit President Eisenhower at Gettysburg, that he would guide me across the battlefield where my Confederate grandfa-ther lay. . . . Or that I might become a friend of President John-son's, who invited me to the White House before last Christmas, questioned me on many subjects, and asked me to swim with him and to stay for dinner." As he once described his response to these familiarities, "I picked up the phone the other day, and the voice on the other end said, 'Hello, Billy, this is Lyndon.' I was nearly speechless."

But this ultimate intimacy with the Oval Office itself began not all that promisingly, actually, with a somewhat burlesque mishap with Truman. At an invitation intitiated by a South Carolina Congressman, one summer day in 1950 Graham and Cliff Bar-rows, along with aide Jerry Beavan, presented themselves in Truman's office, all arrayed in white suits, white bucks, and floral ties. "The President stood and greeted us," says Graham, "and told us he was a Baptist himself. Well, I immediately began trying to preach to him." After a moment or two, Truman inter-rupted him a bit brusquely. "He said he lived by the Sermon on the Mount and the Golden Rule," says Graham, "and then re-peated he was a Baptist —" and then, recalls Graham, Truman added in his clipped piano-wire twang: "If it just weren't for these goddam newspapers after me every day, and that colum-nist Drew Pearson, the sorry s.o.b. . . ." Undismayed, Billy soon blurted, "Would it be all right if we just had a word of prayer before we leave, Mr. President?" and recounts Graham now, "I'm afraid I put my arm around him in my zeal." Truman, find-ing himself abruptly pent in this clasp, bowed his head a small stiff fraction as Billy then addressed the Almighty — "I prayed that God would bless him and his administration, and that God would give him of His wisdom in dealing with all the difficulties in the country and the world" — while Barrows kept up a contrapuntal accompaniment, "Amen. Tell it. Yes, Lord. . . ."

Graham then emerged with Beavan and Barrows into a small tumult of newsmen and photographers on the walkway outside. "They immediately started asking me all kinds of questions — what did I tell the President? What did he say? What had I prayed in my prayer with him? Did the President kneel? — and I just stood there and answered every single thing they asked me. I had no idea you weren't supposed to quote the President in those kinds of things. I told them absolutely everything I could think of. Then they asked me to show them. They all started yelling, 'Kneel down! Kneel down!' Of course, it wasn't quite how it had happened, but —" and Billy and his party obligingly knelt in their snowy suits on the White House lawn and performed a rendition of their visit to a chattering of camera shutters around them.

Truman proved to be so miffed by the whole episode that he ordered that Graham was to be admitted nowhere near his vicinity ever again. He further refused all discreet elicitations, during the Graham crusade in Washington not long afterward, to attend one of the services. Asked about this rather pointed absence, Graham merely pleasantly surmised, "I guess he was just too busy or something." Instead, during that Washington campaign, Graham had to content himself with an audience with General Douglas MacArthur, reappearing after an hour with him to announce, "He is one of the greatest Americans of all time" — an enthusiasm that did not exactly enchant Truman either. For that matter, when Truman had divested MacArthur of his command a year or so earlier, Graham had professed in one message, "Ladies and gentlemen, I am not a politician, I refrain from making statements on political matters" — and then had gone on to dilate further that all Christians in the Orient were "deeply grieved and all feel that Christianity has suffered another major blow."

It may have owed to Truman's deepening irritation over all this that, after Graham ambitiously put forward his own five-point peace plan for Korea, his visa application for a clerical expedition there was very nearly denied. In fact, when the reluctance of South Korean president Syngman Rhee to comply with truce terms began to occasion considerable exasperation with him in Washington, Graham fumed in one crusade sermon, "Isn't it strange to you that we had three great and strong men in the Far East — men whose moral stature and integrity were unquestioned — and we pulled MacArthur back to this country, we pulled the rug out from under Chiang Kai-shek, and now the Communists have maneuvered us almost into a war with Syngman Rhee."

On his part, Graham had abandoned by now all last lingering fancies of any possible overture to Truman. A year or so after that misfortune at the White House, during a crusade in Greensboro, North Carolina, he indulged in the offhanded waggery that along with everyone else present at the Last Judgment would be Hitler, Mussolini, Joe Stalin, "and Harry Truman." To the guffaws from his congregation, Graham then coyly added, "Don't you Democrats laugh. Harry is doing the best he can. The trouble is that he just can't do any better. After all, when a man's been in a haberdashery shop — but I won't say anything more about that. Except, that I have found that after my car has run for a long time, it needs a change of oil. That's the strongest political statement I'm going to make, now." Finally, on the eve of the 1952 presidential election, during one crusade Graham even "drew a rather startling parallel between President Truman and Adam," according to a newspaper account — by pointing out that, in the same way in which all mankind had become a part of Adam's decision to disobey in the Garden, we had all become involved in Truman's commitment to the Korean action: "How many of you voted to go into the Korean War? I never did."

Nevertheless, in 1967, Graham — invincibly officious and impervious to any past dissonances — managed to arrange a fifteen-minute chat with Truman in Independence to "apologize in person" for his indiscretion in that call at the White House some seventeen years earlier. "Truman told me, 'Oh, I knew they hadn't briefed you and counseled you.' We really had a very friendly visit." As it turned out, from that one disastrous offense against the decorums of high station, Graham at least implacably learned his lesson — to the extent that, after an audience with the Queen Mother in London in 1955, not even two *Daily Mirror* reporters breaking through the locked door of his hotel room could prise from him the merest murmur of the pleasantries that had been exchanged.

But whatever his unluckiness with Truman, Graham found himself in an instant and easy consanguinity with his successor, Eisenhower. It had been early in 1952, while Eisenhower was still occupying his office at SHAPE headquarters outside Paris, that Billy had first been conducted into his presence — through the good graces of Sid Richardson. Richardson had earlier impressed him into writing a letter to Eisenhower encouraging him to run for President — Billy first protesting, as he later related, "Mr. Sid, I can't get involved in politics!" to which Richardson rejoined, "There's no politics, Billy. Don't you think any American ought to run if millions of people want him to?" With it put that way, Billy conceded, "Yes, Mr. Sid, I agree he should —" and Richardson snapped, "Well, then, say that in a letter!" Asked now why Richardson might have supposed he would have any influence on Eisenhower, Billy conjectures, "Well, it was right after the Washington crusade, and about half the Congress was there, it was in newspapers all over the country. And Eisenhower was in regular correspondence with Mr. Richardson at that time, of course."

Whatever, not long afterward Richardson received an inquiry from Eisenhower: "Who was that young preacher you had write me? It was the darndest letter I ever got." Richardson replied, as Billy quotes it, "I want to send this young fellow over who's stirring up the country so to talk to you." And with that, Richardson shipped Billy over on the rather giddy mission of personally exhorting General Dwight D. Eisenhower — architect of the destruction of those German legions whose trample over Europe Billy had listened to radio reports of while painting the house for his father that summer twelve years ago — now to run for President of the United States.

He was ushered in to a smile, beaming between flanked gilt-crested flags, as wide and generous as a Nebraska corn prairie. Taking a seat, "I presented to him arguments that I had already written out," Billy recounts, "which mostly came to why any American who was wanted by all that many people should respond." Eisenhower received this particular bit of proselytizing from the young evangelist with an immense graciousness, bestowing on him a warm and benign attention. Billy himself presently began to notice, as he later recorded, "the general was even . . . more charming and more down-to-earth than I had anticipated. He immediatly put me at ease, relating some of his past experiences."

After this genial exchange, how Graham proceeded to abstain from the political din of the 1952 presidential campaign was to sound in his messages curious reverberations of the Republican slogan — "We all seem to agree there's a mess in Washington" — and to declare that "the nation desperately needs a strong spiritual leader" who would insure a "cleanup" in the Capital. It was a testimonial that did not precisely incline toward Adlai Stevenson. With his elegant reflectiveness and celery-crisp wit and cosmopolitan vision, Stevenson seemed, in the flat and sullen weathers of those times, more a dangerously subtle and whimsical mandarin than a sturdy spiritual scoutmaster. As for Billy, he was accorded two more appointments with Eisenhower during the campaign, once at the Blackstone Hotel in Chicago, another session "for a couple of days" at the Brown Hotel in Denver, during which he personally conferred a Bible on Eisenhower, and Eisenhower confided to him that, while he may have been somewhat remiss in his church attendance through his long career as a soldier, he wanted now to align himself with some church, though not until after the election to avoid any appearance of political calculation. "He told me, 'I don't believe the American people are going to follow anybody who's not a member of a church.' I said, 'What denomination are you?' and he said, 'Well, I'm not any. But my parents were River Brethren.' I told him that was fairly close to the Presbyterians from what I'd heard, and recommended to him two Presbyterian churches in

Washington — the reason I recommended those two were because their pastors had supported him. He seemed very grateful."

Then, on a gray winter day after his election, Eisenhower
called Graham up to his suite in the Commodore Hotel in New
York. Now as the President-elect, Eisenhower seemed of a more
heavy humor. He presently sauntered over to a window and,
after gazing out meditatively for a silent while, announced to
Billy that he had concluded it was one of the destinies of his victory to lend a higher spiritual quality to the conduct of the nation's business. To begin in this, he would like Billy to advise him
on "bringing something spiritual, some spiritual note and tone,
into the inauguration ceremony." His eyes suddenly dewing,
Billy declaimed, "General, you can do more to inspire the American people to a more spiritual way of life than any other man
alive!"

Throughout his two terms, Eisenhower kept on his bedside
table at the White House the Bible that Billy had delivered to
him in Denver, while Billy continued to assure him in crusade
messages, as he would go on to assure the Presidents to come
after, that "he has done more than realize our hopes that he
would become a spiritual leader. His prayer on Inauguration
Day, his faithful attendance at church and his participation in
other religious activities have encouraged the entire nation. The
people look upon him not as a politician, but as a spiritual
leader." In one *Hour of Decision* broadcast two months after the
inauguration, Graham went on to compare Eisenhower's first
foreign policy address to the Sermon on the Mount, and finally
even compared, in their capacities as righteous judges, the Lord
Himself to Ike. After making a brief sojourn to the Geneva Conference in 1955, Graham declared that "to see the President of
the United States kneeling in prayer at a church in Geneva
brought tears of joy to my eyes, and I said at the time, 'God will
be with that man at the Big Four Conference.' And He was."

At the same time, Graham himself had begun now to develop
the habit, in their periodic company together on golf courses
and at White House receptions, of casually proffering sugges-

tions to Eisenhower, such as recommendations once during a
White House luncheon on the juvenile delinquency problem.
"We just discussed it," Graham said afterward; "I had some ideas
and I wanted to put them to the President." Eisenhower entertained these extensions of advice with apparent good cheer. Indeed, he even consulted with Graham before his dispatch of federal troops into Little Rock in 1957.

On the whole, those years with Eisenhower proved the balm-
iest of Graham's career up to then. Not until 1969 would he
seem again quite so completely and comfortably suited to the
general temper of the nation. Presided over by a vest-suited rec-
titudinous figure with the starched respectability of a Sunday-
school superintendent, it was one of those orderly and monotone
interludes in the country's experience when, as Harding had
declared some thirty years earlier after World War One,
"America's present need is not heroics but healing; not surgery
but serenity; not nostrums but normalcy." If, also as in that insu-
lar calm during the early Twenties, there was again loose in the
air through the Fifties certain furtive dementias about "the Red
Menace" while deeper social combustions were quietly and profoundly gathering, the Eisenhower years nevertheless passed in
sedate domesticity. To such a time was Graham made to be The
Preacher, and it was then that his evangelism became fully accomplished as a continental institution. By 1958, some ten thousand letters a day were unsacking into his organizational complex in Minneapolis, which had compiled a mailing list of its own
of over a million names.

With the transition to John Kennedy in 1959, Graham's entente with the White House became somewhat more tenuous,
owing not a little to his conspicuous sympathies for Nixon during the campaign. But when the election was over, by December
he had responded with a glad nimbleness to Kennedy's invitation
to a round of golf in Palm Beach, where he wound up spending
six hours with him. With Kennedy's assumption of the presidency, Graham made an occasional appearance at a presidential
prayer breakfast, and persevered in his practice of stopping by
the White House before and after his expeditions abroad. As he

had urged Eisenhower to visit India after his own tour through there, he returned from Latin America in 1962 to recommend ambitiously that Kennedy undertake yet another presidential processional through those parts like the one JFK had mounted only a year before — "I just don't think the President has any conception of the impact of his visit!"

But what finally amounted, in a way, to his moment of closest communion with Kennedy came, as he reported after the shatter of shots that bright November noon in Dallas, when "last week I had such a strong feeling the President should not go to Texas, that I tried unsuccessfully to reach him through Senator Smathers. Senator Smathers wired me that the President would get in touch with me later. Then it occurred to me what a ridiculous thing it was, and I didn't pursue the matter." But what seemed then his dramatically oracular presentiment, he now specifies, "was actually not so much — ah, not so much that he would be harmed, actually. It was more a political premonition. Because I had just been to Dallas, and the political atmosphere seemed not at all favorable to his making a trip at that time." But if he had been endeavoring to convey merely a word of political counsel to Kennedy, he nevertheless declared after the far more fateful circumstance Kennedy met with there, "I was just getting ready to tee off on the golf course when I got the word of the President's death. Then I remembered my earlier fears. The premonition came back to my mind." And he added, "It was a terrible thing, but we must have a terrible shock sometimes to rouse us out of our spiritual neglect and apathy."

He wound up attending the funeral. "I sat with David Brinkley's wife. The way I got the invitation was through George Smathers. He called and said, 'Would you like to go to the President's funeral?' I said, 'Oh, my, it would be a great privilege.'"

Before a month was out, he had already passed a convivial five-hour visit with the new President, Lyndon Johnson, which had rambled on through dinner, and shortly thereafter, he was lauding Johnson as "the best-qualified man we've ever had in the White House" who would "provide moral leadership for the country. The President is a very religious person. He has attended many of our crusades, and he comes from a religious family." In this particular appreciation, Graham seemed as cheerfully oblivious of the bawdier Rabelaisian gustos of John-son's nature as he would prove, a few years after, equally unsens-ing of the cold artifices of his successor — as, indeed, he seemed congenitally innocent of all difficult qualifications that could complicate his most hopeful enthusiasms. At the most, Billy still insists, "Johnson might have said hell or damn a couple of times, but he'd look at me right away and say, 'Pardon me, preacher.' He had this side to him that was very religious — for instance, he loved to tell stories about preachers."

But if Graham had been only politely abided by Kennedy, he was enveloped by Johnson. As Billy himself relates, "I almost used the White House as a hotel when Johnson was President. He was always trying to keep me there," he reports not without delight; "he just wouldn't let me leave." Graham was constantly conducting private devotionals for Johnson at Camp David, and Johnson in turn would produce himself with a magisterial solem-nity at Billy's crusades now and then, reposing in a special flag-hung box. In 1965, when Graham was recovering from a pros-tate gland operation at the Mayo Clinic, Johnson phoned him several times in his room, and in May of the next year, when Gra-ham received the Big Brother of the Year Award at the White House, Johnson stood benevolently grinning at his side. For Billy's part, after Johnson had professed admiration for a pair of soft yellow pigskin golfing shoes he was wearing, "the next time I was in New York, I bought a pair of them in Mr. Johnson's size in every color available — six, I think — and sent them to him."

Bill Moyers, for a long time Johnson's press secretary and con-fidant, and himself a ministerial student once at a dusty little Southern Baptist seminary in Texas, remembers that he noticed between Johnson and Graham "an almost visceral attraction to each other." For one thing, both of them had made their way out of essentially the same Southern out-country obscurities to a na-tional eminence. And perhaps even more, as is often the case with such assertive public personalities, both of them had been raised by lavishly fond, genteel, staunch-willed women married to somewhat crasser men who were rather remote fathers to their sons. As a matter of fact, it had been the ardent and un-lagging aspiration of Johnson's own mother that he be a preacher. "I think he always wondered how he'd have turned out," Moyers speculates now, "what he'd have been like, if he'd been cleaner — if he'd gone the way his mother wanted, the way Billy went." It was as if Billy captivated him, then, as a gallant dramatic image of that unrealized and lost possibility of himself. "But then," observes Moyers with a wry smile, "Johnson looked on *everybody* as an extension, a possibility of himself. I even won-dered often myself — was I his young protégé, did he look on me as sort of his son, a version of his own youth again, or was I just another pair of hands and feet to him?"

In a sense beyond that, though, it was with Johnson that the peculiar nature of the symbiosis at work now between Graham and Presidents came into its full definition. Johnson himself was a personality of a proportion and complexity that would have in-vited Shakespeare: there was not a little of Lear about Lyndon — epic of ego, epic of exuberances and vision and generosities, epic of glooms and paranoias, capable of monumental self-illusions. All he wanted — ferociously — was to be the greatest President in the history of the Republic. But he turned out to be a kind of magnificent anachronism: a last praetorial Roman belonging to the old imperial integrities of duty, intrepidness, endurance, who happened to be lost and uncomprehending now in a subtler, milder season of measured commitment and rea-soned accommodation. Aside from his calamitous obsessions with Vietnam, it was not incidentally his misfortune to have sim-ply appeared at a more neurasthenic moment in the collective sensibilities of the nation — a hypersensitivity induced by the age's nervous ubiquitous media scrutinies — whereby he came to be dismissed for ebullient vulgarities that would have equally undone Andy Jackson or Abe Lincoln. Curiously enough, John-son himself seemed to sulk ponderously over such criticism, act-ing as if his manners did matter, disguising himself in public in the improbable and vaguely suspicious demeanor of an Epis-copal archbishop or an Ivy League dean of humanities.

All of this was precisely why he so cherished Graham. Answering to those same plain integrities from which Johnson acted, Graham gave back to him, as Johnson became progressively beleaguered by Vietnam and by his own misgivings about his actual fitness as a President, mirrorings of esteem and awe that confirmed for him his worthiness and fortitude. Johnson himself would later recall that whenever he "was being called a crook and a thug and all," he would invite Graham for a weekend and "we bragged on each other. I told him he was the greatest religious leader in the world, and he said I was the greatest political leader." As Moyers defines it now, "Billy Graham represented a basic kind of patriotism in this country — an unquestioning, obeying partiotism, a loyalty to the authority of the President. Billy was always uncritical, unchallenging, unquestioning. And this driven man, Johnson, was far more haunted about his deficiencies than anyone ever supposed. He found Billy filled a need. Johnson needed reminding from other people who were formidable that he was formidable." Nothing, finally, endeared anyone to Johnson like that particular reassurance — "and there were none of them around," says Moyers, "none of those impressive individuals, who were every quite so ready to do that as Graham."

Johnson would even sometimes dispatch a jet to loft Graham to his ranch to conduct services for him there, lodging Graham in a bedroom right above his own where, in the middle of the nights, Billy would awake into the measured and resonant rumble of the President of the United States snoring directly below him. On these visits, Johnson would spend the day hugely sweeping Billy along with him from enthusiasm to enthusiasm, "he'd even have me go along with him to count his eggs and his chickens," Johnson lobbing jelly beans into his mouth as he barged on, and with the same swooping expansiveness which produced all the large-hearted disarray of his Great Society benefactions, he would impress Billy into pitching down commodious pourings of buttermilk: "He'd made us all drink that buttermilk, he knew all that buttermilk would help us out."

Mostly, though, they would go whomping dustily over the

countryside in Johnson's Continental convertible — "once we
went for a ride that must have been sixty or seventy miles" —
careening across that terrain at the uncertain marge of desert,
rubbled hillsides under wizened trees and the occasional distant
slow flutter of a windmill, with Johnson periodically braying a
question about a Scripture verse and "I would say, 'It's not quite
like that, Mr. President, let me get my — here — my —'" turning
as he bounced in the seat to scrabble with one hand for his Bible.
It was as if Graham were caught up in Johnson's sheer engulfing
presence as he might be carried by some great blustering of wind
beyond his weight and will. "He said to me once, 'C'mon, Billy,
let's take us a ride,'" and shortly spanking over a lake in a motorboat, "Johnson drove that boat just as fast as he could get it to
go. He drove it absolutely wide open, looking all the while as if
he were half-drowsing. I was just about scared to death."

At the same time, Johnson himself was hardly undiscerning of
the peculiar compulsions, high or low, that happened to be at
play in the souls of other men. "That was Johnson's genius, and
part of his curse too," remarks another of his familiars in Washington. "When it came to dealing personally, psychologically,
with other men, he was like Bach working the organ pipes. But it
was also like he knew almost *too* much about human nature, too
much about the way people are, to have that higher perspective
to handle it." Whatever, in the course of his ministrations to
Johnson, Billy found he had never enjoyed quite so dazing an intimacy with the Olympian magnitudes of power in the Oval Office. "I remember one time when he was trying to get his budget
up," Graham recites, "and he said, 'Billy, you take this budget
here and tell me where I can get ten million dollars out of it. I
mean it. It's just beyond me. You tell me where, and I'll do it.'
And," Graham adds with perfect seriousness, "I'm quite confident he did mean it." During a dinner at the White House with
both Graham and Ruth on the evening before the 1964 Democratic Convention in Atlantic City, Johnson seemed sluggish and
sodden with forebodings of Robert Kennedy somehow spiriting
the convention out of his hands — "He was scared to death Bob
Kennedy would maybe come out with Jackie and just take the

thing by storm," says Billy. "I think I finally managed to set his mind at ease a little about that." Then, Billy continues, "he went down fourteen names with me that he was considering for Vice-President. 'Who do you think?' he asked me. Ruth kicked me under the table then, and Johnson noticed it. 'Now, why'd you kick him?' he asked her. She told him, 'I think Billy ought to limit his advice to you to religious and spiritual matters.' He said, 'Oh, I agree! I agree!' But then when dinner was over and the ladies had gone out ahead of us, he quietly closed the door for a second and turned and asked me, 'All right, what's your choice?' I said, 'Hubert Humphrey.' He just nodded. And you know, I've often wondered since then. . . ."

But Moyers remembers, "Billy, I sometimes noticed while the two of them were talking, seemed to have a touch of secret wickedness." Whenever Johnson, in the late hours of an evening, would lounge back in his chair idly twirling his glasses in one dangling hand, and begin rummaging forth certain more lickerish viscous confidences about other figures of prominence in his low, luxuriously browsing voice, Billy would lean forward listening with a rapt half-smile of unmistakable glee — hardly less a relish, actually, than Johnson's own roguish bemusement perusing those requisitioned FBI reports at night beside his bedside lamp. "It was an obvious delight Billy received," says Moyers, "that you could see in his eyes, from hearing Johnson tell him those little inside stories — and things like, 'You know what Brezhnev told me the other day? You know what Harold Wilson told me once?' He would have Billy completely riveted. And most of all, when he would let him in on state secrets, especially about the war — he'd say, 'Here's how I chose those bombing targets, Billy,' and there'd come this light in Billy's eyes."

As Moyers finally appraises the singular rapport that developed between Johnson and Graham, "Johnson always had a high appreciation of men as symbols. And Lyndon recognized that Billy was a symbol, a representative of a certain important constituency — that great middle of the country of respectable, churchgoing, decent middle-class people — who would see a measure of approval brought to him, Johnson, in the person of Billy Graham. Johnson was also uncannily shrewd about how vicarious identifications work among the American people, and how, when all those people saw Billy at the White House, it was as if they were there, they had been accepted into the Oval Office in the surrogate of Billy. He knew that if Billy were part of the White House ceremony, to that degree he had assimilated Billy's constituency. When he ran into issues particularly sensitive and difficult with that constituency — like the poverty program — he would hoist Billy Graham up the flagpole. Every man became a metaphor to him — a political metaphor, in the classic Greek sense of politics. Westmoreland was his general, his soldier. Fortas was his Jew. Thurgood Marshall was his Negro. And Billy was his preacher. So for a man who lived in symbols like Johnson, if a man comes clothed in symbols like Billy did, you never have to ask that man to do anything for you: he's done everything just by being there. And anybody who could help Johnson without any actual money changing hands he was extraordinarily fond of. So Billy didn't have to do anything to help him, and Billy, in turn, never asked him for a thing. He was helped by being there as much as Johnson was helped by having him there. They were also both quite aware of this exchange that took place in their association and meetings — it was tacit, they never had to mention it. I remember thinking a lot of times as I watched them, it must be the way contracts are worked in the Mafia."

All the while he was dwelling in this special communion with the President of the United States, Graham was also increasingly indulging in other clerical collaborations in ceremonies of authority, such as assisting in the inaugural program for John Connally when he was inducted into the governorship of Texas. Graham had come, in fact, to be greatly entranced by Connally — himself a towering theatrical figure, one of those poor boys who'd crossed over into the company of the merchant princes, with a huge splendid squinting grin and an art for a ferocious, if slightly inexplicit, persuasiveness. Graham even eventually proclaimed, "Connally has the necessary abilities to be President of the United States. But I'm not making an endorsement; I'm just giving advice to the Democratic Party."

Graham's customary way of denoting his selective approval of various other candidates was to invite them up to Montreat for breakfast, as he did with Jesse Helms during his Senate race, or, as with North Carolina's lieutenant governor Bob Scott during his campaign for the governorship, beckoning them up to nearby Asheville for coffee, a chat, a two-stroke golf lesson. Scott, who went on to win the election, recollects now, "I wanted his endorsement, yeah. I wouldn't have asked him really, except I thought as long as he was heppin' them out so much up there at the White House, maybe he could hep out one of the local boys. Him and his people were a little reluctant at first, but he did finally allow me to come up and play a few holes of golf with him." An old colleague of Scott's adds, "I remember when that happened, but did Bob also happen to mention that was the first game of golf he'd ever played in his life? First thing, he sailed one off the tee right off into the rough and he walks over there and sets his ball to tee up right there again. Graham and his people looked at each other a second but didn't say anything."

Actually, Billy had been mightily tempted to enlist himself directly in Nixon's campaign in 1960 — and when he was besieged, in 1964, with some sixty thousand telegrams just in one day, to declare himself for Goldwater, Johnson thought it prudent to deliver to him the small admonition, "Now, Billy, you stay out of politics." In fact, during the rest of that campaign, says Billy, "he pretty well kept me locked up. He even kept me right in the White House on the weekend before the election." Finally, while Johnson and Graham were lolling in the swimming pool at Camp David one weekend when Johnson was feeling particularly embattled, he casually unfurled to Billy the ultimate titillation. "He said to me all of a sudden, 'Billy, you know, *you're* the man to become President of the United States. You're the only one who could bring 'em all together. If you ever decide to run, I'll be your manager." Graham insists, "He was very serious at the time. But of course, I took it as a half-joke. I knew I would be getting out of God's will for my life to even begin considering anything like that."

But simply from his ever-more-conspicuous involvements in the nation's political commerce, there inevitably began to ripple rumors of his being seriously approached to run for the presidency himself. And around February of 1964, word appeared that he was actually pondering a run for the office. "The first person who ever really mentioned it to me," says Billy, "was John Glenn once at the Spacecraft Center in Houston. Of course, I appreciated his saying that, but I certainly didn't take it very seriously." Nevertheless, one Graham source soon indicated, "He is deeply interested in the opportunity for service, and deeply distressed by other things that necessarily are involved in such a decision. He is giving prayerful consideration to the idea," and if he were to accept a draft, "it would be as a Republican."

Shortly thereafter, while Graham acknowledged he had at least mulled the prospect, he announced he had decided against it. It subsequently emerged that about the only significant party who seemed to have soberly promoted this whimsy had been H. L. Hunt — though the *U.S. News & World Report* did indulge in a brief assessment of his possibilities. After he declared his rejection of the notion, one of Graham's more persistent critics, the *Christian Century,* observed, "This denial of an intention nobody except perhaps a few of his entourage suspected he entertained was remarkable. Why should he publicly disavow so improbable a possibility? . . . That he should feel it necessary after such reflection publicly to take himself out of a race few even dreamed he might enter indicates just how far out of touch with political reality a man who stands in front of crowds can get."

In the end, though, Graham had retained at least the minimal canniness to sense that he "would be a terrible flop in politics." Besides that, as Graham noted in 1958 after being approached to run for the Senate, "Why should I demote myself to be a Senator?"

Indeed, he had arrived at an elevation of his own now above all factions and parties, above the scrabblings and caprices of political fortune — as a transcendent high chaplain to each succes-

sive order of authority in the land: an enduring pastoral Ma-
zarin, in jade cufflinks and Countess Mara ties, to the national
community of power.

In that late winter of 1968, a few months after Johnson's abdication and before the inauguration of Richard Nixon, Graham's original presidential patron, Eisenhower, lay dying in a
hospital suite at Walter Reed and Graham was summoned to his
bedside. "I was on my way to Vietnam," says Billy, "and Nixon
asked me to go see him, so I went." On a cold glassy December
morning, Graham was conducted in for his last consultation with
Eisenhower, this time to perform the final service of comforting
and blessing his imminent departure into the shades. "All the old
glories seemed far from him then," recalls Billy. "He was starting
a journey of a totally different kind." Eisenhower said to him in
a dimmed and dwindled voice, his eyes watering, "Billy, give
those ole doughboys in Vietnam a message from me when you
see them. Tell them there's an old soldier back here at Walter
Reed who's pulling for them and wishes he could be there with
them." But then, his eyes welling over, his voice faltering — terrible, indeed, the random dreams and reveries that visit those
last hours of all old generals — he implored Graham, "How can
I know I'm going to heaven? How can I be sure, Billy, absolutely
sure, that my sins are forgiven?" Graham reached out and took
Eisenhower's chill hand, and held it firmly while "I told him his
whole past was forgiven, I assured him he need not worry about
any of his past sins, and I prayed for him." And with that, says
Graham, "he looked up at me with the tears still in his eyes but
with that famous big broad Eisenhower grin, and said, 'Thank
you, Billy. I'm ready.'"

Then, a few weeks later, on Johnson's last weekend at the
White House, Billy was fetched up to attend him as he restlessly
lumbered and loomed through his final empty hours in those
bare offices and halls and imperial chandeliered rooms, spending the last night there with him, and then accompanied him the
next morning out the white-columned portico and on to the inauguration service, standing beside Johnson through the proceedings until the climactic oath and conferral of power to

Nixon, whereupon he stepped forward and delivered the invocation for this new administration. And when Nixon arrived at the White House, Graham was there to greet him in the foyer. Having stayed with Johnson his last night there, he now stayed with Nixon his first night — spanning with his actual presence the shifting and completion of the transition in national governments like the abiding avatar of some unwritten continuing folk covenant and consecration.

With this transition, in fact, ahead of Graham now, for all his amicable associations with Eisenhower and Johnson, was the true high solstice of his ministry and his moment in the life of the country. It had been early in 1952, while he was having lunch with North Carolina Senator Clyde Hoey in the Senate Cafeteria, that a slender, dark, deacon-sober figure had quickly shadowed past their table, and Hoey muttered to Graham, "There goes that young Senator Nixon from California. I'd like for you to meet him." Hoey hailed him over and introduced them to each other. "Yes," Nixon rang, "I've heard about you and I approve of what you're doing. By the way, do you play golf? Would you like to go with me for a few rounds at Burning Tree this afternoon? George Smathers is going to join me there, and if you're free . . ."

Graham accepted with precipitous eagerness. Then after they had finished several holes, Nixon drove Graham back through Washington in the ebbing sunlight of the late spring afternoon to his own house, where they sat, Nixon taking sips from a cup of coffee, Graham cradling a Coke, "talking about things for several hours more. Then he asked me where I was staying, and I told him the Fairfax, and he drove me on back to my hotel."

They struck an immediate mutual affinity, found they hummed to profoundly common frequencies. Both of them neat and energetic young noteworthies from modest but righteous homes, both of them emphatic and didactic of nature, they seemed made up of remarkably the same wall-sampler reverences and homilies. Beyond that, Nixon had now gained, from his recent interrogations as a kind of Cold War Torquemada in committee hearings, an impressive altitude in Washington's firmament of consequence, to the point of being cited now as a possible nominee for Vice-President at the Republican Convention late that summer. Graham himself would remark yet again during a moment of somber reflection in 1958, "You know, it would be a tragedy if through the wiles of Satan, I should be led into anything that might be construed as political. . . ." But, as a mutual acquaintance observed in later years, "Richard Nixon and Billy Graham were simply two pieces cut from the same American apple pie. They were just naturally fated to gravitate together at some point in their lives."

II

At the same time, even through the course of his ascent into the high halls of power, he kept his own immediate world self-contained and detached — out of that abiding dread of ever allowing himself to be actually claimed by the common theater of mere mortality. Throughout his prominent politial vicarages, yet he felt compelled to profess that, while he had been offered ambassadorships and even Cabinet posts, he had only "accepted an invitation to serve on the hospital authority in my own hometown. Other than that, I have not done anything political. I do a lot of little things to try to maybe help a President, primarily in the spiritual and moral area, but I feel that my role is of a preacher, a spiritual influence on whatever President is there."

This apartisan posture that he vigorously affected may have been not a little vital to a general popular geniality toward his crusade ministry. But even in his assumption into the American galaxy of pop-stardom, Graham remained all the while scrupulously wary of ever coming to actually belong to its thrall. When he was blandished by NBC once in 1954 with a proposal to host a "homespun" show patterned after Arthur Godfrey's for $1 million a year over five years, he was, according to intimates, "actually in terror" until he could reject the offer. He maintains, "Why, I could make I don't know how many millions of dollars a

year in television. The offers I've had from Hollywood are astounding. The president of Paramount Pictures once gave this
huge banquet for me with all these big movie-stars there, and
said he'd like to make a movie-star of me. Cecil B. DeMille
wanted me to play some part in *Samson and Delilah,* in fact — an
important supporting part. But I just laughed. I told them I was
staying with God. And Mr. DeMille told me afterward that he
knew all along that I would say that, and he said it had restored
his faith." In the end, in both his celebrity and all his consortings
with the powerful of the land, he seemed engaged more in a
kind of interminable, delicious, but perseveringly chaste coquetry: *I could have it if I wanted it. As long as I don't really want it,
as long as I don't take it, I could still have it if I decided.* . . .

Instead, even as he continued to flourish as a magazine-cover
phenomenon and a ministerial medium to Presidents and commercial potentates, he steadily constructed around him his own
personal institutional universe in which to dwell — his own alternative, improved version of a world, expansive and dynamic
enough to replace that gamier, more treacherous one that he
had forevermore abjured. It was not unlike that compulsion of
certain other public men, who also in their varying ways have
found the common reality inadequate to their hopes or tastes, to
contrive a cosmos of their own intact from any intrusions of
other visions, other wills — the recourse of Howard Hughes, of
other confounded and miscarried men of power like Judge Roy
Hofheinz of Houston, who finally enclosed himself in his Astrodome with its own fantasy culture in its own precisely tuned
climate, all hermetically sealed to obliterate any sabotaging
vagaries of raw nature in reckless flux outside.

With Graham, this inversion into an alter world of his own
handiwork took the form of his personal incorporation into the
Billy Graham Evangelistic Association. From that shoebox
stuffed overnight in Grady Wilson's hotel-room dresser in Portland in 1950, it proliferated in time into a megacomplex of an-
cillary agencies and enterprises with a budget, by the late Seventies, of some $40 million. It amounted to a vast privately ordered
society of Graham's own, complete unto itself — his own com-

munications network, with his weekly *Hour of Decision* broadcasts carried on some 900 stations around the world, his crusades televised three or four times a year over 310 metropolitan areas holding 90 percent of the potential audience, "about the exposure General Mills achieves for Wheaties," as one BGEA official declares; his own movie studio, World Wide Pictures, which has produced some one hundred films, including promotional documentaries, and his own publishing house, World Wide Publications; his own inspirational monthly magazine, *Decision*, distributed in six languages and Braille to some five million readers; a dominion, in fact, with its own population of some eight million souls enrolled on the computers of the Minneapolis headquarters; all this sustained by a self-operating economy, not only of donations, but of subsidiary enterprises like the Grason Company, a mail-order operation offering sacred recordings and sheet music, books by and about Graham, Bibles with prefaces by Graham, miscellaneous gift volumes like *Casseroles I Have Known*, calendars with portraits of team members like Barrow and Shea "in action," small gold lapel crosses, home wall plaques of "rustic plastic" with mottos like "Divine services will be conducted here daily," albums of musical scores from the films produced by World Wide Pictures, recorded readings of the entire New Testament, even "spiritual comic books."

Within this private realm, Graham even presides over something like his own system of providence — dispensing from its treasury intercessions of relief and succor to spots over the earth stricken by calamity, earthquakes in Guatemala and Rumania, famines in Africa, along with various benefactions to missionaries and seminaries, overseas students and halfway houses in Mexico. Roy Gustafson, his old compatriot from the days at Temple Terrace, who was himself eventually inducted into BGEA, recalls that he once approached Graham about a new electrical generating system for a missionary hospital in Jordan, Graham then inquiring, "How much do you think it's gonna take?" and when Gustafson submitted a little uncertainly, "Well, I'm afraid it really can't be done for under twenty-five thousand dollars, Billy," Graham blithely snapped, "Okay. We'll send 'em five thousand dollars a month for five months, do it like that." In distributing these grants of grace about, as Graham instructed Gustafson, "I want you to call me whenever you see a need anywhere, now, Roy, just call me day or night — I have a note pad right beside my bed."

Gustafson himself, before he was brought into BGEA as one of Graham's circle of associate evangelists, had toured for a while with Billy Sunday's old assistant, Homer Rodeheaver, playing "Carnival of Venice" on his cornet at services. Since coming in from that cold, as it were, he has been comfortably established in a bayside villa-home in St. Petersburg, his discreetly sumptuous living room with its sliding glass doors looking out on a shuffleboard court, a dock, and the twinkling of the bay. A large capacious figure with a bland bespectacled face of a soft gardenia-petal texture, a faint blur of white hair over his high sleek forehead, he has rather the look of some reincarnated priest or astrologer from a Mesopotamian temple. Sitting one afternoon in his living room — wearing beltless bagging blue jeans and a butter-yellow polo shirt, cherry-red lounging slippers on his feet — he reminisced amiably about his early days of battering about the country as a freebooting revival cornetist: "A lot of these young evangelists today, they don't know what it really used to be like. When you'd go into a town, it was rough, you never knew what kind of reception you were going to get, you had to worry that the wind didn't blow your tent down." But it seemed a curiously implausible nostalgia of Gustafson's now. Presently there noiselessly pittered into the room on twiglike legs a taut little shivery Chihuahua that looked more like an insect than any mammal, which Gustafson scooped up in one large hand and kept then cuddled between his legs, as he talked on with the precise and sonorous elocution of a radio announcer: "When Billy hires you, he sets you free. He told me back then, 'The only boss you've got now, Roy, is God — God, and me.' "

This free-form arrangement led, in Gustafson's case, to some discomfiture once when he took it on himself to begin acting as a kind of informal BGEA chaplain to the government forces in the field in Rhodesia — this discovered at a press conference there during which another BGEA representative was photographed with a magnum pistol tucked somewhat swashbucklingly into his boot-top. About the ensuing furor, Gustafson merely vows now, "I'll never talk to another press person as long as I live. They just seemed so *sincere*. And then they went and wrote all those stories. . . ." Greatly unnerved by the whole affair, Gustafson was admonished by Graham afterward, "When anybody asks you who you're working for, Roy, you just tell them from now on that you're working for Jesus Christ. That's all you have to tell them."

Along with Gustafson, Graham kept assembled around him his old troupe of associates — Barrows, Shea, Grady and T. W. Wilson. In general, explains another of Graham's retainers, "All of us feel a tremendous responsibility always to uphold in our own lives the kind of integrity that has been the hallmark of Billy's ministry." The other assistant evangelists and aides in BGEA all tended to be selected, not only for their verve and unflappably chipper demeanor, but also for their ability "to make a good appearance." As a BGEA functionary pointed out once, "Not that appearance makes a better man, but it reduces the limitations a man faces if he is to present himself well." What this corps of auxiliaries in BGEA presents, actually, are varied reflections and refractions of Graham himself, like a company of demiclones of his own person and personality.

In fact, all the formidable logistics of Graham's evangelistic conglomerate finally come to an operation monumentalizing his particular vision of life. In the midst of the great national tempests of the mid-Sixties, Graham's World Wide Pictures produced the "contemporary" saga of *The Restless Ones,* narrating the struggles of a backsliding son of good family who becomes disastrously enamored of an "ultrasophisticated" girl, a scenario eventually involving teenage vandalism in a church, a young girl who gets pregnant by a truck driver, a courtroom crisis occasioned by juvenile drinking, a suicide attempt, and, at last, the deus-ex-machina denouement of everyone attending a Billy Graham crusade. Such dramas, on the whole, reflect Graham's sense of what life and mankind's condition are made up of; his vision of how the world and the human heart actually work.

It is in this dialectic of reality, battened fast against any larger possibilities of human experience, that all of Graham's people live as a kind of bureaucratic commune of well-groomed righteousness within the immense preserve of his organization. Their only sense of any mystery at work in life ranges no farther than incessant reports among themselves of wondrous and pleasant coincidences — such incidents as a family of nine arriving for a crusade to find the coliseum filled and the doors locked, only to have a man suddenly thrust his head out of a parted door just as they were leaving to say he had nine spare tickets if they could use them ("Praise the Lord, wasn't that a miracle?") — to, at the most, a certain appreciation for blank dead ends of the terrible: at the mention of a particularly gifted and perceptive writer, Noel Houston, who had turned out a less-than-benign two-part profile of Graham for *Holiday* in 1958, Graham's face briefly took on a grave and remote look — "Yes, and you know, very soon after those articles of his came out, he dropped dead of a heart attack."

Any subtleties or ambiguities beyond this simple sensibility they regard more or less as gossamers of the Devil, himself a creature of infinite sophistication and elegance. Graham himself describes how he has come to sense Satan's nature in his own experience: "Charming. Attractive. Cunning. Sensible. Argumentative. Very sophisticated. Very intelligent." It may be for that reason that anyone with too expansive and adventuresome a spirit and wit is finally, hopelessly alien to Graham's people, as if such natures affronted them with intimations of some lusty unordered energy dimly subversive.

Equally generic to Graham's enthusiasms, and elemental to maintaining the vigor of his evangelism over the years, has been a certain cheerful imprecision in his apprehension of the actual — some lack of a final fine close-focus register in his sense of things. With both himself and his operatives, impressions and reactions are all large and easy and broad-stroke; it's as if they move through some bright cartoon strip of reality. In Graham's invariable Roman-candle excitements about the outcomes of his crusades, there persists a kind of indiscriminately ebullient imperviousness to the precise particulars — after a crusade, he is always, unfailingly, "astonished . . . amazed" by its results, ". . . beyond anything I had ever anticipated!" After every campaign, he will declare it "the most rewarding and thrilling of my ministry . . . the most exciting and dramatic crusade we have ever held."

But it's not really shamming or flimflamming — it is simply his native instinct, as a friend explained once, "to ignore everything that doesn't fit into the pattern of the best and the ideal." Graham's old associate from his student days, Jimmie Johnson, reflects, "The thing about Billy, I don't know how many of us who've been with him he's told, 'You'll never know how much your ministry has meant to me. It made all the difference! If it hadn't been for you — I'd never have gone into evangelism!' And then he'll say, 'I want to kneel right now, right here, and just thank the Lord you came along, that *you were there!*' " With a wry flicker of a smile, Johnson notes, "At least *twenty different people* I've heard him tell that to at one time or another — every time, absolutely sincere. That's just Billy. It's his natural generosity, his extravagance of heart and outlook. He just feels an impulse to give that to you — to *award* that congratulations to whomever has meant anything at all at any point in the wonderful thing that turned out to happen to him." Perhaps more than anything else, it is this congenital, invincible, hearty imprecision of feelings, of perception, that has accounted for almost everything boggling in Graham's public professions over the years.

But also perhaps for that reason, despite Graham's spectacular prosperity as a journalistic phenomenon, the press itself remains to Graham's people, by the very nature and order of its curiosities, an inherently foreign and suspect agent. It has amounted to an excruciatingly gingerly relationship. Their chariness derives, at least in part, out of a certain lamblike naïveté: after the *National Inquirer,* perhaps the most famously cheesy tabloid in the country, ran a story about Billy's early infatuations that considerably distressed his people, Roy Gustafson earnestly inquired of a passing caller, "The publisher is not a believer, is he?" But Graham's own public relations operatives, maintaining beneath their meticulous cordialness an unrelenting wariness of the press, are engaged in a peculiar exertion of polite, unflagging defensiveness, acute to the point of neurosis — at a crusade service one evening, a secretary sitting at the press table, penciling in corrections on Graham's printed sermon text for his press director, quickly clamped both palms over these innocuous notations with a kind of fierce thinly smiling casualness at the idle glance of a newsman beside her.

Within this hothouse insularity of meanings, what would pass as utterly incidental in the exterior world often takes on, by their own abstruse reference points, the most curlicued implications — sets off the most unexpected and eccentric decibels and detonations. This happens most often in their exorbitant sensitivity to any connotations of impropriety or indelicacy. T. W. Wilson managed to take extraordinary umbrage at one particular monograph, purportedly the chronicle of a day in a Graham crusade, that could not have seemed more abjectly admiring, T. W. fuming, "He had these little things in there like Billy in his motel room alone with his secretary" — the only spot from which T. W. could have possibly taken this meaning being a single sentence, *"Graham is in the middle of dictating a note to Stephanie Wills when Cliff Barrows walks into the room."* "He makes out in his book like he was right with us all the time during the crusade," T. W. continued, "but all we saw of him that whole week was he waved to us once. And he wrote all this stuff about the things in Billy's house, thermal baths and whatnot. All he did was, I just drove him up there for a few minutes one morning, couldn't have been more than a half-hour, and he went to the bathroom once, that's all." Somehow T. W. had succeeded in divining, even in this diligently deferential and wholly inoffensive little volume, intonations of malice and ill will.

But if Billy and his company seem to abide in their own rather contracted reality, that isolation is also a kind of reflex to the sheer stupendous public scale of his evangelistic effort. All the diverse energies at work in Graham's personal Christian dominion are mostly orchestrated from the central administrative center in Minneapolis — two blocks, in a somewhat drab downtown section, of aged brick buildings, the main one inherited from Standard Oil in the Fifties, the others reconverted automobile showrooms and garages. However unprepossessing its dim facades, this compound, with a staff of some 470, serves now as something like the combination Vatican and Pentagon of Graham's ministry, plotting and staging all his major evangelistic offensives, deploying the numerous subsidiary minicrusades conducted by his supporting repertory of associate evangelists.

Inside its clinically neat offices, with rubber plants and portraits of Graham and the current President appointed about in a shadowless aspirin-white brightness of fluorescent lighting, the atmosphere is immaculate of any whiffs of cigarette smoke, with a connecting walkway across an alley enclosed against any stray street-funks in its own thermostat-preserved springtime. Within this bastion of pleasantness — the lobbies and corridors electronically monitored by a security system, panels of control buttons to release locked doors — all employees, including the janitors, commence each working day with ten minutes of Bible reading and private prayer, typists, computer programmers, adding-machine operators beseeching the Almighty to "help us this day to do good and accurate work in using this machine in Thy service." Particular "prayer needs" of employees — incidents of illness, the demise of loved ones, the departure of children for college — are announced for general attention over the public-address system, and everyone gathers collectively at least once a week for a service in the compound's chapel.

The operations here — originally designed after Billy Sunday's organization, which in one survey was ranked the fifth most efficient concern in the nation, right after the National Cash Register company — are directed by George Wilson, Graham's former business manager at Northwestern Schools, a spry chubby steward once described by Graham as a kind of carbonated Pepsi-Christian, "more bounce to the ounce than any

other Christian I know." What he is occupied in, Wilson explains, is "dispensing the world's greatest product with the greatest economy to the greatest number of people as fast as possible." As T. W. Wilson once put it a bit more smackingly, "Too
much work done in the name of Christ is rundown, baggy-
trousers stuff. Billy believes in going first class." Accordingly,
Graham's ministry is administered from Minneapolis in a manner that has become a mix of IBM, McCann-Erickson, Sears Roebuck, Blue Cross, and the morning devotionals at Vacation Bible
School.

From these offices there is conducted a gargantuan mail-order
ministry so imposingly efficient that both Republican and Democratic political technicians, even Madison Avenue nabobs, have
made pilgrimages there for enlightenments. Virtually any contact with Graham whatsoever — from responses to the offers of
free books and pamphlets at his crusade services, to the inquirers
who come forward to be recorded at his invitations — instantly
translates onto the BGEA master mailing list. From this list,
some 100,000,000 pieces of mail are sent out each year, with an
annual in-tide of 2,500,000 letters — 100,000 a day after televised crusades. These letters are separated between nondonors
and donors — usually about 77 percent of them, with each dona-
tion averaging about eight dollars, the checks and cash totaled
separately and a report of these totals, along with the number of
contributions, delivered to George Wilson's desk at the end of
each day.

All the names that accrete onto the mailing list — from peti-
tions for counsel or prayer, from crusade conversions, from
every conceivable wafting of induced interest — periodically re-
cieve from Graham himself such appeals as "Paul considered it
just as spiritual to talk about finances as he did about the Resurrection. One fifth of all the teachings of Christ was given over to
money and stewardship. The importance of giving money to the
Lord's work is one of the basic teachings of the New Testament.
Therefore, I make no hesitation to ask you in the name of
Christ, point blank, to continue helping us maintain this extensive ministry." Acknowledgments of contributions are made,

then, within thirty-six hours: "If you don't show gratitude promptly," one official explained, "they stop giving."

Graham's first actual payment for uttering the gospel, when he was still a student down at Temple Terrace preaching in tabernacles and trailer-court missions, came to exactly $2.25, lick-sealed into a plain white envelope and shoved into his clumsily startled hand. He carried it around with him for several days, in fact, for some reason profoundly queasy about even opening it. "I wasn't sure then that a preacher really ought to accept money for preaching the gospel," he recollects. "There seemed too much joy, too much pleasure, just to have the privilege to preach the gospel, for one to get money for it too." He finally pleaded of Dean Minder, "But how can I make a *charge*, accept a *fee*, for preaching God's word?" and Minder quickly assured him "Did the Lord ordain that they who proclaim the gospel should *live of the gospel too?*" After ruminating over that for a moment, Billy withdrew the envelope, now rumpled and linty, plucked off the flap, shook out the $2.25 into his palm, and plumped it into his pocket. Not long after that, an old friend in Charlotte remembers, when a collection was taken for him at one service and the plate brought back to him after his sermon, he quickly scooped out the bills and stuffed them in his coat pocket, whooping, "That's great, I need to make a payment on my car!" When someone once smuggled $300 into his coat during an early evangelistic foray, it even precipitated a tiff with Ruth over whether they would use it to take a holiday down on the Ocean Forest Hotel at Myrtle Beach, Billy stalking about and declaiming, "Well, you can do whatever you want to. I'm going."

But as Graham frequently recites now, "I began to get some very, *very* large love-offerings in those early days" — he winding up with $16,000 after his six-week stand in Portland in 1950. Finally, at the conclusion of a crusade in Atlanta four months later, the Atlanta *Constitution* featured a pair of photographs on its front page, grinning ushers hefting up plump collection sacks in one of them, and in the other, Graham himself about to stoop into his car to head back home, with an equally broad grin on his face. When Graham glimpsed this picture spread, he was appalled. "It absolutely knocked him to his knees in tears," says one intimate. With that, he swiftly improvised a plan to totally incorporate his apostleship and, though Ruth and three of his associates happened to be installed on its board of directors, he put himself on a straight salary.

Since then, he has been careful to maintain an appearance of seemly moderateness in his own material circumstances. Through the Fifties, he abstained from investing in any stocks and bonds, even avoided having a savings account, declaring in 1958, "We intend to leave behind nothing that accrued during my ministry." It was usually the case then that all the money he personally had to his name was contained in his checking account at the bank down in Black Mountain, compiled from his salary, which had been computed to be approximately equivalent to the upper-middle-class figure that would be accorded to the pastor of a leading church in a large city. Even so, a bank clerk was frequently phoning Ruth to mention haltingly that the account seemed somehow sort of overdrawn.

At the same time, though, for all this circumspection in his personal means, neither has it worked out that he has ever been substantially bereft of any of this world's goods. After he was ordained at twenty as a Southern Baptist minister in a pond-side clapboard church in Florida, it had not escaped his contemplations that, not only "could I now conduct funerals, baptize converts, and marry people," but there were "other advantages. I could travel at half-fare on the railway, play golf free at many golf courses, and get laundry and dry-cleaning done at ten percent off." In time, he had also discovered, as Grady Wilson noted of their early days on the road, "about every town we'd go to, the car dealers would always furnish cars for us, the business folk would tell us, 'We'll look after you boys; don't worry about anything.'" However unpresumptuous Graham has kept his own means, he has continued to fare rather painlessly and agreeably on those kinds of consideration from other parties. He was able to return from his sojourn through India in 1956 luxuriously to find his new mountainside home already completed and awaiting him as, largely, the gift of ten businessmen, including the new road curling up to it — he having contributed only an incidental measure out of his proceeds from the sale of his first book, *Peace with God*. His study itself was the present of a contractor whom he had never seen.

"I have tried to make it a practice not to accept gifts of money," he insisted on one occasion, "but there are just so many other gifts —" including, he went on to mention, a new Buick from a local dealer; wardrobes from local haberdasheries, ties from a local department store, with one couple in Texas providing him with a new suit for each crusade. Finally in 1970, he turned out to be, along with one of the ten most admired, also one of the year's ten best-dressed men. He protested on his return from a stay in the Virgin Islands, "I just don't know how it happened. Nearly all my clothes are given to me. I don't think I've bought a suit of clothes for four or five years. I did buy a sport coat once — a yellow coat — because the people on the TV want me to wear more colorful clothes." Beyond that, he also seemed to move through a ceaseless falling manna of golf clubs, stereos, silver services from foreign dignitaries, which have accumulated in a kind of cornucopian conglomerate profusion in storage rooms and showcases at his offices down the slope at Montreat.

As a matter of fact, there was a spot of conversation with the IRS in 1973 over his returns for '65, '66, '69, and '70, the IRS citing what seemed to be appearances for undeclared income from such solicitudes as "construction work performed free of charge . . . decorator's work performed free of charge . . . clothing received as gifts from stores in Charlotte and Asheville." Graham agreeably professed unwitting and inadvertent omission of these items, and since that small awkwardness, Graham says now, "I insist on being audited every year. It's by my own request. I've instructed my lawyers not to contest any gray areas." He allows there may have been a touch of difficulty over this back in 1973, "yes — but I'm not accepting any gifts anymore. See this suit?" — and he briefly plucks up a pinch of his ash-blue worsted trousers, fingering the material — "I've slept in this suit, I guess, about twenty times. I've had it about six or seven years; Ruth bought it for me in Honolulu." Carefully smoothing his pantsleg back out, he adds, "Now, of course, I just got a lot of denim clothes that just came in a couple of days ago from Johnny Cash — about a dozen cardboard boxes, and when I opened them up, they were full of nothing but denim clothes, jackets and jeans and things like that. But I'm not, uh, I'm not gonna declare *that* — I mean, I don't think that's hardly what could be considered undeclared income now."

But contrary to the cliché-cynicism about Graham most familiarly belabored over the years, he is, in the end, hardly a mercenary. A vast number of commentators have found it somehow impossible to account for him without that factor. But if he has chosen in the past not strenuously to abjure the convenient and comfortable either, it is still a failure of perception to understand him in those terms, as a profiteer. He is far more earnest than that, and precisely for that reason, the earthly ease in which he finds himself has persisted as a particular ague of fretfulness in his soul.

According to Ruth, "Bill literally spends hours, *hours,* trying to figure out how not to make money. He has tried harder than anyone else I've ever known *not* to make money." Along with an annual salary of around $39,500 and the income from his newspaper column, *My Answer,* he came by around a quarter of a million dollars from the sale of land left to him by his father. As Graham points out, he would really have no need to own property himself: "I have friends all over the world who are always asking me to come and stay with them" — among them his daughter's father-in-law, a Swiss-Armenian financier named Ara Tchividjian, who has five residences himself in Switzerland, one in the Miami environs, and three in France. Yet Graham has somehow wound up acquiring $420,000 worth of acreages himself in North Carolina, with another home donated to him in California by an admirer. Nevertheless, Graham's family pastor in Montreat declares, "He just drives himself nuts worrying all the time about whether he's got too much."

For one thing, Graham himself acknowledges, "I *can't* make too much money for public relations reasons, as well as spiritual ones. My salary, for instance, and the little else I might be worth, somebody reads about that over in India or a country like that, it seems like a fortune to them, I'm a millionaire." More than that, though, "Ruth and I were talking just the other night, 'What are we going to do with all this? All this property and everything else?' We already have too much. We worry all the time about our standard of living — how much we could do without, how much we *should* do without. I'm not afraid of poverty. I have struggled and struggled to keep my income down, yet I'm always embarrassed by how much I have."

Still, he has not been able to bring himself to relinquish any of those embarrassments. It's as if he continues to defer, in the end, to that dispensation pronounced by Minder decades ago, *"Did the Lord ordain that they who proclaim the gospel should have to live of the gospel too?"* At the most, it has become the same kind of ambivalent and interminably inconclusive tantalization in which he has been caught with those other spells of the world, fame and power — another of the tensions in which he is forevermore hung, his nature split in this instance between the ascetic Puritan pieties and the equally immemorial American mythos of the Gatsbian fancies. At a conference of Christian workers convened one morning in a large urban sanctuary during a crusade, Graham declared from the pulpit, "It seems that everywhere I touch, money, money, money comes!" — he fluttering his fingers about him in the air as he said this, as if magician-like casting forth bouquets and rainbows out of invisibility, summoning with mere finger ripplings blossoms from bare earth — "but like Dwight L. Moody said once, 'God will allow millions of dollars to pass through my hands if none of it sticks to me.' " But privately, he still can not resist musing to visitors, interviewers, "You know, Bill Mead, he's on our board of directors, I was talking to him the other day, and he said I could be worth fifty million dollars if I wanted to be. I'm always just a few strokes of a pen away from being a multimillionaire — just a few signatures, that's all. I'm in a position to get awfully rich, just like that —" and he gave a light wave of his hand "— that easy. And I mean, really, *really* rich."

Beyond this lingering half-beguilement, though, the real difficulty in which his resources have entangled Graham is a larger and more serious liability that is simply implicit in the ambitiousness of Graham's evangelism itself. Out of his innate veneration of the Mass Affirmation, the grandiose means he has mobilized to prosecute his ministry as widely as possible are almost inevitably assumed by many to be the purpose of that ministry in themselves: the means are constantly taken to be the end. Too, the sheer elaborateness of all his resources — the computered solicitation techniques, the investment portfolios, the $40-million-a-year budget — necessarily occasions a certain inescapable awkwardness for anyone purporting to be, after all, merely an apostle of Christ's gospel. Some elemental misrhyme between the two seems to keep nagging. This problem has inevitably produced an inclination — indeed, almost a desperation — to minimize somehow, if not disguise, such unfortunate appearances: specifically, embarrassment over those means has entailed Graham more than once in a certain deviousness, as when he was asked about BGEA's total financial picture by the Charlotte *Observer* in 1977, which prompted him to dissemble by omission — refraining from mentioning his $23 million benevolent fund in Texas on the specious technicality, he later protested, that it was an operation incorporated independently of BGEA.

What it all arises from finally — all the boards and offices and financial machineries — is that central activating principle of Graham's whole life and ministry: the ultimate significance of the mass-reality. As Graham himself happily propounded once, "By using today's mass communications, we can preach to more people in one day than the Apostle Paul reached in a lifetime. I imagine that if Paul could look down here, he is champing at the bit. How he would like to be on television! How he would like to have a radio hour!" It never seemed to occur to Graham that there might be an existential difference of kind between those two ministries precisely for those reasons. On the contrary, as Graham's former public relations director, Jerry Beavan, once declared, "In our crusades and work, we need every instrument of modern mass communications. We've got the greatest product in the world to sell — salvation for men's souls through Christ. Why shouldn't we sell it as effectively as we promote a bar of soap?"

Accordingly, tracing through Graham's official gaugings of his ministry's effect in promoting the redemption of Christ's crucifixion as a commodity equivalent to a package of Lifebuoy, ranging through all the catalogings from BGEA of his evangelism's impact and import over the years, one finds oneself wandering through a kind of infinite abstract maze like some Steinberg landscape of blank numbers, multiple zeroes — 12,000; 39,000; 1,400,000. Beyond donations, even his toll of souls is meticulously computed in Minneapolis, with an electronic imprint for every convert collected over at least the past two decades. As Graham once reported to an assembly of clergymen in London, "We can pull out a card and give the whole spiritual case history of every one of them." More, much of his ministerial effort itself has come to be conducted through computered mailing. During a crusade in Australia, when the response at one invitation threatened to swamp and carry away on a swell of penitents the entire platform on which Graham was standing, he flung up his arms and cried, "Stop, ladies and gentlemen, there is no more room! If you want to give your life to Christ, go home and drop me a letter in the mail, and we will send you the follow-up literature."

By 1958, all such "nondonor" mail — principally letters appealing for all varieties of reassurance and guidance — had come to be processed in Minneapolis through an automatic system, in which all travails of the heart were broken down into about forty categories. Each letter was perused by a BGEA clerk who would underline the operative words with colored pencils — a spectrum of different tints for such preset orders of despair as financial worries, lonesome servicemen, marital discord, wayward children, uncertainty about decent amusements, chronic drinking by spouse, mental problems, doubt of God's existence. The appropriate tape was then selected from the color of the underlining and processed through a robot typewriter, which clat-

tered out the answer, the solace, the admonition, on a form letter machine-signed with Graham's signature. Also offered
through the Grason Company was a device called a Biblegraph,
an arrangement of cardboard discs that could be twirled in com-
binations to find, for each day of the week, Scripture verses for
"the 36 most troublesome questions of modern everyday life."
Among its selection of tribulations were "Is business bad? . . .
Do your children seem ungrateful? . . . Are you harassed by
money matters?" (Monday's comfort on that count being, from
Ecclesiastes, "The sleep of a labouring man is sweet, whether he
eat little or much: but the abundance of the rich will not suffer
him to sleep.") ". . . Do you feel inferior?" (Friday's assurance
offering, from the Psalms, "Though the Lord be high, yet hath
he respect unto the lowly: but the proud he knoweth afar off.")

What is eloquent in all this of the assumptions on which Graham's ministry proceeds is that it supposes one might categorize,
reduce to filing classifications, all the range of the heart's woes
and struggles and hopes. It is a presumption that would more or
less mechanize all human despair and happiness. Indeed, in all
such standardizings of human experience there lies, not incidentally, one more advance of the front of the totalitarian sensibility.

In Graham's case, it is a mass evangelism that operates out of
the pop-metaphysic that the more, the truer and mightier. As a
Graham advocate has explained, "When the average, moral, rep-
utable American . . . sees thousands of respectable, normal
people listening and consenting to all this he hears, and then sees
hundreds voluntarily get up and walk to the front in response
. . . he'll begin to consider the message and the situation with
some sincere, honest interest. It's much easier to say a single
speaker is wrong than to discredit the conviction and decision of
thousands." Another Graham partisan noted after a crusade service that it was "deeply moving to watch the solemn audience
suddenly break up when the invitation was given, like a giant
human anthill stirred to life, as thousands rose from their seats
in the arena or in the farthest stands to go forward . . . like the
blowing of the wind across a field of wheat; this sudden movement in the vast crowd, and then the streams of seekers converg-

ing on the platform — like a movement of the breath of God."
There is something of the Nuremberg mystique at work in such
excitements — the faceless and impersonal grandeur of immense
throngs; regarding the movements of huge crowds as "the
breath of God." Graham himself would appeal in his invitations,
"God has spoken to you as you have seen this great crowd, as
you have seen these thousands and thousands listening to the
word and heard them in singing, the spirit of God has spoken to
your hearts. . . ."

From Los Angeles in 1949, even with his own progressive
insulation within his organization, he truly amplified into a mass
phenomenon, and in the films from all those years — he moving
through countless surfs of multitudes, all the hosts in stadiums
and coliseums — there emerges a kind of dramatic *Geist*
strangely like the fascist epic sensibility; the sanctification and exaltation of great masses. It has been a mission whose meaning,
whose exhilarations, have been cast on the most colossal collective scale. Graham once remarked, "Lenin had only a small
number of followers in Russia in 1917; today the Communists
dominate *eight hundred and fifty million people!* How did they do it?
In *one generation!*" It seemed the simple numerical magnitude
alone was what awed him about that feat. And indeed, Graham's
own effort succeeded in that respect to the extent that, before
long, even huddles of dusty-ankled aborigines were squatting in
the emerald glooms of Fiji and New Guinea jungles listening to
the canned blare of Graham's sermons and altar calls on tapes
played by missionaries. As one Graham observer comments,
"When they discovered that lost Stone Age tribe over there in
the Philippines, I remember I thought immediately, 'Oh, boy.
It's only a matter of time now before Billy Graham reaches the
Tasadi — if he doesn't have a scouting party from Minneapolis
over there already.'"

At the close of one night's service in a 1957 Madison Square
Garden crusade, a reporter had found, standing off in shadows
at the edge of all the spectacle there, a faintly baggy figure with a
bald freckled pate, circular spectacles, and a white stippling of a
mustache — old Mordecai Ham, beholding now what had en-

sued out of that Indian summer tabernacle revival of his near
the railroad tracks in Charlotte over twenty years ago. By that
point, he had wound up somewhat bare on his luck. He had
recently undertaken another revival passage through Charlotte,
where he had phoned some previous marginal acquaintances of
Graham's, a retired couple, "to plead with us," says the wife, "to
come out there one night and stand up at one of his meetings
and say that Ham had converted Billy Graham. We told him we
didn't think we really ought to do that. But he kept calling
back — two or three more times, until he finally left town."
Sometime later, while Grady Wilson was in Nashville, Ham managed to arrange a meeting, and over a table in a hotel dining
room there, Grady recalls, "he sat there with his lips quivering,
tears streaming down his face, and told me, 'Grady, if I had my
life and ministry to live over again, I'd do it differently — I'd *love*
people. But I'm an old man now. And I can't find anybody
who'll let me come and preach in his church.' "

It's in the crusades themselves, of course, that Graham's whole
organizational complex comes into its focused articulation, its
moment of truth. Some five hundred or so invitations a year arrive at the headquarters in Minneapolis, which sifts and winnows
them on the basis of Graham's own schedule, the capaciousness
of the meeting facilities available at the locale, and particularly
the local readiness for the effort — a consideration that usually
requires letters of enthusiasm from state and city authorities to
be included in the application. The truth is, at any indication of
interest from a city that seems especially promising, an advance
man is dispatched to cultivate a larger general concert of eagerness, advising ministerial committees of what they still need to do
to attract a commitment from Graham, gently blandishing the
still reluctant and mollifying any lingering uncertainties, continuing then a close contact with influential laymen and the
prominent clerics in the city. There is posed to them eventually
the grand design, developed over the years for tending to the
costs of a crusade — "The Graham Plan."
All of Graham's crusades operate on a kind of reciprocal con-

tract between the BGEA and the local religious community, something like a short-term franchise arrangement — the total budget for the campaign is conceived by Minneapolis in advance, and then presented for what is usually perfunctory clearance by the local executive commitee incorporated to manage the whole enterprise. The local churches are responsible for raising and administering the funds, attending to all the bills for the facilities, advertising, printing, postage, staff quarters, as well as for arranging the special area delegations at the services, providing the ushers, choir, counselors, prayer-group leaders, even the floral sprays around the podium. On his part, Graham provides himself and his cadre of specialists, his "team" — which usually includes a publicity director, two counseling experts, a business adviser, the choir director and soloist and miscellaneous other entertainers, a pianist and organist, and several assistant evangelists for all the peripheral promotional meetings. Graham's own contingent is salaried from Minneapolis, while two offerings during the crusade and whatever surplus is left afterward are directed back to the BGEA.

The offerings themselves at each service are directed by some local minister or layman: "Let this be a Praise-the-Lord offering tonight! The first night was a faith offering, to make a statement before God of your faith that God would do great things here in this crusade. So let this be a praise offering to the Lord for all he's doing through these services. Be a hilarious giver! It's been such a great time of blessing in the Lord! Now all of you with offering envelopes, hold up your envelopes now. I'm not trying to trap you, I just — yes, that's right, just hold them up for a moment — ahhh, wonderful, wonderful. Now," and to a gentle undertone from the organ, he conducts them through filling out the check blanks enclosed in the envelopes, taking out his own pen and proceeding through it with them, ". . . and now, write in the name of your bank, or the branch bank where you have your account . . . and don't forget to include your account number. . . . All right. Now, sign your name. . . . There! . . . Now, just drop it in the baskets the ushers will pass out among you. . . ."

It is customarily the effort, actually, to muster at least a third of the projected expenses before the crusade ever opens — through contributions from churches, specific personal appeals to local businessmen of means, fund-raising luncheons, "inspirational breakfasts" where Graham himself will personally appear to enlist the goodwill and subscriptions of the "better elements" of the city, as Jerry Beavan once put it. This initial preliminary phase of extensive tilling and nurturing can range from eight months to, with especially difficult cities, two years.

The crusades themselves are occasions that were described by one euphoric matron, during a Graham visitation to Charlotte, as "being together in Christ." It is a kind of cozily perfect world those evenings offer, like previews of Heaven itself: All lost things — car keys, purses, umbrellas — are somehow found; the cigarette and beer signs in the coliseum concourses are all tidily taped over with blank sheets of paper, the concession stands supply only sandwiches and soda pop, Life Savers, chewing gum. During his crusades in Charlotte, Graham himself would wait each night in a backstage lounge before appearing to present his message, pacing and absently nibbling at his nails, now and then receiving callers, the mayor and a Congressman and a textile potentate and other deputations of dignitaries. In the meantime, when the coliseum outside was finally filled, calls clanged up and down the concrete reaches of the entrance lobby, "All right. Bring the ushers in, and lock it down." They were, on the whole, warm and neighborly revival gatherings, Graham convivially confiding before one evening's message that he had actually been asked to mediate a current baseball strike, but had declined, another time whooping, "Mickey Mantle hit two home runs today. Boy, what a guy!" and then went on to submit that what Charlotte really needed was "a great stadium." After his sermon, that evening's leaf-fall of decision cards would be processed in a 3,500-square-foot storage room in the basement of the coliseum, 60 to 75 men and women working until two in the morning among a steady chunk-a-pock chinging of typewriters and adding machines donated by IBM, with attendants from various designated churches bringing them pastries and hot chocolate.

It was probably Graham's monumental ninety-seven-day stand in New York City in 1957 that still constitutes the classic performance of his crusade system. A few years before, he had made a first exploratory foray into the city, intended to touch off, with a few resonant appearances, an ionic field of interest. In time, a substantial enough party of patrons had become intrigued with the prospect — including the Vanderbilts, the Goulds, and the Whitneys, ducal houses that had collaborated in the earlier missions of both Moody and Sunday to the city, and the Phelpses and the Dodges, who had been sponsoring mass revivals in New York since the 1820s — to allow a formal invitation to be extended by the preliminary provisional committee of businessmen and clergy, and for Graham to grant his formal acceptance. He additionally emboldened the assorted social and financial chevaliers of the city, at a private luncheon once the whole effort was underway, "Gentlemen, . . . I walked around Valley Forge one day with President Eisenhower, and he remarked, 'This is where they got it for us. . . .' But now we are threatened with destruction as a nation. Communists have more fervor than Christians. And they have nuclear weapons capable of destroying civilization as we know it today. I wouldn't give the snap of my finger for any of your businesses unless a genuine spiritual awakening takes place in the next few years."

To oversee Graham's adventure into Manhattan, a general executive committee was assembled that constituted something like a high commission of the national respectability then — its chairman Roger Hull, president of Mutual Life of New York, and including Henry Luce, Ogden Reid of *The New York Times*, Chase Manhattan president George Champion, Captain Eddie Rickenbacker, Dr. Norman Vincent Peale; along with, appropriately enough, William Randolph Hearst, Jr., heir of Graham's progenitorial patron in Los Angeles. Out of the ranks of this board of crusade trustees were selected, then, the diverse tactical committees to superintend directly such matters as financing — the chairman of that operation being Howard E. Isham, vicepresident and treasurer of U.S. Steel. When this congenial council nevertheless proved a bit nonplussed at first by the expan-

siveness of the budget presented to them by Beavan, he quickly
disposed of any equivocations with his customary admonition,
"If a corporation can spend eight million dollars on a campaign
to sell a bar of soap, why can't a million or two be spent to tell
the message of God's promise of salvation through His son, Jesus
Christ?" And so the lease was signed with Madison Square Garden.

It took a year, in all, for Graham and his company to gird
themselves for Manhattan — the ambition being, as one Graham
publicist put it, that "the name of Jesus Christ will be for many
the biggest topic of conversation on the streets, in factories and
offices, and on the dimly lit night circuit of such spots as The
Stork Club and Toots Shor's." For his part, Graham now began
casting New York both as the Sodom of modern civilization and
as "our Jerusalem. It is the center of art, culture, and entertainment. The world watches New York, how it eats, drinks, dresses,
looks." For much of the year of prelude, though, Graham himself was withdrawn into the high solitudes of his new mountainside home in Montreat, engaging in what had become his
chronic precrusade agonizings: "We face the city in fear and
trembling," he would periodically proclaim. "I'm prepared to go
to New York to be crucified by my critics, if necessary. When I
leave New York, every engagement we have in the world might
be canceled. It may mean that I'll be crucified — but I'm going!"

However self-conjured a suspense, these professions of foreboding were nonetheless quite authentic with him: in fact, before
such momentous extensions, he would often fall ill — contracting vague pneumonial complaints, bronchial ailments, once an
"acute undetermined infection" in his digestive regions. At the
same time, as his New York encounter approached in May, he
began rigorously to attend to his customary posture of passionate humility, as if banking in himself its prodigious energizing compressions: he even insisted, as the promotional overtures
began to mount in New York, "If I ever succumbed and got the
wrong idea about this publicity or tried to use it for the wrong
purposes, I think I would die. Yes! That's why we never go out
for publicity. Our going to New York is certainly not a demon-

stration of faith in our methods, for we know that New York would be impervious to a merely human effort. I am nothing myself. But we are daring to go because we know that, with God, all things are possible!"

These ceremonies of self-tensing proceeded all the while in a careful seclusion from any disconcerting infringements, out of that unabating wariness — which had prompted him to cancel his television exchange with the clerical skeptic before a Toronto appearance — about subjecting himself to any possible sabotages worked by detached perspectives, any critical complicatings. Instead, if he happened not to be in Montreat, he would simply commune with the Scripture while perfecting his tan in a lounge chair outside some private beach-front cabana, pass afternoons on a golf course, quiet evenings of pizza suppers with a few intimates at a rear table in some small eatery. Finally, with New York only a few weeks away, he took to stalking the steep foot trails above Montreat in his khaki windbreaker with a ski cap on his head, clasping his Bible, wandering alone through woods now blurring into the first green mistings of spring — pausing once on the edge of a bluff open to far distances of sky and mountain ridges, to throw out his arms with clutched fists and cry, "Oh, God! Help me!"

But in fact — despite all these psychic isometric exercises down in Montreat of solitary anguishing, declarations of dire trepidation about the outcome of the whole undertaking — simultaneously, in New York itself, imposing machineries were at work that made it highly improbable, as he permitted himself once to accede, that he would not have "a fair audience ready before we even get there." While Graham remained mostly in semi-isolation — plowing his garden, planting a lawn, applying himself to his daily calisthenics, meditating on his messages and the fearsomeness of what awaited him — Jerry Beavan, out of a bleak office suite with some twenty-five assistants in a Times Square building harboring theatrical agents and dance-band booking companies, was directing an enormous symphonic operation of advance committees and deployments. Troupes of Graham assistants were dispatched to preach in suburban pul-

pits, offices, factories, to high-school students, throughout the
New York environs; salvos of mailings went to four hundred
campuses over the area; movies of past crusades were shown to
local ministerial groups; special Bible classes were set up and
over ten thousand "prayer support" cells activated not only in
New York but over the globe, including one among a rehabili-
tated tribe of headhunters in Assam.

In the meantime, others were synchronizing the efforts of a
medley of committees — the music committee, which collected
volunteers for the choir; the auditorium committee, which han-
dled the maintainance and decoration of the Garden site; the
delegation committee, which managed the reservations for special deputations from other churches and other locales, with
travel agencies like Christian Tours arranging for their importation into Manhattan by special trains and bus caravans from the
distant interiors of the country, 112 of these preordered groups
having been accumulated for the opening night's service; the
ushers' committee; the men's prayer-meeting committee; the cot-
tage-meeting committee; the publicity committee; the young
people's committee; the counseling committee. . . . It was an enterprise, in fact, not unlike a major political campaign blitz, extending all the way down to the precinct level — the whole city
intricately graphed into specific geographic cells, each with its
own committee chairmen for youth, women, men, churches, who
were themselves then assigned to produce other subechelons of
workers of their own. On the whole, the city seemed as exhaustively organized and riddled as watermelon swarmed by wasps.
"After all that priming and preparation," said one observer, "the
real miracle would have been if Graham had actually missed in
Manhattan." But as a BGEA official once proposed of this massive clockwork of action committees, counselors' workshops, ladies'
teas, coordinated prayer programs: "There's nothing pious
about confusion."

What it all came to, actually, were the myriad structures and
strategies of a monolithic exertion, designed "to minimize wastage," as one Graham chronicler has phrased it, all engineered finally to address that most elusive and mysterious of intangi-

bles — the human soul. All those volunteering themselves as counselors to advise the inquirers drawn forward by the invitations were required to fill out an application questionnaire explaining exactly how and why they became Christians, why they aspired to be counselors, and each to furnish three references who would attest to their spiritual soundness. Processed then through a finer second-stage filter of considerations — such as "inability to communicate," an argumentative or prickly disposition, unkempt appearance, halitosis — those emerging approved were then elaborately versed in six two-hour classes on such final niceties as the importance of using deodorants and having handy just before the invitation a few mint lozenges to tuck in before moving on into action. They would then be seeded throughout the congregations every evening, and as Graham finished his message and, his voice ringing over the Garden's eighteen loudspeakers, began to deliver the invitation, this diffusion of counselors would all keep their eyes on their respective captains — wardens stationed in the aisles to scrutinize those stepping forth to answer the altar call, who would signal one of the counselors in his detachment when he spied an appropriate inquirer heading down: that is, one of the same sex, race, approximately same age and cultural cachet. At his captain's nod, the counselor would then peel out after his appointed party. As one Graham partisan described it, "it was absolutely thrilling to see how the counselors and inquirers were placed together — just as smoothly as the running of the engines of a big ship."

As the hour of the crusade's opening approached, Graham and his immediate entourage moved at last into the city to an accompanying fanfare of 650 billboards, 40,000 bumper stickers, over half a million leaflets — all imprinted simply with the service times, the site at the Garden, and Graham's own rather basilisk-eyed visage: as Beaven explained, "When you see an advertisement for a Cadillac, it just says Cadillac and shows you a picture. Billy is like a Cadillac. We don't have to explain." Reviewing now the awesome mobilizations in place before him, Graham himself was enspirited to speculate, "If some poor fishermen and tax collectors, without TV, radio, and airplanes, could turn the world upside down and shake the foundations of Rome, what can we do here in the next few weeks?" Even so, as soon as he was settled into the Hotel New Yorker, which had provided him with a free suite along with free rooms for his closest aides, he was again beset with vague alarms, and quickly phoned Barrows, Grady Wilson, Shea to come to his room and kneel with him for a session of prayer.

Finally, the Tuesday night before it was all to begin, he left the hotel and took a stroll alone — except for a considerable train of newsmen and photographers shuffling down the sidewalk after him — through Times Square's maze of lights, rippling around him now in the gently dissolving drizzle of a warm spring evening. Presently, he wound up outside Madison Square Garden itself, and, his hands plunged into his plastic raincoat, stood off for a while in the noiseless misting watching an evacuation of elephants from a circus that had just closed that night — huge mute shapes moving past in the dark with a slow tremendous deliberation in a kind of primeval rank musk of straw and dung and brutal animal sweat, while scattered and disembodied voices, hoarse shouts, sounded around them. Only a few lights were flaring, with faint glints and winks of gilt, sequins, spangles, silks being hurriedly gathered through the shadows back into trucks — it was like a hasty and covert withdrawal in the night of some alien rowdy gaudy celebration before the coming with daylight of another, more austere reality. And abruptly, they were gone — completely vanished from the dimly shining streets. Almost immediately then, even before Graham had returned to his hotel, other vans began arriving to unload into the vast vacated spaces of the Garden tumbling heaps of flowers to muffle the last effluvia left behind by that lustier departed event.

So the day came at last — Wednesday, May 15. Before leaving his hotel to take the pulpit that evening in the Garden for the first time, Graham received a wire from Roy Rogers prophesying that his preaching would "refresh a very tired city," and as he waited on the podium through the opening hymns with the Niagaral booming of the choir's two thousand voices, before the congregation mounting around him in terraced mesas of people on up to the far flag-hung girders of the arena, he had in his coat pocket a document signed in thumbprints by illiterate tribesmen in Africa testifying to their prayers for New York's regeneration. At the same time, some two hundred professional entertainers had been conscripted into a Bible group headed by Jerome Hines to insure a dependable supply of celebrities each evening, and a special celebrity gallery had been set aside in Box 31 of the Garden, variously populated as the crusade proceeded by Sonja Henie, Pearl Bailey, Gene Tierney, Ed Sullivan, Dale Evans, Dorothy Kilgallen, Walter Winchell. Surveying from the celebrity box this whole huge Noah's Ark pageantry of revival that Graham had brought to pass in the Garden, Perle Mesta effervesced, "Isn't it fantastic! I think he is just wonderful! Certainly we need this. It's all that's going to save the world."

In fact, less than eight years had passed since his emergence out of that tent revival on the corner of Hill and Washington in Los Angeles. Striding now up to the pulpit to begin his crusade in Madison Square Garden, he took his text from Isaiah, resounding the verses over the arena in a voice like the bugle-blast of Judgment Day: "*Ah sinful nation, a people laden with iniquity, a seed of evildoers, children that are corrupters. . . . Your country is desolate, your cities are burned with fire: your land, strangers devour it in your presence. . . . Hear the word of the Lord, ye rulers of Sodom; give ear unto the law of our God, ye people of Gomorrah. . . . If ye be willing and obedient, ye shall eat the good of the land: But if ye refuse and rebel, ye shall be devoured with the sword: for the mouth of the Lord hath spoken it. . . .*" And the message he then delivered, on that first night in New York City, was much the same he had pealed forth in Los Angeles eight years earlier — only a few weeks could have actually passed since then. Regally stalking back and forth behind his pulpit console, one long forefinger lancing high into the air, he announced, "During the Bible days, every time the nation went into a period of spiritual declension, God raised up a prophet. Most of the prophets were bold, daring, and dramatic. They got the attention of the multitudes and then proclaimed the message of the Lord to the cities and the nations! . . . Isaiah, the son of Amoz, came up to the temple that day

clothed with sackcloth and with ashes upon his head and with
the leper's rag upon his upper lip, and with dramatic passion he
began to deliver the message of the Lord to Israel. With flashing
eye and his voice reaching a mighty crescendo, Isaiah shouted:
'But if ye refuse and rebel, ye shall be devoured with the
sword — for the mouth of the Lord hath spoken it!' "

While Graham himself happened to be groomed, in place of
sackcloth and a leper's rag, with the dark-suited distinction of a
carnationed wedding usher, yet he rendered these lines with his
eyes also icily flaming, his own voice vaulting to mighty crescendos. " — How the people must have listened! The whole city of
Jerusalem was stirred as Isaiah the prophet thundered forth the
message of the Lord. And the times in which we live are parallel
to the times that Isaiah lived in. . . . The H-bomb casts its ominous shadow over the whole world. No life on this planet can escape its threat of death and annihilation. Communism continues
her forward march and her avowed pledge to wrest the world
from free men and bring all men under the rule of the hammer
and sickle. . . . Sodom and Nineveh, Jerusalem and Rome —
these and other cities have felt the curse of God's judgment. . . .
Night after night, here in this Garden, I intend to be only a messenger to give God's message to the people of New York!"

Through those evenings, Graham considered himself, as
usual, pitched into a quite direct hand-to-hand duel with Lucifer
for the destiny of New York. Just as he had declared before setting out for an earlier crusade in England, "I seriously doubt if
at any time in my ministry I have so felt the powers of darkness;
it seems as though the demons of Hell have concentrated against
this mission," so he now maintained, as he began striving to
redeem Manhattan, that he had never sensed such satanic opposition and resistance — to the point even of attributing a sudden savage glower of temperature into the nineties to the ruses
of the Devil.

But as it turned out, Graham in a sense never really seemed to
engage New York City itself through those services. For all of his
anticipatory precrusade pronouncements posing Manhattan as
the great Byzantium of America's cultural and civilized life, once

he arrived there, he mostly remained an undeflectably resolute provincial, all his militant simplicities unchanged. Greenwich Village, the evening lobby at the Algonquin, the Guggenheim Museum, the Actors Studio, O'Neill and Ionesco and Arthur Miller on Broadway — it all might as well have been five thousand miles away. The sensibilities out of which he preached were still those of Charlotte and Western Springs, Illinois. He dismissed modern art as "nothing but a splotch. Man is scarcely recognizable. He is portrayed not as we know him, as a creature bearing the image of God, but as a blur, an irregular splotch, something abstract, something uncertain, indistinct." He proclaimed that "our literature, despite its pretense at realism, is marked by a flight from reality." In the midst of even this most cosmopolitan of locales, his rudimentary certitudes from those earliest Temple Terrace days of his resolve and commitment persevered still impervious and intact, delivered now to New York with an eye-blazing jaw-clapping finality.

In his sermons, Graham put the problems of man's modern condition fully enough: "emptiness, loneliness, guilt, and the fear of death. Man is expanding further and further, faster and faster, with mounting dilemmas, problems, confusions, and bewilderments. . . . Our generation is filled with nervous tension, a revolt against all restraints, and a terrible gnawing fear. The whole world is frantically searching for an answer before it blows itself into oblivion." But his own answer to this organ-fugue of angst proved to be itself more like a cornet's flat chipper blare: the all-purpose efficacy of a "decision for Christ" to restore every benighted soul and dispel every real tribulation, no matter whose — housewife, racketeer, governor or President, Elvis Presley ("I read about a rock-and-roll star the other day . . . and someone asked him if all the fame and money had brought happiness, and he replied that he was often miserable and 'lonely as hell' "), even Ernest Hemingway: ". . . Hemingway, who had four wives — Ernest Hemingway, one of the world's great writers, who has been known for his doubtings about God. He got in one plane that crashed, and he got into another plane that crashed and burned. Could it be that God saved Ernest Hemingway so he might know the mercy of Jesus Christ?" Graham then declared, "The lilt and music is gone out of modern life primarily because we can no longer say from the bottom of our hearts, *I believe!* Philosophers, scientists, diplomats, political leaders, and intellectuals are all beginning to say with one voice: *We need God!*"

As Graham propounded it, "We have explored the mysteries of the universe, but have not solved the riddle of our souls. . . . All the scientists, the greatest intellects on this earth — they haven't been able to solve the problem of sorrow." Thus the human heart amounted to no more than a difficulty, a problem to be solved. Specifically, to Graham, all the woes and pains and conflicts of man's state reduced to a mere matter of pathology: the simple virus of sin. "Few people really want to do wrong. But they do it. Few people want to be sinners. But they are. What is wrong? The Bible calls it sin. I know we don't like to face it. We don't like to admit it. We would like to give it some other terminology that would be easier on our egos. But during this crusade, I am going to use Biblical terminology. I do not intend to beat around the bush and skirt the basic issues of life and death."

But in the messages he preached to New York City — from a pulpit resembling a suburban patio with an iron lattice fence around it, elevated like a dais and surrounded by mums and ferns — it seemed to be his import that the Victorian village respectability of the nineteenth century in America more or less constituted the fundamental plan of God for all mankind over all history. His effect was to exalt the ordinary proprieties — a tidiness and hygiene of behavior and habits — to the cosmic magnitude of salvation or damnation: niceness, in the end, was the ticket to immortality. As he explained Heaven and the eternal life, "Are we to think tyrants of history and criminals will end up in the same place as those who live good lives?" It was that simple. His own sense of that life of sanctity, as defined by Christ, he indicated by pointing out once, "It was not easy for Pilate's wife, Claudia, to defend Jesus, since everything for which Jesus stood — his emphasis on purity, his glorifying of marriage, his benediction upon children, his esteem for the home — was

bitterly opposed by the sensuous pagan world of Claudia's day."
It was a didactic rather after the moral sentiment of DeMillean
soap epics — Moses' honest simple Hebrew yeomanry being led
out of Egypt's Hollywood-gorgeous debaucheries. The saintliness that Graham preached was a matter of circumspection; it
was a kind of Messianism of mores.

"If church people would quit gambling, drinking, and lying,"
he proposed, "and would start living as Christ taught, we would
have a spiritual revival that would move the whole world." In the
main, those "basic issues of life and death" that he declared he
would put before New York seemed to consist finally of a catechism of correctness: "A Commandment says, 'Thou shalt not
commit adultery.' A woman commits this sin when she deliberately dresses in such a way as to entice a man. . . . Bad temper.
You explode when things don't go to suit you and kick up your
heels." Anyone contemplating marrying a party outside this
order of piety should "drop them like a hot potato," he advised,
and the Christian wife "should keep herself attractive and give
the husband a big kiss when he comes home from the office instead of yelling at him from the kitchen. Don't gossip. Don't nag.
. . . And you husbands, how long has it been since you sent her
some flowers? They like little things." Most of all, he decreed, a
Christian "leads a disciplined life. The Bible warns about disobedience. Parents are disobeyed, teachers are disobeyed — and if
the State Department asks you not to go to China, you go anyway!"

He would counter interviewers' questions about the glossiness
of his attire with a verse of Scripture that, in fact, pertained not
just to his approach to his wardrobe, but really amounted to the
essential text of his whole ministry's vision: "*Let all things be done
decently, and in order.*" It seemed, at the least, a species of Christianity that could not have been more remote from, for instance,
Dostoyevsky's anguished Christian vision, or Graham Greene's
poor, dingy, God-haunted derelicts. It did not really take a great
sinner anyway, as Graham appraised it, to make a great saint.
"Some of the greatest leaders in the Bible were men that never
rebeled and never sowed their wild oats first. You don't have to

go to the Devil first to find Christ! The gospel can prevent you from getting scarred by sin. You can come to Christ now and save all that!" If there seemed a certain shallow efficiency to this economical approach to the Christian experience, Graham nevertheless insisted, "The Prodigal Son — he would have been a lot better off if he'd never left home in the first place! What a wonderful thing it would have been if he had come to God as a boy — then he would have never gone to the 'far country.' " At the least, it was a far country, Graham assured his congregations, into which he had never ventured. In his invitation calls to repentance, he said, "It's not an emotional experience. It wasn't for me. There may be emotion to it, there may not be. It's primarily a commitment you make with your will, not your mind, not your emotions."

Despite that, his invitation appeals still inclined toward the gothic in their persuasions — he once narrated an instance of a man who had left a revival service with a curse on it all, whereupon the man's wife and daughter died in rapid succession, and he expired shortly thereafter. "We used to have a busy Senator down South. A kindly man wanted to speak with him one morning about eternal things, and he replied, 'If Jesus Christ wanted five minutes with me this morning, he couldn't have it.' The Senator was dead that night." Of God's general disposition, he would bay, "He is not a jolly fellow like Santa Claus. He is a Great Bookkeeper. And he is keeping the book on you! . . . I am a Western Union boy! I have a death message! I must tell you plainly — you are going to Hell! You listen! Don't you trifle with God! Don't you think you can barter! You are a sinner! You have come short of God's requirements! Your punishment is sure!" . . . All the while in these exhortations, as he once confided, *"I would feel as though I had a sword, a rapier, in my hand, and I would be slashing deeper and deeper into the consciences of the people before me, cutting away straight to their very souls. . . ."*

As the choir then began hymning "Just as I Am" behind him, he would step forward from the pulpit and loft one long arm in a wide caressing arc over the far reaches of people around him. "I'm going to ask you to come now — over here, down here, you way up there in the balconies. I want you to come now — " and over the Garden there would stir a sense of some immense shifting and loosening in the multitude banked around him. "That's it, come on now. Your whole life can be completely changed if you just yield to Christ tonight." The spill would begin now, a wide and steady silting of people down the aisles toward the front of the Garden. "If you don't come tonight, you may never come, you may never have another moment like this one. The Bible warns that every time you reject Christ, your heart gets harder and harder. And after a while, he may speak to you, but you'll no longer hear him. I beg you not to commit the terrible sin of refusing to hear his voice. Great battles are going on in many a heart here tonight — as you stand there, a great battle is going on in your soul. It's a battle for eternity. . . ." *It was still, as in those reeling nighttime revivals of his youth, the same heaving dramaturgy, the old struggle joined again against the winsome clay and pipings of this world. . . .* "You can get up and come and stand here and never be the same again. To all the lonely people, Christ says, *Come!* To all those with frustrations and burdens and bewilderments, sins, longings, and boredoms, Christ says, *Come!* To those of you that have a lashing conscience, he says, *Come! Take! Learn! Rest! Come* for the fellowship your heart craves. Learn of the secret of peace your mind seeks! Rest in the confidence your heart desires!" By now, they would even be descending in a heavy continuous float down by escalator from the top tiers, as the host already dammed around the podium gradually welled wider, back into the front aisles.

In the meantime, the mammoth turbines and gears of the event had resumed their turning. At gestures from their captains, the counselors with their small badges and small red instruction manuals in hand trailed one after another unobtrusively after their assigned inquirer down to the front, to be discovered then at Graham's notification — "Now, if you look around, you'll probably find a counselor standing beside you" — poised politely smiling at the inquirer's elbow, giving some of them a slight start. What followed was not unlike a policy agent's consultation with an insurance customer, each counselor con-

ferring sotto voce with his inquirer as he filled out the blanks
and checked the proper boxes on the "decision card" —
"Inquirer's Name: — Define Need: — Type of Decision: 1, Acceptance of Christ as Savior and Lord; 2, Reaffirmation of Faith;
3, Assurance of Salvation; 4, Dedication of Life." Once this clas-
sification was completed, the inquirer was then presented with
his salvation kit — a packet containing a Gospel of John, two
Bible memorization lessons, a form letter from Graham, a list of
additional instructions, and a business reply envelope addressed
to BGEA headquarters in Minneapolis. The note from Graham
went, "In order for you to grow in your Christian life it is necessary for you to . . . 1. Read your Bible daily. . . . 2. Pray every
day. . . . 3. Witness for Christ. . . . 4. Attend church regularly.
. . . Further instructions will follow."

As the inquirers were released from this first induction process
into redemption, special "runners" drafted from such sources as
the Fellowship of Christian Athletes plunged about collecting the
decision cards and then sprinted them off to the main processing
center, an operation that somehow resembled a swim of bees
gathering honey into the hive: in this case, a cavernous room in
the deeps of the Garden. There, this nightly pollen of decisions
was passed through a "statistics section," with each card numbered and coded. A battalion of typists then clattered out notices
to pastors over the area apprising them of the inquirers being
forwarded into their hands.

An attorney in Columbia, South Carolina, remembers that
"when Graham came through here back yonder in 1950, he had
to move from the city auditorium to the football stadium, so
many folks started turning out for the thing all of a sudden. This
owed mostly to a couple of sensational conversions about midway
through his crusade. One of them was the numbers racket king
of South Carolina, a widely renowned figure hereabouts, and the
other one was the state's most notorious bootlegger, who was an
equally fabled celebrity. But it didn't turn out to take too good
with the first one, the numbers king — a few months later, he
was arrested for running a prostitution ring and trying to bribe

half the sheriff's department. But it sure definitely took with the second fella, the bootlegger. No doubt about that. Before Graham came through, he'd been the most spectacular hell-raiser in Columbia's living memory, but after his conversion, he flat quit drinking, quit brawling, quit running around on his wife — and became the most purely *mean* son of a bitch I have ever known of. In fact, he passed on here not long ago, and I went to his funeral, and somebody there said, 'What in the world are you doing at this thing? I sure didn't expect to see you here,' and I said, 'I just want to make sure he's really dead.'"

It occurred once to A. J. Liebling, as he was perusing a Graham crusade in Glasgow in 1955 and noted two young lasses fresh off the heather fretting inconclusively with their own obvious urges toward the altar, that they both "probably took away from the hall with them a sufficient load of guilt to make them unbearable for years. The effects of the crusade on the saved are quite possibly less lasting than the traumata sowed among the almost saved." Indeed, after Graham's passage through Greensboro, North Carolina, in 1951, among the more novel effects reported in a survey of doctors there were crying spells, severe headaches and abdominal cramps "associated with fear of sin," digestive disturbances and loss of energy, disruption of customary sex relationships, "threatened self-mutilation and removal of genital organs because of past sins." Graham himself would allow, "I read criticisms of our work, that many people go away psychologically disturbed. This is the work of the Holy Spirit. He is a disturber."

In all, though, Graham's campaign in New York was an event that, like all his other crusades, seemed to produce conversions that were like thousandfold multiplications of his own. The faces that would collect below him at the invitation every evening were almost unanimously blank of any elation or passion — about the expression of customers in line waiting to get prescriptions filled at a druggist's counter. At the most, these conversions did effect certain sanitations of conduct — as one of Graham's apologists reports, "During and in the wake of every Billy Graham crusade, broken families are reunited, alcoholics are cured of their alcoholism, juvenile delinquents are brought within the influence of the church." After one crusade in Washington, hotels there reported an abrupt anonymous returning of filched silverware. In New York, journalists foraging for specific converts among the some 62,000 decisions tabulated there got from them such explanations as, from a teenage girl in the Bronx, "When Billy Graham said, 'Your sins will condemn you,' I wanted to rid myself of mine" — which she defined, when pressed further, as having once worn a tight sweater and daubing on a touch of lipstick now and then against her parents' instructions. The jubilations of other converts seemed generally on the order of "Since that night I have felt and acted as a Christian should, not drinking, gambling, vulgar talking . . . something I couldn't do for myself, to stop smoking after twenty-five years. It is now five weeks since I've had a cigarette." On the whole, what Graham's evangelism seemed to produce, as more than one witness of his Garden crusade suggested, were more or less popcorn conversions — from tight hard little dull kernels, suddenly, at the conclusion of his sermon, all over the coliseums and stadiums, *pop! pop!* they puff and bloom innumerably into instant popcorn Christians, white, weightless, with rather a papery savor.

Any further impact of the massive effort of a crusade begins to elude substantive computations. In fact, Graham's people have come to maintain that it takes the passing of about four years before a crusade's results can properly be registered, and for the interim they offer such ineffables as "a lift to the general spiritual life . . . a quickening of the spirit in the general area. . . . Probably the most lasting result will be in the lives of hundreds of ministers." Even such testimonials as a change in the expressions on people's faces are put forward: one of Graham's more solicitous biographers reports, "I noticed one young girl with a very hard and scornful expression on her pretty face as the hymns of praise and faith rose around her; but before she left . . . I saw tears in her eyes, and at the last moment she too smiled at us." Graham himself finally submitted as the achieve-

ment of his New York crusade that he now noted smiles instead
of scowls on the faces of the passengers in the subways. It was a
triumph, as it were, of pleasantness.

Nevertheless, by the time of Graham's epic exertion in Manhattan in 1957, his crusades and his message had already begun
to occasion a certain deep unease among some Christian
thinkers — principally, that it propagated a pious simplicity that
finally flattened the true dimensions of good and evil in life, im-
poverished all the true possibilities of human character and
human struggle. It was again that old impulse of American frontier religion to vanquish and order the chaos of the wilderness — which now, in Graham's case, acted to deplete existence
for the sake of that ordering. It was something like a religious
version of the American commander's report in Vietnam, "We
had to destroy the village in order to save it." Graham's was a
gospel, as Reinhold Niebuhr observed after the New York crusade, which cast too absolute and pat a divide between the sanc-
tified and the unredeemed, and thereby worked to abrogate the
"ambiguity of all human virtues, the serious perplexities of guilt
and responsibility, and particularly of guilt associated with responsibility, which each true Christian must continually face."

Graham's rejoinder to Niebuhr after the Manhattan crusade
was the disarming and gracious concession, "I have read nearly
everything Mr. Niebuhr has written, and I feel inadequate before his brilliant mind and learning," but he then added, "If I
tried to preach as he writes, people would be so bewildered they
would walk out." To Niebuhr's complaint about the constricting
simplicity of his vision of the Christian life, Graham offers now,
"There are mysteries in human personality and the human
mind, yes. The brain is extremely complex. I do not believe that
all problems are solved when someone comes to Christ — I
wouldn't say that. But I do think there's a limit beyond which he
won't let a Christian go in iniquity and doubt." During the controversy set off by the God Is Dead theologians in the Sixties,
Graham allowed that perhaps the faith should continue to be
reexamined, "but there are certain things I think we should
settle. . . . While the intellectual God of some people may be

dead, the real and living God is alive. I know, because I talked to him just this morning."

Perhaps Graham's most pertinacious critic during that time of his 1957 New York campaign was religious scholar William G. McLoughlin, Jr., who observed that, at that moment in American culture, "in order to succeed, revivalism must be commercial in its advertising, exploitative in its mechanics, literal in its theology, bland in its pietism, statistical in its measurement" — with the evangelisms of the new American piety during the Eisenhower Fifties necessarily casting "salvation as a way of obtaining peace of mind, peace of soul, and a sense of security 'in these crisis times.'" But, insisted McLoughlin, "Are the means compatible with the ends? It is necessary to do more than ask: Does it spread the gospel? It is essential to know how." Indeed, McLoughlin suggested, "the very term 'mass evangelism' is a contradiction, for every evangelist maintains that man cannot be saved *en masse* but only as individuals." Graham's retort on that count over the years has been to point out that Jesus himself spoke to sizable throngs — to five thousand once at the Sermon on the Mount. Some twenty years after New York, he would unblinkingly acknowledge on one hand that "true Christianity should never be popular; we've simply lived through a very unnatural period in our history." Yet, when he is asked if his mass technologies might not in fact tend to permute the original nature and effect of the gospel message by so depersonalizing and mechanizing it — along with isolating him within those technologies and so breaking some vital personal communion between gospel minister and the individual — Graham will merely assert, "But how else are you going to reach the millions? Television now, it works when Barbara Walters, say, or Dinah Shore uses it. They manage to communicate; they get the message across. There's no way I could go to a million people, one by one. Besides, in a few minutes, even in those large stadiums, they feel alone. They don't even hear me any longer, aren't even aware of me."

But McLoughlin protested that, most of all, crusades like Graham's campaign in Manhattan really came in the end to a gigan-

tic "pep-rally for middle-class church-goers." Graham himself
would later admit that from 40 to 75 percent of all decisions at a
crusade were made by individuals already a member of the sponsoring churches, with most of the others also having been church
members once — and the follow-up censuses usually conducted
six months afterward neglected to distinguish between these re-
activated church folk and what had become of the actually newly
converted. Some five months after the Garden crusade itself
closed, a scan by *The New York Times* found that 64 percent of
those who had come forward were already members of the
churches to which their cards were relayed, and most of the
remaining 36 percent never joined those churches to which they
had been referred. For the most part, Graham's ninety-seven-
day performance in New York City — the most stupendous
evangelistic exercise in history up to that point, with a total of
some two million souls having heard Graham — mostly served to
simply envigorate the church community to a degree.

A considerable portion of the Garden congregations through
those three months, in fact, happened to have been transported
in from ranges of Middle America well beyond New York. Of
the Garden's 19,000 seats, 7,500 were reserved for these out-of-
town delegations, hauled into Manhattan by bus and train from
as far away as Houston, Oklahoma City, Nashville, Richmond,
Louisville, Detroit. Before he had even arrived in New York,
Graham had entreated his listeners on his *Hour of Decision* broadcasts to arrange to take their summer vacations there so they
could attend the services. It turned out that only 7,800 of the
Garden's seats were available to the general citizenry of New
York itself each night, with the rest — 11,200 — accorded to
those delegations out of farther regions, along with the crusade's
own supporting cast of counselors, ushers, choir, guest ministers.
One Graham strategist explains, "One reason we like to try to get
as many people as possible involved and participating in a crusade is that it is a guarantee that that many will be there to start
with, and they'll almost certainly bring others with them —
somebody's singing in the choir, and their family wants to come

along too to see what it's all about, or some fellow serving as an usher will naturally want to bring his family with him."

It largely amounted, then, to a prepackaged host that could be counted on to populate the Garden amply every evening, and what proceeded there was really a curious in-house event. Indeed, after all the grand theatre of Graham's advance on New York City, the actual occasion of the crusade services themselves struck a number of onlookers as oddly prosaic and perfunctory. More than one commentator noted that the crowds at the Garden seemed almost exclusively "churchly," crisp and clean and fresh as mint, carrying Bibles and binoculars. For all of Graham's portentous advance propoundments of New York as the American Pompeii, which he intended to take on even if it meant he would be consumed in the process, his crusade there was more like a peculiar oblique feat of prestidigitation, Des Moines simply brought to Manhattan. After a few weeks, Graham began to enthuse, "It's not the sophisticated city that I first thought it was. They're just plain people here! They respond to the gospel just as the people in Miami or Omaha or Charlotte" — which should have really been no surprise, since a large bulk of them *were* from cities like Omaha and Charlotte. As one young minister later remarked of the impressive size of the congregations there, "My greatest misgiving about Graham is his apparent conviction that a kind of intramural revival within the church serves just as well as a true sweeping revival out in the world. For that reason, I don't think he's ever going to reach the truly lost, the truly destitute and despised and unreconciled of the earth. With him, it's more an inside-the-sanctuary production — a matter of housekeeping within the faith." In all, then, through Graham's ninety-seven-day campaign, he was in New York only in the incidental terms of the setting, the crusade itself taking place there as a kind of huge hologrammic happening.

Graham in New York did make certain cosmetic concessions to the more cosmopolitan sensibilities of his locale, such as installing one black on his headquarters staff midway through the crusade. But Graham's appearances at the Garden were about the sum of his excursions into the city itself. At his hotel, the corridors around him and the lobby downstairs were constantly impacted with his own faithful from all over the nation, industrialists, ministers, governors, oilmen — while he kept to his room, occupied in sustaining his pure and solitary concentration. His absorption was so intense that once, when he was greeted on a crowded elevator with a "Hello, Bill" by a woman with a familiar face, he only mumbled, "Hi," then after getting out halted suddenly to sputter, "Good gracious, that was my wife."

The few instances when he did set out into the thick of New York itself did not turn out all that memorably. He made one processional with aides and newsmen along the Bowery in the muggy late hours of a night, pausing once to stoop over a castaway slumped in a doorway, "Hello, there! I'm Billy Graham." From the dim form below him came a low croak, "Beat it." Undaunted, Graham rejoined, "You have a problem. You won't accept God." After a moment, the man grunted, "So gimme a dime, will you? I'm hungry." Graham did, with the announcement, "I'm going to pray that you'll find God. You'll never regret it," but at the suggestion of an aide, moved briskly on — though when he returned at last to his hotel room, he passed the rest of the night sleepless from what he had beheld.

Aside from a few such haphazard encounters, though, what time outside his room Graham allocated himself between his pulpit performances was mostly invested in such ceremonies as reviewing a Sunday-school parade, speaking at a lawn party held for him by Mrs. Cornelius Vanderbilt Whitney, having lunch once with Jackie Gleason, putting in television appearances with Dave Garroway, Steve Allen, John Cameron Swayze. He did conduct one service on Wall Street during the lunch hour, his voice gonging on a loudspeaker from a makeshift pulpit on the steps of the Subtreasury Building: "Our forefathers gave us a great heritage. Feel in your pockets and pull out a coin. You will see it inscribed, 'In God We Trust.' . . . ." But on the whole, as one witness remarked, "New York was here, Billy Graham was here, but it was as if they simply passed through each other without touching whatsoever, like an optical illusion."

But that peculiar absence of any interplay with his locale had already ceased to matter. It was while he was in New York, on a Saturday night on the first of June, that Graham staged on ABC his first coast-to-coast television presentation of a crusade service. His congregation that evening was suddenly amplified to some seven million souls. When he neared the tentatively scheduled conclusion of his New York effort on June thirtieth, his determination to project the crusade on to Labor Day largely owed to the consideration that subsequent telecasts from the Garden had encompassed an audience of more millions than any other single revival enterprise in history — among them, as it happened, the great-great-granddaughter of the frontier American evangelist Jonathan Edwards, who herself was won by Graham's electronic performance and wrote him afterward, "You seemed to talk directly to me on television."

It was the beginning of Graham's next transfiguration — into a television being. Before that first service translated by the magic radium glows of television into the blue glooms of the new living-room altars over the whole continent, Graham had begun urging his New York gatherings, "Do come Saturday night. We're on TV then. It would be bad for the cameras to swing around and nobody up there." From that point on, his crusades would tend more and more simply to provide the stagework, the settings, the props, for his television productions. To an increasing degree, television itself would become the larger reality.

With that development would come the perfect consummation of the peculiar genius of Graham's technique as a popular evangelist: a massive closed system with its own vision and terms of evaluation and its own independent dynamic for self-perpetuation. With the total expenses for one 1954 Tennessee crusade, for instance, coming to $75,234, the special offerings taken then by prior arrangement exclusively for BGEA and its *Hour of Decision* broadcasts, plus the surplus in general collections after expenses, toted up to $80,497: that is, the crusade returned to Graham's organization more than was expended to finance all of his mission there. From such revenues, BGEA would then begin arranging to mount the next campaigns. Also, the costs of producing a movie documentary about one crusade would be included in the budget of those ordinary expenses to be attended to by general collections there, these documentaries then employed to prompt interest and invitations for further crusades, which would themselves, in turn, be filmed for the same uses later on. From the surplus that accrued in New York itself, $150,000 went to BGEA to fund the televising of a crusade in San Francisco, which, aside from the surplus accumulated there, also drew its own further swell of donations by mail from its televised appeals. Some of the surplus in New York was then reseeded to finance another Charlotte crusade, and a surplus produced from Charlotte went on to help subsidize a campaign in Australia.

It amounted, altogether, to a kind of enormous solipsistic phenomenon — an organization designed to induce and finance and conduct crusades that turned out, for the most part, simply to refresh and enspirit the local church community, beyond that serving to sustain the operations in Minneapolis, which were devoted to engendering more crusades. In a sense, then, a crusade was to produce further crusades, which in turn were to produce more crusades — a sequence continuing on over some three decades, a ministry like an interminable flexing and marshaling for some eventual engagement never quite arrived at, never quite realized. Instead, the means — the crusade system itself — had come to exist for the sake of their own self-propagation. And with Graham's mutation in New York on into television, that circular syllogistic system suddenly registered a quantum leap into its simple perfection: crusades now existed for their televised reproductions; the television event now existed to produce more television events.

But however mirage-like a happening it may have been, New York was still not without its own moments of majesty. On a hot Saturday dusk toward the end of July, under flaring field lights, some hundred thousand people had massed in Yankee Stadium for a special service, the largest assembly ever contained there — their voices thundering the hymn "All Hail the Power of Jesus' Name" against the summer evening sky. To a long detonation of applause, Graham had proceeded with his Bible across the grass of the infield toward the podium at second base with the dark-suited raven-like figure of Richard Nixon striding along with him, the two of them surrounded by a small cluster of security agents and aides. Nixon found himself, emerging abruptly into the grandeur of this mighty whelming of Graham's applause, not a little aswoon as they moved through it together, he presently proposing to Graham that it must be unimaginably gratifying to have accomplished such a host and such a reception. But instantly, out of that unstinting vigilance to any small lethal temptings to vainglory, Graham muttered, "I didn't fill this place, God did it" — and even when he had taken the pulpit, he still felt compelled to protest, "God has done this, and all the honor, credit, and glory must go to him. You can destroy my ministry by praising me for this. The Bible says God will not share his glory with another." . . .

Then, as his closing service in the city, he held a gigantic rally in Times Square, some 120,000 people thronged before him on a Sunday sundown of the Labor Day weekend, and his voice echoed over the endless stretches of people in a twilight air touched with a tint of autumn: "This is the spot that thousands of tourists think of as New York. . . . Tonight, for a few moments, it is being turned into a great cathedral . . . as a symbol of spiritual revival that is now in progress in America. Let us tell the whole world tonight that we Americans believe in God. Let us tell the world tonight that we desperately want peace, but not peace at any price. Let us tell the world tonight that we are morally and spiritually strong as well as militarily and economically. Let us tonight make this a time of rededication — not only to God, but to the principles and freedoms that our forefathers gave us."

But if the actual effect of that crusade on New York itself was somewhat evanescent, Graham left the city declaring, "I feel a great burden has been lifted," and pronounced it all "the biggest, certainly the most important crusade we have ever had." And on his return to Montreat, as he would later report, "the first thing I did was to go up in the woods on the mountain, and thank the Lord for what he had done in New York — for doing what I hardly had the faith could be done."

Nevertheless, once Graham has completed a major campaign like New York — once it is all past — "he tends to get kind of depressed," says his sister Catherine. "I can remember him after one of his crusades not long ago, sitting in our den sort of moody, not saying much to anybody, just slumped there on the sofa spooning at a dish of ice cream."

However illusionary a struggle New York may have proved, through those ninety-seven days some thirty pounds had wasted off him, and Graham maintained afterward, "Something went out of me in New York that I seemingly cannot recover." In fact, over the course of the unremitting tension of his evangelistic exertion through the years since Los Angeles, he has endured myriad falterings and attritions of the flesh — hernias, retina clots, pleurisies, battering headaches, drab brackish nauseas, removal of a salivary gland once, urinary infections, ulcerative colitis, jaw abscesses, tumors on the forehead, "many polyps once all over my body's interior," he relates. At one point, he implored of T. W. Wilson, "T, can you think of anything I've done in my life, anything at all, to deserve these sicknesses?" Consuming pills and vitamins ferociously — once even inadvertently grabbing and gulping from a bottle of hair tonic — yet he has seemed unable to cease, to relent from that almost manic urgency to spend himself on and on before great crowds in distant places: it has continued to propel him on almost blindly. He would constantly insist that he really had to begin preaching less, had to withdraw soon from so much sheer unalleviated furious assertion and pass more time meditating. He protested, "I do not enjoy living in hotel bedrooms, eating room-service meals, hurtling around the world in jet airplanes; I much prefer being at home with my wife and my children." Yet he could never resist that impulsion to be off again: as he noted once, not uncheerfully, "Something is always breaking out somewhere."

Graham's brother-in-law, Leighton Ford, married to his sister Jean and also an evangelist, was for a long time considered Graham's presumptive successor in the campaigns of the BGEA someday. A Canadian, Ford carries a peculiar resemblance to Billy — tall and gangling, he could pass as Graham's leaner younger brother, with the same fresh sharp face and clear gaze, and much the same ringings in his delivery. But Ford confesses now that, after some twenty years at it himself, he has reached the point where, just before he has to leave for yet another extended sojourn somewhere, 'I actually get sick. I'll get physically sick a day or two before. I just can't stand being away from home any longer." But as for Graham, says Ford, "he's just not made that way, he has to be on the move always — to just *go* somewhere, anywhere, but to go, to always be going and coming."

As one of his associates observes, Graham is one of those religious temperaments "who have a sense of woe if they do not preach the gospel." During one of his brief intervals at home in 1956, his eldest daughter, Gigi, happened to answer him curtly one day, "and he spanked me. I then asked him in anger what kind of father he thought he was anyway, always being gone. Tears filled his eyes." But before long, whichever child he might be holding and talking to he would abruptly nudge away — suddenly release them from his hug as if at some secret click within him — and turn immediately back to his sermon study, to his correspondence and plottings for the next crusade. "I did not ask for this assignment that was pressed on me by a sovereign God," he once contended. It has simply been that "they come. Always, they come." And whenever he is plunged into another crusade, he still experiences, he confesses, "this burden, this terrible burden, that I have to preach the *whole* thing *every* night. Many times, I wish the Lord would just take me, because I get so weighted down with the sins of the world, for which I have a constant revulsion."

It seems a desperation in which he will be captured as long as he still has movement and breath, out of that heroic passion of his for universal wholesomeness: he remaining through all the years still somehow that imperishable country boy innocent of his youth — smacking down creamed buttermilk along with a hot dog between sermons, sometimes sprawling out full length

on his motel room rug for a nap as he would in the days of his
boyhood — still that eager and intrepid Candide out of the
North Carolina midlands, striking out even on his expeditions
overseas as the consummate, earnest, sunny American Innocent
abroad, with a staggering obsession to transform and pasteurize
the whole world, as it were, into a Sunday afternoon in Charlotte.

III

It was in 1954, almost ten years after those tours with Youth for
Christ at the end of the war, that Graham sallied forth on his
own first crusade beyond America, a twelve-week stand in England. Graham would later recount, "They had an idea that I
was coming with a Texas sombrero hat, probably shooting two
guns." One reason that impression may have taken some time to
dispel was that he had shipped over with him Roy Rogers and
Trigger, along with an All-American fullback named Don Moo-
maw. Beyond that, though, contemplating this tall gilt-bright figure abruptly appeared among them out of the preserves of the
American righteousness, it struck some Britons, as one columnist
remarked, "whatever wrestling Billy Graham has done with
Satan, there are no claw marks." He was asked at one press conference, "What do you know about the suffering of Christ that
you preach about so often? You have never really suffered, have
you? You have lived fairly well, with most of the comforts of life,
it would seem —" and to this, Graham riposted, "When a Western Union messenger boy delivers a death message to a home,
he doesn't take part himself in all the suffering connected with
that message. He just delivers the telegram, that's all." He
seemed to many to have, himself, a quality of almost startling
cleanliness, and on the whole, he proceeded through that first
crusade abroad in England with "the sincerity, ingenuousness,
the sort of simple charm," as one journalist put it, "that is the

greatest fun about Americans and the quality that makes us love Danny Kaye so."

Nevertheless, a rather sizable furor had been touched off even before Graham had reached England when it was discovered that a promotional brochure for his campaign there, peddled back in the United States for twelve dollars each, not only misspelled the names of eight prominent Britons and flourished a gawky misquotation of Shakespeare, but proposed it as Graham's mission to England to address a national condition there wherein "what Hitler's bombs could not do, socialism with its accompanying evils shortly accomplished." Rumors of a spirited clamor over this suggestion began to reach Graham while he was still reposing aboard the decks of the liner, the *United States,* a day out of Southampton. He quickly got through to the editor of the London *Daily Herald* on a ship-to-shore phone to insist that it was all a simple misprint, what had been meant was *secularism,* not socialism — "It's all a horrible mistake. I never attacked socialism." This explanation, though, sounded faintly clinky to some — Graham having professed only a few months earlier, "Within five years we can say good-bye to England when Aneurin Bevan takes over," and not long after that, having indicated to his radio audience on *Hour of Decision* that he and his team just might set out for England soon to challenge its general drift into "Marxian socialism." Perhaps the most charitable characterization of his hastily devised disavowal from the decks of the *United States* was put forward by one crusade spokesman in London: "You caught him on the high seas without his documents or his advisor." Whatever, that quip about socialism was to prove one of those "momentous indiscretions," as Balzac once recited, "of which they say so picturesquely, 'Yoke five bullocks to your cart!' — you will need at least that to get you out of the mud." For all his earlier exhortations back in the U.S., Graham declared after his arrival in England, "I am not anti-Socialist, anti-Liberal, or anti-Conservative. I am completely neutral in politics," and he finally even offered the sportingly effusive concession in London, "You can say what you like about socialism, but boy, it's done a lot of good here!"

Despite that, two U.S. Senators then in Britain who had been enlisted to appear with Graham his opening night, Stuart Symington and Styles Bridges, phoned around 3:30 that afternoon to say they wouldn't be able to make it after all; they were entailed in a dinner that evening. This news came as the most unnerving of omens to Graham — a portent of a withdrawal at last of that mystic grace he had enjoyed ever since his deliverance forth by Hearst in 1949. Graham himself acknowledges, "I had a terrible sinking feeling," and one friend would later recall, "If ever man was stripped of any confidence in himself, it was dear Billy. He was shaking from head to foot." He began to anguish shrilly that it was all the infernal doing of the U.S. ambassador there, "that fellow Aldrich," and presently was seized by a savage headache — again, that "terrific pain at the base of my skull," as when he had found himself abruptly spilled into those voids of uncertainty shortly before his 1949 Los Angeles crusade. The night itself arrived as a singularly forbidding one — black, raw, haggard with sleet, rain, snow. Transported on to Harringay Arena by the chauffeur and sedan furnished him by the Ford Motor Company, Graham merely sat slumped in the back seat holding hands with Ruth, utterly inert, mute, blank, as if already blasted back into obscurity.

But when they pulled up at Harringay — a vast dank wharf warehouse of a hall in the dingiest reaches of north London — they discovered it engulfed with thousands of people, and a moment later in Graham's dressing room, grinning ruddily, Symington and Bridges, Symington belling, "Billy, we just couldn't let you down." Graham, for his part, was faintly trembling now, panting in soft flurried gaspings like someone just surfacing from deep dark vaults of water. He was restored — returned to grace. And "on the platform," he later exulted, "were bishops of the Anglican Church and religious leaders from all over Britain. In the audience were members of Parliament and other leaders of British life. . . ." Over his next three months there, his accumulation of ranking converts included the First Sea Lord and Chief of Naval Staff, the Admiral of the Fleet, and

Sir John Hunt, leader of Hillary's Everest conquest the year before.

Actually, almost as much as by the "socialism" bumble, English sensibilities had been somewhat affronted at first by all the glare of Graham's advance publicity, with his billboard-sized countenance in rather livid tints melodramatically staring out all over London. But the actual services themselves turned out, as *The Times* remarked in surprise, to be — like those in New York — "very demure." The truth is, Graham was not so unwitting of the particular milieu of his location now in London not to tone himself studiously to it a bit — subduing his customary parrot-hued ties and suits to more sedate serges and woolens, modulating his usual pell-mell breathless clattering alarm-clock delivery to a more measured and deliberate enunciation. Even Barrows at last divested himself of his trombone. In all, Graham carefully Englished himself and his company to a degree while there — even though, when the Archbishop of Canterbury amiably offered after one evening's service, "We'll never see such a sight again until we get to Heaven," Grady Wilson convivially slung his arm around the prelate's shoulders, slightly jostling him, and hooted, "That's right, Brother Archbishop, that's right!"

But during those twelve weeks in England Billy produced an altogether winning and handsome impression — a kind of straightforward Eagle Scout of the American conscientiousness, wholly unpretentious and refreshingly open-natured, as simple and honest as a sunflower. Eventually, even the House of Commons gave a luncheon in his honor, and he wound up being accorded a reception by English gentry at Claridges, presided over by a peer named Lord Luke — though actually subsidized by Sid Richardson — where, amid the wide tinkling of cocktail crystalware, he confined himself to a glass of orange juice. Shortly after his arrival for this occasion, he was approached by an arresting figure in white cravat and swallowtails, to whom Graham bowed and pronounced, "How do you do, my lord?" — the man then dryly replying, "I am your waiter, sir." In time, he was invited to Clarence House for a chat with the Queen Mother — announcing afterward, "If anyone were to ask me who was the most charming person I have ever met, I would say, without hesitation, 'The Queen Mother!' " — and shortly after this, to Windsor Castle for tea with the Queen herself, where on entering, he heartily grabbed and shook the hand of the butler who was reaching to take his hat.

At last he was granted an audience with Winston Churchill, then serving as Prime Minister for his last time and already sinking ponderously into that dim moroseness of his life's final long winter. Actually having to be nudged into the courtesy by one of his private secretaries, he received Graham on a gray afternoon in the Cabinet Room at Downing Street, still a bit grumpish and short of word, standing squat and slightly rumpled behind a long conference table, an enormous unlighted cigar wedged in one blunt hand. "It was one time I was really awed," Graham reports, "though, you know, I had never realized how short he was." After they were seated, Churchill mumbled something about having read of his presence in Great Britain, but his voice seemed only some thick low sound, stirring dully under the great loads of all his time — his eyes bleary like the eyes of an ancient tortoise, he heavy and sluggish, almost as if drowsing, from his long tumultuous passage through over half a century of uproars and splendors and disasters, immense commotions. The large room in which he sat alone now with Graham was strangely murky; "There wasn't a single light on," remembers Graham, only a dingy paleness from the smoky day outside admitted, through bleak windows, over the bare polished expanses of the tabletop. Regarding Graham for a moment with a peer out of the deepest brimstone reaches of experience, out of a weary knowing as old as the Fall, he presently muttered, "What hope do you have for the world? I am an old man without any hope for the world." Graham instantly rang, "I am filled with hope!" — deftly withdrawing then his small slim black New Testament from his coat pocket, he proposed, "Life is very exciting, even if there's a war. Because I know what is going to happen in the future," and as he continued his energetic expounding, Churchill stared at him with a curious fixedness, uttering not a syllable, merely a remote and incredulous fascination in his filmy eyes, as if musing over what was beginning to seem a vague aspiring effort by this glossy young American evangelist now actually to float out the net over him too. . . . Afterward, he grunted only that he had found Graham "a most interesting and agreeable young man." But after this forty-five-minute session with Churchill, on his return to the United States Graham was enspirited to announce, "I am convinced that the Lord has given me a world ministry."

But in Scotland the next year, the response to his efforts — mounted in Glasgow's Kelvin Hall amid a great profusion of camera lights, cranes, trolleys — turned out somewhat nipped. The peculiar indifference to Graham there — even though, as one visitor to Kelvin Hall later reflected, religion has always been more or less the national connoisseurship of the Scots, about what opera is to Italy — may have simply been one measure of the degree to which Graham had reconstituted into a polyethylene blandness all the old fierce theologies brought by his own ancestors from these very heaths and moors: those briny metaphysical potions he was returning to them now, after some two hundred years, reprocessed into a kind of pietistic Kool-Aid. While a BGEA documentary of that crusade was rather ambitiously entitled *Fire on the Heather,* subsequent scrutinies found only marginally perceptible smolderings — in the seven churches accounting for 98 percent of the Protestant membership in Glasgow, attendance did increase from a 56,503 average in 1954 to 67,078 a month after the crusade, though ebbing back to 62,224 a year later; but there was an actual decrease in church members from 203,430 to 202,035 a month after Graham's services.

Whatever, after Scotland, Graham pressed on to the Continent. Before a four-day foray into France, Graham declared with what was beginning to seem by now a singular facility for systematically producing appalling clankers, that France was like "a watch without a mainspring. . . . The French just sin and sin, and get weaker." Like the "socialism" gaffe with England, this required in following days some rather feverish calisthenics

of interpolation. But in later services in Paris, in a tent auditorium pitched in a vacant lot at the Flea Market, he kept demanding of his French audience, "Why are you unfaithful to
your wife?" Altogether, in France he was like some evangelical
Dodsworth out of the plain vanilla virtues of Inner America,
warily sensing himself now among the arabesque dissolutions of
old effete Europe. In turn, when he appeared at the Vélodrome
d'Hiver — brought on by a local Protestant churchman with the
cry, *"Voilà* Beelee!" — it was as if the very milieu there, as he
proceeded to preach amid a gallery of cognac advertisements arrayed around the balconies, simply could not accept him, quite
digest him: the lighting around him fluttered, faltered, flared
wackily, the amplification system gasped in and out, the roof
suddenly began leaking under the batterings of a rainstorm.
Even though his reception there was fairly bouncing — the congregation chanting, "Beelee, Beelee," the impression of one of
them being he was "the famous American clairvoyant," he
swamped by the crowds after his messages with calls of *"Jésus,
Jésus, mon Dieu!"* — yet it had a certain Gallic flair and vivacity in
the midst of which Graham seemed, with his chill Anglo-Saxon
proprieties, a bit dislocated and squeamish. When he was suddenly enveloped and bussed on both his cheeks by a portly Protestant cleric with a great frothing beard, Graham was noticeably
startled and disconcerted, remarking afterward, "His beard tickled. Anyway, he hadn't eaten any garlic." His vague discomfiture
as he moved among the French also happened to be accompanied by a dreary succession of kidney attacks.

In Germany, though, Graham seemed immeasurably more
vigorous and effective. He addressed a throng of some sixty-five
thousand one Sunday afternoon in Nuremberg's stadium, lightning scattering in a darkly heaping sky and thin rain flicking
while he preached from the foot of a megalithic cross, with banners lettered *Jesus Christ Is the Light of the World* rippling everywhere from the amphitheatre's colonnades. In Berlin's Olympic
Stadium, he was introduced with a somewhat Wagnerian
flourish — a two-thousand-voice choir pealing anthems to a blazing of four hundred brasses — and he took the pulpit to exhort

what was advertised later by his corporation as "the largest youth gathering since Hitler," he indeed looking like some bright pale-eyed Teutonic godling against the sheer blue sky. He himself would later report raptly, "The tremendous power of modern Germany is almost frightening. There is every possibility that this nation could turn to God and lead the world in a spiritual awakening." At the least, on Graham's several visits to West Berlin, the authorities on the other side were prompted to loose a continuous rolling concussion of practice rounds from their artillery throughout one night's service, and to bring out tanks on the main thoroughfare on the other side of the Brandenburg Gate when Graham pitched a tent in the Tiergarten, only three hundred yards from the East Berlin divide. But when they demanded that Graham's revival tent be removed from the Tiergarten, Graham not only vociferously refused, but, in those cool black autumn evenings in Berlin, his voice doughtily blared on loudspeakers over the floodlights into the Eastern sector — "Germany's youth are ready to follow a new leader! It has been demonstrated that the new Germany will follow Christ! And if that happens, Germany can lead the world!"

But whether he was in Madison Square Garden or a soccer stadium in Manila, in Santa Barbara or Yugoslavia, the service — the choreographies and religious dramaturgies — remained the same, the same systematic and enclosed occasion duplicating itself again and again against merely a succession of travel-poster backdrops, even in a red-brick bullring once on the dust-blown outskirts of Lima, with twelve thousand Peruvians gnawing on chunks of grilled beef hearts and swigging down corn beer through the hymns and collection and message. It was more as if he were being spirited through a series of foreign slide scenes, posing momentarily in each and then, with a blink, blooming for another moment in the next. In Maracaibo, actually, he had to be rapidly bundled out of the State Legislative Hall when a brief ruction developed outside, howls of *"Yanqui no, Castro sí!"* fists hammering on the closed doors, even a few pistols whamming away into the air. Yet Graham reported after this South American tour, with his compulsively gleeful inexactness, "There was nothing, not one jeer. Not one stone was thrown. There was nothing but warm welcome everywhere. All of it was far beyond anything we had anticipated!" Also, throughout that South American expedition, he had been fairly consistently rebuffed by the Catholic Church, its leaders refusing even to meet with him privately, a disapprobation that resulted in the mayor of one town in Colombia denying him the use of the municipal stadium. Yet on his return, it was as if this particular reaction to his presence had simply never entered his field of notice; one would have assumed from his jubilant reports afterward that, to his perspectives, it had all been a happily unanimous reception he had met with. In the same way, after a short tarry in the Philippines during which Manila's archbishop rather direly admonished all Catholics to stay away from his rallies, Graham would blithely insist, "The Catholic Church has been extremely friendly to me anywhere I have gone."

In all, the immediate and particular realities of the sites through which he passed impinged on him only nebulously. While he was in Bangkok, he was taken for a look at an opium den, and he later recounted, "The place was very clean, I must say — extremely so. . . . It must be a terrible addiction. I thought it was one of the most terrible things we have seen," but he added, "this type of addiction seemed to be far more orderly than the type we have in the United States." In fact, it was orderliness that seemed to particularly preoccupy him in his rangings about the face of the earth. He found South Korea especially congenial on that count — enthusing afterward, "You know, in Korea, when you walk into a classroom, the students will *snap!* to attention. It was wonderful how students bow to the teacher in Korea. They don't sit down until the teacher tells them, they don't stand up until the teacher tells them. *Absolute discipline!*" Indeed, when Graham was addressing one large assembly all hunkering on the ground out in the Korean countryside on a winter afternoon, a policeman could be glimpsed in the distance lustily clubbing back down a youth who had thought to stir to his feet for a moment.

Even more, in these trackings about the globe, Graham

seemed to assume an incidental aspiration to serve as a kind of informal ambassador-at-large of the American ethic. After his passage through Southeast Asia in 1956, he returned to announce that the advance of Communism there had been "slowed down to a walk," and to present such assurances, as he unfolded for the *U.S. News & World Report,* "everyone felt if there's any nation in the world that is friendly to the United States, it's the people of Thailand. We were told everywhere that that's one country that the United States can count on." Of Korea he declared, "You can't help but admire Syngman Rhee. He's a great stalwart giant. He's every inch a Christian, a Methodist, a man with very strong ideas. He is the George Washington of Korea. He is ready to go to war if necessary to reunite his country." Similarly, on a stopover in Formosa, he passed a delicately filigreed evening with Generalissimo and Madame Chiang Kai-shek, during which Madame Chiang informed Graham, as he would later record, "that for a long time now she had ceased to think of earthly things. She said, 'My mind is entirely on spiritual things, and my eyes are on Christ.' I doubt," Graham went on, "if there are two statesmen in the world today that are more dedicated to Christ and His cause than Generalissimo Chiang Kai-shek and his wife." Chiang himself "was smiling the entire time. I seemed to sense that the light of Christ was in his face." Nevertheless, after they had passed a while "discussing spiritual things . . . the Generalissimo pulled a black nightcap from his pocket and put it over his head," at which Graham and his party arose and took their leave.

Despite his ideological exuberances in these jaunts, Graham in time was even granted a dispensation from authorities in Yugoslavia to conduct three services in Zagreb — assuring party officials at a dinner that religion actually made for more dutiful and diligent citizens. Then at a soccer field at a local Catholic seminary on a raining Sunday afternoon, he urged the congregation huddling under umbrellas to "obey those in authority." And in the summer of 1959, after consenting to a stipulation that he engage in no religious exercises while there, he finally succeeded in infiltrating — however briefly, however minimally reduced to little more than just his own person — on into Russia.

With a meager party, he landed in Moscow in a stunning vacuum, for once, of any crowds of flashbulbs — unnoticed, unrecognized, abruptly and utterly anonymous. It was a slightly discomposing and surreal sensation. But he was quickly recollected and enspirited again when, touring the museums of Moscow, he came upon various religious insignia in the galleries of cultural relics, which he took to mean that "religion is still alive here too!" He affected to be astounded to discover the gold crosses atop the Kremlin's church museums, marveling, "Over the heart of the Kremlin — the cross! That's a symbol I never expected to see here. To have the religious spirit in the heart of the Kremlin! It's symbolic of some future date." And on his arrival back in Paris on his way home, he announced, "I could read on the faces of the people a great spiritual hunger, and the sort of insecurity that only God can solve."

But another, considerably warmer, impression he had come away with happened to touch off a minor rumpus when, at a stopover in England, he went on to acclaim the moral earnestness of the Soviets, "the moral purity," in contrast to an unnerving stroll he had recently taken through a London park. He reported admiringly that in Moscow, "I did not see one person walking down the street with an arm around another. We went to a park where thousands of young people were gathered. They held hands, but they were very disciplined." But wandering into London's parks once, as he had earlier declared, "I was so embarrassed, I took my wife out of them." To rather bristling queries by British newsmen then as to what precisely he had beheld, Graham at first could only bring himself to hint at it, stammerously: "I have traveled all over the world, and never seen anything like it," and at last submitted, faintly flushing, "The parks looked as if they had been turned into a bedroom." Finally, just as he was about to board a plane, he managed to blurt it — "We saw two couples in the midst of the sex act in broad daylight." On his arrival back in the States, he further reflected, "It's interesting to me that in the Soviet Union, Cuba, and China, they're trying to build a strong society, a revolutionary society that they hope will ultimately conquer the world. But they don't allow this kind of sexuality. They came to the conclusion that it's a descructive force. . . ."

Of all of Graham's evangelistic extensions abroad, perhaps the most rousingly successful have been to Australia. It turned out to be something like the special country of his own spirit: an open sunny land of hale, tanned, neighborly, uncomplicated folk. The only other country possibly more congenial to his deepest nature has been Switzerland — tidy, fresh, brisk, vigorously hygienic, its national passion a sensible pragmatism, a neat business-like watchwork nation. It has proven perhaps his fondest locale on the planet. But in Australia, they took to him with a great heartiness, and he to them. In one crusade, about half of the country's entire population came out to hear him, and the decisions registered amounted to about 1.25 percent of the whole citizenry.

But in all these coursings about, it was as if Graham were orbiting the globe still securely enclosed within the systems and air locks of his own organization's space capsule. In 1960, from a departure shed at Idlewild on a January afternoon scattered with light whiskings of snow, he boarded his plane for Africa — on a mission which had been entitled "Safari for Souls." From those snow flurries at Idlewild, they then hammered across the Atlantic, beating through a foreshortened flare and wane of dusk into night into dawn, as if speeding now in some time slip through a quickening recession of days, years, centuries, until presently the mottled tremendous flank of Africa began to edge out into the blue haze of the sea below and ease immensely under the wings of the plane — the dark shoreline of that land where back in an unmemoried eon man had his first runtish barking emergence on grassy veldts and savannahs — the plane then making a somewhat reeling and slappy descent down into the glaring swelter of Dakar. And over the next nine weeks, in a fourteen-thousand-mile trek, Graham moved over Africa engaging primordial paganisms and animisms, worships of the sea and thunder and beasts, ancient magics of feathers and dried bats, with his own staunch dry-cleaned churchly sanctitudes and an accompanying pageantry of amplifiers, recorders, generators, and master consoles — his own magics of technology.

It was not always a completely decisive encounter. In Nigeria once, electrical charges somehow strayed from a live wire to a platform railing, which, when Cliff Barrows happened to grasp it, dealt him a jolting eye-glazing kick, and now and then sudden slammings of rain would, with a brief crackle of sparks, snuff out to dead silence the public address system. Beside these occasional disarrayings, Graham also was persistently challenged by Islamic evangelists to healing duels — one proposal being to divide equally between them thirty hospital patients pronounced incurable for a grand public face-off between Christ and Allah. Roy Gustafson, who had accompanied Graham there, remembers, "Boy, those phones started ringing, press people and all sorts, wanting to know what Billy was going to do." But Graham, beginning to feel somewhat harried, would merely snap to all inquiries, "No comment. No comment." Finally, says Gustafson, "we started getting all these wires and letters from people back in the States — particularly the Pentecostal folks — telling us 'Go on! Accept the challenge! Show them that the God of Elijah still lives!' But Billy just kept quoting from Jesus' parable, 'If they hear not Moses and the prophets, neither will they be persuaded, though one rose from the dead.' "

There was also a spot of unpleasantness after Graham arrived in Ghana, where it happened that Prime Minister Nkrumah had begun presenting his own person as "the son of man" and "the Redeemer" and having his mother hymned on occasion, "Blessed art thou among women." Graham was thus greeted there with a rather measured enthusiasm. But more than that, what abruptly thinned the attendance at his services in Accra was his refusal to condemn impending French atomic tests in the Sahara. Graham's own explanation was that, morally, a man who heaves a spear with deadly intent was as iniquitous as a man detonating a nuclear bomb — an equation that, on several counts, did not further endear him to local citizens.

Still, he forged dauntlessly on — down the equatorial steamy-surfed shores of West Africa, the tin-roofed smoky shantytowns

of Lagos with their hard dirt lanes and Coca-Cola signs, multitudes gathering in the speckled shade under plane trees at noon-
day, on to the stark baked red-dust desert towns of the Moslem
north with their thin spiralings of minarets in the hot pale sky:
Graham preaching under thatched platform awnings with a
squinting and faintly pained grin in the sun glare, attired in the
dark wash-and-wear business suits of some vice-president of a
Topeka savings-and-loan office, his hair flurrying in the wind. In
a sense Graham in Africa was venturing now all the way back to
the worn earths of the whole race's genesis — and as it happened, among those yellow scorched plains and mud-cake villages, there transpired one of his most eloquent moments in all
his years of preaching: he recounted to one assembly of tribesmen how, while walking in the woods once with his small son, he
had accidentally trodden on a hill of ants, and when his son
asked if he couldn't help them, Graham had told him no, only if
he could become an ant himself — "So how could mighty God
speak to us little people? God looked down from heaven, and he
wanted to talk to us. But how could he? We so little, he so big.
You know what he did? Now listen carefully. Mighty God became a man — and that's who Jesus Christ was!" But from this
metaphor for God's compassionate intercession in history, Graham would then go on to bring the Calvinist message in a rather
stern and hectoring blare back to these landscapes of mankind's
beginning: "You've told lies, you've committed adultery, you've
done all these bad things. Because when man disobeyed God in
the Garden of Eden, a great wall came between God and man,
men hated each other, and all these evils came into the world,
and eventually death" — elaborately detailing for them then how
nails had been hammered into Jesus' hands and feet, "He bore
our sins in his own body on the tree! All the lies we ever told. All
the things we ever stole. All our lust and evil. All our jealousy
and pride. If you say no to that sacrifice and forgiveness, you will
be judged! You've seen the storm come up. You've heard the
lightning and thunder. God's judgment is like the lightning and
thunder!" And he would then instruct them that they must rup-
ture themselves from "the world, the flesh, the devil. You must

repent! You must learn from your sins, you must quit your lying, you must quit your immorality. You must receive Christ into your heart by faith. You must confess Christ openly — and you must live for Christ and get into a church."

Once in Tanganyika, after presenting this fearsome Protestant catechism to Masai villagers standing in the brilliant sun on the lower slopes of Kilimanjaro, when Graham then asked those who wished to make a decision to raise their hands, not a single arm lifted — they merely stood watching him calmly, impassive and motionless under their rigidly held parasols. He waited a moment, and then leaned forward again, raising high one long forefinger, and knelled in a lower clanging voice, "You have not understood what I said. Now you listen carefully: you have never repented of your sins, you are willing to pay the price even if it means death! Now — lift your hands!" With that, thousands of arms finally sprang into the air.

In between these evangelisms, Graham indulged in a few leisurely outings about the countryside. He tramped once to Victoria Falls, lank and ibis-like in khaki shorts with his New Testament clamped in one hand, and he happened another time to come upon a film crew shooting footage along a river for a movie about the Victorian missionary-explorer David Livingstone: at the invitation of the director, he stretched himself out to be carried in the kind of tented litter in which an enfeebled Livingstone had been transported on into the interior by natives — swung up on the shoulders of the bearers, Graham lay somewhat uneasily flat on his back under the canopy, trying to peer now and then over his chin, his shoes sticking up like rabbit ears out of the other end, floating along in this manner for a few moments until, suddenly, one pole snapped, and he was very nearly spilled into the muddy river-edge aslosh with crocodiles. He preferred, actually, to conduct most of his sightseeing sorties by airplane. Swooping low over veldts eddying with shoals of antelope, zebra, buffalo, tides of wildebeests, he and Barrows in the cockpit of the plane would yelp, "Wahoo! Wahoo!" — Graham finding himself now arrived at the actual terrains of those fantasies of his boyhood when he would lose himself for hours in the woods beyond his father's fields, and he whooped as they skimmed over shambling surges of elephants, "Look, fellas, there aren't many places down there where Tarzan could have swung from tree to tree!"

Actually, most of his congregations, in the cricket fields and soccer stadiums where he preached, were rather soberly dressed townspeople, middle-class professionals many of whom were churchgoers themselves. Once in Addis Ababa, a Coptic patriarch snuffled, "Who is this man trying to bring Christ to our ancient land, which adopted Christianity sixteen hundred years ago? Let him go into the bush and Christianize the heathen." Graham did essay that several times: in Tanganyika once, tieless and in his shirt-sleeves, he wandered with his Bible into a village of mud huts, where a procession of women, their bare breasts bobbling, were toting in five-gallon tins of beer on their heads for a communal dance that was underway. One huge villager with a gourd of beer greeted Graham with the happy bawl, "Boy, we having some party!" After a few minutes, Graham, in a reckless flush of affability, even allowed himself to be momentarily tugged into a few shuffling steps with the dancers — until sudden chill second thoughts overhauled him, at which he delicately detached himself and retreated behind a table that someone had draped in a white cloth for him. He remained deposited there while he regarded the dancing — gaudily daubed figures coiling with fly whisks before him in a drum-battering hip-scooping transport at least unmistakably pagan if not spectacularly obscene — with his hands clasped politely together atop the table, a rather frail smile on his face. Finally, noting some of the celebrants tottering off to plop under a tree, he sidled over to them, and settling himself on the grass with them, produced his Bible, and began reading through a few verses. One of them presently interrupted, "I am too drunk. I do not understand." Graham replied with a cordial grin, "When you have Christ in your heart, you won't have to get drunk again." But he shortly gave it up, submitting to one of his companions as he was leaving, "Somehow I don't think I made much of an impression on them. . . ."

And the more Graham ranged beyond his pulpit services back into the bush — trudging through the dusts of villages in wing-tip shoes and dark slacks and starched white shirts with sleeves rolled to his elbows, his taffy-blond hair closely barbered (some tribesmen in Nigeria called him "the man with his skin peeled off"), proceeding with a resolute pleasantness through wild clatterings of drums, a harlequin tattooing of hides all around him, coming once on a party of Ubangis with their pancake-slabbed lips, all dustily bare-hided with only sprigs of leaves at their groins, the women with slick melon-plump buttocks and bare breasts brown as the earth itself, like strays just rawly lobbed out of Eden themselves and staring at Graham with dark peers — the more he ranged back into such regions of man's primal easy sensual barbarism, perhaps for that reason the more he seemed to be beleaguered by insomnia.

Toward the end of his nine weeks there, lifting out of Nairobi, his plane passed over a school for missionaries' children in whose chapel he had spoken the day before. He glanced down to see them all gathered in their recess field around a message they had spelled out for him with large rocks, *God Bless You All*, waving now and calling to him with unheard cries, their dwindling tiny figures in crisp white-bloused uniforms remote and unreachable and bright over the schoolyard receding below him; and as the plane headed on toward Ruanda Urundi and he leaned back in his seat, he abruptly remembered the white morning steeples and calm lawns of all the tidy little towns across America, his own children back in his mountainside home in North Carolina, and suddenly he was weeping, his cheeks washed with tears.

Nevertheless, as Graham continued in these odysseys, in the late Fifties Governor Price Daniel of Texas proclaimed, "Billy Graham is doing more than anyone I know for this great country of ours by helping other people of the world understand what we believe in." Before Graham embarked on a four-week campaign through India in 1956, he was invited to Washington to consult with Secretary of State John Foster Dulles — a chat during which Dulles himself allowed that he considered the most critical need of the time to be the propagation of a Christian message of discipline "to the masses" as in olden ages. He was specifically intrigued with this venture of Graham's into India, as Graham himself reported later, because "he seemed to feel that, particularly after the recent visit of Messrs. Khrushchev and Bulganin of Russia to India, that America was in need of someone that could appeal to the masses of India."

Still, before his departure, Graham felt obliged to put forward the curious assurance, for a successor to Paul, that he was "not going to proselytize any Hindus." At last, with thermos bottles filled from his room's sink faucet and packed in his luggage so he would be able to drink American water for a while still after his arrival in India, he fared forth from his New York hotel. And over the long flight there, he read in his Bible from Paul's epistle to the Ephesians, *"We all had our conversation in times past in the lusts of our flesh. . . . But now in Christ Jesus ye who sometimes were far off are made nigh by the blood of Christ. . . ."* The speckled wastes of the Sinai Desert emerged under him out of the night in a crimson sunrise, with the pilot slowing the plane's engines as they passed Mt. Sinai, its savage rubbled ridges dazzled in the brimming sun's wash. . . . *"Whereof I was made a minister . . . that I should preach among the Gentiles the unsearchable riches of Christ. . . . Stand therefore, having your loins girt about with truth, and having on the breastplate of righteousness. . . . And for me, that utterance may be given unto me, that I may open my mouth boldly, to make known the mystery of the gospel. . . ."*

But after his arrival in Bombay, he seemed, suddenly translated into that prodigious and ageless land, no more than an incidental and momentary intrusion — the posters advertising his rallies tacked to baobab trees with a kind of hasty and flimsy ephemerality in landscapes endlessly littered with stumpy ruins, the anonymous flotsam of long-receded millennia, with crows scattering off over plains of hot hazed dust under a low smoldering pink sun. In cities that were swarming just as pandemoniously when Babylon and Thebes and Troy were full of voices and multitudes, once even treading with faint shoeprints the mild dirt of the spot where over 2,400 years before Buddha had spoken his first sermon after his enlightenment, Graham moved about in it all, in white shirt-sleeves with opened collar and bleak haircut, like some tall thin apparition somehow briefly strayed from a YMCA church-ground picnic — strolling through millings of people along shade-spattered dirt paths under banyan trees, incandescent blossoms everywhere perfuming the hot air, his flaxen head bobbing amicably in greeting, hands folded politely under his chin.

But in Benares, he found himself stumbling through an interminable twining of rank and sweetly reeking streets like tunnels, repeatedly bumping with a start into the heaving flanks of cows, and finally stood gaping at the soft small roar and glare of corpses being flamed on kindling pyres along the Ganges, dark forms slowly smoldering with an interior luminescence like images in a photograph negative. Then he came on a temple pool of "stagnant, dirty water," where, as he recorded later, "hundreds were washing their clothes, others were bathing, and others were drinking. It was considered holy water. It was almost impossible to believe our eyes." He could not have been more of an alien, plopped here among this mystic indistinguishable mingling of flies and holiness and sensuality — he happening on a shrine to Siva where, after dutifully removing his shoes and proceeding on inside, he suddenly discovered himself in a celebration of luxuriant carnality, priests offering vegetables to phallic effigies with a cyclorama around him of serenely smiling cherubic figures opulently entwining, clinging, "the most awful, obscene drawings and carvings," as he reported it. "This is all done in the name of religion. I think I felt the powers of darkness and heathenism more in Benares than in any city in which I've ever been."

He almost dizzily exulted when he found, in the midst of all this, an enclave of young Christian seminarians, neatly brushed clean-cut lads, "some of the most handsome, dark-skinned young men completely dedicated to Christ." And finally, when he was greeted at a missionary compound by a trilling flock of Indian orphans all now in freshly pressed uniforms, brightly bearing him armloads of flowers, again as when he had passed over that school for missionaries' children in Africa, "I had something very strange and unusual happen. They all had the joy of God on their little faces. And as I walked around the grounds, I could not keep back the tears — in fact, I could hardly talk."

Indeed, even here among the oily pyre smokes and wild slapping and dinning of small Hindu drums, it was still the same affair as Portland and Houston and New York and Charlotte at his after-sundown rallies over the countryside, globes of lights strung over the crowd sitting on grass mats under lowering twilight clouds and he preaching in his Sunday-sober suit from an illuminated platform flickering with moths, crying at the end of his sermon, "Get up out of your seat now and come — just get up from your seat, wherever you are. I want you to come. Over here, back there — yes, that's it, you come on. If you have friends, they will wait on you. The Holy Spirit is speaking to you tonight. You come now. No matter what your trials are, no matter what your sufferings are, you can be *singing* for joy! . . ."

Now and then, the First Calvary Baptist Church theologies he had brought over with him afforded the sensibilities of some Indians certain bogglements: one commentator acknowledged that "Dr. Graham can be dreadfully effective," but went on to report with a measure of amazement that he "propounds the theory that the reproductive act, for instance, is in itself sinful, 'the whole business being a legacy from Adam and Eve.' He insisted that his son, age three, was a liar, and asserted that he himself had wallowed in 'evil' pleasures until, at the age of seventeen, a 'voice' had asked him to spread the divine message." But Graham sustained his customary chipper insensibility to such demurrals — of one particularly venomous editorial about his presence in India, he simply insisted, "A very friendly article!"

Finally one morning, he presented himself at Nehru's office in New Delhi for a scheduled thirty-minute audience. Just before he was ushered on in, Dag Hammarskjöld emerged from a conference with Nehru — seeming to pause for an instant when he glimpsed Graham, but then striding on. Graham would later surmise, "I imagine that he thought he recognized me, or had seen my picture somewhere." But when he was conducted on into

Nehru's office, Graham found him in a somewhat glum and distracted humor. After a short exchange of pleasantries, "we sat down, and then he didn't say anything." A few seconds passed. Graham then commenced expansively to assure Nehru how much he was admired in the United States, how if he had perhaps been sometimes misinterpreted there it was only because few could really apprehend the enormous problems he faced. But as Graham recollected afterward, "when I got through what I considered a rather pleasant speech, he still didn't say anything" — he merely continued to regard Graham with a mute and dour gaze, absently fingering a letter-opener, sighing, glancing now and then at the ceiling. "Then I decided that I would tell him about our tour of India," and in the course of this account, Graham also notified Nehru that "peace conferences are no stronger than human nature, and human nature is diseased. In over three thousand years of history, there have been only three hundred years of peace. Why? It is because man has rejected God's offer of peace through faith in His son, Jesus Christ." When he had finished, Nehru wore if anything an even more morose expression. "He still didn't say a word, and there was a dead silence for a moment." At last, Graham produced his own testimony as to how he himself had been saved, "— and Christ can do that for everybody!" at which Nehru finally betrayed a guttering of curiosity, leaning forward to inquire more exactly into this happening and listening to Graham's explanation with a light smile now on his face. After he left, Graham declared, "I had a very strong impression that he was pro-Christian." (And on his return to the U.S., reporting to Dulles and Eisenhower, Graham would advise that India and Nehru could be lured into a closer affinity with the United States through the device of such special gifts as "a streamlined, air-conditioned train, or a new Cadillac for Mr. Nehru, pure white. Wouldn't it be a wonderful thing if we gave to India a beautiful new train, or Mr. Nehru a white air-conditioned Cadillac?")

But in fact, Graham began to attract throngs, as he ambled over India, soon outnumbering even those that had turned out for Khrushchev and Bulganin during their passage through a

few weeks earlier — a development that did not entirely charm
Nehru, actually, since he had accompanied them in their peregrinations to insure sizable audiences. But if anything, the more
spectacular popular receptions being accorded to Graham now
were simply a testimonial to India's lingering zest for the mystical over the political — one hundred thousand white-gowned
listeners once gathered before him in a vast clearing under date
palms that teenage girls toiling for weeks with wooden hoes and
baskets had transformed into a terraced dirt stadium. And while
his pentecostalisms there remained as astringent as always — *The
soul has a disease. It is worse than cancer or leprosy. God calls it sin. All
of us are afflicted with it. And the Bible says the wages of sin is death,
eternal separation from God in a place called Hell* — yet as he delivered these ammoniacal Calvinist austerities against lavish sultry
swimming gold-and-vermilion sundowns, his figure elevated on
a platform vaguely resembling a pagoda shrine, somehow his
frosty theologies seemed to cease to matter. It was as if he, too,
were gradually being assimilated, gently digested, into that land's
delirious all-devouring polymorphous sense of the divine, Graham himself now being hospitably installed among its some
thirty thousand other gods, in honored company among Vishnu
and monkeys and cows and lotus blossoms — like that moment
in the crammed sweltering courtroom in *Passage to India* when
Mrs. Moore, the kindly British matron who has just departed
back for England, suddenly begins to be transmuted into yet
another of their deities with a low droning plaintive chant,
"*Esmiss Esmoor, Esmiss Esmoor. . . .*"

In village after village, Graham moved through ever-greater
surgings of people, "crowds had gathered to put up a roadblock
to stop us, and the police would not let us through until I had
gotten up and waved to the crowd," arms lifting up to him offerings of oranges and bananas and garlands of flowers, a processional that began to take on a peculiar semblance to the climactic
triumphal entry of Jesus into Jerusalem, palm fronds even
swimming and dancing in the air now throughout his progress.
He remarked eventually, "It's in a sense a terrifying experience
with the crowd pressing in close with their dark faces peering at

you, trying to get us in view. . . . You could imagine that anything could happen if they became excited." Sometimes at night, staying in a provincial hotel, he would find himself in a room with nothing between him and the shuffle of the street immediately outside but a flimsy swinging door, a ragged curtain, and sitting on a rickety bed reading his New Testament in an orange insect-muttering lamplight, he would glance up to discover still forms staring in at him through the curtain gap with a noiseless, unshooable captivation. In some way, it was as if all the customary small organized details of his detachment from the life of the land around him were beginning gradually to dissolve, dissipate — crows would flap into his rooms to rummage in the bowl of fruit on his dresser, pilfer his cufflinks and tie clasps on his bedside table. . . . Before long, a kind of light swoon seemed to settle over him: "I had on a very heavy winter suit and the sun came up and it was very warm. I had not slept very well and I was very tired. . . . I have also felt something else that has been very strange, and that is an expectant faith all the time, continually believing that something is going to happen." In his preaching now, when he mounted the pulpit, he would extend his arm and bow his head and pray "almost a prayer of commanding, a prayer of authority," as he later related with a certain wonder — "I remember I opened my hand as though to come down upon the crowd, and I said, 'Oh God, stop the noise. Quiet the people now.' Immediately a deathlike hush came on the crowd. It was like the breath of God had suddenly fallen. I preached for about an hour and had tremendous power and liberty. People began to run forward and fall upon their knees. . . . A blind man was led by his daughter. . . . Some of them even began to scream to God for mercy; others were saying, 'Jesus, save me. Jesus, save me,' until about three thousand to four thousand people had come. They were falling on their knees like flies. It was almost as if they were being slain by the Lord." It began to seem as if he were reaching now in some private mystic sense, as he mentioned of one flight across a range of mountains near Bangalore, "nearly my fainting altitude. . . . I got very faint. It was sort of a good feeling. My head was swimming. I hardly knew what was going on around me."

Finally, in a shabby little sun-blasted city called Palamcottah, in the languishing southernmost heats of India, Graham arrived one morning to address a convocation in the Christian cathedral there, and found a seethe and billowing of people seemingly convoked out of the sheer bright fever-shimmer of the air itself. As he told it later, "The cathedral was jammed and some five thousand or six thousand people were outside, and the streets were lined with people. An English missionary was fearful that many of them were beginning to accept me as a god. The word had spread all over southern India; the oxcarts were bringing in thousands of people. As we got to the cathedral, our car could not get through. The people were pressing and fighting. Many of them were trying to touch us. I almost thought the car would overturn. They were pushing it and grabbing it." Graham at last had to grapple himself on out of the car, and at his sudden loom now among them, there immediately issued from the moiling of the throng a vast unanimous release of sound like a soft huge moan, "*Ahhhhh. . . .*" He began pulling himself through their midst, moving tall and lordly and luminous in the center of their ravenous gazes, a certain abject violent musk about them in the heat. "Many of them tried to get in my shadow, and I told them time after time that I was not a god but man, but many of them fell down and practically worshiped me as I came by." He struggled on through them toward the cathedral with the slow and dreaming sluggishness of someone moving against a deep undertow, against some terrific opposite gravity, a chill glitter of sweat now on his temples, lifted hands tangling and teeming about him while a kind of ecstatic tongueless sibilation, like locusts or millions of bees, began thrilling everywhere in the air around him. When he was delivered finally into the cool shadows of the sanctuary of the cathedral, he stood there for a long moment, panting and dizzy.

But that was as close as he came to the sun of that mystery. On his return to the United States, he did vaguely indicate, "Sometimes it seems as if I've lived a whole new lifetime in a few weeks," but the experience, the memory, had been reduced to a kind of polite warm tea of amiableness: "The different people everywhere with their common yearnings and needs, you can't forget them. They've made me one of them." His reflections toward the end of the whole trek suggested a boy's letter home during the last days of summer camp: "Everything has been absolutely perfect. I have not been sick one single day. I do not have any cold, sore throat, or stomachache. . . . I have not lost my temper once and try to wait patiently on everybody." Whatever rare metaphysical altitudes he may have briefly and accidentally reeled through in India, "when we came back down," as he had confided of that flight across the mountain range, "I felt much better." When he was asked afterward to assess what had transpired there, he jubilantly narrated, "I don't think that in any place I've ever been, they've had finer platforms for me to speak from, better amplification systems, and finer arrangements." That was about all that was left now of that awesome moment on the hillside of Palamcottah.

It was in 1960 that he finally paid his first visit to the Holy Land, and so arrived at last, like the completion of some spiritual circle, in those calcium-white landscapes from which his whole ministry and vision — those Scripture verses taught him by his mother as she scrubbed him in that Saturday-night tin washtub, those Sunday-afternoon front-porch evocations of Judgment Day by his Uncle Simon, his surrender in Florida, his own crusades, his whole life's very meaning — had first been conceived and uttered: the actual aboriginal geographies of Elijah and Hosea and Isaiah and John the Baptist and Jesus himself, wastes of crags and gulches and blank dust and sun-stunned silences, as if God spoke most directly to mortals only in the medium of breathtaking heat and fierce white sun glare.

Graham happened to make his entry into the Holy Land in a blazing of flashbulbs, and he immediately announced, "Man, I feel as if I belong here!" At a press conference at the Mandelbaum Gate, he explained, "I became a Christian back in North

Carolina at the age of sixteen, and ever since then, I've always wanted to come see where Jesus lived, where he died." Over the following days, he loped buoyantly about those gaunt hills and ruins in a mesh golf cap and sunglasses, with reporters and photographers clambering over the stones after him in a constant whir and snick of cameras. There occurred a brief row over what facilities ought to be made available to him for any public addresses, Ben-Gurion finally wiring from the United States that he would be agreeable to most any arrangements so long as Graham "refrained from mentioning Jesus Christ before a Jewish audience." But Graham himself quickly charmed away this small awkwardness by appearing at a press conference at the King David Hotel to peal in his golden tones, "Shalom," and then proclaim, "I am going to address only Christian audiences. I have no intention of proselyting. In fact, I must be grateful to you for proselyting *me*. For Jesus Christ was a Jew, all his apostles were Jews, and the whole early church was Jewish."

In truth, it was not lost on the Israelis that one of their most vital rapports with the United States happened to lie with the sizable evangelical community there — those ruddy farina-plain gospel folk in Arkansas and Indiana and Nebraska who regarded themselves just as much as a People of the Book, and Israel's re-creation as one happy realization of the prophetic scenario for the Second Coming. Accordingly, Graham was received with particular solicitude by the Israelis. As on a subsequent visit he would be provided a Mercedes limousine to spirit him from the VIP lounge at the airport to his suite at the Jerusalem Hilton and on to visits with Golda Meir and Rabin, so in his first sojourn there in 1960 he was obligingly wafted about by helicopter to the sites he wished to behold, carried in a motorboat over the Sea of Galilee, even helicoptered out to the Megiddo Plain to scan for himself, from a windblown hilltop, the parched scruffy terrain awaiting the inevitable Armageddon of Revelation there someday.

He preached once in a Lutheran church in Jerusalem, with his voice on a loudspeaker outside clangoring over the old stone walls of the streets around. Before long, a considerable crowd had collected outside the church, and when Graham finished his message, he stepped out among them, they then thronging after him as he proceeded on, remembers Roy Gustafson, "through those narrow streets of Jerusalem where the crowds had followed Jesus once. It was the one time I recall when he didn't seem alarmed or bothered by a crowd pulling and pressing around him. In fact, I could tell he was rejoicing" — and as he made his way through the cavelike streets, he kept glancing back over his shoulder with a kind of amazed abstracted smile at the multitude welling after him. Another time, he arranged himself, in a dapper blazer and dark glasses, on a donkey like that which had borne Jesus into Jerusalem before his crucifixion, and let himself be gawkily carried a few jolting yards, his slacks hitched high on his thin shanks and his shoes almost scuffing the ground. Later, he strolled over the weedy brow of the bluff purported to be Golgotha, site of the crucifixion — pausing to read from his Bible, for recording by camera, the story of the crucifixion, lifting his arm to point, with crisp white shirt cuff shooting beyond his coat sleeve, to the road "where they which passed reviled him." Finally, he read again to the camera the story of the resurrection from the supposed site of the tomb, now a small snug scrupulously tended park of raked pathways and tidy flower beds and meditation benches under cedar trees — Graham, standing there with his opened Bible in his dark suit and glimmerous tie, looking as if he had just been transliterated directly out of some varnished suburban pulpit in Fort Worth or Kansas City.

For anyone reared in the religious climes of inland-America communities like the Charlotte of Graham's boyhood, it was indeed as if one had grown up, not only among those neighborhoods of oak lawns and gabled white houses, but also, simultaneously and as intimately, in the land of Canaan, in Galilee and Mt. Carmel and the Judean desert, an unseen inner second country which would abide changeless through all the years. As Graham professed of his first arrival in the Holy Land, "I felt like I'd just landed home. Everything was almost more familiar to me than Charlotte and Mecklenburg County." But yet, as he

tramped cheerfully about those primordial landscapes of his
faith — sere plains rubbled with traces of stone villages from the
time of Abraham; and then those squat rude crypts and cells
from the first dim emergence of Christianity, catacombs holding
in them still some old dank of anonymous dreadful asceticisms
and dark pieties — passing among all this, Graham somehow
suggested more a prosperous pharmacist from Pasadena among
those bleak bitten Biblical hills. He seemed robustly unwitting of
any disparity between his orderly, clinical, odorless sanctitudes
and whatever intimations lingered among those glowering rock-
wastes of the actual fury and anguish and blood and ecstasy that
had taken place in those settings. At the least, he was eminently
unlikely while there to wind up perishing like Bishop Pike in the
wilderness — that uncertain Christian divine, who, abstracted
through his fastidious equivocations into a kind of fine tentative
nebulousness, in the sudden primal glare of the Judean desert
seemed simply to evaporate altogether like a singed spiderweb.
Instead, Graham wound up making another film documentary
of it all, *His Land,* and then incorporating it into the BGEA's program of guided tours.

But through all these expeditions about the reaches of the
world — to France, to South America, to India — even in what
seemed these sensational farthest-flung affirmations of his message and his ministry, he still continued to be ambushed intermittently by the dreads of his old Samson complex: as he confessed once in Japan, "I feel tonight as if my ministry is going to
be very brief. My name has appeared in too many newspapers, it
has been placed on too many posters. There has been too much
praise. . . ."

IV

He would return from these ceaseless campaignings over the
face of the earth to tarry at his mountainside home in Montreat
for only a few weeks, bringing back with him toy stuffed animals

now and then, perhaps a small souvenir for Ruth. She and the children would be waiting just after dawn by the tracks at the railroad station down in Black Mountain as the train from New York pulled creaking in to a brief champing pause, and he would appear once more out of its steams in his crisp ice-white raincoat, wearily grinning. They would ride then back up the narrow drive curling through the steep woods — now in the early morning ringing with a thin chittering of birds — passing through the stone buttresses of their gate to, at last, the house. There, after long weeks among all those foreign cuisines, he would go immediately to the bowl in the kitchen to snatch up and chomp a fresh tomato. Later, for lunch, he would fetch himself a can of vienna sausages or pork and beans from the pantry. And that night, they would eat steaks, with Irish potatoes roasted in the ashes of their hearth. But for the first week or so back there, Ruth admits, "he'd always be a little restless."

Before they had removed themselves up to this retreat in 1956, while they were still lodging down the mountain in their renovated stone-wall summer house, tourists would cluster along their sidewalk to click snapshots of their front porch, some of them even browsing about the yard, plucking souvenir sprigs from their shrubbery, snatches of bark from their trees. More than once, Graham and his family would look up from their dinner table to find grave faces hanging in the window gazing in at them. It reached a point where Graham, to move from one side of his study to the other, would crawl on his hands and knees under the window. Finally they discovered that their small children had taken to charging tourists a nickel to pose for photographs out on the front walk.

But they had withdrawn to their more isolated abode on up the mountain as much, actually, to quarantine their children from the reckless worldly contagions loose in those lower latitudes. The truth is, it had been a fairly subdued community even down the mountain for their young to grow up in, made up mostly of church schools and religious assembly grounds, populated largely by retired ministers and missionaries with few other children about. But when Ruth was asked once if she and Billy ever had any uneasiness about their children eventually entering into those prodigal buckings seemingly endemic with the progeny of divines, she replied, "That's why we keep our children quite secluded now back in the mountains. . . ."

It was a refuge that had to be blasted and bulldozed out of the mountain's sheer slope, and was soon thereafter surrounded by an eight-foot-high electrified fence put up on the recommendation of J. Edgar Hoover and paid for by the president of Sun Oil. It became for them, as Ruth once termed it, "a kind of eagle's nest." For a time, the drive winding up to its gates led past small signs advising, "Vicious dogs. . . . Trespassers will be eaten," and the iron-grill gates themselves, set into stone bulwarks with the look of a Maginot Line fortification, would swing open only at the touch of electric buttons on the dashboards of Graham's cars. The grounds within were patrolled by a security guard — along with, over the years, a succession of enormous dogs padding and flowing through the dappling drifts of leaf shadows.

But for all these formidable barricadings, the house itself was surprisingly demure and sedate, a cozily winsome dwelling of an indefinite style somewhere between Early American cottage and suburban ranch house, with its interior decor largely done in nursery-room colors of yellow and blue and red-gingham. Set on its artificial graded ledge with its immaculately mown side lawn fringed in irises and daffodils, overlooking the far airy distances of the Black Mountains, around it there was no sign of any other earthly habitation in sight — it nestled there utterly alone in immense empty blue spaces of sky.

It was in this pretty solitude, then, that Ruth raised their five children, and to which Graham would return from his forgings among great hosts in remote locales. The youngest daughter, Bunny, would later recollect, "When Daddy was there, we weren't allowed to have friends in the house, and never on Sundays whether Daddy was there or not. No visitors, no TV. . . . If, for some special reason, we were allowed to have guests, we had to memorize three verses from the Bible before we could play." But even while those Sundays were confined to Bible games and Bible stories, it was also the only day in the week the children were permitted candy, soft drinks, gum. In fact, in something like a small analogue of Graham's own sense of the celestial effects of righteousness, their eldest child, Virginia, was set to learning by heart the Sermon on the Mount on the promise of twenty-five dollars and a new bicycle.

But Graham's administerings of discipline, when he was home, tended to be brisk and direct. "As my boys grew up," he once related, "I had to spank them sometimes, but on each occasion, I talked to them first for ten or fifteen minutes, explaining their transgressions. Next, I read the Bible to them. Finally, I punished them. Our daughters got the same treatment." One daughter recalls, "I can remember him whipping me three times — once, because I told Mother I hated her, another time when I kicked my brother in the head, and the third time when I told a lie and wouldn't retract it. But," she adds, "after it was all over, we'd pray together for guidance." For instruction in certain more elemental matters, Graham resorted to keeping a few sheep and goats around the place so that, rather in the same way he had come by his own enlightenments on those affairs, "the kids will learn the facts of life."

Rearing their children in the engarrisoned seclusion of that mountainside, Ruth says, "I was never so much afraid of physical danger for them. Especially the boys — boys need to be aggressive and take physical risks. It was moral danger I was afraid of." As teenagers, they were permitted to attend football games, but no high-school dances. "But, you know," says Ruth, "it was a strange thing with them about dancing; they just never *wanted* to."

There eventually transpired, though, a season of some uneasiness with the elder son, William Franklin, Jr. As a family friend puts it, "Franklin, I'm telling you, that boy was just as wild as when he was captured," and Graham himself allows, "He was into everything you can think of, even having the police chief chasing him." Not altogether unlike his father at sixteen when he would flee through the nights over those dirt back roads around Charlotte, Franklin took to careening over the countryside late into the nights — but with the difference of a six-pack of beer sitting in a paper sack on the floorboard. Pursued once by the police chief on up the mountain road to the Graham place, as soon as Franklin plunged through the entrance gates he simply closed them behind him with his electronic control button, the chief having to retreat then back down the mountain to make a sputterously irate phone call to the Grahams.

Ruth relates how she would often wait up for him until two or three in the morning — "It was just that that was the only time it seemed we ever really talked, when he'd come home at night and we'd sit there." Finally, when he returned late one night to find her yet again sitting with a calm alertness in her robe in a little pool of lamplight in the living room, he barked, "All right, I know why you wait up for me every night. So you can smell my breath." She snapped, "Well, if that's what you think, I'm just going to bed, and I won't stay up to talk to you again. I won't be staying up for you anymore from now on." After that, she would still go into his room in the mornings to wake him. "He'd have his ashtray full of cigarettes," she says — until one morning, "what I did, I just picked up that ashtray while he was lying there still asleep, and I emptied it, very carefully, on the bed all around him." With that, she found his door locked in the mornings. She abided that for about a week, and then, after gently trying his doorknob yet once more, she made her way out of a window onto the roof and began crawling across the gray shingles toward his dormer window "with a glass of water in my hand. I was going to throw the water in there on him to wake him up" — but just as she reached his window, he slammed it shut.

It had devolved to the caretaker to introduce Franklin to hunting, and to the Grahams' family pastor in Montreat to take him fishing, and during his own short interludes at home, Graham began counseling about Franklin with the pastor, Dr. Calvin Thielman — "He was really suffering over that thing there for a while," says Thielman. Franklin had grown now into a large hulking youth with a tumultuous energy and restlessness most reminiscent, actually, of Graham's great blusterous Cyclops of a grandfather, Crook Graham. Roy Gustafson wound up serving as a kind of casual avuncular attendant to him in his later careerings abroad to Europe, and on the flight over, "we'd be sitting there," says Gustafson, "and then after a while he'd say he had to go to the bathroom, and get up — and then just never come back. I'd find him sitting back there in the back of the plane where he'd bought him several drinks, grinning at me and puffing away on a Marlboro." Then on the Via Veneto, Gustafson would sit heavily and uncomfortably deposited at a sidewalk table with him, perspiring a little and smiling patiently and repeatedly removing his eyeglasses to scrub the lens with his handkerchief, while Franklin tossed down slugs of Johnny Walker — "He called it Johnny Rainwater" — and perused the exotic fauna of Rome rippling past them.

Gustafson says now, "He got awfully close to crossing that line where you can't go back. Awfully close." But finally, one evening in a hotel in Jerusalem, "he called me and asked me to come to his room," and hurriedly pattering down the hall, Gustafson found him "sitting there at his desk reading the New Testament. He told me, 'Look in the wastebasket there.' There was a crumpled pack of Marlboros in it. 'And I've given up Johnny Rainwater too,' he said." Gustafson could barely contain his elation, and the next evening, they went out for a comfortable dinner in a small cafe in the cluttered warrens of old Jerusalem, among those ancient walls of the faith of Franklin's father.

When Franklin returned to Montreat, says Graham's family pastor, Thielman, "He wanted to be baptized again" — a ceremony that was conducted in the pool excavated on the Grahams' place. For a while after that, he contemplated becoming a preacher, with Graham reporting once, "I've been told he sounds very much like me." But he soon concluded, "I'd probably just turn out an embarrassment to my father and my father's name." Casting briefly about in a variety of other vague directions, including a beguilement for a while with a career as a tennis pro, he wound up, after marrying, studying business management at a small mountain campus called Appalachian State

University in the upper recesses of North Carolina, living with his wife in an apartment there.

Gustafson reflects, "He's been so perceptive, just so fair in his understanding about his father. He's just a terrific guy." Graham himself happily recounts now, "He never really rebelled against God or against Christ through all that. And I never got after him. Love would always come first. During that time, he would hug and kiss me when he saw me. You need to keep their love at any cost. Because when they come through it, they'll still have that there. When it was over with Franklin, there was no relationship to reestablish; it had been there all along." Recalling a recent visit with Franklin, Graham proudly reported, "He just grabbed my cheeks between those big hands of his and said, 'Dad, I love you.' And before I left, he said, 'Dad, let's have prayer.' . . ."

The younger son, Ned, was shipped over to England when he was about thirteen to a somewhat Spartan school where, Graham recites admiringly, "they were very strict, very disciplined, they would make their boys strip and sit for an hour in ice-cold water in a stone bath for an infraction of the rules. But Ned didn't do too well there. We had to bring him back after a year." He was then entered in a private school in Stonybrook, New York. One morning when Graham was home at Montreat, during the regular staff devotional in his offices down the hill, Graham himself posed to the gathering, "I want you all to pray for me and my relationship with Ned. He's coming home this weekend, and I want to spend as much time with him as I can. It's a difficult time for him. He's doing well, but he's seventeen now, and I just want to be closer to him and give him what strength I can." The truth is, one of Graham's more touching compulsions over the years has been his struggle, however intermittent and distracted, somehow to cross the distance between him and his boys, that gap that with his own father was never closed. After his weekend at home, Ned — a tall, lean youth, muted of word and manner — came down to the offices with a girl friend to bid Graham farewell, and Graham stood and, with a certain abrupt clumsiness, reached for him and hugged him, several repeated large awkward hugs with slappings on the back, and finally pulled Ned's head against his shoulder and held it there as if he were six years old, Graham's eyes briefly dampening.

In turn, all of the children came to seem almost poignantly appreciative of the most elementary solicitudes from their father. Bunny once reported that, about a year after her own marriage in 1970, while Graham was conducting a crusade in Chicago, she asked to see him about a problem and ended up weeping on his shoulder; he had just returned from the White House wedding of Tricia Nixon, and it was only an hour before he had to depart for that evening's service, but "busy as he was, he spent time, he loved me, he prayed with me. That will always be a very special memory, that Daddy would take time from his busy and tired schedule to share the burden with his daughter. . . ."

Actually, it had been his hope and Ruth's for a while that all their children might become missionaries. That did not quite turn out — but they seem, almost uniformedly, dutiful and decorously behaved, wholly clean of any dubious extravagances of spirit. Once, when the spiralings of the Sixties had passed, Ruth explained that all their children "have been brought up with a profound respect for law. I think it's all right for people to argue with the establishment respectfully, but I don't think rock-throwing or abusive language is respectful or shows good sense." Anne, the second daughter, a tall, rangy, corn-blond girl with something of Graham's pale-eyed and slightly hawkish look, has proven perhaps the most intense and assertive of the children — "She loved to read Ayn Rand," remembers Ruth. During the presidential campaign of 1964, Anne touched off a small clamor when she put forward her own endorsement of Barry Goldwater, and during a Graham crusade in North Carolina in 1973, when an uncongenial commentary by a local minister in his church bulletin was subsequently published in the newspaper there, she dispatched a quick letter to the editor: "The naivete of [this minister's] type of criticism amazes me. The critic assumes that because Dr. Graham is a friend and spiritual counselor to kings, queens, presidents and leaders, that he sanctions their various 'policies and practices of government.' . . . The presumption of these critics is immense. . . . Thank God, He works through some of us and in spite of others."

The youngest daughter, Bunny, a somewhat softer-focused figure with long sunny hair and sky-blue eyes and a cream-meringue complexion, is also assured that "God controls our destiny. He sets up kings and puts them down again, the Scriptures tell us. Any man who gets to the White House is therefore God's choice. You must trust His choice. You know He will prevail." Besides that, she said not long after her marriage, "God is helping Ted and me find a new house. We thought we'd found the right one, but God blocked it. We'll know when a house is the best choice for us, because then God will let it happen."

As it turned out, all three of his daughters wound up marrying before they finished college, and in a certain sense Graham succeeded in furnishing them, not only his own particular Christian sense of life, but even their husbands. The eldest daughter, Virginia — who came to be called Gigi — eventually married the son of an expatriate Armenian financier in Switzerland named Ara Tchividjian, who became a Graham convert after reading his first inspirational volume, *Peace with God*. Tchividjian subsequently supplied Graham with a house near Lausanne for his convenience when journeying to the Continent, and in time, Graham received a letter from him enclosing another letter from his son, Stephan, asking Gigi for her hand. She was then only seventeen, a thinnish dark grave girl, and when she read young Tchividjian's letter, she declared to Graham, "This is of God, Daddy!" When Graham announced her engagement to twenty-three-year-old Stephan Tchividjian in March of 1963, he explained, "He is the most dedicated young Christian I have ever met, and the only man in the world to whom I'd give my daughter in marriage at her age." He conducted the service himself, in a fifteenth-century stone church overlooking Lake Geneva, and about a year later, at eighteen, she gave birth to a son, Graham's first grandchild.

Two years after that, he presided at Anne's wedding, at nineteen, to a thirty-year-old prospering Raleigh dentist named

Danny Lotz, a former North Carolina basketball player whom Graham had come across at a Fellowship of Christian Athletes conference. While Anne was recovering from a turn of mononucleosis, she remembers, "Daddy came home and reminded me to look for God's blessing. The blessing turned out to be six feet, six inches tall, weighed two hundred thirty pounds, and visited each weekend while I was confined to the house." Bunny also came by her husband, Ted Dienert, by way of Graham's radio ministry — Dienert the son of the advertising executive who had urged Graham in 1950 to strike out into broadcasting. For that matter, even Graham's younger sister Jean's husband, evangelist Leighton Ford, had come to her through the medium of Graham's ministry back during the Youth for Christ campaigns. Graham had tugged Jean off to one side to announce, "You hold on tight to Leighton; don't let him go. I could walk around the world a hundred times, and I'd never find a fellow I'd rather have for a brother-in-law." Graham officiated at their wedding, too.

Within the private cosmos of his evangelistic institution, then, he has kept his own personal world snugly self-enclosed and self-complete. Even his medical operations were performed on him, whenever possible, by his father-in-law, Dr. Bell — repairing an inguinal hernia of Graham's once, he conveniently went on to take out his appendix as well — and when Graham underwent prostate gland surgery in 1965, "we had the whole Billy Graham organization in prayer during the operation," one associate declared, "those in Minneapolis, in Atlanta, and at the World Wide Film Studios in California." In a sense, even Dr. Thielman, the local Presbyterian pastor, was imported to Montreat through special arrangements to serve as a kind of standing family vicar. An affable, somewhat tousled country fellow out of Texas who was commended to Graham by Lyndon Johnson, Thielman remarks with a drawling smile, "I can remember when I was first introduced to Billy and first spoke to him — my voice went way up high, you know, in a little squeak. Yeah. . . . But he's brought a lot of famous people here to church. Julie Nixon Eisenhower, she was here just this past Sunday. . . ."

Nelson Bell himself came to serve as something like a second compensatory father to Graham. As Graham once allowed, "My own father was a dairy farmer, so on many major issues I went to my father-in-law, because he was a churchman and a missionary and knew the church situation." A tall and rigid-backed figure with a balding bulbed white-fuzzed pate and rimless spectacles, one of those more scholarly and heatless of Protestant fundamentalists, Bell would submit it as his own opinion that "Billy has a keen sense of destiny." At the same time he intervened often to temper Graham's more florid impulses, especially his sporadic tantalizations with the overtures directed at him by political and television entrepreneurs. Once when Billy seemed to become particularly intrigued with petitionings to run for Senator from North Carolina, "Dr. Bell gave it to me," he says, "and gave it to me very strong." Himself having grown up the sort of erect young lad who had played baseball and sung in the choir with equal vigorousness, described as "a good Christian boy, solid, sensible, substantial, dependable," after some twenty-five years in that missionary compound in China, Bell had returned to the United States with a certain hoarfrost of bitterness on him: as he explained once, "After World War Two, we contributed to the success of the Communists. There were men in high places who consistently helped the Communists, calling them 'agrarian reformers.'" Settling in Montreat, he occupied himself for the rest of his years as a surgeon in Asheville while writing endless commentaries with a cold precisioned disputatious intensity in religious periodicals, especially deploring the civil rights campaigns of the Sixties as a subversion of social discipline and order. Someone who heard him speak on several occasions remembers, "Dr. Bell was one of those minds who could make prejudice perfectly plausible." A rigorous Goldwater partisan during the 1964 presidential campaign, Bell was preparing to perform surgery one morning on Eugene Carson Blake, who had become by then one of the most eminent liberal consciences of Protestantism, and just as Blake was sinking into the anesthesia, Bell leaned down to his ear and whispered, "Eugene — in your heart, you know he's right."

One visitor to the Presbyterian assembly grounds at Montreat when Bell was conducting Sunday-morning discourses from the front porch of the World Mission Building still recalls, "He would stand very straight up on that porch above us, always wearing that dark blue suit with the morning light slanting through the leaves and reflecting off his glasses, talking on with that uninterruptible earnestness of his about the danger of Mao Tse-tung and Communism. There was something about him like a pair of scissors. 'My friends —' Snip. '— America —' Snip. '— faces a time of crisis!' He would hold up this shell fragment he had brought back with him from China, apparently from a shell the Communists had used over there. 'My friends, this came from bombs that were made — not by the hands of our enemies — but the hands of America! This is something — I shall never forget.' He was a positively riveting figure. It never occurred to me until years later that he also may have been just a touch of a fascist. But a very commanding presence."

After Bell's death in 1973, says Graham's sister Jean, "I think Billy Frank began turning more and more to Ruth to sort of take her daddy's place. He began to depend on her for that kind of strength he used to get from Dr. Bell."

In that mountainside bower of theirs — secure against all the disheveling vicissitudes of the world below, even kept clean of any intruding snakes by Ruth who, no Eve, expeditiously dispatches with a marshmallow fork any she finds — the two of them have remained through the years like imperishable valentine sweethearts. "I've never heard a cross word between them," says Bunny, "which made me worry sometimes about my own marriage. Ted and I *have* had cross words, and I used to think that was abnormal." Instead, they have maintained a manner between them almost of high-school steadies, a blithe skittering banter and ceaseless light teasing, Ruth fond of citing the time she muffed a curtsey to the Queen Mother, "and Bill — the merciless wretch — said it looked like I had tripped over the rug." Ruth once observed to a stadium congregation in 1976 — after a floral bouquet had been presented to her, at which a vast low

"*Ahhhhhhh*" had rolled over the stands — "During the years, we really haven't had a *chance* to get tired of each other. So I think we'll just hang in there a little longer!" Indeed, it's as if, by holding themselves forever arrested in that stage of their courtship back in the Forties, they have actually managed to move themselves out of time — have thus preserved themselves against all the attritions and complications of time's long seasoning, and so delivered themselves safely at last, untouched, intact, beyond the treacherous gustings of life's dangerous heats and winds. When they retire now in the evenings, they even continue their playful joshing patter in bed — "I'll lie there," says Graham, "and you know how well read Ruth is, she seems to know everything about everything, and I'll lie there and kid her, 'One thing about you, you're just so unread, you're just so out of it.' " Most of all, though, after navigating all the years since the brief duress of that upstairs apartment in Hinsdale, "it's wonderful now just to lie there in bed, the two of us, and hold each other and talk."

Having arrived at this quiescence, Graham seems to have peculiarly taken on a more mellow personal expansiveness: "He used to just shake hands when he'd see me or another member of his family," says Jean, "but now he'll throw those long arms around us and just hug us. The older he's gotten, the freeer and more expressive his body-language has become for some reason." Ruth herself professes, "Bill's just the way now I used to think of as my ideal man. He looks now, he's become just like that man I used to dream about. . . ." But if he has finally realized for her the vision of the ethereal little poem she wrote as a maiden — "*And let his face have character, . . . let him be like Thee*" — the truth is, they have come to look rather like each other, she with the same bladelike sharpness of face and cavernous eyes which have the same deep bright glare when she laughs, as if they had somehow subtly metamorphosed into brother and sister.

Graham still observes a scrupulous politeness toward her, will lug himself to his feet as many as eight times in an hour as she passes through a room where he is sitting with a visitor. For her part, whenever she addresses assemblies of other women, she will attest, "The best advice I've ever known is, your business is not to make your husband perfect, but to make him happy. Study your husband, find out what kind of woman he needs. If you were a man, what kind of wife would you want to come home to? Don't disagree with your husband when he's absolutely bushed at night — or when your hair's in curlers." Graham himself enthuses now, "She has my cup of coffee right there every morning when I wake up. I've never seen her moody. She's always positive. She's always on the upbeat. I've never heard her say, 'I'm tired,' or 'I'm depressed.' I've never known her to lie down in the daytime. She just amazes me. She has no moods at all. She's wonderful. She's always the same!"

But in fact — at middle age and with all her children gone, and taking to wearing, with her still-ample figure, denim jumpsuits with a small lavaliere inscribed in Hebrew, "Pray for the Peace of Jerusalem" — she suddenly pitched herself into such headlong whimsies as plunging on motorcycles over the roads around Montreat, hang-gliding off mountain bluffs, once dangling from a parachute towed by a speedboat in Acapulco. She asserted at one point, "I do love to go fast. To go full speed, with the wind in my face." But in these slightly hectic adventures, she was constantly getting battered in spills and capsizings. Grappling with those oversized motorcycles, she splintered once through a rail fence, again vaulted off a road into a lake when she accelerated instead of braked, another time slid tumbling down a mountain slope. Her hang-gliding apparatus had luckily collapsed before she was fully airborne off the side of a cliff. About all those exploits, she now pipes gaily but a little thinly, "There's no fool like an old fool! But it was just that I realized I was getting on, no longer young." Graham himself surmises wanly, "She figured she had sort of missed out on a lot of things all these years, I guess, so she was trying to make up all of a sudden for things she'd wanted to do but couldn't all that time."

Perhaps out of that same obscure restlessness, she also took to accompanying an itinerant troop of gospel guitarists for a week in their perambulations to jail, and assorted other gamy locales. "A funny thing, and I'm sure wholly unfair," remarks one North

Carolina journalist, "but when all that business happened with Margaret Trudeau tagging about with the Rolling Stones, first thing I thought of was Ruth Graham and that little gang of missionary minstrels of hers." She found herself once in the middle of a small rhubarb during a street service outside a porno shop in Asheville. "Actually, we weren't really going to have a street meeting, we were just going to sing a song or two," she says — but the proprietor phoned the police, and presently a small, portly, elderly patrolman appeared. "He told us, 'Now you'll not leave this spot until my superior comes,' " Ruth narrates a little breathlessly. "That's when I got really mad! I felt like asking that little Christmas pudding whose side he was on, anyway! I finally shoved a tract in his hand, and it just blew his mind!"

Actually, she seemed increasingly disposed to such fitful little public affrays. "I love to watch *60 Minutes*, because I get madder than a hatter," she says, "I don't think people realize we have more rights than we think we do." At a Bicentennial observance in Charlotte's Freedom Park in the spring of 1975, where Graham was to deliver the benediction after an address by President Ford, one young man among a small gaggle of demonstrators happened to wander with his sign — "Eat the Rich, Don't Tread on Me" — near the front row of the audience, where Ruth was sitting. Suddenly the sign was snatched out of his hands — "It just happened real quick, bam!" he later testified — and tucked under Ruth's feet. "It was the element of surprise that was on my side," says Ruth. "I just acted instinctively. Here came this little man holding up his little sign, which was all right, except to stand between me and the President, that was something else — that was a violation of my rights. He had every right to his opinion, but when the President of the United States is speaking, it is definitely not the place to express his opinion." The demonstrator, a young woodcutter, squatted beside her and asked for his placard, but she remained with her white pumps neatly and firmly planted together atop it, smiling serenely. "I just patted him on the shoulder and shook my head. He was a pitiful little character. He really looked rather helpless and harmless." About then, the young demonstrator was closed in upon by policemen and shouldered back to the edge of the crowd. A few days later, he signed a warrant charging her with "simple assault." Ruth, with a faintly harried air now at these complications, averred to newsmen that she wished the whole affair had simply not been reported — "But what he did was disrespectful." The charge against her carried a maximum penalty of fifty dollars' fine or thirty days in jail, but "I would have gone to jail," she states, "rather than pay that fine." She promptly retained two Charlotte attorneys. At the hearing, the case was rapidly dismissed, and afterward, outside the courtroom, when Ruth happened to spy the young protestor emerging into the corridor, she bobbed over to him, smiling pluckily, to bestow upon him a Bible, "which I had inscribed with various passages for him to look up. But he looked like I had offered him a snake," and he stalked on off. Graham himself happened to be off in Texas then conducting a crusade, and he announced from there, "I'm delighted the judge saw fit to dismiss the charges against my wife. It was a blessing to me to watch her attitude during these intervening weeks and how day after day she earnestly prayed for the young man who had brought the charges."

Sometime around 1960, she began to be fretted by a small tight cough that has continued to cling through the years, and which she tries to muffle behind wads of Kleenex snatched hastily from her purse. She still practices that nicely minted decorativeness of expression and sentiment — recounting how she attended a black church once where someone in the choir was singing "in this absolutely seraphic voice," while she noticed on the front pew "a totally grotesque gargoyle of a figure listening with an expression of pure beauty on his face, a beauty that you'd miss in somebody whole." Graham himself professes, "Why, she could look at that blank wall over there, and see an illustration of something, of some truth in the Bible, which I couldn't if I tried for a year." But at the same time, she seems to have taken on a certain overelaborated and slightly pained meticulousness of word and phrasing — a halting and distracted preciseness, that thrall of double and triple consideration of impression and connotation of those who have passed perhaps a bit too much time in solitude and self-contemplation in which, after a while, everything begins to echo a bit too far beyond its immediate apparentness.

Around the time of her fracas over the protestor's sign, while she was visiting at Gigi's home in Milwaukee, she was climbing to repair some playground equipment and fell, suffering a concussion, and was in a coma for several hours. It left her afterward with small white obliterations in her memory — "even the Bible verses I had memorized all my life were gone. Just gone." Gradually, those blank fogs began to clear, the old familiar decors of her life began to reappear, including her Bible verses — "and boy, was I glad to get 'em back!" Then, while Graham was off inspecting the wreckage left by a massive earthquake in Guatemala, she was dizzied one morning by what was later thought to be a small vague heart attack. "But they aren't sure what it was now," says Graham. "Anyway, she's been just fine since then."

She accompanies him somewhat more often on his crusades now — leaning back in a lounging chair in the vacant midafternoons on a little sun-glared motel patio, neatly attired in a pants suit, her eyes closed calmly and her long hands, browned and freckled and strangely rugged, lying flat and perfectly still on the aluminum armrests of the recliner; and her face with its sharp fox's profile, turned now full into the white light of the sun, showing a fragile gauntness, graying and somewhat weathered with the skin taut on her cheekbones and her temples, her high round smooth forehead tanned and faintly dusted with a dim gold down like pollen; she lying absolutely motionless and composed in the empty suspension of the bright voiceless afternoon, her head back and her eyes lightly closed in the thin quiet dry sunlight. . . . *She has no moods at all. She's always the same.* . . .

Of late, she has begun to occupy herself in sedulously, systematically compiling a list of all verses in the Bible holding in them the words *Fear not.*

Graham himself, whenever he is abiding at his mountain-fastness home, usually awakens with the first blue tints of dawn. Decades now after his Los Angeles advent, dwelling within this perfectly self-contained world he has accomplished, he is still spare and flatly tapered, only a faint diminished slump having set in to his shoulders, his long arms in his golfing shirts slightly thinner and his midriff a bit potty, but still shallow and lank of loin. He exercises himself daily — "and I don't jog, I run, on a stopwatch" — and has begun taking lecithin against mutterings of high blood pressure, along with regular administrations of vitamin E. He has also installed at Montreat a thermal bath, five feet deep, in which he languidly eddies about with slow wide spider-like fannings of his arms and legs. As he suns himself along some beachfront in Acapulco or Jamaica between crusades, his tawny chest is just slightly slack, palely furzed, but his large noble maned head and wide sculpturesque hands seem somehow oddly misplaced on his long slat-thin form, too histrionic and imposing. It's as if they are only restored, his hands and head, to their accustomed proper aspect, and he only comes into his natural definition, when he is in his pulpit suits now. But on the road or at home, he still slings his washcloths and towels over the back of his bathroom door.

Awakening at dawn when he is home, after a cup of coffee, he conducts himself in a brief devotional. "I've noticed that if I get up in the morning and, for some reason don't spend time in prayer, get busy with something else first, nothing seems to go right the rest of the day. But if I get up in the morning and have my first thoughts on God, everything crooked from then on is made straight." Immediately after this private communion, he clicks on his television to watch the morning news. After a sturdy breakfast then of grapefruit, Branflakes, grits, an egg, two cups of coffee, his mornings are usually passed in his study, black-framed glasses ledged on his nose, reading five psalms, a chapter of Proverbs, some of the gospels, from a worn Bible thoroughly notched with penciled notations. He also rustles through about six newspapers. Around him in his study is usually a wide spill of books, but most of them are religious commentaries, sermon collections, Bible concordances, along with such secular manuals as *How to Improve Your Golf Game.* He confides, "I haven't read a novel for years" — his last excursions into those regions of the imagination seeming to have been Zane Grey westerns and "one or two historical novels by Taylor Caldwell." He does indulge periodically in biographies and memoirs — Ralph Martin's *Jennie,* "Westmoreland's book on Vietnam, I forget the title." For the most part, though, staff assistants still supply him with those quick-scan digests of pertinent current books, including those that lend themselves as reference material for his own books. As for the theatre, "the last play I saw was — let's see — I guess was when we were taken by some friends in Houston to see *Fiddler on the Roof.*" Mainly, he and Ruth sit at home in the evenings, holding hands on the sofa and watching two telecasts of the evening news and sometimes a detective drama. Ruth declares, "Our house is just loaded with magazines, *Time, Newsweek,* any magazine you could think of." Even so, after Graham once obligingly compiled an essay for a periodical that had sent a request into his office, he then thought to have his secretary drive down to the drugstore in Black Mountain to get a copy of the magazine — "It's something called *Hustler,* I think" — which she dutifully returned with and, without glancing into it, left on Graham's desk; after a few minutes, he came blowing out of his door — "Don't you ever, ever again, bring anything like this into this place!"

Perhaps the only instance of any significant infiltration of the cosmopolitan into his Calvinist rectitudes over the years has been that, since that high-school class party when he had taken a few dislocating gulps of homemade wine out of that jar retrieved from the woods, Graham admits to medicinal sippings of a hot dram of spirits for an ague once in a while, and in fact, "after my many trips to Europe," even began to take a polite glass of wine now and then. "I found they thought nothing of it over there to have a glass or two of wine in the evenings — clergymen, prominent figures in the church. A lot of the top people drink. I don't do it now, because of my blood pressure problem, but there were periods when I did —" He gives then a quick, light grin. "My father would turn over in his grave, I suppose. And that would get me in a lot of trouble from some of the people. But no, I'm not a teetotaler."

Along with that small concession to urbanity, Graham has also managed to develop a certain curiosity, if not quite a connoisseurship yet, about abstract art. "I have studied it from the spiritual point of view. I got interested in it from Arlene Francis, when she asked me once to try looking at it that way." But in general, Graham has remained a creature constitutionally innocent of most perspectives and sensibilities beyond his own earnest reverences, and is prone, if he should happen to find himself engaged in some protracted discussion of such alien matters of art or literature, to bolt from the room and return eagerly ruffling through his Bible, exclaiming, "Now, here in Corinthians, what Paul says is . . ."

So he has continued to live within the inviolate and halcyon calm of his own private universe of reality, personally presiding over his monolithic organization from his Montreat office with its oak-paneled walls mounted with a bronze plaque of the Constitution, a reproduction in tin plate of the Last Supper, which was the gift of a Pontiac dealer somewhere, and a waist-length plaster statuette of a Michelangelesque Moses flourishing high one pointed finger in a gesture fleetingly familiar. The sanctuary of his Montreat home with its eight-foot-high fence has been only rarely breached — once, by a somewhat wolfish mountain lad who came blundering into his study, wailing, "I've come to get you!" whereupon Graham dropped him with a single wild flinging blow, pulled him on outside, and, keeping him pinned to the ground under him, demanded, "Now, what's your trouble?" — at which, the youth commenced simply to weep. His father shortly appeared in pursuit, explained his son was demented, and after Graham conducted a short prayer with them both, authorities arrived and trucked the boy away.

There have also been a number of threats, mostly beginning after the assassination of Martin Luther King, and by 1970 the FBI was maintaining a list of them all. "The threatening letters I get I always turn over to the FBI," says Graham, "and they tell me which ones to consider seriously." During crusades, he usually moves about within an encircling flotilla of several bodyguards. But once in 1963, at the end of a coliseum service in Los

Angeles, Graham was walking with a friend toward an exit tunnel when a tall bony young man, wearing a neatly pressed gray suit, suddenly appeared before him and casually remarked, "I'm going to kill you before this crusade is over." Graham strode on past him with an unfaltering smile, explaining a moment later to his friend, "God's able to take care of me. I've got an invisible shield. . . ."

But the defenses around his home in Montreat, at least, have been not altogether that invisible. Once, an out-of-state television crew made the mistake of proceeding on up to Graham's residence a bit too quickly after the call from the office down the mountain that they were on their way, and as they passed through the just-opened gates, two mammoth dogs immediately surged toward them out of the shadows under the trees. A member of that crew recalls now, "One of them — a strange-looking beast like some cross between a lion and an alligator, with this gigantic tubular body — he grabbed our front tire, sank his teeth into it, and began to just shake us back and forth. I swear to you. This was a full-size station wagon we were in, loaded with cameras and lights and gear, and that animal was shaking it like it was a toy. The steering wheel was yanking back and forth in the driver's hands. Then the driver realized the other dog was on his side and was going straight for his face. He just managed to get the window rolled up in time. It was like something out of *Jaws*. All we could do then was sit there, the steering wheel jerking back and forth and the other dog clicking away with his nails at the shut windows, both of them raising this roar around us that they must have been able to hear all the way down at Black Mountain, until the keeper finally came running and led the things away. When we drove on up to the house and stopped, I had to just sit there a minute or two until my knees quit quaking."

One of their guard dogs, relates Graham's daughter Anne, "became horribly vicious to everyone but me," and had to be put through several sessions at a training school, after which Anne brought it on a leash into the bedroom where Graham lay reading: the dog sat very quietly, very still, merely regarding Graham lying on the bed with an unblinking amber gaze, until Anne let its leash drop — for just a second still, it did not move, and then suddenly was in the air, fell ravening on Graham while he struggled to get a pillow over his head, until Anne and Ruth finally managed to drag the dog, lunging and lashing, off of him.

But if such grim provisions against harm or danger can sometimes take on a blank indiscriminate fierceness of their own, suddenly turning on what they were meant to defend, the real treacherousness attending Graham's security insulations is more profound than that. In the midst of a crusade in 1976, he arrived one morning at a downtown church to address a gathering of local ministers and Christian lay workers, the assembly standing and applauding him as he entered the sanctuary and mounted the dais of the pulpit. At the close of his short chat to this congregation, just as he was turning to leave the podium, a voice called from the back of the sanctuary — "Dr. Graham? Dr. Graham? Could I ask you one question?" Graham paused with his Bible clapped to his chest, and said, "Well, I don't usually answer questions at the end of these meetings —" and then, grinning generously, pointed with a quick peck of his finger "— but I'll answer yours." It was a tall and hefty-shouldered youth wearing an open-collared white shirt, standing in a rear pew, and he hesitated a moment, and then stammered, "This — I've never — this is the hardest thing I've ever done —" A barely audible shuffling of unease stirred over the pews around him, a sudden hush of alarm hung in the air. "— I can't — I don't know how I'm going to be able to get through this —" The youth seemed strangely out of breath. "— But, well, I've read in the press and other places — I mean, they say you wear three-hundred-dollar suits, and I just want to ask if —"

Immediately a general moan arose from the filled pews, at which the youth hung his head, but remained doggedly standing there, while off in a vestibule at one wing of the podium, T. W. Wilson instantly began stalking back and forth in short lunges, one hand whipping away at his coat lapel and his round eyes flaring wide, he furiously and mutterously fuming, "What is this? Where did that fella come from? Who does this character think he is?" But Graham, still wearing his genial grin, only seeming to hang at a slight off-tilt now a few paces away from the pulpit, opened his coat to glance down at the label inside, "Let's see — yes, I got this suit, I think, from J. C. Penney's. As I can recall, the last three suits I've bought have come from J. C. Penney's, and I can assure you, not one of them cost anything like three hundred dollars." There was a sibilation of approval from the audience, one or two sputters of clapping. Altogether, Graham negotiated this small accostment quite gracefully and hand-somely, and strode off the podium to another benediction of applause — but when he reached at last the privacy of the ves-tibule, he was just slightly trembling, a vague and almost imper-ceptible scatter of uncertainty in his movements and the tenor of his voice, as if the concussion of any unexpected unpleasantness, any intimation of an animus toward him, left him always some-how stunned and unnerved.

Then, a few minutes later — while Graham was closed off in a back room of the church conferring with one of his financial pa-trons, a fertilizer tycoon from San Francisco — the youth sud-denly appeared in the nearby alcove where Wilson and a few others were waiting. He had the look somehow of an obscurely spoiled decathlon athlete, large and sturdy and clean of jaw, tan-ned, but with his forehead damp with a light oil of sweat, he panting as if in some dull panic. It was a moment or two before he was noticed: an angular and elongated minister in a black suit peered at him and then said, "Ah, yes. You were the one who asked that question. What I want to know is, just what were you asking?" The youth gulped and began in a stumbling murmur, "Well, I've felt the Lord has told me — all I've been doing re-cently is trying to go around witnessing for the Lord, and —" The minister took a step closer to him, while T. W. watched un-moving with a flat expressionless face. "Yes, but I didn't get your question, see?" the minister continued. "I just want to know what you were getting at. I mean, don't you remember what you asked?" The youth had now a certain impaled look of helpless anguish in his eyes. "I only — I only —" Someone then noticed a note crumpled in his hand, and asked if he would like to have it relayed on to Graham, and the youth quickly surrendered it with a sudden deep breath like a sob: "Yes, if you could, I would really appreciate it, I just want to explain to him —" But the minister in the black suit persisted, "You know what you really need, young man?" The youth stared at him for a moment with a hopeless little grin: "A psychiatrist, you're going to say —" "No, no," said the minister, "let me tell you," and he looped his arm now around the youth's shoulder and took him aside, and T. W. then dipped to one side with one hand draped jauntily from his coat lapel, and quietly nickered, "Never a dull moment!"

The bystander who had taken the note then unfolded it — a labored printing in ball-point pen, *"Dear Dr. Graham I want to Apologize for my Question but I was led of the Spirit. Since my recent Failure* I have asked the Lord to Forgive me and have been Praying for his Forgiveness through Sincere Repentance and Fasting. Have been trying to Find his Will for me Repenting for my Terrible Mistake. *Rebellion."* When the youth had passed this note to him, the bystander had glimpsed, in the palms of the youth's hands, identical deep tattered cross-slashes like stigmata, stained now with Mercurochrome, gashes carved with a clumsy deliberation with what could have been a nail or shard of broken glass.

If anyone should ever happen actually to make a strike on Graham, one senses it will likely be some solitary and agonized soul like the youth in that church that morning — someone abrupting forth as a God-crazed abject specter out of the very fevers and mysticisms of Graham's own religious passion, the very visions in which he himself dwells; at his stadium service that evening, Graham recited with a heavy solemnity from a letter sent him by "a leader of a Satanic coven of witches in Pennsylvania," who reported that he had been converted watching one of Graham's messages on television — a communicant who could hardly have been any less humid and baroque of fervors than the youth in the church that morning.

More significantly, though, it was clear that of all the people gathered there in that sunny sanctuary, that harrowed young man with sweat-prickled brow and cross-gashed palms was at least one truly lost and tormented soul. But the only general concern he seemed to prompt was a fretful embarrassment over the violation of graciousness he had afforded the occasion. When Graham emerged from his conference with the fertilizer manufacturer, one pastor assured him, "A number of people have asked me to tell you, 'Please tell Billy, make sure he knows, we all love him here.'" Graham produced an expansive grin, "Oh, I know that," and gave the pastor an appreciative smack on the back. But as Graham was proceeding on out of the church, someone mentioned to him the youth's note and the ragged slashes in the palms of his hands — and Graham, halfway down the steps of the church, suddenly stopped as if slammed, standing in the calm bright sunlight with a stricken and astonished stare, and then breathed, "Oh, no. Oh, no. God help him —" dangling there though for only an instant before his aides called him on to his car, chunked the doors shut clapping him in behind the tinted window glass, and he was swept on off, back to the privacy of his motel room to await the host in the stadium again that evening.

Some weeks after that episode, Graham was asked if he had not perhaps become so isolated within the sheer structures and schedules of his system of evangelism, it would have been impossible for him to know that youth was the one creature there that morning most desperately in need of being ministered to. "But I have gone straight to people like that at times," he insisted. "After a meeting, I sometimes go back to the office and counsel people until the middle of the night. There was a fellow once, created a disturbance at a meeting, and they took him around back and I talked to him afterward for about thirty minutes. When he faced me, he sobered up considerably. But I have to realize I can't do all of God's work. There were at least five hundred people out there who could have helped that young man — they were specialists."

But while he was waiting in a television station one morning to appear on a local talk show, word reached him that Rod McKuen happened to be there, and as soon as he was ushered on into the studio and, with his rapt eagle peer, spotted McKuen, he in-

stantly headed for him. McKuen — smallish and a trifle podgy of
midriff, in beltless jeans and tennis shoes — seemed momentarily ambushed by the sudden materialization of this legendary
Mount Rushmore figure of righteousness looming over him: he
shuffled and rummaged in his hip pockets until Graham intoned
with a hospitable grin, "I'd like for us to just take off our shoes
together sometimes and just talk." McKuen mumbled, "Let's do
that. I'd like to do that —" so warmed, in fact, that he promptly
scuffled off and brought back to Graham an inscribed copy of
his new book. Such prospects as McKuen continue to be an unerring ministerial instinct of Graham's. His attentions to this particular flock have ranged from Taylor Caldwell to Debbie Reynolds, to whom he expeditiously had a Bible delivered during a
Houston crusade when he learned she was in town. In a somewhat ethereal colloquy with her that was recorded by *Redbook*, he
informed her, "I think that people everywhere have sensed integrity, morality, and all these other qualities in you that give you
a great influence. I believe that right here and now, this [conver-
sation] is sacred in God's sight, in the sense that this may perhaps
give some new patterns to people in their thinking." An especially energetic disciple of Graham's, frequently performing at
crusades, has been Johnny Cash, and Graham reflected once,
"He's been studying the New Testament all the way through,
he's on St. Paul now — he's just finished the letter to Timothy
and he's starting on Titus. I tell you, Paul has become all Johnny
wants to talk about here lately. He thinks Paul, eats Paul, sleeps
Paul, I expect dreams Paul. He even wants to make a movie with
us on Paul now. He wants to play Paul himself. We've had to tell
him we just can't do it if he insists on that, and I hope he'll finally agree not to. I like Johnny a lot, but Johnny Cash playing
the role of St. Paul wouldn't quite — you have to watch out
sometimes, you know, you can lose your balance and perspective
if you get too absorbed in a thing."

But even with all the enclosures around him, Graham has
remained a congenitally generous-hearted soul, possessed still of
a spontaneous blurting goodwill. The family minister, Calvin
Thielman, recalls that when Graham once invited Oral Roberts

along for a conference on evangelism held in Europe, Roberts —
with his faith-healing tent-carnival past — was carefully avoided
by all the other churchmen there as a slightly tawdry curiosity,
he passing most of his time walking about in a little circle of
aloneness. Finally, Thielman noticed him one afternoon in the
hotel lobby waiting rather forlornly for an elevator — and, on
impulse, went over to greet him heartily, then took him by the
arm and proceeded to introduce him to the small clots of other
conferees standing around the lobby. A short while later, Thielman got a call from Graham to come to his room. Graham was
reading in bed in his pajamas, his glasses propped on his nose,
and he looked up at Thielman and said, "What's this I hear about
you and Oral Roberts?" Thielman explained, "Well, Billy, everybody's been avoiding him like he has the mange or something,
but we invited him over here to this thing, and then I saw him
just standing down there by the elevators all alone — I don't
think we ought to leave him to feel like an outcast, that's all."
And Thielman remembers that as Graham looked at him over
his glasses, his eyes suddenly swelled with tears, and he said,
"God bless you for that, Calvin. I can remember when all the big
preachers once would walk away from me, and how that made
me feel. God bless you for doing what you did down there."

V

Nevertheless, Graham is visited at times with dim disquietudes
that he may have become captured now in the large constructions of his own institution. "I do have a feeling sometimes that
this big organization that we've built could be the tail wagging
the dog, yes. It's a constant concern of mine to find some way to
get out from under all this. I find it frustrating, terribly. It's
become so that it's still a full-time job just being Billy Graham,
even if I didn't preach a single sermon or attend any organization meetings. As I look at the world today, it often occurs to me
that the smallest mission worker in the most obscure place in the

world may be making headlines in Heaven, while my work may be way off somewhere on the back pages."

More, Graham is not without vagrant pangs of discomfort about how the course of his ministry — with the extraordinary approval it has enjoyed from the national estate of authority and prestige — actually scans against the original script: that passionate, ascetic young vagabond country mystic who briefly wandered about one of the more remote and fly-blown outskirts of civilization two thousand years ago. "Christ made himself of no reputation," Graham will readily profess. "And if I know my own heart, reputation has not been a factor in my thinking. We have been called to suffer and follow the footsteps of the Man of Sorrows. This world is not a place of bliss for Christians. Paul was stoned and beaten in practically every city he visited. If he presented his credentials for membership, I'm sure many of our churches would reject Paul. He had been in a lot of jails." When he is asked, then, what tribulations he has met with in his own long apostleship, he insists, "There're many kinds of suffering. I have struggles about the absolute concentration of my ministry on the gospel, not getting sidetracked. My entire life has been a struggle — to keep my head above water without accumulating too much of this world's goods. I weep over America. I see judgment coming over this country. Maybe enough are responding, I don't know. But there're different forms of suffering, you see. Ruth and I live almost like prisoners. I remember once when we were with Queen Elizabeth. We were looking out of a window. There was a great crowd standing out by the fence. I asked Queen Elizabeth if she ever felt sometimes she would like to be able to just go down and join them. She said, 'With all my heart.' I said to her, 'That's just the way I feel.' "

Even so, that "you didn't see Jesus going around with the important people, he was with the ordinary people" — as Graham cites now and then in his sermons — seems a matter that does sporadically and mildly fret him. When he is questioned on this particular point, he will contend with a touch of irritation, "When you have your picture taken with Arnold Palmer or Bob Hope or the President out on a golf course, that doesn't mean you're always playing golf with them." But he then adds, "Many people came to Jesus, after all, because he was a celebrity." That would seem a somewhat novel sense of that wandering young Galilean ecstatic, given the circumstance, as Malcolm Muggeridge points out in his chronicle, that "Pilate had never heard of Jesus when he was brought before him." In truth, Muggeridge goes on, "Jesus had no organization, no headed notepaper, no funds, no registered premises, no distinguished patrons. . . . When he said the Son of Man had nowhere to lay his head, it was literally the case. . . . When the disciples were sent out they were instructed to take with them no money or food, neither staff nor spare clothes; to make no arrangements or plans. . . ."

In Graham's case, suggests one religious commentator, "it's become more like the melancholy tale of the rich young ruler." In the midst of a downpour one evening during a crusade service in Mississippi, with lawns of rain drifting down under the stadium lights, Graham himself preached on that young aristocrat mentioned in Mark and Luke who came running to offer himself as a disciple to Jesus: "Handsome, we can suppose, certainly wealthy and young. . . . He came with urgency. He *ran* to Jesus. . . . That was an amazing sight, this rich young aristocrat falling at the feet of the penniless prophet of Nazareth, who was on his way to being an outlaw and was going to be crucified in a short time as a common criminal. But this young man didn't care who saw. He came in the open, publicly, to Christ, and he asked the right question — 'What must I do?' " But retelling this encounter in his sermon that rain-blowing evening, Graham neglected to add how it had actually ended: that virtuous and princely young man who had, himself, dutifully honored all the commandments and proprieties since his childhood, so enthusiastically captivated by Jesus, with an eager goodness about him that immediately touched Jesus himself — *"Jesus beholding him loved him"* — who had then been admonished, *"One thing thou lackest . . . sell whatsoever thou hast, and give to the poor . . . and come, take up the cross, and follow me"*; but at that, he had hesitated, faltered, *"very sorrowful, for he was very rich"* . . . *"and went away grieved,"* Jesus himself watching his retreating figure with a mourning.

It was finally the confoundment, the disappointment, of not only the rich young ruler but all the others who failed in the end to comprehend this figure who somehow stirred them so — Pilate, the Zealots, Judas, even at times his other disciples — that what in fact he meant was not power and distinction and the conventional worthiness, but plainness, simplicity, pity, inglorious and even irrational sacrifice out of a love that passed all understanding. His real call was, as Muggeridge mentions, "to share with him in the public ridicule and obloquy, and, ultimately, in the rage and abhorrence, which so strange an interpretation of the Messianic role must inevitably arouse." Graham himself finally protests, "People are always expecting me to be like Jesus, but we can't be. We're never going to reach that point of perfection in this life. We can't walk in the steps of Christ. Because, for one thing, it's just not the same now as it was in his day, the world is so different. For instance, there's so much technology, and in those days, they didn't have all the technology that we have today. . . ."

But in one commentary during the early Seventies in the religious journal *Katallagete,* a kind of free-form guerrilla gospel minister out of Tennessee named Will D. Campbell put forward the proposition, "Where in the Gospel account of Jesus do we find crusade on the agenda? It's just not there. . . . There can be no 'decisions' for Christ in crusades. There can only be enlistments — by institutions, structures, movements. Their means *are* their ends. Where was there ever anything about Jesus to provoke the imperative to crusade? He turned down the proposition Satan made. And it was the proposition both Jesus and Satan agreed was Satan's to make. The proposition was to bring all peoples to their knees, organizationally. . . . When did Jesus, for that matter, pray for political order? He didn't. And that is precisely the point of false witness: Jesus for us Christians today is not the Jew scorned and rejected by culture, politics, religion. . . . Toward the end, when things began to come into focus about Jesus and what he was actually getting at, his popularity quickly sagged — attendance fell off sharply. Friends looked the other way, denied or betrayed him. And he was tried and executed by the legal and religious authorities of his day."

Whenever Graham happens to find himself pressed on this most notable variance between his own apostleship's fortunes and Christianity's beginning, he will propose, "Oh, I don't believe the Lord is going to let me get by this easily. I am attacked by extreme fundamentalists from the right and extreme liberals from the left. It could easily be that some crisis — Communism, some social upheaval — would arise in which I would have to suffer martyrdom. Remember that Christ was extremely popular the first two years of his ministry. They came from everywhere to hear him and praise him. Then they tore him apart!"

But still Graham's patrons — the industrialists, the financiers, the government dignitaries — attend him. All the thousands in the stadiums have, as yet, hardly fled him. It remains somehow inconceivable that he would ever find himself in the dungeon of Paul and Silas. He has resisted, so far, any call to position himself at such a lonely extreme. He will admit sometimes with a light wry smile that, if Jesus were translated into this day, "He would probably take on the church Establishment — I suppose he would probably even take on the Billy Graham Association." But for all his random twinges of unease about his incorporated mass ministry, its sheer magnitude and self-momentum seem to have claimed him beyond any disengaging; he has simply been annealed now into its patterns and self-reality.

In the end, about all that Graham will seriously concede about his career over the years is, "How I wish I could take back some of the statements made in those early days because of immaturity or a lack of knowledge or experience." Otherwise, in his long labor of certitude, he has developed an almost absolute Plexiglas imperviousness to criticism: "I've never known a moment of despair," he insists. At the most, he has confessed only to the vague, passing puzzlement now and then — "a strange paradox that has often confused and bewildered me," as he once put it — that "we have seen a revival of religious interest throughout the United States, but also an acceleration of crime, divorce, and im-

morality. Within the church there is a new depth of commitment, a new sense of destiny, and a spirit of revival. Yet in the
world there is an intensification of the forces of evil. Fear haunts
the council halls of the nations. Family life is threatened by evil
forces as never before." Among a number of explanations for
that was one offered by a Graham critic after that ninety-seven-
day crusade in New York in 1957: "The United States is the only
country in the world where the current renascence of religious
faith has expended so much of its energy on professional mass
evangelism. . . . But there are other ways of communicating the
gospel. They are not so exciting, so colorful, so likely to be fea-
tured in the mass media. They are slower and more difficult;
they require more courage and perseverance. But they are also
more enduring."

In 1971, during the high flush of Graham's entente with the
Nixon White House, an open letter was addressed to him by that
informal gospel-partisan minister in Tennessee, Will Campbell,
in *Katallagete,* the journal of Campbell's small company of Christian activists, the Committee of Southern Churchmen: "True,
some are 'led to Christ' in the instituted Church today, but it is
done against the stream of five-point grading programs, 'evangelistic crusades' planned and executed more like the Pentagon
than St. Paul. . . . Who spread all these lies about Jesus? He
judges us by what we do to the children, the prisoners, the
whores, the addicts, the scared and bewildered, the poor, the
hungry — to 'the least of them.' . . . But why do we address
ourselves to you, Dr. Graham? Maybe it is because you are our
Baptist brother, and we love you. Early in your career, we
thought, despite your lack of the specialties of the Ivy League we
were then seeking ourselves — erudition and academic degrees — that you were a man preaching more Jesus than culture,
more Gospel than Law. So maybe we are a little hurt now to see
a man we once tried to stand up for become more and more a
man of tremendous power and influence. Maybe it's the use of
that power and influence, in Christ's name, to become a court
prophet, adding your blessing and power to the current Kings of
Israel and Judah — whether in the semi-secrecy of a political

convention corridor or on the golf course, or at the East Room of the White House. . . . We believe that the only way you, or any of us, can *minister* to the White House or the Pentagon is to *prophesy* to the White House and the Pentagon in the tradition of Micaiah, son of Imlah. And you, our brother, have been and will be the prophet summoned to those halls. We shall not."

To this, Graham was moved to dispatch a letter: "Dear Brethren: Normally I do not reply to criticism from any source. I most certainly do not reply to 'open letters' which I sometimes think are motivated by self-seeking publicity or the desire to make a 'point' at the expense of a rather well-known individual. However, I am certain that no such motives would characterize your criticism of me. I am certain that you are completely sincere. I want you to know that I do not take it personally and am not the slightest bit offended. Sometime we might be able to sit down privately and discuss the points you have raised. With warmest fraternal greetings, I am cordially yours. . . ." Somehow it was as if Graham had managed to simply absorb it all into an indistinguishably benign haze of pleasantness. Nevertheless, Campbell promptly replied with a letter thanking him for his note, indicating that he would be indeed eager to sit down with him somewhere, as Graham had suggested, and explore in earnest those questions of Christian discipleship — and he would await Graham's word as to when it would be convenient.

Around that time, on an Easter morning in Nashville — with most of the city's population collected into sprucely groomed congregations in translucent-windowed sanctuaries, among hushed organ tones and rustling church bulletins and small polite coughs — on his own twenty-five-acre hillside homestead several miles outside town, Campbell himself, an ordained Southern Baptist minister with a divinity degree from Yale, was occupied instead at that bright morning hour of church doxologies with hauling stovewood in his pickup truck, now and then depositing precise spits of King Edward tobacco juice into an empty Coke bottle. He had, in fact, already observed Easter. The night before, with a few friends gathered in his log-wall study, set off in a pasture a short distance from his white-frame farmhouse, he had thrummed a few country ballads on his Gibson guitar, with a dingy little Spitz named Leroy plopped beside the alternately pumping toes of his rococo-patterned cowboy boots — *Hello, brother mother, friend of mine* — and then he had presided over a communion service like those he has conducted late at night in the kitchens of black sharecroppers and coal miners and Manhattan radical romanticists and Ku Klux Klansmen alike: "Everybody in this room, now, who believes Jesus Christ is Lord, and that through the grace of his loving sacrifice we have all been freed from the old way of the world and reconciled each to the other, everybody here who knows that, let 'em say, Hallelujah! and drink now to his victory —" and everyone around him then took a long swallow from their lifted glasses of bourbon and water.

Campbell has always tended to scandalize more conventional religious sensibilities as a blasphemer, a heretic, an anarchist, a degenerate. But if, the next morning after that communion service, any sign on Campbell's place that it was Easter or even the Sabbath was largely undetectable, it would be because each day passes for him more or less as a common unceremonious Sabbath. What he is engaged in is a curious sort of earthly, fundamentalist New Testament para-Christianity. A slight and rather unprepossessing figure, with soft shy eyes musing behind horn-rim glasses in a mild mulish face with a lank fringe of hair drooping from his bald pate, usually adorned in a wide-brimmed black Amish hat, he has the prim and archaic look of some member of Brigham Young's wagon train long lost and stranded in a time lapse in these low hills outside Nashville, among his chickens and horses and dogs and goats. But along with his small band of religious irregulars in the Committee of Southern Churchmen, Campbell has long been occupied in an inconspicuous but assiduous ad hoc gospel ministry — his church pulpitless, roofless, unpropertied, uncodified, but catholic in what could be considered the fullest sense. In his clanky ketchup-red pickup truck, often carrying with him no more than his guitar case — in which he packs, with a single change of underwear and socks, a bottle of his Tennessee mash "medicine" — he moves about among the publicans and sinners, the unlovely and wrathful, not only Klansmen but the destitute and despised and dispossessed all over the outlands of the South and in the sleety winter ghettoes of the North.

On his twenty-third wedding anniversary, leaving his wife at home to observe the occasion with their four children, he appeared at the home of a North Carolina Klansman to pass the long night with him before the man's jailing the next morning for refusing to divulge Klan data to the House Un-American Activities Committee; with other Klansmen sitting around him in the small linoleum-floored kitchen around the white kitchenette table with a glass bowl of wax fruit set precisely in its center, Campbell whunked out plushly chorded gospel hymns and hillbilly ballads in the unblinking weary glare of an overhead bulb burning on into the far deep tunnel of the night — "Now, this song coming up, it's kind of powerful material. It's the whole New Testament boiled into one song, really. And its message is, black or white, it doesn't matter *what* we done, Jesus Christ loves us anyway. That's the miracle none of us deserves." When Campbell was asked once, in regard to his ministry to the Klan, "But how in the world do you manage to *communicate* with those brutes?" he replied, "By emptying the bedpans of their sick."

As it happened, Campbell himself, reared on a forty-acre cotton farm in the piny back-brush of lower Mississippi, was intricately involved in the whole long moral saga of the civil rights movement in the South, acting as a circuit-riding strategist and mediator for the National Council of Churches during those now-legendary summers of lightning and travail. But around 1962, he began to suggest about that "the racist is the greatest challenge the church faces today in both the North and the South — the most unlovely and the most in need of love. Certainly the church must not abandon him in its attempts to force him to maturity." It was a notion that tended to disconcert not a few of his liberal colleagues, but Campbell asserts, "I've never been into social engineering, even when I was in the movement. I was, and I am, and I always will be, just a preacher."

Oddly enough, Campbell's theology is at least as stoutly fundamentalist as Graham's — in a sense, they both profoundly answer to the same religious pulses. "Look, all it's about is this," Campbell declares, scrimmaging for a moment through the voluminous litter on his desk until at last he finds his Bible and hefts it forth, his hands then scuffling through its pages — "The thing's so simple, see, it just tears up all that complicated machinery in the heads of the sophisticates. Here, listen to this now —" and he begins reading, from Second Corinthians, without pause or alteration in his easy conversational tone: "For the love of Christ constraineth us . . . that he died for all, that they which live should not henceforth live unto themselves, but unto him who died for them. . . . ' Because God was in Christ, reconciling the world unto himself, not imputing their trespasses unto them —" He glances up. "Get that, now — *not imputing their trespasses unto them,*" and resumes reading, "and hath committed to us the word of reconciliation. Therefore, we pray you in Christ's stead, be ye reconciled to God." Smacking his Bible shut and pitching it back on his desk, he quickly lifts his empty Coke bottle to drop a deft spit of tobacco juice into it. "Now, that's all that the seminaries and the First Baptist Church reverends and the Astrodome Isaiahs really need to pass on to the brothers and sisters. Reconciliation! *Reconciliation to our natures.* Sure, that's a hard idea to accept, that's why the gospel's more drastic than a lot of folks have ever dreamed — our trespasses are not held against us, we are *already* forgiven. Because nobody who truly accepts that, now, is gonna use that pardon as a license to keep on abusing folks or living piggish. It's gotta change his behavior. Nobody can tell me that to abide in grace — what I mean is, to live in acceptance of this gift of reconciliation — isn't far more radical a Christianity than to abide by law. Don't you see how that liberates us all? Black, white, Kluxer, preacher, banker, Teamster, murderer, chairman of General Motors, head of the Ford Foundation — we are *all* bastards, but God loves us anyway."

Proceeding from the same source, Graham and Campbell could hardly have wound up at a more critical cross-tilt to each other. "Will's whole impulse in his ministry," says one colleague, "goes back to that ancient tragic view that all human beings are basically ornery and unreformable creatures, with a Christian being no better than anybody else — a man isn't changed by taking on the vows of Christianity; he's just got some way of dealing with his nature." At the same time, Campbell's fundamentalist perspective — with its old dark pessimism about the congenital perversity of the human species, and its complete trust in all the mysterious supernatural works of New Testament theology, the Incarnation and the Blood Atonement — also gives considerable pause to a number of those who answer to the rationalist humanitarian ethic. Yet Campbell has construed from his primitive fundamentalist vision, with all its dire and heavy metaphysical smokes, a liberation and grace to believe in the race that, peculiarly, would seem a quantum leap beyond the ordinary optimisms and sympathies of the common liberal decency — a kind of ultimate hope and compassion.

Shortly after a middle-aged white deputy sheriff in Alabama, Tom Coleman, had been acquitted of manslaughter by a village jury for the shotgunning of a young white seminarian named Jonathan Daniels who was involved in local civil-rights demonstrations, Campbell proposed in *Katallagete,* "Jonathan can never have died in vain, because he loved his killer — by his own last written words. And since he loved his murderer, his death is its own meaning. And what it means is that Tom Coleman is forgiven. If Jonathan forgives him, then it is not for me to cry for his blood, his execution. Any act on my part which is even akin to 'avenging' Jonathan's death is sacrilege." This pronouncement occasioned some spectacular instances of ideological apoplexy in liberal quarters. Says Campbell, "A whole lot of my civil-rights friends came to me and said, 'Good God, Campbell — you can't be going around saying things like that to those rednecks. You tell 'em stuff like that, "Why, we not holding your deeds against you, fellas, it's all okay, you're forgiven" — man, that just gives 'em *license.*' But of course, that's not true, I told them. What that jury down there in Lowndes County told Tom Coleman was: You are forgiven and congratulated, go thou and kill again, if you want. But what the gospel, what Second Corinthians says, and what we are obliged to say is: Your sins are already forgiven you, brother, go thou and kill no more. That's the difference. And that's all the difference in the world." Therein, Campbell maintains, lies the truly revolutionary premise and promise of Christianity: that the angry, the predatory, the base, the indifferent — the lost — can only be redeemed through inducing in them the transforming realization that they are in fact reconciled to all other men, including even those whom they abuse — that we are all finally of one nature and one flesh and one grief and one hope — and only with this recognition can any real contrition and regeneration and compassion come, and then it is immeasurably more overwhelming.

At a campus seminar once, a professor of theology kept insisting, "But what do you actually *believe*, Reverend Campbell? I mean, what do you actually believe in that's going on *today?*" until Campbell finally barked, "Look, I told you, I believe in Jesus, dammit — *Jesus*. Maybe you've just never quite gotten around yet in your theological studies to actually acquainting yourself with that particular figure of the faith." One among Campbell's plenitude of critics in the formal church sniffed once, "Absolutely nothing seems to be sacred to the guy." But rather, it seems that to Campbell there is simply no distinction between the sacred and the secular.

If the Incarnation meant anything, Campbell believes, it was the accomplishment and annunciation in Jesus of the final closing of any divide between the divine and the temporal, between the holy and the profane, between the church and the street, between heaven and earth. After that, Campbell asserts, it should have been apparent that God, through Jesus, was a presence from that point on quite literally and immediately abiding in every level and every detail of man's tenure in life: that, in fact, the whole history of the faith from Abraham through Moses to Jesus really amounted to a sequence of progressive recognitions that heaven and earth, God and man, were drawing always closer together, with the final fusion realized with the Incarnation in Christ — that was the great climactic instant of merging.

But it is also Campbell's conviction that the organized church ever since has acted to resist and subvert that cosmic event by reasserting the old dichotomy between the divine and the earthly. And this failure of comprehension and of belief constitutes, to Campbell, the original and still single greatest betrayal of Jesus' meaning: when the sacred and the secular were resundered by the traditional church — when the gospel was reextracted out of the common daily dusty welter of humankind — that reopened gap then admitted all the grotesque discords, the limitless monstrous mischiefs throughout the course of Christendom like the Crusades and the Inquisitions and the Hundred Years War, the whole sum of the church's outrages ever since Paul.

"Every time a group of believers has moved from a catacomb or a brush arbor to a steeple," says Campbell, "they have lost something they once knew about Jesus. And they never seem to get it back." Campbell seems, if nothing else, to be trying at least to realize that original implication of Jesus' appearance among men by observing, simply within the circumference of his own life and ministry, no real distinctions between the religious and the profane. It could not come to a more total repudiation, then, of that assumption that righteousness is a matter of mores, of those delicacies and decorums of behavior and language and appearances which make up the common respectability of a community: a case of cultural propriety, as Campbell regards it, exalted to the magnitude of religion.

If Campbell's indiscriminate assimilation of the gospel into not only the commonplace but the vulgar appalls most institutional churchmen, Campbell himself entertains a fine distaste for the official church itself. "Who created this fraud about Jesus," he says, "that Christianity is consecrated water, pews, altar cloths, budgets, computers, decision cards, ordained men, parking lots, Sunday-school boards?" He once reported in *Katallagete*, with some incredulousness, that the Southern Baptist Convention headquarters in Nashville had just adopted an office-security program entailing not only Pinkerton guards but emergency provisions for the use of tear gas, and not long afterward, a Baptist official from that headquarters appeared at Campbell's study late one afternoon for what he had cheerfully proposed as "a little chat about your article." Seating himself with a kind of fastidious politeness amid the cabin's customary dishevelment of cardboard boxes and walking canes and scattered hummocks of cedar shavings from Campbell's perpetual whittling, the official — a small trim gentleman with shell-rim spectacles and a vague haze of sandy hair, attired in a neat pale-blue summer suit — at length began to explain, with an air of meticulous pleasantness, that he knew, of course, that Campbell realized, naturally, that his department really had a *duty*, unfortunately, to protect its premises. Campbell softly interposed, "Protect it from who?" The official, crossing his legs then with a certain preciseness, cleared his throat lightly behind his fist: "Well. Of course, I'm aware you'd have no way of knowing this, Reverend Campbell, but the fact is, we'd had a number of people to report lately that they'd seen undesirables in the building —" Campbell's whittling knife paused: "Undesirables?" The official blinked several times, rapidly: "Well, yes, you know what I mean, the sort —" but Campbell murmured again, "Undesirables? *Undesirables?* Can you tell me, for the love of Jesus Christ, exactly who you think it is that our Lord asked us to reach and to serve?" The official again briefly cleared his throat behind his fist, and submitted patiently, "Reverend Campbell, I don't think you understand what I'm trying to get across, exactly. You see, there's also been some stealing going on —" and Campbell snapped, "Some stealing? But how can they steal? Didn't our Lord tell us, if any man take your coat, give him your cloak also?" Campbell's voice lifted now slightly louder: "Yessir, I *do* understand, I think. Yessir. We've somehow wound up in the position, God help us, where our Savior's church is forced to deal with those very people it was commanded to rescue and minister to as undesirables now, and barricade itself against them — where we have to set apart a group of our fellow men and make sure they stay apart from us even if it takes gas to do it. *Gas.* When you all were discussing this security program, wasn't there *anybody* in that room who jumped up and said,

'Whoa, wait a minute here, brethren, what in the name of our Lord Jesus Christ are we talking about here? *Gas!* What are we saying?' " At that, the official — his face having taken on a faint pink tinge — suggested with a certain brittleness, "Now, I think we might be getting a little bit overzealous here — " and Campbell shook his head. "No, we ain't. We're *supposed* to be zealous on these points. But I'm not blaming you, understand that. If I were in your position, I'd have to feel exactly the same way you do. See, you *got* to protect all that stuff over there — if I had an office building I was in charge of, with all those files that some demonstratin' undesirable might pour ketchup in, all those elevators and wall-safes and typewriters and adding machines, yessir, I'd feel obligated to protect it too, I'd be worrying about some undesirable dropping a pill maybe into the air-conditioning ducts too. But that's sort of my point, see. You enter into a contract with the devices and means and procedures of Caesar — let's don't even say the Devil, let's just say Caesar — then it's caught you, you got no choice; of course you have to act then according to Caesar's terms. I'd have to do the same thing . . . . But those aren't exactly the terms of the gospel, are they?" The official simply stared at Campbell for several seconds, unmoving, and finally Campbell offered, "But it's hard, ain't it? It's hard to get." After a moment, the official said in a small voice, "Yes. Yes, it is. It's very hard to understand, Reverend Campbell," and Campbell answered with a deep-dipping nod, "Yes, I know it is, and I can't say I understand it all myself. It's just the way Jesus said to act, that's all I know." A few minutes later, the Baptist official took his leave, mustering only a wan semblance of his initial cordiality, and Campbell later recounted to a friend, "He just never did manage to get past that institutional mind-lock. It has him — has him probably for the rest of his life."

It is Campbell's appraisal, on the whole, that "the formal institutionalized church has come to act as the single greatest barrier to the propagation of the gospel. That was certainly the case in Jesus' day — who gave him the most trouble? It was the established church, that's who. Jesus Christ wasn't a churchman;

he was outside all the institutions and systems then, and that's precisely what got him in so much trouble all the way around, from the left and the right. There's no real reason to suppose things should be any different today. If they couldn't even understand the man while he was walking around actually trying to tell them, I don't guess it's any surprise they haven't understood him too good since he's been gone. All that's happened is, the official church has just changed into another cultural guise. Somebody once said that any church truly of Jesus would be an instrument literally and constantly being used up in his service — that is, service to those not even in it. But just like every other institution, the church — and I include in that all its adjuncts and accessory operations, conventions and high councils and mass crusades and mailing lists — it's all come to serve perpetuating itself by the trick of identifying its own perpetuation with the survival and advancement of Christ's gospel. That's the great and really unforgivable blasphemy of it."

Campbell is fond of suggesting, "I wouldn't be surprised at all to see a real protest movement directed at the institutional church, in the form of young folks beginning to say, 'Look, man, what if we sort of took in hand that church building down there worth at least three million dollars, and that lot it's settin' on worth probably a quarter-million dollars? What if two hundred of us just went down there and *joined* that thing, you know, and then we all showed up at the very next business meeting, and somebody made a motion, "I move we sell this building and this lot." "Yeah, I second that motion." "All in favor — okay, we sell it." ' *Bam!* They got three million dollars. You ask these young people, who are already thinking along such lines, ask them, 'Well, what would you do with three million dollars that's any different really from what the church was doing with it, or Billy Graham, or the Carnegie Foundation for that matter?' And they tell you, 'Well,' they say, 'you could go down to the jail and sho bail a whole heap of folks out with that. And you could take it and go out and feed an awful big bunch of hungry folks outta three million dollars —' And they talk on like this, and all of a sudden what you're hearing is Jesus talking about releasing the captives, giving meat to the hungry and clothing the naked and healing them that are bruised. And if this kind of challenge ever hits the institutional church, how they're gonna field it I can't imagine."

Of course, more clerics than Campbell have sensed how the primordial reality of that feverish young provincial exalté, who for a few short years preached and ministered and suffered in one of the dustier corners of the earth two millennia ago, has hopelessly come to be perceived only through the accumulated refractions and permutations of numberless subsequent lenses of interpretation. As one of Campbell's colleagues notes, "You can't even *name* him now — can't even just say, *Jesus* — without, immediately, whoosh, all these other associations and connotations, both personal and cultural, all this accrued sediment and static getting in the way. When you say, 'Jesus,' people hear about everything else in the world but him, he's lost in two thousand years of echoes." What Campbell and his colleagues in the Committee of Southern Churchmen seem to be essaying, then, is a kind of thirteenth discipleship time-leaping, two thousand years later, back past all the intervening unscrolling elaborations of catechisms and encyclicals and ecclesiastic jurisdictions, all the way to the simple figure of Jesus himself.

But as much as Campbell ministers to the unnoticed drifts of human slag from industrialization and corporate agglomeration in the country, he also makes regular appearances before Establishment groups — business executives, university dons — in which he brings them tidings of a mentality in American society, pervasive and diffused and found in teak-paneled corporate boardrooms among sensible and civil modulations of language and manners, that has accomplished immeasurably more havoc, he maintains, than any Klan cowpastures lit with burning crosses. "The real enemy is whatever it is that's keeping folks outside and poor and without hope, that makes for emptiness in life and the brutality that always comes out of that emptiness. In the words of a famous ole country song, it's hard to find the blame, it's too smart to have a name; it ain't flesh and blood we fight with, it's powers and principalities. You turn it all into a matter of administration, see — make it all a question of main-

taining a system, a procedure, keeping the machinery functioning — and that way, the hideous mess that functioning machinery might also happen to be incidentally causing in the lives
of human beings, such little problems as that, that's not what's at
issue. The system, the structure — that's what's at stake."

Propounding all this once to a seminar of Atlanta's civic establishment gathered into an auditorium at Georgia Tech,
Campbell remarked as he whittled on his usual stick of cedar
kindling, "In fact, this institution right here and respectable institutions like it all over the country have contributed, unwit-
tingly or not, to incomparably more bloodshed and misery, done
more to maim and murder, than the whole lot of pore old boys
in sheets holding cross-burnings in rented meadows back there
through the Sixties." This was answered by a rather chasmic
hush over the auditorium. "I 'spect some of yawl would disagree
with that right strongly. But I wonder if any of us really have an
idea what crimes are committed in the name of order and progress." Campbell — with his Amish hat resting on the table at his
elbow, looking like some homely hillbilly prophet with his
scraggly scarf of hair hanging limp below his ears — briefly lifted
his cedar stick for a few delicate sniffs of its winy tang. "I buried
a man up in Chicago last Saturday who'd spent thirty years in
coal mines — *thirty years* — and after all that, he literally didn't
even have a shirt we could bury him in. We held this service,
now, almost in the shadow of a statue up there to the notable
railroad free-enterpriser, George Pullman. What I'm telling you
gentlemen is, that man was *lynched*. He was lynched by the system in this country — the kind of system that'd keep a man
toiling for thirty years in a coal mine to keep himself alive and
then leave him without so much as a shirt to be buried in."

What finally strikes one most arrestingly about Campbell, perhaps, is that he seems to have managed somehow to transfer all
the steamy business in the Scriptures directly and inherently into
his time, into the immediate moment in the land. Riding once
along a Mississippi interstate, he presently looked up from the
pilfered motel-room Gideon Bible he was reading to say to the

other passengers in the car, "Yawl wanna hear something? Listen
to this from old Nahum — 'Woe to the bloody city! it is all full of
lies and robbery; the prey departeth not.' That sound anything
like Manhattan or De-troit City? 'The noise of a whip, and the
noise of the rattling wheels, and of the prancing horses, and of
the jumping chariots —' He's talking about the Pentagon there,
listen to this, ye Joint Chiefs of Staff, '— The horseman lifteth
up both the bright sword and the glittering spear: and there is a
multitude of slain, and a great number of carcases; and there is
none end of their corpses; they stumble upon their corpses —'
That's Vietnam, all right, that's My Lai, the prophet's seeing it.
'— They stumble upon their corpses: because of the multitude of
the whoredoms of the wellfavoured harlot, the mistress . . . that
selleth nations through her whoredoms.' Listen, America, ole
Nahum's talking to you. 'Behold, I am against thee, saith the
Lord of hosts! . . . I will discover thy skirts upon thy face —' "
Campbell shook his head softly with a little smile, muttering,
"That's putting it strong enough, ain't it? The CIA in Chile, we
been discovered with our skirts over our face. '— I will show the
nations thy nakedness, and the kingdoms thy shame. . . . And
will set thee as a gazingstock. And it shall come to pass, that all
they that look upon thee·shall flee —' You think that's not the
way the rest of the world looks on America now? '— Thy
crowned are as the locusts, and thy captains as the great grasshoppers, which camp in the hedges in the cold day, but when the
sun ariseth they flee away, and their place is not known —' So
much for Johnson and John Connally and Nixon. 'There is no
healing of thy bruise; thy wound is grievous: all that hear the
bruit of thee shall clap the hands over thee, for upon whom —' "
and Campbell paused again, gently shaking his head again in
awe, and then repeated in a louder, fuller voice, "— '*upon whom*
hath not thy wickedness *passed — continually!*' " For a long moment then, Campbell gazed out through the windshield, and finally murmured, "Brother, if that don't speak to the times. I
don't take all that stuff lightly, I tell you. . . ." After another
moment, he said, "Wonder what would happen if Brother Gra-

ham were to read that out to the notables assembled at one of
those devotional services in the East Room of the White House
sometime."

. . . Mississippi's Amite County, back during Campbell's boyhood there in the Depression, was a countryside of piny scruffy
mule-and-moonshiner hills and gullied roads of pebbly pale-
orange dirt trailing thinly up to isolate paintless tenant shacks
roosting atop shadeless ridges of broom sage, a countryside with
a communal folk past of numberless shotgun-and-woodax violences. Campbell was baptized when he was seven years old, on a
shimmering summer Sunday morning, with the chapped and
horny hands of an itinerant preacher tilting him gently backward into the sluggish current of an olive-brown creek while the
congregation of the East Fork Baptist Church, gathered on the
leafy bank, sang together *"Happy Day, when Jeee-sus washed my sins
away. . . ."* About nine summers later, he mounted the pulpit of
the East Fork Church, having earlier that hot Sunday morning
drunk a can of pineapple juice to lubricate his larynx, and proceeded to preach his first sermon, which he had practiced for
weeks from a sheet of notes tacked to plow handles behind a
mule. When Campbell had finished it, he stood in the vestibule
to receive twittering congratulations, his spirit wheeling in winds
of euphoria.

Even now, the only certification legitimizing his ministry is a
framed document, hanging on the thin-slatted tan walls of his
farmhouse, which "attests to the fact," says Campbell, "that in
1941, when I was seventeen years old, I'd had certain hands laid
on my head, and when they were removed, I was a Baptist
preacher, and it's signed by my daddy, my uncle, and my
cousin." But in time, Campbell found himself at Yale — "See,
even in rural Mississippi the mistaken notion had gotten around
that the birth of a baby to a peasant Jewish girl — a baby who,
without the aid of scholarship or academe, was to turn out to be
the Son of God and, by his public hanging, Savior of the
world — this was such a *complicated* matter that it took seven
years beyond high school, at least, to learn how to tell other folks
about it right." After a pastorate in Louisiana, he moved on to

the University of Mississippi as campus chaplain, then migrated
to the southern office of the National Council of Churches, in
that office escorting the first black children into Little Rock's
desegregated high schools. But it was in his passage through the
turmoils of the civil-rights movement in the South that Campbell
arrived at last at a total disillusionment with all political and institutional intercessions to improve man's condition. "If one does
not believe that, let him go into a tavern in Tennessee and hear
the manager say, following the visit of a thirsty Negro, 'Yeah, we
have to serve 'em, but we break every glass they drink out of.
There ain't no law against that yet.' This may be justice, but it's
not reconciliation."

He concluded, "All institutions — all of them — are fundamentally inimical to what Christ was about on this earth."
What struck him as most malignant was their common reliance,
however benevolent or humanitarian their intents, on the me-
chanistic for reform: "What institutions actually institute, in the
end, is inhumanity, by advancing the illusion that form is substance, the means are the meaning, doing is being, procedure is
redemption — and so they can only further dehumanize the relationships between those they were instituted to reconcile." In
his appearances before civic groups at conferences and seminars,
he admits, "Somebody's always winding up those sessions by
charging, 'Why, good Lord, man, you're telling us here tonight
we ought to forget about every single instrument we've got now
for doing good, including the church. What you're saying, it
seems, is just, *Do nothing!*' And when I hear that, that's when I
know I'm beginning to come through. That's when I say,
'Brother, just nail that down — now you got the message. Do
nothing. Instead, *be* something. Before you start trying to figure
out what you should do about all the world's woes, just *be* what
you say you are — a Christian, a follower of Christ. When that
happens, then you won't have to ask what to do — you'll already
know.' "

But precisely because of his antipatterned approach, Campbell's own ministry tends to elude any hard assessments. He is
called on now and then to perform more formal ministerial of-

fices, like the funeral he conducted for a young mother who had died suddenly of an unsuspected disease: "Toward the close of that service, I felt moved for some reason to ask all those there who felt like it to just stand for a minute, in honor of who Jenny had been and all she had meant while she was among us, and to applaud whatever memories they had of her — for this life now ended that she had spent among us. I really wasn't too sure how they might take this — but they began standing up all over that auditorium, first her friends and then her family and then her husband, getting to their feet and starting to applaud louder and louder, a standing ovation that went on and on, looking at that casket with tears coming into their eyes and still clapping on and on. . . ."

But Campbell's ministry consists, for the most part, of private incidents, haphazard and spontaneous. In the end, he seems simply to act out of some incapacity to detach himself from the pain or despair of anyone touching on his own life. One winter morning, a friend phoned to inform him that the Nashville Housing Authority had dispatched convicts to eject indigent black tenants, who had lapsed in their rent, from the scrappy wooden shanties the Authority had purchased from them for a new expressway's right-of-way — that, in fact, two aged women and an old man were already, at that moment, standing out on the sidewalk amid the tumble of their belongings. Shortly thereafter, Campbell came flurrying through the office door of the Authority director, his black Shaker hat clamped on his head, and while the director stared at him incredulously, Campbell — his face flushed red as a radish and light winking flatly off his glasses — recited the news he had just received and then proceeded to pronounce, from a passage in Matthew, in a voice like a wailing tabernacle pump-organ, "Woe unto you, feller. The scribes and Pharisees, they bind heavy burdens and lay them on men's shoulders, and they will not move them with one of their fingers. Woe unto you, for ye devour widows' houses. *Woe!* unto you, for that day — now, listen to me, feller, this isn't me talking, it's the Lord God Almighty talking —" the director had started to rise from his chair, but sank back down "— for on that day, the Lord God shall set the sheep on his right hand and the goats on his left, and he shall say to those on his left, 'I was hungry and ye gave me no meat, I was thirsty and ye gave me no drink, a stranger and ye took me not in, naked and ye clothed me not — in fact, you, feller, you threw me out of my pore little house on that cold winter morning back there in Nashville — so depart from me, ye accursed, into the everlasting fire prepared for the devil and his angels —' " At this point, the Housing Authority director interposed in a thin voice, "Stop —" A balding middle-aged man sitting behind a metal desk in his dowdy office, he swallowed: "Just stop. Please. Don't preach to me anymore. If you can do anything at all about that rent I have to collect, I'll help move them all back in myself. When do you want me down there?"

Consisting, then, of such extemporaneous moments, Campbell's ministry is mostly a private and antispectacle affair beyond capturing by statistics and flashbulbs and television screens. But Campbell also cultivates this anonymity for its own sake, out of a suspicion that, like other commando clerics discovered by the klieg glare of the media reality, he might find himself eventually alienated and isolated from his own first purposes, appropriated instead into all the gallimaufry of pop relevance. "More guys than one," he ruminates, "have stopped serving and all of a sudden started performing without ever realizing it's happened to them." An acquaintance of Campbell's explains, "It has haunted Will more than once — Good God, what if the networks and the newsmagazines had been around when Jesus was at work? They wouldn't have needed to crucify him, all they'd have had to do was run him on the cover of a national magazine, put him on the Johnny Carson show, interview him on the *Today* show and *Face the Nation*. That would have done it. It's the mirror that kills."

It's a trepidation that prompts Campbell to seem at times almost exorbitantly self-effacing. "If I were to look around and find a bunch of folks following me, I'd fall to pieces. What I'm doing is just my interpretation of the Christian faith, and anybody following me is following a second-hand situation, which means they're in a third-hand condition. It'd scare me silly if anybody started taking me that seriously. There's hardly anything dramatic or messianic about just holding a man's hand whose brother has died, or singing a few songs to a fellow who's about to go to jail, but folks keep exaggerating and romanticizing the damn thing. I used to get all these college students wanting to come down and do what I'm doing, and finally I got up a trick question — I'd say, 'You kind of want to be our *disciple*, is that right?' And they would say, 'Yeah, yeah, that's right. That's what I want to be.' Then I'd say, 'Well, that's too bad. See, I don't want any disciples. I'm terrified of 'em.' "

Campbell, though, is sometimes oppressed by the consideration that "in all these years, I can't really point out one thing I've actually, personally accomplished." Of course, that would largely be because he is operating almost exclusively in the invisible — beyond convert data files and attendance records and decision counts, on that interior front of the human heart itself, which, Campbell would insist, is the only real and lasting one anyway. But it also makes any sequence of effect between his work and its results impossible to trace: rather, those effects would only brim back forth into life seemingly sourceless, like artesian wells. The most that might be projected is that communities of simple unsystematized existential discipleship like that of Campbell and his committee — tending, out of universal concerns and urgencies, one's own garden, the immediate neighborhood of one's own life — could proliferate through multiplying personal impingements on through society.

"But I can't afford to even fantasize about that," says Campbell. He merely continues to move about in an inauspicious discipleship to a peculiar call which, however imponderable its final promise of efficacy, he realizes it would be spiritual suicide to deny. Campbell admits it may all come in the end to no more than the benediction contained in the last refrain of one of his own ballads: "O yea. They gonna love me when I'm dead. They gonna come in from miles around — the old Hartmann Funeral Home in McComb City — stand 'round my coffin all night. And they'll say, 'Ole Will was a good ole boy. He just had some crazy ideas. . . .' "

After Campbell's open letter to Graham had brought from him that amiable acknowledgment — "I am certain that you are completely sincere. Sometime we might be able to sit down privately and discuss the points you have raised" — Campbell then had responded that he would certainly welcome that opportunity and, knowing how full Graham's schedule must be, just to let him know when it would be convenient.

He never heard from him again. Graham merely declared to the Southern Baptist Convention once around that period, "I've even heard of pastors who think nothing of using profanity. . . . Some of our radical groups in this country are even being led by so-called clergymen. Where many of these men get the 'reverend' in front of their names, I don't know. Certainly, they don't get it from God."

VI

Meanwhile — for all his self-detachment into his own institutionalized ethos and his constant insistence that "it would be a tragedy if through the wiles of Satan, I should be led into anything that might be construed as political" — yet irresistibly, Graham continued his political extensions and punditries vigorously on through the Sixties. While in 1963 he discounted the Peace Corps as an enterprise "almost completely materialistic in its aims," his misgivings about the materialism of such political adventures seemed to have evaporated by 1967, when, at the behest of President Johnson, he occupied himself for about a week making phone calls to Congressmen personally to urge them to support LBJ's Poverty Program. Indeed, he pitched himself into this political exercise to the extent of accompanying Sargent Shriver, whose helicopter had come beating down out of the sky to alight on his side lawn at Montreat, on an OEO promotional foray through a neighboring Appalachian county.

Then in 1966, he proclaimed that he had detected "a great wave of conservatism" gathering now through both the Republican and Democratic parties, and during that year's turbulent summer, he called on President Johnson to identify publicly "those extremist groups who are teaching and advocating violence, training in guerrilla tactics, and defying authority. . . . The FBI and the President know who they are and what they are up to. Now the people need to know. Congress has no more urgent business than to pass laws with teeth in them." In 1968, to a prayer-breakfast of motel franchise owners in Memphis, he declared that "guerrilla war is now being planned by the anarchists," and the next year, it was his propoundment that the war moratorium demonstrations in Washington were the handiwork of "radicals and those seeking to overthrow the American way of life" — announcing that "extremists" intended to launch terrorist operations on October 1 to undo order in the nation.

If the phenomenon of mass revivalism throughout America's past has largely depended on a general popular sense of uncertainty and embattlement, by no means the least extraordinary of Graham's feats is that he has succeeded in sustaining his ministry in such a dramatic tension through almost three decades. For one thing, reports an associate, Graham himself "personally operates on a constant sense of crisis in his own life. Even the smallest little things he sees and interprets in the most drastic terms — for instance, if he's riding on an airplane and something begins to sound a little out of the ordinary with the engines, he sits right up, 'Listen, did you hear that?' and immediately, we're all on the brink of disaster in that plane." Equally in his evangelism, ever since his national inception in Los Angeles in 1949 when he was declaring, "Unless the Western world has an old-fashioned revival, we can not last," he has maintained an unabating incantation of imminent apocalypse. In 1951, he was trumpeting, "The day of crisis has not passed. We seem to be moving toward a climactic battle which will settle the destiny, if not the annihilation, of the human race," and still in 1956, "The Day of Judgment is near. The signs all point to the fact that this may be the hour," and still again in 1961, "This Christmas is the most precarious in history. The world hangs on the edge of an abyss." Moving always in this context of Armageddonal crisis also had a way of lending his own ministry, as he presented it, no negligible pertinence: before setting out on one European tour, he announced that his mission was "more important than any diplomatic or political mission. This year, weapons for mass destruction will reach the peak of perfection. We have reached the point of no return in our destructive philosophy and strategy. . . . I have never undertaken a mission in my life for which I felt more inadequate and unqualified and in need of prayer. I think it will possibly be one of the most crucial weeks of my entire ministry."

In fact, in this obsessive litany over the years — once even appropriating a sag in the stock market as an apocalyptic omen, "Americans are at the edge of an abyss and about to fall in, our days are numbered, the hour glass is already turned over" — there seems to emerge after a while almost a lust for the Götterdämmerung, an impatience for the holocaust.

In 1963, he dismissed the recently negotiated Test Ban Treaty as nothing but "a false hope. Many world leaders today are consciously aware that we are on the brink of a world catastrophe and impending judgment. There is a growing universal awareness that, as a society, we have our backs to the wall." To a college assembly in 1965, he proclaimed, "We are like a people under sentence of death, waiting for the date to be set. History has reached an impasse. Something is about to give." Indeed, by now it would have seemed something would have to, given the accumulating compressions of what one critic called twenty years of terminal emergency in Graham's preaching. But with undiminished urgency he was contending in 1966, "I think the world is heading for a gigantic disaster. I think we are on a collision course with China," and in 1970, "I personally think we might be approaching the end of our history," and still in 1977, "The atomic clock at the University of Chicago was recently moved from twelve minutes before midnight to nine minutes until midnight. How much longer can the world have until destruction comes? We see time collapsing all about us."

Whenever it is suggested to Graham that it has come to seem by now a rather protracted alarum of impending judgment and calamity, he submits, "Maybe enough have been responding to forestall it, I don't know — like Jonah warning Nineveh it would be overthrown in forty days, and then, one hundred fifty years later, it did finally fall. It's been only a critical holding action, that's all." But it's as if Graham in his forensics has simply abided in a historical attention span of no more than a few months' duration, a moment of suspense simply repeated over and over again through the years without real connection or continuity. "Yes, I've been criticized for being repetitious," he allows, "but I am consoled by the fact, pointed out once by a very eminent theologian, that Jesus repeated himself five hundred times." In a sense, though, for Graham time has indeed collapsed. As one of his aides explains, "Billy just lives totally absorbed in today. That's why, in every one of the crusades I've been with him, this one was the most critical, the one that would start the worldwide revival. He'd work and preach and give himself to that crusade as if he'd never had one before and would never have one again. It's what gives him his tremendous concentration and energy." But at the same time, to the extent to which Graham seems to live and perceive almost totally in the motion and din of the instant, he is supremely a creature of the peculiar catatonia of the pop age — that frantic ceaseless interruption of any longer, evolving, more comprehending sense of time and sequence in experience, which some have cited as an intrinsic part of the totalitarian conditioning of a people: the capturing of the individual in the moment, isolated from any larger, fuller sense of what is actually happening to him.

Whatever, it has simply been Graham's nature that "unless there was some crisis somewhere," says his old friend, Stephen Olford, "Billy couldn't preach. In the midst of one crusade, I remember him walking down the street one afternoon and buying four newspapers just in the space of one block, looking for a crisis. He'd snatch one up and rummage hurriedly through it, then pitch it away and grab another. A fellow walking along with us finally turned to me and whispered, 'Stephen, he's thrown

down every one of those newspapers — he can't find a crisis anywhere; he's not going to be able to preach tonight.' "

In his beginning years, this running oratorical suspense of
momentary catastrophe was cast primarily in terms of the Cold
War conflict. Then, as that public tension began to wane, Graham proceeded to rearticulate his evangelism's crisis dynamic
into the increasing complications in the nation's own inner life
and moral order — the racial throes, the estrangements and
angers of youth, all the yawings and dislocations of the Sixties.
"The United States is in the worst state of spiritual decline and
immorality in its history," he began to say in 1963, and in 1970,
he was declaring, "Take the twin problems of pornography and
drugs, along with the rebellion and disrespect for authority rampant all over the country today, and in another five years, we've
had it, in my opinion." He advertised a particular foreboding
over the Supreme Court's restrictions on religious observances in
public schools: "This is a dangerous thing for America. . . . It is
interesting to note that as soon as prayer was taken out of the
schools that drugs, sex permissiveness, and even crime entered
the schools."

But in all his commentary on the course of the nation's condition, Graham seemed always to be dwelling oddly at one remove,
one lagging and denerved synapse apart, as it were, from the
actual smack and heat of the realities themselves. While his congregations have always tended to be fairly thin of communicants
from George Wallace's order of blue-collar jacquerie, Graham's
spokesmen would insist that he had a special effectiveness with
factory folk, steelworkers, laboring people, owing to his "air of
authority. Authority is the word. This is what the working man is
looking for, because he is used to it" — and it persisted as a puzzlement, as one Graham confidant put it, that "so many of them
have stayed unresponsive." This strangely askance fix on the ac-
tualities has been attributed by one critic to the fact that Graham's faith is of that order described by Bergson, a certitude
tending "not so much to move mountains as to see no mountains
really to move." Graham himself has put it, instead, as "to be
able to sleep in the storm — that is peace." But it's as if, in his

long enterprise to invest his ministry and message with a journalistic currency, he has succeeded in acquainting himself with everything while finally understanding nothing.

Industriously undertaking to verse himself in the new Rimbaudian geist of youth in the Sixties, he appeared at a counterculture festival in Canada once wearing dark glasses and a baseball cap, indicating afterward that he had "learned a lot, they're asking the right questions," then in 1969 briefly navigated the sidewalks of Sunset Strip, again costumed in baseball cap and dark glasses, and finally, with his camouflage this time muttonchop whiskers, inserted himself for about half an hour in a student demonstration in New York City, emerging from this with the conclusion that "student radicals are very dangerous to the security of our nation." Accepting an invitation to address a rock festival in Hollywood, Florida, Graham gamely wired, "I really dig this generation of young people" — a vernacular that somehow seemed to fit him about as appropriately as those muttonchop whiskers he had assumed in New York. Graham's own divining of the angers and nauseas at work through those times he indicated once when he announced that "we are in danger of entering an era of cynicism as we had in the 1920's and 1930's. This is a real danger. People are wondering if anything or anybody is sincere, they're beginning to suspect everything. For instance, my children were watching television last night and saw a commercial — and they chuckled. They didn't even believe the announcer giving the commercial."

But it was a time in the life of the country — in the Sixties after the assassination of Jack Kennedy — when it seemed some cellar door had suddenly been nudged ajar, loosing over the land a berserkness out of the chaos of old night, uproars and strange sorceries. Hints of sulfur hung in the air then, intimations of seismic fissurings in American society widening beyond the span of any true voice. The American regulars like Ronald Reagan and J. Edgar Hoover could not have been more uncomprehending of the American mystics like Allen Ginsberg or Norman Mailer, Lyndon Johnson could never have understood LeRoi Jones or Bob Dylan. With those rifle cracks in Dallas, in fact, it seemed that old schizophrenic conflict in the American psyche between the sober Plymouth disciplines and the dark lyricisms of the frontier had once again been joined — the ever-recurring struggle with the mystery of who we actually are.

It took the form, this time, of a tumultuous recoil of rage among a quickened citizenry at sensations of some progressive totalitarian deadening of the nerves of the nation's soul, a slow euthanasia principally being worked through the distant monstrousness in Vietnam being bureaucratically conducted in the guise of the *Our Town* virtues. For almost a decade, marches spilled through the streets of Boston and Chicago and San Francisco in a seethe of flags and banners and storming of voices below the cast-concrete-and-plateglass towers of government and corporate offices from which, pent behind high windows, pale figures gloomed in white shirt-sleeves, looking down — night marches surging through the dark streets of the nation in a vast dirgelike chanting, *"Ho-Ho-Ho Chi Minh! The NLF is going to win,"* bearded faces under long tattered hair resembling, in the myriad muttering of their candles, the faces of Picts, Goths, John Brown, Whitman, while far above their beating voices somewhere in the dark heavens a jet's thunder dwindled in fading booms on across the wide night. . . . The memory of all the grand angers of those times has come to taste now rather like flat champagne left overnight from some barely remembered revel. But for almost ten years, the land was full of such scenes, a kind of hallucinatory theatre of portents. . . .

One of those warm seasonless evenings in Los Angeles: Republican seigneurs are gathering at the Beverly Hilton Hotel for an inspirational banquet, a congregation of bald burnished heads and tuxedos, women in vaporing chiffon and trailing Arabian fragrances; Governor Reagan arrives, tall, boxy-shouldered, waningly but still staunchly handsome in a certain parched way with his genial eye-crinkling grin. In the large banquet hall of dusty pinks and rose with candles glimmering over tables covered in heavy white linen, the Los Angeles County Sheriff leads everyone in the Pledge of Allegiance, a small orchestra produces a somewhat diminished-sounding "Star-Spangled Banner," and with that, everyone settles down to their quenelle of English Channel sole in wine sauce, in a mellow fellowship pulsing in puffs of bright voices over the candelabra to the strings of Manny Harmon's vest-pocket orchestra playing "Fascination," "The Sound of Music," "Theme from *Dr. Zhivago.*" Finally, at the head table, Art Linkletter takes the microphone to make the introductions: "On my extreme left — I don't know why I should say extreme left, *moderate* left — it's all a family party anyway, isn't it?" . . . At that moment, in the dark hills of the Big Sur, some three hundred miles to the north, where a rock festival is about to begin, another host is gathering as the last ghost of the day dims away on the rim of the sea, a numberless convocation of spectral youths with long filmy hair, coming down everywhere out of the mountains of the night. . . . At the Beverly Hilton, Reagan takes the lectern and begins in a voice with a crisp Post-Toasties-cornflakes rustle of conscientiousness: "What will be the spirit of this land and its people when we mark soon the two hundreth anniversary of its founding? We must unleash the full power and the many benefits of the free, competitive enterprise system if we are to take the fullness of tomorrow's promise. If we've all been lumped together in what they call the Establishment, then we've got to work together. Because there are those abroad in the land working day and night to alienate our young people." . . . Countlessly they continue to come filtering down out of the mountains as if called by some unseen horn of evening, like a legion of lost young angels arrayed in the attire of Pawnees, Ché Guevara, Bowery derelicts, Davy Crockett, trudging in endless procession along both sides of the narrow highway carrying knapsacks and bedrolls, guitars, unlit lanterns, tin pots, jugs of wine, while a line of glimmering headlights, several miles long, eases through them. It seems an unaccountable materialization out of the night: like some immense suddenly discovered evacuation from a doomed city, a gathering together of some secret population of unknown tribes out of these dark mountains, moving now to a mysterious appointment and confrontation somewhere. . . . Over the banquet room in the Beverly Hilton there is a soft scattering of small coughs, a momentary

shivering of the candle flames over the tablecloths like the passing of a light random wind, as Reagan, both arms gripping the
lectern, concludes: "The party of the Seventies will not confuse
charity with justice, compassion with centralism, equality with
conformity. The party which will be relevant to the Seventies is
the party which will lead the way to a renewed commitment to
integrity and morality. Our forefathers wove God into the very
fabric of government. We must do no less." And the crowd rises
to their feet with hurrahs and whistling, napkins twirling in the
air, and then they stand with bowed heads, chins snuggled down
into black ties and hands folded before cummerbunds, the can-
dlelight dreaming over the soft hair of the gowned women, as the
minister's voice rings the benediction over them: "The Lord
bless you and keep you. The Lord make His face to shine upon
you and be gracious unto you. The Lord lift up His countenance
unto you, and give you peace. Both now, and forevermore." . . .

If the Sixties became something like America's own time of the
Troubles, throughout that period it was Graham's message — as
he called once through a hand-held megaphone to the seasonal
beach bacchanal at Ft. Lauderdale, "I believe the young people
of this generation are searching for something to believe in.
They are looking for a song to sing! They are looking for a
slogan to say!" That seemed more or less to constitute his understanding of the nature of the disillusionments and despairs of
the time — as if it were all merely a free-floating adolescent restlessness casting about for some available cause with which to exercise itself. He reported that a group of students had entreated
their university chaplain, as Graham quoted them, "What can we
march for? What can we demonstrate for? We don't have a
cause. What would you suggest?" and Graham proposed, "How
wonderful if we could get them to march for Christ with love in
their hearts!" A close version of what he might have been hoping
for would have seemed the Jesus Movement, but of that somewhat irregular and free-form phenomenon Graham only remarked with a grudging indulgence, "The Jesus thing is now

receiving a great deal of publicity, and whether this publicity is
going to have an adverse reaction, I don't know. As long as it was
unpublicized, it was doing quite well, but when the cameras
begin to come on the scene, the young people become unnatural
and distorted." As an authentic Christian passion for youth, Graham inclined more to the manner of righteousness celebrated in
the "Explo-'72" commemoration in Dallas — a revival festival
with Day-Glo posters featuring such slogans as "Things Go Better with Jesus!" and "You Have a Lot to Live and Jesus Has a Lot
to Give!" — all of which Graham hailed as "a religious Woodstock." When he returned to New York in 1969 for another
crusade, this one conceived in a corporate dining room of Mutual of New York during a luncheon that included RCA president Elmer Engstrom and Richard Nixon, Graham contrived for
the campaign the extra embellishment of "America's largest coffeehouse" in a rented loft — exclusively a coffeehouse, actually,
where up to a thousand youths could dance to "Christian rock"
amid swooping strobe lights and video screens flashing *Jesus* and
Love — and the services themselves in Madison Square Garden,
with its color-coded plastic seats and hydraulic pulpit on a stage
muffled in synthetic ferns, took on the surreality of a Tower of
Babel cacophony of sensibilities, "Do your own thing!" mixed
with "Devote your life to Jesus," and "Turn on and tune in to
Jesus" somewhat uneasily counterpointed with "A mighty
fortress is our God."

Throughout the Sixties, Graham's own apprehension of the
corrupt, the false, the evil at play in life remained confined to a
spectrum of such vices, as he recited once in 1969, as "the bar-
tender who sells beer to minors, the barbiturate peddler and the
drug pusher who infest campuses, the income-tax chiseler, the
insurance faker, the college grad whose diploma is won by crib-
bing rather than cramming, the professor who allows himself to
be intimidated into giving superior grades to inferior students. . . ."

And how Graham finally addressed the two greatest moral
travails of that momentous decade — civil rights and Vietnam —
was with a Christian vision constituted still of those almost mar-

tial Roman fortitudes of duty and order and discipline. He continued to evangelize a kind of Wehrmacht Christianity. Indeed,
during one service on a warm October afternoon in 1960 in
front of the Reichstag in West Berlin, he orated, "The young
people of this generation who cannot remember much about the
war are searching for a flag to follow, a leader to believe in. Let
that flag be the Christian flag! Let that leader be Christ!" —
which came out, as conveyed by his interpreter, "Lasst Christus
euer Führer sein!" As he further elaborated during a crusade
back in the United States, "All over this world tonight, young
people are seeking security. They want a master! They want a
center of life! I believe Jesus Christ can become that master! Just
as Hitler was able to get the youth of Germany, and Mussolini
was able to get the youth of Italy, and the Communists were able
to get the youth of Eastern Europe!" This may have struck some
as a slightly unsettling proposition, but as he declared in the autumn of 1966, "We see on television how excited the Red Guards
in China are about something that's false. Why can't we get excited about the truth?"

It was, with Graham, still consummately the old Crusader impulse, the Crusader mentality: to combat the infidels with their
own stern instruments of conquest, to hack away and have at
them with clashing swords and shields. "We are losing the battle
to the Russians because they are more dedicated, more disciplined," he declared in the Fifties. "I once asked an army
officer which he had rather have on the field of battle — courage
or obedience. He flashed right back, 'Obedience!' " He was even
prone to pose Christians now and then as something like celestial
commandos, spiritual marines: "If the United States marines and
infantry trained like the Christians in this country, we would
have lost the war to Germany, we would have lost the war to
Japan — we could be licked by Costa Rica."

Central and enduring in Graham's somewhat Prussian species
of Christian piety through the Sixties was a rigorous authoritarian ethic. One commentator in 1957 had noted that Graham's
theology seemed curiously askew to the "mystic and antinomian"
principles of Paul's own Christian understanding, which held

"the law itself as one source of evil" — instead, Graham seemed to perceive evil as simply a matter of "breaking the law, like going through a red light." From his very beginnings, for that matter, he had evidenced a special reverence for the mystique of authority: "Billy always loved, almost worshiped, his teachers," his mother remembers, and he would declaim in 1965, "There is defiance of law on all levels — children disobeying parents, students disobeying teachers, and now, people against policemen," as if all three came to the same thing. "Without law," he declared, "we will have chaos." It was, of course, still that old instinct of frontier pentecostalism to subdue the rampant in nature as being sin itself, only with that nemesis of the wilderness's chaos now transferred into society. Graham even once announced to an assembly of one thousand policemen in New York City that they were "God's agents for punishment." It was his conviction as well that "when capital punishment is administered equally, it's proven to be a deterrent."

In fact, his vigor on this particular aspect of righteousness once prompted him to recommend, in South Africa in 1973, "I think when a person is found guilty of rape, he should be castrated. . . . That would stop him pretty quick." To the considerable uproar produced by this suggestion, Graham eventually issued a statement from Montreat: "My comment on rape was an offhand, hasty, spontaneous remark at a news conference that I regretted almost as soon as I said it. I meant to come back to it before the conference was over and correct it, but got sidetracked on other issues. . . . I unfortunately used a word which in our sex-oriented culture, was emotionally charged and did not clarify my true thoughts." But by way of further clarifying his true thoughts, he could not resist adding, in this peculiar unapology, "It is interesting that the thought of castration for some people stirs a far more violent reaction than the idea of rape itself. Perhaps this is part of our permissive society's sickness."

Along with these burly rectitudes, Graham's Christian vision also consisted of a kind of Spartakiad virtue of sturdy clean-cut haleness. "I think a Christian ought to look like a Christian," he proclaimed in 1958. "I've seen so many Christians slouch around. That's not God's way. None of this sissy, effeminate sort of business we've got now with these long sideburns and all the rest." It was a classically American mutation of Christianity, the Teddy Roosevelt canon of hardy robustness. "The Bible says leisure and lying around are morally dangerous for us," Graham asserted. "Sports keeps us busy — athletes, you notice, don't take drugs" — it was 1971 when he advanced this precept. "The Bible reveals that Saint Paul was an avid sports fan," he suggested, "because he used so many illustrations from the Olympics in his letters." In fact, Christ himself — from Graham's constructions of him over the years as "a real he-man, a real man who had a square jaw and strong shoulders, the most perfectly developed physical specimen in the history of the world, he would have been one of the great athletes of all times!" — tends to evoke someone between Jack Armstrong and Bruce Jenner.

With these reverences making up Graham's Christian sensibility, then, it was no accident that he always entertained a special enthusiasm for the astronauts — those lean, competent, flawlessly healthy, imperturbable and more or less interchangeable heroes of the new American mythos, the heatless Ulysseses of the technological order, creatures of the new evolutionary intelligence of the race, minimal and efficient of emotions and words, with the initiatives and decisions and ultimate control of their feats coming from elsewhere, their part in it as individuals only to perform excellently and dutifully with an impervious machine-like precision.

Nevertheless, in all of Graham's political assertions over the years, without question his handsomest hour came with his early pronouncements against segregation. In the already enfevered times of 1960, he declared, in explaining his refusal to include South Africa in his African tour that year, "To keep the races in total separation is a policy that won't work and is immoral and un-Christian. The segregated churches and church institutions in America are becoming known to people all over the world. They cannot believe it. They can't take it in. They're astonished to hear that Christian institutions bar a man on the basis of color. The greatest need in the South today is contact between the races, and the church in the South should lead the way toward bettering racial relationships."

Actually, when Graham had first arrived as a student at Wheaton in 1940, he had brought with him a racial perspective still intact from his Charlotte boyhood, and had to be instructed by a Wheaton anthropology professor that utterly no scientific grounds existed for his assumption of Negro inferiority. But almost a decade later, during his early revival tours, "he was still a very intense segregationist," remembers Stephen Olford. Once, when Olford was scheduled to address a Christian laymen's breakfast in some far point of Florida, "I had to travel through the night by car," he relates, "and the driver was a Negro. Halfway along the journey, he started getting dozier and dozier, the car started swaying from one side of the road to the other, so I had him pull in at this little cafe for coffee. I sat down, but the black driver went over to a little trap window at the rear of the place, a hole, to be served. I was furious. The next day, I caught up with Billy, and standing there on the sidewalk I told him about it, and he said, 'So what?' We had the most terrific argument right there on the street. Everything I said, he kept referring to the footnotes in the Scofield Bible about how Ham had been cursed by God to be servant to servants and all that dimwitted business. I almost thought it was going to end up in a fistfight. Finally he shouted, 'Stephen, if it weren't for you wretched Britishers, we wouldn't have any Negroes in this country anyway; we wouldn't have this mess!' He was absolutely impossible on the subject."

But by 1953, when he happened to notice before the first service of a Chattanooga crusade a webbing of ropes dividing white and black seating sections, he began stalking about in a fume of exasperation snatching them all down. A pair of ushers came hurrying toward him, aghast, one of them hissing, "No, no, please, Reverend Graham, this will be misunderstood," and Graham clipped, "Either these ropes stay down, or you can go on and have the revival without me. We're just not going to have ropes in our meetings" — though he then added the somewhat mitigating consideration, "In my opinion, they'll go with their own people anyway; they'll probably be afraid to sit anywhere else."

His ardor on the issue may have still been a bit qualified. While he insisted in 1956, "Most of the ministers I know in the South feel that segregation should be ended now on buses, in railroad and bus stations, hotels and restaurants," he then appended the reservation, "Most of them feel it is far too early to implement school integration in some sections of the deep South. They seem to feel the day will come when both races will be psychologically and spiritually ready for it, but that time has not yet come." Yet even with his extenuations, it was still a commendable assertion at a time of racial tensing in the country when it could hardly have seemed a propitious stance to strike. This posture of his continued to provoke intermittent cracklings of ill humor, South Carolina's colicky segregationist governor George Bell Timmerman protesting in 1958, "I was shocked to learn that Billy Graham had been invited to use our State House property for a rally. As a widely known evangelist and native Southerner, his endorsement of racial mixing has done much harm," and he went on to insist that Graham's preaching on the capital lawn would violate the separation of church and state, posing it to "Graham's conscience as to whether he will trespass upon state property." In this instance, Graham simply shifted his integrated service into the fastness of the Fort Jackson parade ground.

In fact, however much Graham's turn of conscience on the obvious indecency of segregation owed to his simple natural generosity of spirit, it was also as much a reflex to what was actually the larger national respectability at the time — he quickly sensed, with that same unerring instinct for the Establishment seemliness that had afforded him such discomfort in his brief association with the neolithically fundamentalist Northwestern Schools, the simple shabby tackiness of segregation now. Indeed, his commitment on the matter was cued, at least in part, by a private appeal from Eisenhower in 1956 for him to exercise his influence to help temper the crisis — after this, "I went back to my hotel room and knelt in prayer, asking God to help me make any contribution I could toward the easing of racial tensions." He subsequently made special mollifying processionals into such combustible communities as Clinton, Tennessee, and Little Rock. "But Graham's bravest and finest service to those troubled times," testifies one former civil-rights partisan, "was just his insistence on holding all those open, integrated crusades back then — there's no way to estimate how much difference they probably made in things in the end."

Even in this, though, it was as if he were proceeding in some lapse of final focus from the actual texture and tissue of the reality itself — he invariably equivocated on the true vitals of the travail. While he was contending in 1956, "There is the argument that Jesus never specifically denounced slavery, but such reasoning is silly, because he constantly emphasized neighbor love, and every violation of it is a sin," yet even in that profession Graham appended his double-edged hedge: "Most Negro leaders have told me that they really do not want to intermingle with whites. They just rebel at laws and ropes that bar them. As someone has said, 'Take the dare out of it, and ninety percent of the problem is solved.'" In 1960, he maintained, "The Bible most certainly approved of master-and-servant relationships, but not along racial lines. But the Bible also recognizes that each individual has the right to choose his own friendships and social relationships. I am convinced that forced integration will never work. The Supreme Court can make all the decisions it feels are necessary, but unless they are implemented by goodwill, love, and understanding, great harm will be done." Also, Graham explains now, "I think around the early Sixties, during the sit-ins, I began to have my doubts about the methods that were beginning to be used." In 1961, he cautioned, "I feel the Freedom Riders made their point and had a right to do so, but now there is a possibility they may go too far," and two years later, while he was still conceding that "the greatest need of the moment is for people of both races to act like Christians toward each other in personal contacts," he was also contending that "the extremists" were trying "to rush things." To a convention of Baptists in Atlantic City that same year, he declared, "I've never understood how, in the church, you can say, 'This church is for one race only,'" but later executed one of his didactic double-passes by adding, "I doubt the wisdom" of the civil-rights offensives then in the South.

As it happened, what was underway then — with Birmingham, Saint Augustine, Montgomery, the Mississippi summer of 1964 — was a struggle to purge the whole nation of its primal collective crime of slavery at last, through a kind of elemental ceremony of catharsis in the crucible of the South, where that old guilt still lingered most palpably and brutally. But Graham expounded, "I don't understand the playing up of racial tension in the South. The greatest racial tension is really in the North. Things happen up there and get put on the back pages of newspapers. The same things happen in Birmingham, and they get all over the front page." Finally in 1965, Graham forged down to Alabama — again on an inspiration from the White House, when "Johnson asked if I'd be willing to tour the state" — and his message to the citizens there was "all laws must be obeyed no matter how much we may dislike them," while he assured them that "it is wrong for people in other parts of the country to point an accusing self-righteous finger at Alabama. To single out one state as a whipping boy often becomes just a diversion to direct attention from other areas where the problem is just as acute." Speaking in the football stadium in Dothan, he persevered in this particularly staggering naïveté — Alabama was "well on the way to solving its problems by itself, if the extremists both to the left and the right can be controlled." Passing through Montgomery, he paid an abbreviated and somewhat strained call on Wallace, whom he seemed to regard as a slightly disreputable article: "We had a social visit," he indicated somewhat flatly afterward, "and I enjoyed it very much." And while he was in Montgomery, he repeated that Alabama could actually be an exemplar to the rest of the nation "if the Ku Klux Klan will quiet down, if the extremists in the civil-rights organizations will give Alabama time to digest the new civil-rights laws, and if the politicians will not try to exploit the situation" — thus indiscriminately equating somehow King's SCLC with Wallace and the Klan.

What seemed to disconcert Graham most about the movement, though, were its untidy affronts to the ethic of discipline and order. During the sit-ins of 1960, he complained in a press conference in Atlanta, "I do believe we have the responsibility to obey the law. No matter what that law may be — it may be an unjust law — I believe we have a Christian responsibility to obey it. Otherwise, you have anarchy." (Though in the summer of 1968, he termed LBJ's assignments of Secret Service men to presidential candidates after Robert Kennedy's assassination a recourse that was "illegal, but right.") He began to suggest increasingly through the Sixties, "I am convinced that some extreme Negro leaders are going too far and too fast. I am also concerned about some clergymen of both races that have made the race issue their gospel. This is not the gospel!" It was as if Graham's whole perspective on the crisis reduced more or less to that Scripture text which still served as the essential coda of his entire ministry, his life: "Let everything be done decently, and in order." As he seemed to see it, "The difficulties arising from racial tension should be a challenge to individual courtesy."

If there was another figure during that time who could have also been considered the conscience of America, as John Connally had termed Graham, it was Martin Luther King, Jr. In a sense, the two of them — Graham and King — were like the antipodal prophets of that continuing duality in the American nature between the Plymouth asperities and the readiness for spiritual adventure, between the authoritarian and the visionary. King's own moral urgency, born as directly out of the Scriptures, had happened to find its articulation in the South's racial ordeal — that brief, simple, passionate pageantry of good and evil and violence which has about it now almost the poignance of a lost innocence: a few short summers of danger and belief with grave processions moving down tawdry little main streets in a hot brassy sunlight with a huge choiring and clapping, while

state troopers and sheriffs' deputies, faces blank and depthless as
tin, waited for them on the quiet shaded courthouse lawns with
shotguns and billy clubs and dogs; King himself striding along in
the midst of all this in tie and shirt-sleeves with his coat neatly
slung over one arm, a stocky and rather unheroic figure, with a
peculiar expression on his round bland vaguely Oriental face of
an almost abstract remoteness.

But King was more than a strategist of confrontation: he became, in the oldest and truest sense, a national prophet. The genius of his otherwise baroque and ponderous metaphors was
that they were the rhetoric of the human spirit gathering itself to
terrific and massive struggle. And his moral vision — with its essential assumption that there exists in every man, however gut-
teringly, a natural identification with all other men, and therefore no man could indefinitely continue to brutalize another
human being without eventually feeling himself suffer, that indeed a man could be vitally touched and even redeemed as a
human being when his violence was met with love — was, in fact,
a vision that by its very nature addressed itself not only to racism
but, with poverty and Vietnam, to a general national malaise: a
habit of easy brutality, the rupturing of that natural connection
between all men by the glib and orderly barbarisms of progress
and affluence and institutions, and the infinite and subtle chem-
istries of the material life in reducing men to clay, with affluence itself having become like the iridescent decay of our civilization — in all, a national loss of soul. In the end, King was
engaged in nothing less than a regeneration of the entire country's moral life: a national New Birth. He felt the nation could
survive on no other terms.

The greatest subversions of his effort were those immemorial
confoundments of all prophets: cyncism, dogmatic reverence for
technicalities, less urgent consciences, lesser hopes, lesser visions
of humankind. He simply could not be comprehended, not only
by J. Edgar Hoover, but by many in America. Indeed, it's possible his vision was one that finally presumed too much about
man. But even in his later labor to accommodate the ramifying
mood of exhaustion and despair and fury in the black commu-

nity, yet he could not bring himself to relinquish his belief in the efficacy and necessity of nonviolence: to him, there were really no other choices. Even before his death, many were already saying he was an anachronism, and now in retrospect, it's almost as if his death were a personal enactment of the end of the nonviolent experiment, as if he were necessarily extinguished with its waning — perhaps the most purely moral spontaneous popular adventure in the nation's experience. And the conflagrations then in Watts and Harlem and Newark and Detroit that followed that quick rifle-clap in the spring dusk at Memphis were like flash detonations of a desolation again for an old hope irretrievably lost, a dread of the future that final effacement portended. One of King's old movement horsemen, James Bevel, himself a Byzantine mystic with simmering pitchblende eyes, sat at a small breakfast meeting with a deputation from the OEO about a month after King's murder, they having come to question him about what they might expect from SCLC now, and Bevel told them in his thin tense voice, "King was the moral leader in this country. Of everybody, blacks and whites, he was the leader. Now all black people knew that instinctively. And in another five years, everybody else would have known it. That's precisely why he was busted. He could not be permitted any longer. Frigid, impotent people have to do that. In order to arm, in order to use violence, in order to prosecute a war like Vietnam, in order to allow the sacrifice of people for an economic system, you have to be frigid and impotent. You see, you are all, you whites in the management of this country, an extension of Robert E. Lee's ego."

After King's mighty sermon on the steps of the Lincoln Memorial in 1963 — "I have a dream. . . . I have a dream that my four little children one day will live in a nation where they will not be judged by the color of their skin, but by the content of their character. I have a dream!" — Graham himself was prompted to remark, "Only when Christ comes again will the little white children of Alabama walk hand in hand with little black children." After a time, he did concede that demonstrations had "served to arouse the conscience of the people," but

then felt constrained to add, "I have been holding demonstrations myself for fifteen years — but in a stadium where it was
legal." He continued to admonish that civil-rights campaigns
"have the pattern of defiance of authority." In August of 1966,
he made a brief skim by helicopter over the charred and rubbled
streets of Watts after the first eruption there, and when back on
the ground declared it his conclusion that the rioters had been
"exploited by a small, hard core of leftists," and again exhorted
Congress to "curb this kind of thing." A little later into that summer of flames over the nation's ghettoes, he again demanded
that Congress drop all other legislation instantly and "devise new
laws to curb the type of violence that is going on in California, Illinois, and Massachusetts. . . . We need new, tough laws." That
seemed largely to be the terms in which he perceived the whole
crisis: he was curiously insensible of anything more profound
underway in the country. His response to King's stabbing in a
Harlem bookstore in 1958 had been, "Thank God, Martin
Luther King was not stabbed by a white person, or we might
have seen racial war with blood flowing down the streets."

Then in 1965, he publicly appealed to King to "call on civil
rights leaders to declare a moratorium on demonstrations until
the people of the North and West have an opportunity to digest
the new Civil Rights Act." It was his pronouncement on the tur-
moil in Selma, with Colonel Al Lingo's Cossack-like charge of
mounted state troopers in a haze of gas and flailing of clubs
through marchers on the Pettys Bridge, that "most of the people
on both sides in Selma are professing Christians. There are more
churches in Selma per capita than in almost any other city in
America. Certainly we ought to be able to meet together and
discuss our mutual problems in a spirit of Christian love, understanding, and brotherhood." And even some eight years after
King's assassination, he was still pointing out, "Yes, he had his
demonstrations out in the streets, while I had mine as lawful
religious services in stadiums."

Graham says now, "I knew King. I'd been with him on several
occasions — I even had him come to New York for our Fifty-
seven crusade, and he stayed with us for two days and spoke to

the whole team and delivered a prayer at one of the services. Yes. I thought he was a man filled with as much charisma mixed with intellect as any man I'd ever met. In nineteen sixty, when I was on my way to South America, I had a black man with me, and we happened to meet King at the Miami airport, and we decided to spend two days in Puerto Rico. Flying over, he asked me to call him Mike. That's what all his close friends called him, you know. We had a wonderful two days of fellowship and discussion there. I told him, 'I certainly am not going to ever condemn you for your street demonstrations. So let me do my work in the stadiums, Mike, and you do yours in the streets. I don't expect you to condemn me for my stadium demonstrations.' And he told me, 'Billy, I realize that what I'm trying to do will never work until the heart is changed. That's why your work is so important.' And he said to me that, whenever he tried to deliver an old-style sermon now, he said, 'You know, I just can't preach the gospel any longer. Something's left me.' Later on, during the Baptist World Alliance in Brazil, I even gave a party for him one night in Rio at the Copacabana. . . . I have to say, though, that in time I became mixed up in my thinking about him. I became concerned about the people who were around him. I think it was because of Hoover, and all the things he kept warning me about in regard to King."

But nothing, perhaps, so finally and dramatically defined the difference between Graham and King as prophets to the American conscience as their respective ministries through the tribulation of Vietnam. As early as 1965, King had protested, "I'm not going to sit by and see war escalated without saying anything about it. It is worthless to talk about integration if there is no world to integrate," and finally, in the spring of 1967, he declared that the United States had become the "greatest purveyor of violence today. . . . If America's soul becomes totally poisoned, part of the autopsy must read, *Vietnam*. . . . A nation that continues year after year to spend more money on military defense than on programs of social uplift is approaching spiritual death." Graham himself could say of his own gestures against

segregation, "My belief in the social implications of the gospel
has deepened and broadened. It is my conviction the evangelist
must not hedge on social issues. I have made the strongest possible statements on every social issue of our day" — and even
more compellingly, "Let us not forget that faith without works is
dead. God will say of some of us, 'When you spread forth your
hands, I will hide my eyes from you; even though you make
many prayers, I will not listen, for your hands are full of
blood.' " But as it happened, his public apostleship throughout
the campaign in Vietnam, up to its very end, proceeded as a
peculiar split exertion — half a strenuous labor to keep himself
detached from the increasingly virulent controversy over its
moral implications, and half a constant covert commendation of
the enterprise. "All through this period," he would profess, "I
have not been sure whether our involvement was right or
wrong — I don't want to get involved on either side," while he
would simultaneously note, "The stakes are much higher in Vietnam than anybody realizes. The stakes are extremely high for
the Western world. Every American can be proud of the men in
uniform who are representing our nation on that far-flung battle
front. They are paying a great price for the victory they are almost certainly winning there."

"What you always have to keep in mind about Graham, in everything," one veteran observer summarizes, "is that ambiguity,
that dichotomy he's always seemed to live in. He simply has two
natures. There's his private, personal nature, which I think still
remains his true one — warm, amiable, spontaneous, wholly
without pretense, even gullible, strangely vulnerable, quick to
like and eager to be liked. But then there's his second nature, his
pulpit nature, which is what most people know him by — imperious, strict, autocratic, authoritative, dogmatic. He is a completely transformed being in that pulpit personality. That's the
one he gets his opinions from. But he still gets his feelings, I
think, from the other, from his personal nature, including his
desperation for approval and the reassurance of favor from the
powerful. But of course it's been the opinions of his pulpit nature, all those harsh stern traditional abstractions, that have won

and provided him that approval. Over all these years, it's hard to understand how he's kept from going completely schizoid. But that double and contradictory temperament in him has made for everything finally tragic — well, not quite that, say pathetic — about his story. For one thing, I believe it's because of that perpetual disjunction between his personal nature and his pulpit opinions that he's never really seemed to quite understand what's truly going on in the world. . . . Now, on the race question, he reacted at least in some measure with his personal nature. But on Vietnam, it was all pulpit."

From his public dawning in 1949, it was not only that he had confirmed so resoundingly the common American folk decencies that he came to enjoy such goodwill from the nation's proprietorial community. More particularly, he had also proved a galvanizing drum major of all the Cold War sanctitudes — indeed, the Cold War had, in America then, no more avid an evangel. "No man with Christ in his heart," he proclaimed, "could be a Communist." After sallying forth to Korea in 1952 in the manner of Cardinal Spellman to enhearten the front lines spiritually, Graham returned with a supply of reprints of *A Book Signed in Blood*, a testimonial by several hundred North Korean and Chinese prisoners who had signified with fingerprints stamped in blood their vows not to return north, which so awed Graham that he personally presented a copy to Eisenhower. It was peculiarly appropriate that the main medium of his ministry should have come to be termed *crusade:* it was much that old lusty mix of martial and pious gustos, the cross and the sword — only addressed now, instead of to Islam, to Marxism.

Actually, ever since Plymouth and the Mayflower Compact — "Haveing undertaken, for the glorie of God, and advancemente of the Christian faith and honour of our king & countrie, a voyage to plant the first colonie in the Northerne parts of Virginia . . . in the presence of God, and one of another, covenant, & combine ourselves togeather into a Civill body politick; for our better ordering, & preservation & furtherance of the ends aforesaid" — it has tended to be an endemic assumption of the American righteousness that Americans had come into an anointment as God's new Chosen People on earth, with America's own multiple manifest destinies, whether social or economic, really indivisible from God's general design for the whole race of man. Some three hundred years even before Vietnam, that sometimes meant dispatching cholera-infected blankets, as did Cotton Mather, to an inconveniencing nearby tribe of Indian heathens. But there have been few of America's wars which it did not regard more or less as crusades of its manifest destiny baptized from on high — from the decree of the Revolutionary War, "to assume among the powers of the earth, the separate and equal station to which the Laws of Nature and of Nature's God entitle them . . . appealing to the Supreme Judge of the world for the rectitude of our intentions," through the Civil War with Lincoln's declaration at Gettyburg that "this nation, under God, shall have a new birth of freedom, and that government of the people, by the people, for the people, shall not perish from the earth," on to the high Wilsonian spirituality of the sentiments for World War One.

Graham acted to reaffirm this folk-American assumption, and with his Vietnam pronouncements, his effect was to disarm any misgivings among his own constituency about that exploit. His importance in the life of the nation has finally been, not so much that of a precipitating agent, but that of a great reassurer — reflecting back to Inner America a bracing, splendid image of its conventional uprightness, and so, especially in the case of Vietnam, securing and fortifying that earnestness. Whatever suspicions might have begun to stir along the Elm Streets and Sunday-morning pews over the land about the decency of that undertaking, in Graham there was reassurance that Vietnam was of course correct and admirable. Says one critic, "There's no question that all his integrated crusades made a considerable difference among his constituency of the great middle citizenry throughout the civil-rights years. One can only wonder what would have been the effect on that same citizenry, and the difference in the domestic sufferance of Vietnam, if he had spoken out on that with the same alarm King did."

That was never very likely, however. From the very beginnings of his evangelism, it was his message that "we were created for a spiritual mission among the nations," and on the steps of the Capitol in 1952, he proposed, "We must maintain strong military power for defense at any cost." It was eminently after the Cromwellian style of piety: iron and sanctity, prayerfulness and pikestaves — as Graham admonished the cadets at The Citadel once, "It is time to keep our power dry and pray at the same time." Before long, in fact, he had begun conducting devotional services at the Pentagon, presiding at the Christmas observance there in 1962, and delivering prayer messages at West Point and Annapolis, while continuing to caution that the United States must maintain "the strongest military establishment on earth."

Throughout all this, he was also incessantly propounding the inveterate malevolence of the Soviets. In October of 1957, he announced that he had it "on good authority" that a faction in the Kremlin was demanding an attack on the U.S. within two years, and in 1960, declared that Soviet submarines were "sitting off our coast with atomic warheads on their rockets that can penetrate fifteen hundred miles." In a Philadelphia crusade the next year, he reported that "there is a possibility Russia has already created the neutron bomb — the ultimate weapon." It was still as if, in this persevering recital of dire speculations, he somehow actually half-longed for the fulfilling resolving Armageddon. Conjuring the prospect of a Soviet missile strike in 1957, he added, "It would be most unfortunate if the President in his forthcoming speeches should say anything that would give the American people a false sense of security." At the same time, such was his political subtlety that he heartily recommended during Krushchev's tramp about the U.S. in the autumn of 1959 that he be dragooned into a church: "I certainly hope that President Eisenhower will invite him to church Sunday. Khrushchev is his house-guest, and if he should refuse to go, it will put Khrushchev on the spot." In a Confederate Memorial Day service at Charlotte's shade-speckled Elmwood Cemetery, Graham confessed to an impatience that "everytime Khrushchev growls, we tremble," adding with what seemed an improbable truculence, in all, for a disciple of the gentle Nazarene, "I often wonder what Theodore Roosevelt, Abraham Lincoln, Jefferson Davis, and Robert E. Lee would have done with a man like Khrushchev." But then, as Graham mentioned once in 1961, while it was always his hope there would be no war, actually he had never seen anything in the Bible that was really adverse to war. He specifically requested an interview, finally, with the Asheville *Citizen-Times* in the summer of 1961 in order to observe that citizens had become indignant because "we have suffered defeats, and because of Communist threats and infiltration. But they are now tired of being shoved around and are ready to fight if there has to be a showdown. . . . We oughtn't to give another inch to Communism."

Graham purports now, "The first time I ever heard about Vietnam was Kennedy, when we were sitting around in the locker room at the Seminole Golf Club in Florida before he was inaugurated President. 'We've just got to do something about Vietnam,' I remember him saying. That always colored my thinking afterward." It became inevitable, then, that out of his rigorous and enduring Cold War chaplaincy, he was saying of Vietnam as early as 1965, "So steady, so deadly has been the encroachment of Communist tyranny on the West that we have been in danger of being hypnotized into a state of unawareness. Communist China is the most dangerous enemy of freedom in the world." In personal Christmas letters to the fourteen servicemen from North Carolina in Vietnam that year, he assured them that Americans were "proud of what you men are doing to help keep Asian Communism from engulfing all of Southeast Asia." Along with Johnson and what was still the orthodox perspective in Washington then, Graham's response on Vietnam answered to the abiding World War Two eschatology, the Munich analogy, the Churchillian principle, as the definitive moral metaphor by which to divine and negotiate the tensions in history and world conflicts foreverafter — thus in the lesson Hitler left the Western democracies, as some have suggested, could he yet manage to incinerate civilization. As Graham presented it to a student assembly at a college near Montreat, Vietnam was, in effect, a repetition of Europe in the late Thirties — "The war in Europe seemed very far away, too."

The companionability between Johnson and Graham grew ever warmer as Vietnam smoldered on. Johnson himself, of course, acted in Vietnam from those old American-eagle integrities that were eminently Graham's also: steadfastness, resoluteness, unflinching and indissuadable certitude. As Bill Moyers indicates, "Nobody could ever make Johnson feel he was right quite like Billy Graham could." In fact, at a Washington prayer breakfast with Johnson in 1966, Graham even offered the Scripture passages in respect to the Vietnam difficulty, "Think not that I am come to send peace on earth: I came not to send peace, but a sword. . . ." "I come to send fire on the earth." Though these happened to be Jesus' warnings about the ordeals and strife that would necessarily ensue from any true Christian commitment in an enduringly barbarous world, and hardly a sanctification for the mayhems visited on each other by the societies of that world, Graham elaborated, "There are those who have tried to reduce Christ to the level of a genial and innocuous appeaser. But Jesus said, 'You are wrong — I have come as a fire-setter and a sword-wielder.' There were thousands of people in Christ's day who could not understand what he meant when he said he would set fire to the earth. They were good-hearted, kind people who were anxious to have a better world. They were idealistic, but they were ignorant of the deep-seated disease of human nature. They looked at the world through rose-tinted glasses."

Graham himself set out for a direct perusal of Vietnam, at the invitation of General Westmoreland, during the Christmas of 1966 — delivering a sermon on his arrival to some two thousand persons at Saigon airport assembled in a puddled, rain-sodden soccer field, with helicopters churning in the air around him, jets battering in and out. Saigon, by then, had already begun to take on a certain look, actually, of lurid and dingy phantasmagoria — a labyrinth of moiling ramshackle streets under a sullen wet sky strung with electric wires, weltering low to a weary mire as if life

had been reduced there to a meager vicious unhoping minimum
of the human spirit: it suggested less a capital city than some
enormous police detention compound, with a quality about it unnatural and transitory and dully doomed, a ceaseless fine skimming hysteria of motorbikes shrilling through its gaseous streets
among the heavy shuffle of army trucks and jeeps, while sibilant
profusions of teenage girls with lavishly daubed kewpie faces
thronged like parakeets on the downtown terrace bars daintily
sipping Coca-Colas as they brightly stared at clamorous tables of
sun-scorched Americans in Ban-Lon golf shirts — all of it finally
giving one some dim nausea that the United States, in all its
intrepid earnestness, was committing an incalculable crime and
obscenity against the human spirit in that place. But Graham, still
possessing his impeccable neatness even in a khaki safari shirt
now, forged on doughtily over the shabby and savaged terrains
of Vietnam, ethereally unheeding — on Christmas Eve, conducting a service at An Khe in the central highlands with Bev Shea
carilloning to ten thousand troops holding twinkling candles
in paper cups, "I Heard the Bells on Christmas Day"; preaching
aboard the carrier *Kitty Hawk* in the Tonkin Gulf on Christmas
Day; then lifted clatteringly on back to the Vietnam mainland to
join Bob Hope in a show there. At Long Binh, he diverted the
five thousand troops gathered to hear him with an anecdote
about the man who had gone bear-hunting without a rifle and,
after half an hour, came running out of the woods back toward
the cabin where two companions were waiting: said Graham, his
voice barraging over the loudspeakers with bumps of artillery in
the distance, "They heard him hollering, 'Open that door! Open
that door!' They looked out and saw a big bear chasing him.
They opened the door, but just before he got there, the man
stepped aside and the bear ran in. The man shut the door and
shouted through the window, 'Skin that one, and I'll go get another!'" Beaming, Graham then cried to his grimed and hel-
meted congregation, "You might work that on Charlie sometime!"

On his arrival back in the United States, one perception he reported he had come by about what was actually transpiring in

Vietnam was that the troops were "extremely religious. . . . They all seemed to have two things, a Bible or New Testament, and a camera." He went on to cordially testify, "You almost have to see them to feel their spirit. . . . I talked to one boy who had been a protestor when he was in college. He was drafted, and a month later his commanding officer said he was the best fighting man he had." Shortly after that, during the political ado over Romney's remark about having been "brainwashed" on his own sojourn through Vietnam, Graham professed with a vibrant assurance, "I underwent the same briefings as Mr. Romney, and I wasn't brainwashed. I even lived with General Westmoreland for a time. All the men were trying to do was give us the facts, I didn't feel like they were trying to sell me a bill of goods."

But it had at least struck Graham in Vietnam that the effort there might likely be an unexpectedly protracted and difficult one. He began describing Vietnam as "one of the greatest dilemmas in U.S. history in Southeast Asia" — but how he constructed that dilemma as a moral issue was "We either face an all-out war with Red China or a retreat that will cause us to lose face throughout Asia." Again, in the desperate and terminal way he compulsively posed things, it was as if he were nudged almost by some dim lust for the apocalypse. At the least, he betrayed an unusually bellicose readiness for a showdown, an enthusiasm in which Jesus himself, as Graham increasingly cast him now, assumed more the balefulness of a celestial Siegfried than the Man of Sorrows. Only a few days before Christmas of 1968, Graham decreed of "the peace issue" that many parties "completely misunderstood" the idea of peace as presented in the gospels: "Jesus said, 'I didn't come to bring peace, I came to bring a sword,' and until Christ comes again, we're going to have convulsions and wars. War is sinful, yes. But as long as you have human nature so wild as it is, you're going to have to use force." By now, though, Graham had also begun to take pains to always attach to such remarks the curious double-dip demurral that "I've always been careful not to take any real position on the war, you understand." But still the only active moral difficulty in the situation, he explained in 1969, was that "the President and the administration are going to have to soon make a decision whether to admit we have failed in this commitment, or that they must win this commitment."

But after a second tour through Vietnam, even that incidental apprehension disappeared: on his return again, he declared he was confident the war would be ended before 1969 was out, "There is no question — the war is already won militarily." This was, of course, a not uncommon mirage in other circles at the time, and Graham, for his part, robustly concurred in it. "Right now, seventy-three percent of the Vietnamese people are under South Vietnam's government," he proclaimed, and the U.S. troops there "know why they are fighting in Vietnam, and they believe what they are doing is right." At the same time, he felt obliged to produce again one of his peculiar non-sequitur disavowals: "I don't," he asserted, "comment on Vietnam. Because it's a complicated problem. . . ."

Nevertheless, he had by now evinced at least enough of an appearance of a personal inclination on the question to have begun encountering in his crusade circuit certain fitful distractions — such as, during a 1967 service in London, a hooting surge of demonstrators toward the platform unfurling banners saying "Think about Vietnam." After demonstrators had swarmed after his swiftly accelerating car on the campus of UCLA once, he was given enough pause to concede, "Vietnem is difficult, confused, complex, and perplexing. I can make no moral judgments on the question of whether we should have troops there in the first place" — but went on to add that, since the United States happened to be already entailed there, "we should see it through to a satisfactory conclusion." More and more, though, it became his instinct to repair to a detached transcendence: as he has since come to describe it, "My position was I had a higher cause."

Even so, after Martin Luther King's early outcry against the mission in Vietnam, which scandalized the curias of authority at the time, Graham himself responded, "Surely Negroes are divided about the war as the rest of us are, and it [King's denunciation] is an affront to the thousands of loyal Negro troops who are in Vietnam." Before long, he was further propounding that antiwar protests "so exaggerate our divisions over the war that they could make Hanoi confident that it will eventually win. Then, what is already anticipated as a long war will be even longer —" What it came to, he averred, was simply that protestors were "giving comfort to the enemy." While it began to seem that Graham was almost systematically articulating the White House's own exegesis through those years, in fact he never needed to be prompted from the Oval Office into dispensing these sentiments — they also happened to be eagerly, fulminously his own. In 1970, with Nixon now President, it occurred to Graham, as an answer to the dinnings of protest continuing over the land, to mount an Honor America Day celebration in Washington on the Fourth of July — something like his own rendition, set on the steps of the Lincoln Memorial too, of that memorable spectacle there seven years earlier when King had delivered his legendary exhortation, only this commemoration — conceived in part by *Reader's Digest* chief Hobart Lewis and to be choreographed by Walt Disney Productions Inc., with Bob Hope acting as emcee — exalting another American ethic, now in Nixon's ascendancy: a pageantry to the old Puritan values. As Graham explained it, "There is just too much negativism. There are too many people knocking our institutions — the government, the church, the flag." While he hotly denied that the rally was to commend either Nixon or the war, he did allow that "atheists and agnostics" had not been invited to the ceremonies "because they don't believe in God." When the day arrived, Graham, with his blond Templar Knight's visage brassy with sweat in the July sun, rang a call — for all its oratorical ambition yet somehow clankingly less heart-whelming than King's — for reverence for U.S. institutions: "Honor the nation! . . . And as you move to do it, never give in. Never give in! Never! Never! Never! Never!"

But through the nation's immense moral struggles in the Sixties — its violent trial of conscience on racism, the amplifying guilt and outrage over Vietnam — popular weathers of despair with the country's institutions and processes had gathered over the course of that epiphanic decade past any dispelling, any repeal. No amnesia was possible now that would extinguish the new consciousness and political kinetic loosed into the nation's life during those years. For that reason, the nation was hardly likely — however sedated and suspended the moment seemed with Nixon — to recede placidly back again into the mild anesthesias of the Eisenhower years in which Graham had taken his national conception. But with those tensions of disillusionment in profound flux over the land, it was as if we had become locked into a lethal paralysis with the Vietnam adventure, an increasingly perverse obsession that, while progressively immobilizing the nation, at the same time steadily deepened all those angers and desperations. It began to seem it would prove, in the fate of America, the Tragic Distraction — prompted perhaps by another split impulse, split character through the nation's past, owing to the circumstance that we had come to front on two oceans, and so two perspectives of ourselves: the European ocean, bourn of our origin, its other shore still sensed as our source, a world seasoned in an autumnal measured temperateness, restraints still felt most strongly in our Eastern cities closest to it both in latitude and heritage; but then the Pacific, terminal of that two-hundred-year brawl on across the continent, a yet open and limitless expanse terrifically tempting to a nation still unresolved, still restless and turbulent with that everlasting *Not-Yet* in its spirit. The war with the Japanese, if it had not actually been partly induced by the draw of this last boundless prospect of the Pacific, at least did nothing to diminish that half-dreaming urge of engagement with the Pacific now as the new theater, the new West of our destiny. However much this may have been at work in the nation's eventual implication in Vietnam, though, it began to be gradually sensed that it could become, in fact, the war that destroyed the Republic.

Not the least of the depredations that war began to visit back on America was the solemn, overwhelming banality of its rationales as its squalidness and folly grew ever more apparent — the banality of the vision necessary for the nation to assume to continue to believe in it and prosecute it: the baseness of its presumptions about the human spirit and human history, and the profusely voluble deadness this began to blow into the language of our leaders, into the thought of the land, into its nerve sensings of good and evil. Graham himself in his dogged evangelism for that increasingly dubious crusade was devout to the point of finally even being impelled, after the disclosures about My Lai, to dismiss the import of that slaughter: out of what seemed an unfailing capacity of his to trivialize the awesome — a disposition to banalize the fearsome and mysterious that was like the stunning triteness of Alan Shepard swacking a golf ball on the face of the moon, a mundaneness which constitutes in itself a kind of elemental violence against human experience — Graham submitted, "We have all had our My Lais in one way or another . . . with a thoughtless word, an arrogant act, or a selfish deed."

To increasing appeals that he address himself to the methodical ravagement being performed in Vietnam, Graham pointed out that "it's all over the world, this business of civilians being killed. There is tragedy everywhere. Violence is something worldwide. I deplore the suffering and the killing in the war, and I pray it can be ended as soon as possible, but we also have to realize that there are hundreds of thousands of deaths attributed to smoking. . . . A thousand people are killed every week on the American highways and half of those are attributed to alcohol. Where are the demonstrations against alcohol?" Thus through this equation rendering Vietnam's enormity of violence into more or less a commonplace, Graham added the further diminution that "if I understand correctly, they had three hundred or so civilian casualties in North Vietnam, which is about one-half of what the Syrians say they had last week from Israeli bombs." It was as if moral evaluations of suffering reduced to a mere matter of such arithmetic — "the mathematical morality," as one religious writer commented after this numerical comparison of Graham's, "of the mass reality. As if there could be such a thing as addition, numerical relativity in human misery."

As tumults of protest magnified on across the nation, Graham finally posited at a news conference that it wasn't really Vietnam that was touching off the uproar, "but a Satanic spiritual power

of evil that is stirring up all the hatred and dissent in this country" — as if an explanation of demonology, exterior and supernatural forces, were the only recourse he was left with when a reality became inexplicable in any other way outside of a meaning
he could not afford to accommodate. It happened to be at that
same press conference that Graham disclosed that he had at last
been constrained to barricade his mountainside home behind a
high wire fence, and had acquired for the grounds within two at-
tack-trained police dogs.

Finally, when Nixon launched his bombing storm of North
Vietnam during the Christmas of 1972, Graham was publicly
implored by a large community of religious leaders to urge
Nixon to reconsider what he was doing. Graham somewhat tes-
tily retorted that he was a "New Testament evangelist, not an
Old Testament prophet," and insisted again that "all through
this period, I have not been sure whether our involvement was
right or wrong. . . . I don't want to get involved on either side."
Anyway, he snapped, "I am no more chaplain to the White
House than Cardinal Cushing was during the days of President
Kennedy. . . ." Even though Nixon had in fact notified him several hours ahead of his Cambodian incursion, Graham maintained now, "I'm not one of his confidants. I'm not one of his
advisors. I'm just a personal friend, that's all. In no way would
he ask me military strategy. He's never even discussed it with me.
If I have something to say to President Nixon, I'll do it privately,
and I won't announce it from the housetops with a lot of publicity."

Actually, Graham relates now, "Nixon along that time — well,
the truth was, he called me once shortly after Dr. Bell died to
express his condolences, which was during the B-52 strikes on
North Vietnam, and I took that occasion to tell him — Johnson
asked me and Cardinal Spellman once what we thought he
should do in the war, and the Cardinal spoke right up, 'Bomb
them! Just bomb them!' — but I told Nixon now, 'Now, I don't
want to say anything to you about Watergate; I'm not going to
get into that. But about this bombing of North Vietnam — even
my father-in-law was uncertain about that. There're a lot of people

who've been very strong for you who just don't understand —'
and he told me, 'Billy, it's going to shorten the war.' You see, he
knew we had to get out of there, he really meant for us to be out
a year after he took office. He told me even before he was inaugurated, 'Billy, everything we have is over there — all our resources, our economy — and all that's happening is, it's going to
be destroyed, and we're going to have to destroy that country if
we don't find a way to get out.' So the bombing of North Vietnam that some people raised such a hue and cry about, it was to
get out, to *shorten* everything — but not just pick up and run.
Bombing North Vietnam was to show the North Vietnamese that
we meant business about a *just* peace."

Indeed, Graham's primary misgiving about the terror underway in Vietnam seemed to remain the disgruntlement, "I
doubted from the beginning our sending American troops anywhere without the will to win. We entered the war almost deliberately to lose it." He cited, on the other hand, the admirable
decisiveness of the Soviets: "You see, when the Russians went
into Czechoslovakia, they went with such overwhelming power,
there was no battle. Nobody was killed." He offered then the
somewhat uniquely guttural sentiment for a divine, "I don't
think we should fight these long-drawn-out, half-hearted wars.
It's like cutting a cat's tail off a half-inch at a time."

But as criticism gathered still louder around him about his
long complicity in touting the Vietnam enterprise, Graham eventually protested in a letter to the *Christian Century,* "I have been
extremely careful not to be drawn into the moral implications of
the Vietnam war" — which struck a number as a curious disclaimer for the national preacher hailed by Connally as the conscience of America. Actually, for all his disinclinations to entertain appeals that he publicly declare himself on Nixon's
Christmas bombings, during that time Graham had pitched himself into a North Carolina campaign for highway safety, with the
pronouncement that "selfishness, anger, carelessness, neglect,
and pride are all symptoms of a spiritual disease the Bible calls
'sin.' Accidents, injuries, and fatalities are only the result."

Nevertheless, the cries deploring his Vietnam apologias began to assume proportions of a small furor by 1973, and Graham finally decided to issue a fuller and definitive statement of, as it were, firm equivocation: "In regard to the conflict in Southeast Asia . . . I have avoided expressions as to who was right and who was wrong. . . . During all this time, though, I have repeatedly indicated my hope for a rapid and just peace in Southeast Asia. I have regretted that this war has gone on so long and been such a divisive force in America. I hope and pray that there will be an early armistice." Even so, again he had to note that "Biblical truth . . . would indicate we will always have wars on the earth, until the coming again of the Prince of Peace. Nevertheless, I have never advocated war. I deplore it! I also deplore all the violence everywhere throughout the world that evidences man's inhumanity to man." After this proclamation, one of Graham's ministerial critics was moved to remark, "I tell you, following the public professions of Billy Graham over the years — not just on Vietnam, but on segregation, on political issues, the whole long catalogue of his commentaries — is like trying to find your way through the infinitely interwobbling reflections of a museum of trick mirrors. But I'll tell you something else. I think that's the reality Graham actually lives in. It's what he has as a gallery of opinions and ideas."

Years after the passing of the national delirium of Vietnam, one morning in the carpet-muted clock-ticking calm of Graham's executive office quarters down the mountain in Montreat, Graham himself, settled in his wingback chair, essayed an amiable retrospective on it all now: "It was a very difficult thing. I saw it from so many angles. I'm still not sure, frankly. Let's suppose, for instance, if somebody were attacking me, or say somebody was attacking Ruth, I don't know what I'd do, I can't say I wouldn't use violence to stop it. Certainly the American climate at first was for stopping those people and meeting our commitments. I thought at least — I mean, we went in there and started it, and even Kissinger, he was always pushing for bombing Hanoi and Haiphong; it was Nixon who was trying to hold him back. But equally devout Christians could be on different sides of the question. The whole question became a very difficult gray for me. I was just privy to too many conversations on both sides. I would listen to General Westmoreland, Abrams, Zumwalt — I was like a babe in the woods, I didn't know what was really going on. And then I'd listen to others. Especially when I'd go into Britain or Sweden, I'd get great criticism. In northern Italy once, we had a press conference in Turin, and a very vigorous reporter kept after me, he said, 'Now, somebody's wrong in this thing. Both sides can't be right, can they? So which side is wrong? Just tell us — which side are you on?' Well, by then I had decided, I told him, 'Now, as a world evangelist, for me to try to go around the world and try to say what is morally right over here, and what is morally wrong over there, I'm just not going to get involved in that kind of thing.' I continued to pray about Vietnam — I prayed about it, and prayed about it, and I couldn't seem to get any leading finally except just to stay out of the whole matter."

But when it had all been brought to its inconclusive and ambiguous cessation with the Paris accord, Graham's principal ruefulness still seemed to be, as he snapped to one inquiry, "We should never have gotten into a no-win land war in Asia." After agreeing to take part in a ceremony in Charlotte's coliseum commemorating the end of the war, a service held on a chill wet January day, Graham did not appear until midway through the program, produced a few incidental and not particularly enspirited remarks, "Men still have the seed of war in their hearts. . . . We will not turn our swords into plowshares until that seed of war has been eliminated," and with that, quickly departed into the dim and drizzling afternoon.

But if Graham seemed somewhat distracted that day, one reason might have been that he had already begun to sense himself caught in a beleaguerment far larger than the harrying complications over Vietnam — a duress that would turn out, over thirty years now after his strugglings of heart through those nights in Florida, long years after his ordeal of doubt with Templeton, to be the climactic crisis of his life.

As he lounges in the wingback chair in his office now at the end of the day, behind him the shadows of the cedars outside vaguely stir and murmur in the white gauze curtains, float and shift without sound in the long declining afternoon.

—*"I just couldn't understand it. I still can't. I looked up to him as the possibility of leading this country to its greatest and best days. Sometimes, when I look back on it all now, it has the aspects of a nightmare. . . ."*

III

Tribulation and Deliverance

His beguilement over the years with the sirens singing in the national empyrean of power, his own gradual Assumption up into those high altitudes through Hearst and Luce and Eisenhower and Johnson, reached its apogee with the presidency of Richard Nixon. As one religious essayist has put it, "Here was this truly God-enraptured country youth once appearing out of the back provinces, who really had the passion and presence to be a young Amos coming forth as a prophet to the land pronouncing the Word of God to the courts and councils of the mighty, and somehow he wound up instead a court priest of Caesar's." But it had always been one of Graham's particularly fervent fancies, as he explained it once, to have the nation's political parties nominate "men who lead wholesome family lives and who have faith in God." No one seemed to him to have answered his ambitions in this regard quite like Nixon.

What Graham had always envisioned as the ideal society on earth, the perfect government, was a kind of Puritan autocracy. "We need to rehabilitate that much-abused way of life called Puritanism," he notified one gathering of Charlotte's Executive Club. "The times require the Puritan spirit of self-control, industry, honesty, conscientiousness, and patriotism." And he was constantly proposing, "We stand at the brink of a new age — God's age: a theocracy whose ruler will be the King of Kings and the Lord of Lords." At times, in fact, he seemed reluctant to wait on the unfolding of that eschatological development, orating to one crusade audience in Los Angeles in 1963, "There are almost enough people here tonight to have a march on Washington. And if they keep throwing the Bible out of the schools, we might just do that."

It was still, of course, that dream as old as the Conquistadors, to accomplish on these new shores a City of God. What most affronted Graham about the Supreme Court's restraints on prayer in public schools was that they seemed an effort to "secularize" the nation: "God honors a nation that honors God. The Supreme Court has misinterpreted our forefathers' intentions. . . . Personally, I think that the few atheists who object to Bible reading in schools should be overruled by the majority." What especially endeared the government of Formosa to Graham, as he expounded after one visit there, was the "thrilling" fact that Generalissimo and Madame Chiang and most of the top people are spiritually-minded Christians. . . . Madame Chiang and "Generalissimo Chiang get up every morning at five o'clock for prayer." At the end of history, Graham insisted, Christ himself would return to reign on earth as a king, because "God's perfect form of government is a monarchy" —'while, other than this overhaul of the world's political system, there would still be "hotels and cities and airplanes and ships sailing the sea."

It was as if Nixon now posed to Graham the exhilarating prospect of an actual realization of that old Cromwellian urge for a society of righteousness over the land — a kind of second, continent-wide Plymouth order in America. From their first encounter that spring afternoon in Washington in 1952, there had evolved an especially rapt synergy between them. Nixon — vigorously sober, monumentally ambitious but yet remarkably chaste of any of those muskier extravagancies and flairs of most men of power, indeed seeming almost clinically clean of any ribaldries or vulgarities, who had nevertheless managed to deliver himself up into the highest reaches of American public life — appeared to Graham a singular fulfillment of all his own sensibilities and rectitudes. In October of 1959, still a year away from Nixon's certain presidential candidacy, Graham returned from an interlude of golf with him to report to a crusade congregation in Indianapolis, "I think Christians ought to get into politics. Mr. Nixon is probably the best-trained man for President in American history, and he is certainly every inch a Christian gentleman."

All along, Nixon may have held within him a certain peculiar extra property, an odd furtive permutability, like some shy taut polite church usher who, in personal midnights of trouble, could shadow into a warlock. But he seemed smitten with Graham in the same way he was later captivated with John Connally: they were both spectacularly in possession of all those personal graces and magics which Nixon had long ago realized, with a cold pang of resignation in the pit of his spirit, that nature had somehow left him irredeemably devoid of — self-assurance, charm, self-possession, a dramatic public presence, simply likability — and which he had then, with that bleak recognition, consigned the rest of his life laboring to simulate as passably as possible. Nixon's regard for Graham, marveled one assistant in those days, approached "almost a personal relationship." But Nixon also seemed fascinated with Graham, not only as a resplendent personification of all that he had been left without — that missing ideal half of himself — but as a brilliant totem image galvanized into life of what he himself esteemed as the essential American integrity and goodness, the American character. When he flew to Asheville in 1956 to address a series of meetings at the religious retreats riddled through those mountains, Nixon declared with a deeply belling earnestness, "No man has done more for the cause of goodwill and brotherhood throughout the world than Billy Graham, not just in terms of a minister, but as a good American who lets the peoples of the world see what Americans are at their best."

While Graham's lasting bedazement with the magneticisms of power may have suggested a political variation of the final poignance of The Rich Young Ruler, there was also something about his equally abiding eager innocence throughout his relationship with Nixon that somehow strikingly evoked, more than anything else, Herman Melville's moral fable *Billy Budd*. Having grown up a glad and careless creature of nature, the truth is Graham had remained, for all his Calvinist forensics, still something like an only slightly-spoiled version of Melville's "Handsome Sailor," the "welkin-eyed Billy." . . .

A virtue went out of him, sugaring the sour. . . . Nor unaware was he of the peculiar favorable effect his person and demeanor had upon the more intelligent gentlemen of the quarterdeck. . . . Billy was yet by no means of a satirical turn. The will to it and the sinister dexterity were alike wanting. To deal in double meanings and insinuations of any sort was quite foreign to his nature. . . . With little or no sharpness of faculty or any trace of the wisdom of the serpent, nor yet quite a dove, he possessed that kind and degree of intelligence going along with the unconventional rectitude of a sound human nature, one to whom not yet has been proffered the questionable apple of knowledge. . . . Billy, like sundry other essentially good-natured ones, had some of the weaknesses inseparable from essential good nature: like his sense of fear, his apprehension as to aught outside of the honest and natural was seldom very quick. . . . Much of a child-man . . . giving no cause of offense to anybody . . . yet a child's utter innocence is but its blank ignorance, and the innocence more or less wanes as intelligence waxes. But in Billy Budd intelligence, such as it was, had advanced while yet his simple-mindedness remained for the most part unaffected. . . . He had none of that intuitive knowledge of the bad which in natures not good or incompletely so foreruns experience. . . . [He had not that] distrust keen in proportion to the fairness of the appearance . . . the young sailor never having heard as yet of the "too fair-spoken man." . . .

Melville's other protagonist in this classic parable of innocence and evil is the ship's master-at-arms, Claggart, who belongs to a species of perversity before which Billy Budd's fresh and simple goodness is peculiarly unsuspecting and helpless:

It folds itself in the mantle of respectability. It has its certain negative virtues serving as silent auxiliaries. It never allows wine to get within its guard. It is not going too far to say that it is without vices or small sins. There is a phenomenal pride in it that excludes them. . . . [It] partakes nothing of the sordid or sensual. It is serious . . . not only neat but careful in dress. . . . An uncommon prudence is habitual . . . for it has everything to hide. . . . Though the man's even temper and discreet bearing would seem to intimate a mind peculiarly subject to the laws of reason, not the less in heart he would seem to riot in complete exemption from that law, having apparently little more to do with reason than to employ it as an ambidexter implement for effecting the irrational. That is to say: Toward the accomplishment of an aim which in wantonness of atrocity would seem to partake of the insane, he will direct a cool judgment sagacious and sound. These men are madmen, and of the most dangerous sort, for their lunacy is not continuous but occasional, evoked by some special object; it is protectively secret, which is to say it is self-contained, so that when, moreover, most active it is to the average mind not distinguishable from sanity . . . whatever its aims may be, and the aim is never declared, the method and the outward proceeding are always perfectly rational. . . .

As Melville describes it, it is also a nature of evil with a clear faculty for "apprehending the good, but powerless to be it." And while "the form of Billy Budd was heroic . . . the moral nature seldom out of keeping with the physical make," Claggart himself "in an aesthetic way saw the charm of it, the courageous free-and-easy temper of it, and fain would have shared it. But he despaired of it."

Despite Graham's great ardor for the superrealities of Heaven, his indifference to the spells of worldly power and circumstance had never proven quite that of Jesus blandished on the mountaintop by Satan with prospects of earthly importance, and Graham recounts now, "Mr. Nixon always liked to call on me, for some reason, as an authority on national and world affairs." Especially with Nixon, it was like some dark enchantment — he had always seemed to act as some malign, hexing agent in Graham's life, producing over the years some of Graham's most hapless, graceless public moments. But this never seemed to occur to Graham, not even to the very last — it was like some phenomenon wholly outside his moral and perceptual scan.

I

After his jaunt through the Holy Land in 1960 — where he had paused once to assert, when asked about the possibility of Kennedy, a Catholic, becoming President, "I just can't get involved in a political discussion" — Graham returned to the

United States and, only a few months before the Republican convention, put in an appearance at the annual session of the Southern Baptist Convention, held that year somewhat improbably in the sequined seashore Babylon of Miami Beach. At a press conference there, Graham — sleekly tanned from his tarryings in Galilee and the Judean desert, wearing now a rich dark blue suit and lightly chewing on a wad of gum — announced, "This is a time for a man of experience and world stature, and not a novice." He had added this observation after just insisting again that he was endeavoring to stay as distant from politics as possible — "although I have deep personal convictions about this election." He was asked then if his "deep personal convictions" about the election had anything to do with his long close amity with Nixon, and he grinned — "Might be." It began to take on almost the dainty ceremony of a coyly transparent coquetry. "The next four years will be the most crucial in world history," he expanded on, "and we need a President of world stature and experience. This is," he repeated, "no time to experiment with a novice."

It was more than a little clear, in these circular sentiments, whom he was actually commending. And on through that 1960 campaign of Nixon's against Kennedy, Graham continued to occupy himself in the curiously rarefied exercise of trying to manage to smuggle across his will for the outcome somehow without appearing to indulge in any overt political commitment — to exert his persuasions on the final issue of it all obliquely and tacitly: an exertion not incomparable to a fastidious celibate struggling to effect a conception without any actual carnal grappling. But in this exquisite dual labor, Graham soon approached excruciatingly close to outright dissembling.

That August, when Democratic nominee Jack Kennedy called on Graham to sign a pledge along with other clerics that they would not make religion an issue in the campaign, Graham refused — with Grady Wilson, in announcing this refusal, going on to mention, as reported in the Charlotte *Observer,* that they had been informed that when the Graham team was recently in flight to Spain, Catholics there had conducted a midnight mass with prayers that the military plane bearing Graham over would crash before it arrived. Two days after he had rejected Kennedy's appeal, Graham further proposed, from Switzerland, that religion "definitely will be a major issue" — though he again appended his customary polite disclaimer that he intended himself to stay utterly out of politics. He had, in fact, removed himself out of the country at this point, as he explained it, to avoid betraying his own profound personal preferences — so formidable the temptation to do so that he had to resort to such an extraordinary recourse, which became an eloquent enough testimonial in itself.

From Bonn then, he disclosed that he had personally assured Nixon and Kennedy both by letter that he would not raise the religious issue in his own sermons, "but from newspaper reports, it is obvious that religion is an issue. . . . It will definitely be a major issue whether we like it or not. It will go much deeper than in 1928." The election, he elaborated from Geneva, "poses certain problems for Prostestants because the Roman Catholic Church is not only a religious institution but also a secular institution with its own ministers and ambassadors. A man's religion cannot be divorced from his person, and Kennedy himself has faced up to this." In the meantime, Graham's father-in-law, Dr. Bell, was presenting the matter in a busily circulated tract called *Protestant Distinctives and the American Crisis,* "The election of Sen. Johnson as vice-President will mean that Sen. Mansfield, a Roman Catholic, will be in line to become majority floor leader of the Senate. Mr. John McCormack, another Roman Catholic, is floor leader of the House. These are all good men, but this will indicate how completely political leadership will be in the hands of men whose church has its headquarters in the Vatican."

All the while, Graham's side-signalings continued — all his formally enunciated disavowals of involvement accompanied by mute and strenuous gesturings and tiltings to denote his actual urges. He returned to the U.S. in October with the proclamation again that this particular presidential selection was "the most crucial in American history" — adding again his customary feint, "My main task is just preaching the gospel," but indicating once more that, this time, he would be voting himself out of "deep personal convictions." Around late October, though, Graham seemed to conclude that all this industriously allusive miming of his sentiments might still not be enough. While insisting with an unblinking solemnness, "I have never said anything that would lead people to believe that I would support Nixon," he declared nevertheless that he was finally considering an actual endorsement in the campaign — "I've been praying and thinking about it for some time. I have never endorsed a political candidate, but I do have some strong convictions about this campaign that are deeper than any other since I have come of voting age." He only demurred from this last full open pitch into the campaign when advised by Nixon himself that perhaps it would be more prudent if he refrained — his already obvious implicit sympathies would remain more compelling, anyway, if he sustained his appearance of elevation above the common ruck of it all. Graham subsequently announced, "I have prayed a good deal about this matter, and I have reached the conclusion that my main responsibility is in the spiritual realm and that I shouldn't become involved in partisan politics."

Instead, he persevered in his effort of inference and implication, a kind of energetic attitudinal striptease. An article that he was inspired to write for *Life,* in which he fondly mused on what he had found to be Nixon's qualities as a human being over the years, was aborted only when Kennedy's people got word of it and, incredulous, protested to Luce. What Graham then hastily came up with as a substitute — his enterprise in this endeavor almost inexhaustibly resourceful and tenacious — was a commentary entitled merely "We Are Electing the President of the World." In this, he posed the election as "the most crucial our nation has ever confronted. . . . Even now we are wrestling with the forces of anti-Christ on a worldwide scale," and against this rather cosmic sounding, he then explained, "Certainly we should not decide on the basis of which candidate is more handsome or charming. . . ." There was little question who would have been the beneficiary of that cautionary distinction. "Neither should we follow the dubious path of tradition and say, 'I'll vote for my Party, right or wrong.' This is bigotry at its worst. . . ." It was also rather conspicuous to whose advantage this recommended liberality would tend — styling bigotry as an issue in that election not of religion but of party, with Republicans happening to be massively outnumbered in the general electorate. Graham went on, "There are those who say that American elections are won by the side that is better organized and more ruthless. . . . Still others say that the candidate that can spend more money will win the election. Some say elections can actually be bought. I have a greater faith in the American people than that." This, put forward in the context of the controversies at the time about Kennedy's wealth and political funding and the implacable efficiencies of his campaign, also had its own built-in compass tilt. Thus Graham managed to deliver yet another cryptogram advertisement for Nixon.

Ultimately, in the final high heats of the campaign, Graham abandoned all but the last token affectations of detachment and delivered the invocation at a rally for Nixon in Columbia, South Carolina. "Governor Jimmy Byrnes down there asked me to come and lead the prayer," Graham says, "but I told him I wasn't sure I should, I didn't want it to look too much like I was coming out for Nixon. Byrnes said, 'Well, Billy, just say you're doing it for me. We really need to have you at this thing.' So I went."

If Kennedy, watching Nixon's churlishly grudging concession on television the morning after the election, could sniff, "The man simply has no class," one can only speculate what he might have muttered contemplating Graham's demeanor through those following days. Almost a week and a half after the voting, Graham was still doggedly averring, "I understand there is to be a recount of votes in Illinois, Nixon may win there. And they may recount the votes in New Mexico. Those Mississippi electors could still be important. Technically, you know, the President isn't chosen until December nineteenth."

Despite that, by the first of December, Graham had accepted with chipper nimbleness Kennedy's invitation to play golf in Palm Beach — a politic civility, actually, so considerable and consequential a national icon of the Main Street values had Graham become by then: whatever his guised gambits during the campaign, his congregation over the country had nevertheless become so sizable that Kennedy, having won by a mere fractional measure, promptly recognized, as would Johnson after him, that he would need to enlist that constituency of Graham's for an effective prosecution now of his Presidency. As for Graham, with what seemed his endlessly adaptable agreeableness, he was soon offering that Kennedy's election "indicated there wasn't as much religious bigotry as some people thought." This was a rather startlingly abstracted and genial observation, considering Graham's own diligent attentions to that particular popular impulse through the campaign. But he now benignly pronounced that Kennedy's election "helped relations between the churches. . . . Certainly a better understanding between Protestant and Catholic churches in the United States has emerged." By the following spring, he had even decided, owing to Kennedy's resistance to federal aid for parochial schools, that "in some ways, he's turned out to be a Baptist President."

Throughout Nixon's subsequent political eclipse, though, Graham continued to attend him — meeting him for quiet dinners, afternoons on the fairways — on after his California gubernatorial defeat, then the shots in Dallas, on through Goldwater's debacle, then the throes of Vietnam and the tremendous capsizing of Lyndon Johnson. Finally, toward the end of 1967, as Nixon began his virtually necromantic self-exhumation and reanimation back into political relevancy, making reappearances at Republican banquets and party sessions, Graham commenced drumming him about in public again as "the most experienced Republican for the type of conflict we have today." Then, while Graham was visiting with Nixon in his Florida home in January of 1968, Nixon enlisted him in what he purported were his final deliberations on whether to commit himself to the race for President — Graham's pastorship to these ponderings conducted as the two of them took long strolls, watched football games on television together, huddling now and then for periods of Scripture study and prayer. Before Graham left, Nixon said, "Billy, you still haven't told me positively whether I ought to run or not," and Graham replied, "Well, if you don't, you'll worry for the rest of your life whether you should have, won't you?"

Not long afterward, while insisting that he was "studiously trying to avoid political involvement this year," Graham introduced Nixon's two daughters to his audience during a Portland crusade with the flourish, "There is no American I admire more than Richard Nixon." And so he resumed, with undiminished eagerness, his curious political shadow dance of 1960 once more. In August, he declared that he intended to reconfirm, on one of his upcoming *Hour of Decision* broadcasts, his absolute determination to stay disengaged from all political commerce. Whether that radio avowal ever came to pass, though, was, a few weeks later, rather ineffably academic, when he wound up at the Republican Convention in Miami passing most of his time in Nixon's headquarters — the extent of his incorporation into the transactions there indicated when one of Nixon's adjutants complained that a North Carolina Congressman had defected to Reagan after relaying assurances of support through Graham — "It's okay to lie to another politician, but you just don't lie to Billy Graham. That's going too far."

Shortly after Nixon's nomination, then, Graham had him put in an appearance at a crusade in Pittsburgh, introducing him with acclaim for his "generosity," his "tremendous constraint of temper," and his "integrity in counting his golf score," even hailing him, it was reported, as a man on the whole more "realistic" than Jesus, and entreating his congregation to "pray for Richard Nixon and America." Departing this service, Nixon gravely confided to newsmen, in coronas of camera lights, "This was one of the most moving religious experiences of my life."

It was while his campaign against Humphrey was quickening on through the autumn that Nixon arranged to drop by Charlotte one afternoon for tea with Graham's mother. As she stood watching on the side porch with Graham's sister Catherine, his cavalcade came sweeping on up to Frank Graham's brick squirelike house on Park Road with a great blattering uproar of motorcycles around Nixon's glassy gray Lincoln Continental, the other cars discharging a spill of security agents over the lawn among

the shrubbery while Nixon made his way up to the front stoop
with its potted geraniums. When Graham's mother appeared at
the door and opened the screen to admit him, his greeting to her
was that his visit was in return for Graham's visit the year before
to his own mother when she was ill — an illness of which she
shortly expired, with Graham having conducted her funeral. It
was not the most sprightly of entrees, and Mrs. Graham, still
quite hale and brisk herself, received this dubious pleasantry of
Nixon's with a rather spare smile. With Secret Service men outside deployed in their graphite-gray suits and dark glasses
among the camellias and under the crepe myrtles, inside they all
deposited themselves politely about Mrs. Graham's small azured
front parlor, among the genteel brocades and antimacassars, the
marble coffee table in its middle holding an open Bible and cop-
ies of Graham's inspirational books. With other Secret Service
men distributed bulkily about them, on frail side-chairs and in
the kitchen, they then proceeded to partake of oatmeal cookies
and sip Russian tea — Nixon after a moment mustering the
quip, as Mrs. Graham later recollected, that "it was good for him,
maybe he'd have to get along with the Russians, and it might
help him if he liked their tea." Beyond the living room's drapes,
some two hundred people had now collected about the edges of
the front yard, and while they stood staring at the house, Nixon's
campaign aides hurriedly shuffled out among them small cards
with the portrait and signature of Nixon. Inside, Nixon — sitting
at the other end of the settee from Mrs. Graham, plopped somewhat awkwardly against a pink satiny pillow with his teacup in
his hand, an almost abjectly uncomfortable little grin on his
face — eventually invoked once again the appropriateness of his
call after Graham's services to his own mother. They sat in silence for a long moment.

"How long have you lived in this house?" Nixon then ventured.

"Forty-two years."

"Umm."

After another brief hang of a pause, Nixon extracted forth the
witticism, "You know, here I sit in your red brick house. Some-

day I'll have you come and visit me in my white columned house. . . ."

Presently Nixon arose to take his leave. As they all hesitated together on the front stoop for the photographers, with Nixon clasping Mrs. Graham's hand, he again muttered, "Billy, you know, came to see my mother, so I said I'd —"

"Bless your heart," she quickly, deftly intercepted this third recital.

She stood then watching Nixon in his neat dark suit pulling himself through the crowd with double-handed snatches at the palms outstretched around him, and she allowed herself the light surmise, "I do believe he'll make it."

As for Billy himself, he was still insisting as late as September that he would make no endorsements or indulge in any projections about the outcome of the election. Nevertheless he suggested that the American popular mood was "swinging slightly to the right. . . . A big segment of the population is very committed and aware. They are not out there carrying placards and demonstrating. They are not vocal radicals. They don't believe in taking what they want by violence. But they're out there across the country . . . a great unheard-from group somewhere, both black and white, who are probably going to be heard from loudly at the polls." It was that kind of hopeful promoting that conveys itself through the sleight-of-hand of a general situational assessment. And in this, Graham provided perhaps the first annunciation of the Silent Majority — the warmth of his evocation of this host deriving not a little, perhaps, from the circumstance that they also tended to be his own constituency.

If any uncertainties had still managed to survive these assiduous transmissions of his true enthusiasm, Graham in October had Julie Nixon down to Montreat for an appearance, and at last, he let it be known that he was once again contemplating an endorsement. His abstaining from an endorsement in 1960, he had since had occasion to reflect, could have actually cost Nixon the presidency — a speculation that hardly dispelled the headiness of the tantalization this time. He ruminated in some interviews, "I might find I will. . . . This country is going through its greatest crisis since the Civil War. Many people who just don't known how to cast their vote might accept what I have to say. . . . I do believe I could influence a great number of people." He even turned up then in the studio gallery at one of Nixon's series of carefully orchestrated question-and-answer television performances, his arresting figure reposing with a wordless smiling attentiveness in the front row. Once again, dizzily, luxuriously, he almost surrendered himself to it — but still refrained. Nixon then, in the last of those simulated television interview productions, to an inquiry from his solicitous interlocutor Bud Wilkinson, blurted with an odd bashful stammer of his eyelashes that, yes, he felt he could report now that Billy Graham was supporting him. And finally Graham could not resist announcing, only four days before the election, that he had indeed voted for Nixon by absentee ballot. Nixon aide Harry Dent later declared, "That was all I needed. I used it in all our TV commercials right down to the end."

Two months later in the cold glitters of that January noon when Nixon assumed the office of the presidency, it was Graham who delivered the inaugural prayer — intoning thanks that "in Thy sovereignty, Thou hast permitted Richard Nixon to lead us at this momentous hour of our history."

II

It was during the season of Richard Nixon in the life of the Republic that Graham came most spectacularly into his fulfillment. Through Nixon now, that American folk ethic that had uttered them both — those pieties of discipline, prudence, order, propriety — had come to be translated at last, it seemed, into the governing and the directing of the whole nation's affairs. Graham began to preside so frequently at devotional services in the Nixon White House that one Washington waggery soon went, "The administration that prays together stays together."

His assimilation into the Nixon presidency had already been well underway, in fact, at that convention in Miami when, after Nixon's nomination, Graham wound up sitting in Nixon's penthouse suite among the smoggy late-night deliberations over Nixon's vice-presidential selection: Graham himself, whatever initial uncertainty he might have felt to find himself in such a political locker-room session, soon pitched into the proceedings with his own effusive recommendation of Mark Hatfield: "He's a great Christian leader. He's almost a clergyman. He's been an educator, and he's taken a more liberal stand on most issues than you, and I think the ticket needs that kind of balance." Whatever the slight aeriality of his political counsels, after the inauguration Graham came to dwell in an easy immediate intimacy within the Nixon White House community. He was even presented with special appeals before long for his intercession in such problems as relatives in Russia who were refused immigration clearance, and Graham, out of his instant natural flushes of large-heartedness, would pluck up the phone and dial from a small address book: "Yes, this is Billy Graham calling; is Henry there? Well, tell him to call me the minute he comes in." Once he withdrew into the seclusions of Nixon's compound at Key Biscayne to flex and tone his spirit with prayer and meditation for an upcoming crusade. He also flew out now and then to San Clemente, sometimes taking Grady Wilson along, to lend his presence to such occasions as board meetings of the Richard Nixon Foundation, or simply for turns of golf with Nixon and then convivial loiterings around Nixon's pool at sundown. The nature of the fellowship on those private visits tended toward a playfulness lasting from their camaraderie in the Fifties, Nixon twitting Grady Wilson, after a golf game which Wilson won by consistently sinking long putts, "Greedy Grady. Greedy Grady. How's Greedy Grady, huh?" and with a faintly rictus-like smirk, swacking Wilson on the stomach, "Greedy Grady, but what about that tummy of yours, huh? That's got to come down, that tummy, huh?" When Graham returned to Africa some ten years now after his first processional through in 1960, this time it was in an official delegation to the inauguration of Liberia's chief of state, with Graham himself there as Personal Representative of the President of the United States.

So that long symbiosis that had begun with Hearst, Luce, Sid Richardson, Eisenhower was now consummated. Graham became, in truth, something like an extra officer of Nixon's Cabinet, the administration's own Pastor-without-Portfolio. While both he and Nixon eminently answered to the same proprieties, Graham proved as comfortably settled among the sanctitudes of all the limousine authoritarians then of Nixonian Washington. In 1970, he eagerly choired with Agnew in rebuking "the news media for imposing a leadership of the American public which they do not want, and for making heroes from radicals, both black and white. . . . There is a militant black group [the Black Panthers] with less than 1,500 members in the country today, and yet they get on national TV almost daily. But if we fill that stadium every night with young people, the crusade would not make national television as news." When eggs were lobbed at Nixon after his rancorous San Jose peroration during the Congressional campaign, Graham did not hesitate to fulminate from Lisbon, "Those who engage in these acts should feel the full force of the law. America needs new tough laws to deal with these incidents."

Then, shortly after Nixon's Cambodian raids and the ensuing eruptions at Kent State and other campuses over the nation, Graham agreeably allowed Nixon to make an appearance at a crusade he was conducting in Knoxville, Tennessee, "to show the younger generation that the President is listening to them." It was to be a public emergence of Nixon's, however, in a track of the country that already happened to be a fastness of the conventional American pieties — a facing of the people in one of his own political backyards, set moreover in the bastion of the University of Tennessee's football stadium, and additionally accommodated by a Tennessee statute forbidding disruption of any religious service. On a warm Thursday evening in May, with a battery from the local Fellowship of Christian Athletes guarding the platform on the twenty-yard line, Nixon and Graham entered the stadium together, striding over the synthetic-grass field as a roar rolled over the grandstands — a month or two later, watching this moment replayed on video tape in a studio over a thousand miles away, Graham murmured appreciatively, "Boy, they really gave him an ovation."

But in fact, for all the event's massive insulations, protests shortly began to sputter about the stadium — though of a rather modest variety, mostly placards lettered with Scripture verses of reproof, a brief kneel-in along one edge of the field for the Vietnam dead. Even so, when one demonstrator was tussled down out of the stands and then hauled by his long hair on along the length of the stadium, there broke out a storming of applause. Graham presently arose to introduce Nixon with the remark, "I'm for change — but the Bible teaches us to obey authority," and Nixon then took the pulpit to amplify on that: "I am proud to say that the great majority of America's young people do not approve of violence. The great majority do approve, as I do, of dissent. . . ."

At one point in this discourse, Nixon submitted the strangely intriguing observation, "We can have what can be described as complete cleanliness and yet have a sterile life. . . ." But as he went on — "If our young people are going to have a fulfillment beyond simply material things, they must turn to those great spiritual resources that have made America the great country that it is" — a small uproar began to develop in the stands, scattered choruses of "Bullshit! Bullshit! Politics! Politics! Peace now! Peace now!" with the rest of the stadium commencing to boom back at these fitful little clamors — all of which, with the cameras taping the occasion kept focused with a steadfast obliviousness simply on the proceedings on the platform, created the illusion, in the video reality, of a continuing ovation. During all this, Nixon faltered only once, "If I could have your attention for just a moment —" that the only guess of what was actually happening in the stands, Nixon finally grinning, "I'm just glad that there seems to be a solid majority on our side tonight rather than the other" — at which Graham, as he regarded it all later on video in a cork-tiled studio, gave a small chug of a chuckle. When Graham at the end of his sermon that night delivered the invitation call, protesters who tried to get onto the field were halted and frisked by police, relieved of their signs, with some forty-seven of them eventually arrested for violating that Tennessee statute against "disturbing a religious assembly." But when the evening recurred in its national television broadcast several weeks later, none of the dissonance happened: it became a unanimously triumphant occasion.

Not long after Knoxville, Graham was asked about the simple propriety of Nixon's presence in the pulpit at that crusade service in Tennessee, and Graham tautly replied, "Now, if Mr. Nixon had been running for election, I could understand the charge of politics. But he is the President. I wouldn't think you'd call the President political." Not a few questioned whether Graham could actually be that stunningly credulous, but he was still insisting as late as 1972, to any suggestion that Nixon might be entailing him as a political property and enhancement, "Nixon has told me many times, 'Billy, at all costs, you stay out of politics. . . . Your ministry is more important to me than my election.' . . . And he would never, *never* try to use me politically."

Whatever, so thoroughly digested into Nixon's administration had Graham become by the next presidential campaign, he dispensed with any further apolitical niceties altogether and announced, before the end of August of 1972, that he intended to vote for Nixon — going on to propose jauntily that Nixon would likely carry every state except, perhaps, George McGovern's own South Dakota. Watergate, at that point, still seemed little more than a mere stirring of shadows off at the far edges of Nixon's serene dominion now, only an idle rumor of a distant faint commotion in the brush. To McGovern's suggestion that Nixon's government would prove one of the most corrupt and immoral in history, Graham flourished the spirited dismissal that McGovern "is desperate, and he is tired." Instead, Graham celebrated Nixon again as "a man with a deep religious commitment. . . . I know the President as well as anyone outside his immediate family. I have known him since nineteen-fifty, and I have great confidence in his personal honesty. I voted for him because

I know what he's made of. He was just born to be President."
Graham's energy in these exhortations eventually produced another of those abrupt astounding little gaucheries that had
always seemed to attend his long infatuation with Nixon: on the
Today show, he suggested that the "Explo-'72" religious youth
festival in Dallas was meant to be sabotaged by the calculated
release at the same time of the film *Marjoe,* the confessional
documentary of a teenage evangelistic huckster, which, Graham
indicated, had been financed by "a Jewish businessman" for
McGovern.

Inevitably, Graham delivered the sermon at the first Sunday
morning service in the White House of Nixon's second term.
That private compact he had elatedly struck twenty years before
with the inviting appurtences of earthly eminence — *I felt that
God had given me an open door. Because of my friendship with people
like Luce and the others, eventually even Presidents, it would open doors
that otherwise wouldn't be opened* — had arrived at its full accomplishment. But at least one other political notable then,
North Carolina governor Bob Scott, reflects, "I don't know, I
used to be a great Graham admirer, but I can remember when
we were up in Washington once at one of those presidential
prayer breakfasts of Nixon's. They had all those guards around
in those silly little uniforms Nixon had designed for them,
played 'Ruffles and Flourishes' when Nixon came in, all those
trumpet fanfares they used back then. And then Billy came
through the door with all his own entourage, and you'd have
thought he was some high office-holder there himself — running around greeting everybody with his great grin and shaking
everybody's hand just like Nixon. It just seemed he'd gotten
caught up in that aura of power — just completely caught up in
it all."

In October of 1971, the local reputables in Charlotte had conceived a citywide fete for him, a Billy Graham Day, to which they
invited down Nixon himself. For Graham, that blue sun-dazzled
autumn day was to become something like the high meridian of
his ministry and his meaning over the years in the life of the na-

tion — a commemoration, a celebration that seemed to affirm the magisterial triumph at last of all the decencies and respectabilities of his long evangelism of righteousness. Wires of tribute and acclamation flurried in for the occasion from that great diverse constellation of the famed that had become, wondrously, Graham's own habitation now — from Arnold Palmer and from Prince Rainier ("Grace joins me in sending our heartiest congratulations"), from Haile Selassie and Pat Boone, from Bob Hope, Lawrence Welk, General William Westmoreland, Dan Rowan, Randolph Scott, James Stewart, Pearl Bailey, Robert Stack, Reagan, Dale and Roy Rogers. Deputations of other notables, industrialists, Congressmen, came skidding in by jet from all over the country throughout the whole day before. At a reception for Graham on the eve of the affair at Charlotte's Carmel Country Club, sponsored by the Holiday Inns of America Inc., Graham moved affably among the rustling of admirers collected in a large long suburban-colonial banquet room of pale dove-green walls with cake-icing molding and crystal chandeliers, a scintillation of candle flames purring everywhere over the sheen of the parquet floors — having paused once to marvel to a bystander "When I started preaching twenty-five years ago, people associated evangelism with emotionalism and nonintellectualism. Religion itself was back-page copy. But now, just look at all this!"

Yet it was an occasion in which there already impended the dim shape of what would soon emerge as the most staggering dislocation in the Republic since the Depression, if not the Civil War: the pattern, the shadow of that nightmare, still a year or so away, was already lurking in that bright and glistening day. An administration advance man had stipulated in private White House memos that he would "have to make all of the decisions" about the logistics of the event, since the notions of the Graham Day steering committee in Charlotte were "totally impractical in terms of benefit to us." The Secret Service had been conducting a surveillance of nearby campuses for some three weeks beforehand, and as one of H. R. Haldeman's aides later explained, "We had very serious intelligence reports received of likely disruptions, violence, and people going to be hurt." But a large part of this intelligence, it subsequently turned out, seemed to consist simply of a report from the Charlotte police chief that certain diversions and stunts had been plotted at a conclave of a local irregulars calling themselves the Red Hornet Mayday Tribe, more a collection of cultural fantasticks than political insurrectionists. Nevertheless, as the Watergate Hearings disclosed, Haldeman's aide had dispatched a memo from Charlotte to the White House on the day before Nixon's arrival for the Graham festivity: "Re: Charlotte demonstrations, the most recent intelligence that has been received . . . we'll have demonstrations in Charlotte tomorrow. . . . They will be violent, they have extremely obscene signs," and in the margins by these notifications Haldeman had scrawled "good" and "great."

The memo further inquired as to whether procedures should continue on "our plan to prevent demonstrators from entering the coliseum," and Haldemen initialed his approval, with the footnote, "As long as it is local police and volunteers doing it — *not* our people." The actual preoccupation of the White House, as John Dean was later to indicate, was always to provide Nixon with a handsome and becoming public manifestation against which instances of opposition would assume a character of the scandalous and perverse, while still insuring, out of that White House determination mentioned by Dean to "purge the crowds" at all Nixon appearances, that it would be a public assertion kept fiercely, if discreetly, quarantined from any muddling intrusions.

But if the pathology of Watergate had already quietly begun its metastasis in that Charlotte occasion, Graham himself was ebulliently oblivious. On that day, his sun had never been higher — a Friday, dawning lyrically soft and clear and burnished, that was turned by Charlotte into a kind of Sabbath, with all school children granted a holiday, all cases in traffic and domestic-relations courts suspended, businesses simply closing up and releasing their personnel for the afternoon. As Graham stood with Senator Strom Thurmond and other dignitaries in the Air National Guard lounge at the local airport, waiting for the arrival of Nixon and his party, he kept up a cozy chatter —

still somehow the invincible country boy, slightly giddied by the breathtaking circumstances in which he found himself now, arrayed in a suit of fluorescently shimmering checks with cuffs on his coat sleeves and buckle loafers under his belled trousers, and happily fretting to Thurmond once, "This suit is a little louder than I thought it was. I bought it at Finchley's in New York especially for today, but I didn't know the blue checks would light up so in the sun." At last, as Graham proceeded out with the others to cluster together in the sunshine with coattails blowing, the brilliant blue-and-white imperially crested presidential jet eased ponderously to its precise stop with an immense whining of its ceasing engines, and with a sudden scamper of Secret Service agents over the tarmac in a steady electronic cricketry of walkie-talkies, out emerged John Connally, nine members of the North Carolina Congressional delegation — including Senator Sam Ervin — and finally, with Pat, Nixon himself, baring his grin, flinging high an arm.

All this while, though, around the coliseum where citizens were arriving for the affair, small skirmishings had already begun to break out — one youth arrested, as a police sergeant later explained, for whooping indelicacies about Baptists "in front of quite a few old ladies waiting to get in," another swooped upon when he brandished a placard lettered "Jesus and Caesar Weren't Best Friends." A local police major, approached by newsmen, merely snorted, "We're not going to have any agitators if we can help it. And I'm not going on any legal basis whatsoever." Those Secret Service agents who were spotted by reporters simply mumbled, "Go away. . . . No speaka English." But most of those occupied in shunting off selected parties in the crowd were men in anonymous civilian suits wearing red armbands with "marshal" stamped on them: no one seemed to have any notion exactly from where they had come. They had devised, inside the coliseum, a special exit chute of ropes and barrels, down which they propelled the suspect with shoves on back outside. One girl was so ushered out after she was noticed laughing at an officer struggling with another teenage girl. A theology student from nearby Davidson College, who had been roosting in his seat for an hour, was promptly bundled out when he quietly made to slip on a black armband. One young man with a heavy beard who was bluffly refused entrance, along with his wife and one-year-old daughter, turned out later to be a wounded Vietnam veteran who'd grown the beard to mask the scars left when his jaw had been shattered by a Viet Cong bullet. From testimony in the long civil suit that followed the curious security operations of that day, the presiding judge concluded that the criteria of exclusion seemed to be: "People advocating peace in Vietnam . . . opposing the Administration . . . long-haired people, mostly young . . . people distributing pamphlets . . . people holding pamphlets that had been handed to them by others . . . people opposing close affiliation of church and state . . . people who asked questions . . . people suspected of fitting into any of the above descriptions."

Meanwhile, Graham and Nixon were proceeding from the airport to the coliseum in a motorcade with a helicopter slapping low overhead, the gallery along the downtown sidewalks banked twelve deep, the two of them standing together in the White House limousine. Graham later fondly recalled, "He and I rode along with all these thousands of people on each side of us . . . and he even told me how to wave. For example, he said to touch them with the palm turned backward. . . ." When the motorcade arrived at last at the coliseum, there was a welling of cheers from those still outside, with only a sputtering undertone of chants, "Ho, Ho, Ho Chi Minh, the NLF is gonna win," and Graham and Nixon were whisked expeditiously on inside the coliseum, a kind of gargantuan cupcake of concrete and glass where some 12,500 citizens were congregated now, with its high girdered flag-looped spaces suddenly ringing and clashing with the blare of the Third Army band smacking into "Ruffles and Flourishes" and "Hail to the Chief" as Graham, with Ruth, and Nixon, with Pat, strode up onto the stage, arranged themselves in front of the garnet backdrop curtain.

When the cheering began to ebb, Graham stepped to the lectern to respond reverberantly, "Thank you and God bless you. . . . A prophet is *not* without honor in his own country. . . . Mr.

President, I grew up with these people who are here today, and they are the finest people in America —" for which they all then mightily applauded. Within the vaults of this arena now, there was no murmur of the scrimmagings still sporadically proceeding outside beyond its locked doors. "— And if all Americans were like the people of the Piedmont section of the Carolinas, we would have little of the problems we have today in this country. . . . In our home, we also wrestled with poverty, if you go by today's standards, except we didn't know we were poor. We did not have sociologists, educators, and newscasters constantly reminding us of how poor we were. We also had the problem of rats. The only difference between then and now is we did not call upon the government to kill them. We killed our own!" This observation was answered with another billow of cheers, applause, with Nixon permitting himself a small approving nod. At one point, Graham declared that Nixon, this man sitting there beside him now as President of the United States, "has taught me many lessons. . . . I remember once I made a suggestion to him. He looked me in the eye and said, 'Billy, that *wouldn't be moral!'* At that moment, he was the preacher and I was the sinner —" At this, Nixon merely gazed flatly and unblinkingly ahead, sitting as still in his dark suit as a paraffin effigy.

After a bronze plaque was presented to Graham, Bev Shea arose and commenced to unroll his deep baritones over the coliseum in "How Great Thou Art," while Graham's mother — sitting off at the left of the stage, a figure of frost and snow wreathed in a pale fur stole, with her butterfly-wing spectacles glinting — reposed now behind the loom of the bronze marker, almost invisible. And finally Nixon himself took the lectern, sounding in the low clanging carborundum chambers of his voice, "You have contributed to America and the world one of the greatest leaders of our time — the top preacher in the world!" He expounded on, "It is the character of a nation that determines whether it survives. It is the spiritual and moral strength of its people . . . each individual American. It comes from his home, it comes from his school, but most of all, it can and must come from his church, his religious faith. . . ."

In the meantime, outside, the scatter of scufflings continued. One mother who had arrived with her nine-year-old son had happened to motion cheerfully to one youth being shoveled away from an entrance, whereupon she was immediately clamped upon, her purse grabbed and rummaged through. "It was the most frustrating thing. My child just wanted to see the President and Billy Graham — he thinks they're superstars. I'm just a nice, gray-haired, everyday mother. I kept trying to explain to them, *'But I'm nice! I'm nice!'* But a man said, 'Get her on out of here.' "

Finally, Nixon and Graham made their way out of the coliseum for a special reception a short stroll away in Ovens Auditorium, and Nixon by simple reflex extended his hand to one young bystander with the greeting, "Glad you could come" — at which the youth barked, "You're a murderer. You speak platitudes." Nixon instantly, limply dropped his hand as if its nerves had just been cut. He and Graham stalked on along the walkway, both grinning a bit flatly now as howls and hooted obscenities began to rise around them, sign flapping in the air, "Stop the Bloody War . . . The Church and State, a Holy Alliance?" — both of them, in dual reflection, finger-pronging a quick V-sign once or twice, with Pat and Ruth following behind, their faces somewhat starched and bitten.

They were delivered on into the calm of the Starlight Lounge in Ovens Auditorium — the security there so forbidding that even some of the ushers from local churches couldn't get in, with Bob Scott, the governor of the state, recollecting, "I even had to get somebody to identify me before they'd let me though." Graham and Nixon found arrayed for them, among the scarlet roses and chandeliers, a Belshazzarian spread: biscuits stuffed with filet mignon, Danish lobster with hot butter sauce, crabmeat patty shells, fruit punch, along with sandwiches neatly cut in the shape of a cross and, under two dangling glass doves, a monumental thirty-pound cake in red icing sculptured as a Bible, with "We Love You Billy" scrolled on one side and "For God So Loved" on the other. For all these operatic provisions, though, the reception puttered on for only about twenty minutes. Gra-

ham accompanied Nixon back to the airport. Nixon's party —
Connally, the Congressional delegation, Pat — trailed back up
into the presidential jet, and Nixon, giving a last parting high
waggle of his arms, disappeared after them, with the cabin doors
then snuggling shut, the jet wauling on away from the terminal,
skimming off the runway and taking the air, vanishing off into
the quiet autumn afternoon sky.

But from the measures to filter out all possible unpleasantness from that day, there shortly ensued a somewhat less
exalted series of litigations with some twenty petitioners, a
suit whose docket sheet was the largest in Charlotte legal history.
A Haldeman aide admitted during his testimony in Charlotte,
"We kept the people out, yes. There were thousands who wanted
to attend, and a few who wanted to disrupt. But the day went in
an orderly fashion." One reason it did, as was disclosed during
the trial, had been the clandestine recruitment through the
Washington VFW office of some thirty regulars from the local
Stonewall Jackson VFW post — this brigade of volunteers, led by
a tankish stalwart named Ernie Lee Helms, turning out to be the
"marshals" who had mysteriously materialized that day. Helms
himself professed, "I did feel a little honored to be able to help
that day. I felt like, well, Ernie, you're finally doing something
good."

Taking the stand at one point was the "official tailor" of the
Red Hornet Mayday Tribe, a chap with a flaring aureole of red
hair who confessed he also occupied himself part-time as a
Volkswagen mechanic, and who offered, to an interrogatory
from a Secret Service defense attorney, that the red cape in
which he had earlier presented himself to give a deposition,
along with blue tights and baseball cap, allowed him to "leap
over fourteen defense attorneys" on a motorcycle. Outside the
coliseum on Graham Day, he had been waving a black silk flag
with a red star framing a marijuana leaf insignia, and the Secret
Service lawyer asked, "What'd it mean?"

"Man, that's like asking Picasso to talk about one of his paintings."

Haldeman's aide further testified on the special logistics for that day, "It was not just another presidential visit. It was in some respects a religious ceremony . . . honoring a distinguished American, Reverend Billy Graham." But the trial, as it proceeded, turned out to be a rather vaudevillean, tinny aftermath to the seeming splendor of that occasion for Graham. Among those listed as potential witnesses was Graham himself, who was termed by an attorney for the national VFW office, also a defendant, as "an expert witness in the field of mob violence from the circa of the Crucifixion to the present." It was a vaguely burlesque awkwardness in which Graham found himself now caught — if only tentatively, by his coattail — from his conscription into the processes of Nixonian politics.

A federal grand jury finally dismissed all charges and complaints — a resolution not all that innocuous, actually, with several jurors remarking afterward that they trusted the dismissal would serve to instruct any other potential demonstrators that they would not be much cherished in Charlotte. The Charlotte News then proposed in an editorial, "A few people did have their rights violated by the heavy-handed scheme that excluded spectators as well as potential disrupters. But the damage done to any individual was of a low order, the sort of thing we all encounter in our lives —" an indulgence and bland equanimity that was itself a part of the mentality of a totalitarian conditioning: equating the elemental outrages of democratic decencies that had characterized the White House scenario for the event with the incidental inconvenience of an incorrect speeding ticket.

Following that commemoration in Charlotte, when Graham was asked about all the attendant disarray, he merely rejoined, "I'm sorry, I haven't heard about it. I was a guest of honor that day, and stayed out of those things. It's unfortunate if it did happen, but I'm sure it was not deliberate. Anyway, you can't blame it on the President."

But almost immediately after the pageantry of that affirmation of his ministry on that October day, there followed for Graham a sudden astonishing dissolution of all its sunny glory — pitching him into his life's most desperate winter of uncertainty.

Long years before, of course, there were many, of far less righteous sensitivities than Graham, who had seemed to catch whiffs of some peculiar dank about Richard Nixon — a must about his presence of some void of petty avidity. As early as 1955, Graham had felt obliged to comment of these recurrent suspicions, "I disagree with those who say Mr. Nixon is not sincere. I believe him to be most sincere, and like President Eisenhower, he is a splendid churchman." But even aside from the wolverine ferocity of Nixon's first Congressional campaign against Helen Gahagan Douglas, aside from his Cold War Congressional hearing scourges and his peculiar aura of drab officiousness, there were some who simply questioned what could ever really be assumed about the amplitude of soul of anyone who, for instance, could direly advance the lumberous silliness, as did Nixon in the mid-Sixties, that the Marxist Du Bois Club had so named themselves deliberately to disguise themselves as the Boys Club. But it was as if Graham, in his confederation with Nixon, proceeded in a kind of perceptual and moral glaucoma. During the 1968 campaign, he put forward the incensed complaint that Humphrey advisor George Ball had been "hitting below the belt" when he made certain uncharitable inferences about Nixon's regard for principle, Graham asserting that he himself knew of absolutely nothing to suggest that Nixon was "tricky." As Graham expostulated, "He has a great sense of moral integrity. I have never seen any indication of, or agreed with, the label that his enemies have given him of 'Tricky Dick.' In the years I've known him, he's never given any indication of being tricky."

Indeed, in *Nation's Business* in 1969, Graham produced a commentary entitled "The Answer to Corruption," in which he offered a quote of Nixon's from an address in North Dakota: "We have seen too many patterns of deception . . . we all have witnessed deceits that ranged from the 'little white lie' to moral hypocrisy, from cheating on income taxes to bilking insurance companies. . . . We sorely need a new kind of honesty that has been too often lacking, the honesty of straight talk." From these homilies of Nixon's, Graham then projected that "in parts of Asia, graft is a way of life. . . . They don't know any better. Their religion lacks a God of judgment who punishes evil," and he went on to propose of America's own moral lot, "I believe there is hope. . . . As much as any man, President Nixon knows the hearts of Americans. I have known him for many years and, after many conversations, I am convinced his greatest concern is that America have a moral and spiritual renewal. . . . President Nixon has introduced a Sunday service at the White House. . . . Once a year, the President himself heads a Presidential prayer breakfast for thousands of business and political figures from all over America. Anyone attending, as I have, cannot help but be impressed."

If he was ever pricked himself by any vague discomforts about certain inexplicable little gaps and misalignments in Nixon's nature, his apologies for him nevertheless over the years had an almost poignant intrepidness about them. "I've heard people say, 'I don't like Nixon.' I have never understood this, because he is one of the warmest and most likable men I've ever known. With his Quaker background, he may be reticent about speaking of his religious life, but the President doesn't mind people knowing he has deep religious convictions — though he's not very good at articulating them publicly. . . . I know that he is a devout person and a man of high principles, with a profound philosophy of government. I have always thought he had the qualities to make an American Churchill in time of crisis." Still as late as 1972 Graham was insisting, "I've been fairly close to two or three Presidents, so I know something of what they feel, and it's just really beyond a man to deal with. But I think Mr. Nixon is coming as close to it as anybody. Contrary to what people think about him, he is a true intellectual. We haven't had an intellectual in the White House in a long time. Kennedy was no intellectual — I mean, he was written up by the Eastern press as an intellectual because he agreed with the Eastern Establishment. But Nixon is a true intellectual, and he is a student, particularly a student of history. In that respect," Graham then bravely propounded, "he's a DeGaulle type." Graham will still raptly report, "He just read all the time, was studying all the time. He had a world dream, a world plan. He told me once, 'Billy, if Russia and China ever get together, the rest of the world is going to go Communist. But if we can just drive a wedge between them, we can save the world.' "

Once, when Grady Wilson went along with Graham for one of his leisurely retreats with Nixon, Nixon began to reminisce on his own conversion as a youth in California — and suddenly snatched Wilson's arm in a tight clutch, leaning into him with a confidential hunching of his shoulders to mutter, "Pray for me. I'm a backslider." But Graham's serene enduring insensibility to any dingier complexions in Nixon's nature took on, after a while, the quality of some blank bewitchment. Any glimmerings, any hints of a possible falseness or insufficiency in his appreciation of Nixon's character, he would always strenuously contrive to discount.

But as the successive revelations of Watergate ineluctibly glared ever closer to the Oval Office itself, Graham came to be absorbed in a critical struggle of his own, in a way the most mortal he had ever experienced. It was a struggle now, after all the years of his evangelism of certitude, against a demolition of all his simple hale assurances of what righteousness consisted of, those certitudes to which — ever since that agonized night in Florida when he had repudiated the musics of the earth — he had committed his life, his very being.

At the same time, to the degree that Graham had since then come to constitute the apotheosis of the native American rectitude, in his ordeal of uncertainty now he was also engaged, in a larger sense, in a trial and crisis of the American conscience itself.

III

In the end it came, as it always does, to the immemorial parable, as old as Othello and Don Quixote and Oedipus, as Pilate's question, as old finally as the flattering hisses in the Garden — that continuing moral mystery of the fair and the false, truth and counterfeit: the everlasting mirror-play of appearances between health and malaise, reality and illusion, innocence and evil, life and death.

It remains the most desperately important dramatic game that we ever play. But it's as if we still perceive with only one eye, in the flat and undimensioned caricatures of a cartoon strip: honorable men are civil and sober, and sober and politely civil men of circumstance and responsibility, whatever their occasional indiscretions, "are not criminals at heart," as Ronald Reagan kept reminding everyone during the disclosures of Watergate. It poses the prospect that there might be nothing left for Middletown America but to landslide into madness if it ever came to sense, to glimpse for only an instant, the true dark anarchic abyss of possibility always just a blink away from the simple innocent shines of a Norman Rockwell scene.

But well before Watergate — certainly with that surprisingly prosaic and potty collection of prim sulky uncles who appeared for civilization's judgment at Nuremberg — we should have begun to suspect at least that evil does not move among us now in those forms and guises by which we've popularly recognized it for so long over our past. No longer does it present itself as, say, Richard the Third, humped and shadowy and shuffling. Neither is it so easily theatrical as white-hooded specters milling in the glare of a flaming cross, or muddily glowering behemoth black Caligulas in Africa. At its most profound now, it tends more to speak in muted and sensible modulations of language with Kleenex textures of civility in its voice, wears circumspect vest suits and shell-frame glasses, carries an attaché case. It dwells among graphs, charts, statistics, policy profiles, program reports — that whole paper universe of bureaucracies, research centers, government agencies, corporations, which are collectively accomplishing, in their application to life of systems and techniques as the final medium and definition of human experience, a strange new brutalization of mankind.

Watergate, in fact, amounted only to an incident, a metaphor of a larger and endemic condition of our age. Nowhere in all

those elaborate electronics and softly spooling tapes and sober
respectabilities of the Nixon White House did there turn up one
good stout medieval conscience with a lusty sense of good and
evil, a fine old lively dread of brimstone. There was only a passion for processes and appearances. The evil of our time is not
even necessarily aware of its malignity — all it is aware of is efficiency, methodology: there are no real problems or struggles of
the human spirit, there are only the questions, Will it work, and
How will it look? As Jacques Ellul has suggested, the world of
simple nature in which the race so long strived has now been re-
placed almost wholly by an environment of technology. And for
corporate, urban, electronic man, technique alone has become,
not only practically, but morally the sole *Why* of what we do.

There was some speculation during the latter stages of Watergate that it might turn into the serendipitous blessing of a
kind of national political catharsis, larger than the actual particulars of the case: a communal ceremony, almost in the ancient
sense of Greek drama, of pain and shame and confession and
expiation, which, however accidentally occasioned, would renew
our covenant with our beginnings and our knowledge of our
own national meaning. For indeed, it finally remains a truth
about America that, despite all else, few nations have ever been
conceived in such brave belief and audacious spirit and expansiveness of proposition. But if Watergate began to seem it might
act as a kind of Lent in the nation's life — if nothing else, it was
both the confirmation and climax of the real distresses that had
convulsed the Sixties — it was the reaction of the Nixon White
House to undertake to reduce this portentous moment to a mere
skirmishing of public-relations ploys, mounting an offensive to
trivialize the import of it all. How nice, mused Mary McGrory
during that time, if Nixon would merely say, just once, *I'm sorry
this has happened.* But then, words like "contrition," "expiation,"
"catharsis" are really glossolalia to the methodologies of leadership by technique. So chic, so easy and cheap it became over the
years to deplore Nixon, and never more so than during those
days: yet how insistently he depressed all impulses to demur
from that voguish aversion — again and again, he sank the heart

of any beginnings of goodwill and reappraisal. He was a man of formidable faculties, that was always clear. But one was always left with the other, old familiar apparition: that Richard Nixon remained in his soul, above all else, the ultimate technician: a technician of law, technician of argument and justification, most devoutly a technician of appearances, all his own values and reverences and gratifications those of the technician — the master Mordred of all technicians, with a finely perfected facility, as in those solitary legal-pad computations of his large Historical Decisions, for finally detaching himself from all personal and incidentally human considerations.

Through those months before the Senate Watergate Committee, Nixon's White House orderlies were not only unabashed when confronted with the chroniclings of their attempts on the integrity of the law — they deemed to go one measure further and vigorously insist, elaborate with a hardy sanctimoniousness, on the absolute spanking-bright propriety and normalcy of it all. It stupefied: at instants, it succeeded in producing a strange sensation that the center of all gravity had disappeared. It was, in fact, consummately after the Madison Avenue dialectic. Interspersed through the televised testimony of Nixon's associates during the Watergate hearings was a highly solemn commercial for an insurance company that, with a quick and almost imperceptible sleight-of-hand, transsublimated a glimpse of the venerable chambers in Philadelphia where the patriarchs signed the great documents that founded the Republic, to similarly antique quarters where, the churchly overvoice intoned, there had transpired the "founding" of the insurance company — "men banded together to help a new nation." That commercial, and all the robust rationales and explications of Nixon's White House, were constituted of precisely the same synthetic tissue: semi-truth, pseudo-truth, polyester truth.

Watergate, however, hardly ended the commerce in it. The fact is, it remains just as pervasively the currency of the nation's new technological and corporate order: it has become interchangeably the stuff now of political statement, and all those commercial anthems about "helping to build America" from savings-and-loan associations, the little humanitarian homilies with which IBM and ITT and GM christen themselves, "Helping to put information to work — for people . . . People building transportation — to serve people," all the little sixty-second TV ad pastoral lyricisms about calendar-picture hamlets and deer in green glades from none other than the colossi of earthly defilement, in all of which it seems words and meaning, language and intent, are being elementally sundered, fissured, never to be fused again. What it all is, of course — these blithe little flimflams of altruism from oil companies and power conglomerates, the systematic lunatic inflations of excitement over laundry bleaches and mouth washes and bathroom tissue and margarine — is simply, at bottom, lying. Watergate is, indeed, still with us.

But as in all the dapper explanations of Nixon and his executives, through the whole myriad cycloramic distention of reality continuing around us there blows some final, thin, dead chill from that source of all evil: the Void. Hannah Arendt, as she watched, a decade and a half after Nuremberg, another of the holocaust's prim and fidgety clerks quibble with perfect correctness that he was, as Nixon's men liked to put it, only a "conduit" dutifully following "the game plan," contributed a classic recognition toward a new apprehension of evil in this age — its essential, dreadful banality. In fact, banality itself — in its debasement of sensibility and distinctions, its dulling of consciousness — is the very action of evil.

Because evil is finally neuter. It is cut off not only from God, but from the quicks of all life and passion — save perhaps the small cold fever of self-interest. In the end, evil is simply the advance of emptiness — an advance that, like cancer, has the appearance of a robust, bustling vitality. But its effect is a progressive, discreet etherizing of all the true nerves of experience and meaning.

Sensing its persistent gentle infiltrations, we know somewhere in our blood and brine that it should be met, instance by instance, with fury. But it cannot finally be engaged — one meets instead with impalpability, insubstantiality. That is because it is itself antisubstance — imprecision, indistinctness — the suck and sough over life of the great hole of nothingness. It is a kind of disembodied vandalism against us, unconfrontable. And so one is left, after so many existential short-circuitings of anger, at last singed out: through innumerable little mufflings, we are existentially disarmed, preempted, conditioned to be conducted, one by one, softly on into the final deep white fog, to be assimilated at last without pain or even notice into some new, undefined, unknown twilight of computered Touch-Tone barbarism.

Already, for that matter, it's as if we have come to exist primarily in the totalitarian pop-reality of an electronically homogenized mass society — a culture of the instantaneous and simultaneous and endlessly various in which nothing lingers beyond its brief flash of celebrity, any memory past the moment fades, all outrages and excitements are ephemeral: where are the scandals, the sensations of yesterday? It is the age of the Pop-Metaphysic: the more widely and spectacularly any matter registers to the general eye, the more real it is: the more exclusively private and solitary a matter, the less real — nothing really happens except as it happens and counts in the public, popular notice. The only important verities of our lives now lie in the fitful commotions of the collective experience; we live most fully in the stadiums, the talk shows, the convention halls, elections — and when off alone, seem only a vague, tentative ghost of a self, suspended in a parenthesis and limbo of solitude. In this way, however unpremeditated the process, the individual life — that old solitary portion of the human heart that is the part that needs, sometimes disruptively, the truth; that needs sometimes irrationally to be free; that is also the contrary and troublesome part perhaps, but also happens to be the only part of us that can love — is gradually being extinguished. However impersonal the process, the end of it all is monolith, sameness: the extinction of the individual in every active and meaningful sense save for a last mere pretty illusion that he is still an individual — but finally not even that. Even that ceases to matter.

The deepest crisis of our time, as it has always been, remains then the crisis of awareness — the crisis of appearances and perceptions, of a nervous alertness. Because the mummifications of the heart and the small annihilations of the spirit — the coma, the Void — of the next totalitarianism is coming upon us with the innocuous, pleasant familiarity of a McDonald's commercial chorale. Germany would have been only a sudden, lurid premonition of history — a brief, fantastical foredream — of what will ultimately transpire in all human society decades later quite sedately and perfunctorily. It is being effected not so much by government or even by that corporate estate that has invested itself with all the instrumentalities for it, but by the whole cosmos of technology itself, which has simply accumulated on its own and blindly begun to arrange and accomplish it; in that way a new order's technology has always tended to preoccur and then tug history along after it.

Here, at least, it will be utterly and endemically American, spankingly decent and sanitized, totally devoid of any of the swaggers or blusters of the German or Stalinist precedent. It will have far more to do here with Disneyland and suburban shopping malls and Kiwanis luncheons on Wednesday afternoon at the local Holiday Inn. It is coming not in jackboots and helmets, but in polymer Dacron Fortrel leisure-suits. It will be choired by Doublemint-fresh, relentlessly glad and grinning youths like the Up With People Chorus, belting out like thronging bells on Easter morning "I Believe" and "You'll Never Walk Alone" for Teamster conventions in Denver and Miami Beach. It will arrive, not with a thunderclap, but to the quiet blue murmuring of the evening network news. When that final long twilight falls, it will be to the gentle whiskings of automatic lawn-spinklers up and down the ranked clipped lawns of suburbia. It will stroll right in through the front door, wearing the congenial, wholesome, reassuring grin of Fred MacMurray.

Neither, for that matter, does goodness appear among us in the bright mien by which we've long presumed to recognize it. Frequently, it's as if there is no way for it to move about in this age other than with the air of a fugitive, vaguely disreputable, almost guiltily — like one of Graham Greene's shabby, God-haunted castaways. Watergate became, if nothing else, a sudden season of sheet-lightning epiphanies on the new aspects of the malign and the honorable in our time — one of those manifestations, in the person of Senator Sam Ervin, being that goodness comes sometimes blunderous, flawed, even at times buffoonish. He could not have been more bereft of the metallic efficiencies and glosses and precisions of the Nixon executives who appeared before him — that impermeable confidence and glib machinery which had carried them far, very far indeed, and which they had good reason to suppose was all that was needed to carry them finally as far and high as was worth going in this society. But then they bumped into something.

Invoking passages from the Constitution and the Old Testament, musing aloud on the incorrigible vagaries and ironies of the human animal, Ervin would gaze about the far corners of the chamber with his tilting nodding pumpkin-like head, seemingly addressing the walls and chandeliers, everything around him but the actual witness before him — what he was engaged in actually was a three-way conversation in which the witness was only the third party and he merely the second party, Ervin conducting them both in a rapt and fascinated colloquy, his long tapering gnarled hands stiffly flagging up and down and his eyebrows furiously fanning, with the other last party, invisible but larger than them both and that particular moment: sheer history itself, right and wrong, the truths of honor. And all the excellent technologies of appearance and sophistry of the White House, confronted in the end with something absurdly archaic, rudimentary, plain and unassuming, inefficient, sluggish and even unregardful up to now, startlingly could not prevail against it. What had happened, in effect, was that IBM and the J. Walter Thompson Agency had abruptly encountered an Old Man of the Woods.

Watergate proceeded, then, like a kind of classic theatre, a high moral drama of illusion and reality, pride and power and waste and ruin, the interplaying faces of innocence and guilt. And in it all, now, was Graham himself caught.

In the spring of 1973, shortly before the Watergate hearings were to commence, Graham was asserting, "I don't think anyone, even the President, knows the whole truth. . . . I have known him a long time, and he has a very strong sense of integrity," and in November of 1973, even after the close of the Senate hearings, Graham was still stoutly proposing that the Watergate scandals would affect Nixon only in the pleasant sense that they would "probably make him a stronger man and a better President." Nevertheless, his insistences on Nixon's chasteness began to take on a slightly hectic tone. Asked once if Nixon might not at least have indulged in indirectly facilitating the cover-up here and there, Graham rather enigmatically retorted that the first cover-up had actually taken place in the Garden of Eden when Adam and Eve "realized their sin and tried to hide themselves with fig leaves from God." Then that December, not long after the disclosure that some eighteen minutes had been blotted out of·one of the most pertinent Oval Office tapes, Graham emerged from yet another of his White House prayer breakfasts to announce ringingly that Nixon was in splendid spirits, "in complete control of himself. I was quite surprised in view of the situation. He was chipper, full of fun. He was the life of the party." Even so, at that prayer breakfast, Graham now reflects, "I knew something was not quite right, I felt something was wrong. Because he couldn't seem to look me in the eye."

Indeed, the devotional Graham had delivered that morning happened to be composed of meditations on repentance and forgiveness — it may have begun to intrigue even Graham himself by now that Watergate could possibly develop into that essential scenario in his religious dramaturgy of conviction and penitence and redemption, a kind of political altar call. Whether or not that had tempted him into his edifications that morning, a certain estrangement between him and Nixon set in immediately afterward — Nixon's reaction, in his embattlement, seemed to be to recoil and detach himself even from Graham now. While in the flush days of 1970 a Nixon aide had declared, "Others may have trouble getting through the White House switchboard, but not Billy; Billy can get through right away," after that little December devotional of his, Graham did not hear from Nixon again for some four and a half months — "I did call twice, just to let him know that I was praying for him, but I couldn't get through."

It seemed to baffle him. "I don't know what my relationship is now," he once allowed, and finally offered the game speculation, "I heard from a friend of the President that he didn't want to get Billy Graham involved, so maybe he just wanted to keep me entirely out of it." But Nixon's abrupt reluctance even to chat with Graham intimated more a profound discomfort, a curious shyness, at the prospect of having to confront Graham's simple persevering innocence — that awkwardness being yet another superfluous and insupportable distraction to dispense with in the elemental terms of his own struggle now.

For that matter, Graham himself was increasingly occupied in grappling with his own private goblins. Soon he began declaring that the U.S. was gripped in a "spiritual and emotional crisis" which was like "a huge monster creeping across the country, engulfing all before it" — an expostulation that as much hinted a vast cold shadow of misgiving and dread creeping now across the open sunny landscapes of Graham's own certainties. Toward the end of 1973, all he would still allow publicly was that "many of Mr. Nixon's judgments have been poor, especially in his selection of certain people," but, he insisted, "the President has not been formally charged with a crime. Mistakes and blunders have been made. Some of them involved moral and ethical questions. But at this point, if I have anything to say to the President, it will be in private."

But Watergate was unmanageably proliferating now with a kind of rampant and implacable volition of its own. In the course of this, the President's financial records were disclosed — the provisions from government funds for the plusher enhancements of his retreats at San Clemente and Key Biscayne, the singular meagerness of his own disbursements to charities or religious work, which carried a connotation perhaps more astounding than any other so far: of a sheer base venality. Graham remarks now, "I just couldn't understand it. He'd never seemed to me to really want things like that, he never wanted clothes or fancy things around him or money or anything like

that. He never even had any money on him. He even borrowed a
few dollars from me once to put into a collection plate. But then
all that came out about what he'd spent on his places — I could
hardly believe it." With this particular revelation, Graham was
obliged to acknowledge publicly, "I was surprised at the small
amount he reported giving to charities in relation to his income,"
and when Nixon phoned to express condolences on the death of
Dr. Bell, reports Graham, he mentioned to him at one point,
"You know, maybe you ought to just give San Clemente to the
government. And Key Biscayne too, if you want to know the
truth," and after a short dead pause, Nixon retorted, "Yes. Yes,
I've already thought about that. . . ." Still, the only indications
of any deeper interior unease that Graham would evince
through that time would be fleeting asides now and then in his
crusade services — "And we have seen in these past few weeks
how morally *weak* we really are in this country!"

But in fact, he had come to find himself now lurching through
a bewildered twilight filled, it seemed, with multiplying phan-
tasms. "Of course I knew Watergate was bad, was immoral," he
recounts. "I knew that from the first. But Nixon always had a
disdain for immorality, I thought. I never dreamed, just never
dreamed, when he assured all those people he hadn't had anything to do with the cover-up — I just could never conceive of
him breaking the law deliberately. And all those people around
him, Haldeman, Erlichmann, Dwight Chapin — they seemed to
be people who were so clean. They were even Christian Scientists, you know — family men, clean-living, with an active interest
in their church. All of them seemed so upstanding." But as those
persistent intimations of corruption continued to wink unmistakably behind all the deacon-like decorums and Quaker probities
of Nixon's White House, Graham was finally slung in a harrowing personal limbo beyond all the familiar, orderly assumptions
of his lifetime — a vertigo in which he dimly sensed now possibilities of the human heart and human experience, of good and
evil, abysmally more complicated, more mysterious, than his vision had ever embraced.

Insomnia again began to harry his nights. "We could tell he

was in some distress," says a member of his family. "He had always seen in Mr. Nixon such a gracious, generous, upright man, such an admirable man, you know. He was in great confusion. On visits, he would pace back and forth, from one room to another and back again, his mind way off on the thing, gnawing on his fingernails. He kept on saying, *There're two men there. There're just two men there.*' . . ."

At last, in the spring of 1974, the tape transcripts of Nixon's private Oval Office sessions were released.

Curiously, almost immediately on surrendering the tapes but before their publication, Nixon phoned Graham, one last time, in Phoenix, where Graham was in the midst of a crusade. "I got the call in my hotel room one morning about six-thirty A.M.," Graham later related — "He just wanted to say hello." But that seemed all — merely a tentative, vague, brief, and finally pointless last contact just before the exposure at last of his actual conversations through all that time.

A few days later, Graham issued the pronouncement, "I just didn't know that he used this type of language in talking to others. . . . I rarely have ever heard Mr. Nixon use even words like 'damn' or 'hell,' and even when he did, he would look over at me and say, 'Excuse me, Billy.'" At the same time, in these public commentaries on the tapes, Graham still could not resist laboring to trivialize as more or less ordinary the seeming arrantness of Nixon's malfeasances of the presidency that those transcripts unfolded: "It would appear that there was a great deal of maneuvering. It reminded me a little of a smoke-filled room at political conventions." He did concede, "One cannot but deplore the moral tone implied in these papers. . . . What comes through in these tapes is not the man I have known for many years," but he submitted, "I have known five Presidents, and I suspect if we had the transcripts of their conversations, they too would contain salty language. . . . Though we know that other Presidents have used equally objectionable language, it does not make it right." In these expositions of Graham's, it was as if the whole affair still amounted only to an indelicacy of language, as if he were accosted not by the nihilism of spirit and

principle disclosed in those White House colloquys, but merely
by their offense against proprieties: it was an offense of manners,
not matter. Beyond that, while Graham declared, "I would be
neither [Nixon's] friend nor God's servant if I did not point out
what the righteousness of God demands at such a time as this,"
he presented then one of his chronic obliquely mitigating qualifications: that the White House dialogues really described "a nation confused by years by the teaching of situational ethics," and
the nation "now finds itself dismayed by those in government
who apparently practiced it" — another of his curious little perceptual and moral malapropisms, as if Nixon had ever really
been a part of the situational-ethic sophistication: it had always
been rather the political technology of situational amorality.
Nevertheless, Graham doggedly proclaimed that Nixon remained "my friend, and I have no intention of forsaking him
now. Nor will I judge him as a man in totality on the basis of
these relatively few hours of conversation under such severe
pressure."

Such were Graham's public professions following the release
of the tapes. In fact, privately, they had left Graham blasted. He
had been reluctant to approach them, delaying and deferring it
until finally one afternoon, he closed himself off in his study,
and began making his way through *The New York Times*'s extensive reprint of the transcripts. And after a while, he began weeping. . . .

"I'd had a real love for him. He'd always been very attentive to
his friends, he never forgot a birthday. He seemed to love his
country, love his children, love Pat. His thoughtfulness — there's
a reason why so many people were loyal to him for so many
years. I'd thought he was a man of such great integrity. I really
believed, I really looked upon him as the greatest possibility ever
for leading this country on into its greatest and finest days. He
had the character for it. I'd never, ever, heard him tell a lie. But
then the way it sounded in those tapes — it was all something totally foreign to me in him. He was just suddenly somebody else."
And when Graham at last finished tracking through those confidential exchanges between Nixon and his operatives, he be-

came physically, retchingly sick — a nausea that clung in his vitals through the rest of that afternoon.

Through the following days, according to his intimates and his family, he seemed lost in some blank abstraction, a heavy slowness hanging to his movements as if he had just suddenly entered for the first time into the earth's dull and massy pull. His mother remembers that his very face seemed to dim — "There just wasn't that usual glow in Billy's face. It was like the light had gone out."

Graham maintains now of his concord with Nixon over the years, "All along, I'd only wanted to be a pastor to him" — but his nausea, after reading through those transcripts, seemed as much that of a half-recognition of what had actually been at play in his own long enthralled communion with power and high position: it was like a sudden glimpse of the other side of the proposition on the mountaintop; a closing at last of the contract; and all those exhilarations of his over the past thirty years from Luce and Richardson through Eisenhower through Johnson had assumed now, in the illuminations of the Nixon tapes, abruptly a different and unbearable implication. There were moments then in which, Graham confides as he recollects it all years afterward, "I thought like Wesley when he said: *'When I look into my heart, it looks like hell.'* "

Through those last reeling weeks in the summer of 1974 before Nixon's resignation, Graham kept proclaiming, "Those tapes revealed a man that I never knew; I never saw that side of him." But now, as if in a mere second reflex to extricate himself somehow from the appalling unseemliness of the whole situation — out of that unfailing instinct of his for the peril of wandering outside the general respectability — Graham began to profess that he had not really had a truly private conversation with Nixon in about two years; they had just met in public several times. Finally in July, he simply removed himself to Switzerland for an international congress on world evangelism — repairing to that orderly, placid, tidy, sanitary little nation which had always been the special country of his spirit. It was August before he ventured back into the United States, immediately on his return checking into the Mayo Clinic with a "gum infection," while in Washington, Nixon's administration now was going down like the enormous collapsing of the *Hindenburg.*

After Nixon then disappeared into the palmy oblivion of San Clemente, Graham was released from the Mayo Clinic, and he shortly issued another statement: "I feel sorry for President Nixon and his family. . . . I shall always consider him a personal friend. His personal suffering must be almost unbearable. He deserves the prayers of even those who feel betrayed and let down. . . . We should let President Nixon and his family have some privacy now."

But, with not quite three years having elapsed since that day of celebration with Nixon in Charlotte, "It was the lowest," one associate recalls, "that I've ever seen Billy."

IV

Nevertheless, after the passage of only a few weeks, he was again forging through another crusade with a seemingly undaunted and reverberant urgency — heartily booming that unless the United States soon made a total commitment to Christ, it "may be finished." Suddenly, uncannily, it was as if nothing had really happened.

Despite Watergate, despite Vietnam, it was again, still, the same pulpit dramatic of breathless Armageddonal suspense of his public annunciation in Los Angeles thirty years ago, the same stentorian pieties and assurances. Barely six months after Nixon's fall, Graham was maintaining once more, in a "Prayer for the President" published in the *Ladies Home Journal,* that "we acknowledge Thy sovereignty in the selection of our leaders. We remember the responsibility Thou hast placed upon each individual to honor those in authority and to pray for those in authority," again hailing that divine dispensation whereby the Lord Himself "alone hast given us our prosperity, our freedom, and our power." And the following April, he rematerialized in Wash-

ington along with the first green brimmings of spring, to deliver
the opening prayer for a session of the Senate — intoning with a
certain amorphousness, "Forgive us if we have compromised our
ideals" — and finally appeared at the White House again for a
long visit with Gerald Ford, during which, Graham related afterward, "the President read the Bible and prayed with me." Not
long after that, Graham pleasantly allowed, "the President called
and asked me to ride with him to the reception for the Liberian
president. I asked him if that wouldn't be looked on as political,
but he assured me it wouldn't." Then in July, he participated in
a telethon to raise funds for the Democratic Party. And when the
merchant tanker *Mayaguez* was waylaid by Cambodian raiders,
Graham could not refrain from addressing himself with his old
zest to this confrontation: "What will the American response be?
The Scriptures say there will come a day when the weak will say,
'I'm strong,' those little nations will twist our tail and kick us and
beat us, and there is nothing we can do about it, and we've already reached that stage. I'm just glad I'm not President — I tell
you, something would be done about it!"

So he had survived. He had somehow delivered himself even
out of that deepest private midnight of doubt and dislocation
with his message and enthusiasms undeflected, intact. This self-
willed resurrection and triumph over what would have seemed a
final disillusionment constituted, in the end, his most monumental feat of certitude. And he had managed it more or less the
same way he had resolved every other real crisis through his life.
As, after his rejection by Emily Cavanaugh some forty years earlier, he had simply etherized the pain of the experience by di-
minishing it to a mere incidental happenstance — "I'd forgotten
her in a week, and was dating other girls in two weeks" — so now
he seemed to reduce Watergate to no more than an unhappy accident: his final regret seemed simply the mild reflection, "I just
wish the whole thing had never happened." Whatever, he was
soon insisting, "We've just been too emotional about it." At the
same time, he discounted the intimacy of his own involvement
with Nixon, thereby exorcising all the unsettling implications of
that involvement that he had briefly sensed while reading the

transcripts: "I wasn't really one of his confidants, either to have a game of golf or to sit down and have a serious discussion. I didn't really move at the level with Nixon that the press thought I did."

Also in that way he had survived every serious beleaguerment of his devout assumptions — the two admired school officials in Florida discovered in "serious moral defection," then Templeton's skepticisms — he emerged from the violences visited on his sturdy simplicities by Watergate, not by pursuing any larger suspicions it might have prompted about the true complexities of the human heart, but by retreating even more conclusively into yet a further contraction of reality — abstracting himself even more distantly out of all temporal and earthly circumstance. During one crusade not long after Watergate, as he was riding to his motel, he abruptly proposed of all the pomps and glamours of the earth, "It's not going to last. None of it's going to last. It's all a shadow, a vapor, a sounding brass and tinkling cymbal." He seemed to have receded even more deeply into that Eternity Thrall to which he gave himself up in Florida, that absorption into the infinity of God, a preoccupation with only the timeless and universal and last ultimate measurements, which only further pales and dwindles all life immediately around: a kind of existential anemia, an Eternity Sickness, in which one finds a nothingness at the heart of all merely human experience. "We're told we're citizens of another world," he explained. "Now, we're enjoined to pray for those in authority, and this means even Brezhnev, pray for those in authority so we can lead a peaceable life. But we don't belong to this world, we belong to a higher world, and the Bible says the world and all the lusts thereof shall pass away."

Having thus spirited himself out of the whole catastrophe, as it were, he quickly became disposed to a benevolent solicitude for those who hadn't, whom it had consumed. "After Haldeman's conviction, I was in Washington, and I called him at his hotel to come by his room." And not long after Nixon's withdrawal into the confines of San Clemente, "I tried to reach him while I was in California and was unsuccessful," Graham reported. "But then he phoned me back one day later, and we talked for three minutes. I asked him if I could come and see him, and he said it was not convenient. He said he was in pain from his leg and that he had a lot of work to do." Then that October, when Nixon was rushed to the hospital in a coma, sinking at last near a final obliteration of what had happened to him, Graham urged prayer for him — "He has already suffered far more than any of us can comprehend."

Finally, some eight months after Nixon's resignation, Graham passed two and a half hours with him at San Clemente in a candlelit dinner, the two of them retiring afterward to Nixon's study to pray together for a while. And Graham reappeared from this reunion to declare that Nixon had actually become "deeply religious" since his resignation. "Most of our conversation was on religion. We talked a lot about the Bible. I think he has some regret he'd let his friends down. . . . He had no recriminations, no rancor. He's suffered a lot, but religiously he has grown."

It was as if now, in his own regeneration from the desolations of Watergate, Nixon too had been rejuvenated for Graham more or less to his prior self. He began to suggest before long that Nixon's only real culpability had been an inordinate concern for his friends: "He was just trying to protect his friends, I think, who were guilty. But he just had this great sense of loyalty to them." After a time, he was attributing all those otherwise inexplicable aberrations in Nixon to, in part, the aides around him: "I've been told that some of Nixon's people, like Haldeman, said after his second inauguration, 'Now maybe we can get him out from under the influence of Billy Graham.' I don't know. But I can remember hearing somebody say once, 'Those people around him are going to destroy him.' " As to the popular mood about Nixon after Watergate, Graham still submits it as his own political perception that "if he had not been pardoned, and then had been acquitted in a trial, you know — then it would have turned this country inside out. The country would have turned viciously on those who tossed him out."

Through Nixon's exile in San Clemente, Graham continued to

telephone him — as he reported one afternoon in 1976, "Just last night, for some reason, I felt a burden for him, just a burden to call him." But, Graham added, "he returns my calls about half the time, about half the time he doesn't." In fact, Graham curiously suggests now in retrospect, with a strangely touching poignance, "I think I always thought a great deal more of him than he thought of me."

But for his part, he avows, "I still love him, yes, to this very day. If Christ didn't love us when he saw our sins, none of us would have any hope, would we? I loved him as I love Grady, as I love Cliff, and I still do." At the most, he concedes, "Maybe I was naïve and was used by some others," but he insists, "I can't think that of Nixon. I just can't believe that he exploited me or took advantage of me."

In fact, Graham continues, "He was even afraid that if I were dragged into it with him, I would be destroyed too. He deliberately tried to keep me out of it. Or else, it would have destroyed me too."

For a year or two afterward, Nixon's demeanor toward him, Graham indicates, remained an uncomfortable contriteness. "Shame? My goodness, man, I never saw him but that he wouldn't apologize. Every time I saw him, he apologized to me again; it was the very first thing he'd mention — 'Billy, I don't know why I used that kind of language. I really thought I was a better man than that; I didn't think I was that kind of man. I can't explain it, it really disappoints me.'" Then, after reports began to sift into the press about Kennedy's extradomestic rompings, Graham eagerly posited that at least one of Nixon's redeeming virtues was that "he didn't have nude women running around in the private quarters of the White House."

Nevertheless, there have lingered certain small repeating afterconcussions. "It was very hard for me to get to Woodward and Bernstein's *The Final Days,* I don't know why," Graham admits. Then, in *Esquire* of November 1976, a former Nixon speechwriter, Benjamin Stein, reported on a small birthday dinner for Julie Nixon Eisenhower that he had attended with Nixon and a few other close associates — at which Nixon, mixing himself a scotch and water, had established himself in a large easy chair to recite with a progressive glee and animation, "[Ford] should have said, a week before July Fourth, 'Look, I'm going up to Camp David to work on this speech.' He didn't actually have to work on it. He could go swimming or do anything. But people would have thought he was working on it. Then he could have given it and he could have locked up the nomination right then and there — Am I wrong? . . . Amin? He's just a goddam cannibal. A goddam cannibal asshole. . . . The whole U.N.'s a bunch of goddam jackasses. . . . Did any of you ever talk to L.B.J.? God, you should have. People said that my language was bad, but Jesus, you should have heard L.B.J.!" Graham offered around that time, "I understand how there's a piece that's come out about him at some dinner party not long ago, drinking and using profanity and all those things like that again. I haven't seen it yet, but —" And he merely shook his head softly, vaguely, in a weary wondering bafflement. "I don't understand it. The last several times I've seen him, I thought he — I mean, I really had the feeling he'd gotten over all that. But this thing now that's just come out, if it's true —"

In the end, actually, he finds himself still compelled to accede, "I don't really know what happened. Some have said there was just a split personality thing there, but I don't know. It's still a mystery to me." One quiet autumn afternoon some three years after Nixon's fall, Graham reclined in a spacious chair in the vaulted-ceilinged conference room of his offices in Montreat, and listened to a visitor — the two of them sitting alone in the enormous room over by a picture window — read to him that passage in Melville's *Billy Budd* on the peculiar nature of the evil to which the master-at-arms, Claggart, had belonged:

"It folds itself in the mantle of respectability. . . . It is not going too far to say that it is without vices or small sins. . . . It partakes nothing of the sordid or the sensual. It is serious . . . not only neat but careful in dress. . . . Though the man's even temper and discreet bearing would seem to intimate a mind peculiarly subject to the laws of reason, not the less in heart he would seem to riot in complete exemption from that law, having apparently little more to do with reason than to employ it as an ambidexter implement for effecting the irrational. . . . These men are madmen, and of the most dangerous sort, for their lunacy is not continuous but occasional, evoked by some special object . . . so that when, moreover, most active it is to the average mind not distinguishable from sanity. . . . Dark sayings are these, some will say. But why? Is it because they somewhat savor of Holy Writ in its phrase 'mystery of iniquity'?"

Graham stared for an instant — still in his loose slouch in the chair, his hands folded together across his middle. Suddenly he whipped forward, a bright shine in his eyes, and cried with an eager spearing of his finger, "You know — you know, that sounds like it could have come right out of the Scriptures! That's almost *exactly* how Paul described it in Second Timothy! Did you know that?" He was asked if he himself had ever actively encountered this variety of evil at any point throughout his career. "Yes! Yes, I certainly have. I've known men who were absolutely moral in their behavior, moral in all their relations, lived what seemed to be Christian lives — but deep down, they were just like what Melville is talking about there" — and he pointed with another sling of his forefinger — "they seemed perfectly rational, but ever so often, a tiger would come out of their hearts. They were insane in just the way Melville's saying there, but they seemed perfectly rational. Absolutely rational!" And he was then asked if, at any point over the years, he had not sensed anything of that — any inkling, any whiff at all — in Richard Nixon. Graham stared for a blank instant again, and then blinked, lightly, twice. He sank softly back in his chair, his face now drab of all expression. Then he gave a small vague smile. "No. No. None whatsoever — I know a lot of people say they did, but I just never did. Never."

He paused a long moment. He cleared his throat, faintly. "Of course, though, I've come to my own conclusions about it now. About what actually happened. I don't know if I'm really ready to reveal it yet —" But then, after only another small hang of hesitation, he presented it — how he has come at last to account for it all: reporting in a quiet, easy, almost perfunctory voice "— I think it was sleeping pills. Sleeping pills and demons. I think there was definitely demon power involved. He took all those sleeping pills that would give him a low in the morning and a high in the evening, you know. And all through history, drugs and demons have gone together — demons have always worked through drugs. Even the Greek word for them both is the same. My conclusion is that it was just all those sleeping pills, they just let a demon-power come in and play over him. . . ."

Thus he has made his final peace with it: it had all been an exterior, artificial, demonic, chemical intervention. The fault had lain, not in Nixon, but in the dark stars and dark winds of the otherworld.

Indeed, increasingly now he seems to have relegated all the confounding in life to the simple workings of the supernatural. It had always been an inclination of his, actually — in the Fifties, he would offer, "My own theory about Communism is that it is master-minded by Satan. I think there is no other explanation for the tremendous gains of Communism in which they seem to outwit us at every turn, unless they have supernatural power and wisdom and intelligence given them." But now, it's as if he has come to ascribe to the extranatural, the extrareal, almost everything truly amiss in the world — "Now in Cambodia," he asserted, "that's a Satanic thing happening over there. The Khmer Rouge, that Satan's power at work."

In a way, since Watergate, his politics have become pure theology: his passion for a theocracy — that old dream of the Conquistadors and Puritans of a City of God — has become, if anything, only more compelling: "Every type of government has been permeated with corruption, evil, and greed," he declared not quite a year after Nixon's abdication, "but there's one type we have not tried. That is a theocracy, with Christ on the throne and the nations of the world confessing him. I love America, but I am not an ambassador for America, I represent a higher power. I am an ambassador for Christ, and someday his flag will wave over every nation of the world."

It has been the reflex, for that matter, of any society in a time of bewilderment and seeming helplessness before portents of chaos, to begin to turn, like Rome in its long last dissolution, to the explanation of imponderable preternatural forces outside one's own immediate truth and being and volition — "a tendency in the average citizen, even if he has a high standing in his profession," as Paul Tillich notes in *The Future of Religions*, "to consider the decisions relating to the life of the society to which he belongs as a matter of fate on which he has no influence . . . a mood favorable for the resurgence of religion but unfavorable for the preservation of a living democracy." If something not unlike that phenomenon seems now astir across the land, Graham himself presents its great emblematic figure.

Indeed, it has been the case since 1949 that, as one of his associates declared, "never having been sullied himself by defeat or tragedy, eternally optimistic and enthusiastic, Billy Graham *is* America." And through the transitions of the Fifties and Sixties, he had served to keep and sustain the old simple familiar center of the American innocence. During Vietnam, he gave back to Inner America resonations of the rectitude of that campaign. And in his own passage through the duress of Watergate, he was also enacting in the most profound symbolic sense an ordeal of the American righteousness itself. Watergate worked no less trauma on the conventional reverences of folk America. What center was there even left to keep and hold, if that center as so consummately represented by the Nixon presidency had not only failed, but proven elementally false? Watergate, climaxing the trial of Vietnam, seemed to leave over the land some exhaustion, some break of spirit. As one worthy and patriotic business elder put it afterward, "We all know that people steal; there're scoundrels even around a President — nothing like that has ever surprised me before. But for the *President of the United States* to *lie* to the people, to manipulate government and the Constitution to protect himself from his crimes and mischiefs — that's the end of the system. The Ark of the Covenant's been violated. There's nothing sacred anymore, I see a total breakdown of values coming; nobody can believe anybody anymore.

It's all over with. We're just a big Costa Rica now." It became the last wilderness in American life — a disorder now at the very center of those folk integrities of soberness, propriety, respectability we had been defending against the wilderness all along.

And shortly, there were indications that Inner America had come to terms with it all in much the same manner as did Graham: by a withdrawal and retrenchment into the extrareal. Precisely to the successive concussions of Vietnam and Watergate have some attributed the subsequent evangelical phenomenon rife across the land, detecting in that signs we are entering a second kind of Middle Ages, a curious new sort of electronic, suburbanized medievalism. Graham himself presides now as the Abrahamic patriarch, the elder statesman of that pandemic evangelical mystique over America, with its profuse second generation of TV gospelteers in gumdrop-bright synthetic suits: an uncannily pervasive elation conglomerately claiming pro football coaches and governors, Walter Hoving of Tiffany's and former Manson demonics, converts as implausibly disparate as Chuck Colson and Eldridge Cleaver and Graham Kerr, the Galloping Gourmet — a rampant mass-happening that, if not shaping into the next great American Religious Transport, is like the forming of a whole interior alter-culture, with its own Christian Yellow Pages and its own Christian broadcasting network, its own Christian talk-shows emceed by ruthlessly cheerful personalities like pentecostal Merv Griffins, with their guests of Christian entertainers such as one devout chap occupied in a Yo-Yo ministry, "using my talent to witness for the Lord" at conventions and in prisons, and even Christian nightclubs with paintings of Jesus in the ferny entrance parlors, where the audiences sit sipping Fresca or Hawaiian Punch as they listen to gospel quartets, Christian comedians, watch Christian magicians.

One morning while he was in southern California, Graham appeared to address a Christ rally of college students, convoked in a campus auditorium of an architecture that could have been best classified as suburban mod Hajji Baba, the walls ranked with archways framing brown corrugated panels resembling the crinkly ribbed paper sheets in chocolate candy boxes, while the

students who were massed there, under a low ceiling star-
stippled with pink lights, had a look about them peculiarly
lingering, it seemed, from the storms of the Sixties — that look
of Anglo-Saxon and Celtic tribal aborigines, thistly beards and
long blond hanks of hair, clothed in serapes and limp dingy
jeans with thong-wrapped boots. Only now, as if this were what
the marchings and urgencies of those young Rousseauian legions
of the Sixties had finally looped into, they were standing, singing
like a winding of wind in a cavern, *"Father, I adore thee. . . . Oh,
how I love Jeees-us,"* with their arms everywhere stretched up into
the air, a high thicket of arms all over the auditorium held stiff
and motionless, hands uplifted in a pose of almost ancient-Egyp-
tian formal rigidity, a gesture of supplicatory expectancy: an
oddly spooky ceremonial somehow in that clinically abstract
motel-chic auditorium, a touch of the primevally ecstatic and
orgiastic about it. . . . Graham arrived then, attired in an impeccable light-blue suit, to a standing ovation, he answering the
uplifted forefingers of their one-way-to-salvation salutes with his
own vaguely awkward air-jabbings, and when he arranged himself finally at the lectern and announced the Scripture text for
his remarks that morning, there was wide rustling and ruffling
of Bible pages among the ponchos and Zuni head-sashes over
the auditorium. And Graham declared once more, as he had
exhorted those throngs years ago in Berlin — this assembly before him now lending an unexpected inflection to those exhortations — "Most of you want somebody to tell you what to do.
Because you're insecure inside, you need security, you need discipline, you need a master!" At one point he recounted for them,
in rather protracted detail, stories of spectacularly grisly martyr-
doms around the world, Christians tortured in Lebanon, arrow
executions in Africa — "The first arrow went through his right
eye! Then they forced open his mouth, and shot an arrow
through the roof of his mouth! And it came out, here, through
the back of the neck. . . . That's what Jesus meant when he
talked about denying self to take up the cross. That's dying for
Christ!" And he went on then to present a call that had the
sound of a summons to the catacombs again: "The last bastion of

free Christianity is in the United States, and it'll be gone within ten years. . . . You and I are a colony of believers!"

Thus Graham, in his private ordeal of Watergate, hardly wound up, like Billy Budd, destroyed, hanged from the main-yard, his "agony . . . over now." Yet Graham's self-deliverance out of that trauma to his certitudes, his own arrival at a peace again, was not altogether without its costs. If it proved his life-time's most heroic triumph over despair, this time it exacted what seems a certain abiding toll — indications still that he may have suffered a deeper hit than he supposed, than he quite re-covered from.

Of Watergate, Graham says now, "I've had periods like that when I've felt God was removed from me. I've always been afraid God would remove his hand. But he tests us, to make sure we walk by faith, not feeling or understanding." Nevertheless, Graham has continued to dwell in that tension in which he com-menced his ministry long years ago, the Samson dread — he who was consecrated by Jehovah as a Nazarite with a superhuman might to chasten the profane and unrighteous, but who then compromised that consecration, "and all his strength went from him," as Graham would frequently recite. "And that could hap-pen to me, God could take his hands off my life without my knowing it at first, everything would seem the same, but my lips would turn to clay, everything would begin to collapse around me, and all that remained of the whole thing would be ashes." . . . When someone once asked Graham how he had managed to sustain such a bearing of formidable assurance for so long, he replied, "It's just an order I've received from Christ. I am con-vinced that the reason some ministers are cracking up is that they have no authority. I have to be consumed with my message in order to deliver it — it can be just a dead set of words other-wise." Some three years after the denouement of Watergate, then, he was still proposing that the blessing did not seem to have been withdrawn from him yet, "I don't believe God has lifted has hand from me yet" — reporting with some gratifica-tion that on a recent excursion to Northern Ireland, "I went into a pub on Sunday morning in no-man's-land, and they received me, and clapped and applauded me, and sang a song to me."

Still, he continues to live in the unease that, somehow, the anointment might be removed from him: "I've been very frightened all these years — just terrified. People have expected me, for instance, to be more of an authority on everything than I've really been able to be. And I'm still scared. I'm sure terrible traps are being set for me all the time. I probably will fall before it's over with."

Since his resolution that all the unnerving aberrancies of Watergate really owed to the mischiefs of the infernal, it's as if Graham's own sense of the Satanic at work around him now has become almost obsessive. In his Montreat office one afternoon, he recounted a recent crusade service where "some two thousand people came forward at the invitation, and I happened to look down and see a man standing down there, nicely dressed, with a neatly trimmed beard — but with the most evil face I've ever seen, right down there in front of me, doing this —" and Graham leapt suddenly from his chair, hunching his shoulders up around his neck, and began swaying back and forth in a crabbed humped crouch with his long hands lifted up to shield the sides of his face, as he grimaced maniacally, his eyes dully rolling upward and plunging about the ceiling: a truly startling and hair-raising mummery, an abrupt grotesque transformation of his bright noble form that was strangely stunning, obscurely horrifying. Then, just as quickly, he sat back down again, utterly recomposed, matter-of-fact. "That's what he was doing. And I couldn't help but wonder if he weren't trying to cast some Satanic spell over me, or over what was happening there."

Graham went on from this to confide, "I have the feeling that Satan's constantly laying land mines for me, and if I step on them, they'll blow up. I'm sure I'm a prime target. I walk on eggshells." And then after a moment, still comfortably lounging in the chair with his legs crossed and hands folded together, with a slow, musing, mild smile he proposed, "I'll have my crucifixion. I know that. It's going to come. I'm very frightened now by the high visibility of evangelicals in the country, and there are going to arise, in my judgment, a lot of false prophets, Elmer Gantrys, to take advantage of that, and I'll be included among them — it'll be some kind of a frame-up. I can already sense hostility in areas that I never sensed it before. I am hated in some areas. Why, I even have to watch what I say on the telephone now. I even watch what I say to my wife at home. They've got this electronic equipment now, microphones that they could aim at you from some mountaintop around here five miles away —" and fleetingly, there is a bizarre impression that he now somehow imagines himself being ambushed like Nixon, through the same perverse medium of electronics "— and they could pick up absolutely everything you're saying in your own bedroom. I even watch what I say to my wife in our own bedroom now."

Much of this dull foreboding seems to be visited on him out of the circumstance, as Graham explains, that "when you become a visible person, you know, you become a target. To have become a well-known clergyman, the head of a large organization, a friend of leaders in all walks of life — to be almost in a category in yourself, like a movie-star or a politician, organizations wanting to use your name — well, there are times now when I feel like I'm about to be devoured. By the adulation as well as the hostility." Ironically, after his prosperity as a public being through all the years, with his own long avidness for the media reality as the validation of his ministry's worth, it has become now like a peculiar vengeance of the pop celebrity.

In the midst of one crusade not long after Watergate, Graham and his small party were seated in a restaurant for lunch along a wall far in the back, but even as he was lodged unnoticed in this remote alcove, throughout the meal Graham's casual chatting proceeded, oddly, as more or less a continuation of those litanies in his stadium services of the eclectically famous and auspicious: they seemed to populate his private conversation just as compulsively and ubiquitously — "Jim Copley, a very good friend of mine, whose family owns newspapers all over the country, you know. . . . You mention speaking to crowds, now, Jack Kennedy once gave me a book on that, I can't recall the title right off, but he told me, 'Here, Billy, you ought to read this.' . . . Herbert

Stein, he used to be with, ah, in the White House, you know, he took us to that club up there on that hill one night when we were last out there. . . . By the way, Chuck Colson sent me a copy of his book the other day with the flyleaf inscribed, 'To my spiritual grandfather.' Seems the fella who counseled with him when he had his conversion experience had been converted at one of my crusades. . . ." Presently he confided — almost thirty years now since he had been flown over by Sid Richardson for his first audience with Eisenhower at SHAPE headquarters out of Paris — "Now, David Eisenhower: that's a brilliant young man. He's got that great smile of his grandfather's, you know. He's got a great future; he's going to go a long way. Right now he's writing that biography of his grandfather, but I've advised him just to let it be a personal record of how he remembers his grandfather. But we're going to hear a lot from that young man someday!" Then at the end of the lunch, after a last sip of coffee, Graham stood, lifting himself to his imposing tallness, and began making his way out — it had been only two years now since Nixon's fall — walking swiftly through an instant aisle of sudden stares at the tables he passed, conversations halting in midsentence, daiquiris and bloody marys pausing in midair, a running corridor formed by his passage of surprised arrested sound and motion which as quickly dissolved again behind him into turnings and chattering voices, "You see that? . . . There goes Billy Graham, my God. . . . Would you look, quick, look going there . . . ," while with this wake following at his back, he stalked evenly and resolutely on, a spare semblance of a half-smile set obliviously on his upthrust jaw.

"My life has always been a sacrifice of privacy," Graham says. But especially for the past several years now — as it happens, since Nixon's own humiliation and banishment, and with that, the sudden fall of the high sun of Graham's own golden season in the life of the nation — Graham reports that he has noted, "Whenever I enter a restaurant now, any public place, I can see the mockery in their eyes. I can see the hostility. I can see people punch, nudge each other, whispering among themselves — *Watch out, here comes Billy Graham. Be careful, don't get converted.* I'll be very happy when my time comes to go to Heaven."

In fact, Graham declares he has found of late that it has become far easier for him to talk to vast hosts of people than to individuals: he has come to feel comfortable, natural, only before crowds. But even so, Roy Gustafson recalls with a certain incredulity that when Graham arrived in Jerusalem once on his way back from addressing a succession of great throngs in Hong Kong and Taipei, among the most mammoth of his career, "he came barging into my hotel room, still with his hat on, and chewing on some gum, and the very first thing he said to me, flipping open his coat lapel, was, 'Sears and Roebuck, Roy. Eighty-five dollars.' Here he was, coming from just speaking to maybe the largest crowds in all his years of evangelism — hundreds and hundreds of thousands of people — and all he wants to talk about is how cheap he was able to get this new suit. And for the whole time we were together there in Jerusalem, he didn't have one thing to say, not one mention, of those huge crowds he'd had out there in Taiwan and Hong Kong."

In time past, this would have been an unthinkable indifference in Graham. But it's as if he has come to only incidentally remark now those immense stadium hosts; they have somehow flattened into a familiar indistinguishable sameness as commonplace as incidents of weather, through which he merely moves now reenacting himself and his message endlessly — as also, having tracked back and forth over so much of the surface of the earth since his boyhood's rapt dreaming over those pictures of distant landscapes, he has come to complain, "The glamour of travel is just gone; it's not there anymore": after beholding and enthusing over so many spectacles and wonders, pyramids, cataracts, Himalayas, Acropolises, the whole pageantry of the splendors of this world seems to have waned for him now to a monotonous idle interchangeableness.

Asked what, in his long haunted preoccupation with the tragedy of Samson, he most dreads actually happening to him, Graham pronounces, "For the passion to be gone — like it happened with others in their old age in the Bible. For the fire to go, to die, and then backsliding perhaps, a scandal. Because as you become older, you can lose the passion, the certainty." But as Chuck Templeton, Graham's old compatriot during the days of the Forties, now suggests, "Billy has had to be in the presence of so many people, at the center of so much mass attention — because that's where he's made his life and his ministry, in the mass public — and when you are tired, or fatigued, or worried, or discouraged, or unsure, yet you still have to be what they expect: you still have to be vital, you have to be dynamic, you have to be confident, you still have to carry that personal charge of authority. Billy has been in the public theatre now for almost thirty years — that's longer probably than any other single public figure of comparable stature of our age, certainly any evangelist or politician or reformer. Can you imagine, *thirty years* of living in that kind of a demand and tension? With anyone, that has to begin taking its due sooner or later. And I've noticed the last times I've seen Billy, on television or even just among people, for the first time there were signs of a professional glibness that was just never there before."

It began to seem as if the final cost of his survival of those sabotages worked by Watergate on his lifetime's canon of assumptions had become a last contraction and ossification totally into those certitudes, an arrival at last at entropy — the absolute solution. And the result began to hint itself, to more and more observers, as a vague but surprising inertness came over him. A former magazine editor now teaching in a Southern university, who had himself acquired through a number of encounters a considerable esteem for Graham, remarks now, "You know, the last time I watched him in one of his crusades on television, something was missing — he just wasn't connecting like he used to. He wasn't hitting somehow. There was something gone — something had shorted in the circuits."

In fact, after all these years, his insomnia seems to have become only intermittent, to be waning — "I carry with me all the time Librium if I ever get too tense at night," he says. At the same time, though, no longer does he awake in that cool ethereal hush just before dawn. "I'm just not a morning man any longer, it seems. It's usually seven or eight before I get up, and that's usually when my wife wakes me with a cup of coffee." Neither, for that matter, does he still entertain his old glee for golf: "I have to shake hands with everybody there on the course, and then as I go through the locker room." Instead, "what I call a holiday now is just to go to a place that's fairly isolated, in the sun. I love the sun" — and so he will pass an afternoon simply reposing, motionless, in its white clean bleak light, in a solitary and bright silence.

Now in his autumnal latitudes of middle age, his appearance has taken on — like some faint alteration left from that one momentary brush with unimagined shades of corruption, from which he managed to salvage himself but with a vague imprinting of it left — a faint, incongruously raffish look, the merest touch of a look of an old pirate, with his frosty eyebrows bristling over his slightly sunken fierce pale eyes, his grin jutting under an eagle-beak nose now slightly bulbed on the end. It's the slightest, but most astonishingly transmogrifying shift — its effect rather that of an archangel abruptly beginning to assume hintings of an old reprobate brigand. It's almost like a final subterfuge of that one part of him — the body, the incorrigible and irredeemable beast, belonging still to the goat world of the Devil — to taunt him with one last mockery. In fact, Graham declares, for a time "I was actually growing horns — polyps or whatever they were — these horns out of my mouth, out of my forehead."

While Graham confesses to an occasional sensation that he is "in a kind of jail now," he adds, "Modern communications can change all that." And in fact, Graham has begun to ponder what would be his ultimate translation out of life on into the pop reality — a mutation into, exclusively, a television evangelism: the final metamorphosis of the man into the medium.

Already in his 1969 New York crusade at the Garden, a closed-circuit television relay to another audience nearby had elicited a higher proportion of respondants at the invitation than came forward from the congregations in the Garden itself. More and more, his crusades tended to serve simply to supply the set-

tings and props for their television reproductions, and as he ex-
uberantly assured everyone at his crusade services, in the television renditions of his crusades "we purchase only *prime* evening
time!" He increasingly seemed to come by his definitive sense of
a crusade's actual effect by, as with that service with Nixon in
Knoxville, watching its video replay a week or so later in a television studio. As one BGEA tactician explained in 1975, Graham
had begun selecting as the locales for his crusades more mod-
erate-sized communities, requiring far less preliminary cultivation and staging than megalopolises like New York and Chicago,
which facilitated producing more crusades a year — or "television opportunities," as he put it — while still furnishing coliseums and congregations for an atmospheric of grandeur that
would be absent in any conventional studio.

In 1970, Graham mounted, from Dortmund, Germany, a
monolithic television crusade transmitted on a closed-circuit network onto billboard-sized screens distributed through some ten
nations — from Great Britain to Norway to even Yugoslavia —
his magnified colossal image preaching, for seven nights, to a
pan-European congregation totaling some 840,000 souls, with
15,813 conversions tallied. It was a brief passage into a woozily
vaster dimension, in itself an almost mystical experience, like
that of the first earthling to circle the moon. Then in 1976, he
began deliberating an offer from ABC, his original broadcasting
patron, which would have facilitated his ministry's almost total
incorporation into television. While he was meditating on this
prospect, Graham pleasantly reported, ABC was putting up a
special custom-constructed tower near his mountainside home so
he could receive network programming unavailable to him from
Asheville. In his crusade services, he would announce, "Whether
you believe it or not, we've got some wonderful people at the top
of these networks!" Graham's family pastor at Montreat, Calvin
Thielman, insisted at the time, "I just can't believe he's taking
that ABC thing seriously. If he decides to go into that, I'll be the
most surprised person in the world." But it continued to tanta-
lize him extravagantly. In his study with Ruth one afternoon, he
went on dandling the proposition, "It would be a great, great op-

portunity. I could reach so many more thousands and thousands of people." Someone asked him, "How much bigger do you want it all to be, Billy? It isn't big enough now? Is it worth being allied for the first time with another corporation?" and Ruth interposed, "Well, I certainly hope you won't do it, Bill. You know my feelings; I think it would be a mistake. I know what Daddy would have told you about this, and I think you do, too —" but Graham only fretted, "Well, yes, but it would open up such a wonderful new opportunity. . . ."

Along with that, as if entering himself now into that immemorial last ambition of the powerful and notable — that impulsion, as ancient as the pharaohs, for an imperishable perpetuation of one's occurrence in life, one's works and meaning — Graham has begun building at Wheaton, to provide a kind of ultimate expansion of his ministry on through time and a statistical universe, a fourteen-million-dollar Billy Graham Center and Library. As one of its promotional brochures poses it, "There are two billion 700 million persons sharing our planet who have not yet heard the Gospel of our Lord Jesus Christ. . . . To help meet this urgent need God has given Mr. Graham and other Christian leaders a vision of a unique international hub from which Biblically trained leaders can go forth in these critical days to carry the whole Gospel to the whole man to the ends of the earth. The Billy Graham Center at Wheaton will belong to the world" — and thereby will Graham himself, with his message of sanctity and wholesomeness, belong to the world, for the ages. It is to be, this memorial pyramid of his ministry, a great auto-battery-shaped edifice of tannish brick with long thin arched windows like Popsicle sticks extending from ground to roof, terraces around with fountain reflection pools, and set out in that Illinois suburban prairie of vanished wheat and corn — its architecture, on the whole, that common architecture of polytech campuses and off-expressway motels and IBM office parks and medical clinic complexes, that coast-to-coast profusion of clean and instant-minted buildings of a regionless harshly geometric neatness, the architecture of the American totalitarianism should it come. The Billy Graham Center will be composed of an Institute of Evangelism, where "key church leaders from the Third World — Africa, Asia and Latin America — will be offered advanced training"; a Laymen's Bible Training Institute; a Conference Ministries Program, in which "pastors, students, and laymen may study methods and strategies for spreading the Christian message" — all of this with a Display-Exhibit Area "highlighting the many-faceted ministry of Billy Graham," which will lead on into "a small theatre where a specially prepared motion picture with dramatic highlights from Mr. Graham's ministry will climax with a brief, compelling presentation of the Gospel by Mr. Graham"; and then the Library itself, and the Billy Graham Archives, where "students may study original sermon manuscripts, thousands of master tape recordings of radio and crusade messages"; and finally the Graduate School of Bible Communications and Missions, which will produce yearly "up to 500 young men and women to go forth with the Gospel of Jesus Christ," and the Billy Graham School of Communications "to provide more advanced training in television, radio, journalism, satellite transmission of the Gospel."

It bodes to be, altogether, Graham's final Ozymandian monument, an international evangelical Vatican in America's plain heartland.

In truth, he has at last perfectly accomplished himself, seems to have succeeded in removing himself wholly out of time — preserved inviolate now like an image held in crystal. To his own national congregation and multitudinous others across the reaches of America — after the disillusionments and disarray of the years since those quick clapping shots in Dallas which seemed to split the sky of the country's life ever after — Graham has become the only familiar American paragon left: the last hero of the old American righteousness.

Appearing for a television talk-show one midmorning during a 1976 crusade, Graham was greeted in the hall of the station by a young girl who was a program assistant, he towering over her with his cordial kingliness while he chatted with her, leaving her virtually breathless as she watched him walk on: "He's just the most fantastic person I've ever met." But as he waited in an office with the woman who was to interview him, he seemed, as usual, somewhat uncertain and awkward, the woman asking him, "Should I call you Dr. Graham or what?" to which he quickly intoned, "Please don't. Just call me Billy, please. All I have are just honorary doctor's degrees, you know. Bob Hope and I have both gotten doctor's degrees, but we don't use them. You know, Bob Hope is a wonderful human being. . . ." When the woman then asked him, "Do you mind if I smoke?" Graham instantly flagged up one hand, "No, not at all, certainly not. Go right ahead. You know, my son is married to the daughter of a large executive in a tobacco company. . . ." Conducted on to the outdoor studio for the start of the program, he stepped up onto the stage in the morning's brilliant sunlight and stood for a moment, a strikingly gallant figure against the flawless blue sky, genially grinning at the ladies in the small bank of bleachers before him, one of them twittering softly, "Isn't he a gentleman! What a splendid gentleman!" When the interview was finished, he dismounted the stage in a flurry of handshakes, and proceeded on through a garage-like room pooled in cords and cables, with a sizable portion of the audience simply tumbling on after him, pursuing him with a steady lapping of entreaties — "Dr. Graham, could I just ask you, what do you feel about abortion?" — as they trampled softly on after him, "Dr. Graham — Dr. Graham, do you think this generation will see the Second Coming?"

So he abides. Still, forever, the departures for distant cities, unfolding himself out of cars into the deafening shrill of jets in the savage sleepless nights of airports, proceeding across late-evening lobbies in which there seems to hang a clangoring staleness of the Void, that dull mausoleum miasma of airport lobbies that holds in it drab exhaustions somehow hinting a final end of America's old existential travail for its truth in mere coma now, that travail itself forgotten in a new urban and technological Ice Age of the spirit. . . . Then the peace of the plane: a Friday evening flight filled with thirtyish middle-echelon corporation executives in synthetic Cellophane-weight suits or cranberry jackets with knit butterscotch slacks, who after a week in

motels in Denver or Houston or Cleveland are now returning
bleary and rumpled and faintly sour to their weekend families,
their weekend lives, in those placeless outer suburbs of Atlanta
or Philadelphia or Dallas that are populated by other executives
like themselves in computer and chemical conglomerates, neighborhoods designed, with their ranks of small-scale imitation
Tudor and Barcelona split-levels, much like the motels they have
just left, which are in fact like expanded motel enclaves, where
they have lived only a couple of years, soon to move to another
neighborhood just like it somewhere else on the continent to stay
there for a few more years before moving yet to another: that
single continental indistinguishable suburbia which was pre-
figured by that deserted housing development in Temple Terrace through which Graham long ago wandered the grieving
warm nights. In the plane cabin's dim glows now, they sit up and
down the aisle with their drinks in a quietly clamoring suspension high in the faint-starred American night — and presently
discover Graham's presence on the plane with them: he arises
once and strides along the length of the aisle with his composure
of splendid decency and wholesomeness, clean and fresh and
hopeful as a never-ending May morning, greeting them as they
fumble somewhat abashedly with their miniature bottles and
plastic tumblers on the miniature trays — "Hello. Hi. God bless
you" — and they are left awed, moved: "I don't care what anybody says, he's a super guy. A tremendous man."

At a staff breakfast one morning before the commencement of
another crusade, Graham arose to dispense assorted ruminations
to the company around him, in the course of which he happened
to cite the instance in the Old Testament when King Heze-
kiah — "a godly man" — was surrounded by the Assyrians, "and
he turned to Isaiah, the prophet," recited Graham, "and Isaiah
did a wonderful thing. Isaiah told him: 'Be not afraid. Be not
afraid.' "

In a certain respect, of course, this was also the service that
Graham himself had been performing for the leaders of his day

since Eisenhower. But then, as he had professed on the side veranda of his mountain home that April morning not long after Nixon's fall, "Never again. I mean —" and his small cough of a laugh then "— I've had my turn getting mixed up in politics, you can be sure of that. Oh, no, never again." Several months later, during a crusade in San Diego, he was asked, after his return from a service at Camp Pendleton the day before, if he had dropped by San Clemente, which had been only some twenty-two miles away, and Graham's face momentarily flushed, he gave a quick grin, "Oh, goodness sake, naw — not at all. In fact, I never even thought about it while I was up there. No. I don't know when's the last time I've seen him, actually." He still seemed somewhat uneasy about lingering recollections of that old enthusiasm of his. He was asked during a television interview in San Diego why he guessed he had not been invited to appear at either of the nominating conventions this time, and he submitted with a flat smile, "Well, I suppose they might have thought I'd be representing Mr. Ford or Mr. Carter or Mr. Reagan." As it happened, during that San Diego crusade the Rupublican Convention was also underway in Kansas City, and Graham offered one night, "I suppose everybody here is a Democrat, since the Republicans are watching the convention," and he then chuckled, "but no, no, let's not get into that. . . ."

The night of the nomination itself, Graham noted only, "I'm sure that everyone will pray that God's will will prevail in November, and that God's choice will serve us for the next four years" — without happening to mention that Julie Nixon Eisenhower was in the audience that evening, she having made an early unobtrusive entrance with Ruth from a field-level side door in the stadium. Before the service had begun, one newsman at the press table down on the field called to Graham's public-relations manager, Don Bailey, when he floated past once, "Hey, Don, isn't that Julie Eisenhower sitting up there with Mrs. Graham?" Bailey paused for just an instant, seemingly on the tip of his toes, grunting, "Hunh? —" and then, with a certain funereal soberness on his countenance, furtively motioned the newsman over a few dozen yards from the press table, and mumbled to him, "Look. Obviously you know that's Julie Eisenhower sitting up there. Obviously, I'm not going to stand here and try to tell you that's not Julie Eisenhower. It's not that we have anything to hide, or are ashamed of anything, or anything like that. But she just wanted to be able to come out and attend a service and listen to Mr. Graham preach, that's all, and if word got to those fellas over there at the press table, every camera and reporter in the place would be converging on her. So I'd appreciate it if you'd just do us a favor and not say anything about it to the rest of 'em at the table over there — okay?"

Even so, it was an invocation that continued to confront Graham — *Now about President Nixon, Dr. Graham, could you tell us . . .* It seemed for a long while as if he would never really have total peace, total release from it: he would have to endure it forever rising up to accost him yet again wherever he went: that specter of misfortune out of his past to be with him from now on, ever recurring — the David Frost interviews, then Haldeman's book, then Nixon's own — it would never leave his heels, like Bill Sikes's dog in *Oliver Twist*.

Nevertheless, that spring of 1976 as the presidential season began to stir more briskly, Graham could not resist announcing once again that, while he meant to stay "totally out of any partisan politics," he could not help but be convinced that "people are going to demand moral integrity and some spiritual strength in public leaders in a way they have not done before." Graham himself, of course, had all along served to secure that center of the conventional integrities for the American establishment while the nation had passed through struggle and reorderings. And sitting on his side porch, he noted, not without a certain rich resonance in his voice, that the some forty million evangelicals now in the country "would be enough to turn a presidential election" — a fact, he added enigmatically, that he was "sure Mr. Carter has not been unaware of" — but he stipulated that any efforts to mobilize this new potential political property "would be very detrimental to America and to the church. I would fight that — to organize an evangelical political bloc." Even so, he later publicly went on to propose, with a curious unflappable detachment, that with the recent raft of scandals in government, many "may vote their moral and religious convictions above any other issue." For his part, Graham allowed as to Ford and Reagan and Carter, "It's a refreshing thing to have candidates come along and talk about their devotion to God, especially if they back it up with their lives" — adding then that he had "prayed with all three of them" on different occasions. Preparing to set out for the crusade in San Diego, Graham proclaimed, "We need to know what political leaders believe religiously, morally, and sociologically. . . . Their beliefs and philosophy are going to be a determining factor in many of the great decisions a President has to make."

Incredibly, it was as if he were entering once again into all the towings of the old entrancement. And after addressing a Christian workers' conference one morning during that crusade in San Diego, Graham paused on the sidewalk outside before getting back in his car to beckon over a journalist from Atlanta who had accompanied him, a huge grin suddenly unfurling across his face. "Well, you might be interested to know that I got a call from your former governor this morning. That's right — it's the first call I've gotten from him since his nomination. He called me in my room early this morning, said he just wanted to ask how the crusade was going — he told me, 'I just want you to know that Rosalyn and I are praying for your meetings out there.' I've known him since he was governor, you know. He's a friend of mine, has been for some time. Well then —" He started to duck on into his car, but then straightened again. "Of course, I've heard, and I don't know if it's so, but I understand that when he had his conversion experience walking with his sister that Sunday in the woods down there, it was just after he had listened to his pastor preach from a sermon of mine once. That's what I understand — that very Sunday morning the pastor preached this sermon he had heard me preach somewhere, Carter was sitting there in the congregation, and then it was that afternoon that

Carter had his experience." And with that, his spacious grin still wrapped across his face, he plunged into the car, and was gone, off again.

V

So, thirty years now after his advent in Los Angeles, only two years having elapsed since Watergate, he surged on through that San Diego crusade with an undaunted eagerness, his thumbs taped in plastic Band-Aids to protect them against his nail-gnawing — proceeding, even against what might have seemed a panoramic debris left by the failure and inadequacy of his whole lifetime's assumptions and vision, still with his heroic assurance: the indestructible American Innocent. To prime and brace his lungs, his wind, for the delivery of his message now, he would sit up straight while riding somewhere with T. W. or Grady and, staring straight ahead through the windshield, blankly bellow, again and again, "YES! NO! YES! NO! NO! YES!"

He awakens from his afternoon nap in his motel room, and after a last sip at a cup of wan tea, descends in the elevator, bends into the back seat of the car that is waiting, and begins the ride to the stadium, settled low in the seat, his shoulders slightly humped, mostly gazing out of the window with a forefinger curled over his lips. . . .

Meanwhile, the stadium escalators are steadily lofting the multitude on up into the dimming sky, a continuous floating of quiet files of still figures up into the heavens of dusk, up to the high parapets of the stadium under the flaring batteries of lights, spilling them out then into the huge spaces of the stadium's titanic concrete geometries lit with random lingering blurs of the westering sun, while now a distant sound of splendor, the singing of the choir, faintly and eerily thrills through the enormous vaulted walkways filled with the hushed shuffling of numberless feet. . . . Down on the field itself, brilliant-lit, a profusion of

pastel suits ripples about the grass around the platform, an Epis-
copal priest in a hay-green leisure suit with a clerical collar, the
crusade director himself striding about with his walkie-talkie in a
suit the color of a banana Popsicle, as the musical prelude rings
over the filling stands with the sound of the organ renditions at
suburban cafeterias on Sunday afternoons.

And then he comes on once again — stalking swiftly over the
grass under the field lights blazing in the night sky, his Bible
cuddled in one hand against his chest and his chin resolutely
lifted: a tall and radiant figure with — from a distance now, but
only the smallest distance — still that immaculate glamour of
Sunday-morning sanctitude, that look of a blond valorous prince
out of a Nordic fairy tale, with that rangy lankness still of a plain
country-grown American Candide. He takes his place once more
on the podium among that evening's gallery of miscellaneous notables, San Diego city councilmen, state senators, commanding
officers from nearby naval bases — the sensation here on the
platform something like sitting in a dazzlingly lit furniture
showroom that has somehow been translated into the center of
this stadium field, all deeply carpeted, shoefalls noiselessly absorbed into the mustard-yellow layers of rug, with upholstered
easy chairs of the same yellow, a self-contained parlor, only without walls, open to the night and the surrounding loom of stands.
Through the preliminary proceedings, Graham sits with crossed
legs, nervously biting at his fingernails with tiny snicks of his
teeth, bows his head momentarily and closes his eyes in a short
prayer. . . .

Finally he swoops on up to the pulpit, a master console
custom-made for him by IBM, waiting for the ovation booming
around him to subside, and declaring then with that unrelenting
vigilance, "All the applause, of course, and all the wonderful
things that are said, will be stored up in Heaven and given to
whom it belongs — Jesus!" which brings yet another wash of
applause.

And so once more, transliterated out of all time now — *It's almost as if I'm not even aware of the thousands and thousands of people
out there. I'm preaching just to the first six inches in front of my face. I*

feel almost totally alone. And even if nobody responded, if no one came, I would still preach — towering solitary against the night, his profile struck with a bright glistering edge against the field lights, with a fierce arctic brilliance in his pale eyes, he begins: "I believe we could have a great spiritual awakening that could turn this country around, and turn the world around!" His hands thrown back on his hips palms downward, his voice barges with its vaguely autocratic clang over the steeps of the stadium: "You're not here by accident tonight. Tonight could be the most decisive moment you ever live. But you must choose! Choose! Choose! *Choose!*"

After these thunderclaps, he sweeps one hand in a long wide slow stroke over the expanse of the stands: "Just look at the graves there'll be in just sixty years. . . . But all of you out there, you have a tremendous hope. . . . We're seeing an increase in earthquakes, floods, famines on scales we never heard of before — drugs. And there's an increasing possibility of World War Three. Civil wars, and fighting, and revolution, and terrorists' groups are making atomic bombs. It seems the world's almost out of control! And then there're all your personal problems — boredom, children in rebellion, bad health, an unfulfilled longing in your own soul for something else. . . . The psychologists tell us that every person has three instincts — hunger, sex, and herd, the social instinct. Hunger and sex can be temporarily satisfied, but herd can be satisfied only by Christ! You can get total fulfillment and total gratification in the herd instinct from Christ! . . . Now, nowhere in the Bible are we told to pursue happiness — we're told to do our *duty*." And forty years now since those nights of listening to music from far ballrooms on the car radio while parked on that drive in front of the gutted mansion in Charlotte, he does not name Pauline, he merely recounts, "Yes, I thought I loved her. I'd cry about it. But I knew I had to end it. Finally, I went and told her. She cried and I cried. I remember, as I drove back down that long driveway that night afterward, I could hardly see it for the tears in my eyes — but I'd have fouled up my life forever! The price you have to pay is to surrender your will and your ego and your

mind to God. Man cannot come to God by his mind alone —
there is a cloud, a veil over the intellect," and Graham passes his
spread hand over his face "— a veil. I know something of the
terrible way that Bertrand Russell and George Bernard Shaw
died. Why? Because they had no spiritual life — life was a bore
to them. But for a Christian, whatever your circumstances, whatever it is, if you're in Jesus, you can *rejoice!* Corrie ten Boom,
when the Germans invaded Holland, her sister was killed, her father was killed, her whole family lost, but not one time, *not one
time,* did God forsake her. No matter what the problem, she
always had a shine on her face! But I think of Hemingway, Ernest Hemingway, how he finally just gave up in despair and blew
his brains out. But we're not living in the darkness of a Nietzsche, or a Sartre, or a Camus or Hemingway. We're not living in
that darkness. We can have cheer, and *joy,* and satisfaction, and
peace, there's *hope,* there's joy, there's purpose, there's *meaning*
for the Christian." And as he had first decreed to himself in that
midnight of desolation on the golf green in Florida; as, for over
thirty years now, he had been telling all the thousands in India
and New York and Africa and Australia and Korea; as he had
told them in the South during the agonies of the Sixties; as he
had assured Eisenhower, Churchill, Nehru, the kings and
queens and prime ministers of the earth; as he had told Nixon;
as he had been proclaiming to the troubled spirit of Inner
America for over a generation now; he cries, "No matter what
the problem, there's a *shine* on our face! — Because the world
and all the things thereof, it's not going to last. None of it is
going to last. The things of this world are all a vapor. . . ."

On one of the last nights in San Diego, a Korean girl is led to
the microphone and left there, a small and wispy figure, to recite
in a gladly ringing voice the tale of how, during the Korean War,
her father had warned her not to look directly at the bomb
glares, "but I was only five years old," and so, one day, glanced at
a detonation, "and I have been blind ever since, which shows the
punishment sometimes of disobedience," after which, her father,
"who became discouraged," took her and her younger sister and
pitched them both into a winter river to drown, she being re-

trieved, though, shortly afterward — "and I am so thankful," she then chimes, "to God for all that He's done, the love of God which saved me from the river and many other trials," and with that, this slight figurine of a blameless innocence blasted and left blank-eyed by the deep furious mysteries of evil, begins to sing in a pretty crystal voice, in what seems suddenly a cheerful sweet barbarity of mindless piety, *"The love of God is greater far than tongue or pen can ever tell, it goes beyond the highest star, and reaches to the lowest hell — O love of God! How rich! And pure! How measureless and strong. . . ."*

And finally, as the choir begins hymning once again, *"Just as I am, without one plea . . . O Lamb of God, I come,"* he calls over the soft surfing of their voices, one long arm swinging over the reaches of the stadium, "Something deep down inside of you is speaking to you, urging you, telling you that you need to come down tonight. It's the Holy Spirit, wooing you to give your life over to Christ, who died for your sins. You may never have another moment like this one. If you don't come tonight, you may never come. . . ."

And in the dark stands around him, there is a kind of mute answering chorus, as in those scribbled notes always slipped into the collection plates at each service, an accompanying mass hosannah in which he takes on his final definition beyond everything else, the final truth of his presence and his meaning in the maelstrom of the mind of his multitudes: *"Please Dr. Graham, pray for my alcoholic husband. God has blessed me by giving me 7 more years through surgery. . . . Dear Billy Graham, At age 15 am going on with God. I can't explain it — but God has put such a burden and a love on my heart for you and the whole team. You're the greatest Worldwide Evangelist this world has ever known! I wish you, your wife, and your family the very best of God's Goodness! . . . God Bless Billy Graham, and America. . . . Dear Dr. Graham — I request that you, in your personal prayers, join my wife and me and hundreds of our Christian friends everywhere beseeching the Lord to bring our son to full mental health. He was born with a brain dysfunction and even now at the age of twelve has never spoken a word. . . . Things are looking up Billy!*

We'll never be able to thank you and God enough. Your both fantastic! See ya in heaven — God bless ya. . . . My 8 yr. old grandson is talking baby talk a lot and is very high strung — Not bad enough to have a tumor on brain also has to have cysts even in the neck. Please Pray for them? . . . Thank you Jesus for Dr. Graham & Crusade — How I love him. How I love you. . . . Your type of work is 'the greatest'. P.S. I, also wish that Dick Nixon would have 'fought' it to the end instead of 'giving up!' . . . Dear Billy Gram. Would you like a treat on a sailboat ride for a couple hours while you stay here. You and your wife and couple others are invited. I have a 24' sailboat in Davis Mariner. If interested call this number, It's my pleasure. Just a friend in Christ . . . Dear Jesus, My Lord and Savior, I believe you can deliver me from out of all my personal problems and trials. That you will control my will in exchange for yours. I yield my self completely to you. Lord pour out your spirit upon me. I desire to give you my very best. Life is not dull or dreary with the song you have put in my heart. I hope to please you. . . ."

He looms over the pulpit's star-spray of gladioli and ferns, his pale phosphorescent raincoat having been draped back over him, still calling, "That's it, come on now. Father, mother, young person — you can find a new life tonight by a complete surrender to Jesus Christ. You come on. There's still time. You come. . . ." And they continue to ripple down all over the stands, collecting in a wide hushed lake of uplifted faces below his tall bright form, as he folds his arms across his Bible and bows his head once more with the fingertips of one lifted hand lightly spread across his brow.

Finally, he arrives back in his motel room and closes the door. The drapes are drawn against the night outside, enclosing a lamplit carpeted muffled hush abruptly far from all the heavings of great hosts, the anthems and grandeurs of the stadiums. It could, in fact, be a room now anywhere in the world — the wrapped glasses on the tiny tray atop the desk, the shadowed glaze of the television screen, the framed prints over the walls of vague piazzas and placeless seashores. At last, after a brief clinking and rustling about in the white bleak glare of the bathroom, he snaps out the light, and he then stretches out his long gangling length under the bedcovers. His eyes stay open for a while in the darkness as he waits for sleep — waiting to resume his navigation through that gape before him again of the night.

Notes

The peculiar problem one encounters with the literature on Graham that has collected over the years is that it has remained, for all its expansiveness, largely parochial, repetitive, and thin. It somewhat calls to mind Chesterton's remark about H. G. Wells's immense body of work — to the effect that it reminded him of some vast stretch of sea that was only two inches deep. A certain prevailing interest of advocacy in all considerations of Graham, as mentioned in the author's note, has probably much accounted for this. For some reason, no writer with larger, disinterested curiosities and instincts has ever seemed able to muster the spirit or appetite for anything more than an occasional magazine run at him.

Whatever, in the magazine journalism, by far the richest and most alive is Noel Houston's two-part series in 1958 for *Holiday,* "Billy Graham" — it strongly suggests that Houston, who died in 1958, six months after his story's appearance, could well have produced the definitive, fully felt and fully thought biography of the man and the phenomenon. Also notable are John Corry's 1969 *Harper's* piece, "God, Country, and Billy Graham," and Harold Martin's 1963 profile for the *Saturday Evening Post,* "Billy Graham." For consistently discerning appreciations of Graham and his meaning, though, nothing approaches Ken Woodward's exercises in *Newsweek* since the sixties.

As for newspaper coverage, none has been so exhaustively detailed and varied and alert as that of the two, and uncommonly excellent, newspapers of Graham's hometown, Charlotte — the *Observer* and the *News.* In those files, particularly instructive and astute is a 1958 series by John Borchert of the *News,* the intermittent coverage by Kays Gary of the *Observer,* and a 1977 series by the *Observer*'s Mary Bishop.

Among the biographies, John Pollock's 1966 authorized account, *Billy Graham,* is however unrelentingly promotional, perhaps the most ambitiously thorough as sheer circumstantial record, and Stanley High's 1965 study, *Billy Graham,* even though also a long commendation, is not without a special perceptiveness. The most effective and impressively researched of the critical biographies is, without question, William G. McLoughlin, Jr.'s, 1960 *Billy Graham: Revivalist in a Secular Age.*

It should be kept in mind, though, that the following log of references is more a sample selection of supportive sources — simply to offer the reader some further substantiation of authenticity — and is by no means a complete tabulation of all sources, often multiple on an item, which have backgrounded the writing of this story. Such a total listing would range ponderously beyond the practicable or useful. I have elected to cite on a given specific most frequently the references to it by Graham's admiring biographers — Pollock, High — precisely because of their sympathetic bias. But in particular, the citations of quotes (which are denoted in a shorthand version) are seldom, it should be stressed, the sole source or support for their use — in many cases, they are cited as supplementary to primary sources, and some of them, in turn, were later expanded on and supplemented in the course of the interviews. But when not mentioned in the following compendium, remarks and particulars can be assumed to have come directly from those interviews and the author's own reportage.

PAGE

12 Telegrams offering eyes: "Billy Graham's Journey," *Newsweek* (Feb. 16, 1959), p. 93.

Letters asking for kidney stone: Dr. L. Nelson Bell, "Billy Graham, My Son-in-Law," *Ladies' Home Journal* (Aug., 1958), pp. 103–110.

Notes slipped into collection plates: from in-house BGEA report compiled in 1977 and provided to author.

"Better off playing with lightning": Letters column, the Charlotte *Observer* (June 24, 1974).

PAGE

13–14   Graham's explanation of his sense of Jesus: John Corry, "God, Country, and Billy Graham," *Harper's* (Feb., 1969), pp. 33–39; Billy Graham, "The Man Called Jesus," the *Reader's Digest* (July, 1972), pp 90–94; John Pollock, *Billy Graham* (London: Hodder and Stoughton, 1966).
"Young people are searching": John Borchert, the Charlotte *News* (Sept. 24, 1958).

22   Barefoot, living on stolen provender: Borchert, Charlotte *News* (Sept. 9, 1958).

25   "I never hated anyone": Ibid.

28   Trudged, heavily pregnant, to gather butterbeans: Warren Barnard, Charlotte *News* (Jan. 27, 1973).

28   "Committed the unpardonable sin": Borchert, Charlotte *News* (Sept. 9, 1958).

29   "Just as I turned off Park Road": Ibid.
"Never heard him use slang word": Kays Gary, the Charlotte *Observer* (Aug. 29, 1962).

29–30   Abstaining from letting them know his prosperity: Stanley High, *Billy Graham* (New York: McGraw-Hill, 1956), p. 103.

33   A fancy he had been meant to preach: Borchert, Charlotte *News* (Sept. 8, 1958).
"Dawned on me when a letter came": High, p. 107.
"Now you take Melvin": Brochert, Charlotte *News* (Sept. 9, 1958).

34   "Whenever we'd be somewhere together": Pat Borden, Charlotte *Observer* (April 5, 1972).

36   "Never realized how far apart we'd grown": Susan Jetton, Charlotte *Observer* (Sept. 21, 1968).

37   "Just doing what he's supposed to be doing": Brochert, Charlotte *News* (Sept. 9, 1958).
"I went to London to hear Billy Frank": Roy Covington, Charlotte *Observer* (month undated, 1957).
"Now exactly where is this Korea?": Billy Graham, "God Is My Witness," *McCall's* (April, 1964), pp. 122–25.

38   "Came to my office with tears in his eyes": Charlotte *Observer* (Oct. 2, 1958).

40   "He prayed for me faithfully": Gary, Charlotte *Observer* (Aug. 29, 1962).
"Mr. Graham went away": Rita Simpson, Charlotte *News* (Feb. 23, 1971); Sue Titcomb, Charlotte *News* (Jan. 10, 1963).

41   "Today for lunch": Sue Titcomb, Charlotte *News* (Jan. 10, 1963).

45   "Acres of hard red clay": Margaret Shannon, the Atlanta *Journal* and *Constitution* Magazine (Oct. 9, 1977); George Burnham, *Billy Graham: A Mission Accomplished* (Westwood, N.J.: Fleming H. Revell, 1955), p. 36.
A daily laboring to dusk: Brochert, Charlotte *News* (Sept. 8, 1958).

46   Recited Scripture as she scrubbed him: George F. Hall, "Billy Graham in Moshi," the *Christian Century* (March 23, 1960), p. 366.

48   On Sundays, forbidden to read comics, play: Graham, *McCall's* (April, 1964).

49   Whippings for chewing tobacco, squirming in church: High, p. 106.
Such Old Testament verses as: Brochert, Charlotte *News* (Sept. 8, 1958).

59   "Folks spent every night singing in choir": Graham, *McCall's* (April, 1964).

60   So energied, parents took him to doctor: Brochert, Charlotte *News* (Sept. 9, 1958).

61   "Could see no point in going to school": Graham, *McCall's* (April, 1964).
"Never actually any question of his graduating": Noel Houston, "Billy Graham," *Holiday* (Feb., 1958), pp. 62–65.

63   "When one big fella came at me": Graham, *McCall's* (April, 1964). (Only, in this account, Graham has it as a "stick" he picked up, not a milk bottle.)

PAGE

66   Any fancy for spirits extinguished by his father: "The New Evangelist," *Time* (Oct. 25, 1954), pp. 54–60.

67   "Mother and father were reluctant to discuss": Graham, *McCall's* (April, 1964).
"A pretty rough character": Ibid.

69   "Understood little, and resented my parents": "Billy Graham: The Man at Home," the *Saturday Evening Post* (Spring, 1972), pp. 40–47.
Through one hundred volumes before he was fifteen: John Pollock, *Billy Graham* (London: Hodder and Stoughton, 1966).
Had dispatched Gibbon's: Ibid., p. 6.

70   Running taxis into ditches: Graham, *McCall's* (April, 1964).
Driving down sidewalk: Covington, Charlotte *Observer* (Sept. 24, 1958).

71   Clocked up almost three hundred miles: Pollock, *Billy Graham*, p. 4.

73   "Hope you can come up this weekin": Houston, *Holiday* (Feb., 1958).
"Tendencies to become wild": Graham, *McCall's* (April, 1964).
"Reason I didn't commit sexual immorality": Ibid.

78   "Aw, probably some fanatics": Houston, *Holiday* (Feb., 1958); Terry Taylor, Charlotte *News* (Aug. 23, 1975).
Clatters of gunfire, millworkers killed: Charlotte *Observer* (Feb. 6, 1977); Vernon W. Patterson, "The Prayer Heard Round the World," *Decision* (Oct., 1975), p. 3.

79   "We fasted all day": Houston, *Holiday* (Feb., 1958).

80   Ham presiding at bonfire of dubious literature: Edward Ham, *Fifty Years on the Battle Front with Christ* (Nashville: The Hermitage Press, 1950), p. 117.
Street altercations often attended his presence: Ibid., pp. 110, 112, 113.
Livid anti-Semite: Brochert, Charlotte *News* (Sept. 8, 1958); Houston, *Holiday* (Feb., 1958).
"More strength to your arm": Ham, *Fifty Years on the Battle Front with Christ*, p. 151.

80–81 An "agency in International Jewry": Ibid., p. 261.

83   Flung a finger at Billy, "You're a sinner!": High, p. 35.

84   "I felt very ittle emotion": Graham, *McCall's* (April, 1964).
"The Lord did speak to me about certain things": Pollock, *Billy Graham*, p. 7.

86   "It is not something you do for yourself": AP dispatch, Charlotte *Observer* (March 6, 1966).
"Concept of conversion is not unusual": Graham, *McCall's* (April, 1964).

87   "I tried to be courteous and kind": Ibid.
"Sir, don't do that. I'm a Christian": Pollock, *Billy Graham*, p. 10.

91   Would begin his rounds with a prayer: High, p. 108.

92   Housewife had to empty a pitcher of water: Pollock, *Billy Graham*, p. 10.

95   "I was a sinner! And no good!": Houston, *Holiday* (Feb., 1958).

98   Insomnia to harrow his nights from then on: High, p. 18; Graham, *McCall's* (April, 1964).

100   "Leave and throw away your life at a little country school": Pollock, *Billy Graham*, p. 12.

106   Cross-handed golf grip, zestful dish-washer: High, p. 74.

109   Jell-O his most cherished savor: Pollock, *Billy Graham*, p. 16.

110   "I have something to tell you, Billy": Ibid., p. 16.

111   Indicated he seemed spiritually frivolous: High, p. 75.

113   "I learned something of the crucified life": Graham speech to Trinity graduating

PAGE

class, quoted on inside cover of booklet by W. T. Watson, "The Bible School Days of Billy Graham" (Dunedin, Fla., n.d.).

113   Autumn's cool weather: Graham, *McCall's* (April, 1964).

114   "Lord, if you want me, you've got me": Charles T. Cook, *The Billy Graham Story* (Wheaton, Ill.; van Kampen Press, 1954), p. 29; High, p. 77.
  "How does one know God's call?": Graham, "God Is My Witness," *McCall's* (May, 1964), p. 118.

116   "They sat me with her family": Mary Bishop, Charlotte *Observer* (Feb. 6, 1977).

117   "Serious moral defections": Pollock, *Billy Graham,* p. 15.

118   "It was the best, if most difficult": Graham, *McCall's* (April, 1964).

119   "They are free in a way": William G. McLoughlin, Jr., *Billy Graham: Revivalist in a Secular Age* (New York: Ronald Press, 1960), p. 154.
  Haze of flies around shirt: as reported in unpublished monograph by John Pollock and provided to author by BGEA.

120   "When I was seventeen, eighteen, nineteen": "Billy Graham: The Sickness of Sodom," *Time* (July 11, 1969), pp. 65–66.
  "You'll never make it to the top": Sherwood Eliot Wirt, *Crusade at the Golden Gate* (New York: Harper & Brothers, 1959).
  "A terrible tyrant": Borchert, Charlotte *News* (Sept. 24, 1958).
  "Will damn your soul": AP dispatch, Charlotte *News* (Oct. 2, 1959).
  "In the Soviet Union, Cuba": "Billy Graham: The Sickness of Sodom," *Time* (July 11, 1969).

121   "Can be a driving dynamo": Pollock, *Billy Graham,* p. 254.
  "I am true to my wife": Bob Slough, Charlotte *News* (Oct. 18, 1958).
  Haunted by story of Samson: George Burnham and Lee Fisher, *Billy Graham and the New York Crusade* (Grand Rapids, Mich.: Zondervan, 1957), p. 161; High, p. 17.
  Pulled by his own appeals: High, p. 77.
  "He has doubts, but not for long": Ibid., p. 59.

122   Remarks on death: "The Preaching and the Power," *Newsweek* (July 20, 1970), pp. 50–55; Billy Graham, "Through the Valley of the Shadow," the *Reader's Digest* (April, 1971), pp. 107–110.

123   "Heard another preacher preach": Bob Saiṇ, Charlotte *News* (Dec. 27, 1949).
  "Didn't start preaching just to show a girl": Houston, *Holiday* (Feb., 1958).
  "Pessimists": AP dispatch, Charlotte *Observer* (March 14, 1966).
  "I don't think the function of the playwright": "Billy Graham: The Sickness of Sodom," *Time* (July 11, 1969).

124   "What would have happened to Lee Harvey Oswald?": UPI dispatch, Charlotte *Observer* (March 31, 1964).

126   "Father, mother with gray hairs": McLoughlin, *Billy Graham: Revivalist in a Secular Age,* p. 126.
  "At the invitation": Edward B. Fiske, in Charlotte *Observer* (June 15, 1969).
  Had to wade through a swim of hounds: Pollock, *Billy Graham,* p. 15.

127   First single-handed invitation call: Ibid., p. 20.

129   Baptized with his converts: Harold Martin, "Billy Graham," the *Saturday Evening Post* (April 13, 1963), p. 17.

132   *One day, there'll be many:* High, p. 77.

133   Offer of subsidy while caddying: Pollock, *Billy Graham,* p. 23.

134   In clomping plowboy brogans: High, p. 112.

PAGE

135   Students remember him red of eye: Gerald Strober, *Graham: A Day in Billy's Life* (London: Hodder and Stoughton, 1977).

136   "Most devout girl on campus": Brochert, Charlotte *News* (Sept. 11, 1958).
"Mother had always hoped we wouldn't look like the pickings": High, p. 118.
"I remember the light in her face": Brochert, Charlotte *News* (Sept. 11, 1958).
"That the Lord would let her be a martyr": John Pollock, *A Foreign Devil in China* (London: Hodder and Stoughton, 1972).

137   "Hearing gunshots somewhere in the distance": Linda Raney and Joan Gage, "Mrs. Billy Graham: Teaching Children to Believe in God," the *Ladies' Home Journal* (Dec., 1972), p. 84.
Thumbtacked newspapers over walls: Pollock, *A Foreign Devil in China*, p. 105.
Would read to them from Dickens, Uncle Remus: Ibid., p. 88.
Put on minstrel shows: Ibid., p. 89.
Awoke with rats coiling over them: Ibid., p. 85.
Mrs. Bell would retire with a migraine: Ibid., p. 85.
Sang at funeral, Bell wrote afterward: Ibid., pp. 91–92.

138   Denied sugar on porridge: Ibid., p. 84.
Consigned books to flames: Ibid., p. 162.
Ruth's *amah* had supplied small girls to teahouses: Bell, the *Ladies' Home Journal.*
Sang, *"There is a fountain":* Pollock, *A Foreign Devil in China*, p. 83.
"Daddy, I'm such a sinner": Ibid., p. 87.
"The chinese have not changed": Ibid., p. 112.

139   "She has just always been that way": Herbert Weiner, "Billy Graham: Respectable Evangelism," *Commentary* (Sept., 1957), pp. 257–262.

140   Talked for first time under tree: Pollock, *Billy Graham*, p. 25.
"Just met a wonderful girl": Graham, *McCall's* (April, 1964).
"If you wish to give me the privilege": High, p. 122.

141   "Our attraction was spiritual": Graham, *McCall's* (April, 1964).
"Didn't have enough time to go to ball games": Pollock, *Billy Graham*, p. 26.
How can I sit through all this?: High, p. 87.
"Daniel was prime minister": Ibid., pp. 87–88.

142   Flinging his arm wide: Ibid., p. 123.

144   Some thirty-five souls who worshiped in basement: Martin, the *Saturday Evening Post.*

145   Convened at a local dining retreat: Pollock, *Billy Graham*, p. 30.
Red, blue, and amber stage lights: George Beverly Shea with Fred Bauer, *Then Sings My Soul* (Old Tappan, N.J.: Revell, 1968), p. 87.
"From the friendly church": High, p. 140.

148   Had forged through about every state: McLoughlin, *Billy Graham: Revivalist in a Secular Age*, pp. 40–41.
Home no more than two or three months: Burnham, *Billy Graham: A Mission Accomplished*, p. 155.
"Who's him?": undated biographical memorandum on Graham in files of Charlotte *News-Observer*, circa mid-fifties.
"Looks just like a movie star": Ansley Ketchin, Charlotte *Observer* (Aug. 1, 1955).
"Have both had to be dedicated": George Cornell for AP, Charlotte *Observer* (April 8, 1960).

149   "Neither your father nor I feel": High, p. 120.
Never saw even the blink of a tear: unpublished monograph by Pollock provided to author by BGEA.
"You get used to it": Dorothy Wallace, Charlotte *Observer* (April 12, 1967).

PAGE

150 "Typical of our forefathers' ingenuity": Bell, the *Ladies' Home Journal.*
Blue shutters, hooked rugs, calico dolls: Titcomb, Charlotte *Observer* (April 27, 1964); Marjorie Marsh, Charlotte *News* (April 23, 1966).
Dogs had to be chained: Charlotte *Observer* (April 12, 1967).

150–151 Had children listen to his broadcasts: Graham, *McCall's* (May, 1964).

151 "There's nothing greatly stimulating": Borchert, Charlotte *News* (Sept. 11, 1958).
Sewing, reading, gardening: Charlotte *Observer* (April 12, 1967).
"Since I don't enjoy housework": Brochert, Charlotte *News* (Sept. 11, 1958).
Her light would be burning: unpublished Pollock monograph from BGEA.
"Had felt called for mission work": Bell, the *Ladies' Home Journal.*

152 "Of the woman, God said": Ann Sawyer, Charlotte *News* (Oct. 13, 1958).
Polishing shoes of other ladies: Burnham, *Billy Graham: A Mission Accomplished,* p. 142.
"Not right to go off and leave them": Barbara Brawley, Charlotte *Observer* (May 16, 1957).

152–153 Encounters with strip-teaser: High, p. 181.

153 "Wait till we get to Heaven": Ibid., p. 131.
"Unquestionable physical charm": Bell, the *Ladies' Home Journal.*

154 "I should like to see Bill oftener": Borchert, Charlotte *News* (Sept. 11, 1958).
Barrows converted at eleven: Cook, *The Billy Graham Story,* p. 78.

155 "God moved over these children": Donald E. Hoke, "Harvesting at the Revival," in *Revival in Our Time* (Grand Rapids, Mich.: Van Kampen, 1950), p. 47.
"No escape from life": Wirt, p. 102.
Waked by mother's soprano: Shea, p. 18.
"Impressed by the life-expectancy charts": Ibid., p. 45.

156 "Line which made me uncomfortable": Ibid., p. 16.
"For sacred singing, however": Ibid., p. 69.

159 Like boys' summer-camp japeries: Lee Fisher, *A Funny Thing Happened on the Way to the Crusade* (Carol Stream, Ill.: Creation House, 1974), pp. 16–17.

160 With bands, magicians, a hundred pianos: High, p. 140; Pollock, *Billy Graham,* p. 33.
"Used every modern means": McLoughlin, *Billy Graham: Revivalist in a Secular Age,* p. 38.
A bare little office: Mel Larson, "Tasting Revival," in *Revival in Our Time,* p. 24.

161 Carried a disquieting familiarity: McLoughlin, *Billy Graham: Revivalist in a Secular Age,* p. 38.
Such interests as William Randolph Hearst: High, p. 142; Pollock, *Billy Graham,* p. 35

162 Styled delivery after Winchell and Pearson: High, p. 89; Pollock, *Billy Graham,* p. 85.
Reharsed poses before mirror: Jim Shumaker, Charlotte *Observer* (Jan. 8, 1975).

164 Interest by Hearst had grown to such a point: Pollock, *Billy Graham,* p. 35.
Had entourage kneel on runway: High, p. 215.

166 "If they had realized what the war had meant": Pollock, *Billy Graham,* p. 36.

167 Traveled 750,000 miles: McLoughlin, *Billy Graham: Revivalist in a Secular Age,* p. 41.
Restored with check for seven thousand dollars: Pollock, *Billy Graham,* p. 40.

173 An enthusiasm about him personally: McLoughlin, *Billy Graham: Revivalist in a Secular Age,* p. 43.

175 Riley phased into anti-Semitic, anti-Catholic evangelism: Ibid., pp. 41–42.
Riley's charge to Graham: Graham, "God Is My Witness," *McCall's* (May, 1964); Pollock, *Billy Graham,* p. 42; High, p. 145.

176 Hailing trustees as "Dear Gang": Pollock, *Billy Graham,* p. 44.

Beating over the country ten months out of year: McLoughlin, *Billy Graham: Revivalist in a Secular Age,* p. 42.

178 "Enamored of intellectualism": Graham, *McCall's* (May, 1964).

182 "Terrific pain at the base of my skull": Pollock, *Billy Graham,* p. 51.

183 "Much confession was made": J. Edwin Orr, "Preparing for the Revival," in *Revival in Our Time,* p. 36.

How a brown cow could eat green grass: Pollock, *Billy Graham,* p. 53.

184 "Voice of commanding authority": undated biographical memorandum in Charlotte *News-Observer* files, circa mid-fifties.

"Don't care what the scientist has to say": sermon by Billy Graham in *Revival in Our Time,* p. 144.

"You may laugh at me down here": John Kilgo, Charlotte *News* (Oct. 16, 1958).

186 Canceled colloquy with critic: AP dispatch, Charlotte *Observer* (Sept. 7, 1967).

191 With names of virtuosos on balconies: High, p. 147.

Headed by Hollywood Togs president: McLoughlin, *Billy Graham: Revivalist in a Secular Age,* p. 45.

192 Sudden unloading of rain: Graham, *McCall's* (May, 1964).

Sacred duets, organist, gospel-violinist: Cliff Barrows, "Singing during Revival," in *Revival in Our Time,* pp. 40–41.

"If we're not guilty of one thing": as in sermon reported by Willmar L. Thorkelson, "Billy Graham Draws Throngs," *Christian Century* (Oct. 25, 1950), pp. 1270–1271.

194 Local radio personality named Stuart Hamblen: Hamblen background from Lewis Gillenson, *Billy Graham and Seven Who Were Saved* (New York: Pocket Books, 1968), pp. 171–194.

196 Long-distance runner named Louis Zamperini: Zamperini background from Pollock, *Billy Graham,* p. 63; High, pp. 149, 255–266; *Revival in Our Time,* pp. 16–17.

A gentleman named Jim Vaus: Vaus background from Gillenson, pp. 89–116; High, p. 149; Pollock, *Billy Graham,* p. 59; *Revival in Our Time,* p. 17; Houston, *Holiday* (Feb., 1958).

198 "Have heard the radio story of Mr. Truman": sermon in *Revival in Our Time,* p. 122.

"Area marked out for first bomb . . . more rampant in Los Angeles . . . a desperate choice . . . if Rome could not escape . . . world divided into two camps . . . may be God's last great call": Ibid., pp. 70–80.

199 "I want you to see Amos": Ibid., pp. 124–125.

201 *Puff Graham:* High, p. 148.

"Hearst papers gave me publicity": "Heaven, Hell & Judgment," *Time* (March 20, 1950), p. 72.

Then *AP,* then *UPI:* McLoughlin, *Billy Graham: Revivalist in a Secular Age,* pp. 49–50.

"That God uses the press": Graham, *McCall's* (May, 1964).

202 "You've been kissed by William Randolph Hearst": Pollock, *Billy Graham,* p. 59.

"Judgment Day is fast approaching": "Billy Graham Today," *Newsweek* (Sept. 2, 1963), pp. 74–75.

"Rarely do I find an atheist": "Sickle for the Harvest," *Time* (Nov. 14, 1949), pp. 63–69.

"Why, in Los Angeles": Sain, Charlotte *News* (Dec. 27, 1949).

204 "The weaker I became physically": Graham, *McCall's* (May, 1964).

Again pacing caverns of insomnia: Ibid.

"Better get out here fast": Pollock, *Billy Graham,* p. 61.

Attendance had totaled 350,000: McLoughlin, *Billy Graham: Revivalist in a Secular Age,* p. 51.

Heaviest smog in city's history: Orr, in *Revival in Our Time,* p. 38.

PAGE

205   Then sank back down, shaken: Larson, in *Revival in Our Time*, p. 271.

214   "Preaches the life of certitude": Donald Meyer, "Billy Graham — and Success," *New Republic* (Aug. 22, 1955), pp. 8–10.
"The Eisenhower era was a time": Graham, *McCall's* (May, 1964).
"Could have just patted man on back": Fiske in Charlotte *Observer*, (June 15, 1969).
"Like the rich fool in Luke": McLoughlin, *Billy Graham: Revivalist in a Secular Age*, p. 83.

215   "Yearning remains for something deeper": Weiner, *Commentary*.
"A Baptist uneasy in his Buick": the *New Republic*.

216   Clouds would hang at bay: Pollock, *Billy Graham*, p. 71; Jerry Beavan, "New England Revival," in *Revival in Our Time*, p. 66.
Just as the newspapers were in a free-for-all: Houston, *Holiday* (Feb., 1958).

217   Sapphire-blue suit, cowboy belt: "Personality" profile, *Time* (Nov. 17, 1952), p. 47.
Sombrero, blue suede shoes: Wirt, p. 46.
"Nothing in Bible which says I must wear rags": E. J. Kahn, "The Wayward Press," the *New Yorker* (June 8, 1957), pp. 117–123.
Four or five showers a day: "The New Evangelist," *Time* (Oct. 25, 1954).
"Gets the poison out": Pollock, *Billy Graham*, p. 71.
Four meals daily: "The New Evangelist," *Time* (Oct. 25, 1954).
Stalking the room in pajamas, baseball cap, before mirror: "Personality" profile, *Time* (Nov. 17, 1952).

218   Joke about mother-in-law: Dick Young Jr., Charlotte *News* (Sept. 22, 1958).
Through "painful cultivation": Houston, *Holiday* (Feb., 1958).
"Now, T. K. Chesterton says": Graham, "The Cure for Discouragement," the *American Mercury* (Aug., 1955), pp. 96–100.
Heaven a cube-shaped affair: Richard Rovere, "Letter from Washington," the *New Yorker* (Feb. 23, 1952), p. 78.

219   "Going to have a new body": sermon in *Revival in Our Time*, p. 148.
"Will be weeping and wailing": "Heaven, Hell & Judgment," *Time* (March 20, 1950).

220   Survey in Seattle: "Billy Graham's Seattle Campaign," *Christian Century* (April 23, 1952), pp. 494–496.
Moody had first developed such devices as: McLoughlin, *Billy Graham: Revivalist in a Secular Age*, p. 17.
From Billy Sunday, Graham grafted pattern: William G. McLoughlin, Jr., "Billy Graham," the *Nation* (May 11, 1957), pp. 403–410.
So many reserved church parties once: McLoughlin, *Billy Graham: Revivalist in a Secular Age*, p. 58.

221   Dropped to knees in pajamas: Pollock, *Billy Graham*, p. 81.
"Lord, you know I'm doing all that I can": Ibid., pp. 81–82; Brochert, Charlotte *News* (Sept. 16, 1958).
"Won't be seeking you out": High, pp. 163–165; Brochert, Charlotte *News* (Sept. 16, 1958).

222   Two special sections added: McLoughlin, *Billy Graham: Revivalist in a Secular Age*, p. 61.

223   "Have read the reports in the press": Interview, "New Crusade in Europe," *U.S. News and World Report* (Aug. 27, 1954), pp. 82–90.
"People will respond to a smile": Houston, "Billy Graham," *Holiday* (March, 1958), pp. 80–81.
Mentioning reporters' names to congregations: Kahn, the *New Yorker*.
"When one hundred prominent Americans": Graham, UPI, Charlotte *Observer* (April 20, 1962).

224 "All started here 14 years ago": "Protestants: Crusader in the Coliseum," *Time* (Sept. 6, 1963), pp. 53–54.
"Make it a point to keep up with the news": Graham, *McCall's* (May, 1964).

225 "Message for these crisis days": McLoughlin, *Billy Graham: Revivalist in a Secular Age*, p. 110.
Kilgallen, Kempton comments: Kahn, the *New Yorker*.
Enjoyed the largest audience: Shea, p. 132.
In some seventy-three newspapers: "Billy Graham: Young Thunderer of Revival," *Newsweek* (Feb. 1, 1954), pp. 42–46.

226 Sixty percent of his congregations women: Linda Blandford for the London Sunday *Times*, in Charlotte *Observer* (June 4, 1966).

227 "First of all, he was handsome": Charlotte *News* (Oct. 8, 1958).

228 Great nemesis was vanity: High, p. 22.
Colics of ill temper: "Personality" profile, *Time* (Nov. 17, 1952).
"My name has been printed": Charlotte *Observer* (Jan. 8, 1958).

229 Originally a Wall Street broker: The data on Maguire is from "Maguire of the Mercury," *Newsweek* (Aug. 25, 1952), p. 49; "Trouble for the Mercury," *Time* (Dec. 8, 1952), p. 42.

231 "Story of the free-enterprise system": McLoughlin, *Billy Graham: Revivalist in a Secular Age*, pp. 98–99.
A $50,000 bequest from two enthusiasts: Pollock, *Billy Graham*, p. 101.

232 "Willing to go to any end": UPI dispatch, Charlotte *Observer* (Oct. 3, 1959).
"Whether the story of Christ is told in a huge stadium": Clarence Hall, "The Charisma of Billy Graham," the *Reader's Digest* (July, 1970), pp. 88–92.
"A prominent Asheville businessman": Sain, Charlotte *News* (Dec. 27, 1949).
"A higher-type social strata": Rovere, the *New Yorker*.
"A perpetually guilty conscience": McLoughlin, the *Nation* (May 11, 1957).

234 "Highest of moral principles": "Billy's Apostles," *Newsweek* (June 23, 1969), p. 65.
"To the urban masses": McLoughlin, *Billy Graham: Revivalist in a Secular Age*, p. 17.
"Great power for good": Ibid., p. 204.

235 "God bless the Holiday Inns": Corry, *Harper's*.
"Best blueprint of government": Graham, "The Answer to Corruption," *Nation's Business* (Sept., 1969), pp. 46–49.

236 "No union dues": McLoughlin, *Billy Graham: Revivalist in a Secular Age*, p. 99.
"Would not stoop": Ibid., p. 100.
"America is under the pending judgment": AP dispatch, Charlotte *Observer* (June 22, 1951).
"Communism is creeping": Charlotte *Observer* (Nov. 23, 1947).
"Crack troops" be turned loose: McLoughlin, *Billy Graham: Revivalist in a Secular Age*, p. 113.

237 "In favor of building the strongest possible military": Charlotte *Observer* (Oct. 23, 1951).
Note from Eisenhower: Charlotte *Observer* (Dec. 6, 1951).
"Licked before the Communists get here": Thomas L. Robinson, Charlotte *News* (July 8, 1957).
"Needs a show of strength": Richard T. Stout for the Chicago *News* World Service, in Charlotte *Observer* (June 16, 1960).
"Paul was influential": Houston, *Holiday* (March, 1958).

238 "Eleven hundred social-sounding organizations": McLoughlin, *Billy Graham: Revivalist in a Secular Age*, p. 112.
"Then let's do it!": Ibid., p. 112.
"McCarthy . . . gone too far": Charlotte *Observer* (Oct. 25, 1951).

PAGE

"Communism is far worse": Charlotte *Observer* (Dec. 6, 1951).
Comparable to Nero's fiddling: McLoughlin, *Billy Graham: Revivalist in a Secular Age*, p. 112.

239   "Go loyally on in their work": "Still in Business with the Lord," the *Nation* (June 30, 1969), p. 814; McLoughlin, the *Nation* (May 11, 1957).
Standing in his shorts, discoursing: Gary, Charlotte *Observer* (Sept. 24, 1958).
"Hope they have a golf course": Kilgo, Charlotte *News* (Oct. 16, 1958).
"The Apostle Paul . . . said": Bob Quincy, Charlotte *Observer* (May 12, 1974).
"Golf demands control of temper": Bob Myers, Charlotte *News* (Sept. 20, 1968).
In his own game: Gary, Charlotte *Observer* (Sept. 24, 1958).

240   Would return to dictate sermon: Charlotte *News* (April 4, 1958).
Inaugurated new schedule of flights: George Burnham and Lee Fisher, *Billy Graham and the New York Crusade* (Grand Rapids, Mich.: Zondervan, 1957), p. 156.
Esso president proposed: Porter Munn, Charlotte *Observer* (Oct. 11, 1958).
Salesman of the year: UP dispatch, Charlotte *Observer* (March 1, 1958).
Horatio Alger award: Charlotte *Observer* (May, date unclear, 1965).
First devotional in Congress: AP dispatch, Charlotte *Observer* (April 27, 1950).
Sam Rayburn declared: Pollock, *Billy Graham*, p. 93.

242   "Evangelism's a tremendous factor": Interview, *U.S. News and World Report* (Aug. 27, 1954).

243   Pondering commitment at Montreat: Pollock, *Billy Graham*, p. 94.

244   "Only forty of these cards!": Houston, *Holiday*, (March, 1958).
Established headquarters on Pennsylvania Avenue: "Newsmakers" section, *Newsweek* (Dec. 19, 1955), p. 44.
Installed teletype: *Newsweek* (July 20, 1970).
"The U.N. is not willing": AP dispatch, Charlotte *Observer* (Dec. 11, 1961).
"Businessmen better get on their toes": Richard Maschal, Charlotte *Observer* (Nov. 5, 1971).

245   Testimony on bomb shelters: AP dispatch, Charlotte *Observer* (Jan. 29, 1962).
"Church getting too involved in politics": UPI dispatch, Charlotte *Observer* (Nov. 6, 1964).
"Church's duty to lead": Sam Covington, Charlotte *Observer* (Oct. 25, 1958).
"Have really stayed out of politics": Covington, Charlotte *Observer* (April 2, 1972).
"Remember the worst part of history": Corry, *Harper's*.
Phoned John Volpe: AP dispatch, Charlotte *Observer* (May 14, 1970).
Zoo bond issue: AP dispatch, Charlotte *Observer* (May 4, 1972).
Petition for zoning change: Paul Jablow, Charlotte *Observer* (March 29, 1966).

246   "Taxes make it imperative": Charlotte *Observer* (Jan. 19, 1966).
"I retract the statement": UPI disptach, Charlotte *Observer* (March 22, 1962).
"Feel free to kick me": UPI dispatch, Charlotte *Observer* (Dec. 31, 1971).

247   Inquiring if churchman irate: Strober, p. 61.
Confided to one Jewish journalist: Weiner, *Commentary*.
Encouraged Israel to hold steadfast: UPI dispatch, Charlotte *Observer* (Dec. 26, 1967).
When denied visa by Jordan: Brochert, Charlotte *News* (Dec. 5, 1959).

248   To avert "difficulties": Shea, p. 118.
"Is doing more harm to the cause": Charlotte *News* (March 4, 1966).
"Love Bob Jones Senior": "Boycotting Billy," *Time* (March 18, 1966), p. 66.
Submitted citation from Paul: High, p. 152.
"Few or many may be saved": Graham, *McCall's* (April, 1964).
"Peculiarly American brand of evangelism": Weiner, *Commentary*.

249   Newspaper scribe undertook to explain: Phyllis Battle for INS, in Charlotte *Observer* (Aug. 26, 1957).
Only programs he tended to watch: Houston, *Holiday* (March, 1958).

251   "Averaged between twenty-five and forty Congressmen": "Rockin' the Capitol," *Time* (March 3, 1952), p. 76.
Such unlikely acolytes as: Charlotte *Observer* (June 16, 1960).
Discounting reports he had inspired Clement: R. Covington, Charlotte *Observer* (Aug. 22, 1956).
"Every effort not to let it appear I favor": Houston, *Holiday* (March, 1958).
"Swimming in the nude at the YMCA": "Billy's Political Pitch," *Newsweek* (June 10, 1968), pp. 62–63.
"McCormack is the best friend": Houston, *Holiday* (March, 1958).
"I would say Daniel": the *Saturday Evening Post* (Spring, 1972).

252   "Never could I have dreamed": Graham, *McCall's* (April, 1964).
"Picked up the phone the other day": Titcomb, Charlotte *News* (Dec. 17, 1963).
In white suits: Martin, the *Saturday Evening Post.*

253   To be admitted nowhere near him: Charlotte *Observer* (Feb. 1, 1952).
"Guess he was just too busy": *Time* (March 3, 1952).
Audience with MacArthur: AP dispatch, Charlotte *Observer* (Feb. 23, 1952).
Dilated on Christians in Orient: McLoughlin, *Billy Graham: Revivalist in a Secular Age,* p. 115.
Put forward his own peace plan: Pollock, *Billy Graham,* p. 74.

253–254   Visa application nearly denied: AP dispatch, Charlotte *Observer* (around Dec. 2, 1952).

254   "Isn't it strange to you": McLoughlin, *Billy Graham: Revivalist in a Secular Age,* p. 116.
Present at the Last Judgment would be: Ibid., pp. 243–244.
Parallel between Truman and Adam: Ibid., p. 114.

255   "Mr. Sid, I can't get involved": Graham, "God Is My Witness," *McCall's* (June, 1964), p. 62.

256   "To agree there's a mess" . . . insure a "cleanup": McLoughlin, *Billy Graham: Revivalist in a Secular Age,* pp. 110, 117.
Eisenhower confided wanted to join church: Pollock, *Billy Graham,* p. 96.

257   "General, you can do more to inspire": Ibid., p. 96.
"Our hopes he would become spiritual leader": Frank Van Der Linden, Charlotte *Observer* (Nov. 4, 1953).
Compared Eisenhower foreign policy address to: McLoughlin, *Billy Graham: Revivalist in a Secular Age,* p. 117.
Compared as righteous judges: R. Covington, Charlotte *Observer* (Oct. 20, 1958).
"To see the President kneeling": Charlotte *Observer* (Aug. 5, 1955).

258   "We just discussed it": R. Covington, Charlotte *Observer* (Aug. 9, 1955).
Consulted Graham before Little Rock: Hall, the *Reader's Digest.*

259   Recommended Kennedy make another processional: AP dispatch, Charlotte *Observer* (March 14, 1962).
"Last week I had such a strong feeling": Harold Hammond, Charlotte *News* (Nov. 23, 1963).
"Just getting ready to tee off": Ibid.
Johnson "the best qualified man": Titcomb, Charlotte *News* (Dec. 17, 1963).

260   Conducting devotionals for Johnson: AP update (March 1, 1966) to biographical sketch (July 1, 1960) in Charlotte *News-Observer* files; AP dispatch, Charlotte *Observer* (July 19, 1965).
Johnson phoned him at Mayo Clinic: AP dispatch, Charlotte *Observer* (Sept. 10, 1965).
Big Brother of the Year award: AP dispatch, Charlotte *Observer* (May 11, 1965).
"Bought a pair . . . in every color": Jetton, Charlotte *Observer* (Sept. 20, 1968).

PAGE

262   "Was being called a crook": Charlotte *Observer* (May 20, 1965).
Would dispatch a jet to loft Graham: UPI dispatch, Charlotte *Observer* (Nov. 22, 1965).

265   Assisted in Connally inaugural: AP dispatch, Charlotte *Observer* (Nov. 25, 1963).
"Connally has the necessary abilities": AP dispatch, Charlotte *News* (Jan. 16, 1963).

266   As with Lieutenant Governor Bob Scott: Jablow, Charlotte *Observer* (Nov. 2, 1968).
Sixty thousand telegrams in one day: Strober, p. 94.
"Billy, you stay out of politics": AP dispatch, Charlotte *Observer* (Dec. 23, 1964).

267   "He is deeply interested in the opportunity": AP dispatch, Charlotte *Observer* (Feb. 1, 1964).
Acknowledged had mulled the prospect: UPI dispatch, Charlotte *Observer* (Feb. 2, 1964).
Promoted by H. L. Hunt: AP dispatch, Charlotte *Observer* (May 2, 1963).
"Why should I demote myself": Houston, *Holiday* (March, 1958).

268   Countess Mara ties: Robert Johnson, "Will the Real Christians Please Stand?" the University of North Carolina *Daily Tar Heel* (April 3, 1973).
Attended Johnson as he restlessly lumbered: R. Covington, Charlotte *Observer* (Jan. 17, 1969).

270   "It would be a tragedy if": Houston, *Holiday* (March, 1958).
"Homespun" show patterned after Arthur Godfrey: AP dispatch, Charlotte *Observer* (Jan. 29, 1954).
"Could make I don't know how many millions": AP biographical sketch (issued July 1, 1960) in Charlotte *News-Observer* files.

271   Budget of $40 million, nine hundred stations, "the exposure General Mills achieves," *Decision* to five million readers, eight million souls enrolled: Robert Hodierne, Charlotte *Observer* (Feb. 6, 1977).

272   A mail-order operation offering: Houston, *Holiday* (March, 1958); McLoughlin, *Billy Graham: Revivalist in a Secular Age*, p. 197.

274   "Appearance reduces the limitations": Strober, pp. 59–60.

278   Commence with ten minutes of Bible reading: High, p. 167–168.
Sunday organization ranked fifth most efficient: Houston, *Holiday* (March, 1958).
"More bounce to the ounce": Pollock, *Billy Graham*, p. 365.
"Dispensing world's greatest product": Ibid., p. 243.
"Work done in the name of Christ": Corry, *Harper's*.

279   100,000,000 pieces of mail sent out: Hodierne, Charlotte *Observer* (Feb. 6, 1977).
Donations average eight dollars: Strober, p. 102.
"Paul considered it just as spiritual": Houston, *Holiday* (March, 1958).
First payment came to $2.25: High, p. 79.

280   "Did the Lord ordain that they": Ibid.
Ushers hefting up collection sacks: Bishop, Charlotte *Observer* (Feb. 7, 1977).
Ruth, three associates on board: McLoughlin, the *Nation*.

281   Abstained from investments, savings account: Houston, *Holiday* (March, 1958).
Clerk mentioning account overdrawn: High, p. 127; R. Covington, Charlotte *Observer* (Sept. 29, 1958).
"Now conduct funerals, baptize": Graham, *McCall's* (April, 1964).
To find new home awaiting him: Martin, the *Saturday Evening Post;* High, p. 126; Borchert, Charlotte *News* (Sept. 11, 1958).

281–282   "Not to accept gifts of money": Charlotte *News* (Oct. 15, 1958).

282   "I just don't know how it happened": Simpson, Charlotte *News* (Jan. 28, 1970).
Spot of conversation with IRS: Gary and Polly Paddock, Charlotte *Observer* (June 30, 1973).

PAGE

283 Salary, sale of land left by father: Hodierne, Charlotte *Observer* (Feb. 6, 1977). $420,000 worth of acreages: Ibid.

285 "If Paul could look down here, he is champing": McLoughlin, the *Nation.* "Got the greatest product in the world": Martin, the *Saturday Evening Post;* Brochert, Charlotte *News* (Sept. 16, 1959).

286 Electronic imprint for every convert: McLoughlin, *Billy Graham: Revivalist in a Secular Age,* p. 152. "There is no more room": Pollock, *Billy Graham,* p. 191. Underline words with colored pencils: Brochert, Charlotte *News* (Sept. 15, 1958). Such orders of despair as: McLoughlin, *Billy Graham: Revivalist in a Secular Age,* p. 151. The Biblegraph: Ibid., p. 219.

287 "When the average, moral American": Pollock, *Billy Graham,* p. 180–181. "Deeply moving to watch the solemn audience": Ibid., p. 207.

288 "Lenin had only a small number": Interview, *U.S. News and World Report* (Aug. 27, 1954). In Fiji and New Guinea jungles: Martin, the *Saturday Evening Post.* Ham standing off in the shadows: R. Covington, Charlotte *Observer* (June 8, 1957).

289–290 Operation of Graham's crusade system: McLoughlin, the *Nation* and *Billy Graham: Revivalist in a Secular Age,* p. 165; High, pp. 153–154; Strober, p. 25; Houston, *Holiday* (March, 1958).

290 To muster a third of the expenses: McLoughlin, *Billy Graham: Revivalist in a Secular Age,* pp. 164–165.

291 "The better elements": Ibid., p. 252. All lost things found: Borchert, Charlotte *News* (Oct. 4, 1958): Charlotte *Observer* (Oct. 14, 1958). Taped over with blank paper: Brawley, Charlotte *Observer* (May 16, 1957). Concession stands supply: Charlotte *News* (Sept. 22, 1958). Would wait in backstage lounge: Bill Arthur, Charlotte *Observer* (April 9, 1972). Asked to mediate baseball strike: S. Covington, Charlotte *Observer* (April 9, 1973). "Mantle hit two home runs": Donald MacDonald, Charlotte *News* (Oct. 3, 1958). "A great stadium": Charlotte *News* (Oct. 1, 1958). Decision cards processed: Carol Moore, Charlotte *News* (April 7, 1972).

292 Patrons who were intrigued: McLoughlin, *Billy Graham: Revivalist in a Secular Age,* p. 159. "I walked around Valley Forge": Burnham and Fisher, p. 124–125. Executive committee was assembled: "Mighty City Hears Billy's Mighty Call," *Life* (May 27, 1957), pp. 20–27; Houston, *Holiday* (March, 1958). "If a corporation can spend eight million dollars": Houston, *Holiday* (March, 1958).

293 "Jesus Christ will be biggest topic": Burnham and Fisher, p. 185. Cast New York as Sodom: Milt Freudenheim, Charlotte *Observer* (May 16, 1957). "The center of art": "Billy Graham's 'Invasion,' " *Newsweek* (May 20, 1957), pp. 66–70. "Face the city in fear": Cornell for AP, in Charlotte *Observer* (March 145, 1957). "To be crucified by my critics": Burnham and Fisher, *Billy Graham: Man of God* (Westchester, Ill.: Good News Publishers, [no printing date]), p. 27; "Billy Graham's 'Invasion,' " *Newsweek* (May 20, 1957). "Acute undetermined infection": AP dispatch, Charlotte *Observer* (March 1, 1963). "If I ever . . . got the wrong idea about": Weiner, *Commentary.*

294 While perfecting his tan: S. Covington, Charlotte *Observer* (April 2, 1972). Stalking foot trails in windbreaker: Burnham and Fisher, *Billy Graham: Man of God,* pp. 24–25. "God! Help me!": Ibid., p. 25. "A fair audience ready before": "The New Evangelist," *Time* (Oct. 25, 1954).

Plowing garden, planting lawn: Cornell for AP, in Charlotte *Observer* (May 12, 1957).
Calisthenics, meditating: Helen Parks, Charlotte *News* (April 18, 1957).
Out of Times Square office suite: Houston, *Holiday* (March, 1958).
Troupes of assistants dispatched, "prayer" cells: Ibid.

295   Christian Tours arranged importation: Ibid.
"Nothing pious about confusion": S. Covington, Charlotte *Observer* (Jan. 21, 1972).
"Minimize wastage": Pollock, *Billy Graham*, p. 109.

296   Such as "inability to communicate": "God in the Garden," *Time* (May 27, 1957), p. 46.
Versed on such niceties as: High, p. 234.
"How the counselors and inquirers were placed together": Pollock, *Billy Graham*, p. 129.
650 billboards, 40,000 bumperstickers: Houston, *Holiday* (March, 1958).
"An advertisement for a Cadillac": "The New Evangelist," *Time* (Oct. 25, 1954).
"If some poor fishermen": UP dispatch, Charlotte *Observer* (May 17, 1957).
Provided him free suite: Houston, *Holiday* (March, 1958).
Beset with vague alarms: Shea, p. 151.

297   Sidewalk stroll the night before: "Mighty City Hears Billy's Mighty Call," *Life* (May 27, 1957).
Watching circus evacuate: *Ibid.;* "Billy in New York," *Time* (May 20, 1957), p. 104.
A wire from Roy Rogers: Kahn, the *New Yorker*.
Had thumbprints of tribesmen: Weiner, *Commentary*.

297–298   Entertainers headed by Jerome Hines: Houston, *Holiday* (March, 1958).

298   Special celebrity gallery: "Crusade Windup," *Time* (Sept. 9, 1957), p. 60.
Populated by: Shea, p. 149.
Perle Mesta effervesced: R. Covington, Charlotte *Observer* (June 4, 1957).
"Ah sinful nation": sermon in Burnham and Fisher, *Billy Graham and the New York Crusade*, pp. 51–53.
"Every time the nation went into . . . declension": Ibid., pp. 54–55.

299   "How the people must have listened!": Ibid., pp. 55–56.
"So felt the powers of darkness": High, p. 64.
Attributing sudden glower of temperature to: UP dispatch, Charlotte *Observer* (June 19, 1957).

300   "Man is scarcely recognizable": Burnham and Fisher, *Billy Graham and the New York Crusade*, p. 62.
"Our literature": Ibid.
Put the problems of man's condition as: Ibid., pp. 55–60.
"Read about a rock-and-roll star": Ibid., p. 72.
"Hemingway, who had four wives": McLoughlin, *Billy Graham: Revivalist in a Secular Age*, p. 128.
"The lilt and music is gone": Burnham and Fisher, *Billy Graham and the New York Crusade*, pp. 60–61.

301   "Explored the mysteries of the universe": Ibid., p. 57.
"Few people really want to do wrong": Ibid., p. 63.
"Know we don't like to face it": Ibid., p. 65.
Pulpit resembling a suburban patio: "Mighty City Hears Billy's Mighty Call," *Life* (May 23, 1957).
"To think tyrants of history": Charlotte *Observer* (June 17, 1957).
"Not easy for Pilate's wife": Graham, commentary in Charlotte *Observer* (Dec. 25, 1966).

302   " 'Shalt not commit adultery' ": Burnham and Fisher, *Billy Graham and the New York Crusade*, p. 110.
"Bad temper": Ibid., p. 166.

PAGE

"Drop them like a hot potato": Ibid., p. 115.
"Keep herself attractive": Ibid., pp. 116–117.

303 Left revival with curse on it all: Bill Hughes, Charlotte *News* (Oct. 9, 1958).
"A busy Senator": Burnham and Fisher, *Billy Graham: Man of God*, p. 30.
"Not a jolly fellow": Charles Kuralt, Charlotte *News* (May 22, 1957).
"A Western Union boy": Houston, *Holiday* (Feb., 1958).
"Feel as though I had a sword": McLoughlin, *Billy Graham: Revivalist in a Secular Age*, p. 124.
"Going to ask you to come now": Cornell for AP, in Charlotte *Observer* (June 3, 1957).

304 "To all the lonely people": Burnham and Fisher, *Billy Graham and the New York Crusade*, p. 68.
Descending by escalator: Weiner, *Commentary*.
"Inquirer's Name": Wirt, p. 86; "The New Evangelist," *Time* (Oct. 25, 1954).

305 Packet containing: McLoughlin, *Billy Graham: Revivalist in a Secular Age*, p. 401.
Special "runners" drafted: Charlotte *News* (April 4, 1972).

306 The more novel effects reported were: McLoughlin, *Billy Graham: Revivalist in a Secular Age*, p. 247–248.
"I read criticisms": Pollock, *Billy Graham*, p. 260.
Faces collected below him blank: Houston, *Holiday* (March, 1958); Weiner, *Commentary*; "Dedicated Deciders in Billy Graham's Crusade," *Life* (July 1, 1957), pp. 86–91.
"Broken families reunited": High, p. 63.
Hotels reported silverware returned: Charlotte *Observer* (March 4, 1954).

307 "I wanted to rid myself of mine": "Dedicated Deciders in Billy Graham's Crusade," *Life* (July 1, 1957).
"Since that night I have felt": High, p. 213.
Impact eludes computations: "Crusade's Impact," *Time* (July 8, 1957), pp. 57–58.
"A quickening of the spirit": "Crusade Windup," *Time* (Sept. 9, 1957).
"In the lives of ministers": Pollock, *Billy Graham*, p. 145.
"I noticed one young girl": Ibid., p. 121.
He now noted smiles: AP dispatch, Charlotte *Observer* (Aug. 30, 1957).

308 "Ambiguity of all human virtues": Dr. Reinhold Niebuhr, "Liberalism, Individualism and Billy Graham," *Christian Century* (May 23, 1956), pp. 640–642.
"Have read nearly everything Mr. Niebuhr has written": Houston, *Holiday* (Feb., 1958).
"Things we should settle": Charlotte *News* (April 8, 1966).
"Talked to him just this morning": UPI dispatch, Charlotte *Observer* (March 1, 1966).

309 "Revivalism must be commercial": McLoughlin, "The Revival of Revivalism," *Christian Century* (June 24, 1959), pp. 743–745.
"Pep-rally for middle-class church-goers": McLoughlin, the *Nation*.

310 Reserved for out-of-town delegations: Ibid.
As far away as Houston: "Billy Graham's 'Invasion,'" *Newsweek* (May 20, 1957).

311 Carrying Bibles and binoculars: "Mass Conversions," *Christian Century* (May 29, 1957), pp. 677–679.
"Not the sophisticated city that I first thought": R. Covington, Charlotte *Observer* (June 7, 1957); AP dispatch, Charlotte *Observer* (June 26, 1957).
Installing one black on staff: "Crusade's Impact," *Time* (July 8, 1957).
Corridors impacted with his faithful: Burnham and Fisher, *Billy Graham and the New York Crusade*, p. 98.
Once greeted on elevator: Ibid., p. 143.

312 Processional along Bowery: "Crusade's Impact," *Time* (July 8, 1957).
Such ceremonies as: Houston, *Holiday* (March, 1958).
One service on Wall Street: Burnham and Fisher, *Billy Graham and the New York Crusade*, pp. 126–127.

PAGE

312–313 Telecasts encompassed more millions than: Ibid., p. 138.

313 "You seemed to talk directly to me": Ibid., p. 100.
"Do come Saturday night": Houston, *Holiday* (Feb., 1958).
With the total expenses of one Tennessee crusade: McLoughlin, *Billy Graham: Revivalist in a Secular Age,* p. 201.
The costs of a movie documentary: Ibid., pp. 61–62.
From the surplus in New York: Ibid., pp. 201–202.

314 Voices thundering the hymn: Burnham and Fisher, *Billy Graham and the New York Crusade,* p. 140.
Nixon striding with him: Ibid., pp. 139–140.

315 "I didn't fill this place": Ibid., pp. 140–141.
Times Square rally: Ibid., pp. 189–190.
"First thing I did was to go up in the woods": AP dispatch, Charlotte *Observer* (Sept. 27, 1957).

316 Myriad attritions of the flesh: High, pp. 18, 176; Pollock, *Billy Graham,* pp. 94, 135–137, 184–185, 190, 232, 245; Bell, the *Ladies' Home Journal;* "Billy Graham: Young Thunderer of Revival," *Newsweek* (Feb. 1, 1954); Charlotte *Observer* (March 12, 1965; Sept. 22, 1966; July 11, 1967; Nov. 28, 1967); Charlotte *News* (Sept. 19, 1968; Jan. 16, 1975).
Implored of T. W. Wilson: Corry, *Harper's.*
Gulped from bottle of hair-tonic: Bell, the *Ladies' Home Journal.*
Insisting had to begin preaching less: Charlotte *Observer* (May 22, 1964).
"Do not enjoy living in hotel bedrooms": Graham, *McCall's* (April, 1964).
"Something is always breaking out": "Protestants: Crusader in the Coliseum," *Time* (Sept. 6, 1963).

317 "He spanked me": unpublished Pollock monograph provided by BGEA.
Would abruptly nudge away: Ibid.
"Did not ask for this assignment": Graham, "What Ten Years Have Taught Me," *Christian Century* (Feb. 17, 1960), p. 180.
"They come": Graham, *McCall's* (April, 1964).
"Wish the Lord would just take me": "The Preaching and the Power," *Newsweek* (July 20, 1970).

318 "Idea I was coming with a Texas sombrero": Interview, *U.S. News and World Report* (Aug. 27, 1954).
Shipped over with him Roy Rogers: AP dispatch, Charlotte *Observer* (Feb. 18, 1954); "Billy Graham: Young Thunderer of Revival," *Newsweek* (Feb. 1, 1954).
"What do you know about the suffering": Brunham, *Billy Graham: A Mission Accomplished,* p. 133.

419 "The sort of simple charm": "Crusade for Britain," *Time* (March 8, 1954), pp. 72–74.
Brochure peddled for twelve dollars: Pollock, *Billy Graham,* p. 113, 116.

319 Insisted all a misprint: McLoughlin, *Billy Graham: Revivalist in a Secular Age,* p. 104.
"We can say good-bye to England": Ibid., p. 102.
To challenge its drift into: Ibid., p. 102.
"Caught him on the high seas": Ibid., p. 105.
"I am not anti-Socialist": Ibid.
"Can say what you like about socialism": Ibid., p. 222.
"Ever man was stripped of confidence": Pollock, *Billy Graham,* p. 119.

320 All the doing of the U.S. ambassador: Houston, *Holiday* (Feb., 1958).
Seized by savage headache: High, p. 176.
Night forbidding, transported by furnished chauffeur: Houston, *Holiday* (Feb., 1958).
In back seat holding hands: Graham, *McCall's* (May, 1964).
"On the platform were bishops": Houston, *Holiday* (Feb., 1958).

Accumulation of ranking converts: Ibid.

Affronted by publicity: Ibid.

Times remarked in surprise: Ibid.

320–321 Subdued his wardrobe, Barrows forsook trombone: Houston, *Holiday* (Feb., 1958); Pollock, *Billy Graham,* p. 127.

321 "That's right, Brother Archbishop": Graham, *McCall's* (May, 1964).

Commons gave honorary luncheon: Houston, *Holiday* (Feb., 1954).

Claridges reception funded by Richardson: Pollock, *Billy Graham,* p. 117.

Confined himself to orange juice: High, p. 175.

"I am your waiter": Bell, the *Ladies' Home Journal.*

"Who was the most charming person": Graham, *McCall's* (June, 1964).

Shook hand of butler: Martin, the *Saturday Evening Post.*

Churchill nudged into the courtesy by: Pollock, *Billy Graham,* p. 131.

322 "I am filled with hope!": Ibid., p. 131.

Profusion of camera lights: "When Billy Graham Saved Scotland," R. B. Robertson, *The Atlantic* (June, 1957), pp. 39–45.

323 Subsequent scrutiny of seven Glasgow churches: the *Nation* (Feb. 8, 1958), p. 110.

France "without a mainspring": "Billy in Germany," *Time* (July 5, 1954), p. 48.

"Why are you unfaithful": UPI dispatch, Charlotte *Observer* (May 13, 1963).

"*Voilà* Beelee": "Billy's Conquest," *Newsweek* (July 12, 1954), p. 68.

Gallery of cognac advertisements: High, p. 188.

Lighting around him fluttered: Houston, *Holiday* (Feb., 1958).

324 Congregation chanting, "Beelee": "Billy Graham in Paris," *Time* (June 20, 1955), p. 53.

Bussed by portly cleric: Ibid.

Succession of kidney attacks: "Billy's Conquest," *Newsweek* (July 12, 1954).

In Nuremberg's stadium: Burnham, *Billy Graham: A Mission Accomplished,* pp. 134–135.

Two-thousand-voice choir pealing anthems: "Billy's Conquest," *Newsweek* (July 12, 1954).

"Tremendous power of modern Germany": "The Conquest of Berlin," *Newsweek* (Oct. 10, 1960), p. 98.

Loosed practice rounds of artillery: Pollock, *Billy Graham,* p. 136.

Refused to remove Tiergarten tent: AP dispatch, Charlotte *Observer* (Sept. 29, 1960).

325 Blared into the Eastern sector: UPI dispatch, Charlotte *Observer* (Oct. 30, 1960).

In Lima bullring: "Billy in Catholic Country: He Collides with Clergy," *Time* (Feb. 23, 1962), pp. 77–78.

Bundled out of Maracaibo state hall: AP dispatch, Charlotte *Observer* (Jan. 24, 1962).

"There was not one jeer": "Triumph of Tolerance," *Newsweek* (Feb. 26, 1962), pp. 58–59.

Rebuffed by Catholic church: "Billy in Catholic Country: He Collides with Clergy," *Time* (Feb. 23, 1962).

Colombia mayor denied stadium: "Triumph of Tolerance," *Newsweek* (Feb. 26, 1962).

326 Manila archbishop admonished Catholics: "Billy in Manila," *Time* (Feb. 27, 1956), p. 76.

"The place was very clean": Burnham, *To the Far Corners: With Billy Graham in Asia* (Westwood, N.J.: Revell, 1956), pp. 99–100.

Communism "slowed down to a walk": AP dispatch, Charlotte *Observer* (March 20, 1956).

"Can't help but admire Syngman Rhee": Burnham, *To the Far Corners: With Billy Graham in Asia,* p. 129.

327 She "had ceased to think on earthly things": Ibid., pp. 111–112.

Assured party officials, "obey those in authority": "Billy's Communist Rally," *Newsweek* (July 24, 1967), p. 71.

PAGE

In a vacuum of any crowds: "Billy in Moscow," *Time* (June 29, 1959), p. 40.
"Religion still alive here": Ibid.
"Over the . . . Kremlin — the cross!": UPI dispatch, Charlotte *Observer* (June 15, 1959).

328   Acclaimed "moral purity" of Soviets: "Billy in Moscow," *Time* (June 29, 1959).
"So embarrassed" in London parks: "People" section, *Time* (June 22, 1959), p. 36; AP dispatch, Charlotte *Observer* (June 9, 1959).

329   From departure shed on snowing afternoon: Tom McMahan, *Safari for Souls: With Billy Graham in Africa* (Columbia, S.C.: the *State-Record* Company, 1960), p. 14.
Reeling descent into Dakar: Ibid., p. 14.
Stray wire shocked Barrows: Ibid., p. 26.

330   Nkrumah had his mother hymned: Ibid., p. 27.
What thinned Accra attendance: AP dispatch, Charlotte *Observer* (Jan. 26, 1960).
Wash-and-wear suits: McMahan, *Safari for Souls; With Billy Graham in Africa*, p. 12.

331   "How could mighty God speak to us": "Mission's End," *Time* (March 28, 1960), p. 63.
"You've told lies, done all these bad things": McMahan, p. 105.
"You've seen the storm come": Ibid.
Merely stood watching him under parasols: "Mission's End," *Time* (March 28, 1960).

332   Carried on litter, nearly spilled: McMahan, pp. 61–62.
Would yelp in plane cockpit: Ibid., p. 52.
"Where Tarzan could have swung": Ibid., p. 9.
Congregations soberly dressed townspeople: AP dispatch, Charlotte *Observer* (Jan. 24, 1960).
"Trying to bring Christ to our ancient land": "Mission's End," *Time* (March 28, 1960).

333   Wandered into mud-hut village: AP dispatch, Charlotte *Observer* (Feb. 29, 1960).
"We having some party": "Mission's End," *Time* (March 28, 1960).
Settled on grass with them: AP dispatch, Charlotte *Observer* (Feb. 29, 1960).
Replied, "When you have Christ": "Mission's End," *Time* (March 28, 1960).
"With his skin peeled off": "Moslems vs. Billy," *Time* (Feb. 15, 1960), p. 86.

334   Beleaguered by insomnia: "Mission's End," *Time* (March 28, 1960).
Saw missionaries' children below him, wept: McMahan, p. 66.
Governor Daniel proclaimed: Burnham and Fisher, *Billy Graham and the New York Crusade*, p. 172.
First consulted with Dulles: Pollock, *Billy Graham*, p. 163.
Christian message "to the masses": McLoughlin, *Billy Graham: Revivalist in a Secular Age*, p. 119.
"Not proselytize any Hindus": AP dispatch, Charlotte *Observer* (Jan. 16, 1957).
With thermos filled from sink: Burnham, *To the Far Corners: With Billy Graham in Asia*, p. 13.

335   Read from Ephesians: Ibid., p. 16.
Pilot slowed plane at Sinai: Ibid., p. 16–17.
Stumbling through rank streets: Ibid., p. 74.
Watched corpses burning: Ibid., p. 73.

336   Temple pool of "stagnant, dirty water": Ibid., p. 43.
Happened into a shrine to Siva: Ibid., p. 79–80.
"Dark-skinned young men completely dedicated": Ibid., p. 69.
Greeted in missionary orphan compound: Ibid., p. 65–66.

337   "Graham can be dreadfully effective": P. Lal, "Billy Graham in India," the *Nation* (April 7, 1957), pp. 276–277.
"Very friendly article": "'Billy in India," *Time* (Feb. 13, 1956), p. 72.
Surmised of Hammerskjold's glance: Burnham, *To the Far Corners: With Billy Graham in Asia*, p. 57.

PAGE

Found Nehru glum: Ibid., p. 61; Houston, *Holiday* (Feb., 1958).
Expansively assured Nehru: Ibid.
Fingered letter-opener, glanced at ceiling: Houston, *Holiday* (Feb., 1958).

338 "Christ can do that for everybody!": *Ibid.*
"Strong impression he was pro-Christian": Burnham, *To the Far Corners: With Billy Graham in Asia*, p. 58.
Such special gifts as: Ibid., p. 72; Bishop, Charlotte *Observer* (Feb. 8, 1977); McLoughlin, *Billy Graham: Revivalist in a Secular Age*, p. 119.
Outnumbering those for Khrushchev: High, p. 190.
One hundred thousand gathered in dirt stadium: Ibid., p. 196; Interview, "Asia Can Be Won," *U.S. News and World Report* (April 6, 1956), pp. 67–71.
The soul has a disease: Burnham, *To the Far Corners: With Billy Graham in Asia*, p. 147.

339 "With the crowd pressing in close": Ibid., p. 49.
Forms staring into his room: Ibid., p. 71.
Crows flapping into room: Ibid., p. 34.

340 "Had not slept very well . . . something about to happen": Ibid., pp. 92, 155.
"I opened my hand . . . upon the crowd": Ibid., pp. 53–54.
"Nearly my fainting altitude": Ibid., pp. 70–71.
"The cathedral was jammed": Houston, *Holiday* (March, 1958).

341 "Tried to get in my shadow": Ibid.
"Everything absolutely perfect": Burnham, *To the Far Corners: With Billy Graham in Asia*, pp. 155–156.

342 "Had finer platforms": Interview, *U.S. News and World Report* (April 6, 1956).
Entered Holy Land to flashbulbs: McMahan, p. 88.
"Shalom": Ibid., pp. 90–91.

343 Provided Mercedes: Strober, pp. 127–128.

345 Made film documentary, instituted tours: Dot Jackson, Charlotte *Observer* (Nov. 16, 1969).
"Ministry going to be very brief": Burnham, *To the Far Corners: With Billy Graham in Asia*, p. 124.
Brought back stuffed animals: Pollock monograph provided by BGEA.

346 Tourists clicking snapshots: High, p. 126.
Plucking sprigs from shrubbery: Joan Rattner Heilman, "Billy Graham's Daughter Answers His Critics," *Good Housekeeping* (June, 1973), pp. 82–83.
Children charging tourists: Ibid.
"Why we keep our children secluded": Battle, INS, in Charlotte *Observer* (Aug. 27, 1957).
By eight-foot-high fence: Heilman, *Good Housekeeping*.
On recommendation of: Bishop, Charlotte *Observer* (Feb. 6, 1977).
Signs advising: Fiske for *The New York Times*, in Charlotte *Observer* (June 15, 1969).

347 "When Daddy was there": Heilman, *Good Housekeeping*.
Set to learning Sermon on the Mount by: "The New Evangelist," *Time* (Oct. 25, 1954).
"Had to spank them sometimes": Graham, "Joy of Family Life," *Good Housekeeping* (Oct., 1969), p. 103.
"Remember him whipping me": Heilman, *Good Housekeeping*.

348 So "kids will learn the facts of life": Pollock, *Billy Graham*, p. 167.

350 "He sounds very much like me": Kay Bartlett for AP, in Charlotte *Observer* (May 18, 1975).
Career as tennis pro: "Billy Graham: The Man at Home," the *Saturday Evening Post* (Spring, 1972).

351 But "busy as he was": Pollock monograph provided by BGEA.

352   Hoped children would be missionaries: Houston, *Holiday* (March, 1958).
"Brought up with a profound respect for law": Charlotte *News* (April 4, 1972).
Anne touched off clamor: Pollock monograph from BGEA.
Her letter to editor: "Evangelist's Daughter Replies to Critical Article," the Raleigh *News* and *Observer* (Sept. 18, 1973).
"God controls our destiny": Heilman, *Good Housekeeping.*
"Helping Ted and me find a new house": Ibid.

353   "This is of God, Daddy": Ibid.
"He is the most dedicated young Christian": Charlotte *Observer* (March 31, 1963).
Conducted the service himself: AP dispatch, Charlotte *Observer* (May 3, 1963).
At eighteen, gave birth to son: Charlotte *Observer* (March 12, 1964).
A . . . Raleigh dentist: AP dispatch, Charlotte *Observer* (May 2, 1966).
"Reminded me to look for God's blessing": Pollock monograph from BGEA.

354   Repaired hernia of Graham's: Bell, the *Ladies' Home Journal.*
"Whole organization in prayer": Sue Creighton, Charlotte News (Sept. 27, 1965).
"My own father was a dairy farmer": Pollock, *A Foreign Devil in China*, p. 237.
"Billy has a keen sense of destiny": Burnham and Fisher, *Billy Graham: Man of God*, p. 9.
"Dr. Bell gave it to me": Pollock, *A Foreign Devil in China*, p. 238.

355   "A good Christian boy": Ibid., p. 26.
"We contributed to the success of the Communists": Ibid., p. 230.
Deplored civil rights campaigns: Ibid., p. 242.

356   "Never heard a cross word between them": Heilman, *Good Housekeeping.*
"Bill — the merciless wretch": High, p. 131.

357   "Best advice I've ever known": Charlotte *Observer* (April 22, 1967).

359   Demonstrator wandered near Ruth: Fran Schumer, Charlotte *Observer* (May 21, 1975).
"Happened real quick": Phil Whitesell, Charlotte *News* (Aug. 30, 1975).
"Right to his opinion, but": Schumer, Charlotte *Observer* (May 21, 1975).
Pumps atop sign, "patted him on the shoulder": Ibid.
Shouldered to the edge of the crowd: Charlotte *Observer* (May 29, 1975).
Charged her with "simple assault": Charlotte *Observer* (May 25, 1975).
Wished it hadn't been reported — "but": Schumer, Charlotte *Observer* (May 21, 1975).
Bobbed over to him, smiling: Whitesell, Charlotte *News* (Aug. 30, 1975).

360   "Delighted the judge saw fit": Ron Alridge, Charlotte *Observer* (Aug. 30, 1975).

361   Thought to be a heart attack: Chicago *Daily News* Services, Charlotte *Observer* (Feb. 16, 1976).

362   Spill of books, most of them religious: "Billy Graham: The Man at Home," the *Saturday Evening Post* (Spring, 1972).
How to Improve Your Golf Game: Burnham and Fisher, *Billy Graham: Man of God*, p. 14.
Holding hands through two telecasts of news: Strober, p. 111.

364   Mountain lad came blundering into study: Pollock, *Billy Graham*, p. 246.
FBI maintaining list of threats: "The Preaching and the Power," *Newsweek* (July 20, 1970).
When young man appeared before him: AP dispatch, Charlotte *News* (Sept. 6, 1963).

365   Dog became "horribly vicious," attacked Graham: Pollock monograph from BGEA.

369–370   Bible delivered to Debbie Reynolds: *Redbook* (May, 1961), p. 34.

371   "Christ made himself of no reputation": Burnham and Fisher, *Billy Graham and the New York Crusade*, p. 137.

373   About rich young ruler in Mississippi sermon: Strober, pp. 147–153.

374   "Am attacked by extreme fundamentalists": Houston, *Holiday* (March, 1958).

PAGE

375 "Paradox that has often confused . . . me": Graham, *Christian Century* (Feb. 17, 1960).
"Only country in world where the current renascence": McLoughlin, *Christian Century*.

394 "Radical groups . . . led by so-called clergymen": "The Preaching and the Power," *Newsweek* (July 20, 1970).

395 "Almost completely materialistic": AP dispatch, Charlotte *Observer* (Aug. 23, 1963).
Making phone calls to Congressmen: Jetton, Charlotte *Observer* (Nov. 22, 1967).
Shriver alighting by helicopter for joint OEO tour: Jetton, Charlotte *Observer* (May 14, 1967); "Billy Graham: The Man at Home," the *Saturday Evening Post* (Spring, 1972).
"Great wave of conservatism": UPI dispatch, Charlotte *Observer* (Nov. 19, 1966).
To identify "extremist groups": David Lawrence, Charlotte *Observer* (July 25, 1966).
"Guerrilla war being planned": Corry, *Harper's*.

396 "Radicals seeking to overthrow the American way": UPI dispatch, Charlotte *Observer* (Nov. 15, 1969).
"Extremists" intended to launch terrorism: UPI dispatch, Charlotte *Observer* (Aug. 25, 1969).
"Day of crisis has not passed": Charlotte *Observer* (Dec. 6, 1951).
"Day of Judgment is near": Carlton Ihde, CDN, in Charlotte *Observer* (Nov. 13, 1956).
"This Christmas is the most precarious": Graham for UPI, in Charlotte *Observer* (Dec. 17, 1961).
"More important than any diplomatic . . . mission": Charlotte *Observer* (March 14, 1955).
"Never undertaken a mission . . . for which I": Pollock, *Billy Graham*, p. 156.

396–397 Appropriated sag in stock market: UPI dispatch, Charlotte *Observer* (June 4, 1962).

397 "At the edge of an abyss . . . days are numbered": Charlotte *News* (June 4, 1962); UPI dispatch, Charlotte *Observer* (June 11, 1962).
"A false hope": AP dispatch, Charlotte *Observer* (Aug. 23, 1963).
"On the brink of a world catastrophe": AP dispatch, Charlotte *News* (Aug. 26, 1963).
"A people under sentence of death": AP dispatch, Charlotte *News* (Aug. 26, 1963).
"World is heading for a gigantic disaster": AP dispatch, Charlotte *Observer* (Dec. 31, 1966).
"Am consoled by the fact that Jesus": Graham, *McCall's* (April, 1964).

398 "In the worst state of spiritual decline . . . in history": "Protestants: Crusader in the Coliseum," *Time* (Sept. 6, 1963).
"Take the twin problems of": UPI dispatch, Charlotte *Observer* (May 27, 1970).

399 "As soon as prayer was taken out of schools": Maschal, Charlotte, *Observer* (Nov. 5, 1971).
"Authority is the word": Pollock, *Billy Graham*, p. 209.
"Able to sleep in the storm": Meyer, the *New Republic*.
Wearing dark glasses, baseball cap: James H. Bowman for Chicago *Daily News* Service, in Charlotte *News* (around Aug., 1969).
On Sunset Strip: John Dart for News World Service, in Charlotte *Observer* (Sept. 11, 1969).

400 "Student radicals very dangerous": AP dispatch, Charlotte *Observer* (May 19, 1969).
"I really dig this generation": AP dispatch, Charlotte *Observer* (Dec. 27, 1969).
"In danger of entering an era of cynicism": Julian Scheer, Charlotte *News* (Nov. 11, 1959).

403 To Ft. Lauderdale bacchanal: UPI dispatch, Charlotte *Observer* (Aug. 5, 1961).
"What can we march for?": Graham, *McCall's* (June, 1964).
"Jesus thing is now receiving great publicity": "Billy Graham: The Man at Home," the *Saturday Evening Post* (Spring, 1972).

Such slogans as "Things Go Better with Jesus": UPI dispatch, Charlotte *Observer* (June 18, 1972).

As a "religious Woodstock": AP dispatch, Charlotte *Observer* (June 11, 1972).

Crusade conceived in corporate dining room, "America's largest coffee house": "Billy's Apostles," *Newsweek* (June 23, 1969), p. 65.

404   Strobe lights, video screens, "Do your own thing!" mixed with: Philip Tracy, "Billy Graham Plays the Garden," *Commonweal* (July 25, 1969), pp. 457–459.

Such vices as: Graham, "The Answer to Corruption," *Nation's Business* (Sept., 1969), pp. 46–49.

"Young people . . . are searching for a flag": Pollock, *Billy Graham*, p. 217.

"They want a master!": Borchert, Charlotte *News* (Sept. 24, 1958).

405   "See . . . how excited the Red Guards . . . are": Earl Larimore, Charlotte *Observer* (Dec. 7, 1966).

"Losing the battle to the Russians": Borchert, Charlotte *News* (Jan. 8, 1958).

"Once asked an army officer": Meyer, the *New Republic*.

"If the . . . marines trained like the Christians": Cornell for AP, in Charlotte *Observer* (June 15, 1957).

Askew to Paul's "antinomian" principles: Weiner, *Commentary*.

"Defiance of law on all levels": AP dispatch, Charlotte *Observer* (Aug. 15, 1965).

406   "God's agents for punishment": "Hiring for God," the *Nation* (May 26, 1969), p. 653.

Capital punishment "proven deterrent": UPI dispatch, Charlotte *Observer* (March 22, 1973).

"Guilty of rape, he should be castrated": Lin Menge, the Rand *Daily Mail* (March 24, 1973); UPI dispatch, Charlotte *Observer* (March 23, 1973).

"My comment on rape was . . . offhand": Charlotte *News* (April 2, 1973).

"Christian ought to look like Christian": Borchert, Charlotte *News* (Oct. 1, 1958).

"Leisure . . . morally dangerous": "Are Sports Good for the Soul?" *Newsweek* (Jan. 11, 1971), pp. 51–52.

407   "Separation is a policy that won't work": AP dispatch, Charlotte *News* (April 4, 1960).

"Segregated churches . . . are becoming known over world": AP dispatch, Charlotte *News* (April 7, 1960).

"Greatest need in South is contact": Borchert, Charlotte *News* (April 1, 1960).

408   Had to be instructed no grounds existed for inferiority: Strober, p. 55.

"Most . . . ministers in the South feel": Graham, "Billy Graham Makes Plea for an End to Intolerance," *Life* (Oct. 1, 1956), p. 138.

409   "Shocked to learn that Billy Graham had been invited": Charles Wickenberg, Charlotte *Observer* (Oct. 12, 1958).

Posed it to "Graham's conscience": UPI dispatch, Charlotte *Observer* (Oct. 23, 1958).

Shifted service to Fort Jackson: Charlotte *Observer* (Oct. 25, 1958).

Cued by Eisenhower appeal: Pollock, *Billy Graham*, p. 224.

"Went back to my hotel room and knelt": Graham, *Life* (Oct. 1, 1956).

To Clinton, Tennessee: UPI dispatch, Charlotte *Observer* (Dec. 11, 1958).

To Little Rock: UPI dispatch, Charlotte *Observer* (Sept. 14, 1959).

410   "But such reasoning is silly": Graham, *Life* (Oct. 1, 1956).

"Approved of master-and-servant relationships": Graham commentary for UPI, carried as "No Solution to Race Problem 'At the Point of Bayonets,' " in *U.S. News and World Report* (April 25, 1960), pp. 94–95.

"Freedom Riders made their point": AP dispatch, Charlotte *Observer* (July 9, 1961).

"For both races to act like Christians": Cornell for AP, Charlotte *Observer* (Aug. 16, 1963).

"Extremists" trying to "rush things": AP dispatch, Charlotte *Observer* (Aug. 29, 1963).

"How, in the church, you can say": UPI dispatch, Charlotte *Observer* (May 25, 1964).

"I doubt the wisdom": Charlotte *Observer* (June 27, 1964).

411   "Playing up of racial tension in South": Titcomb, Charlotte *News* (Oct. 11, 1963).

"All laws must be obeyed": AP dispatch, Charlotte *Observer* (April 19, 1965).

Alabama "well on the way": AP dispatch, Charlotte *Observer* (April 25, 1965).

"Had a social visit": AP dispatch, Charlotte *Observer* (June 17, 1965).

"If the Ku Klux Klan will quiet down": Rex Thomas, Charlotte *Observer* (June 21, 1965).

"Have the responsibility to obey the law": AP dispatch, Charlotte *News* (Nov. 28, 1960).

411–412   On assignments of Secret Service men: AP dispatch, Charlotte *Observer* (June 6, 1968).

412   "Some extreme Negro leaders are going too fast": Graham for UPI, in *U.S. News and World Report* (April 25, 1960).

"Should be a challenge to individual courtesy": Ibid.

414   "Only when Christ comes again will white children": "The Preaching and the Power," *Newsweek* (July 20, 1970).

Had "served to arouse the conscience": AP dispatch, Charlotte *Observer* (April 27, 1965).

"Have the pattern of defiance": Lawrence, "Billy Graham's Plea to President Johnson," *U.S. News and World Report* (Aug. 7, 1967), p. 92.

"Exploited by a small, hard core of leftists": AP dispatch, Charlotte *Observer* (Aug. 18, 1965).

"Devise new laws to curb . . . violence": AP dispatch, Charlotte *Observer* (Aug. 15, 1965).

415   "Thank God . . . King was not stabbed by white": R. Covington, Charlotte *Observer* (Sept. 22, 1955).

Publicly appealed to King to: AP dispatch, Charlotte *Observer* (Aug. 15, 1965).

416   "Belief in the social implications . . . deepened": Graham, *Christian Century* (Feb. 17, 1960).

"That faith without works is dead": Graham, *Life* (Oct. 1, 1956).

417   "Not sure whether our involvement was right or wrong": Fiske for *NYT* News Service, in Charlotte *Observer* (Jan. 21, 1973).

"Stakes are much higher in Vietnam than anybody realizes": AP dispatch, Charlotte *Observer* (Dec. 29, 1966); AP dispatch, Charlotte *Observer* (Dec. 30, 1968).

418   "No man with Christ in his heart": Martin, the *Saturday Evening Post*.

Returned with a supply of reprints: Van Der Linden, Charlotte *Observer* (Nov. 4, 1953).

419   U.S. "created for a spiritual mission": McLoughlin, *Billy Graham: Revivalist in a Secular Age*, p. 142.

"Must maintain strong military": Ibid., p. 145.

"Time to keep our powder dry": AP dispatch, Charlotte *Observer* (Jan. 13, 1957).

"For prayer and soul-searching": Charlotte *Observer* (Oct. 11, 1957).

Devotional services at Pentagon: "Rockin' the Capitol," *Time* (March 3, 1952).

Christmas observance there, messages at West Point: AP dispatch, Charlotte *Observer* (Dec. 18, 1962).

"Strongest military establishment": AP dispatch, Charlotte *Observer* (July 31, 1965).

420   That Kremlin faction demanding attack: UP dispatch, Charlotte Observer (Oct. 28, 1957).

Soviet subs "sitting off the coast": Hannah Miller, Charlotte *Observer* (May 30, 1960).

"Russia has already created the neutron bomb": AP dispatch, Charlotte *Observer* (Sept. 1, 1961).

"Unfortunate if the President . . . should say": UP dispatch, Charlotte *Observer* (Oct. 28, 1957).

"Hope that President Eisenhower will invite him to church": AP dispatch, Charlotte *Observer* (Sept. 27, 1959).

"Everytime Khrushchev growls": Miller, Charlotte *Observer* (May 30, 1960).

Never saw anything in Bible adverse to war: John C. Dills for AP, Charlotte *Observer* (Aug. 10, 1961).

"We have suffered defeats": Ibid.

421 "So deadly has been the encroachment": AP dispatch, Charlotte *Observer* (July 31, 1965).

"Proud of what you men are doing": AP dispatch, Charlotte *Observer* (Dec. 10, 1965).

"War in Europe seemed very far away": AP dispatch, Charlotte *Observer* (Dec. 8, 1965).

421–422 Offered Scripture at LBJ prayer breakfast: Clayton Fritchey, "The Issue (and Some Miscellaneous Trimmings)," *Harper's* (May, 1966), p. 32.

422 Delivered sermon at Saigon airport: AP dispatch, Charlotte *Observer* (Dec. 22, 1966).

423 Bev Shea carilloning to troops: Shea, p. 163.

Aboard *Kitty Hawk*, joined Bob Hope: AP dispatch, Charlotte *Observer* (Dec. 28, 1966).

Anecdote about bear-hunter: AP dispatch, Charlotte *Observer* (Dec. 23, 1966).

Troops "extremely religious . . . to feel their spirit": Charlotte *News* (Dec. 30, 1966).

"Underwent the same briefings as Mr. Romney": UPI dispatch, Charlotte *Observer* (Sept. 10, 1967).

424 "One of the greatest dilemmas": Charlotte *Observer* (Feb. 15, 1965).

"Peace issue completely misunderstood": Jackson, Charlotte *Observer* (Dec. 21, 1969).

"Have to soon make a decision": UPI dispatch, Charlotte *Observer* (March 31, 1968).

"The war is already won": AP dispatch, Charlotte *Observer* (Dec. 30, 1968).

425 "I don't comment on Vietnam": Jackson, Charlotte *Observer* (Dec. 21, 1969).

Surge of demonstrators in London: AP dispatch, Charlotte *Observer* (June 30, 1967).

"Vietnam is difficult, confused": AP dispatch, Charlotte *Observer* (Feb. 1, 1967).

"Negroes divided about the war": "Graham Denounces Dissenters," *Christian Century* (May 17, 1967), p. 645.

Protests "exaggerate our divisions": Ibid.

426 As answers to protests, to mount Honor America Day: "The Preaching and the Power," *Newsweek* (July 20, 1970).

"Too much negativism": Saul Friedman, Charlotte *Observer* (July 3, 1970).

"Because they don't believe in God": Ibid.

"Never give in!": "The Preaching and the Power," *Newsweek* (July 20, 1970).

428 "Have all had our My Lais": as quoted by Alexander J. McKelway in Letters column, Charlotte *Observer* (Oct. 18, 1971).

"All over the world, . . . civilians being killed . . . thousands of deaths attributed to smoking . . . where demonstrations against alcohol": Fiske for NYT News Service, in Charlotte *Observer* (Jan. 21, 1973); "Quote of the Week," the *New Republic* (Jan. 6 and 13, 1973), p. 11.

"Three hundred or so civilian casualties in North Vietnam": Fiske, Charlotte *Observer* (Jan. 21, 1973).

"Satanic spiritual power": S. Covington, Charlotte *Observer* (Oct. 14, 1970).

Had to barricade his home: Ibid.

429 "Not an Old Testament prophet": AP dispatch, Charlotte *Observer* (Jan. 4, 1973).

"I am no more chaplain to White House": Ibid.

Notified by Nixon of Cambodia incursion: Strober, p. 47.

"Not one of his confidants": AP dispatch, Charlotte *Observer* (Jan. 4, 1973).

430 "Doubted our sending troops . . . without the will to win": Fiske, Charlotte *Observer* (Jan. 21, 1973).

"Careful not to be drawn into the moral implications": "Graham Denounces Dissenters," *Christian Century* (May 17, 1967).

Pitched into highway safety campaign: AP dispatch, Charlotte *News* (May 31, 1968).

"Avoided expressions as to who was right": Heilman, *Good Housekeeping.*

432 "Never gotten into a no-win land war": "The Preaching and the Power," *Newsweek* (July 20, 1970).

Graham at commemoration of war's end: Henry Eichel, Warren King, Bill McGraw, Charlotte *Observer* (Jan. 29, 1973).

435 "Men who lead wholesome family lives": "Billy's Political Pitch," *Newsweek* (June 10, 1968).

"Need to rehabilitate . . . Puritanism": Charlotte *News* (March 15, 1966).

"At the brink of a new age": Stewart Spencer, Jr., Charlotte *News* (Nov. 28, 1964).

"Enough people . . . to have a march": AP dispatch, Charlotte *News* (Sept. 9, 1963).

436 "Court has misinterpreted our forefathers": UPI dispatch, Charlotte *Observer* (March 31, 1964).

"Atheists . . . should be overruled by the majority": Burnham and Fisher, *Billy Graham: Man of God*, p. 54.

Fact that "Generalissimo and Madame Chiang": Interview, *U.S. News and World Report* (April 6, 1956).

"Perfect form of government is a monarchy": Fiske, Charlotte *Observer* (June 15, 1969).

Would still be "hotels and cities": Ibid.

"Christians ought to get into politics": UPI dispatch, Charlotte *Observer* (Oct. 15, 1959).

437 "No man has done more for the cause of goodwill": UP dispatch, Charlotte *Observer* (Aug. 5, 1956).

439 "Can't get involved in a political discussion": AP dispatch, Charlotte *Observer* (March 18, 1960).

440 Sleekly tanned, "for man of experience": Bill Lamkin, Charlotte *Observer* (May 21, 1960).

Grinned, "Might be": Scheer, Charlotte *News* (Oct. 26, 1960).

"Next four years will be the most crucial": Lamkin, Charlotte *Observer* (May 21, 1960).

Grady Wilson going on to mention: Charlotte *Observer* (Aug. 8, 1960).

441 Further proposed from Switzerland: AP dispatch, Charlotte *Observer* (Aug. 10, 1960).

From Bonn, he disclosed: AP dispatch, Charlotte *Observer* (Sept. 13, 1960).

He elaborated from Geneva: UPI dispatch, Charlotte *Observer* (Aug. 20, 1960).

Bell in tract presenting the matter: Lamkin, Charlotte *Observer* (Oct. 27, 1960).

Election "the most crucial": AP dispatch, Charlotte *Observer* (Oct. 6, 1960).

441–442 Voting from "deep personal convictions": Borchert, Charlotte *News* (Oct. 13, 1960).

442 "Have never said anything that would lead": Scheer, Charlotte *News* (Oct. 26, 1960).

Demurred when advised by Nixon: Charlotte *News* (Oct. 31, 1960).

"Have prayed a good deal": Ibid.

443 "Understand there is to be recount": Charlotte *News* (Nov. 19, 1960).

Accepted Kennedy's invitation: Don Oberdorfer, Charlotte *Observer* (Dec. 1, 1960).

444 "There wasn't as much religious bigotry": UPI dispatch, Charlotte *Observer* (Dec. 20, 1960).

Election "had helped relations between churches": AP dispatch, Charlotte *Observer* (Jan. 17, 1961).

"Turned out to be a Baptist President": UPI dispatch, Charlotte *Observer* (May 18, 1961).

Continued to attend Nixon: Fiske, "Closest Thing to a White House Chaplain," *The New York Times Magazine* (June 8, 1969), p. 27.

PAGE

"Most experienced Republican": AP dispatch, Charlotte *Observer* (Dec. 31, 1967).
Ponderings conducted as they: Bishop, Charlotte *Observer* (Feb. 8, 1977).

445   "Trying to avoid political involvement": UPI dispatch, Charlotte *Observer* (March 13, 1968).
"No American I admire more": Charlotte *Observer* (May 27, 1968).
Intended to reconfirm disengagement: UPI dispatch, Charlotte *Observer* (Aug. 4, 1968).
"All right to lie to another politician": Charlotte *Observer* (Aug. 18, 1968).
Acclaim for his "generosity": "Evangelists: The Politicians' Preacher," *Time* (Oct. 4, 1968), p. 58.
More realistic than Jesus: Barry Farrell, "Billy in the Garden," *Life* (July 4, 1969), p. 2B.

445-446   Nixon's call on Graham's mother: also from Tom Seslar, Charlotte *Observer* (Sept. 12, 1968); S. Covington, Charlotte *Observer* (Sept. 12, 1968); Kay Reimler, Charlotte *News* (Sept. 11, 1968).

447   Would make no endorsements: Jane Roehrs, Charlotte *News* (Sept. 19, 1968).
Mood "swinging slightly to right": Ibid.
Julie Nixon at Montreat: Charlotte *Observer* (Oct. 18, 1968).

448   "I might find I will": Washington *Post*–Los Angeles *Times* News Service, Charlotte *Observer* (May 14, 1968).
"People who just don't know how to cast their vote:" "Billy's Political Pitch," *Newsweek* (June 10, 1968).
Could not resist announcing: Charlotte *Observer* (Nov. 1, 1968).
Dent later declared: "The Preaching and the Power," *Newsweek* (July 20, 1970).
Delivered inaugural prayer: Fiske, "Closest Thing to a White House Chaplain," *The New York Times Magazine* (June 8, 1969).
Washington waggery soon went: "Praying Together, Staying Together," *Time* (Feb. 7, 1969), pp. 15–16.

449   "Is Henry there": Strober, p. 62.
Withdrew to Key Biscayne before crusade: "Evangelism: Mellowing Magic," *Time* (June 27, 1969), p. 48.
Nixon twitting Grady Wilson: Bishop, Charlotte *Observer* (Feb. 8, 1977).

450   Choired with Agnew in rebuking: AP dispatch, Charlotte *Observer* (Feb. 26, 1970).
"Should feel the full force of the law": AP dispatch, Charlotte *Observer* (Nov. 1, 1970).
Allowed Nixon to make crusade appearance: Strober, pp. 78–79.
"To show the younger generation": "The Preaching and the Power," *Newsweek* (July 20, 1970).
Accommodated by Tennessee statute, battery from FCA: Garry Wills, "How Nixon Used the Media, Billy Graham, and the Good Lord to Rap with Students," *Esquire* (Sept., 1970), p. 119.
Entered stadium together: Ibid.

451   "Really gave him ovation": "The Preaching and the Power," *Newsweek* (July 20, 1970).
Modest protests sputtered: Wills, *Esquire*.
"I'm for change": "The Preaching and the Power," *Newsweek* (July 20, 1970).
Nixon took the pulpit to amplify: "The Presidency: In Praise of Youth," *Time* (June 8, 1970), p. 13.
Scattered choruses of: Wills, *Esquire*.
"Glad there seems a solid majority": "The Preaching and the Power," *Newsweek* (July 20, 1970).

452   Protestors frisked: Wills, *Esquire*.
"If Nixon had been running for election": "The Preaching and the Power," *Newsweek* (July 20, 1970).

" 'Billy, . . . you stay out of politics' ": David Frost, *Billy Graham Talks with David Frost* (London: Hodder and Stoughton, 1972), p. 66.

That he intended to vote for Nixon: AP dispatch, Charlotte *Observer* (Aug. 13, 1972).

McGovern "desperate," Nixon "with deep religious commitment": AP dispatch, Charlotte *Observer* (Nov. 3, 1972).

453   *Marjoe* financed by "a Jewish businessman": Johnson, University of North Carolina *Daily Tar Heel* (April 3, 1973).

Sermon first Sunday of Nixon's second term: AP dispatch, Charlotte *Observer* (Jan. 22, 1973).

454   Wires of tribute from: Emery Wister, Charlotte *News* (Oct. 21, 1971).

Reception sponsored by Holiday Inns: Jetton, Charlotte *Observer* (Oct. 15, 1971).

Would "have to make all of the decisions": Michael Schwartz, Charlotte *Observer* (June 8, 1974).

Secret Service conducted surveillance: Paddock, Charlotte *Observer* (Oct. 18, 1971).

455   Plotted by Red Hornet Mayday Tribe: Nancy Brachey, Charlotte *Observer* (May 2, 1972).

Memo to White House: Charlotte *News* (Aug. 2, 1973).

Friday dawned soft and clear: Gary, Charlotte *Observer* (Oct. 16, 1971).

School children granted holiday: Charlotte *Observer* (Oct. 13, 1971).

Cases suspended, businesses closed: Bill Arthur, Charlotte *Observer* (Oct. 14, 1971).

456   In shimmering suit, happily fretted to Thurmond: Gary, Charlotte *Observer* (Oct. 16, 1971).

Arrested for whopping indelicacies: Brachey, Charlotte *Observer* (May 1, 1972).

"Not going to have any agitators": Charlotte *Observer* (Oct. 16, 1971).

"Go away": Ibid.

Were men with armbands stamped "marshal": Ellison Clary, Charlotte *News* (March 2, 1972).

Exit chute of ropes: Cathy Packer, Charlotte *News* (April 26, 1975).

When noticed laughing at officer: Packer, Niki Scott, Charlotte *News* (April 24, 1975).

Theology student bundled out when: Paddock, Charlotte *Observer* (Oct. 16, 1971).

457   Vietnam veteran refused entrance: editorial, Charlotte *Observer* (Oct. 22, 1971).

Judge concluded criteria of exclusion as: Bradley Martin, Charlotte *Observer* (Aug. 1, 1973).

Motorcade with a helicopter, gallery twelve-deep: Henry Woodhead, Charlotte *News* (Oct. 16, 1971).

"He even told me how to wave": "Billy Graham: The Man at Home," the *Saturday Evening Post* (Spring, 1972).

Undertone of chants: Charlotte *Observer* (Oct. 16, 1971).

Third Army band playing as: Arthur, Charlotte *Observer* (Oct. 16, 1971).

Graham responded: S. Covington, Charlotte *Observer* (Oct. 16, 1971).

458   "If all Americans were like the people of the Piedmont": Ibid.

"We also had problems of rats": Ibid.

Answered with billow of cheers: John Osborne, "The Rev. Billy's Day," the *New Republic* (Oct. 30, 1971), pp. 11–13.

" 'Billy, that *wouldn't be moral* ' ": Ibid.

Shea arose to sing: Woodhead, Charlotte *News* (Oct. 16, 1971).

"You have contributed to America . . . the top preacher": Charlotte *News* (Oct. 16, 1971); Gary, Charlotte *Observer* (Oct. 16, 1971).

"Character of a nation determines whether": Arthur, Charlotte *Observer* (Oct. 16, 1971).

459   "My child just wanted to see": Brachey, Charlotte *Observer* (May 1, 1972); Woodhead, Ed Freakley, Charlotte *Observer* (Oct. 16, 1971).

Nixon extended hand, youth barked: Brachey, Charlotte *Observer* (April 24, 1975).

PAGE

Howls rose around them: Mary Estes, Charlotte *News* (Oct. 16, 1971).

Signs saying: Gary, Charlotte *Observer* (Oct. 16, 1971).

Finger-pronging V-signs: Osborne, the *New Republic*.

A Belshazzarian spread of: Gary, Charlotte *Observer* (Oct. 16, 1971); Estes, Charlotte *News* (Oct. 16, 1971); Frank Barrows, Charlotte *Observer* (Oct. 16, 1971).

460   Docket sheet largest in Charlotte history: Packer, Charlotte *News* (April 19, 1975).

"We kept the people out": Allen Cowan, Charlotte *Observer* (Sept. 7, 1974).

Recruited through Washington VFW: B. Martin, Charlotte *Observer* (Aug. 9, 1973).

Stonewall Jackson post, led by: B. Martin, Charlotte *Observer* (Aug. 3, 1973).

"I did feel a little honored": Packer, Charlotte *News* (May 1, 1975).

"Official tailor" of Tribe, who offered: Packer, Charlotte *News* (April 24, 1975).

460–461   "In some respects, a religious ceremony": Brachey, Charlotte *Observer* (May 2, 1975).

461   "Expert witness in the field of mob violence from the Crucifixion": Packer, Charlotte *News* (April 19, 1975).

Jurors remarked afterward: Scheryl Gant, Charlotte *Observer* (July 12, 1975).

"I haven't heard about it": Maschal, Charlotte *Observer* (Nov. 5, 1971).

462   "Disagree . . . Nixon is not sincere": McLoughlin, *Billy Graham: Revivalist in a Secular Age*, p. 118.

George Ball "hitting below belt": Charlotte *Observer* (Sept. 30, 1968).

463   "Heard people say, 'I don't like Nixon' . . . has deep religious convictions . . . a man of high principles": Graham, *McCall's* (June, 1964); Hall, the *Reader's Digest* (July, 1970).

"So I know something of what they feel": "Billy Graham: The Man at Home," the *Saturday Evening Post* (Spring, 1972).

464   Nixon reminisced about his own conversion: Bishop, Charlotte *Observer* (Feb. 8, 1977).

472   "Has a very strong sense of integrity": David Broder for Washington *Post*–Los Angeles *Times* News Service, in Charlotte *Observer* (April 28, 1973).

"Probably make him a stronger man": AP dispatch, Charlotte *Observer* (Nov. 22, 1973).

First cover-up when Adam and Eve: Arthur Vesey for Chicago *Tribune*, in Charlotte *Observer* (Aug. 26, 1973).

Nixon "chipper, full of fun": Sherman Harris, Charlotte *News* (Dec. 17, 1973).

"Billy can get through right away": "The Preaching and the Power," *Newsweek* (July 20, 1970).

472–473   "Did call twice, . . . but I couldn't get through": Dart for Washington *Post*–Los Angeles *Times* News Service, in Charlotte *Observer* (Aug. 17, 1974).

473   "Don't know what my relationship is": Ibid.

U.S. gripped in "spiritual . . . crisis": S. Covington, Charlotte *Observer* (June 15, 1973).

"Nixon's judgments have been poor," but: NYT News Service, Charlotte *Observer* (Dec. 23, 1973).

474   "Surprised at the small amount": Knight Newspaper Wire, Charlotte *Observer* (Dec. 28, 1973).

475   "Just wanted to say hello": Cornell for AP, in Sumter (S.C.) *Daily Item* (May 30, 1974).

"Didn't know he used this type of language . . . appear was maneuvering": R. Covington, Charlotte *Observer* (May 9, 1974).

"One cannot but deplore": Cornell for AP, Charlotte *Observer* (May 29, 1974).

"Too would contain salty language": Charlotte *Observer* (May 2, 1974).

"Does not make it right": Cornell for AP, Charlotte *Observer* (May 29, 1974).

476 "Neither [Nixon's] friend nor God's servant if": Ibid.
Nixon remained "my friend": Ibid.

477 "Tapes revealed a man I never knew": Dart for Washington *Post*–Los Angeles *Times* News Service, in Charlotte *News* (Aug. 17, 1974).
Removed himself to Switzerland: Washington *Star-News,* in Charlotte *Observer* (July 18, 1974).

478 Into Mayo Clinic with "gum infection": Charlotte *Observer* (Aug. 7, 1974).
"Feel sorry for President Nixon": Martha Rainey, Charlotte *News* (Aug. 9, 1974).
U.S. "may be finished": AP dispatch, Charlotte *News* (Nov. 5, 1974).

479 Opening prayer for Senate session: Charlotte *News* (April 10, 1975).
Long visit with Gerald Ford: Bartlett for AP, in Charlotte *Observer* (May 18, 1974).
"President read the Bible . . . with me": Strober, p. 79.
Participated in Democratic telethon: Charlotte *Observer* (July 3, 1975).
"What will the American response be": Strober, p. 144.
"Just been too emotional about it": Bishop, Charlotte *Observer* (Feb. 8, 1977).

480–481 "Tried to reach him while I was in California": AP dispatch, Charlotte *News* (Sept. 17, 1974).

481 "Already suffered far more": Bob Wisehart, Charlotte *News* (Oct. 30, 1974).
At candlelit dinner with Nixon, declared afterward: Charlotte *Observer* (March 19, 1975); Bartlett for AP, in Charlotte *Observer* (May 18, 1975).

482 Nixon "didn't have nude women running around White House": Mary Bishop Lacy, Charlotte *Observer* (Dec. 31, 1975).

485 "Communism is . . . master-minded by Satan": McLoughlin, *Billy Graham: Revivalist in a Secular Age,* p. 139.
"Type we have not tried . . . is theocracy": Strober, p. 110.

489 "Reason some ministers are cracking up": Graham, *Christian Century* (Feb. 17, 1960).

493 Easier to talk to vast hosts: Bishop, Charlotte *Observer* (Feb. 7, 1977).

496 TV relay elicited more respondents at invitation: "Evangelism: Mellowing Magic," *Time* (June 27, 1969).
Smaller locales facilitated more crusades: Strober, p. 32.

502 Nixon specter continues to confront Graham: Shannon, the Atlanta *Journal and Constitution Magazine* (Oct. 9, 1977).
To stay "out of any partisan politics," but: Cornell in AP dispatch (dated May 26, 1976).

503 "Refreshing to have candidates . . . talk about . . . God": Ibid.
"Need to know what political leaders believe religiously": Ibid.

504 Blankly bellow, "YES! NO": Bishop, Charlotte *Observer* (Feb. 6, 1977).

508 Answering chorus from stands around him: from 1977 BGEA in-house report provided to author.

In addition to the volumes mentioned in the foregoing citations, the following also provided backgrounding for this account:

Adler, Bill, editor, *The Wit and Wisdom of Billy Graham* (New York: Random House, 1967).
Allan, Tom, editor, *Crusade in Scotland* (London: Pickering & Inglis, 1955).
America's Hour of Decision (Wheaton, Ill.: Van Kampen, 1951).
Ashman, Chuck, *The Gospel According to Billy* (Secaucus, N.J.: Lyle Stuart Inc., 1977).
Barnhart, Joe E., *'The Billy Graham Religion* (Philadelphia: United Church Press, 1972).

Billy Graham Talks to Teenagers (Grand Rapids, Mich.: Zondervan, 1958).

Brabham, Lewis F., *A New Song in the South: The Story of the Billy Graham Greenville, S.C., Crusade* (Grand Rapids, Mich.: Zondervan, 1966).

Calling Youth to Christ: Messages by Billy Graham (Grand Rapids, Mich.: Zondervan, 1947).

Cash, W. J., *The Mind of the South* (New York: Alfred A. Knopf, 1941).

Cook, Charles T., *London Hears Billy Graham* (London: Marshall, Morgan & Scott, 1954).

Hutchinson, Warner, and Cliff Wilson, *Let the People Rejoice: An Amazing Week in New Zealand* (Wellington, N.Z.: Crusader Bookroom Society, 1959).

Kilgore, James E., *Billy Graham The Preacher* (New York: Exposition Press, 1968).

Kooiman, Helen W., *Transformed: Behind the Scenes with Billy Graham* (Wheaton, Ill.: Tyndale House Publishers, 1970).

Larson, Mel, *Young Man on Fire: The Story of Torrey Johnson and Youth for Christ* (Chicago: Youth Publications, 1945).

Levy, Alan, *God Bless You Real Good (My Crusade with Billy Graham)* (New York: Essandess Special Editions, 1969).

Mitchell, Curtis, *Billy Graham: The Making of a Crusader* (Philadelphia: Chilton Books, 1966).

—— *Those Who Came Forward: Men and Women Who Responded to the Ministry of Billy Graham* (Philadelphia: Chilton Books, 1966).

Morison, Samuel Eliot, *The Oxford History of the American People* (New York: Oxford University Press, 1965).

Morris, James, *The Preachers* (New York: St. Martin's Press, 1973).

Settel, T. S., editor, *The Faith of Billy Graham* (Anderson, S.C.: Droke House, 1968).

Streiker, Lowell D., and Gerald S. Strober, *Religion and the New Majority: Billy Graham, Middle America, and the Politics of the 70s* (New York: Association Press, 1972).

Thayer, George, *The Farther Shores of Politics* (New York: Simon and Schuster, 1968).

Tocqueville, Alexis de, *Democracy in America* (New York: Knopf, 1945).

INDEX